THE PELICAN HISTORY OF ART

EDITED BY NIKOLAUS PEVSNER

Z 5

PAINTING IN BRITAIN : THE MIDDLE AGES

MARGARET RICKERT

MARGARET RICKERT

PAINTING IN BRITAIN
THE MIDDLE AGES

PENGUIN BOOKS
MELBOURNE · LONDON · BALTIMORE

Penguin Books Ltd, Harmondsworth, Middlesex
Penguin Books Inc., Baltimore, Maryland, U.S.A.
Penguin Books Pty Ltd, Melbourne, Victoria, Australia

★

Text printed by R. & R. Clark Ltd, Edinburgh
Plates printed by Lund Humphries & Co. Ltd, Bradford
Made and printed in Great Britain

★

TO

FRANCIS WORMALD

*

CONTENTS

LIST OF PLATES   ix

ABBREVIATIONS   xx

FOREWORD   xxi

MAPS   xxiv–xxvi

INTRODUCTION   I

    Chart Showing Interrelationships of Medieval Schools of Art   4–5

CHAPTER 1: *Hiberno-Saxon Art in the Seventh, Eighth, and Ninth Centuries*

    Historical Background   9
    Text   10
    Summary   25
    Notes   26

CHAPTER 2: *Anglo-Saxon Art from the Late Ninth to the Middle of the
    Eleventh Century*

    Historical Background   33
    Text   34
    Summary   52
    Notes   53

CHAPTER 3: *Early Romanesque Art (1050–circa 1110)*

    Historical Background   59
    Text   59
    Summary   72
    Notes   72

CHAPTER 4: *Romanesque Art of the Twelfth Century*

    Historical Background   75
    Text   75
    Summary   101
    Notes   101

CONTENTS

CHAPTER 5: *The Thirteenth Century*

Historical Background   105
Text   105
Summary   129
Notes   130

CHAPTER 6: *The East Anglian Period*

Historical Background   137
Text   137
Summary   160
Notes   161

CHAPTER 7: *The International Style in England (1350–1425)*

Historical Background   165
Text   166
Summary   188
Notes   189

CHAPTER 8: *The End of the Middle Ages in England*

Historical Background   195
Text   195
Summary   213
Notes   214

CHAPTER 9: *Evaluation*   215

GLOSSARY   227
BIBLIOGRAPHY   233

The Plates

GENERAL INDEX   239
INDEX OF MANUSCRIPTS   250

LIST OF PLATES

The measurements given for manuscripts are of the whole page when not otherwise indicated

1 Hiberno-Saxon (Northumbria?): Decorative Page, from Book of Durrow. Seventh century (second half). $9\frac{5}{8} \times 6\frac{1}{8}$ in. MS. A.4.5, fol. 174 verso. Trinity College, Dublin

2 (A) Hiberno-Saxon (Northumbria?): Symbol of St Matthew, from Book of Durrow. Seventh century (second half). $9\frac{5}{8} \times 6\frac{1}{8}$ in. MS. A.4.5, fol. 245 verso. Trinity College, Dublin

2 (B) Hiberno-Saxon (Northumbria?): Symbol of St John, from Book of Durrow. Seventh century (second half). $9\frac{5}{8} \times 6\frac{1}{8}$ in. MS. A.4.5, fol. 76 verso. Trinity College, Dublin

3 (A) Anglo-Saxon: Great Buckle, Sutton Hoo Treasure. Seventh century (first half). $5\frac{1}{4} \times 2\frac{1}{8}$ in. Department of Medieval Antiquities, British Museum

3 (B) Anglo-Saxon: Hanging Bowl Escutcheon, Sutton Hoo Treasure. Seventh century (first half). $2\frac{5}{8}$ in. diameter. Department of Medieval Antiquities, British Museum

3 (C) Anglo-Saxon: Gold Clasp, Sutton Hoo Treasure. Seventh century (first half). $2\frac{1}{2} \times 2\frac{1}{8}$ in. Department of Medieval Antiquities, British Museum

3 (D) Hiberno-Saxon (Northumbria?): Decorative Page, from Book of Durrow. Seventh century (second half). Detail approx. actual size. MS. A.4.5, fol. iii. Trinity College, Dublin

4 Northumbrian (Lindisfarne): Cruciform Page, from Lindisfarne Gospels. 698-721. $13\frac{1}{2} \times 9\frac{3}{4}$ in. Cotton MS. Nero D.iv, fol. 26 verso. British Museum

5 Northumbrian (Lindisfarne): Text Page, from Lindisfarne Gospels. 698-721. $13\frac{1}{2} \times 9\frac{3}{4}$ in. Cotton MS. Nero D.iv, fol. 95. British Museum

6 (A) Northumbrian (Lindisfarne): Canon Table Page, from Lindisfarne Gospels. 698-721. $13\frac{1}{2} \times 9\frac{3}{4}$ in. Cotton MS. Nero D.iv, fol. 15. British Museum

6 (B) Irish (Iona and Kells): Canon Table Page, from Book of Kells. 760-820. $13 \times 9\frac{1}{2}$ in. MS. A.1.6, fol. 2. Trinity College, Dublin

7 (A) Northumbrian (Lindisfarne): St Matthew, from Lindisfarne Gospels. 698-721. $13\frac{1}{2} \times 9\frac{3}{4}$ in. Cotton MS. Nero D.iv, fol. 25 verso. British Museum

7 (B) South Italian(?): The Scribe Ezra, prefixed to Northumbrian Bible. Late sixth century. $19\frac{3}{8} \times 13$ in. Codex Amiatinus 1, fol. v. Biblioteca Medicea Laurenziana, Florence

8 (A) Irish (Northumbria?): St Luke, from Gospel Book of Chad. Early eighth century. Miniature $9\frac{3}{4} \times 7\frac{1}{4}$ in. Fol. 109 verso. Cathedral Library, Lichfield

8 (B) Northumbrian (made at Echternach?): St Matthew, from Echternach Gospels. Eighth century (first half). Miniature $10\frac{1}{4} \times 7\frac{5}{8}$ in. MS. lat. 9389, fol. 18 verso. Bibliothèque Nationale, Paris

9 (A) South English: St Mark, from Cutbercht Gospels. Eighth century (last quarter). Miniature $10\frac{1}{4} \times 8\frac{1}{2}$ in. MS. lat. 1224, fol. 71 verso. Nationalbibliothek, Vienna

9 (B) Irish: St Mark, from Gospels. c. 750-60. Miniature $9\frac{1}{4} \times 7$ in. MS. 51, p. 78. Stiftsbibliothek, St Gall

10 (A) Northumbrian: David as a Warrior, from Cassiodorus, *Commentary on the Psalms*. c. 725. Miniature $14\frac{3}{4} \times 10\frac{3}{8}$ in. MS. B.ii.30, fol. 172 verso. Cathedral Library, Durham

10 (B) Canterbury: David as a Musician, from Canterbury Psalter. Mid eighth century. $9\frac{1}{4} \times 7$ in. Cotton MS. Vesp. A.i, fol. 30 verso. British Museum

11 (A) Canterbury: St Matthew, from Gospels. c. 760. Miniature $12\frac{1}{2} \times 10\frac{1}{8}$ in. Codex Aureus, fol. 9 verso. Royal Library, Stockholm

11 (B) Mercian(?): St Matthew, from Rome Gospels. c. 800. $13\frac{1}{2} \times 10\frac{3}{8}$ in. MS. Barb. lat. 570, fol. 11 verso. Biblioteca Apostolica Vaticana, Rome

12 Mercian(?): XPI Page, from Rome Gospels. c. 800. $13\frac{1}{2} \times 10\frac{3}{8}$ in. MS. Barb. lat. 570, fol. 18. Biblioteca Apostolica Vaticana, Rome

13 Irish (Iona and Kells): XPI Page, from Book of Kells. 760-820. $13 \times 9\frac{1}{2}$ in. MS. A.1.6, fol. 34. Trinity College, Dublin

14 Irish (Iona and Kells): St Matthew, from Book of Kells. 760–820. 13 × 9¼ in. MS. A.I.6, fol. 28 verso. Trinity College, Dublin

15 Canterbury: Decorative Text Page, from Bede, *Ecclesiastical History*. Late eighth century. Detail approx. actual size. Cotton MS. Tib. c.ii, fol. 5 verso. British Museum

16 Canterbury: St Luke, from Gospels. *c.* 800. 18½ × 13⅝ in. Royal MS. 1 E. vi, fol. 43. British Museum

17 Mercian: St Luke, from Gospel Book of Cerne. 818–30(?). 9⅛ × 7¾ in. MS. Ll.1.10, fol. 21 verso. University Library, Cambridge

18 (A) Unknown (Winchester?): Daniel, from Embroidered Stole. 909–16. Detail actual size. Cathedral Library, Durham

18 (B) Unknown (Winchester?): Peter Deacon, from Embroidered Maniple. 909–16. Detail actual size. Cathedral Library, Durham

19 Unknown: Presentation of the Book to Pope Gregory, from Rabanus Maurus, *De Laude Crucis*. Tenth century. 16½ × 13½ in. MS. B.16.3, fol. 1 verso. Trinity College, Cambridge

20 (A) Unknown (Winchester?): Æthelstan Presenting the Book to St Cuthbert, from Bede, *Life of St Cuthbert*. *c.* 930. 11½ × 7⅞ in. MS. 183, fol. 1. Corpus Christi College, Cambridge

20 (B) Winchester: Christ Enthroned, from Æthelstan Psalter. Tenth century (first third). Approx. actual size. Cotton MS. Galba A.xviii, fol. 21. British Museum

21 (A) Canterbury: Beatus Initial, from Bosworth Psalter. Late tenth century. Initial 6¾ × 3⅞ in. Additional MS. 37517, fol. 4. British Museum

21 (B) Ramsey Abbey(?): Beatus Initial, from Psalter. Late tenth century. Initial 6¾ × 5¼ in. Harley MS. 2904, fol. 4. British Museum

22 Glastonbury(?): Christ and St Dunstan, prefixed to Composite Volume. Mid tenth century. 9¾ × 7¼ in. MS. Auct. F.4.32, fol. 1. Bodleian Library, Oxford

23 Canterbury or Sherborne Abbey?: God the Son, from Sherborne Pontifical. *c.* 992–5. 12½ × 8 in. MS. lat. 943, fol. 5 verso. Bibliothèque Nationale, Paris

24 Canterbury or Sherborne Abbey?: Crucifixion, from Sherborne Pontifical. *c.* 992–5. 12½ × 8 in. MS. lat. 943, fol. 4 verso. Bibliothèque Nationale, Paris

25 Winchester: King Edgar offering Charter to Christ, from New Minster Charter. Dated 966. 8⅛ × 6⅜ in. Cotton MS. Vesp. A.viii, fol. 2 verso. British Museum

26 Winchester or Ely: Annunciation, from Benedictional of Æthelwold. *c.* 975–80. 11½ × 8¼ in. Fol. 5 verso. Devonshire Collection, Chatsworth

27 Winchester or Ely: Death of the Virgin, from Benedictional of Æthelwold. *c.* 975–980. 11½ × 8¼ in. Fol. 102 verso. Devonshire Collection, Chatsworth

28 (A) Canterbury(?): Christ in Majesty, from Gospels. Late tenth century. 12¼ × 9¼ in. MS. B.10.4, fol. 16 verso. Trinity College, Cambridge

28 (B) Canterbury(?): Historiated Initial with Majesty, from Gospels. Early eleventh century. 13¼ × 10¾ in. Royal MS. 1 D. ix, fol. 70. British Museum

29 (A) Glastonbury: 'Vita', from Leofric Missal. Before 979. 8⅞ × 5⅞ in. Bodley MS. 579, fol. 49 verso. Bodleian Library, Oxford

29 (B) Winchester: Death of the Virgin, from Benedictional of Archbishop Robert. 990–1037(?). 12⅝ × 9⅛ in. MS. Y.7, fol. 54 verso. Bibliothèque Publique, Rouen

30 Ramsey Abbey(?): Crucifixion, from Psalter. Late tenth century. Miniature 9¼ × 7⅜ in. Harley MS. 2904, fol. 3 verso. British Museum

31 Ely(?): Nativity, from Missal of Robert of Jumièges. 1006–23. 13¼ × 8¾ in. MS. Y.6, fol. 32 verso. Bibliothèque Publique, Rouen

32 Canterbury: Illustration to Psalm VII, from Psalter. *c.* 1000. Miniature 4¼ × 9¾ in. Harley MS. 603, fol. 4. British Museum

33 Canterbury: Illustration to Psalm CIX, from Psalter. *c.* 1000. Miniature 4¼ × 9 in. Harley MS. 603, fol. 56 verso. British Museum

34 (A) Canterbury(?): Ploughing, from Hymnal. Early eleventh century. Miniature 1¼ × 4 in. Cotton MS. Jul. A.vi, fol. 3. British Museum

34 (B) Canterbury: Ploughing, from Astronomical Treatises. Early eleventh century. Miniature 2¾ × 7⅝ in. Cotton MS. Tib. B.v, fol. 3. British Museum

35 Canterbury: Building the Tower of Babel, from Ælfric, *Metrical Paraphrase of Pentateuch*. Eleventh century (second quarter). 12⅞ × 8¾ in. Cotton MS. Claud. B.iv, fol. 19. British Museum

36 (A) Winchester: St Luke, from Grimbald Gospels. Early eleventh century. 12¾ × 9¾ in. Additional MS. 34890, fol. 73 verso. British Museum

36 (B) Winchester: St John, from Grimbald Gospels. Early eleventh century. 12¾ × 9¾ in. Additional MS. 34890, fol. 114 verso. British Museum

37 (A) Winchester: Knut and Ælfgyfu, from New Minster Register. 1020–30. 10⅛ × 5¾ in. Stowe MS. 944, fol. 6. British Museum

37 (B) Winchester: Crucifixion, from New Minster Offices. 1023–35. 5 × 3⅞ in. Cotton MS. Titus D.xxvii, fol. 65 verso. British Museum

38 (A) Unknown: Aldhelm and Nuns of Barking, from Aldhelm, De Virginitate. Late tenth century. Miniature 3⅝ × 6¼ in. MS. 200, fol. 68 verso. Lambeth Palace Library, London

38 (B) Malmesbury: 'Luxuria', from Prudentius, Psychomachia. Beginning of eleventh century. Miniature 4¼ × 7⅝ in. MS. 23, fol. 21 verso. Corpus Christi College, Cambridge

39 (A) Bury St Edmunds: Christ Victorious, from Bury Psalter. Eleventh century (second quarter). Detail approx. 9 in. high. MS. Reg. 12, fol. 28. Biblioteca Apostolica Vaticana, Rome

39 (B) Bury St Edmunds: Psalmist on Mt Sion, from Bury Psalter. Eleventh century (second quarter). Detail approx. 9 in. high. MS. Reg. 12, fol. 22. Biblioteca Apostolica Vaticana, Rome

40 Canterbury: Historiated Initial with David and Goliath, from Psalter. c. 1012–23. 11½ × 8¼ in. Arundel MS. 155, fol. 93. British Museum

41 Canterbury: St Benedict and Monks of Canterbury, from Psalter, c. 1012–23. 11½ × 8¼ in. Arundel MS. 155, fol. 133. British Museum

42 Croyland(?) or Ely(?): Christ Triumphant, from Psalter. Eleventh century (second quarter). 10½ × 6¼ in. Douce MS. 296, fol. 40. Bodleian Library, Oxford

43 Winchester(?): Crucifixion, from Weingarten Gospels. Eleventh century (second quarter). 11½ × 7½ in. MS. 709, fol. 1 verso. Pierpont Morgan Library, New York

44 Canterbury(?): Noah's Ark, from Cædmon's Poems. Eleventh century (second quarter). Miniature 9 × 7¾ in. MS. Junius 11, p. 66. Bodleian Library, Oxford

45 Winchester Style (Fen Country?): St John, from Gospels. c. 1050–60. 10 × 6¾ in. MS. BB.437, 439, p. 166. Monte Cassino Library

46 (A) Canterbury: Historiated Initial with Scenes from the Life of St Cesarius, from Martyrology. c. 1100. Detail 4½ × 3¾ in. Arundel MS. 91, fol. 188. British Museum

46 (B) Canterbury: St Michael, from Martyrology. c. 1100. Initial 3¼ × 2¼ in. Arundel MS. 91, fol. 26 verso. British Museum

46 (C) Canterbury: Zodiac Sign 'Virgo', from Martyrology. Twelfth century (first decade). Initial 3½ × 3 in. Cotton MS. Vitellius C.xii, fol. 139. British Museum

47 (A) Anglo-Norman: Landing Horses, from Bayeux Tapestry. c. 1073–83. Detail 1 ft 9 in. × 2 ft 11 in. Town Hall, Bayeux

47 (B) Anglo-Norman: Battle of Hastings, from Bayeux Tapestry. c. 1073–83. Detail 1 ft 9 in. × 2 ft 11 in. Town Hall, Bayeux

48 (A) Unknown: St Matthew, from Gospel Lectionary. Mid eleventh century. 6⅝ × 4⅜ in. MS. Lat. liturg. f.5, fol. 3 verso. Bodleian Library, Oxford

48 (B) Canterbury: The Psalmist between an Angel and a Devil, from Psalter. Eleventh century (second half). Detail 6¼ × 3½ in. Harley MS. 603, fol. 17 verso. British Museum

49 (A) Hereford(?): Scenes from Life of St Lawrence, from Troper. Mid eleventh century. 6⅜ × 3⅝ in. Cotton MS. Caligula A.xiv, fol. 25. British Museum

49 (B) Hereford(?): St Luke, from Gospels. Mid eleventh century. 7¾ × 4 in. MS. 302, fol. 60 verso. Pembroke College, Cambridge

50 Unknown: David, from Psalter. c. 1050. 10 × 6 in. Cotton MS. Tib. C.vi, fol. 10. British Museum

51 Unknown: David and Musicians, from Psalter. c. 1050. 10 × 6 in. Cotton MS. Tib. C.vi, fol. 30 verso. British Museum

52 Winchester: Crucifixion, from Psalter. c. 1060. 12 × 7½ in. Arundel MS. 60, fol. 12 verso. British Museum

53 Winchester: Crucifixion, from Psalter. Eleventh century (third quarter). 12 × 7½ in. Arundel MS. 60, fol. 52 verso. British Museum

54 Canterbury: St Augustine, from Augustine, De Civitate Dei. Early twelfth century. 13¾ × 9⅞ in. MS. Plut. XII. 17, fol. 3 verso. Biblioteca Medicea Laurenziana, Florence

55 Canterbury: Clerics Discussing, from Augustine, De Civitate Dei. Early twelfth century. 13¾ × 9⅞ in. MS. Plut. XII. 17, fol. 4. Biblioteca Medicea Laurenziana, Florence

56 (A) Norman(?): Historiated Initial, from Jerome, Commentary on Isaiah. c. 1100. Initial 6 in. high. Bodley MS. 717, fol. vi verso. Bodleian Library, Oxford

56 (B) Durham(?): Initial with Robertus Benjamin, from Augustine, Commentary on Psalms.

Before 1088. Initial $7\frac{3}{8}$ in. high. MS. B.ii. 13, fol. 102. Cathedral Library, Durham

57 (A) Durham(?): Initial, from Augustine, *Commentary on Psalms*. Before 1088. Initial $4\frac{1}{2} \times 4\frac{1}{4}$ in. MS.B.ii.13, fol. 68. Cathedral Library, Durham

57 (B) Norman(?): Initial, from Carilef Bible. 1088–96. Initial $4\frac{3}{8} \times 5\frac{5}{8}$ in. MS. A.ii.4, fol. 87 verso. Cathedral Library, Durham

58 Norman(?): Beatus Initial, from Carilef Bible. 1088–96. Actual size. MS. A.ii.4, fol. 65. Cathedral Library, Durham

59 (A) St Albans(?): Sobriety, from Prudentius, *Psychomachia*. Early twelfth century. Approx. actual size. Cotton MS. Titus D.xvi, fol. 17 verso. British Museum

59 (B) Durham(?): St Cuthbert's Horse Finds Bread for the Saint, from Bede, *Life of St Cuthbert*. Early twelfth century. Actual size. MS. 165, fol. 11 verso. University College, Oxford

60 St Albans(?): Crucifixion, from Florence of Worcester's Chronicle. c. 1130. Miniature approx. $8\frac{1}{2} \times 5\frac{3}{4}$ in. MS. 157, fol. 77 verso. Corpus Christi College, Oxford

61 St Albans: Adam and Eve Driven from Paradise, from Albani Psalter. 1119–46. $10\frac{7}{8} \times 7\frac{1}{4}$ in. Page 18. Library of St Godehard, Hildesheim

62 (A) St Albans: Beatus Page, from Albani Psalter. 1119–46. $10\frac{7}{8} \times 7\frac{1}{4}$ in. Page 72. Library of St Godehard, Hildesheim

62 (B) St Albans: Initial to Psalm LXV, from Albani Psalter. 1119–46. Initial $7\frac{1}{4}$ in. high. Page 193. Library of St Godehard, Hildesheim

63 (A) Canterbury: St Luke, from Dover Bible. Twelfth century (third quarter). Initial $4\frac{1}{4}$ in. diameter. MS. 4, fol. 191 verso. Corpus Christi College, Cambridge

63 (B) Unknown: St Mark, from Mostyn Gospels. Early twelfth century. $10\frac{3}{8} \times 6\frac{5}{8}$ in. MS. 777, fol. 24 verso. Pierpont Morgan Library, New York

64 Bury St Edmunds(?): Ascension, Decollation of the Baptist, from Bury Gospels. Early twelfth century. $16\frac{1}{4} \times 10\frac{3}{4}$ in. MS. 120, fol. 5 verso. Pembroke College, Cambridge

65 Bury St Edmunds: St Edmund Feeding the Hungry, from *Life of St Edmund*. 1125–50. $10\frac{3}{4} \times 7\frac{1}{4}$ in. MS. 736, fol. 9. Pierpont Morgan Library, New York

66 Bury St Edmunds: Fight with the Danes, from *Life of St Edmund*. 1125–50. $10\frac{3}{4} \times 7\frac{1}{4}$ in. MS.

736, fol. 7 verso. Pierpont Morgan Library, New York

67 (A) Unknown: Scenes from Infancy of Christ, from Bible Picture Leaf. Mid twelfth century. Detail $7\frac{3}{4} \times 11$ in. Additional MS. 37472. British Museum

67 (B) Unknown: Scenes from the Passion from Bible Picture Leaf. Mid twelfth century. Detail $7\frac{3}{4} \times 11$ in. MS. 661. Victoria and Albert Museum, London

68 (A) Hereford(?): Boethius in Prison, from Boethius, *De Consolatione Philosophiae*. Twelfth century (second quarter). 8×5 in. MS. Auct. F.6.5, fol. 1 verso. Bodleian Library, Oxford

68 (B) Hereford(?): St Michael, from Lansdowne Psalter. Mid twelfth century. $8\frac{7}{8} \times 5\frac{3}{8}$ in. Lansdowne MS. 383, fol. 168 verso. British Museum

69 (A) Master Hugo: Prophet Amos, from Bury Bible. 1121–48. Initial approx. $3\frac{5}{8} \times 3\frac{3}{4}$ in. MS. 2, fol. 324. Corpus Christi College, Cambridge

69 (B) Canterbury: Prophet Daniel, from Lambeth Bible. Twelfth century (second half). Initial $3\frac{1}{2}$ in. diameter. MS. 3, fol. 284 verso. Lambeth Palace Library, London

70 Canterbury: St Matthew, from Dover Bible. Twelfth century (third quarter). Initial $5\frac{1}{4} \times 4$ in. MS. 4, fol. 168 verso. Corpus Christi College, Cambridge

71 Canterbury: Portrait of the Scribe Eadwine, from Eadwine Psalter. c. 1150. 18×13 in. MS. R.17.1, fol. 283 verso. Trinity College, Cambridge

72 (A) Canterbury: Illustration for Psalm LI, from Eadwine Psalter. c. 1150. Miniature $5 \times 11\frac{1}{2}$ in. MS. R.17.1, fol. 90 verso. Trinity College, Cambridge

72 (B) Canterbury: Illustration for Psalm XV, from Eadwine Psalter. c. 1150. Miniature $5\frac{1}{2} \times 11\frac{1}{2}$ in. MS. R.17.1, fol. 24. Trinity College, Cambridge

73 Canterbury: Moses and Israelites, from Lambeth Bible. Twelfth century (second half). Miniature $10\frac{1}{8} \times 8\frac{5}{8}$ in. MS. 3, fol. 258. Lambeth Palace Library, London

74 Unknown: Apostles, from Apocalypse Paintings. Mid twelfth century. Detail approx. 5×12 ft. North Chancel Wall, Church of St Mary, Kempley, Gloucestershire

75 (A) Cluniac(?): Adam and Eve, from Wall Paintings. c. 1125. Figures approx. 4 ft high. West Wall of Chancel, Hardham Church, Sussex.

75 (B) Cluniac(?): Praying Saint, from Wall Paintings. Twelfth century (first half). Detail approx. 2 ft 6 in. high. North Wall of Nave, Clayton Church, Sussex

76 Canterbury: St Paul and the Viper, Wall Painting. Mid twelfth century. 5 ft 9 in. × 5 ft 6 in. East Wall, St Anselm's Chapel, Canterbury Cathedral

77 Ramsey Abbey(?): St John, from Bede, *Commentary on the Apocalypse*. Twelfth century (third quarter). 10⅝ × 7 in. MS. H.6, fol. ii verso. St John's College, Cambridge

78 Unknown: Madonna and Child, prefixed to Augustine, *Commentary on Psalms*. Twelfth century (second half). 10⅜ × 6½ in. Bodley MS. 269, fol. iii. Bodleian Library, Oxford

79 Italo-Byzantine(?): Virgin Enthroned, from Psalter. Twelfth century (third quarter). 12¾ × 9 in. Cotton MS. Nero C.iv, fol. 30. British Museum

80 Winchester: Adoration of the Magi, from Psalter. 1150–60. 12¾ × 9 in. Cotton MS. Nero C.iv, fol. 12. British Museum

81 York(?): Sacrifice of Abraham, Bible Picture, from Psalter. c. 1175. 11⅜ × 7¾ in. MS. U.3.2. Hunterian Museum, Glasgow

82 St Albans: Illustration for Terence, *Comedies*. Mid twelfth century. Detail 6½ × 8½ in. MS. Auct. F.2.13, fol. 125 verso. Bodleian Library, Oxford

83 (A) Winchester: Initial for II Maccabees, from Bible. c. 1160–70. Initial 4¼ × 3½ in. Fol. 363. Cathedral Library, Winchester

83 (B) Winchester: Initial for Jeremiah, from Bible. c. 1160–70. Initial 4⅜ × 5 in. Fol. 148. Cathedral Library, Winchester

84 (A) Winchester: Initial for Zephaniah, from Bible. c. 1160–70. Initial 4⅜ × 4¼ in. Fol. 209. Cathedral Library, Winchester

84 (B) Winchester: Initial for Joshua, from Bible. c. 1160–70. Initial 5¼ × 5¼ in. Fol. 69. Cathedral Library, Winchester

85 (A) Winchester: Initial for Daniel, from Bible. c. 1160–70. Initial 4¾ × 4⅜ in. Fol. 190. Cathedral Library, Winchester

85 (B) Winchester: Initial for Isaiah, from Bible. c. 1160–70. Initial 4⅜ × 4⅝ in. Fol. 131. Cathedral Library, Winchester

86 Winchester: Scenes from Life of David, from Bible Picture Leaf. Twelfth century (third quarter). 22⅝ in. × 15¼ in. MS. 619. Pierpont Morgan Library, New York

87 (A) Durham(?): Initial for Corinthians, from Pauline Epistles. 1153–95. Detail 15 × 5¼ in. MS. A.ii.19, fol. 87 verso. Cathedral Library, Durham

87 (B) Durham(?): Initial for II Kings, from Pudsey Bible. 1153–95. Detail approx. 9 × 3 in. MS. A.ii.1, fol. 173. Cathedral Library, Durham

88 (A) Unknown: The Unicorn, from Bestiary. Late twelfth century. Miniature 4⅛ × 4⅛ in. MS. Ashmole 1511, fol. 14 verso. Bodleian Library, Oxford

88 (B) Radford Priory(?): Tiger, from 'Worksop' Bestiary. Before 1187(?). Miniature 3½ × 4 in. MS. 81, fol. 35. Pierpont Morgan Library, New York

89 St Albans or Westminster(?): Christ in Majesty, from Westminster Psalter. c. 1200. 9 × 6¼ in. Royal MS. 2 A. xxii, fol. 14. British Museum

90 (A) St Albans: Symbol of St Matthew, from Glossed Gospels. c. 1200. Approx. actual size MS. B.5.3, fol. 4 verso. Trinity College, Cambridge

90 (B) St Albans or Westminster(?): Annunciation, from Westminster Psalter. c. 1200. 9 × 6¼ in. Royal MS. 2 A. xxii, fol. 12 verso. British Museum

91 Canterbury: Illustration for Psalm LI, from Psalter. c. 1200. Miniature 6⅜ × 11½ in. MS. lat. 8846, fol. 90 verso. Bibliothèque Nationale, Paris

92 Canterbury(?): Trinity, from Lothian Bible. c. 1200. 14 × 10 in. MS. 791, fol. 4 verso. Pierpont Morgan Library, New York

93 Canterbury: Methuselah, Panel from Stained Glass Window. Late twelfth century. 5 ft × 2 ft 5 in. Clerestory, South-west Transept. Canterbury Cathedral

94 (A) Unknown: Beatus Page, from Psalter. Early thirteenth century. 12 × 8¼ in. Lansdowne MS. 420, fol. 12 verso. British Museum

94 (B) Durham(?): St Cuthbert, from Bede, *Life of St Cuthbert*. c. 1200. 5⅜ × 3⅞ in. Additional MS. 39943, fol. 1 verso. British Museum

95 (A) Canterbury: Medallion, from Stained Glass Window. c. 1220. Detail approx. 3 ft diameter. Trinity Chapel, Canterbury Cathedral

95 (B) Croyland Abbey: Guthlac Receives the Tonsure, from *Life of St Guthlac*. c. 1200. 6 in. diameter. Harley Roll Y.6. British Museum

96 Canterbury: Genesis Initial, from Bible of Robert de Bello. 1224–53. 10⅞ × 7⅞ in. Burney MS. 3, fol. 5 verso. British Museum

97 Canterbury: Biblical Scenes, from Stained-Glass Window. *c.* 1220. Detail approx. 11 × 7 ft. Corona. Canterbury Cathedral

98 W. de Brailes: Scenes from Genesis, Bible Picture Leaf. *c.* 1230–50. 9⅞ × 6⅞ in. MS. 330. Fitzwilliam Museum, Cambridge

99 (A) W. de Brailes (signed): Portrait of W. de Brailes, from Last Judgement. *c.* 1230–50. Detail 1¼ in. diameter. MS. 330. Fitzwilliam Museum, Cambridge

99 (B) W. de Brailes: Christ Walking on the Water, from Bible Pictures. *c.* 1230–50. 5¼ × 3⅞ in. MS. 500, fol. 20. Walters Art Gallery, Baltimore

99 (C) W. de Brailes: Initial with Trinity for Psalm CIX, from Psalter. *c.* 1230–50. Actual size. Fol. 111. Sir Sydney Cockerell, Kew, Richmond

100 Peterborough: Beatus Page, from Psalter of Robert de Lindesey. 1214–22. 9½ × 6 in. MS. 59, fol. 38 verso. Society of Antiquaries, London

101 Canterbury(?): Genesis Page, from Bible of William of Devon. *c.* mid thirteenth century. 12⅜ × 8 in. Royal MS. 1 D. i, fol. 5. British Museum

102 Salisbury(?): Crucifixion, from Psalter. *c.* mid thirteenth century. 12 × 8⅛ in. MS. lat. 6, fol. 5. All Souls College, Oxford

103 Evesham: Crucifixion with a Bishop as Donor, from Psalter. Mid thirteenth century. 12⅜ × 8 in. Additional MS. 44874, fol. 6. British Museum

104 Salisbury(?): Virgin and Child, from 'Missal of Henry of Chichester'. Mid thirteenth century. 12½ × 8 in. MS. lat. R.24, fol. 150. John Rylands Library, Manchester

105 Salisbury(?): Virgin and Child, Painted Roundel. Mid thirteenth century. 2 ft 6 in. diameter. Chapel of the Bishop's Palace, Chichester

106 Matthew Paris (signed): Virgin and Child, from Matthew Paris, *Historia Anglorum.* Before 1259. 14 × 9⅜ in. Royal MS. 14 C. vii, fol. 6. British Museum

107 (A) Matthew Paris: Alban watching Amphibalus Kneeling before the Cross, from *Lives of Saints Alban and Amphibalus.* Mid thirteenth century. Detail 4¼ × 6¼ in. MS. E.1.40, fol. 31. Trinity College, Dublin

107 (B) Matthew Paris, assistant: Brihtwold Bishop of Winchester Relates his Vision, the Young Edward praying, from *La Estoire de Seint Aedward le Rei.* Thirteenth century (third quarter). Detail 5¼ × 7¾ in. MS. Ee.3.59, p. 11. University Library, Cambridge

108 Matthew Paris: Heads of Christ and the Virgin, from Matthew Paris, *Chronica Maiora.* Mid thirteenth century, 14¼ × 9⅝ in. MS. 26, fol. 281. Corpus Christi College, Cambridge

109 (A) Court Style(?): Majesty, Wall Painting. *c.* 1230. Figure 3 ft 4 in. high. Vault, Chapel of the Holy Sepulchre, Winchester Cathedral

109 (B) Court Style(?): Deposition, Wall Painting. *c.* 1230. Detail 4 ft 11 in. × 7 ft 6 in. East Wall, Chapel of the Holy Sepulchre, Winchester Cathedral

110 (A) Matthew Paris: Head of Christ, from Matthew Paris, *Chronica Minora.* Mid thirteenth century. Miniature 5¾ × 6 in. MS. 16, fol. 49 verso. Corpus Christi College, Cambridge

110 (B) Matthew Paris(?): Head of a King, Wall Painting. Mid thirteenth century. Over life-size. Cloister, Windsor Castle

111 St Albans(?): St John and the Angel, from Apocalypse. *c.* 1230. Miniature 4½ × 8¼ in. MS. R.16. 2, fol. 27. Trinity College, Cambridge

112 St Albans: The Apocalyptic Woman, St Michael and Dragon, from Apocalypse. Mid thirteenth century, 10¾ × 7⅝ in. MS. 524, fol. 8 verso. Pierpont Morgan Library, New York

113 (A) Canterbury: St John and the Angel, from Apocalypse. *c.* 1270. Miniature 4½ × 5¾ in. Douce MS. 180, p. 33. Bodleian Library, Oxford

113 (B) Canterbury: St John and the Angel, from Apocalypse. Thirteenth century (third quarter). Miniature 4½ × 6 in. MS. 209, fol. 39. Lambeth Palace Library, London

114 (A) Court Style: Gesso Head imitating Cameo, from Frame of Retable. Thirteenth century (last quarter). 1 in. across. South Ambulatory, Westminster Abbey

114 (B) Court Style: Feeding the Five Thousand, from Retable. Thirteenth century (last quarter). Detail approx. actual size. South Ambulatory, Westminster Abbey

115 (A) Master Walter of Durham: The Incredulity of Thomas. Detail of Wall Painting. *c.* 1300. 8 ft 9 in. high. South Transept, Westminster Abbey

115 (B) Court Style: St Peter, from Retable. Thirteenth century (last quarter). Approx.

actual size. South Ambulatory, Westminster Abbey

116 (A) Worcester(?): Kings, from Fragment of Worcester Embroideries. 1236–66. Detail 12⅞ × 10½ in. Edward VII Gallery, British Museum

116 (B) Court Style(?): Richard Cœur de Lion, Tile from Chertsey Abbey. Thirteenth century (second half). 16 in. square. Edward VII Gallery, British Museum

117 Unknown: Crucifixion, Madonna, Saints Peter and Paul, and Martyrdom of Stephen, Clare Chasuble. Before 1284. 3 ft 3½ in. × 2 ft 8 in. Victoria and Albert Museum, London

118 London (?): Beatus Page, from Tenison Psalter. Before 1284. 9½ × 6¼ in. Additional MS. 24686, fol. 11. British Museum

119 East Anglian: Ornamental Text Page, from Windmill Psalter. Late thirteenth century. 12⅝ × 8¼ in. MS. 102, fol. 2. Pierpont Morgan Library, New York

120 East Anglian (Peterborough): Beatus Page, from Peterborough Psalter. c. 1300. 11¾ × 7⅝ in. MS. 9961–2, fol. 14. Bibliothèque Royale, Brussels

121 East Anglian (Ramsey Abbey): Martyrdom of St Thomas Becket, Bible Picture, from a Psalter. c. 1300. 10 × 6⅝ in. MS. 302, fol. 8. Pierpont Morgan Library, New York

122 East Anglian (Peterborough or Norwich): Virgin and St Christopher, from Peterborough Psalter. Early fourteenth century. 13⅝ × 9¼ in. MS. 53, fol. 16. Corpus Christi College, Cambridge

123 East Anglian(?): Adoration of the Magi, from Queen Mary's Psalter. Early fourteenth century. 10⅞ × 6⅞ in. Royal MS. 2 B. vii, fol. 112 verso. British Museum

124 East Anglian (Artist of Queen Mary's Psalter): St John and the Angel, from Apocalypse. c. 1320–30. Miniature 5¼ × 5 in. Royal MS. 19 B. xv, fol. 5 verso. British Museum

125 East Anglian (Norwich): Illustration to Psalm CIX, from Ormesby Psalter. c. 1310–25. 14⅞ × 10 in. Douce MS. 366, fol. 147 verso. Bodleian Library, Oxford

126 (A) East Anglian (Gorleston): Resurrected Christ appearing to David, from Gorleston Psalter. c. 1310–25. Detail approx. 4 in. square. MS. 13, fol. 52 verso. C. W. Dyson Perrins, Malvern

126 (B) East Anglian (Norwich): Grotesques, from Ormesby Psalter. c. 1310–25. Detail

3½ × 10 in. Douce MS. 366, fol. 131. Bodleian Library, Oxford

127 East Anglian (Gorleston?): Angel with the Sickle, from Apocalypse. Early fourteenth century. 14¼ × 8⅛ in. MS. K.4.31, no. xliii. Trinity College, Dublin

128 East Anglian (Midlands?): Initial with Christ blessing, Border with Grotesques, from Book of Hours. c. 1308. 9½ × 6 in. MS. 242, fol. 29. Fitzwilliam Museum, Cambridge

129 East Anglian: Beatus Page, from St-Omer Psalter. c. 1330. 13⅛ × 8¼ in. Additional MS. 39810, fol. 7. British Museum

130 (A) East Anglian: Ascension, from Psalter of Robert de Lisle. Before 1339. Miniature 11 × 7¼ in. Arundel MS. 83, fol. 133 verso. British Museum

130 (B) East Anglian: 'The Three Living', from Psalter of Robert de Lisle. Before 1339. Miniature 4⅝ × 3¾ in. Arundel MS. 83, fol. 127. British Museum

131 (A) East Anglian: Beatus Initial, from Luttrell Psalter. c. 1340. Detail 7⅞ × 9⅝ in. Additional MS. 42130, fol. 13. British Museum

131 (B) East Anglian: Marginal Scene and Grotesque, from Luttrell Psalter. c. 1340. Detail 7 × 9⅝ in. Additional MS. 42130, fol. 169 verso. British Museum

132 (A) London (St Bartholomew's, Smithfield?): Fox Killed by Geese, from Smithfield Decretals. Mid fourteenth century or earlier. Detail 3⅞ × 5¾ in. Royal MS. 10 E. iv, fol. 48 verso. British Museum

132 (B) London (St Bartholomew's, Smithfield?): Monk and Lady in Stocks, from Smithfield Decretals. Mid fourteenth century or earlier. Detail 2⅞ × 6⅝ in. Royal MS. 10 E. iv, fol. 187. British Museum

132 (C) London (St Bartholomew's, Smithfield?): The King's Messenger, from Smithfield Decretals. Mid fourteenth century or earlier. Detail 2¼ × 5⅝ in. Royal MS. 10 E. iv, fol. 302 verso. British Museum

133 London(?): A Tournament and Grotesques, from Treatise of Walter de Milemete, c. 1326–7. 9⅝ × 6¼ in. MS. E.11, fol. 68. Christ Church Library, Oxford

134 Unknown: Creation of the Birds and Animals, from Holkham Bible Picture Book. Fourteenth century (first half). 11¼ × 8¼ in. Additional MS. 47682, fol. 2 verso. British Museum

135 Canterbury(?): Christ in Majesty, Embroidered Panel. Early fourteenth century.

3 ft 3½ in. × 16½ in. Victoria and Albert Museum, London

136 Unknown: The Syon Cope. *c.* 1300. 9 ft 8 in. × 4 ft 10 in. Victoria and Albert Museum, London

137 Unknown: Embroidered Cope. Early fourteenth century. 10 ft 7 in. × 4 ft 10 in. Museo Civico, Bologna

138 (A) Unknown: Crucifixion, St Michael, and Angels, from Syon Cope. *c.* 1300. Detail approx. 2 ft high. Victoria and Albert Museum, London

138 (B) Unknown: Coronation of the Virgin, from Vatican Cope. *c.* 1300. Detail approx. 27 in. high. Museo Sacro, Biblioteca Apostolica Vaticana, Rome

139 Unknown: Scenes from the Life of the Virgin, from Embroidered Altar Dorsal. Fourteenth century (first quarter). Detail approx. 10½ × 13 in. Victoria and Albert Museum, London

140 East Anglian(?): Crucifixion with Peter and Paul, Centre Panels of Painted Retable. Early fourteenth century. Detail 4 ft 6 in. × 3 ft. Thornham Parva Church, Suffolk

141 (A) East Anglian(?): Nativity of Christ from Painted Panel. *c.* 1325–30. Detail approx. 3 ft square. Musée de Cluny, Paris

141 (B) East Anglian(?): Education of the Virgin, from Painted Panel. *c.* 1325–30. Detail approx. 3 ft square. Musée de Cluny, Paris

142 Court School (Master Thomas?): Two unidentified Kings. Sedilia Paintings. *c.* 1308. Each panel 9 ft × 2 ft 8 in. South Side of Choir, Westminster Abbey

143 (A) Influence of Peterborough(?): Scenes from the Passion, Wall Paintings. Fourteenth century (second quarter). Approx. 22 ft long. North Wall of Nave, Peakirk, Northamptonshire

143 (B) Influence of Peterborough(?): Wheel of the Five Senses, from Wall Paintings. Fourteenth century (second quarter). Detail approx. 6 ft high. East Wall, Tower, Longthorpe Manor, Northamptonshire

144 York School: Peter de Dene Stained Glass Window. *c.* 1310. Detail approx. 16 × 10 ft. North Aisle, York Minster

145 (A) Unknown: St Peter, from Great East Window. *c.* 1349. Detail approx. 9 × 3 ft. East Wall, Choir, Gloucester Cathedral

145 (B) Unknown: Knight, from Clerestory Window. *c.* 1344. Detail approx. 4 ft high. Choir, Tewkesbury Abbey

146 York School: Coronation of the Virgin, and other Subjects, Stained Glass Window. *c.* 1338. 54 ft 3 in. × 25 ft 3 in. West Wall, Nave, York Minster

147 Unknown: Coronation of the Virgin, and other Subjects, Great East Window. *c.* 1349. 78 × 38 ft. East Wall, Choir, Gloucester Cathedral

148 (A) Italianate-English: Creation, from Psalter. Fourteenth century (second half). 8⅜ × 4⅞ in. MS. Pal. lat. 537, fol. 36. Biblioteca Apostolica Vaticana, Rome

148 (B) Italianate-English: The Angel Gabriel, from Carew-Poyntz Hours. Fourteenth century (second half). 7⅛ × 4⅝ in. MS. J.48, fol. 62 verso. Fitzwilliam Museum, Cambridge

149 (A) 'Bohun MSS Style': Scenes from the Life of Christ, from a Bohun Psalter. *c.* 1370–80. Initial 4⅛ × 5¼ in. Egerton MS. 3277, fol 123. British Museum

149 (B) 'Bohun MSS Style': Christ Carrying the Cross, and Adoration of the Magi, from Psalter. Late fourteenth century. Miniature 4⅞ × 2½ in. Additional MS. 16968, fol. 20. British Museum

150 (A) Italianate-English: Scenes from the Passion, from the M. R. James Memorial Psalter. Late fourteenth century. Miniature 4⅜ in. square. Additional MS. 44949, fol. 4. British Museum

150 (B) Italianate-English: Head. Detail of Wall Painting from St Stephen's Chapel. Fourteenth century (third quarter). Head 2⅝ in. high. Edward VII Gallery, British Museum

150 (C) 'Bohun MSS Style': Head, from Bohun Psalter. *c.* 1370–80. Detail 1⅞ × 1¼ in. Egerton MS. 3277, fol. 46 verso. British Museum

151 (A) Court School: Seraph from Last Judgement, Wall Painting. Fourteenth century (third quarter). Detail approx. 4 ft wide. Chapter House, Westminster Abbey

151 (B) Italianate-English: Story of Job, Wall Painting, from Stephen's Chapel, Westminster. Fourteenth century (third quarter). Detail approx. 10¾ × 12¼ in. Edward VII Gallery, British Museum

152 English (Court School?): Richard and his Patron Saints, Left Side of Wilton Diptych. 1380–90(?). 14½ × 10½ in. National Gallery, London

153 English (Court School?): Madonna among Angels. Right Side of Wilton Diptych.

1380–90(?). 14½ × 10½ in. National Gallery, London

154 London (Thomas Rolf?): Crucifixion, from Lytlington Missal. 1383–4. 20¾ × 14⅛ in. Fol. 157 verso. Westminster Abbey Library

155 London (Westminster?): Coronation of a King, from *Liber Regalis. c.* 1382. 10½ × 7 in. Fol. 1 verso. Westminster Abbey Library, London

156 (A) London (Whitefriars?): Trinity and Baptism, from Carmelite Missal. 1393–8. Initial 4½ in. square. Additional MS. 29704–29705, fol. 36 verso. British Museum

156 (B) London (Whitefriars?): Birth of the Virgin, from Carmelite Missal. 1393–8. Initial 4½ in. square. Additional MS. 29704–5, fol. 138 verso. British Museum

157 'Johannes': View of Venice, from Marco Polo, *Li Livres du Graunt Caam. c.* 1400. Detail 9¼ × 12½ in. Bodley MS. 264, fol. 218. Bodleian Library, Oxford

158 Unknown: Kings and Prophets, from Painted Ceiling. Fourteenth century (last decade). Single figures approx. 4 ft 9 in. high. Lady Chapel, St Helen's Church, Abingdon

159 (A) East Anglian(?): Resurrection and Ascension, from Painted Retable. Late fourteenth century. Detail approx. 2 ft 10½ in. × 3 ft 5 in. South Choir Aisle, Norwich Cathedral

159 (B) East Anglian(?): Christ before Pilate, fragment from Painted Panel. Late fourteenth century. Detail 12¾ × 11 in. No. 706. Fitzwilliam Museum, Cambridge

160 (A) Siferwas School(?): Group of Men from Last Judgement, Wall Painting. Late fourteenth century. Detail approx. 4 ft square. Chapter House, Westminster Abbey

160 (B) Meister Bertram School(?): Apocalypse, Wall Painting. Before 1400. Detail approx. 4 ft square. Chapter House, Westminster Abbey

161 John Siferwas: Crucifixion, from Sherborne Missal. 1396–1407. 21 × 15 in. Page 380. Duke of Northumberland, Alnwick Castle

162 Unknown: Portrait of King Richard II. Fourteenth century (last decade). 7 ft × 3 ft 7 in. South Side of Nave, Westminster Abbey, London

163 John Siferwas: Lord Lovell and John Siferwas, from Lovell Lectionary. Before 1408. Miniature 11¾ × 7¼ in. Harley MS. 7026, fol. 4 verso. British Museum

164 Unknown: Sketches of Birds and Animals from Pepysian Sketch Book. Late fourteenth century. 9¾ × 7¾ in. MS. 1916, fol. 11 verso. Pepysian Library, Magdalene College, Cambridge

165 John Siferwas: Detail of Marginal Border, from Sherborne Missal. 1396–1407. Detail approx. 12½ × 9 in. Page 388. Duke of Northumberland, Alnwick Castle

166 'de daer': Annunciation, from Beaufort Hours. 1401–10. 8½ × 5¼ in. Royal MS. 2 A. xviii, fol. 23 verso. British Museum

167 Herman Scheerre(?): Crucifixion, Single Leaf from a Missal. Early fifteenth century. 14¾ × 10¼ in. A. Wyndham Payne, Dartmouth

168 (A) Associate of Herman Scheerre: Creation of the Animals, from Bible, *c.* 1410. Initial approx. 3½ in. square. Royal MS. 1 E. ix, fol. 3 verso. British Museum

168 (B) Herman Scheerre(?): Baptism of Christ, from Bible. *c.* 1410. Initial approx. 4 in. square. Royal MS. 1 E. ix, fol. 262 verso. British Museum

169 (A) Herman Scheerre(?): Pietà, from Book of Hours. 1405–13. 5⅞ × 4⅞ in. MS. Lat. liturg. f.2, fol. 10. Bodleian Library, Oxford

169 (B) Unknown: Portrait of Geoffrey Chaucer, from Hoccleve, *De Regimine Principum.* Early fifteenth century. Miniature 3 × 1½ in. Harley MS. 4866, fol. 88. British Museum

169 (C) Unknown Follower of Herman Scheerre: Prince Henry and Hoccleve, from Hoccleve, *De Regimine Principum.* Before 1413. Detail 5⅜ × 4 in. Arundel MS. 38, fol. 37. British Museum

170 Bury St Edmunds(?): Chaucer Reading, from Chaucer, *Troilus and Criseyde.* Early fifteenth century. 12½ × 8⅜ in. MS. 61, fol. 1 verso. Corpus Christi College, Cambridge

171 John Thornton of Coventry: Apocalypse, Stained Glass Window. 1405–8. 72 × 31 ft. East Wall, Choir, York Minster

172 (A) Master Thomas (signed) of Oxford: Prophet Nathan, and Fragments including Hand of Jesse, from Jesse Window. *c.* 1393. Detail 3 ft 2 in. × 2 ft 1 in. West Window, Thurbern's Chantry, Winchester College Chapel

172 (B) Master Thomas of Oxford: Prophet Amos, from Jesse Window, 1380–6. Detail approx. 3 × 2 ft. South Aisle, Choir, York Minster. Formerly in Antechapel, New College, Oxford

173 (A) Master Thomas of Oxford: Prophet Zephaniah and St James. Stained Glass Panels from Winchester College Chapel, Clerestory. *c.* 1400. Detail approx. 5 ft 9 in. × 1 ft 9 in. each panel. Victoria and Albert Museum, London

173 (B) John Thornton of Coventry: David, from Great East Window. 1405–8. Detail approx. 3 ft high. East Wall, Choir, York Minster

174 (A) Unknown: David Playing Bells, from St-Omer Psalter. Fifteenth century (second quarter). Initial $3\frac{5}{8} \times 3\frac{3}{4}$ in. Additional MS. 39810, fol. 87. British Museum

174 (B) London(?): The Author Writing, from Christine de Pisan, *Le Livre des fays d'armes*. Dated 1434. Miniature $4\frac{3}{8} \times 5\frac{1}{8}$ in. Harley MS. 4605, fol. 3. British Museum

175 (A) Bury St Edmunds: King Henry VI receiving the Book, from Lydgate, *Life of St Edmund*. 1433–4. Miniature $4 \times 4\frac{3}{8}$ in. Harley MS. 2278, fol. 6. British Museum

175 (B) Unknown: Richard the Hermit, from *Desert of Religion*. Fifteenth century (second quarter). Detail $6\frac{1}{2} \times 3\frac{3}{4}$ in. Cotton MS. Faustina B.vi, pt. 2, fol. 8 verso. British Museum

176 Bury St. Edmunds(?): The Earl of Salisbury receiving the Book, from Lydgate, *The Pilgrim*. Mid fifteenth century. Miniature $7\frac{1}{8} \times 5$ in. Harley MS. 4826, fol. 1★. British Museum

177 Oxford(?): Bishop Bekynton receiving the Book, from Chaundler, *Works*. 1457–61. $10\frac{1}{6} \times 8$ in. MS. R.14.5, fol. 8 verso. Trinity College, Cambridge

178 Oxford(?): Crucifixion with Bishop as Donor, from Abingdon Missal. Dated 1461. $14\frac{1}{8} \times 9\frac{1}{2}$ in. MS. Digby 227, fol. 113 verso. Bodleian Library, Oxford

179 Unknown: Tournament, from *Ordinances of Chivalry*. *c.* 1470. $9\frac{5}{8} \times 6\frac{5}{8}$ in. MS. 775, fol. 2 verso. Pierpont Morgan Library, New York

180 Ely(?): Life of St Etheldreda, Painted Panels. *c.* 1425. Each panel 3 ft $10\frac{1}{2}$ in. × 1 ft 9 in. Society of Antiquaries, London

181 East Anglian: St Leonard and Female Saint, from Painted Screen, formerly in St John Maddermarket, Norwich. 1451. 3 ft 4 in. × 2 ft $5\frac{1}{2}$ in. Victoria and Albert Museum, London

182 East Anglian: Two of the Nine Orders of Angels, from Painted Screen. After 1480. Each panel approx. 2 ft $3\frac{1}{2}$ in. × 7 in. Barton Turf Church, Norfolk

183 East Anglian: Apostles Philip and Paul, from Painted Screen. 1490–1510. Each panel approx. 1 ft $7\frac{3}{4}$ in. × $5\frac{3}{4}$ in. Cawston Church, Norfolk

184 (A) William Baker (in part): Miracle of the Candle, from Wall Paintings. 1479–88. Detail 4 ft 10 in. × 6 ft 4 in. North Wall, Eton College Chapel

184 (B) William Baker (in part): Healing of the Knight's Brother, Wall Painting. 1479–88. Detail approx. 4 ft 10 in. × 3 ft. South Wall, Eton College Chapel

185 Unknown: Doom, Wall Painting. *c.* 1500. Approx. 22 ft wide. Chancel Arch, St Thomas, Salisbury

186 John Prudde (documented): Saints Thomas of Canterbury and Alban, from Stained Glass Window. 1447–50. Each panel 4 ft 5 in. × 1 ft $8\frac{1}{2}$ in. East Window, Beauchamp Chapel, St Mary's Church, Warwick

187 'John Glazier': Saints Etheldreda, Catherine, and Sativola, from Stained Glass Window. 1440–50. Each light 6 ft $9\frac{1}{2}$ in. × 1 ft $3\frac{1}{2}$ in. South Window, East Wall, Antechapel, All Souls College, Oxford

188 (A) Norwich School: Visitation, from Stained Glass Window. *c.* 1440. Detail 2 ft 6 in. × 1 ft 8 in. East Window, St Peter Mancroft, Norwich

188 (B) Norwich School: Donor Portrait, from Stained Glass Window. Late fifteenth century. 2 ft 7 in. × 1 ft 6 in. East Window, East Harling Church, Norfolk

189 (A) York School: Miracle of St William, from St William Window. *c.* 1421. Detail 2 ft 2 in. × 1 ft 6 in. North Choir Transept, York Minster

189 (B) York School: St Christopher, from Stained Glass Window. *c.* 1440–50. 4 ft 6 in. × 1 ft 10 in. East Window, All Saints in North Street, York

190 York School(?): Last Supper, from Stained Glass Window. *c.* 1430–40. Detail 4 ft 6 in. × 2 ft 6 in. East Window, Choir, Priory Church, Gt Malvern

191 York School(?): Bishop Wulstan, from Founders' Window. *c.* 1460–70. Detail 7 ft 6 in. × 2 ft 6 in. North Clerestory, Choir, Priory Church, Gt Malvern

192 London(?): Prince Arthur, from Magnificat Window. 1501. Detail 4 ft 2 in. × 2 ft. North Transept, Priory Church, Gt Malvern

ACKNOWLEDGEMENTS FOR THE PLATES

ACKNOWLEDGEMENTS are made for permission to reproduce the following: Plates 8A, 10A, 18A, 18B, 47A, 47B, 56B, 57A, 57B, 58, 65, 66, 76, 77, 81, 86, 87A, 87B, 93, 95A, 97, 102, 119, 140, 154, 159A, 161, 162, 164, 165, 177, 180, by courtesy of the Victoria and Albert Museum – Plates 67B, 117, 135, 136, 138A, 139, 173A, 181 (V. and A. Crown copyright) – Plates 26, 27, 38B, 61, 62A, 62B, 69A, 69B, 73, 83A, 83B, 84A, 84B, 85A, 85B, 114A, 114B, 115B, by courtesy of the Warburg Institute – Plates 38A, 113B, by courtesy of Dr G. Zarnecki and the Courtauld Institute of Art – Plate 134, by courtesy of the Courtauld Institute of Art, and reproduced from the Holkham Bible Picture Book by permission of the Dropmore Press Ltd – Plates 29B, 31, by courtesy of the Bibliothèque Nationale, Paris – Plates 74, 145A, 145B, 189A, 189B, 190, 191, 192 (National Buildings Record and Sydney Pitcher) – Plates 105, 109A, 109B (National Buildings Record and C. J. P. Cave) – Plates 182, 183 (National Buildings Record and E. C. Le Grice) – Plate 75, A and B (Helmut Gernsheim, reproduced by permission of Miller's Press, Lewes) – Plates 115A, 151A, 160, A and B, 187 (Crown copyright) by permission of the Controller of H.M. Stationery Office – Plates 146, 147, 171 (Walter Scott) – Plates 172A, 188, A and B (Dennis King) – Plates 98 and 159B, by courtesy of the Victoria and Albert Museum. Reproduced from the original in the Fitzwilliam Museum, Cambridge, by permission of the Syndics – Plates 99A, 128, 148B, reproduced from the original in the Fitzwilliam Museum, Cambridge, by permission of the Syndics – Plate 110B, by permission of Mrs Eileen Tristram, the owner of the copyright, from Supplementary plate 18 in *English Medieval Wall Painting (XIII century)*, by E.W. Tristram, Oxford University Press, 1950 – Plate 142 (R. P. Howgrave-Graham) – Plate 143A (E. C. Rouse) – 143B (St A. F. St John, Rector of Peakirk and Glinton) – Plates 144, 172B (W. J. Green) – Plate 158 by courtesy of the Oxford Architectural and Historical Society – Plate 173B (G. Bernard Wood) – Plate 184, A and B (Country Life) – Plate 185 (Harold Allen. Copyright by the Vicar of Sarum St Thomas) – Plate 186 by courtesy of Philip B. Chatwin.

ABBREVIATIONS

Anc. Lib. Cant. and Dover	Ancient Libraries of Canterbury and Dover
Archaeol. Jnl	Archaeological Journal
Art Bull.	Art Bulletin
Brit. Mus. Quart.	British Museum Quarterly
Bull. de la S.F.R.M.P.	Bulletin de la Société Française de Reproductions de Manuscrits à Peintures
Burl. Mag.	Burlington Magazine
Jnl Brit. Archaeol. Assn	Journal of the British Archaeological Association
Jnl Brit. Soc. Master Glass-Painters	Journal of the British Society of Master Glass-Painters
Jnl Roy. Soc. Antiq. Ireland	Journal of the Royal Society of Antiquaries of Ireland
Jnl Warb. Court. Insts	Journal of the Warburg and Courtauld Institutes
N.B.R.	National Buildings Record
New Pal. Soc.	New Palaeographical Society
Pal. Soc.	Palaeographical Society
Proc. Brit. Acad.	Proceedings of the British Academy
Proc. Camb. Antiq. Soc.	Proceedings of the Cambridge Antiquarian Society
Proc. Royal Irish Acad.	Proceedings of the Royal Irish Academy
Proc. Soc. Antiq.	Proceedings of the Society of Antiquaries
R.C.H.M.	Royal Commission on Historical Monuments
Roy. Acad. Arts Exhib. Brit. Prim. Paintings, Cat.	Royal Academy of Arts Exhibition of British Primitive Paintings, Catalogue
Roy. Soc. Lit. Trans.	Royal Society of Literature, Transactions
Summary Cat.	A Summary Catalogue of Western Manuscripts in the Bodleian Library
Walpole Soc.	Walpole Society

FOREWORD

THE *preparation of the material for this book, which had to be done largely in England, has incurred deep obligations to friends and associates on both sides of the water. The Administration of the University of Chicago, by granting for purposes of research generous periods free of teaching, and the Chairman, Dr Ulrich Middeldorf, and my colleagues in the Department of Art at the University, by assuming additional academic responsibilities on my behalf, have made possible the necessarily frequent visits to England and the Continent during the past five years. The University also contributed towards the purchase of the many photographs needed. Of my personal and academic associates in America who have assisted materially in the preparation of the book, I am especially grateful to Miss Winifred VerNooy, Reference Librarian at the University of Chicago, and the staffs of the various libraries there for timely help with difficult problems. My former student, Mr Frank Horlbeck, who gave me faithful clerical and research assistance over a period of more than two years, has my sincere thanks. My friends Miss Lucile Gafford and Mrs Rose Jameson who carefully read the text of this book, the one in typescript the other in proof, made many valuable suggestions as to content and form from the point of view of the 'intelligent lay reader'. And my friends, Arthur and Alfred Thurner, stood by loyally as expert typists helping on more than one occasion to meet a dead-line for the delivery of manuscript.*

On this side of the Atlantic there have been too many helping hands to permit naming them individually. The staffs of the Reading Room and the Department of Manuscripts and the Photographic Department at the British Museum never failed to meet the unusual request and to attempt the impossible in order to facilitate maximum results in minimum time. Dr Otto Pächt and the Librarian and Staff of the Bodleian Library, and the Librarians of University Library and of many of the colleges at Cambridge also have been exceedingly helpful in making their resources available to me.

In the task of assembling the hundreds of photographs from which the final selections for reproduction were made, I gratefully acknowledge the unfailing courtesy and helpfulness of the many libraries and museums to which I applied for photographs and for permission to reproduce them. Among these I should like to thank especially the following: the Trustees of the British Museum, from whom I obtained almost one-third of the photographs used in the plates of this book; the Director of the Victoria and Albert Museum, where I found excellent photographs not only of objects in the Museum but of a large number in other collections; the Directors of the Warburg and the Courtauld Institutes who gave me access to their photographic files and allowed me to select from them any prints which would serve my purpose. For permission to reproduce photographs of objects in their collections, thanks are due to the following libraries, galleries, and museums: the Walters Gallery, Baltimore; Museo Civico, Bologna; Bibliothèque Royale de Belgique, Brussels; the Fitzwilliam Museum, Cambridge; University Library, Cambridge;

Musée de Cluny; Trinity College Library, Dublin; Cathedral Library, Durham; Biblioteca Medicea Laurenziana, Florence; Library of St Godehard, Hildesheim; the National Gallery, London; the John Rylands Library, Manchester; the Library of Monte Cassino; the Pierpont Morgan Library, New York; the Bodleian Library, Oxford; Bibliothèque Nationale, Paris; Biblioteca Apostolica Vaticana, Rome; Bibliothèque Publique, Rouen; Stiftsbibliothek, St Gall; the Royal Library, Stockholm; Nationalbibliothek, Vienna. The following individuals and governing bodies also have kindly given permission to reproduce photographs of objects in their possession or under their care: His Grace the Archbishop of Canterbury and the Church Commissioners; the Dean and Chapter of Canterbury; the Trustees of the Chatsworth Settlement; the Bishop of Chichester; the Dean and Chapter of Gloucester; the Dean and Chapter of Lichfield; His Grace the Duke of Northumberland; the Dean and Chapter of Norwich; the Dean and Chapter of Westminster; the Dean and Chapter of Winchester; the Dean and Canons of Windsor; the Dean and Chapter of York; the Society of Antiquaries, London; the University of Glasgow; the Master and Fellows of Corpus Christi College, Cambridge; the Master and Fellows of Magdalene College, Cambridge; the Master and Fellows of Pembroke College, Cambridge; the Master and Fellows of St John's College, Cambridge; the Master and Fellows of Trinity College, Cambridge; the Provost of Eton College; the Warden and Fellows of All Souls College, Oxford; the Dean and Students of Christ Church, Oxford; the President and Fellows of Corpus Christi College, Oxford; the Master and Fellows of University College, Oxford; the Warden and Fellows of Winchester College; the Vicar of St Helen's, Abingdon; the Vicar of Barton Turf; the Rector of Cawston; the Vicar of Clayton; the Rector and Churchwardens of East Harling; the Vicar of Hardham; the Vicar of Malvern; Canon John Waddington, Vicar of St Peter Mancroft, Norwich; the Rector of Peakirk and Glinton; the Vicar of Tewkesbury; the Rector of Thornham Magna cum Parva; the Vicar of St Mary's, Warwick; the Vicar and Churchwardens of All Saints, North Street, York.

For personal kindness and assistance in countless ways, my special thanks go to Sir Sydney Cockerell, friend and counsellor over many years; to Mr C. W. Dyson Perrins who during a whole wonderful afternoon allowed me to browse among his treasured manuscripts; to Mr E. Clive Rouse who shared with me on various occasions his exceptional knowledge and experience in wall paintings and lent me his own lists of churches where paintings had been newly discovered; and to Mr A. Wyndham Payne, the fortunate owner of the magnificent new 'Herman' miniature, who enthusiastically supported my desire to make this miniature public first of all in this volume.

Finally, my greatest single debt is to Francis Wormald to whom by his permission I have dedicated this book. His initial encouragement to me to undertake a task for which he himself was eminently qualified and subsequently his unfailing generosity with information, suggestions, and criticism have contributed no small measure of whatever merit the book may possess.

A few notes of explanation should be made regarding some features of the text. The historical summaries at the beginnings of the chapters make no claim to being either comprehensive or balanced as to their historical contents. They are intended to serve merely as a framework for placing names and events connected with the works of art discussed. The exposition of artistic influences shown in the form of a chart likewise is necessarily imperfect and limited in its application. Only the general trends could be shown and many exceptions to these must be assumed. The maps are intended mainly to illustrate two characteristic features of medieval art in Britain, namely the persistence throughout the Middle Ages of certain main centres of production, such as Canterbury and Winchester, and the emergence of different local centres under divers influences in successive periods. And the glossary, as is noted elsewhere, has been compiled solely with the purpose of clarifying technical or unfamiliar terms as used in this volume.

It is evident that in a volume covering so long a period of time, many examples of the pictorial arts have had to be omitted. Those which are included were chosen partly because of their quality but mainly because they furnish the best evidence for illustrating the development of successive styles. Much of this material and most of what has been omitted is dealt with fully in other sources and these are generally referred to in the footnotes. In the case of manuscripts, the supplementary illustrative material is particularly important, for a single manuscript may show a considerable variety of styles within its pages and a facsimile or monograph reproducing it completely will furnish the reader with a much clearer idea of the manuscript as a whole than can be obtained from only one or two plates.

Books referred to in the footnotes by a short title are listed in full in the Bibliography at the end of this volume. Magazine articles also, where mentioned in the footnotes without sources, will be found with complete references in the Bibliography.

The University of Chicago, and London, England, 1953

Scale of Miles

0   50   100

Melrose Abbey • •Lindisfarne

N
O
R
T
H
U
M
B
R
I
A

Jarrow
Hexham• • •Monkwearmouth
•Chester le Street
Durham

•Whitby

•Ripon

M E R C I A

Croyland Abbey
Lichfield• Thorney Abbey• EAST

•Ely ANGLIA

Worcester•
Hereford• Sutton Hoo

Abingdon• E S S E X

Malmesbury• •London

Glastonbury• W E S S E X KENT

• Cerne
Abbey S U S S E X

Exeter•

•Trewhiddle

Map to accompany Chapters 1 and 2

Scale of Miles

0   50   100

Durham

Rievaulx

Fountains   York

Croyland Abbey

Thorney Abbey

Peterborough   Ely

Hereford   Bury St Edmunds

Kempley

St Albans

Malmesbury   London

Glastonbury   Waverley   Canterbury

Hardham

Winchester   Clayton

Coombes   Hastings

Exeter   Lewes Priory

Map to accompany Chapters 3 and 4

Map to accompany Chapters 5 to 8

INTRODUCTION

MEDIEVAL painting, in England as elsewhere in western Europe, must be viewed through a special lens to be understood and appreciated on its own merits. By the criteria of Renaissance painting, medieval artists fell far short of successful accomplishment, for they knew nothing of correct anatomical modelling, foreshortening, or vanishing point perspective. In medieval painting, figures are almost always strongly outlined whether painted and shaded with colours or sketched with a pen. A three-dimensional representation of a figure, therefore, scarcely exists in medieval art, not because the artist did not know that natural objects had depth but because he did not wish to imitate nature. Figures in groups, by the same token, have no real spatial relation to each other: those which are not in the front row are indicated by their heads showing above the others, as though they were standing on a higher plane. Settings, whether indoor or outdoor, are not of any importance until nearly the end of the Middle Ages when influence of the Italian Renaissance began to affect medieval style. Even then, in England settings for scenes scarcely served to do more than help identify a figure or explain a story. And English medieval painting does not in any of its forms ever show an interest in true perspective.

What then are the principles and purposes of English medieval painting? To this fundamental question there is no answer that would be applicable to the whole span of its development. However, by examining the art period by period and noting relationships to what precedes and what follows, it is hoped that the continuity of successive principles and purposes will appear and that this will lead in the end to some understanding of the art.

At the outset, certain basic facts may furnish some slight preparation for this study. These can be stated briefly.

The *dates* of the Middle Ages in Europe are usually given as *c.* 800–*c.* 1400, from the so-called Carolingian Renaissance of learning and art in central and western Europe generally, to the beginning of the true Renaissance of classical art and literature in Italy. In the British Isles, medieval art began as early as the late sixth century, with Celtic and Saxon art, and lasted until nearly 1500 when Flemish art well-nigh swept it away.

The *subject matter* of medieval art in general, or at least of that portion of it which has come down to us, is overwhelmingly religious, but there is also much detail interpolated by individual artists, which is drawn both from nature and from fantasy. The religious subjects are taken from the Bible – the Old and the New Testaments as we know them, together with many so-called apocryphal writings which are commonly excluded from the modern Bible – and from religious commentaries. There are also pictures illustrating the lives of the saints. In England, the subject matter follows in general the chronological development on the Continent, the earliest painted illustrations being of the Gospels and the Psalms. In the later Middle Ages secular material becomes much more important and in the fifteenth century in England the great literary works of Chaucer, Gower, Lydgate, and Hoccleve appeared in a number of illustrated copies. English medieval painting was

I

always more narrative than didactic and displayed considerable originality in the treatment of familiar stories.

The *forms* of medieval pictorial art are many, but, both in importance and in number, illuminated manuscripts hold first place, and England was no exception to this rule. Only a very small number of English panel paintings survive, and even fewer wall paintings have come down to us in anything like their original style, most of them having been repainted at least once and thereby ruined for stylistic purposes. A good deal of early stained glass still exists at Canterbury and at York, and there are even larger amounts of later painted glass, all of which has suffered more or less from breakage and removal and bad restoration. A considerable number of examples of *opus anglicanum* (English embroidery) are scattered over Europe, chiefly Italy and south France and Spain, and some still can be seen in England, but judging from the number of fine embroideries recorded in inventories, those that remain must represent only a small part. Finally, of the coloured floor tiles made in England there remain only a pitiful few. In view of the fragmentary representation of English medieval painting that has survived, the task of evaluating it as a whole is particularly difficult.

The *techniques* used in medieval painting are, in general, two – painting and drawing – and English artists both early and late preferred line drawing to painting with the brush and heavy pigments. Early line drawing was done in the brown ink of the script or in red as in the rubrics (headings or annotations) of the text. Thin colour in bright or pale hues might be added to enhance the line pattern in drawings, but rarely did it completely obscure the line. Towards the beginning of the eleventh century, ink of other colours – green and occasionally blue – began to be used both in text and in illumination. About the same time, these same pale colours began to appear in shading or decorative patterns enhancing the outlines of figures and draperies. Occasionally the coloured red or green line followed the brown contour line, enlivening or strengthening it. This double use of outline with colour was a distinguishing feature of early English medieval art.

Painting in manuscripts, usually called illuminating because, originally, of its effect in 'lighting up' the text resulting from the use of gold and colours, was most often done in flat, pure colour which might or might not be overpainted with fine lines of white or with deeper or lighter colour tones for the purpose of suggesting modelling or of producing a decorative surface pattern. Gold grounds were usual in fine manuscripts; the painting was not done over the gold, but rather the gold was laid on with size around the areas which were to be painted, and it was burnished before the painting was done so that the burnishing of the surface might not damage the colour. Usually a heavy black line was drawn around the painted figures to tidy up the edges, which sometimes overlapped the gold ground slightly, and to set the painting off from the background. Gold grounds were often tooled in patterns as well as burnished; the effect of the gold ground was to increase greatly the brilliance of the colour scheme.

The technique of panel painting was tempera, probably often mixed with oil, applied on a smooth plaster ground. Gold grounds were usually introduced in this form of painting also. In general, the procedure in English panel painting was as described for manuscripts. English wall painting was not done, for the most part, in true fresco technique, which consists of applying the colour on wet plaster, but in tempera either on a bare wall or on dry plaster. The execution of surviving wall paintings, like their technique, is usually rather rough and shows little modelling of the figures but, at least judging from their present state, places strong emphasis on the outlines. A curious use of very dark, almost black, underpainting of flesh can be seen in many examples where the outer layer of paint has flaked off. This was common but not universal and, when used, it would appear that the faces had been modelled.

The technique of stained glass consists of three processes: the making of the coloured glass; the cutting of pieces from it according to a pattern and joining them together to compose the figures and details, in the manner of a jigsaw puzzle; and the painting with brown enamel, mixed with some glass, of features and of shadows on the glass panels, which were then fired to fuse the surface painting with the glass base. These last two processes may have been done by separate craftsmen; but in medieval England the glass-makers were known as 'painter-glazers' and formed a single guild. The process of making the glass itself is too complicated to describe in detail here, but it consisted essentially of mixing chemicals with silica and other substances under great heat to infuse the colour into the molten glass itself. In England a curious fact is known about the glass that was used for windows: most of it was shipped in from the Continent, and only the cutting, glazing, and painting were done locally.

The *colours* used in medieval painting were chiefly the following: two blues, light and the darker ultramarine which was ground lapis lazuli; vermilion, lake or madder reds, and pink made by mixing these with white; verdigris and, later, a dark, bluish mixed green; yellow in small amount, brown, and white. Other colours introduced into English painting at various times, perhaps under foreign influence, are purple, violet and grey. Mixed colours appear most frequently in later work, but some of the heavier colours used in the early Winchester painting also appear to be mixed and are probably to be explained by influences from Carolingian and thus ultimately from classical painting sources.

The *centres of production* of English painting in the Middle Ages, particularly in the early centuries, were the great monasteries, but it is by no means certain that all the artists were monks. Few names of painters survive and these usually do not indicate the status of the artist although often they do suggest the place of his origin. Of the two thirteenth century illuminators whose names and work are known, one was a monk (Matthew Paris) and the other (William de Brailes) appears to have been a clerk who lived or worked in the illuminators' quarter (Catte Street) in Oxford. At Westminster in the late fourteenth century a lay scribe and illuminator were brought in to write and illuminate a fine missal for Abbot Lytlington. London must have been a centre of much artistic production of all kinds but only late in the thirteenth century do we have a recognizable London style, and this seems to stem from, though it is not always identical with, the Westminster or Court style. The other main centres of English art production in successive periods are marked on the three maps (pp. xxiv, xxv, xxvi).

Continental contacts with England were numerous throughout the Middle Ages but seldom operated in one direction only, as the diagram on the following pages shows. These influences can best be understood individually in the discussions of the different

Chart showing by means of lines (*a*) the principal centres, beginning with Canterbury, where art was produced in medieval Britain and indicating the continuity of these 'schools' through the centuries; (*b*) the principal foreign centres with which British art shows contacts during the Middle Ages; and (*c*) by means of arrows, the direction in which the main currents of influence passed between these insular and continental centres. The left side of the Chart covers, in centuries, the period before 1200. The right side of the Chart covers,

in half-centuries, the more prolific period between 1200 and 1500. Whereas
the early part of the Middle Ages in Britain presents few producing centres
and far-flung foreign contacts, the latter part shows many producing centres
with strong influences coming from comparatively few foreign sources and
closer stylistic connexions between various local centres. It is evident that any
attempt to represent by graphic means such complexity of interrelations
over more than a thousand years can only be selective and approximate.

periods, but the increase in their complexity and scope is clearly indicated even in the diagram, and their appearance in the development of English styles is to a large extent a reflection of general trends in chronological developments in other aspects of English medieval history.

Periods of Development

Hiberno-Saxon and Anglo-Saxon	650–1066	Chapters 1 and 2
Romanesque	1066–1200	Chapters 3 and 4
Gothic	1200–1500	Chapters 5 to 8

Hiberno-Saxon manuscripts had first to formulate their idiom, then bring it into line with Continental idiom. The period of formulation encompasses many different mixtures of the three basic components: Irish calligraphy and calligraphic ornament; Anglo-Saxon geometric and animal ornament as found in jewellery designs; Mediterranean figure types and foliage forms, chiefly the acanthus and the vine. Since both Anglo-Saxon and Celtic art were from their very nature wholly linear, whatever Mediterranean forms – whether figure or foliage – went into the Hiberno-Saxon mill came out as linear pattern. The outcome of the Hiberno-Saxon artistic activity was the clear statement for all time of the essential linear and decorative character of English art.

The bringing of the Hiberno-Saxon style into line with Continental developments means, in simple terms, its exposure to the great Carolingian Renaissance (784–850) during the latter part of the English formative period. The process consisted of receiving into the Insular style a considerable amount of Mediterranean art in the diluted form which resulted from its having passed through the hands of Carolingian copyists. This material included both figure work and ornamental motifs. The decorative style stemmed not only from the acanthus and other classical motifs, but also, in the Carolingian style known as Franco-Saxon, these motifs combined with the Celtic interlace and animal heads which had been introduced from the British Isles. There is little doubt that it was this long-familiar and well-loved interlace and other decorative motifs of Franco-Saxon designs that made the style so acceptable to the Saxon illuminators of the Winchester School. It was a much more surprising feat for them to adopt whole-heartedly, and often with such meticulous respect for their model, the foreign technique of figure painting, which involved the modelling of faces and draperies in shaded pigments. In the full tide of sophisticated Continental painting style, the Saxon artist's obvious delight in occasionally expressing himself in terms of line is easily understood. His unique achievement in these cases is that he has employed his linear technique not to reduce the figure to pattern, as formerly, but to embody, by means of the merest linear suggestion, all the physical monumentality and spiritual dignity of the painted Continental figures which furnished his models. Whatever Anglo-Saxon art produced subsequently – and it was much and of high quality – it never surpassed the consummate skill displayed in the noble renderings of the figures in these drawings.

But Anglo-Saxon style had still another adjustment to make to Continental art before its powers reached complete maturity. The arrival, under what circumstances is not known, of the Utrecht Psalter in Canterbury about the year 1000 was certainly one of the most momentous events imaginable for the future of English drawing. The technique of this manuscript from the Carolingian school of Reims is light and sketchy outline drawn swiftly without calculation and without correction. This type of line was unknown to Hiberno-Saxon illuminators, but at once it struck a spark from their descendants at Canterbury because of the sureness and speed of the technique which, though so different from Celtic line, nevertheless evoked the same degree of dynamic excitement. So the sketchy, broken line took its place beside the firm contour line as a means of dealing with the human figure; the one spun out tales of human actions with the dizzy speed of a moving picture reel, the other grasped firmly but with acute sensitiveness the nobility of the human body and spirit. Needless to say the two techniques did not remain separate, nor were they confined in their application to any single place or time in English pictorial art.

The Romanesque period again brought Anglo-Saxon art abruptly face to face with Continental work, but this time the contact was with more nearly contemporary art than was previously the case. However firmly rooted and sure of itself Saxon art had become before 1066, the Norman influx, by sheer mass of newcomers with new ideas, must have stirred it into new life. Moreover, in Europe great events were afoot – the Crusades and journeys to strange and distant lands, in which Englishmen and Normans alike took part. There were not only the budding Romanesque art in France and its parents in north Italy, but in south Italy and Sicily and beyond, in the East itself, all the riches of Byzantine art were opened up to the western artist. Thus, while the first phase of Romanesque art in England was concerned with formulating again its idiom under Norman influence, as at Canterbury and Durham, in the second part of the period it was engulfed in another strong wave of Mediterranean modelled figure painting style, this time more violent than before, because Byzantine art was closer to its classical figure origins than Carolingian art had been. St Albans first received this style, but it was at Canterbury that it emerged triumphant in a superb dynamic linear rendering, while from Bury St Edmunds came a monumental if somewhat more controlled version. At the end of the twelfth century, St Swithin's at Winchester produced a Bible that surpassed all previous English Bibles in the boldness and scale of its decoration and in the variety and vigour of the styles of its figure painting.

The Gothic period, which was ushered in on the heels of the Winchester Bible, was a long and very fruitful and peculiarly significant time for English art. Across the Channel the French Gothic flame, burning fiercely, was spreading northward and eastward; would the Channel prevent its sweeping England too? In the end, it was not the Channel that saved English art, but the sturdiness of the English temperament, which refused to surrender to fads but insisted on taking time to weigh the new elements and consider what, if anything, it wanted of them. So it was that while a vaulted chevet was admitted to Henry III's new choir at Westminster, the walls were covered with diapered ornament brightly painted with gold and colours. The new French style of small-scale books with tiny miniatures containing minute, unmodelled figures left its mark on certain groups of English manuscripts of the early thirteenth century, notably at Canterbury. There too in this period the Cathedral itself was filled with stained glass close in style to that of the French cathedrals, which fact, as in France, soon affected the design of the illuminated pages in manuscripts. At the same time, a monumental drawing style, fostered at St Albans under the influence of the earlier Byzantine wave, emerged independent of the exquisite if somewhat formal French style, in the work of Matthew Paris and his school. Thus the French Gothic style, tasted but not swallowed whole, in the end left only a slight impress on English work of the mid thirteenth century: the rich output of psalters and also apocalypses, illuminated by English artists, is nearly always distinguishable from French work. In the third quarter of the thirteenth century, it is true, the two styles, French and English, again draw close together under the common influence of medallion stained glass designs; but this phase was of short duration in England.

By the end of the thirteenth century, and almost simultaneously, two of the most internationally famous forms of English art made their appearance: East Anglian manuscript illumination and *opus anglicanum*, as English embroidery was called, both superb types of English decorative design and craftsmanship. The East Anglian manuscript style may have received some initial stimulus from the borderland of present France and Belgium, where illumination was being done with comparable verve, but its fundamental features are those which are most typical of English medieval art as a whole – love of nature, of the whimsical, and of rich decorative pattern. Coupled with these in East Anglian work is the delight in narrative and the incidental. The influence of this style was felt on other forms of English art, notably embroideries and stained glass, and even spread outside England, as far as Cologne and Bohemia.

Manuscripts in East Anglian style were produced almost down to the middle of the fourteenth century, but both the motifs and the design tended increasingly to coarsen. However, it was in this later phase particularly, and possibly under new Flemish stimulus, that interest in nature produced some of those series of scenes from daily life that, used as illustrations for books on medieval history, have made English fourteenth century art known far and wide in modern times.

The mid fourteenth century itself is a sterile period in England, but when better times came in the third quarter of the century, East Anglian style still showed signs of life, but lacked vigour. This was supplied by a strong graft of north Italian figure painting which resulted in the group of fine manuscripts made for members of the Bohun family, and which subsequently appeared in the style of the Court School.

At the end of the fourteenth century other Continental influences passed across the Channel: from Bohemia, perhaps via Cologne or Westphalia; from Gelderland; from Burgundy; from Paris; and at the end of the fifteenth century, from Bruges, the very hub of Flemish Renaissance art. But by this time East Anglian art had taken refuge in showy rood screens and broad windows filled with rather strongly coloured, painted figure glass, the raw material for which was largely shipped in from abroad. An occasional clear note echoing the glory of earlier English linear art is still sounded from East Anglia and the Midlands, but London Court art of the late fifteenth century is more foreign than English.

HIBERNO-SAXON ART IN THE SEVENTH, EIGHTH, AND NINTH CENTURIES

*

HISTORICAL BACKGROUND:
INVASIONS AND INTERNAL STRUGGLES

POLITICAL

PRE-SAXON PERIOD

Celtic invasions of Britain and Ireland third to second centuries B.C.; brought in late La Tène art (chiefly metalwork).

Belgae settled in south-east Britain middle of first century B.C.; perhaps introduced art of enamelling.

Roman occupation A.D. 43–410; late Roman and provincial Roman art; especially architecture, sculpture, and mosaics; metalwork (silver and pewter).

SAXON PERIOD

Angles, Saxons, and Jutes settled in various parts of Britain 400–600; they were pagans, and drove out the Roman Britons, many of whom had become Christians. Principal kingdoms were Kent, Northumbria, East Anglia, Mercia, and Wessex; art chiefly metalwork (chip carving and cloisonné enamel).

Northumbrian Supremacy: under Kings Oswald (633–41) and Oswy (654–70).

Mercian Supremacy: established by the invasion of Northumbria 740; Offa King of Mercia 'Rex Anglorum' (757–96); conquered Kent 775; close relations with Rome.

West Saxon supremacy: Egbert, King of Wessex (802–39); conquered Mercia at Battle of Ellendun 825; became supreme in South England from 830; Viking raids began in South England 835.

MONASTIC FOUNDATIONS

St Patrick established Celtic Christianity in Ireland fifth century; Irish monks were missionaries; founded monasteries at St Gall (Switzerland), Bobbio (north Italy), and elsewhere on the Continent.

Missionaries from Rome to south England: St Augustine at Canterbury 597–604; Manuscripts and other art objects brought and sent from Rome: St Augustine's Gospels (Camb., Corpus Christi Coll., MS. 286).

Irish monks to Northumbria: St Aidan from Iona to found monastery of Lindisfarne 635: Irish scribes and Irish script brought into Northumbria.

Synod of Whitby 664 established authority of Roman Church over Celtic Church in north of England; Irish influence waned and Canterbury influence increased in Northumbria; St Cuthbert at Melrose, Hexham, and Lindisfarne 664–87. His relics moved because of Danish invasions to Chester-le-Street, to Ripon, and finally to Durham 875.

9

Eadfrith, Bishop of Lindisfarne 698–721. Wrote Gospels of Lindisfarne, in honour of St
    Cuthbert (Brit. Mus., Cott. MS. Nero D.iv).
Theodore of Tarsus, Archbishop of Canterbury 668–90.
    Art objects imported which introduced Roman and perhaps Eastern influences.
Benedict Biscop founded Wearmouth and Jarrow monasteries in Northumbria 674–82;
    Brought 'furniture, vestments, relics, pictures, and a library of valuable books' from
    the Continent.
Ceolfrid, successor to Benedict, Abbot of Wearmouth and Jarrow 688; Made several jour-
    neys to Rome, on one of which he carried the Bible known as the *Codex Amiatinus*
    (made at one of these monasteries) as a present to the Pope.
Venerable Bede, monk, first at Wearmouth then at Jarrow *c.* 681; Wrote *Ecclesiastical
    History of England* 731, earliest illuminated copy of which was made probably at
    Canterbury in the late eighth century; also wrote *Life of St Cuthbert* of which a
    number of illuminated copies were made.
Chad (Ceadda) Bishop of Lichfield (Mercia) 669–72.
    Gospels of St Chad (so-called), Lichfield Cathedral, early eighth century.
St Guthlac founder of Croyland Abbey *c.* 697–714.
    Long cycle of illustrations from his life (Brit. Mus., Harl. MS. Y.6), *c.* 1200.
Willibrord, second English missionary to Friesland, founded Abbey of Echternach near
    Trier 698.
Aldhelm, studied at Canterbury; Abbot of Malmesbury, Bishop of Sherborne 705–09.
    Wrote for nuns of Barking Abbey *De Laude Virginitatis*, of which several illuminated
    copies were made.

*

CHRISTIAN Art in England traditionally begins with two specific dates: 597 when St
Augustine established a monastery at Canterbury in the south of England; and 635 when
St Aidan, coming from the Irish foundation at Iona off the coast of Scotland, founded a
monastery on the island of Lindisfarne off the coast of Northumbria. These two monastic
centres with their respective orbits of influence in north and south England set the stage
for the development of English pictorial art.

The earliest form of this art is found in illuminated manuscripts, for the missionaries
had need of books and what they did not bring with them had to be made, that is, the
text had to be copied by any monk who could read the Latin passably well and was
reasonably skilled in the art of writing. The books most needed at first were biblical texts
to be used for reading scriptural passages in the church ritual, primarily the four Gospels
and the Book of Psalms. A Gospel Book with pictures believed to have been made in Italy
and sent to St Augustine at Canterbury (Camb., Corpus Christi Coll., MS. 286) probably
furnished one of the texts later copied there; at any rate, the pictures in this manuscript
influenced the illumination of manuscripts made later at Canterbury, as we shall see.

But the earliest Hiberno-Saxon[1] illuminated manuscript was made not at Canterbury
but in the North of England or, as others maintain, in Ireland or at the Irish monastery of
Iona. There is no record as to whether St Aidan brought manuscripts with him when he
settled at Lindisfarne, but he may have done, for the Irish monks were famous as scholars
and are known to have copied books. What is not known is whether they illuminated

their books, and since no early painted illumination and no fine early examples of any other form of pictorial art can certainly be identified as of Irish origin, their skill as artists is problematic. Thus the earliest known example of insular illumination, the famous Gospel Book of Durrow[2] (Dublin, Trin. Coll. Lib., MS. 57 [A.4.5]) now generally dated in the middle or second half of the seventh century, has for many years been the centre of lively controversy as to the sources of its decorative style.

The illumination in the Book of Durrow (Plates 1, 2, and 3D) is of four types: (1) five pages with symbols of the Evangelists[3] within decorative borders; (2) five pages containing only decorative patterns, one at the beginning of the manuscript and one before each of the four Gospels; (3) decorative text pages, of which the six most elaborate introduce important parts of the text; (4) three folios filled on both sides with the Eusebian Canon Tables[4] arranged in columns, each page bordered with interlace and cable pattern.

The first and third leaves[5] of the Book of Durrow as it is now bound are decorative pages: fol. i verso, a cruciform page facing fol. ii which contains the four symbols; fol. iii, a page of spirals bordered by interlace which probably introduced the Gospel of Matthew (Plate 3D). The symbol of Matthew is now found at the very end of the book (fol. 245 verso; Plate 2A). The original scheme of arrangement of the various types of decorative pages can be seen in the other three Gospels where the page with the symbol comes first in order, followed by the page of decoration on the verso of a leaf facing the ornamental next page which begins the Gospel text. Even in the original arrangement of the manuscript, a very curious inconsistency occurred in the order of the pictures of the symbols of the Evangelists: the order, Matthew, Mark, Luke, John, which is usual and is the text order of the Book of Durrow, is different in the Durrow pictures, Mark and John being interchanged. It would seem that the painter of the symbols and the text writer were following different copies.[6]

The five pages with the symbols of the Evangelists (see Plate 2) are remarkable for the simplicity and clarity of the drawing of the figures and for their total lack of life-like character. The symbol of Matthew, the winged man, who is represented here without wings, is a reduction of the human draped form to the absolute minimum of representational means: he has a head in full-face view with large eyes, prominent ears, and wig-like hair, and he is completely enveloped in a shapeless mantle, like a paper dress on a paper doll, which conceals his body except for the feet which extend from beneath it in sharp profile view. The same anomalous treatment of the figure in a combination of front and profile views is seen in the eagle, symbol of John (Plate 2B). Both the feathered body of the eagle and the cloak and hose of the man are utilized for the display of simple geometric patterns in colour.[7] The man's cloak is further stylized by outlining it with a heavy double line which continues unbroken even at the hem of the garment.

Of the pages filled entirely with decorative patterns, only one contains animal ornament (fol. 174 verso; Plate 1). This faces the opening text page of the Gospel of John. The bands of elongated biting animals (so-called lacertines) seem to be all of one breed, but so varied in their positions and in the resulting curves which they form in the design as to suggest at first glance three different types. The animal has an elongated head and a biting snout, two legs, of which the hind one is so flexible below the thigh joint that it can be twisted into a knot and tied behind the creature's neck. The animals in the short vertical bands have shorter bodies and more prominent ears; the others have extremely elongated eel-like bodies, and those in the two inner horizontal bands have the foreleg placed very far back from the head. The possibilities of contorting this beast into different patterns are great, and depend only on the degree to which the body is extended with its head flattened, or pushed together as in the cramped position of the leading beast in the vertical bands. The black background shows up the pattern with niello-like sharpness. This is also found in the centre medallion, where closely plaited interlace with flat wide bands forms circles and triangles which enclose at three different points smaller circles containing stepped patterns. The centre of the great circle, and the exact centre of the decorated part of the page, is a small medallion containing an even-armed Greek cross. The colours are red, green, and yellow; no gold at all is used.

Another type of all-over pattern fills a page with spiral motifs arranged in varying numbers and designs within interconnected circles (Plate 3D). This page is bordered with interlace in a four-strand 'stopped-knot' design (see below).

Finally, there are the pages of decorative text which in Durrow contain fairly simple calligraphic pen ornament, designed to enhance the script.[8] Little colour is used on these pages, except for two special types of ornament: the S-chain patterns in red connecting the large initial with the block of text, and the myriads of tiny red dots used to outline the initials, to connect text and initial, and to form a solid background for the first two or three text lines. The whole of the decoration on these decorative text pages can be thought of only as the work of a scribe; and for this reason, as we shall see, they throw some light upon the knotty problem of the origins of the Hiberno-Saxon style as represented in the Book of Durrow.

Into the formation of this highly complex art, artistic impulses from at least five distinct sources – Ireland, the Mediterranean, the Britons, the Picts, and the Anglo-Saxons[9] – undoubtedly entered in varying degrees, but oddly enough, evidences of the early stages of their fusion, which should precede the Book of Durrow, are lacking. Thus in spite of a great deal of exhaustive research ranging far afield into little known Continental material,[10] no certain and complete evidence has been or perhaps ever can be produced as to the exact source, or even as to the predominating influence in the development of the Hiberno-Saxon style.

Two pieces of evidence which have been most recently brought to bear on the problem weigh, the one on the side of Irish origins, the other on the side of English (Northumbrian). And because they seem not to be mutually incompatible, they will both be considered briefly here.

One of the arguments concerns specifically the decoration of the text pages. Early examples of such calligraphic ornament in Irish manuscripts are, it is true, very rare, although the Irish monks were noted for their learning and their assiduous copying and dissemination of books.[11] However, one early ornamented Irish manuscript has survived, the Psalter or so-called Cathach[12] of St Columba. Its date, based on both legendary-historical and paleographical grounds, is now thought to be shortly after the middle of the sixth century – if it is actually the copy made by St Columba before 561.[13] At least four ornamental elements found in Durrow can be seen in their rudimentary beginnings in the earlier manuscript: the practice of graduating the sizes of the letters from the large initial to the following text letters; the introduction of simple spirals and trumpet patterns as terminals of the letters; the use, though rare, of open-mouthed animal heads as terminals; and the frequent use of the S-chain both as filling and as external ornament for the initial letter.[14] These ornamental features of the Cathach text are rudimentary and crude, but colour (rubric red) is introduced in addition to the ink of the text and the intention obviously is to create calligraphic ornament. It is noteworthy that the means of decoration are not those found in the initial letters of late classical manuscripts.[15] Such as it is, this ornamental text art seems to be unquestionably Irish.

The other source of recent evidence is furnished by the very important ship burial excavated at Sutton Hoo in East Anglia in 1939.[16] The date of the burial is tentatively placed as 655–6, and many of the objects seem to have been family or tribal heirlooms, so that their date would probably fall in the earlier part of the seventh century at latest – perhaps in the time of King Redwald (d. 624 or 625). The correspondence between patterns included in the decoration of the various objects and the four chief motifs found on the decorative pages of the Book of Durrow is striking: the interlace is represented in very similar forms on the great gold buckle[17] (Plate 3A); the animal ornament is found at the tip of this buckle and also in the border of the gold clasp set with garnets and glass[18] (Plate 3C); the spirals are found on the escutcheons of the hanging bowl[19] (Plate 3B); the stepped patterns and the diagonal fret are used also on the gold clasps and other jewellery, notably the purse mountings.[20] Moreover, the patterned cross design, as on fol. i verso in the Book of Durrow, occurs on the silver bowls of the Sutton Hoo find, though not with the interlace pattern.[21] Thus it appears that much of the ornament of the Book of Durrow can be traced to Anglo-Saxon metalwork of the first half of the seventh century. The incorporation of these ornamental motifs, in colours corresponding to those of gold, rubies, and glass enamels, into the decorative pages of a manuscript, seems to be the explanation of the marvellously complex decorative style in the Book of Durrow. Whether this assimilation was the accomplishment of Irish illuminators or Anglo-Saxons trained by the Irish is not clear, but since there is evidence of writing and of ornamenting the text in earlier Irish manuscripts,[22] it would seem likely that they also had an important if not a determining part in the evolution of the decorative manuscript pages. But it is highly improbable that this development would have come about except for the stimulus of fresh contacts with such rich and varied patterns in colour as are displayed in the Sutton Hoo and other Anglo-Saxon metalwork.[23]

The Book of Durrow, though the simplest and most restrained of the Hiberno-Saxon manuscripts, displays a perfection of technique and a mastery of design that could hardly be expected in the earlier stages of an artistic development. It must be assumed, therefore, that the technique of calligraphic decoration in some form was already familiar to the illuminators before this superb specimen was produced.

Between the Book of Durrow and the Lindisfarne Gospels (Brit. Mus., Cott. MS. Nero D.iv), written by Eadfrith,[24] Bishop of Lindisfarne (698–721), not many years can have intervened. The decorative style which was maturing in Durrow is applied in the Lindisfarne Book to the five cruciform pages and six pages of decorative text on a more lavish scale and with a mingling of the different types of motifs, but the work shows the same kind of calligraphic skill as does Durrow. The link between Durrow and Lindisfarne is too close to be the result of the mere influence of the earlier book on the later and seems to indicate craftsmen trained in the same scriptorium. The Lindisfarne Gospel Book, measuring 13½ by 9¾ inches, contains, in addition to the decorative pages mentioned above, sixteen pages of Canon Tables under decorated arcades and four remarkable pages with the 'portraits' of the Evangelists together with their symbols. It is these two latter features chiefly that distinguish the decoration of the book as a whole from that of Durrow.

The scale and elaborateness of the calligraphic decoration on the text pages is evident in the page (fol. 95) reproduced on plate 5. It is partially surrounded by a border, which stops on each side of the large initial monogram INI (Initium) and consists of panels containing stopped knot and plaitwork designs, diagonal stepped patterns, and biting animal interlace. Many of these same patterns are found in the bars of the initial monogram, while the terminals are filled with spiral or trumpet motifs. In the Book of Durrow the interlace and trumpet patterns constitute the only decoration of the initials. Red dots are used profusely in Lindisfarne as in Durrow, not as a solid background, however, as in Durrow, but for tracing interlace, diamond, and even animal patterns between the letters. The red dots also follow the contours of the letters, as in Durrow. The S-chain patterns used in Durrow to connect the large initials with the text are omitted in Lindisfarne. One very significant feature which occurs in Lindisfarne and not in Durrow is the animal or bird heads[25] which are used as terminals of the border, and also in some of the letters, as the two E's on plate 5. The increase in the number and variety of the patterns introduced on any one page is accompanied by a greater variety and richness in colour: in addition to the red, green, and yellow of Durrow, a good deal of purple and blue is found. On fol. 95 both these colours are used for filling some of the letters, and in the d in the centre of this page there has even been experimenting in overpainting with purple on blue.

One of the finest of the cruciform pages, especially as to colour, is fol. 26 verso (Plate 4).[26] The prevailing tone is a shimmering blue which together with soft pink is used for the ribbon animals in the field surrounding the cross; clear, light green and bright red are used for the patterns within it and for some of the ribbon interlace in the lower part of the field. The outline of the cross is soft purple. The border bands are purple and green; the corner ornaments are yellow with the pattern outlined in brown. The other border ornaments are red, green, and yellow. The technique of this page is unbelievably fine. Each strand of the interlace is carefully painted with both edges reserved in the plain vellum[27] so that the upper ribbon passes cleanly over the under strand. The background of the pattern in the cross is purple; that of the field is black. The effect of this meticulous technique and consummate skill is a sparkling liveliness of pattern, where the strands weave in and out in a rich and varied network within which animals and birds are entangled and over which the flickering variations of colour pass like cloud shadows across the sun. There is rhythm, balance, and rich variety; but the central pattern of the cross stands out strongly defined by its clear purple contour set off by the reserved edges of plain vellum. In the centres of the arms and at their crossing there are small uncoloured roundels, suggesting rivets or bosses, each containing a tiny cloisonné-like cross; in the central medallion is a rosette. It is difficult to imagine a more exquisite piece of all-over decoration. It is a *chef-d'œuvre* of barbaric ornamental design, yet it is tempered and controlled by a symmetry and orderliness in the principal lines of the pattern that are not barbarian in origin but derive from Mediterranean art.[28]

Mediterranean influence is even more startlingly evident in concept, in technique, and above all in colour on the folio which immediately precedes this one (fol. 25 verso; Plate 7A), containing a full-page 'portrait' of the Evangelist Matthew with his symbol, the winged man. The Evangelist is clothed in a dull purple gown, painted spottily between the curved lines, which were reserved in the vellum when laying on the paint and afterward filled with colour to indicate drapery folds. His mantle is bright green and the heavy lines on it are bright red. The technique is completely linear but the contour line is irregular to suggest the folds of drapery around the figure. The feet are bare and very pink, and the thongs of non-existent sandals can be seen on them; the mat on which the feet rest is attached to the wooden brace of the stool, inches from the ground; the book is a solid block with no indication of separate pages. The curtain is heavily painted with deep folds and zigzag edges, and the rings at the top are carefully threaded on a rod attached to the frame of the miniature. The symbol of Matthew appears above and behind his head, the body partially obscured by his halo. The symbol holds a trumpet which he is blowing, and a book.[29]

The decorative treatment of the details of hair and beard, wing feathers, drapery folds and formal geometric ornament on the bench and on Matthew's gown betray the same delight of the artist in ornamental design which characterizes the pages of the Book of Durrow; but the figures cannot be accounted for by the style of the symbols in the earlier Northumbrian manuscript. Obviously the Lindisfarne picture echoes a different type of model, one with its roots in representational rather than in ornamental tradition.

This other prototype was apparently the so-called *Codex Amiatinus*,[30] the first quire of which contains introductory textual matter and on fol. v a 'portrait' of the scribe Ezra with the books of the Bible (Plate 7B); the preceding leaf (fol. iv) containing the Prologue is a purple-stained leaf. It is still not fully agreed whether this picture itself originally formed part of a South Italian manuscript[31] and was brought to Northumbria and inserted in the manuscript written at Jarrow, or whether the picture is a Northumbrian copy of such a miniature. Its present condition is very bad, much of the paint having flaked off, but a close examination shows the technique to be wholly that of painting with thick, opaque pigments; gold and silver, badly deteriorated, also are used. There is no evidence at all of Saxon or Irish motifs in the decorative details. The staring eyes and hard drapery folds and the general lack of competent figure modelling suggest a well-intentioned but ungifted Continental artist.[32]

As to the relation of the St Matthew of the Lindisfarne Gospels to this figure there is no doubt; the details of the pose and the accessories, with the omission of the bookcase and table, correspond as exactly to the Ezra picture as is possible. Here is the explanation of the sandal thongs, the floating rectangular mat under Matthew's feet (which is supported on legs in the Ezra picture and is clearly a footstool), the block-like book, the cushion, and the drapery folds. But the technique in the Lindisfarne miniature is a translation of the painted modelled style into the linear idiom of the insular artist. It is clear that into the Hiberno-Saxon, i.e. Northumbrian, decorative style as represented most typically in the ornamental pages of the Lindisfarne Gospels, a new element has been introduced, namely the human figure rendered intentionally with a semblance of its natural form, and that here two separate, co-existent artistic worlds have met: the Mediterranean with its heritage of classical culture and representational form, and the barbarian with its long history of abstract, dynamic linear pattern. That these two fundamentally opposed methods of artistic expression could co-exist and be successfully combined not only within the covers of the same book but within the same page design is a foreshadowing of the susceptibility of the English artist to alien influences and of his willingness to tolerate and even adapt to his own purposes any acceptable new elements which came his way.

Finally, a brief word as to the Canon Tables in the Lindisfarne Gospels (fol. 15; Plate 6A). They are of a very different design from those in Durrow: the large arch supported on a flat profiled column with base and capital, enclosing other arches resting on similar columns, is reminiscent of Eastern manuscript design. But the ornament of the arches is completely Northumbrian, consisting of the characteristic Lindisfarne biting birds in the arch and shafts of the columns and of interlace on the capitals and bases. Other pages of Canon Tables vary somewhat in motifs and in their arrangement, the chief difference being the substitution for the biting birds of animals in ribbon ornament design or occasionally in pairs. The designs on facing pages correspond in motifs and arrangement. The Canon Table pages display a certain monotony in design as we shall realize when we compare them with the Canon Table pages in the Book of Kells (Plate 6B).

Several other manuscripts can be associated with the Lindisfarne style. One, a fragment of the Gospels in Durham Cathedral Library (MS. A.ii.17) has an elaborate text page (fol. 2)[33] which looks closer to Durrow than to Lindisfarne. In the Durham Gospels, as in the Book of Durrow, the decorative emphasis is on the relation between the ornamental initial letters and the remainder of the text, a relation which is expressed primarily by means of the graduated sizes of the letters and the S-chain pattern. The animal ornament[34] is combined, however, with the trumpet and interlace on the same page, as in Lindisfarne, and the ornament is richer and more elaborate than in Durrow. The colours are purple, yellow, and green. Folio 383 verso in the Durham fragment contains a full-page Crucifixion, the draped figure of Christ in frontal position suggesting an Eastern prototype; Longinus and Stephaton and two feathered[35] angels flank the cross. The Durham manuscript is usually dated in the first quarter of the eighth century, but may be even earlier.

Very close to Lindisfarne in its decorative pages, and not unrelated to the Durham Crucifixion in the style of its Evangelist pictures, is a defective Gospel Book, known as the Gospels of Chad, now in Lichfield Cathedral.[36] On the fine cruciform page (fol. 3 in the manuscript) the trumpet pattern is combined with a running band of Lindisfarne birds; fol. 110 verso of this manuscript has animal interlace on a cruciform page closely resembling fol. 26 verso in Lindisfarne, but with less distinction in the Lichfield manuscript between the patterns within and outside the central cross design. It is dated in the early eighth century, perhaps about the same time as Lindisfarne.

The two surviving pictures of Evangelists, Mark on fol. 71 verso and Luke on fol. 109 verso (Plate 8A), in the Chad Gospels are far removed in style from those in Lindisfarne; the differences are due not only to a different type of original but to a rendering of the figure in a different idiom. The figure of Luke is designed almost entirely in a series of curves. The hair consists of rope-like twists, the hanging locks terminating in spirals; the ears are C-spirals, as are the nostrils; the chin has a deep cleft dividing it into two symmetrical curves. The patterns of the drapery folds are broad uniform bands of colour with the edges reserved in the vellum. The only variation in this complete symmetry is in the feet which, oddly enough, are seen, one in profile, the other in front view, and in the heads of the two staffs. From one of these sprout conventionalized leaf forms on interlacing stems which issue from the double scroll, while the other staff has a simple head with a cross and a circle containing a rosette. The symbol of the Evangelist, the calf, is in a curious position: its front legs are partly obscured by the halo, as in Lindisfarne, its horns extending over the decorative border, while its wings are under the border, the tips showing in the margin – forming in itself a kind of interlace design. The Chad Evangelists are fine Irish versions of figures that suggest Coptic prototypes; we can see similar examples of this style also in later Irish manuscripts.[37]

An interesting comparison can be made between the St Luke of the Chad Gospels and the symbol of Matthew – a wingless man – in a manuscript illuminated by a Northumbrian artist probably at Echternach, near Trier, in the first half of the eighth century (fol. 18 verso; Plate 8B).[38] In the Echternach miniature the representational concept of the human figure and its draperies and appendages is not so much translated into pattern as eliminated altogether, the figure being reduced to a masterly arrangement of ornamental motifs; if the head, hands, and feet were removed, we should never suspect that a human figure was intended. Compared with the earlier stylized Evangelist symbol of Durrow, it is, however, much more sophisticated and impressive, And in spite of the ridiculous crossed eyes and the yellow hair sprinkled with brown dots, there is a tenseness of expression in the face which contrasts with the wide-eyed blankness of the Chad Luke. The animal symbols in the Echternach Gospels, though highly stylized, also have this dynamic quality as compared with the Chad symbols.[39] The calf (fol. 115 verso) is actually walking; the lion (fol. 75 verso) rears up on his hind legs, with darting tongue, bared claws and an angrily coiled tail. The background of the animal symbol pages is divided by red lines into irregularly spaced rectangular patterns which set off effectively the lively creatures. The colours are yellow, red, and purple, the two latter in two shades; no green is used at all. The technique is superb, and this and the simplicity of the designs would seem to date the Echternach Gospels early, close to Durrow and perhaps even before the Lindisfarne Gospels.

Though the Lichfield and the Echternach Gospels differ somewhat from each other in the style of their Evangelist pictures, both these manuscripts display such marked contrasts to the Lindisfarne Gospels with regard to the Evangelists and their symbols as to indicate that an entirely different prototype must have inspired them. In fact, Benedict Biscop, founder of the monastery of Monkwearmouth in 674, is known[40] to have brought back with him from repeated visits to Italy, pictures and manuscripts for this monastery and neighbouring Jarrow. The Ezra in the *Codex Amiatinus* may have been one of these, but it is evident that there were also other Early Christian or Byzantine pictures, from which Irish artists in Northumbria drew their inspiration.

With the figures in the Lichfield and Echternach manuscripts it is interesting to compare another Northumbrian manuscript in Durham (Cathedral Library, MS. B.ii.30), Cassiodorus's *Commentary on the Psalms*, containing two full-page pictures of David, one as a warrior (fol. 172 verso; Plate 10A), the other as a musician.[41] The warrior figure is standing frontally but is not symmetrical; the hair and drapery are stylized in hard, linear patterns, but there is a softness in the contours and a grasp of the proportions of the body which an Irish artist would never have attained. Clumsy as the figure is, the intention is unmistakable here, as in the Lindisfarne Gospels, to suggest the modelled figure by means of a linear technique, not to transform it completely into pattern. The ground on which David stands ends with two animal heads of Northumbrian type, and blocks of stepped pattern and interlace fill the panels let into the border of the page; the red-dotted circles which pepper the background are purely ornamental space-filling. The inventiveness and skill of the decorator's art has by no means been supplanted by his interest in the new representational form.[42]

About the same time as Irish and Northumbrian illuminators were experimenting with the rendering of the human figure, artists in the south of England were combining decorative and figure styles. At Canterbury where, at the coming of St Augustine in 597 and subsequently, books from Italy were arriving, the classical figure style underwent a much less drastic change, as compared with its prototype, than in Northumbria. A gospel book traditionally said to have been sent to St Augustine by Pope Gregory[43] may have been influential in setting the style. At any rate, as early as the mid eighth century several manuscripts were produced at Canterbury which show evidence not only of classical models but of a considerable degree of sympathy with and understanding of the figure style. A comparison of David as a musician in a Canterbury Psalter (Brit. Mus., Cott. MS. Vesp. A.1, fol. 30 verso; Plate 10B) with David the warrior (Plate 10A) in the Durham Cassiodorus will demonstrate the differences. In the Canterbury Psalter, David is seated on a cushioned throne surrounded by musicians and dancers, in a crowded composition which more than fills the space between the columns under the arch, so that the figures are cramped by the architecture. The poses of David and of the other musicians, the vigorous clapping of hands by the two dancers in the foreground, and the general liveliness and movement of the scene, in spite of its tight linear rendering, reflect the representational content of such a manuscript as the St Augustine Gospels. But the modelling itself[44] is done with heavy, rich colours and strong linear high-lights and shadows, contrasting markedly with the flat, decorative rendering of the Cassiodorus David. Particularly the face of David in the Canterbury Psalter shows modelling with green shadows under the eye and on the upper lip, and pink patches on the cheek, though the other features are painted with brown lines. He wears a red tunic, a brownish mantle, and pale blue stockings. Gold is used freely in the framework and for details of the miniature, enriching the heavy colour.

Many of the decorative elements in the Canterbury Psalter, such as the trumpet pattern in the arch of the David miniature and in the column panels, can be traced in large part to Irish and Northumbrian sources. Animal ornament also is present in Canterbury work but in a new form: single birds and confronted beasts are framed in medallions[45] which are used in place of bases and capitals of the columns; the Eastern rosette motif is combined with the whorls of the trumpet scroll; and most significant as new elements are the two symmetrical acanthus-type plants which never grew from Northumbrian roots.[46]

The initials introducing individual psalms are of two types, and evidently come from two different sources. On the page opposite David as a harpist (fol. 31) is an initial letter D introducing the psalm *Dominus illuminatio*, which encloses two figures clasping hands and each holding a spear, probably David and Jonathan; and on fol. 53 is another initial letter D enclosing a picture of David surrounded by sheep and goats, holding his hand in the mouth of the lion which, as a shepherd, he miraculously dominated. Both of these pictures within initials are examples of the so-called historiated initial, and certainly the earliest examples known either in England or on the Continent.[47] They may thus be an English invention, and this might partly account for their persistent popularity during the whole later history of English illumination.

Other initial letters introducing psalms are purely ornamental and not illustrative and are much more Hiberno-Saxon in designs and motifs. The scrolls, the stopped-knot interlace, panels of geometric design and animal head terminals and everywhere red dots thickly sprinkled combine with naturalistic animals in a variety of forms, placed in heraldic positions chiefly in profile view. Some of the bands of ornamental letters which give the first line of a psalm (fol. 64 verso) are in gold on a purple ground; others are in colour on the uncoloured vellum.

The Canterbury Psalter is an almost unique example of the well-balanced blending of the two antipodal styles, Hiberno-Saxon and Mediterranean, the success of which is a tribute to the ability of the artist.

Slightly later (*c.* 760) and even closer in some respects to its Italian or Byzantine original are the Evangelist pages of the large *Codex Aureus* in the Stockholm Royal Library,[48] of which fol. 9 verso is reproduced in plate 11A. In this miniature,[49] apart from the hard, linear technique, the only features which betray its twofold heredity are the interlace pattern on St Matthew's chair and on the lintel of the arch, and the general tendency to formalize the patterns of the drapery and of the looped curtains. Again, like David, the figure is placed within an architectural setting which, it is true, has lost its structural solidity though it retains the architectural details of columns with capitals and bases. But the spatial tradition is present, as is the use of paint in a technique of light and shade, especially in the facial modelling, and the figures of both Matthew and his symbol are solid and imposing and full of dignity. The ribbon pattern in the arch might have come straight out of a Byzantine manuscript or mosaic.

The Celtic ornamental style with its animal and geometric motifs, however, was by no means replaced by motifs taken from late classical models. Two other manuscripts from Canterbury, both of *c.* 800, furnish ample evidence of the modified Celtic forms in use there. One containing a portion of the Gospels[50] (Brit. Mus., Roy. MS. 1 E. vi, fol. 43;

Plate 16) formerly at St Augustine's Abbey, Canterbury, has Canon Tables decorated with patterns which may be traced to the Northumbrian style, including animals and interlace patterns in red dots as in the Lindisfarne Gospels; there are also framed roundels containing single or confronted animals (fol. 4)[51] such as are found in Vesp. A.I. The colours are red, light bluish-green, yellow, purple, and gold. The arches as shown on this page have lost all semblance of architectural forms and have become mere bands of ornament with roundels of interlace at the top. Lion masks occur occasionally in the decoration as on fol. 6 and in the initial[52] on fol. 42. One of four purple pages in Roy. I E. vi, fol. 43 (Plate 16), has a remarkable half-length representation of the symbol of Luke in the tympanum of the arch, and a bust of the Evangelist in a medallion above it. Elaborate gold and silver lettering is used for the first words of the Gospel of Luke, which are distributed over the space beneath the arch.[53]

Another manuscript usually ascribed to Canterbury, a late eighth century copy of Bede's *Ecclesiastical History*[54] (Brit. Mus., Cott. MS. Tib. C.ii) contains ornamental text pages in a style very close to those in Roy. I E. vi. Folio 5 verso (Plate 15) illustrates well the mingling of the Northumbrian and South English styles. The initial letter D is divided into framed panels containing various kinds of ornament including interlace and foliate animal scroll, and ends in a metallesque interlace which is a continuation of the framing bands of the initial. Enclosed in the centre space is a field divided by a flowering rod into four quarters, alternately red and green, in each of which a lively little toy animal with knotted tail yaps fiercely or grins foolishly. Many of the decorative text letters which follow the initial are formed by animals which bite at the adjacent letter or rear their heads pertly above the framework of the background which is also red and green. It is a gay style, very much softened by its contacts with the south, but with the loss of its northern intensity it has become distinctly weakened. Its final phase we shall see later, in the Rome Gospels of *c*. 800.

For the South English figure style, it is important to look at one more example (Vienna, Nationalbib., MS. lat. 1224) which is certainly not later than 800 and perhaps as early as *c*. 770. This is the so-called Cutbercht Gospels, written by Cutbercht, a South English scribe, perhaps in Salzburg itself where the manuscript is known to have been in the first half of the ninth century. Folio 71 verso (Plate 9A) shows the Evangelist Mark with his symbol.[55] The type is that of the Lindisfarne Evangelists; but the style, though linear, carries over more of the modelled figure technique. The face shows traces of modelling in the form of triangular blotches on the cheeks, and the huge eyes have a marked intentness of expression. The drapery folds form a rich and lively pattern; one little fold even flips up at the hem. It is probable that there is Continental influence here, mingling with the South English style, as we have seen nothing so free as this in insular manuscripts.[56] But the columns and the base of the architectural framework retain their interlace and animal patterns, and in the centre of the lower band is a panel with the interlocked bodies of two animals which recall similar designs in the Canterbury manuscripts.

Of about the same date or slightly earlier (*c*. 750–60) is a Gospel Book in the library of the monastery of St Gall, an Irish foundation. This manuscript (No. 51, Plate 9B), which is purely Irish in style, was probably written and illuminated in some monastery in Ireland.[57] The figures show certain affinities with the Lichfield Evangelists but, as we shall see, are much closer both in style and in iconography to its slightly later and much more sumptuous successor, the Book of Kells. The decoration in St Gall 51 consists of one full page of varied ornament – plaitwork, trumpet pattern, geometric designs, and animal interlace – each kind confined within rectangular panels on the page, the centre rectangles forming a cross.[58] There are also ornamental text pages at the beginnings of the gospel books, and these too are surrounded by a formal patterned frame within which the large ornamental initials and a few words of text are placed. In addition, there are four Evangelist portraits: three, Matthew, Luke, and John,[59] wiht their symbols; the fourth Evangelist (Mark, p. 78, Plate 9B) is seated in the centre of the page surrounded by a decorative border, in the four corners of which are all four of the symbols. It is questionable whether all the pictures are by the same artist; two of the Evangelists, Mark and John, have something of the squat stolidity which we shall see in the Kells figures.

The finest of the figures is Mark. He is represented in strictly frontal and nearly symmetrical position, and it is impossible to determine whether he is seated or standing, but no chair is visible. The head is large and round and is joined to the shoulders without any neck. The hair is in ropy, yellow locks curling at the ends (cf. the Luke of the Chad Gospels, Plate 8A); the yellow beard is sprinkled with red dots. The eyes are enormous with a pin-point pupil, and they give the face an intent almost eerie expression. In the drapery of the dark green mantle and the reddish-brown gown showing only a little at the bottom, the folds are indicated by a heavy dark brown line beside a light yellow line; this is obviously an echo of a painting technique by which the highlights and shadows were to be suggested. The figure, in fact, recalls a prototype closest to the Christ in Majesty of the earliest Carolingian manuscript of the Ada group, the Godescalc Gospels,[60] dated 781–3. The decorative panels on the Mark page of the St Gall Gospels have black or dark brown backgrounds, as in Durrow. The symbols of the Evangelists in the corners of the frame are of a different type from any yet seen and are closest to some of the various forms in Kells. The lion and the calf at the bottom, with symmetrical winged bodies and crossed paws in frontal position and heads in profile, recall similar treatment in Durrow, as does the patterning of the feathers.

In addition to the Evangelists there are two gospel illustrations, both at the end of the Gospel of John – a crucifixion with Longinus and Stephaton and two angels, as in Durham A.ii.17, and a Last Judgement, with a half-length Christ, two trumpeting angels, and twelve half-length figures – apostles – below.[61] In all the designs of the St Gall Gospels, there is even greater insistence on symmetry and formality than in the Lichfield figures, and this must be due, it would seem, to fresh contacts with an Eastern style. This same characteristic is one of the striking features also of the Book of Kells, to which we now come.

The Book of Kells (Dublin, Trin. Coll. Lib., MS. A.I.6) takes its name from the monastery of Kells (County Meath), a Columban foundation. It is believed to have been carried there from the parent monastery of Iona, where it was largely written and illuminated, by monks driven out by the Vikings in the early ninth century. The date of its production lies between 760–70 and 815–20.[62] It is not completely finished, some pages having the border only drawn in and many of the ornamental motifs either left uncoloured or painted in a different and obviously later technique. Several hands collaborated in the decoration,[63] and there seem to be indications in the different types of colouring and technique that all of them may not have been contemporary. The scheme of illumination, though partially resembling St Gall 51 and having many elements in common with both Lindisfarne and Durrow, is more elaborate as well as more lively and exciting than any of these.

There are six main types of decoration in the Book of Kells: (1) Canon Table pages, some under arcades with beasts, i.e. the symbols of the Evangelists, in the tympana (Plate 6B); (2) pages containing only Evangelist symbols; (3) portraits of Christ and of the Evangelists, each on a separate page (Plate 14); (4) miniatures representing the Virgin and Child, the Temptation of Christ, and the Betrayal of Christ; (5) cruciform pages, preceding each of the gospels; (6) decorative text pages (Plate 13) including not only extremely elaborate initial monograms and first words, but verse initials composed largely of animals and human figures combined with decorative motifs; there are also line-endings often consisting of animal or human figures. Such a wealth and variety of decoration is impossible to describe adequately; only an examination of the original pages[64] can give any idea of the amazing intricacy and richness and the inexhaustible inventiveness of its detail.

Perhaps the best way to arrive at a basis for evaluating the good and bad qualities of the Book of Kells is to compare the various types of decoration with similar pages in other manuscripts of the Hiberno-Saxon group, especially the Lindisfarne Gospels, the chief rival of Kells in beauty and richness.

Plate 6B illustrates one of the best 'beast canon' pages (fol. 2) which were painted by two hands, one greatly inferior. This manner of decorating the arches of the Canon Tables does not occur in any other manuscript of the group and undoubtedly comes from a Carolingian model of the Ada school. Nowhere in any surviving Carolingian manuscript, however, are the symbols of the Evangelists organized into such a compact design as in Kells, where they completely fill the tympanum space and, together with the other decorative elements, make up a rich and beautiful page. Many of these elements are familiar components of the Hiberno-Saxon style: the stopped-knot interlace, the trumpet pattern and whorl, the stepped pattern (seen in one small lozenge in the centre of the middle capital) the lacertine animals in dizzy coils, and the 'Lindisfarne birds' (middle column). But there are also newcomers: the main arch is bordered with a rope-like twist and filled with Northumbrian vine scroll[65]; and at the bottom of the central text columns there are loosely drawn, curved sprays tipped with trefoil flowerets or perhaps grapes.[66] More novel still, and stemming from Irish rather than Northumbrian taste, is the running pattern of human figures and birds, each of the latter viciously gripping in its beak the leg of the man above. The same interlacement of limbs and tails and feathers is seen in the admirably designed tympanum figures and the beautifully disposed bird and interlace ornaments in the top corners and at the bottom of the outer text columns. The symmetry of the page design as a whole and the careful matching of the types of ornament in corresponding panels is not characteristic of barbaric decoration and is to be traced, perhaps, partly to Northumbrian (cf. Plate 6A), partly to Carolingian sources. The firm drawing and cloisonné-like patterning of the animals goes back to the technique of Durrow, as does the amazing fineness of the geometric patterns. But the colour, especially the overpainting in thick white and yellow pigment (the latter closely resembling the colour and richness of gold) and the mixing of blue and green with enamel-like translucence, as also the rich reds and browns and purples, come either from Carolingian painting or from the East. Often this colour has been applied (later?) to the fine-line spiral and other linear patterns, thus obscuring them or allowing them to appear only where the paint has flaked off.

Folio 28 verso (Plate 14) contains the figure of the Evangelist Matthew apparently standing but perhaps seated, for there is a throne under an arch; he is seen frontally with symmetrically designed drapery decorated with flat squared or dotted patterns. The hieratic character of the figure, the throne with its lion back and its decorated cushion – the ox and the eagle heads appear one on each side, to complete the Evangelist symbol roster – suggest the Byzantine features of Ada School Evangelists.[67] The figure stands out with monumental dignity, closely framed by bands of fine spiral ornament which turn at a sharp angle just below his shoulders and end at the sides in a square filled with spirals of symmetrical C form. The fact that these bands terminate at the bottom in decorative roundels suggests the possibility that the artist was still adapting the square capitals and round bases of columns, which are normal architectural features in the designs of the Hiberno-Saxon Canon Tables, to the purposes of his design: if the shafts of the columns had continued the line of the arch, they would have joined the framework border, and the rich designs of both would have suffered from their proximity. As it is, the insertion of space with the boldly painted animal heads and the draped cushion open up the background and appear to place the figure behind the framing bands. This is indeed something new in the Hiberno-Saxon figure concept, and may come from the Ada tradition. The contrast between the fine-line decorative technique and the bold painting of the figures gives a superb balance to the page, which is a consummate example of Irish artistry intelligently combined with a magnificent figure style. There is no suggestion of grotesqueness in the stylization of the figure, as we saw it in, for example, St Gall MS. 51 (Plate 9B).

Contrasting sharply with this Matthew page is the miniature representing Christ Betrayed,[68] illustrating St Matthew's Gospel (fol. 114). Illustrative scenes from the life of Christ are not usual subjects in Carolingian manuscripts, and the question arises whether the Kells artist had access to some Syrian prototype such as the Rabula Gospels[69] where such scenes do occur. The introduction of an unmistakable vine pattern springing from a vase, in the tympanum, and its rambling, unsymmetrical design further suggests such a source, rather than the more byzantinized forms as found in Ada Group manuscripts. The miniature of the Virgin and Child[70] on fol. 7 verso seems to be by the same hand; this subject, also rare in Carolingian manuscripts, occurs in another Eastern manuscript of the Rabula style, the Etchmiadzin Gospels.[71] The predominance of purple and yellow – representing gold – in these pages of Kells supports the theory of direct Eastern influence.

The XPI monogram page (fol. 34; Plate 13) displays this same oriental richness in pattern and colour. Besides the usual geometric motifs exquisitely drawn and for the most part free of overpainting, angels with spread wings are introduced into the ornament, and also two human heads, one forming the terminal of the loop of the P, the other finishing the spiral ornament in the upper part of the field. Tucked into the right loop of the lower tip of the letter X is a group of well-observed naturalistic animals including two rats nibbling a round wafer – the Eucharistic bread? – while two cats sit watching them. Above, or behind, the cats are two more animals, apparently also rats, who await their turn at the food. The meaning of these figures has been interpreted symbolically,[72] but since no other symbolism has been recognized in the manuscript, the rats and cats may only record the artist's observation of these most familiar household animals. At any rate, the beautifully drawn little creatures serve as a healthy reminder of the humanness of the artist whose almost magical skill in the spinning of his endlessly varying patterns on a page like this leaves us breathless and dizzy.

It is apparent that there are many differences between the illustrative content and style of the Book of Kells and the Lindisfarne Gospels, especially where human figures are concerned. These may largely be traced to the differences in the models available to the artists of the two manuscripts. But there is one less obvious though more fundamental difference even in the decorative style as displayed on the pages of calligraphic ornament such as are common to the two manuscripts. This is not primarily a difference in the motifs used nor even in the patterns which are evolved from them; but it is rather a psychological difference based on the orderliness and consistency and clarity of the Lindisfarne pages as contrasted with a kind of wildness and incongruousness in many of the pages of Kells. Lindisfarne is a marvel of balance between movement and stability, and this gives the design a tremendous dynamic power. In Kells, the control is released and the designs with their bizarre motifs work themselves up into a frenzy of excitement that sparkles and crackles and dazzles and bewilders the beholder. Unlike the Lindisfarne book, Kells is full of whimsies and enigmas. Some pages are hideously ugly as to colour and overloaded as to design; others contain some of the most incredibly fine and intricate calligraphic ornament executed with inconceivable skill. Thus the two greatest exponents of Hiberno-Saxon art, though rivals in the high degree of their accomplishment, will always stand apart, each in its own niche: the only real basis of choice between Lindisfarne and Kells must be a matter of the temperament of the beholder.

The quality of the best pages in the Book of Kells is even more apparent when other Irish manuscripts of about the same time and later are compared with it. Of these, five are well known:[73] the Book of Dimma (Dublin, Trin. Coll. MS. 59) of the second half of the eighth century; the Book of Mulling (MS. 69 of the same collection) of the same time; the Book of Armagh (MS. 52) dated 807–45; the Mac Regal (Rushworth) Gospels (Oxford, Bod., MS. Auct. D.2.19) before 820; and the Gospels of Mac Durnan (London, Lambeth Palace Library) late ninth to tenth century, given, according to an inscription, to Christ Church, Canterbury, by King Æthelstan (d. 940). Although these manuscripts vary among themselves as to the amount and quality of the ornament and the style of the Evangelist figures, all are inferior in drawing, in colouring – one, the Book of Armagh is done with pen and ink only – and most of all in the richness and variety of the decoration.

Not earlier than c. 800 and, according to Kendrick,[74] perhaps of Mercian origin, is the so-called Rome Gospels, an example of the final phase of the South English style, which, like the Hiberno-Saxon, was becoming exhausted in the early ninth century and rapidly losing the vigour of its earlier robust form. Two pages from this manuscript (Vat. Lib.,

MS. Barb. lat. 570) are illustrated in plates 11B and 12. The seated Evangelist Matthew[75] on fol. 11 verso (Plate 11B) is a feebly-drawn figure with a weak, pink face and tidy blue hair and beard. He is surrounded by a rich border divided into panels, red, green, purple, and yellow, of interlace and animal and bird ornament, intertwined or confronted, but without the sharply incised crispness of the Northumbrian ('Anglian') beasts, or the wiry liveliness of the Canterbury-Merovingian animals. The birds look like hung game, and the confronted animals, instead of glaring and snarling at each other, gnaw contentedly on their own legs or graze peacefully nose to nose. The monogram XPI page (fol. 18; Plate 12) is a maze of intricate patterns of every sort, including naturalistic leaves and fruit, which covers the page with a filmy web of dainty prettiness. Evidence of the complete disruption of the tradition of surface pattern is the partial interpenetration of the hook of the P and the I in the monogram, thereby breaking the calligraphic rhythm of the letters and the smoothness of the flat surface pattern. The colours are muddy and harsh, and in spite of some good drawing in the ornament, the design is discordant and lacking in unity.

Indubitably Mercian in origin, according to Kendrick,[76] is the Book of Cerne (Camb., Univ. Lib., MS. Ll.i.10), a collection of Passion narratives from the four Gospels together with hymns and prayers, written for a certain Bishop Ethelwald, whose name is mentioned in the text, probably the holder of the see of Lichfield 818–30.[77] At the beginning of the passages from each Gospel is an Evangelist and symbol page. The Luke page (fol. 21 verso; Plate 17), which is typical in arrangement, with the symbol under the arch and the portrait in a medallion above, is similar in design to the Luke page in Roy. 1 E. vi (Plate 16). The Evangelist busts are also very much alike in the two manuscripts, especially Matthew and Mark in the Book of Cerne (fols 2 verso and 12 verso) and the Luke of 1 E. vi. Moreover, the forepart of the ox in the Book of Cerne is so like the half length ox in the tympanum of Roy. 1 E. vi as to seem to be copied from it; and the hind quarters are so absurdly clumsily drawn in relation to the head and front quarters that they must have been added from the Cerne artist's imagination.[78] The colouring is strong and harsh; the body of the ox is purple, its feet blue. The decoration on the Evangelist pages includes lion masks (fol. 31 verso) and curious nondescript plant and animal ornament.[79] The decorative letters of the first words of text on the opening Gospel pages are composed of animal heads and tails, but two different styles can be distinguished[80] (fols 32 and 43). Folio 43 represents the type closest to Tib. c.ii and Roy. 1 E. vi; the other type is smothered in patterns of red dots, the most common motif being a pyramid composed of dots. Yellow and red in addition to blue and purple are used and there is some gold in bands on the decorative text.

Summary

From an examination of the principal examples of pictorial art produced in England and Ireland during the period from the end of the seventh to the first third of the ninth century, three facts are evident:

1. There is a consistent predilection for decorative art, first in the metalwork, then in the calligraphic ornament of the manuscripts. Most of the motifs used in the decoration

are formal, that is, geometric patterns or stylized animals; but there is an important importation in the form of the 'naturalistic' vine scroll, with or without birds and animals of the naturalistic type. The variations which are evolved out of these comparatively few motifs are the measure of the decorative ingenuity of Hiberno-Saxon art.

2. Very early in the development of this art, there appears a willingness on the part of the artist to accept the human figure as introduced from various Christian Continental sources, but on his own terms: he refuses to copy it slavishly or to learn and adopt the painter's technique of trying to represent the figure as a solid form.

3. The result of the fusion of the two foregoing factors was the formulation of a new linear idiom as applied to figure subjects. This idiom varied locally according to (a) the special type of model known to the artist and (b) the skill of the individual artist.

It is noteworthy that in this period Irish and Anglo-Saxon traits can, at least to a limited degree, be distinguished: in figure types, the Irish artist is inclined to translate the details of human form – as hair, eyes, noses, feet and hands, drapery folds – into sheer linear pattern; the Anglo-Saxon artist, recognizing the fundamental differences between figures and decorative patterns, applies his linear technique to the problem of catching and expressing the human qualities of the figure as presented in his models. Thus the ultimate rendering in Celtic representational form, often hideous and grotesque as figure style, was still fine as ornament, while the Anglo-Saxon artist progressively develops his ability to grasp the liveliness of bodies and draperies in movement and the emotional intensity which they express. The Irish style, lacking the moderation and control of the Northumbrian, could merely spin itself out in a bewildering confusion of hybrid decoration incorporating indiscriminately human and ornamental motifs, while the Anglo-Saxon style of South England under fresh stimulus from the Continent was preparing the way for the emergence of a new linear technique to be applied to figure representation.

NOTES TO CHAPTER I

p. 10   1. This term is intended to suggest the twofold character of the art of this period. An alternative designation could be Anglo-Irish. There is not necessarily in either term any indication of precedence of one element over the other.

p. 11   2. It still belonged in the seventeenth century to the monastery of Durrow (Co. Offaly) which was founded by St Columba c. 553. On fol. 12 verso there are two colophons, one of which states that the book was written in twelve days by Columba in memory of the holy priest, Patrick. Lowe dates the Book of Durrow to the eighth century and describes it as 'copied from an exemplar in the hand of St Columba . . . to judge by the two inscriptions . . .' E. A. Lowe, *Codices Latini Antiquiores* (Oxford, 1934

seq.), II, No. 273. Henry (*Irish Art*, 68, n. 1) finds this late dating surprising in view of the fact that Lowe seems to accept the authenticity of the colophon. No monograph has yet been published on the Book of Durrow.

3. The symbols of the Evangelists are the four Beasts described in Ezekiel 1 and Revelation 4; they were assigned individually to the authors of the four Gospels by St Jerome in the fifth century. They are: Matthew – winged man (angel); Mark – winged lion; Luke – winged bull; John – eagle. On the folio now numbered ii all four symbols are grouped round a cross filled with interlace design and surrounded by a diagonal fret border. Reproduced Åberg, *Occident and Orient*, figure 75. The other four symbols

are on separate pages, one at the beginning of each Gospel.

4. These tables are a concordance of references to corresponding passages in the different Gospels, compiled by a monk, Eusebius of Caesarea, in the early fourth century.

5. These pages are badly damaged probably from water which, as late as the seventeenth century, was poured over the book and used as a cure for sick cattle.

6. Henry (*op. cit.*, 67 ff.) explains this inconsistency by assuming that the symbols were added after the text was written, in Ireland, from a different manuscript which preserved the order of an older version of the Gospels than the Vulgate which is the form of the text. This explanation she uses as evidence that the painting is Irish, though the text may have been copied in Northumbria.

7. Similar patterns are found in the millefiori glass used on later Irish metalwork, as the Tara Brooch and the Ardagh Chalice. *Op. cit.*, 118 ff. Plates 45-7. The symbol of Matthew in the Book of Durrow has been likened to a figure on the handle of a bronze vessel found at Moklebust, Norway, probably insular in origin. See Doran, 'The Enamelling and Metallesque Origin of the Ornament in the Book of Durrow', 143. Two noticeable differences, however, are the wig-like hair and the position of the feet, both suggesting Egyptian figures. The Matthew and the Luke symbols on the page containing all four symbols (fol. ii) also show these Egyptian traits particularly well. For Coptic influence on the symbols see Hovey, 'Sources of the Irish Illuminative Art', 105 ff.

8. Similar but more elaborate text pages occur also in the later manuscripts (see Plates 5 and 13).

9. Åberg, *op. cit.*, 15. This whole section (15-129) contains the clearest summary thus far published of the various theories held by scholars, who tend to separate into two camps on the basis of favouring Irish or Anglo-Saxon influence as the predominating factor in the development of the Durrow style.

10. Parts 2 and 3 of Åberg's study deal with ornamental motifs and compositions, chiefly the interlace, of Lombard Italy and the Merovingian kingdoms. For the animal ornament of Durrow and related manuscripts see the monumental study by Bernhard Salin, *Die altgermanische Tierornamentik. Typologische Studie über germanische Metallgegenstände aus dem IV. bis IX. Jahrh. nebst einer Studie über irische Ornamentik, übersetzt von J. Mestorf*. 2. Aufl. (Stockholm, 1935). On Continental sources of English

ornament in the pre-Norman period as a whole, see Brøndsted, *Early English Ornament*.

11. See P. W. Joyce, *A Social History of Ancient Ireland*, 2nd ed. (London, 1913), I, 410 ff. Bede in his *Ecclesiastical History* remarks on the reception of English scholars in Irish monasteries (Book III, Chapter 27. Trans. A. M. Sellar (London, 1907), 204.)

12. See H. J. Lawlor and W. M. Lindsay, 'The Cathach of St Columba', *Proc. Royal Irish Acad.*, XXXIII (1916), 241-331 and plate 33. A Cathach was a book which was carried before an army going into battle, in the hope of bringing victory.

13. According to legend, St Columba copied the Psalter without permission from one borrowed from St Finnian and a dispute ensued which culminated in the Battle of Cul Dremhne in 561 and led to the exile of St Columba from Ireland and therefore, indirectly, to the founding in 563 of the monastery at Iona. For a colourful account of the copying episode and its dire results, see Manus O'Donnell, *Life of Columcille*, paras 167-201. Trans. A. O'Kelleher and G. Schoepperle, *Betha Colaim Chille* (Urbana, 1919), 177-201. The story is told in briefer form by D. Chrétien, *The Battle Book of the O'Donnells* (Berkeley, Cal., 1935). The early dating of the Psalter is accepted by Lowe on paleographical grounds: *op. cit.*, 41. Lindsay, *op. cit.*, 402, says: 'There is no known reason to prevent the script of the Cathach from being as old as St Columba's time.'

14. See Nordenfalk, 'Before the Book of Durrow', Figures 7, 8, 12, 14, 15, and 17. See also Oakeshott, *Sequence of English Medieval Art*, chapter III, and especially Appendix I and II in which the evidence of Irish and Anglo-Saxon sources has most recently been summarized, with diagrams illustrating special motifs. p. 13

15. Cf. Nordenfalk, 'Before the Book of Durrow', figures 9-11 and 13.

16. British Museum, *The Sutton Hoo Ship Burial, a Provisional Guide* (London, 1947). See also R. L. S. Bruce-Mitford, 'The Sutton Hoo Ship Burial', *Proc. Suffolk Inst. Archaeol.*, XXV, Part I (1949).

17. Cf. also the interlace on seventh century Northumbrian high crosses, as Ruthwell and Bewcastle. Saxl and Wittkower, *British Art and the Mediterranean*, 15-18. It occurs also on an early Irish slab at Fahan Mura (Donegal) probably of the second half of the seventh century. See Françoise Henry, *La Sculpture irlandaise* (Paris, 1933), 15 ff., plates 14 and 15. For an analysis of the Celtic version of the interlace known as the breaks or knot type, see Allen, *Celtic Art in Pagan and Christian Times*, 257-78.

Lethaby believes the source of the knotted and plaited work may be Coptic. See W. R. Lethaby, 'The Origin of Knotted Ornamentation', *Burl. Mag.*, x (1907), 256.

p. 13   18. Even closer and almost identical with the Durrow animals are those on the Crundale sword pommel, dated first half of the seventh century, by Salin, *op. cit.*, 328 ff., and also by Baldwin Brown, *The Arts in Early England*, v, 385. The design of the Crundale pommel is compared with the Durrow animal design in the *Sutton Hoo Provisional Guide*, figure 15. On the Crundale pommel, see British Museum, *Guide to Anglo-Saxon Antiquities* (London, 1923), 11, figure 6.

19. The arrangement of these spirals varies somewhat from that in Durrow. Even closer in design is a hanging bowl escutcheon from Hitchin now in the Victoria and Albert Museum. See Françoise Henry, 'Hanging Bowls', *Jnl Roy. Soc. Antiq. Ireland*, LXVI (1936), 209–46, especially plate XXXII. In her most recent book, Mlle Henry maintains her earlier conviction that these bowls were made in Ireland, though nearly all were found in Saxon graves. See Henry, *Irish Art*, 36 ff., especially 37, n. 1. Kendrick, on the other hand, stoutly maintains the British origin of these bowls. *Anglo-Saxon Art*, 51 ff.

20. *Sutton Hoo Provisional Guide*, plates 18 and 20.

21. Two are reproduced in the *Provisional Guide*, plate 15, b and c. Closer to the cross with interlace, as on fols i verso and ii (see note 3 above) is the Fahan Mura slab (see note 17 above).

22. One of the clearest statements of this idea that Celtic illuminative style was the result of Irish calligraphic skill and the development of Anglo-Saxon metalwork is found in an article by Clapham, 'Notes on the Origins of Hiberno-Saxon Art'. He says in part: 'No one doubts . . . that the learned Irish missionaries brought with them proficient scribes and that the Northumbrian scribes were trained in turn by them' . . . 'In any case all the available evidence goes to show that the Irish came to Northumbria without any form of Celtic art-expression and left it capable of producing the highest forms of Irish Christian art', pp. 56 and 57.

23. Cf. Åberg, *op. cit.*, 123–9, and G. L. Micheli, *L'Enluminure du haut moyen-âge et les influences irlandaises* (Brussels, 1939), 15.

24. This manuscript is sometimes called the Durham Book from the fact that it was preserved in St Cuthbert's shrine there from the late tenth to the twelfth century. The evidence of authorship is given in a tenth century colophon which, because of its late date, has been suspect. The grounds for accepting it are, as Bruun remarks, that if the writer were inventing his facts he would probably have attributed the writing of so sumptuous a manuscript to a better known person than Eadfrith, perhaps St Aidan the founder of Lindisfarne. Bruun, *Celtic Illuminated Manuscripts*, 49 ff. Millar (*Lindisfarne Gospels*, 4) finds no reason for rejecting or even questioning the facts in the colophon. On the acceptability of the colophon, see also Baldwin Brown, *op. cit.*, 334 ff.

25. A bird of prey constitutes one of the fittings p. of the shield in the Sutton Hoo treasure. See *Provisional Guide*, Plate 4C. Bird heads also occur on the gold buckle and on the purse mounting in the same.

26. Reproduced by Millar in colours which represent fairly accurately the original, as the frontispiece to his monograph.

27. On other folios this is not always true. Cf. fol. 95 (Plate 55) where the knotted interlace in both initial and border is painted over in a solid block with considerable loss of delicacy and brilliance.

28. The most noticeable of these symmetrical elements are the C-scrolls of the ribbons in groups of p. four within the cross. C-scrolls are also used in the trumpet patterns in Durrow, but with less perfect symmetry.

29. So also the other symbols, with the possible significance of suggesting the source of the Evangelist's inspiration.

The meaning of the head peeping from behind the curtain is not clear. In the earliest surviving picture of a seated Evangelist (a sixth-century Gospel Book now in the Cathedral of Rossano, Calabria) a female figure, usually interpreted as an allegorical representation of Divine Wisdom, is holding out a book to the Evangelist Mark in a similar manner as in Lindisfarne. Reproduced A. Muñoz, *Il codice purpureo di Rossano* (Rome, 1907), plate XV. It seems possible that the Matthew miniature may be following such a prototype. For another explanation of its source in an ivory panel carved with the legend of St Mark (now in the Museo Archeologico, Milan), see Carl Nordenfalk, 'Eastern Style Elements in the Book of Lindisfarne', *Acta Archaeologica*, XIII (1942), 161. The Lindisfarne Evangelist pictures were perhaps taken from more than one source, as is suggested by the labelling of the symbol in Latin ('imago hominis') and of Matthew in a mixture of Latin and Greek ('O AGIOS MATTHEUS'). In the picture of Mark (fol. 93 verso) it has become 'O AGIUS MARCUS'.

30. Florence, Biblioteca Laurenziana, MS. Amiatinus 1, c. 700. Presented at the close of the ninth century to the Monastery of Monte Amiata, near Siena. It was one of three manuscripts ordered to be written by Ceolfrid, Abbot of Jarrow, 690–716, and was the one chosen by him to take to Rome for presentation to the Pope.

31. Nordenfalk, 'Eastern Style Elements', 157, says the Ezra is 'almost an exact copy of a similar illustration in Cassiodorus's famous Codex grandior'; Burkitt describes the text of the *Codex Amiatinus* as perhaps that approved by Cassiodorus for his monks at Vivarium in South Italy. F. C. Burkitt, 'Kells, Durrow and Lindisfarne', *Antiquity*, IX (1935), 34. According to Burkitt, the Lindisfarne text was not copied from *Amiatinus* but, like *Amiatinus*, from a parent manuscript brought from South Italy, of which Durham A.II.17 has preserved nine leaves. *Op. cit.*, 36.

32. On fol. 796 verso of the *Codex Amiatinus* is a Majesty in a poor linear style which was copied perhaps from some better Continental miniature of this subject. (Reproduced Kendrick, *Anglo-Saxon Art*, plate XLII.) If this is Jarrow art, the Ezra is far from it, as also are the Lindisfarne Evangelists.

33. Reproduced E. Heinrich Zimmermann, *Vorkarolingische Miniaturen* (Berlin, 1911), plate 221. See also pp. 124 ff. and 259 ff. Folios 103–11 are a fragment of an earlier Gospels. See note 31 above.

34. The animal head is the long-nosed biting type as in Durrow (Plate 1). An interesting feature which perhaps points to the intermediate chronological position of this manuscript between Durrow and Lindisfarne is the bird heads in the whorls which could easily have developed out of the Durrow geometric whorl, as on fol. iii (Plate 3D). A similar bird head with biting beak joined to a body with wings, constitutes one of the characteristic motifs of Lindisfarne, as fol. 26 verso (Plate 4). Cf. also Millar, *op. cit.*, 22.

35. The cloisonné-like treatment of the feathers and the staring faces are close to the St Matthew symbol of Durrow, but the striped draperies suggest the Chad Evangelists. See below.

36. Perhaps written in Wales; it was in the church at Llandaff in the early eighth century and at Lichfield from the tenth century. Lowe, *op. cit.*, No. 159. Page 5 is reproduced in Zimmermann, plate 245b.

37. Notably St Gall MS. 51, the Book of Kells, and others.

38. Paris, Bib. Nat. MS. lat. 9389. The Abbey of Echternach was founded in 698 by Willibrord, the second English missionary to Friesland. He was of English birth but educated in Ireland. The manuscript is clearly the work of a Hiberno-Saxon scribe and illuminator, and shows no evidence of Continental influence. Masai, *Essai*, p. 133, dates this manuscript between Durrow and Lindisfarne, i.e., c. 710; Nordenfalk places it shortly after Durrow, i.e. before or about 700. Carl Nordenfalk, 'On the Age of the Earliest Echternach Manuscripts', *Acta Archaeologica*, III (1932), 57–62.

39. Page 219 of the Lichfield Gospels contains all four symbols (reproduced Zimmermann, plate 245a). The calf, symbol of Luke, is exactly as in the Evangelist portrait but turned sidewise as though standing on its hind legs. The other Echternach symbols are reproduced *op. cit.*, plates 255b and 256.

40. Bede, *Ecclesiastical History*, Book IV, Chapter XVIII. Trans. A. M. Sellar (London, 1907), 257ff., and n. 3.

41. Folio 81 verso, reproduced Zimmermann, plate 247. p. 18

42. In Northumbrian sculpture of the seventh to eighth century, such figure types are even more strikingly rendered. Especially the Ruthwell Cross (early seventh century) shows the influence of figure art such as that brought in by Benedict Biscop. See Kendrick, *Anglo-Saxon Art*, 119 ff., on this 'Anglo-Saxon Renaissance'. Another suggestion as to the origin of the figures on the Ruthwell Cross and also of the Evangelists of Northumbrian manuscripts is the influence of Romano-British sculpture. Fritz Saxl, 'The Ruthwell Cross', *Jnl Warb. and Court. Insts*, VI (1943), 1–19.

43. Camb., Corpus Christi Coll., MS. 286, still dated by most recent writers in the sixth century, probably not earlier than the latter half of the century. It contains two miniatures: fol. 125, twelve gospel pictures from the Passion of Our Lord (reproduced *Pal. Soc.*, series 1, plate 34); fol. 129, the Evangelist Luke seated under an arch containing his symbol, and flanked by a series of six gospel scenes on each side (reproduced *op. cit.*, plate 44). The technique though linear is based on antique representational style such as is found in early Christian manuscripts, like the Rossano Gospels of the sixth century. Cf. A. C. Haseloff, Review of Muñoz, *Il codice purpureo di Rossano . . ., L'Arte*, X (1907), 468.

44. This technique certainly does not come from St Augustine's Gospels, however early this may be dated, though some details of the David miniature resemble it, e.g., the rendering of the throne and cushion, the arch filled with decorative patterns and

the plant motifs on each side of the arch. In place of
the gospel scenes between the columns flanking the
throne, the Psalter miniature uses a flat panel of
decoration bordered by plain bands. All sense of
space has of course been lost in the Psalter, as in the
Gospels.

p. 19   45. Traced by Brøndsted to Merovingian manuscripts, *op. cit.*, 100 ff.

46. A book cover of the seventh century at Stonyhurst College has as a central motif a similar type of
acanthus spray stylized and much simplified. Reproduced Kendrick, *Anglo-Saxon Art*, plate XLIII, figure
1. The plant ornament as found on the Ruthwell
and Bewcastle Crosses is the vine used in a running
scroll pattern and was probably introduced from the
Near East. See Brøndsted, *op. cit.*, 35–42.

47. In Carolingian manuscripts, the Sacramentary
of Drogo is probably the earliest example, dated
mid ninth century. On the schools of Carolingian
illumination see Adolph Goldschmidt, *German Illumination*, I (New York, 1928), and Amédée Boinet,
La Miniature carolingienne (Paris, 1913).

48. According to an inscription on fol. 11, it was
bought by the ealdorman Ælfred from some pagans,
who almost certainly had stolen it, and presented by
him to St Augustine's Abbey, Canterbury. Brøndsted says *c.* 775, on the basis of vine patterns and
early Carolingian ribbon; *op. cit.*, 123.

49. Only one other Evangelist miniature survives,
John on fol. 150 verso (reproduced Zimmermann,
plate 283). There are four leaves of Canon Tables
under arches (fols 5–8); on fol. 6 busts of the four
Evangelists appear in the two capitals and bases of
the columns (*op. cit.*, plate 280). Alternate text pages
are stained purple – probably the earliest appearance
of purple pages in an insular manuscript. But cf.
Codex Amiatinus, p. 15 above.

50. Perhaps part of a Bible of St Gregory. See
M. R. James, *Anc. Lib. Cant. and Dover*, LXV.

p. 20   51. Zimmermann, plate 290.

52. *Op. cit.*, plate 292c.

53. It has been suggested that this leaf and fol. 30
with a full-page miniature of Mark framed by an
acanthus border both may be late ninth-tenth century additions, Sir George Warner and J. P. Gilson,
*Cat. of Western MSS in the Old Royal and King's
Collns* (London, 1921.) Kendrick, however, dates
the whole manuscript tentatively to the time of
Archbishop Wulfred (805–32) but attributes it to
Mercia, *Anglo-Saxon Art*, 162. Carolingian influence
in the figure of the Evangelist is evident. For the

relation of this manuscript to the Book of Cerne,
see below, p. 25.

54. Kendrick calls this manuscript Mercian also,
op. cit., 168

55. Other Evangelists are reproduced by Zimmermann, *op. cit.*, plates 297, 299, and 300.

56. Saxl compares the St John with the portrait
of Virgil in Vat. MS. lat. 3867, Saxl and Wittkower,
op. cit., plate 6, e and f, and page 19.

57. Zimmermann, 101 ff. According to Zimmermann, the manuscript is not found in the earliest St
Gall catalogue, *op. cit.*, 240.

58. Page 6 of the manuscript; reproduced *op. cit.*,
plate 187a.

59. Pages 2, 128, 208; reproduced *op. cit.*, plates
189 and 191a.

60. Paris, Bib. Nat., MS. Nouv. Acq. 1203; reproduced Goldschmidt, *op. cit.*, plate 25. It is interesting
to note bands of knotted interlace in the border of
the page, very similar to those on the St Gall manuscript page.

61. Reproduced Zimmermann, plate 188.

62. Henry, *Irish Art*, 149. Zimmermann dates it
much earlier, in the beginning of the eighth century,
op. cit., 234. Masai dates it late eighth century, *op. cit.*,
133. Kendrick dates it by implication *c.* 800, *Anglo-
Saxon Art*, 147. The most precise stylistic and iconographic evidence for dating the Book of Kells is
given by Friend, 'The Canon Tables of the Book of
Kells'. Friend places the greater part of the illumination between the years *c.* 795 and 806 (*op. cit.*, 639).
He explains the beast Canon pages as copies from a
Carolingian model of the Ada School, which was
perhaps also copied by the artist of the Carolingian
manuscript Harl. 2788 in the British Museum.

63. Henry distinguishes at least four, *Irish Art*,
144 ff.

64. The original is not generally available for examination but a facsimile of the manuscript has been
published: Alton and Meyer, *Codex Cenannensis,
The Book of Kells*, with many colour plates and a
text volume containing a study of the ornament (III,
27–52). Many pages are reproduced by Robinson,
Celtic Illuminative Art, plates XI–LI. See also Sullivan,
The Book of Kells.

65. For a detailed discussion of this important
motif in English ornament see Brøndsted, *op. cit.*
Two examples of the Kells vine scroll are reproduced *op. cit.*, figure 71.

66. Bruun describes this and other like motifs as phyllomorphic innovations in Kells, *op. cit.*, 21 ff. Robinson identifies these trilobed forms as 'pendent bells attached to the flabellum, similar to those in use in the Coptic Church for protecting the Eucharistic elements', *op. cit.*, plate XIII. As used on plate 6B of this book they certainly are meant to be the flowers or fruit of a growing vine.

3 67. Cf. Friend, *op. cit.*, plates XX and XXI.

68. Reproduced in colour, Alton and Meyer, *op.cit.*

69. See R. Garrucci, *Storia dell' arte cristiana*, III (1876), plates 128–140.

70. Alton and Meyer, *op. cit.*, reproduction in colour.

71. Josef Strzygowski, 'Das Etschmiadzin-evangeliar', *Byzantinische Denkmäler*, I (Vienna, 1891), plate IV. For an interesting suggestion of the Egyptian Isis and Horus as a prototype, see H. Rosenau, *Burl. Mag.* LXXXIII (1943), 228–31.

4 72. Robinson suggests that this little scene may be an allusion to unworthy receivers of the Eucharist and the impending judgement awaiting them, *op. cit.*, plate XL.

73. See Henry, *Irish Art*, 150–3, with bibliography and references to reproductions.

74. Kendrick, *Anglo-Saxon Art*, 147.

75. The other three Evangelists, fols 50 verso, 79 p. 25 verso, and 124 verso (Zimmermann, plates 313b and 314) have heads of the same type, and similar poses. Only the Matthew page has been completed with the patterned border. Zimmermann places this manuscript in the South English group, *op. cit.*, 140 ff.

76. Kendrick, *Anglo-Saxon Art*, 165.

77. Herbert, *Illuminated Manuscripts*, 85, identifies Ethelwald as the Bishop of Lindisfarne (724–40). Zimmermann (*op. cit.*, 295) says there was a Bishop Ethelwald in Cerne in the eighth century. It is not known when the manuscript was at Cerne Abbey (Dorsetshire). See also Kuypers, *The Book of Cerne*, pp. xii–xiv.

78. The pen drawing of the ox in the margin is a late copy by an even less expert artist.

79. Kendrick, *op. cit.*, plate 68.

80. Zimmermann, plate 293.

CHAPTER 2

ANGLO-SAXON ART FROM THE LATE NINTH TO THE MIDDLE OF THE ELEVENTH CENTURY

*

HISTORICAL BACKGROUND:
POLITICAL UNITY UNDER THE SUPREMACY OF WESSEX

POLITICAL

Raids of Vikings and Danes

Æthelwulf, King 839–58: fought the Danes; made two journeys to Rome with his youngest son, Alfred, 853–5; married as his second wife Judith, daughter of Charles the Bald, Emperor of Germany (875–7).

Alfred (b. 849), King 871–99: fought the Danes and finally settled with them (878) to remain north of Watling Street and keep out of Wessex; from c. 884–5 to the end of his life engaged in literary activities, in which Grimbald, monk of St Bertin at St Omer and Asser of St David's, Wales, joined him; translated Gregory's *Pastoral Care* of which an illuminated copy was made during his lifetime (Bod. Lib., MS. Hatton 60); sponsored the beginnings of the Anglo-Saxon Chronicle.

Edward the Elder (son of Alfred), King 899–925: built New Minster Abbey (Winchester) which was consecrated in 903, and appointed as abbot there the monk Grimbald; his second wife was Ælfleda (d. 916) who ordered the embroidered vestments for Frithestan, Bishop of Winchester (909–31).

Æthelstan (son of Edward the Elder), King 925–39: 'Rex totius Britanniae'; gave the Frithestan vestments to the shrine of St Cuthbert at Chester-le-Street c. 935; his five half-sisters married foreign princes, of whom one was the future Emperor Otto I, founder of the Holy Roman Empire (962–73); many foreign gifts to Æthelstan and many manuscripts given by him to monasteries.

Edgar (younger son of Edmund, Æthelstan's half-brother), King of Mercia 957–9; King of 'all England' 959–75; gave a charter to New Minster in 966, of which the original illuminated copy is Cott. MS. Vesp. A.viii.

Æthelred the Unready (son of Edgar), King 979–1013; dispossessed by Swegn Forkbeard, King of Denmark; married Emma daughter of Richard I, Duke of the Normans; died in exile in Normandy.

Knut, King of Denmark 1014; King of England 1016–35; married first Ælfgyfu; then Emma widow of Æthelred 1017.

Edward the Confessor (son of Æthelred and Emma), King 1042–66 (5 January).

MONASTIC REFORM

On the Continent: Cluny and its dependencies; Abbot Odilo (994) established Cluny as the Mother House of an Order of Benedictine monasteries; reform also in Lorraine and Flanders.

In England:

Dunstan (b. 909), Abbot of Glastonbury *c.* 943–57; exiled 957–8 in Ghent at St Peter's (Blandinium), which had been reformed in 937; Bishop of Worcester and London 958; Archbishop of Canterbury 958–88; manuscripts made for him show both Glastonbury and Franco-Saxon stylistic connexions and brought both of these influences to Canterbury.

Æthelwold, monk at Glastonbury under Abbot Dunstan *c.* 946; Abbot of Abingdon *c.* 954; close connexions with Fleury; Bishop of Winchester 963–84; refounded Ely, Thorney, and Peterborough Abbeys under reformed Benedictine Rule; manuscripts made for him show strong, direct Continental influences, particularly from Fleury (reformed 926–44 under Odo, Abbot of Cluny).

Oswald, monk at Worcester; studied at Fleury till 958; Bishop of Worcester 961; Archbishop of York 972–92; founded Ramsey Abbey *c.* 968.

Robert of Jumièges (Normandy), Bishop of London, 1044–51; Archbishop of Canterbury 1051–2 (expelled); ordered a manuscript in Winchester style to be made for him and presented it to the Abbey of Jumièges (Rouen, Bib. Pub., MS. Y.6).

Stigand, Bishop of Winchester 1043–52 and Archbishop of Canterbury 1052–70 (deposed by William the Conqueror).

*

THE century and a half covered by this chapter is a period of great names in both church and state. If King Alfred had not succeeded in checking the invasions of the Vikings and Danes in Wessex, Anglo-Saxon civilization would have been wiped out. And if a settlement with the invaders had not been made, the important steps taken by Alfred in internal political organization, in establishing a school for the education of both courtiers and churchmen at his own court, in encouraging the writing and translating of books, and in countless other ways fostering Anglo-Saxon culture, would not have borne fruit. Moreover, he had personal contacts with the Continent, beginning perhaps even with early journeys with his father to Rome and certainly continuing through his stepmother Judith, daughter of Charles the Bald, and most important of all, through the arrival at his court of the monk Grimbald,[1] sent by Fulk, Archbishop of Reims. These were crucial in opening the way for the introduction of the influence of the Carolingian Renaissance on England. Foreign contacts were further developed through monastic channels, especially by the sojourn of English monks like Dunstan and Oswald in Continental monasteries. Here the results of the earlier transmission of classical culture were available to learning and here the Continental example of regeneration in religious spirit and reorganization in the administration of the Benedictine Rule were already in practice and could be carried back to English monasteries. The immediate results for the development of art in England were revolutionary; without these fresh strong impulses from the vigorous Continental styles which sprang up under the influence of the Carolingian Renaissance, Anglo-Saxon art probably would have suffered a lingering death by attrition.

In the pre-Conquest Anglo-Saxon period, as in the preceding Hiberno-Saxon period, illuminated manuscripts furnish nearly all the surviving material for the study of English pictorial art.

Alfred's own patronage of learning in the later years of his reign left few traces on art. The original copy of his translation into Anglo-Saxon of St Gregory's *Cura Pastoralis* made under his sponsorship and supervision in 890–7 and sent by him to the Bishop of Worcester,[2] is still preserved (Bod. MS. Hatton 60). Its decoration is simple enough: the initial letters[3] terminating in open-beaked bird or crested animal heads with gaping or biting mouths are in a style which was unmistakably carried over from that of the Rome Gospels (Plate 12) or from the later and cruder Book of Cerne.[4] The initials of the *Cura Pastoralis*, therefore, while offering nothing new in decorative elements, furnish valuable evidence of the survival of a local style[5] through the violent period of the Danish troubles.

Even more important for reconstructing the style of the Alfredian period is the famous Alfred Jewel in the Ashmolean Museum at Oxford.[6] The half-length figure in cloisonné enamel on the face of the jewel shows a certain similarity to the type of the Evangelist Luke in the Chad Gospels at Lichfield (see Plate 8A) and also to the half-length Evangelists in the Book of Cerne (Plate 17). But the cloisonné technique is not English, and this, in combination with the further fact that the enamel has been trimmed to fit the mount, suggests the possibility that the enamel might be earlier[7] than the mount and perhaps was imported from some Continental source.

The mount is even more important than the figure; for it supplies a link between the earlier decorative style of Mercia and the new Continental elements that are to appear in the decades immediately following Alfred's reign. The all-over surface granulation and the beading of the mount recall the use of multiple dots as decoration in the Book of Cerne and in the so-called Trewhiddle[8] metal style; and the animal head terminal is an old Saxon ornamental motif which goes back even to the Sutton Hoo treasure.[9] On the other hand, the fleuronné ornament on the reverse of the Jewel is a rough version of the symmetrical acanthus[10] spray found in the earlier Canterbury Psalter (Plate 10B); but it is also found in a more finished form, probably under direct Frankish influence, on the slightly later Durham vestments, which are our first major example of tenth century pictorial art.

The Durham or St Cuthbert vestments consist of an embroidered stole and maniple, now preserved in Durham Cathedral Library; they can be dated between 909 and 916,[11] and were given by King Æthelstan to St Cuthbert's shrine at Chester-le-Street probably *c.* 934. They are remarkable as introducing a wholly new figure style which bears unmistakable relationship to that of Carolingian manuscripts, particularly those of the School of Tours.[12]

The bands are long and narrow (only about $2\frac{3}{8}$ inches wide) and are bordered by a woven braid in gold and red patterned with tiny acanthus leaves and paired animals in repeated series of seven. Between these borders are full-length figures of prophets and saints standing on conventional bits of rocky ground which, together with the acanthus sprays introduced above the head of each, separate the figures from one another. Of the original sixteen major and minor prophets, twelve survive (Plate 18); they are well-proportioned, dignified figures seen in three-quarter or front view. The drapery is rich in folds similar to those of sixth century mosaics as at Sant' Apollinare Nuovo in Ravenna, but the figures themselves have lost most of the formality of the earlier Byzantine types.[13]

The softness of the Durham prophets' hair and beard, the easy gestures and well-balanced poses, and the free-hanging, sometimes lightly fluttering drapery ends seem to be derived directly from Carolingian rather than from Byzantine models; and the curling, fleshy acanthus leaf ornament also probably comes from Carolingian manuscripts.[14] The colours, which now appear almost uniformly as soft tans, were originally rich and varied. Gold is used with the coloured silks in the combined technique of weaving and embroidery.[15] The vestments are a priceless relic of an early manifestation of that English skill in embroidering which was famous later all over Europe by the name of 'opus anglicanum' (see Chapter 6 below). They also are one of the earliest manifestations of the full and direct impact of the Carolingian Renaissance on English art.

The fleshy acanthus leaf in the Durham embroideries finds its way into the ornamental initials of manuscripts. Perhaps the earliest example is in the Durham Ritual already referred to:[16] the acanthus leaf is held in the mouth of a winged beast whose tail is in turn bitten by another animal head forming the terminal of the initial letter. The technique is drawing in line of varying thickness with some suggestion of shading on the leaf. Heavier and fleshier in form and shaded with white lines on colour are similar acanthus leaves and animal or bird heads used as terminals of the initials[17] in a manuscript copy of Bede's Life of St Cuthbert (Camb., Corpus Christi Coll., MS. 183). A different use of the same acanthus motif, which is closer to the symmetrical type of sprays in the Durham embroideries, is found in some of the border panels of the miniature on fol. 1 in the Bede manuscript (Plate 20A). This motif, which sometimes resembles even more closely a vine leaf with attached bunches of grapes, is worked into running scroll patterns enclosing at intervals lively figures of birds and animals – the so-called inhabited scroll. The colours are white for the pattern and dark red for the ground, which is bordered with yellow.

The miniature itself in the Bede manuscript is painted in a style that is remarkable for England at this time. It represents King Æthelstan offering a book (presumably this very manuscript which he actually did present to St Cuthbert's shrine c. 934) to St Cuthbert who stands before a chapel. Both figures are stiffer in pose and the draperies are more stylized than are the prophets of the Cuthbert vestments, but the resemblance in type of figure, especially of St Cuthbert, is extraordinarily close. In contrast to the brilliance of the gold and colour mingled in the embroideries, the miniature appears even flatter and heavier, with thick opaque colours, chiefly red, purple, and blue, against a plain vellum background. The architecture shows the curious rising perspective characteristic of Carolingian painting, but the artist has put in every tile and every stone with no less care than he drew the graceful border designs in which he took such obvious delight. Both the miniature and the initials in this important manuscript, especially the fine P on fol. 5 verso, are, as Professor Wormald points out, 'a thoroughly Continental production'.[18]

The explanation of the sudden appearance of Continental influences in the south of England, in both figure and decorative styles, may lie, partly at any rate, in the introduction of Continental models by gifts to Æthelstan or others of his court. Some of these importations have survived, and many more undoubtedly have perished or remain unrecognized. The best documented Continental manuscript gift to Æthelstan is a late Carolingian Gospel Book with Evangelist portraits, which, according to an inscription, was presented to him by Emperor Otto I and his mother Mechtild, perhaps in 929 on the occasion of the marriage of Otto to Æthelstan's sister Eadgyth.[19]

Another Continental manuscript which belonged to Æthelstan, a Psalter (Brit. Mus., Cott. MS. Galba A.xviii) has some initials in Franco-Saxon style, others in pure insular style,[20] and four miniatures which were inserted (fols 2 verso, 21, 120 verso, and 85 now a loose leaf in Bod. MS. Rawl. B.484) and may have been copied from Continental models. They were painted by at least two artists, both presumably English, perhaps at Winchester to which the manuscript was given by Æthelstan.[21] The better of the artists painted fol. 21 (Plate 20B) which contains a full-page miniature within a narrow border decorated with acanthus sprigs and, on the two upper corners, heads with curly leaves issuing from their mouths. Within the rectangular frame are two mandorlas, the inner filled with a fine figure of Christ in Majesty holding the Cross in his left hand. He is clothed in a blue mantle, except for the right arm and the side displaying the wounds. At his feet is a rect-angular red-brick building with a yellow-tiled roof, similar to that in the Cuthbert minia-ture (Plate 20A). The solid, cushioned throne, the heavy drapery, and the firmly seated figure with protruding knees are clearly copied with some degree of understanding from a Carolingian original, perhaps of the Ada School, as suggested by the large head and wide-open staring eyes. The figure of Christ is impressive and monumental. The other figures in the 'choirs of martyrs and virgins', though of the same general type, show little differentiation among themselves except in dress and in the colour of their hair. The wings of the angels in the corners of the rectangle are designed to fit well into the triangular spaces. The all-over pattern of the composition is further emphasized by the use of a black ground, against which the soft, dull colours – blue, green, brown, and yellow – stand out effectively. Very little red is used, and no gold at all.

Another miniature painted in a modelled technique forms the frontispiece of a manu-script probably from Canterbury[22] in Trinity College Library, Cambridge (MS. B.16.3) and must be a close copy of a Continental, probably a Fulda,[23] archetype by an English artist in the tenth century (Plate 19). The curious domical arches with the draped curtain and the columns with acanthus leaf capitals, under which Rabanus Maurus and his fellow monks are presenting the book to St Gregory, are Carolingian features; and the idea of the presentation picture occurs first in medieval art in the Tours School.[24] The figures are broad and stocky with great round eyes and solemn expressions. The enormous gesturing hands and the tight linear folds of the drapery betray the English artist's propensity for exaggeration and for pattern. The scale of the miniature – the book measures $16\frac{1}{2}$ by $13\frac{1}{2}$ inches – is unusually large for a book of this kind and suggests a derivation from wall painting or mosaics, and the type of composition, with depth of space indicated by the curtain twisted round the column and by the overlapping of figures and architecture, together with the total lack of any decoration either within or without the miniature, further bears out the effect of monumental painting. The picture is a solemn and pains-taking copy, totally lacking in originality, but valuable none the less for the transmission of a pictorial conception which was to bear fruit in the next generation of English art.

The monumentality which characterizes the Rabanus Maurus miniature helps to ex-plain another figure, very similar in type, which is prefixed[25] (fol. 1) to Bod. MS. Auct.

F.4.32 (Plate 22), a drawing of Christ adored by a kneeling St Dunstan. The date of the drawing may be before 957, while Dunstan was still in Glastonbury.[26]

The magnificent, fully draped figure of Christ and the solemn, intent face with its large eyes, firm, curved lips, and even the little vertical lines on the upper lip seem to be derived from some model[27] similar to the figures in the Rabanus Maurus miniature. The flying fold of drapery in the St Dunstan drawing can be paralleled in the billowing ends of the curtains in the other. The prostrate figure of St Dunstan with his enormous hands and tightly drawn drapery might be derived from the Rabanus Maurus group of monks. The technique is purely linear, yet solidity of the figures has been admirably achieved by the firm, rounded contour line. The only colour used is solid red for the halo, and touches of it in the garments of Dunstan. The Carolingian prototype of such a style (as, indeed, also of Galba A.xviii) is to be sought in the Ada School and its later derivatives.[28]

Dunstan returned from exile in Ghent in 958, to become Bishop of Worcester and then Archbishop of Canterbury in 959. Probably towards the end of his life in 988, or perhaps later, the early part of the Pontifical now in Paris (Bib. Nat., MS. lat. 943), was written for him at Canterbury[29] and illustrated with four drawings – a Crucifixion within an acanthus frame (fol. 4 verso; Plate 24) and three identical figures probably representing the Trinity (Plate 23). The stylistic relation between these drawings, especially the Trinity figure, and the Christ with St Dunstan is exceedingly close: the linear patterns in the drapery[30] are identical in the two miniatures as are the heavy figures with large hips and enormous hands. The faces have the same large eyes and heavily marked eyebrows and the same tense, solemn expressions. The feet of the Christ in the Bodleian manuscript are hidden by clouds and the truncated figure appears, therefore, exaggeratedly heavy in proportions as compared with the Christ in the Paris miniature. The Paris figure stands on the frame of the picture, the foot actually extending slightly over the edge, thus appearing even more firmly rendered and more solidly posed than the Christ of the St Dunstan miniature.

The Crucifixion from the Dunstan Pontifical (Plate 24) is drawn in brown and red and seems to be by the same hand as the Trinity figures. There are features in this miniature which relate it to the earliest phase of the Winchester style, as we shall see it in a painted form in Brit. Mus., Cott. MS. Vesp. A.viii (see Plate 25). The angels with trim wings and flying heels, the stiffly fluttering drapery ends, and the filleted heads are very like those in the Vespasian manuscript, and the round spots on shoulders and thighs can only come from the painted technique of shading these parts of the body to suggest their roundness, or else from the influence of sculpture.[31] The Crucifixion is a superb example of the Anglo-Saxon artist's ability to convey by pure line the monumentality of the painted human figure.

The appearance in the latter half of the tenth century of this monumental style of outline drawing of figures following Continental models is not entirely new in the south of England. Two centuries earlier at Canterbury a similar translation of painted figures into linear ones had occurred (cf. Plates 10B and 11A) combined with an initial style based on a mixture of linear ornamental motifs from Hiberno-Saxon and Continental, perhaps Italian, sources. Likewise, in this same Pontifical of St Dunstan a type of ornamental initial occurs which combines animal heads taken from the Canterbury and Mercian repertoire and the Celtic interlace with a simple version of the Carolingian acanthus leaf.

This hybrid type of initial is not unique nor is this its first appearance in English manuscripts. The beginnings of the style reach back to the early tenth century – the Durham Ritual which, as we have seen, introduced the acanthus leaf into the stock of motifs available for designing decorative initials. The acanthus leaf also occurs modestly in the border of Corpus Christi Coll. MS. 183 (Plate 20A) and more boldly in some of the initials. Shortly after the date of this manuscript, in the second quarter of the tenth century, the initial style incorporating the acanthus motif suddenly flowers out in a psalter (Bod., MS. Junius 27)[32] containing 152 initial letters using many different combinations of this motif with others – animal heads and winged beasts, interlace and even some human heads – all painted in heavy colours. The style thus evolved in the Junius Psalter sets off a whole series of manuscripts with decorative initials which combine in varying proportions the insular and the Continental elements, but which tend steadily towards greater size and sumptuousness and heavier and more lush acanthus ornament, doubtless under the full impact of Continental (Franco-Saxon) influence.

The initial type described above is already well developed in a psalter called, from a later owner, the Bosworth Psalter (Brit. Mus., Add. MS. 37517) also believed to have been written for Archbishop Dunstan at Canterbury.[33] The fine initial B introducing the first psalm (fol. 4; Plate 21A) shows clearly the lines of the drawing, but the ornament has been filled in with dull colour – red, blue, green, violet, brown, and yellow, but no gold. At the junction of the two loops of the B is a mask; this motif, which occurs in the Book of Cerne and earlier, becomes a distinctive feature of the large B of the Beatus in English psalters; the fully developed form can be seen in Harl. MS. 2904 (Plate 21B) of slightly later date. In the Bosworth Psalter initial both the letter itself and the foliage ornament which fills it consist of rather stringy bands, usually double, weaving in and out in a kind of interlaced acanthus scroll, and occasionally breaking in sharp 'elbows', and terminating in either a thick bunchy leaf or a bird or animal head. The initial is painted against the plain vellum and touches in several places the adjoining text letters, thus demonstrating its calligraphic purpose of enhancing the text, as in the earlier Hiberno-Saxon ornamental text style.

Up to this time, outline drawing partly in brown, partly in rubric red, as in the Dunstan Pontifical, and outline filled in with colour, as in the Bosworth Psalter initials, have been, as we have seen, the two usual techniques in English pictorial art. About the end of the tenth century two changes occur in the manner of combining colour with line: one seems to be connected with the introduction of the use of different coloured inks for the writing of the text; the other, with the transference of certain effects of the painted figure style which was being introduced into England through fresh contacts with Continental manuscripts. The two new techniques will be distinguished in this book as coloured outline, where the line is in different coloured inks, and tinted outline, where the drawing in brown ink is shaded with colour. The two techniques do not remain separate in English work but are often combined and thus present considerable variety in style. The earliest example

E

of the coloured outline technique is probably the Leofric Missal; and of the tinted outline, the Harleian Psalter.

The so-called Leofric Missal (Bodley MS. 579) is one of those composite manuscripts which, as we have seen, were common in England in the tenth century. It consists in great part of a Gregorian Sacramentary which was written in the diocese of Arras or Cambrai in the early tenth century;[34] an English calendar and Paschal tables almost certainly written at Glastonbury before 979;[35] and some introductory matter at the beginning, probably added by Leofric, Bishop of Exeter 1050–72, at the time the manuscript was rearranged and given by him to the Cathedral of Exeter. The late tenth century text written in coloured inks, on fols 38–59, and three coloured outline drawings included in it are the parts which concern us here. Folio 49 shows two very lively figures drawn in blue or red outline within a border of linear acanthus leaves placed against a blue or a green background; fol. 49 verso (Plate 29A) contains a crowned figure, 'Vita', holding a scroll which bears the 'good numbers' of the Easter Tables; and fol. 50 has a corresponding figure, 'Mors', horned and nude, holding the 'bad numbers'.

The figure 'Vita' on fol. 49 verso (Plate 29A) is drawn with much the same monumentality, especially as to the upper part, as the Christ and St Dunstan (see Plate 22), but the technique of the line is totally different. In place of the firm, continuous contour outline and the almost unbroken drapery lines often running in parallel groups, the Leofric figure is sketched lightly with a ragged line which appears even more broken because of the different colours with which it is drawn – red, green, blue, and purple. The roughened hair and beard, the drapery folds thrown loosely about the body, the fluttering ends, and the irregular hem-line flipping up around the feet all give the figure an effect of lightness and instability as though it were poised in air and shaking itself, stirring the draperies and allowing the breeze to catch them. It is a remarkable style, both for the quality of the line and for the effect produced by the combination of delicate colours against the plain vellum of the page, and it seems to have originated, not in the heavy coloured Franco-Saxon initials contained in the earlier, Continental part of the manuscript, but in some other Carolingian style which developed in the school of Reims.[36] By whatever channel or under whatever circumstances this style entered England, the outline drawn in colour as in the Leofric Missal seems to be an invention of the English artist; we shall see how the fashion spread in English manuscripts of the early eleventh century.

The other new use of colour with outline, the tinted outline style, is perhaps first seen in the magnificent drawing of the Crucifixion, preceding a psalter (Brit. Mus., Harl. MS. 2904, fol. 3 verso; Plate 30), otherwise decorated only with more or less elaborate initials in very beautiful, heavy acanthus style (fol. 4, the B of the *Beatus*; Plate 21B).[37] This fine manuscript, formerly believed to have been written at Winchester, more recently has been shown to have been made for and probably at Ramsey Abbey between 974 and 986, perhaps for St Oswald its founder.[38]

In the Crucifixion (Plate 30) the figure of Christ is drawn in brown line shaded with soft, pale red; the hair and the drapery edges are accented with black and shaded in the deep folds with brown. The mouth, halo, and wounds are touched with pale red wash. The *suppedaneum* for the feet of Christ is blue. The Virgin has a veil and dress shaded blue in the folds; the dress is patterned with blue and red ornament; her mantle is outlined in brown accented with touches of black. John has a blue-shaded gown with a red-patterned border; his mouth is touched with red. The essential difference between this tinted outline technique and the coloured outline of the Leofric figure is that here the outlining is all done in brown line accented in places with black, and the internal detail – as features, shading, and pattern – is put in with colour, red and blue. The effect is that of a sketch with colour notes for painting: the figures have both solidity and delicacy. It is, in fact, almost an illusionistic technique which gives an impression of modelled forms painted in colour without using the technique of modelling in heavy pigments. This method of drawing is an amazing accomplishment for an English artist of this early date, when we consider what he was doing with the human figure barely two generations earlier (cf. Plate 20). While it is obvious that a new conception of the human form has been introduced into English art, perhaps from some noble Continental model,[39] nevertheless the Harleian Crucifixion could only be the work of a consummate original artist who was creative enough to be able to grasp the essentials of the modelled form and to translate them into this effective outline style.

Nor has the artist missed the emotional significance of the picture: the Virgin's head is bowed and half-concealed in her mantle which she clutches convulsively with clenched hands; John stands with eagerly upturned face, holding with outstretched arm the scroll on which he has written his testimony, 'This is the disciple who bears witness'; and between and above the two towers the cross bearing the powerfully proportioned figure of the dead Christ with drooping head and slightly sagging body – a God in human form. Truly nothing finer of its kind had yet been produced on the Continent or in England; it is the English artist's clear pronouncement as to the Romanesque art which is to come.

Romanesque elements are also present in the splendid initial B of the Beatus introducing the Psalter (Plate 21B), though the technique is painting with rich colour and gold, in contrast to the delicate tinted outline of the Crucifixion miniature on the facing page. The colours are all shaded: green with yellow for the mask; yellow with green, pink with violet, green with yellow, and greenish blue with a darker tone for the acanthus leaves. The effect of shading is due, however, to the use of superficial lines of a colour contrasting with the ground colour, rather than to any real modelling of the forms by areas of colour. Nevertheless, the total impression is rich and heavy as compared with the Bosworth Psalter initial illustrated on the same plate. It is noteworthy that in the Harleian B interlace is used, together with large animal heads, in the Franco-Saxon manner, and the acanthus foliage is kept separate, as in the Continental style, not combined with the acanthus stems as in the Bosworth initial. The general interlace principle, however, is applied in the Harleian initial, where the tips of the leaves often pass over or under the stems. The panels containing more conventionalized designs of acanthus leaves painted against a dark background, in their design recall a similar use of them in outline in the large P of the Corpus Christi College Life of St Cuthbert (see note 18 above). But the style in the Harleian initial is bolder and firmer in drawing and the effect is infinitely richer, owing to the strong colouring. The initial style of the Harleian Psalter is wholly in the manner of late tenth century art as developed at Winchester, which we must now examine.

Winchester from 963 onward was the scene of Bishop Æthelwold's vigorous reforms of the Old and the New Minster following the pattern of Continental Cluniac monasteries, especially Fleury with which he had had close contacts while Abbot of Abingdon. Continental influence, it is true, was already present at Winchester at least from the time of Grimbald, first Abbot of New Minster in 903; it was evident stylistically in the St Cuthbert embroideries and in the manuscripts associated with King Æthelstan (see above). But it is not until the second half of the tenth century that the full force of Carolingian art under Æthelwold's sponsorship of the production of manuscripts resulted in the development at Winchester of the famous Winchester style.

The reform of New Minster by Æthelwold and its refoundation under a new charter granted by King Edgar in 966 was the occasion for the making of the first known Winchester manuscript in the new manner (Brit. Mus., Cott. MS. Vesp. A.viii). It contains only one miniature (fol. 2 verso; Plate 25) representing King Edgar between the Virgin and St Peter offering his charter to Christ who appears in the clouds surrounded by fluttering angels. The composition is painted on purple vellum now much faded and is surrounded by a complete decorative border consisting of a framework from the centre of which curling, hybrid leaves of the acanthus-vine type spread outward over the two bands. The technique is basically linear, though pale colour is used as a wash over parts of the composition, both figures and decoration. The figures are firmly outlined in the manner of the Pontifical of Dunstan, and the drapery folds are indicated by lines of varying width. Shading is suggested in the draperies by means of contrasting coloured lines, as white and black on blue or red ground, black on green, blue on white, red and green on pale yellow, and red on gold. The features are drawn in brown with a touch of red on the lips. The gestures are vigorous and the draperies are loose and fluttering. Edgar is seen in a somewhat curious and puzzling position, with his right side, roundly shaded on the hip, towards the spectator and his head flung back over his right shoulder. His left leg is seen from the back, the sole of his gold shoe showing. The liveliness of the composition as a whole suggests a Tours or St Gall model, of such a subject as David and the Musicians.[40] The border motifs are found in later Tours manuscripts, as the Lothaire Gospels (Paris, Bib. Nat., MS. lat. 266, dated 840–3); or perhaps an even better example is the Sacramentary of Drogo of the School of Metz.[41]

Some fifteen years later,[42] and obviously under the impact of further direct Continental influence, the new foliate border style, which appears somewhat tentative still in the New Minster Charter, bursts forth in all the exuberance and lushness of a plant fully adapted to a new and congenial soil. The splendid Benedictional[43] made for and probably at the order of Bishop Æthelwold of Winchester c. 975–80 is decorated as lavishly in gold and heavy colours as any late Carolingian manuscript.

The miniatures of the Benedictional of Æthelwold seem to come from two different prototypes. This difference in style is evident both in border decoration and in figure compositions, and is well illustrated in plates 26 and 27. Fol. 5 verso (Plate 26) contains a very beautifully composed Annunciation, bordered by a solid frame which suggests the division into panels and the chamfered corners of a carved ivory frame.[44] Within the panels are acanthus leaves with curled tips, placed sometimes vertically, sometimes horizontally or even aslant. In the centre of each side is an ornament of acanthus leaves springing from a small central medallion and extending laterally to curl over or under the plain bands of the framework. The principle used in the arrangement of these ornaments is that of the borders of Vesp. A.viii (Plate 25); they suggest sections of this frame cut off and applied to the panelled border in the Benedictional. The figure composition of the Annunciation is completely contained within or behind the frame, some of the curling leaves overlapping it. This is true also with a few minor exceptions, such as feet and wing-tips, in Vesp. A.viii. The Annunciation figures are very similar in facial and drapery types, but more graceful and elegant, with rich patterns in the Virgin's dress and on the halo, sceptre, and wings of Gabriel. The elaborate, domed baldacchino under which the Virgin is seated, the architectural setting, the cloud background, and especially the dignity and monumentality of the figures point to an ultimate Byzantine source, probably via Carolingian manuscripts of the Ada School.[45] The style, though flat and linear, is evidently based on a good painted original: the patterns of the drapery folds and swirls[46] suggest a painting technique. The colours are pale: blue, green, madder red, brown, cream, and fawn. The shading is in thick white or madder lines. The facial modelling is in white on brownish flesh tone. The gold is not burnished but is sometimes tooled or overpainted with colour.

Plate 27 (fol. 102 verso: Death of the Virgin) exemplifies the second type of design in these miniatures. The frame is an arch supported by 'columns' whose capitals and bases are composed of acanthus leaves curling on a frame. An ornament contrived out of the same elements crowns the arch, and the space within the gold bands that define both the arch and the columns is filled with a pattern of detached conventionalized acanthus leaves. This arched frame seems to develop out of the more architectural arches of fols 1–4, against which are placed the groups of Confessors, Virgins, and Apostles. The arches derive from Evangelist or Canon Table pages of the Carolingian Ada School. The combination of this richly ornate acanthus filling with the ornaments, as on capitals, bases, and arch crowns, results in the rectangular border frame with corners and intermediate medallion ornament as found on many other pages, while the arched frame continues to be used also, as in plate 27. The lushness of the foliage and the variety of ways in which it is used in the frame constitute the typical characteristics of the Winchester ornament. The text pages facing the miniatures in the Benedictional always have borders of similar design.

Plate 27 illustrates well the figure composition of the developed Winchester style. A crowded group fills the upper part of the space, with the Virgin lying on a bed suspended between the capitals of the arch, and beside her, three attendant women. Both the figures and the bed are superimposed on the frame; above them, four angels and the hand of God holding the crown are seen behind the arch, and below are the Apostles, also behind the frame except on the extreme right. The crowded composition, like the acanthus motifs, weaving in and out of the frame, is in the typical English decorative manner, conditioned by an inherent love of all-over ornament and especially of the intricacies of interlace. In rectangular framed miniatures sometimes the frame disappears altogether behind the figures. The rich patterns of the draperies further confuse the figures with the border motifs. The faces are monotonously alike; the modelling is conventionalized. In spite of the emotion shown by the women and some of the Apostles, it is evident that the Winchester artist was carried away by the new wealth of ornamental material rather than by an interest in the representational possibilities of his figure groups.

In discussing the Benedictional of Æthelwold we have spoken of the typical Winchester style. Recent textual research, however, seems to indicate that manuscripts illuminated in this style were made for and possibly at other centres than Winchester itself. The textual contents of the Benedictional of Æthelwold include features distinctive to the monastery of St Etheldreda at Ely,[47] which was refounded by Æthelwold in 973. The stylistic relation of some of the features in the Benedictional to the earlier New Minster Charter, however, and the fact that Winchester was the centre of strong, direct contacts with Continental sources which might have furnished other features, still would seem to point to Old Minster, Winchester, as a more likely place for the production of this style than the more remote, newly re-established monastery at Ely. The most plausible explanation of the production of the Benedictional, therefore, seems to be that it was made at Winchester for the use of Æthelwold particularly at Ely, and the chances would be, in that case, that the manuscript would be deposited at Ely where, as we shall see, it may have influenced a later generation of illuminators.

Another manuscript in the Winchester style (known as a benedictional but actually a pontifical) found its way to Normandy and is now in Rouen (Bib. Pub., MS. Y.7). It was executed perhaps at New Minster, Winchester.[48] Only three miniatures now remain: those for Easter, Pentecost, and the Death of the Virgin (fol. 54 verso; Plate 29B). There are also some acanthus-framed text pages, arranged, as in the Benedictional of Æthelwold, so that the miniature and the text on facing pages are framed with borders of the same design, whether arched or rectangular. The figure types and the heavy painting in colour are very similar to the Benedictional of Æthelwold, though the style seems firmer and the drawing sharper than in the Æthelwold manuscript. In type of composition Rouen Y.7 follows that of fol. 102 verso rather than 5 verso of this manuscript, but the foliage is more plastically rendered than on fol. 102 verso. The colours are those of the Æthelwold Benedictional – dull green, red, blue shaded with white and black, violet, and a very little bright green; the foliage of the border is placed against a black ground which sets off the heavy colours.[49]

Two manuscripts decorated in the Winchester style show evidence of being made for and probably at Christ Church, Canterbury. One of these (Camb., Trin. Coll., MS. B.10.4),[50] a gospel book preceded by Canon Tables, has five full-page miniatures with Christ in Majesty and the four Evangelists with their symbols all under richly decorated arches, painted in a style similar to that of the two Benedictionals. In the Christ in Majesty (fol. 16 verso; Plate 28A) the rich foliage ornament, the monumental figure types, the fluttering draperies, and the heavy colours and magnificent gold are all characteristic of the Winchester style. But the type of leaf is closer to that of the New Minster Charter (Plate 25); that is, a narrower, lobed leaf with a wiry stem which winds in and out between the double bars of the frame in a manner very like that of the Charter. The figure technique is more linear than in the Benedictional, with the drapery folds making a rich surface pattern. The style of the Trinity Gospels, therefore, seems to bear out the suggestion of a possible direct origin in the New Minster manuscripts.

The other Winchester style manuscript, also a gospel book (Brit. Mus., Roy. MS. I D. ix) which was executed for and probably at Christ Church, Canterbury, has four fine illuminated pages framed with Winchester borders and enclosing decorative initials which introduce the first words of the Gospels. Folio 70 (Plate 28B) represents the border style. The colours are mainly dull red of two shades, grey and brownish green; in the background of the initial a bright, pure green is used. The gold is rich and heavy and reddish in hue, as in Winchester manuscripts. The initial letter containing the Christ in Majesty is a rare example for its time of the so-called historiated initial,[51] a form of illumination which was particularly popular with Canterbury illuminators and elsewhere in England after the Conquest.

The so-called missal, which is actually a sacramentary, of Robert of Jumièges (Rouen, Bib. Pub., MS. Y.6) probably was written for use at Ely[52] between 1006 and 1023. It was given by Robert as a memorial of himself to the monastery of Jumièges in Normandy, while he was Bishop of London (1044–50).

The general stylistic dependence of the Missal of Robert of Jumièges on the style of the Benedictional of Æthelwold is clear; in fact, it appears that the designs of the overloaded borders and the scheme of placing matching designs on facing pages, as well as the general type of composition, may actually have been taken from the earlier Benedictional which, as we have seen, was made for use at Ely. But the strange flat-headed types of figures, the restless draperies, and most of all the sketchy technique and pale, thin, but brilliant colouring have little in common with the typical Winchester style. The elements of the Nativity composition (fol. 32 verso; Plate 31) are spread about loosely under the arch, with no spatial relation either to the arch or to the columns which support it (cf. Plates 26–28, and also Plate 29B), and the background is treated in the 'illusionistic' technique of pale washes of streaky colour in the manner of the Carolingian style of Reims.[53] The background colours are violet under the arch, yellow shaded with red, and green around the Virgin's bed, and stronger (lake) red in the lower part of the miniature; Mary wears a bright green dress, with the folds shaded with blue, and she has a blue veil. The bedding is orange shaded with red, the bedstead is gold; the coverlet is white shaded with blue and the pillows are red and green patterned with white. The angel wears a yellow gown shaded with red, and a white mantle shaded with blue. The wings are extraordinarily beautiful, with the large feathers green, the smaller ones, red, yellow, and gold tipped and edged with green and blue. The haloes are gold. The faces are painted with a flat, pinkish white, and the features are drawn in brown; there are red areas above the eyes and around the nose, lips, jaw, and chin. The technique is minute in the handling of detail and the colour is unimaginably varied and sparkling. There is a lightness of touch, both in the drawing and in the painting, which is not found in either of the Winchester style benedictionals, nor, indeed, in either of the Winchester style manuscripts probably made at Canterbury (see above). It is obvious that some new element has entered the Winchester style and that this element has little to do with the monumental, heavy painted figure style of the Carolingian Ada school.

In fact, there is evidence of the presence in Canterbury,[54] perhaps as early as the second half of the tenth century, of a Carolingian manuscript of quite a different type, illustrated in an amazing linear style without colour, the famous Utrecht Psalter. The importance of this Psalter to the Canterbury illuminator is evident from the fact that it was copied there no less than three different times, each time in the current English style.

The earliest of these copies is Brit. Mus., Harl. MS. 603, which was begun about the year 1000 and is in many respects the most important and interesting of the three. It was not all done by the same hand: Folios 28–49 are written in a different script from the preceding and following parts, and the few illustrations in this part are by a different and later hand of the second quarter of the eleventh century,[55] and perhaps were even copied from a different prototype. Folios 1–27 verso (fol. 4; Plate 32) and 50–7 verso (fol. 56 verso; Plate 33) both follow the illustrations of the Utrecht Psalter very closely, even though these two sections of Harl. 603 were apparently done by two different contemporary artists. From folio 58 to the end, yet another hand is at work departing strikingly from the original in the picture compositions but clearly displaying the tremendous effect of the Utrecht style on later English draftsmen (Plate 48B). The vigour of the linear style with its extremely active, attenuated figures, swinging draperies, and dramatic gestures, which seems to have been evolved largely out of copying the Utrecht Psalter, becomes a key feature – almost a hall-mark – of later English illumination.

As for the two artists who followed the original most closely, the first (Plate 32), while copying the composition in all of its details, goes further in the matter of treating them as decorative features:[56] his trees and architecture are elaborated, his hills are multiplied into a swirl of curves and countercurves; the spears and arrows are accentuated; a weathercock is carefully perched atop a building. Everything swings and whirls in a dizzy pattern, closely knit and with no empty space. But the most striking difference from the original drawing in the Utrecht Psalter which is done wholly in brown ink, is the use of colour for the line – red, green, brown, and purple, employed arbitrarily for details, according to the whim of the artist in weaving his decorative pattern. This will be recognized at once as the coloured line technique which we have seen in the drawings of the Leofric Missal (Plate 29A).

Folios 50–7 verso, one complete gathering (Plate 33), are certainly copied by another hand:[57] the artist of these pages has stayed so close to his original that scarcely a penstroke is wanting in the copy. Such meticulous duplication of the swift illusionistic style in the Utrecht drawings can result only in a tightening and hardening of the free sketchy line. Thus flying folds which are only suggested in the original by a zigzag line become flatly pressed pleats; details which are sketched in lightly in the original are given firm contours, as in the ground line and the shading.[58] The action in the original composition is retained but the vibrant aliveness has vanished. Two details will illustrate this artist's typical pre-occupation with decoration: the star has become a jewelled ornament, and the spring from which the river rises has turned into a Celtic scroll.

The characteristics of the English linear art that developed under the direct influence of the Utrecht Psalter are made abundantly clear by a comparison of two miniatures of about the same time – early eleventh century – representing the occupations of the month of January in the calendars prefixed to two different manuscripts of uncertain provenance (Brit. Mus., Cott. MSS Jul. A.vi, a hymnal and calendar, fol. 3; Plate 34A; and Tib. B.v,

Astronomical Treatises, fol. 3; Plate 34B).[59] The scene in both miniatures represents winter ploughing. Manuscript Jul. A.vi is much closer in style to the Utrecht Psalter: the drawing is in brown with touches of green, and is firmer and less nervous than most of Harl. 603; the figures are not extraordinarily attenuated, although the heads are rather small, and they are almost always seen in profile. In Tib. B.v flat profiles are used also; in fact, the composition of the miniature in Jul. A.vi is duplicated in every detail except the border in Tib. B.v, but the technique is that of painting: the oxen are modelled with white highlights in lines and spots, as is also the drapery of the figures. The technique seems to be taken over from the illustrations in the prototype from which the text of this manuscript was copied.

Thus in these two early calendar illustrations two distinct contemporary techniques are represented, reflecting two different Carolingian prototypes.[60] The technique of coloured outline drawing in Jul. A.vi seems to have developed in connexion with the use of different coloured inks for the text initials, as in the Leofric Missal; Tib. B.v, on the other hand, could represent that kind of painting technique which, when transferred to line drawing, resulted in the tinted or shaded outline of Harl. 2904. The painting technique continues to appear alongside the outline drawings during succeeding periods.

From St Augustine's Abbey, Canterbury,[61] comes an illustrated copy, dating from the second quarter of the eleventh century, of Ælfric's *Metrical Paraphrase of Pentateuch and Joshua* (Brit. Mus., Cott. MS. Claud. B.iv) with miniatures drawn in firm, continuous contour lines, partially painted with shaded colour in the earlier part. Folio 19 (Plate 35), representing the building of the Tower of Babel under the supervision of God the Father standing on a ladder, is typical of the painted style. The composition though framed is not confined within the border but pushes out over the edges. The figure drawing is crude but very vigorous, and the artist's fondness for detail is shown in the way each phase of the construction, from the iron work on the door to the laying of the tiles on the roof, is depicted with meticulous exactness, though with considerable naïveté. Also, the interest of the artist in the patterned effects inherent in brick and tile work and in the arrangement of different shaped areas set off by colour is obvious, even though here, as in other instances, he seems to be following some earlier painted prototype in his illustration. These two characteristics – interest in exact detail and love of pattern – are traditional in English art from its earliest appearance, and are to become more firmly established as time goes on.

Meanwhile at New Minster, Winchester, as at Canterbury, a linear type of composition was developing in the early eleventh century, side by side with the Winchester painted style which it was soon to supersede. Four manuscripts can be assigned to this place and date, all very close in style though differing in technique, and all dependent on the earlier style of the New Minster Charter (Vesp. A.viii; Plate 25).

The first of these, the so-called Grimbald Gospels (Brit. Mus., Add. MS. 34890)[62] has a scheme of decoration similar to that of the Benedictional of Æthelwold, that is, pages with heavy borders surrounding miniatures and text which use the same design on facing pages. At the beginning of each gospel in the Grimbald manuscript there is an Evangelist picture and a decorative text page. The Evangelist Luke (fol. 73 verso; Plate 36A)[63] and the decorative text page opposite have frames formed by silver bands enclosing red, green, and grey-blue acanthus leaves, and gold medallion ornaments from which rather stiff leaves extend in pairs. The Evangelist picture, like the text opposite, is on the uncoloured vellum ground; the curtain is suspended from one of the decorative leaves of the border and is looped over a gold hook attached to the silver bar of the framework. The Evangelist's face, hands, and feet are outlined with red and washed over with pale, flat, pinkish colour. The draperies are patterned richly with dark and light linear folds on green or blue grounds. The symbol of Luke – a red calf with green wings and brown tail and hooves – holds a gold ink horn in its mouth. The style is linear but the line is not of the nervous, sketchy type of the Utrecht Psalter and Harl. 603. The square-jawed heads, the large round haloes, the heavily swinging drapery ends are derived rather from the style of the Charter of King Edgar (Plate 25). The heads of the Evangelists are all in exactly the same position and almost identical, as can be seen in the miniature on folio 114 verso (Plate 36B).[64] The border on this page, however, and on the text page opposite, is divided by gold and silver bands into panels and medallions containing figures instead of acanthus leaves. Across the top are three medallions with identical Majesty[65] figures, except for the cruciform halo of the centre figure, representing the Trinity; each medallion is supported by four angels with spread wings. Kings, apostles, and saints occupy other medallions and panels, and in the centre at the bottom are two angels holding a number of figures – souls of the dead – in a napkin. The figures in the medallions and panels on the text page opposite (fol. 115) also are kings and saints; the centre top medallion contains a Madonna and Child supported by angels, while seraphim fill the corner roundels. The subjects of the two pages are parts of the same idea: Christ, or as represented, the Trinity, in judgement on the one side, and the Incarnation of Our Lord on the other. The theological scheme suggests a Continental origin, since nothing of this kind has hitherto appeared in English illumination, but no known Carolingian or Ottonian manuscript has been found to supply the prototype.[66]

The three other early eleventh century manuscripts associated with New Minster are illustrated in pure outline, but the figures still hark back to those of the Edgar Charter, in pose and gesture and especially in the continuous outline technique used for contour and drapery folds. The edges of the draperies swing more freely than in the earlier Charter, and the figures are lithe, and the heads thrust forward with something of the eagerness of the Utrecht Psalter style, which may well have spread from Canterbury to Winchester. Plate 37A (Brit. Mus., Stowe MS. 944, fol. 6) shows King Knut and his first wife Ælfgyfu presenting an altar cross, while Christ above in a mandorla between the Virgin and St Peter (cf. Vesp. A.viii) blesses the gift; beneath the altar is a group of monks. The manuscript, known as the *Liber Vitae*, is a register of New Minster and can be dated *c.* 1020–30. The technique is continuous brown outline tinted and shaded with colour.

The two other manuscripts illustrated in a very similar tinted outline style (Brit. Mus., Cott. MSS. Titus D.xxvi and xxvii) were written by Abbot Ælfwin (Ælsinus) for the monks of New Minster about the same time as Stowe 944.[67] Titus D.xxvi, a collection of prayers, hymns, and other material, contains on fol. 19 verso a full page drawing of St Peter adored by a monk. St Peter, who resembles very strongly the same figure in the *Liber Vitae* miniature (Plate 37A), is shown between columns which support a trefoiled canopy. The drawing is in brown, shaded lightly with green, blue, yellow, and red.[68] Titus D.xxvii, the New Minster Offices (1023–35), contains a miniature (fol. 65 verso; Plate 37B) of the Crucifixion with the Virgin and a bearded St John. The outline, which is very broken, is in red or brown accented with black in the drapery folds and in other details, such as ornament on the drapery (cf. Harl. 2904). Green is used outside the figure contours giving the effect of shadow; it is also used to deepen the folds. The personified Sun and Moon,[69] the jewelled haloes, and the careful labelling of everything suggests an Eastern prototype perhaps via a Carolingian manuscript, but the tinted outline style is typically English. In the New Minster manuscripts the true profile head is used only rarely.

Somewhat earlier than the New Minster manuscripts just discussed and of unknown provenance is a copy of Aldhelm's *De Laude Virginitatis* forming part (fols 66–112) of a composite manuscript now in the library of Lambeth Palace (MS. 200). The prologue to this work is accompanied by a drawing of Bishop Aldhelm presenting his book to the nuns of Barking (fol. 68 verso; Plate 38A). It is dated late tenth century or *c.* 1000.[70] The drawing is not in the style of Harl. 603 as derived from the Utrecht Psalter, but is closer to the Christ and St Dunstan drawing in Bod. MS. Auct. F.4.32 and the Sherborne Pontifical. The figures have the monumentality of the Winchester style in the Benedictional of Æthelwold and somewhat similar draperies are delineated with a stiff, wiry line. In the Aldhelm text there are a number of delicately coloured initials composed of beast heads and acanthus leaves within interlace.

The technique of coloured outline is nowhere more effectively and charmingly used than in three late-tenth or early-eleventh century copies of Prudentius's *Psychomachia*, all of which follow one prototype, possibly a fifth century classical manuscript. The earliest, according to James,[71] and certainly the best is Cambridge, Corpus Christi Coll., MS. 23 (fol. 21 verso; Plate 38B). The figures are solid and well-proportioned and they stand in plausible contrapposto, though their feet and ankles seem scarcely adequate; draperies hang full and heavy yet reveal something of the form underneath; folds are indicated merely by two conventionally parallel lines, but the edges swing free with light puffs at the hem. Colour – red, green, blue, and brown – is used indiscriminately for bodies, drapery or foliage. The line is clean-cut and sure and appears to be drawn directly on the vellum without preliminary sketch. The Cambridge *Psychomachia* came from Malmesbury and may have been made there.[72]

Of the two early copies of the *Psychomachia*[73] in the British Museum, Cott. MS. Cleop. C.viii is closer both in quality and in date to the Corpus manuscript, and the same cycle of pictures is repeated in a style still unaffected by the Utrecht Psalter. In some of the pictures, profiles are used freely. The other copy in the British Museum, Add. MS. 21499, James says, may be slightly later;[74] it was probably planned to contain the same cycle of illustrations, plus two more not in the Corpus copy. The Additional manuscript once belonged to Bury St Edmunds.[75] Though following in large part the classical manner of drawing, as in Corpus 23 and Cleop. C.viii, Add. MS. 21499 contains one figure in unmistakable Utrecht style (fol. 26 verso).

One of the most interesting and, as we shall see later, one of the most influential of the Canterbury productions of the early eleventh century is Brit. Mus., Arundel MS. 155,[76] which contains illustrations in both the painting and the tinted outline technique; on one page the two techniques are found within the same miniature (fol. 133; Plate 41). Another page (fol. 93; Plate 40) shows a very vigorous scene of David slaying Goliath in an historiated initial, and is surrounded by a border of the general Winchester type.

The miniature on fol. 133 represents St Benedict with a kneeling monk under his feet. These two figures are painted in heavy, rather streaky colour: Benedict wears a purple tunic with gold ornaments and a gold cape. He is seated under one of two arches enclosed within the larger arch supported by columns which are partly painted, partly gold. Very strange and ugly acanthus leaf ornaments stick out awkwardly from the capitals of the columns. The background both behind Benedict and above in the tympanum of the arch is streaked with colour to suggest sky, in the manner of Reims manuscripts and also as in the Missal of Robert of Jumièges (Plate 31). Much of the technique of the Benedict figure is linear in spite of the painting; the drapery folds over his knees are both linear and painted; his face has the features drawn in, but his beard and hair are painted as a soft mass. The other half of the miniature is wholly in a tinted outline technique. It is an interesting experiment, but more interesting than beautiful, and it is evident that the drawing has more life and character without the paint.

The historiated initial on fol. 93 (Plate 40) is composed as a picture behind the frame of the initial letter: a considerable part of Goliath's body is cut off by the letter. The drawing is full of life and the action is vigorously if rather awkwardly portrayed, with David apparently standing on Goliath's arm with one foot while the other seems to be tangled in some manner with the giant's spear. The relative size of the two figures is clearly suggested, and the realistic manner in which David saws off the head of his enemy leaves nothing to the imagination. The colour both of the initial and of the framework border is applied with a brush in heavy lines and swathes. The acanthus ornament which springs from the bands of the frame is stiff and meagre, and the curious shape of the outer part of the frame gives it the appearance of a Victorian picture frame. All in all, the decorative elements of Arundel 155 leave much to be desired both in motifs and in design. But the artist qualifies better as a figure painter than as a decorator, and is at his best in the expressive pen-drawn figures. It is extremely interesting and valuable to be able to see, as in the Benedict miniature, the relation of the two techniques, and the type of line that approximates most closely to the painted technique of a modelled figure in this style.

By the second quarter of the eleventh century, Anglo-Saxon drawing had come into its own, with all the swiftness and vitality of the Utrecht Psalter style but with a firmer, cleaner-cut line. The psalter in the Vatican Library (MS. Reg. lat. 12) made for Bury St Edmunds 'not earlier than 1032',[77] is one of the finest examples of this style. There are fifty drawings in the margins, often running into the text, executed mainly in brown and red outline, with an occasional touch of green. On fol. 22 (Plate 39B) there is a picture of David which, in the dignity and poise of the figure and in the vitality of the line, is unsurpassed in early English drawing. There is a suggestion of the figure style of Arundel 155 here, as shown in the St Benedict on fol. 133 (Plate 41); but the technique is more skilful in the David. Except for the sketchy quality of the line there is little resemblance in this figure to the typical Utrecht style. However, in the other drawing reproduced (fol. 28;

Plate 39A) the flat broad head of the Christ and the more distorted poses and lively gestures are vivid reminders both of the Harl. 603–Utrecht style and of the drawings in Arundel 155. The artist of all the drawings in the Vatican Psalter was probably the same person; the differences in the style of the drawings could be accounted for by the various models which might have been available to him.

In the Vatican Psalter the *Beatus* page has the usual initial B with a framework border painted in a rather coarse version of the Winchester style.[78] The initial is filled with foliage terminating in large animal heads; and in a roundel on the upright of the B is a tiny figure of a monk writing, possibly the scribe or illuminator of the manuscript.

More linear in style and less rich in colour than the painting in Arundel 155 is a psalter (Bod. MS. Douce 296) made in the second quarter of the eleventh century possibly for Croyland Abbey (Lincs.).[79] Folio 40 (Plate 42) has a full-page miniature of Christ treading on a lion and a dragon, framed by a border of gold bands and waving acanthus leaves. The figure is extremely attenuated and is outlined in reddish brown. The tunic is tan, shaded lighter and darker with colour applied in broad swathes to indicate the shadows and high-lights of the drapery folds; the mantle is a dull blue, also shaded in the deep folds. The exaggerated height, the long swinging curves of the drapery, the tall cross-headed lance piercing the lion's mouth, and the narrow, bearded head of Christ with pinched features and crossed eyes give an effect of nervous tenseness but have none of the monumentality of the Christ of Harl. 2904 (Plate 30). The technique is interesting in its use of painted colour to accentuate line.

Two eleventh-century Gospel Books in the Pierpont Morgan Library (MSS 708 and 709) are illustrated[80] in much the same style as Douce 296. Morgan MS. 709 appears to be closer in date to the Douce Psalter, and perhaps is not much before 1050; it is believed to have been made at New Minster, Winchester.[81] There are five miniatures: a Crucifixion (fol. 1 verso; Plate 43) remarkable for its emotional power, and four Evangelist portraits. The figures of John and Mary in the Crucifixion are exaggeratedly tall and the drapery over the angular bodies is drawn with long swinging lines, very much in the spirit of Douce 296. The cross is a crooked tree trunk with thick lopped branches. The kneeling woman who convulsively clasps the foot of the cross, and the personified Sun and Moon with faces half covered by their raised arms, give the picture a dramatic force which is climaxed in the tense expression on the face of Christ and the impulsively tender gesture of Mary who holds up her mantle to staunch the blood from his side. The colours are chiefly pale yellow patterned and shaded with brown, blue, soft green, and brick red; gold is used only for haloes, for dress trimmings, and for the frame.

The last of the manuscripts to be assigned to the first half of the eleventh century is a copy of Cædmon's Poems in the Bodleian Library (MS. Junius 11). It is copiously illustrated with figure drawings[82] and decorative initials in two or more different styles. Its attribution and date are exceedingly controversial.[83]

The first style seems to be a rather crude derivation from a painted style, and some of the drawings echo compositions that might be found in Carolingian Bibles of the Tours School.[84] From page 49 onwards the artist appears to have come under the influence of the Utrecht style (page 66; Plate 44). The figures suddenly become more attenuated with flat heads, thin legs, and large flat feet, and although sometimes they show more liveliness, the heavy contour line and the stolid poses and the interest in architectural setting which are characteristic of the first style are still recognizable. Later in the manuscript, from page 73 onwards, this Utrecht influence dominates, with its typical sketchy outline technique in colours – red, brown, and green. It is difficult to be certain whether these three styles indicate three separate hands or one hand passing through different stages of development. Page 66 (Plate 44), with a picture of Noah's Ark, represents the second or middle style with elements of the stolid Carolingian figure types and the painstaking drawing of architectural detail and the ragged but continuous contour line. However, there are also the lightness of touch – no colour is used here – and the naive informality which characterize the Harl. 603 illustrations.[85]

The story of Noah's Ark, like the structure itself, is represented in several stages and suggests a strip narrative running from bottom to top. At the left, below, Noah stands at the oar ready to propel the 'Viking' type of craft, but God in the centre has other plans, as witness the two seraphs in the upper corners. At the right Noah's wife is being difficult and refusing to enter the Ark. In the middle stage all is serene with the animals. In the centre of the upper stage Noah releases the dove and on the right it is about to nip off the sprig of green. The story is told solemnly enough but with childlike simplicity. The design seems to follow some prototype which the artist has not bothered, or known how, to adapt either to his space or to the formal composition of a miniature in a frame. His greatest skill shows in the decorative elements both of design and of detail. The fine dragon's-head prow of the ship was to his taste, and the architectural details and even the wings of the seraphs display that love of linear pattern which is characteristic of the Anglo-Saxon artist.

Summary

The key to the pictorial art of the earlier part of this period lies in two successive waves of Continental influence, mainly from two Carolingian schools: the Ada School with its Byzantine tradition of painting and modelling of monumental figures, which took root most strongly at St Swithin's, Winchester; and the Reims School and especially its most remarkable production, the Utrecht Psalter, with its sketchy, linear style and intense vitality, which exerted its most direct influence at Canterbury. In the early eleventh century these two influences became mingled and diffused to other centres, chiefly in East Anglia and the Fen country. The result of the fusion of the painted and the outline techniques is a variety of gay and charming outline styles using colour with line; this is the outstanding invention of the Anglo-Saxon artist of this period. The surprising thing is that the figures themselves retain so much diversity in type, for the solidly conceived figures of the Ada style are handled in this technique equally effectively with the lightly sketched, impressionistic figures of the Utrecht Psalter type. It is this facility with types and techniques that gives the work of this period its freshness and originality.

4   1. See *Liber Vitae: Register and Martyrology of New Minster and Hyde Abbey*, ed. by Walter de Gray Birch. Hampshire Record Soc. (London, Winchester, 1892), p. ix and n. 4.

5   2. Kendrick, *Anglo-Saxon Art*, 215.

3. Several are reproduced, *op. cit.*, plate 101.

4. Especially fol. 43 (reproduced Zimmermann, plate 293) which differs markedly from other more Celtic decorative forms as on fol. 32 (reproduced on the same plate).

5. Two other examples of the animal style are found in the Durham Ritual (Durham Cath. Lib., MS. A.iv.19) late-ninth or early-tenth century, and Bod. MS. Auct. F.4.32. Initials from both manuscripts are reproduced in Plates II and III of Wormald's excellent study, 'Decorated Initials in English Manuscripts'. The initial from MS. Auct. F.4.32 is labelled in error MS. Hatton 60.) See also *New Pal. Soc.* I, plate 82. To this manuscript, the fine drawing of Christ and St Dunstan was added later (see below). The development of decorated initials in English manuscripts cannot be pursued in detail here. In addition to the article just cited, a good discussion will be found in Kendrick's *Late Saxon and Viking Art*. One other early manuscript should be mentioned, however, in connexion with the survival of the South English-Mercian animal ornament, that is, Royal MS. 5 F. iii in the British Museum, a copy of Aldhelm's *De Laude Virginitatis* the initials of which (see Wormald, 'Decorated Initials', plate IIIc), though related to the two Bodleian manuscripts mentioned above, show evidence of Continental influence, perhaps of the School of Metz, as in the Sacramentary of Drogo (Boinet, *La Miniature carolingienne*, plates 86–90). This same Continental source will be referred to again later on in this chapter.

6. Reproduced and discussed in a booklet, entitled *The Alfred and Minster Lovell Jewels*, published by the Department of Antiquities, Ashmolean Museum, Oxford, 1948; see also Kendrick, *Anglo-Saxon Art*, 216 ff. and plate 101. The association of the jewel with Alfred is still controversial.

7. And therefore closer in date to the Chad Evangelist? On the possible Continental source of the enamel, see Saxl and Wittkower, *op. cit.*, 19, figures a and c. On a possible Coptic source for the two flowering rods, see O. M. Dalton, 'A Note on the Alfred Jewel', *Proc. Soc. Antiq.*, 2nd series, xx (1904), 71 ff.

8. Particularly the silver mounts for a drinking horn from the treasure deposited *c.* 875 at Trewhiddle, Cornwall. Kendrick, *Anglo-Saxon Art*, 185, plate 78. Brøndsted discusses the style in detail and reproduces many more examples, *op. cit.*, 127 ff. and 149 ff.

9. As on the mounts from the great shield. *Provisional Guide*, plate IV.

10. Brøndsted calls it vine, but the stylized curling leaves rather suggest the acanthus.

11. Inscriptions embroidered on the ends of both vestments record the fact that Ælfleda (second wife of King Edward the Elder, son and successor of Alfred) ordered them for Frithestan, Bishop of Winchester (909–31). Ælfleda died in 916, hence the work must have been begun and perhaps was finished between 909 and 916. For a description and complete reproduction of the embroideries, see Baldwin Brown and Christie, 'St Cuthbert's Stole and Maniple at Durham'.

12. Cf. the First Bible of Charles the Bald, Paris, Bib. Nat., MS. lat. I, fol. 192 verso – a prophet standing on conventional clouds or rocky ground, holding a scroll. Reproduced Wilhelm Koehler, *Die karolingischen Miniaturen: Tours* (Berlin, 1930), plate 87b.

13. Cf. also Saxl and Wittkower, *op. cit.*, 19, n. 8, where a figure of Christ from MS. grec 510 in the Bibliothèque Nationale, Paris, is compared with a prophet on the stole.

14. Especially those of the School of Tours: First   p. 36 Bible of Charles the Bald (Paris, Bib. Nat., MS. lat. I), fols 327, 327 verso, and 387 (Koehler, plates 83, 84, and 87e). On Anglo-Saxon vine scroll ornament, see E. Kitzinger, in *Antiquity*, x (1936), 61 ff.

15. The technique is described in detail by Mrs Christie in the article cited in note 11 above.

16. Durham Cath. Lib., MS. A.iv.19. Mynors, *Durham Cath. MSS.*, 25; Wormald, 'Decorated Initials', plate IIc.

17. One of the best is reproduced, *op. cit.*, plate IId. The colours are red, yellow, and blue.

18. *Op. cit.*, 116. The P is reproduced on plate IV, a. The motifs consist of short acanthus leaves arranged horizontally within the loop of the letter, and a vine with grapes running vertically in the upright shaft.

p. 37   19. The book was afterwards given by Æthelstan to Christ Church, Canterbury (James, *Anc. Lib. Cant. and Dover*, xxv) and is now in the British Museum, Cott. MS. Tib. A.ii. The Evangelist Mark (fol. 74 verso) and some ornamental text are reproduced in colour by J. O. Westwood, *Paleographia Sacra Pictoria* (London, 1843–5), plate preceding p. 99. The style of three of the miniatures (Mark, Luke, and John) is that of the Reims School, but the manuscript was written for use in the Abbey of Lobbes in the diocese of Liège. J. A. Robinson, *The Times of St Dunstan* (Oxford, 1923), 60.

The belief that this manuscript was one of two books on which Anglo-Saxon kings took oath at their coronation has recently been shown by Wormald to be without foundation. See 'The So-Called Coronation Oath-Books of the Kings of England', *Essays in Honor of Georg Swarzenski* (Chicago, 1952), 233 ff.

20. See Wormald, 'Decorated Initials', 115. The ornament consists solely of animal heads and interlace, no acanthus; the initials were apparently unaffected by the Franco-Saxon initials in the Continental part of the book.

21. According to a sixteenth-century inscription. See Millar, *Eng. Illum. MSS I (X to XIII Century)*, 2.

22. James, *Anc. Lib. Cant. and Dover*, 529.

23. Cf. Vienna, Nationalbib., Cod. 652 (theo. 39), a copy of Rabanus Maurus with a miniature showing the presentation of the book to Gregory as in Trin. Coll. MS. B.16.3. The Vienna manuscript came from St Stephen's monastery, Fulda, and dates from between 831 and 840. Goldschmidt, *German Illum.* I, No. 55A.

24. For example, the First Bible of Charles the Bald. Koehler, plate 76.

25. The text is composite and was written partly on the Continent, partly in Wales.

p. 38   26. Dunstan is garbed as a monk and not as a prelate, and this may (but need not) indicate a date before 959 when he became Archbishop of Canterbury.

27. It needs hardly to be explained that artists of this period show no evidence of working from living models, even in so-called portraits.

28. See Saxl and Wittkower, *op. cit.*, plate 20, No. 8. See also Wormald, *Eng. Drawings*, No. 46.

29. See *New Pal. Soc.*, Series I, plate 111; Wormald (*Eng. Drawings*, No. 54) dates the manuscript 992–5. It was written for use at Sherborne Abbey,

hence it is commonly known also as the Sherborne Pontifical.

30. Kendrick (*Late Saxon Art*, 45) notes the closeness of the drapery to that of a tenth century ivory Christ on the Cross in the Victoria and Albert Museum, thought to be Winchester work. Reproduced, M. H. Longhurst, *English Ivories* (London, 1926), frontispiece in colour. One notable difference between the three miniatures and the ivory is the succession of pointed folds below the waist in the manuscript.

31. There is a striking similarity between these angels and two carved angels in the Saxon church at Bradford on Avon, which are dated by Kendrick *c.* 950; *Late Saxon Art*, 220 and plate 103. Kendrick calls them 'exercises in a new linear style of such an airy lightness and grace that we know them to be connected with the figure drawings on the Cuthbert stole and in later manuscripts of the developed Winchester style'. The carved angels are even closer in drawing and in conception to those in the Paris Crucifixion. In this connexion the stylistic relationship between Mary and John of the Crucifixion and the figures of the Cuthbert stole and maniple (plate 18) cannot be mistaken. However, in the drawings the drapery patterns, especially the edges, are lighter and richer than in the vestments, and their relation to the body is more marked as in the sculptured angels.

32. For reproductions, see Wormald, 'Decorated Initials', plate IV. He describes these initials as portions of inhabited acanthus scrolls as found in Cambridge Corpus Christi MS. 183, 'snipped off' and twisted into initial form. A sister manuscript in respect to the designs of the initials, which are uncoloured, is the Helmingham Hall *Orosius*. *Op. cit.*, plate va.

33. Kendrick, *Late Saxon Art*, 35; Wormald, 'Decorated Initials', 110. The calendar was added after Dunstan's death (988) as is shown by the inclusion of his feast. This calendar has been identified as of Glastonbury origin, with Canterbury modifications. See Abbot F. A. Gasquet, and Edmund Bishop, *The Bosworth Psalter* (London, 1908).

34. On the dating, text, and other details, see Warren, *The Leofric Missal*. See also Madan, *Summary Cat.*, No. 2675.

35. Wormald, *Eng. Drawings*, No. 49.

36. The Reims style came to Canterbury via the Utrecht Psalter, probably in the very late tenth century, but there is no known connexion between the

Leofric Missal and Canterbury. Its style, therefore, may have come from parallel Continental sources affected by the Reims style.

37. G. F. Warner, *Illum. MSS in the British Museum*, plates 7 and 8. Both initial and Crucifixion are reproduced in colour.

38. Niver, 'The Psalter in the British Museum, Harley 2904'.

39. Such as the ivory crucifix in the Victoria and Albert Museum; see note 30.

40. Cf. Boinet, *op. cit.*, plates 113 and 144.

41. *Op. cit.*, plates 86, 87, and 90.

42. That is, at almost exactly the same time as the Harleian Psalter, *q.v.*

43. A monograph on this manuscript was published for the Roxburghe Club by Warner and Wilson, *The Benedictional of Saint Æthelwold*. The text and drawings of all the miniatures were published by Gage, 'St Æthelwold's Benedictional'. The manuscript is treated in all discussions of early English illumination. See especially Homburger, *Die Anfänge der Malschule von Winchester im X. Jahrhundert.*

44. Homburger, *op. cit.*, 10 ff.

45. Such as the Gospels from Lorsch, miniatures from which were copied in a Reichenau manuscript shortly before 969 (Sacramentary of Gero, Darmstadt Landesbib., Cod. 1948). Reproduced Goldschmidt, *German Illum.*, II, plates 17 and 18. A similar Carolingian prototype may have been present at Winchester.

46. The curious 'padded' fold at the hem of the Virgin's gown (seen also on fols 51 verso and 64 verso of the Benedictional) is found in another Reichenau style manuscript, the single leaf of a *Registrum Gregorii* (Chantilly, Musée Condé). Reproduced, *op. cit.*, plate 8; this manuscript was made at Trèves in 983. Other Reichenau manuscripts use the acanthus frame border also, as the Gospels of Poussay (Paris, Bib. Nat., MS. lat. 10514), of the last quarter of the tenth century. Reproduced, *op. cit.*, plate 22.

47. Tolhurst, 'Two Anglo-Saxon Manuscripts of the Winchester School', 41 ff.

48. On the grounds of liturgical evidence. See H. A. Wilson, *The Benedictional of Archbishop Robert*, Henry Bradshaw Society, XXIV (London, 1903).

49. A seventeenth century inscription records the ownership of the Rouen manuscript by Robert, Archbishop. There is still some controversy as to whether this was Robert, Archbishop of Rouen (990–1037), or Robert of Jumièges, Archbishop of Canterbury (1051–2), who owned the Missal (Rouen Y.6). On stylistic grounds, it hardly seems possible that the Rouen Benedictional can be far removed in date from the Æthelwold manuscript, and the earlier Archbishop Robert, therefore, seems to be indicated as the original owner. The evidence for the identity of the owner is reviewed by Homburger, *op. cit.*, 49, n. 2.

50. The evidence, according to Millar (*op. cit.*, 74) is twofold: the manuscript was given to Trinity College by Thomas Nevile, Dean of Canterbury, among many others which came from Canterbury; and the initial I (fol. 59 verso, reproduced plate 15) is of a type not found in Winchester books, but common to Canterbury. Kendrick also assigns the Gospels to Canterbury: *Late Saxon Art*, 16.

The Winchester style of miniature and border may have been introduced into Canterbury during the archbishopric of Æthelgar who was Abbot of New Minster 965–77 and succeeded Dunstan as Archbishop of Canterbury in 989. See Millar, *op. cit.*, 75.

51. That is, a decorative initial letter containing a p. 45 figure subject, as distinguished from decorative human and animal figures without iconographic meaning. The historiated initial was a fundamental feature of English illumination even as late as the fifteenth century (see below, Chapter 8). The earliest known examples are found in the Canterbury Psalter, Cott. MS. Vesp. A.i.

52. Tolhurst, *op. cit.*, 27–41. Evidence for the dating is the absence of the mass for St Alphege who was martyred in 1012 and in 1023 was translated at Canterbury. Earlier it had been assigned to Peterborough on the basis of the calendar. See Atkins, 'An Investigation of Two Anglo-Saxon Calendars'. For the text of the Missal, see H. A. Wilson, *The Missal of Robert of Jumièges*, Henry Bradshaw Society, XI (London, 1896).

53. Homburger, *op. cit.*, 68, suggests the possibility of a translation from painting to linear technique which parallels that in the Utrecht Psalter but is independent of its influence. Cf. on this point, Saxl and Wittkower, *op. cit.*, 30 ff., illustrating this stylistic translation from the Carolingian MS. Harl. 647 into the English MS. Harl. 2506 containing the same text. See below, note 59. Harl. MS. 2506 is comparable in quality and in technique to Harl. 2904 and could be by the same artist.

54. The evidence, which rests mainly on the

inclusion in the manuscript of a copy of a charter connected with Reculver Monastery, near Canterbury, which was dissolved in 949, is discussed by Walter de Gray Birch, *The Utrecht Psalter* (London, 1876). The Utrecht Psalter is reproduced in facsimile by E. T. De Wald (Princeton University Press, n.d.). The manuscript is fully treated in every study of Carolingian illumination. For its relation to the English copies, see Birch, *op. cit.*, chapter III.

p. 46   55. Millar, *op. cit.*, plate 22; see also Wormald, *Eng. Drawings*, No. 34.

56. Cf. De Wald, plate vi.

57. Compare fol. 56 verso (Plate 33) and fol. 64 verso of the Utrecht Psalter: reproduced *op. cit.*, plate ci.

58. A study of the variations of style in the Utrecht Psalter itself (which certainly is not all by the same hand) is beyond the scope of this book, but two points should be noted. The Anglo-Saxon artists of Harl. 603 who copied the model most closely (fols 1–27 verso and 50–7) reflect differences in style in the originals (cf. fol. 4, plate 32 and fol. 21, and De Wald, plates vi and xxxiv). And secondly, certain miniatures in the Utrecht Psalter have been partially retouched in a style very suggestive of an Anglo-Saxon copyist. E.g. fol. 24 (De Wald, plate xxxviii). This kind of sharpening of the line is different from the shading in ink done in whole sections of the Utrecht Psalter (as fols 30–4) which De Wald notes. The shaded retouching is in the style of the Reims School. Some of the linear retouching may have been done by the Anglo-Saxon copyist, and may explain the almost unbelievably close correspondence between the original and the copy.

p. 47   59. Manuscript Jul. A.vi was in Durham in the fifteenth century: Mynors, *op. cit.*, No. 21. Herbert thought this manuscript was copied from a French original in Northumberland. Herbert, *op. cit.*, 114. Many miniatures in the Utrecht Psalter, as in Harl. 603, however, contain similar occupational scenes, and as far as subject goes, the scenes illustrating the calendar could have been derived from this source. Cf. Wormald, *Eng. Drawings*, plate 2. No earlier 'occupational' calendar is known in England.

As for Tib. B.v, the main part of the text was copied from a Carolingian manuscript of Cicero's *Aratus* (Harl. 647 in the British Museum), which was known to have been in Canterbury from the late tenth century. Its illustrations were certainly copied in Tib. B.v (cf. Saxl and Wittkower, *op. cit.*, 30), but owing to affinities with the Winchester calendar,

Saxl thinks the manuscript was painted in Wessex. Harl. 2506 is another copy of the same work with illustrations in the fine monumental style of Harl. 2904.

60. A psalter written in two columns, in Latin and Anglo-Saxon (Paris, Bib. Nat., ms. lat. 8824), has the spaces at the ends of verses on fols 1–6 filled in with small pictures illustrating the text. They were evidently done by the scribe while writing, since the letters of the text which follows the pictures often overlap them, while those of the text preceding do not. The style is that of the Utrecht Psalter. The manuscript once belonged to the Duc de Berry (cf. fol. 186). There is no indication of its original provenance. Wormald, *Eng. Drawings*, No. 55.

61. James (*Anc. Lib. Cant. and Dover*, p. lxxxiv) identified it with a Genesis in English listed as No. 95 in the Medieval Catalogue of St Augustine's (fol. 3, col. 2), *op. cit.*, 201. Millar, *op. cit.*, 80, and Kendrick, *Late Saxon Art*, 24, accept the St Augustine provenance.

62. Homburger, *op. cit.*, 70, n. 1, questions the Winchester origin of this manuscript. The letter from Fulk, Archbishop of Reims, recommending the monk Grimbald to King Alfred (which connects the manuscript with Grimbald) is a late eleventh century copy, says Homburger, and therefore was inserted later.

63. Reproduced in colour, Warner, *Illum. MSS*, plate 9.

64. The head and symbol of Matthew are reproduced by Kendrick, *Late Saxon Art*, plate vii; the text page, plate vi. The Mark picture is missing and perhaps was never included, since the text of Matthew ends on fol. 45 and that of Mark begins on the verso of this same leaf.

65. A very similar figure is found in the initial Q (fol. 70) of Royal ms. I D. ix decorated at Canterbury in Winchester style. See plate 28B. The angels, however, seem to be inspired by those in the Charter, and the Majesty figures also are close to the Christ in Vesp. A.viii; the three identical figures of the Trinity are found in the Dunstan pontifical (Paris, 943).

66. A gospel book of *c.*1000 in the library of York Minster has three surviving Evangelist pictures which are close in style to those in the Grimbald Gospels. Its place of origin is unknown. See J. P. Gilson, *Description of the Saxon Manuscript of the Four Gospels in the Library of York Minster* (York, 1925). The Evangelist Mark is reproduced in colour, Oake-

shott, *op. cit.*, plate 16. See also Wormald, 'The Survival of Anglo-Saxon Illumination', 3 ff.; he dates it late tenth century.

67. See W. de Gray Birch, 'On Two Anglo-Saxon Manuscripts', *Roy. Soc. of Lit. Trans.*, Series II, xi (1878), 463–512.

68. The Last Judgement on fol. 6 verso–7 seems to be more in the Utrecht style. Millar, *op. cit.*, plate 25b (fol. 7). See also Wormald, *Eng. Drawings*, No. 33, and plate 16.

69. Millar (*op. cit.*, 19) notes this as their first appearance in English manuscripts. On the iconography of the Trinity with the Virgin and Child, (fol. 75 verso) see Kantorowicz, 'The Quinity of Winchester'.

70. *Pal. Soc.*, Series II, plate 191. Wormald, *Eng. Drawings*, No. 43, dates it late tenth century. The manuscript belonged, as indicated by a pressmark, to Waltham Abbey at one time.

71. *Proc. Camb. Antiq. Soc.*, VII (1888–91), 51–7, plates X and XI. For a complete study of all the Prudentius manuscripts, see Richard Stettiner, *Die illustrierten Prudentiushandschriften* (Berlin, 1895; Plates, 1905).

72. See dedicatory verses on fol. 2 verso of the manuscript. Wormald, *Eng. Drawings*, No. 4. Goldschmidt called the drawings of Faith and Charity in this manuscript some of 'the most charming drawings mediaeval art has produced'. Adolf Goldschmidt, 'English Influence on Mediaeval Art', *Med. Studies*, II, 719.

73. Reproduced, Millar, *op. cit.*, plate 26; Brit. Mus., *Reproductions from Illuminated Manuscripts*, I, plate VII; *Pal. Soc.*, Series I, plate 190. See also H. P. Mitchell, 'Flotsam of Later Anglo-Saxon Art', *Burl. Mag.*, XLIII (1923), 104–17.

74. Herbert, however, considered it earlier, i.e. late tenth century; *op. cit.*, 111. Wormald also dates it 'late tenth century with later additions', *Eng. Drawings*, No. 24, plate 6a.

75. M. R. James, *On the Abbey of St Edmund at Bury* (Cambridge, 1895), 71.

76. A psalter preceded by Easter Tables illustrated with a partially coloured drawing (fol. 9 verso) of St Pachomius receiving them from an angel. The manuscript can be dated *c.* 1012–23. See Warner, *Illum. MSS*, where the miniatures are described in detail and the *Beatus* page is reproduced in colour (Plate 10). See also Wormald, *Eng. Drawings*, No. 26, plate 22.

77. According to a note in the Easter Calendar. See *New Pal. Soc.*, Series II, plates 166–8. Wormald, *Eng. Drawings*, No. 56 (with bibliography), and plates 26–8. p. 50

78. Reproduced *New Pal. Soc.*, Series II, plate 166. p. 51

79. Niver, *op. cit.*, 684. The Litany indicates a date after 1031. Madan dates Douce MS. 296 before 1036 and suggests Ely for its provenance, *Summary Cat.*, No. 21870. The B of the *Beatus* in Douce 296 (fol. 9) is a thinly painted linear version of the one in the Benedictional of Æthelwold.

80. For MS. 708, see Chapter 3 below.

81. Harrsen, 'The Countess Judith of Flanders and the Library of Weingarten Abbey', 3. Morgan 709 has had an exceptionally interesting history. It was procured for Judith of Flanders, wife of Tostig, perhaps by Tostig's uncle Ælfwius who was Abbot of New Minster from *c.* 1063 to the Norman invasion, in which he and twelve of his monks disguised as soldiers fought and lost their lives. Judith carried the Gospel Book with her when she fled to the Continent with her husband. Later, after his death, when she married Guelph IV and founded (1094) the Benedictine monastery of Weingarten on Lake Constance, the Morgan Gospels were among her gifts to the monks there. Thus it happened that a Winchester manuscript of the first half of the eleventh century helped to set the style which developed into the magnificent Weingarten illumination of the late twelfth century. See also Hanns Swarzenski, *The Berthold Missal* (New York, 1943), 1 ff. and 8 ff.

82. All the miniatures are reproduced by Henry Ellis, 'An Account of Cædmon's Metrical Paraphrase', *Archaeologia*, XXIV (1832), 329–40, plates lii–civ. See also Charles Kennedy, *The Cædmon Poems* (Princeton, 1916): English translation with introduction by C. R. Morey, and plates much reduced in size. For the latest and best reproduction, see Gollancz, *The Cædmon Manuscript*, a facsimile of the manuscript with a fine colour plate of page 84 as the frontispiece.

83. Millar, *op. cit.*, 76, dates it *c.* 1000 and accepts James's identification of the manuscript as No. 304 in the Medieval Cat. of Christ Church, Cant.: James, *Anc. Lib. Cant. and Dover*, pp. lxxxviii and 51. Herbert, *op. cit.*, 118, dates it *c.* 1035 and gives Winchester as its provenance on the grounds of the portrait of Ælfwin on fol. 2, whom he identified as Abbot of New Minster 1035–57. Kendrick, *Late Saxon Art*, 104 ff., and Wormald, 'Decorated Initials', 121, date

the manuscript in the second quarter of the eleventh century on the grounds of its containing Scandinavian Ringerrike ornament combined with Winchester acanthus motifs. Gollancz, *op. cit.*, vii ff., points out, in support of the Winchester origins of the Cædmon, a manuscript which he finds similar in style, having Winchester connexions: Rouen, Bib. Pub., MS. A.27 (368), the Llanalet Pontifical. The Rouen manuscript was noted and two illustrations of it were published by John Gage, 'The Anglo-Saxon Ceremonial of the Dedication and Consecration of Churches, Illustrated from a Pontifical in the Public Library at Rouen', *Archaeologia*, xxv (1834), 235–74. See also Talbot Rice, *English Art*, plate 70a. Wormald finds no connexion between the style of the Rouen manuscript and the Cædmon and has recently expressed his opinion privately that 'the whole thing is probably a Canterbury produc-tion'. The Winchester connexion really rests on rather shaky evidence, namely the fact that there was an illuminator named Ælfwin there at about the right time. Stylistically, all the Cædmon drawings might very well be Canterbury work.

84. Both the Vivian and the Moutier-Grandval Bibles contain similar bands of continuous narrative. See Koehler, *op. cit.*, plates 50, 69, 70, and 74.

85. Wormald says that this second artist's style 'appears to be a derivative' of that of the Leofric Missal and the Malmesbury *Prudentius* (Plate 38B). The similarities are chiefly in the drapery with its ropy folds and pleated edges, in the survival of a certain 'classical' solidity of figure forms, and in the persistent profiles. The Cædmon is certainly later, however, and much less fine in quality than the Corpus Christi College *Prudentius*.

CHAPTER 3

EARLY ROMANESQUE ART

⟨ 1050 – *CIRCA* 1110 ⟩

*

HISTORICAL BACKGROUND:
TRANSITION FROM ANGLO-SAXON TO NORMAN

POLITICAL

Edward the Confessor, King 1042–66 (5 Jan.).

Harold Godwinson, King 6 Jan.–14 Oct. 1066; Battle of Hastings.

William I, Duke of Normandy, King 1066–87; reorganization in government and Church; systematized feudalism; Domesday Book.

William II (son of William I), King 1087–1100; first Crusade 1096; capture of Jerusalem 1099.

Henry I (son of William I), King 1100–35; Duchy of Normandy annexed to England; organized internal government.

ECCLESIASTICAL

Stigand, Saxon Bishop of Winchester 1043–52; Archbishop of Canterbury, 1052–70; great fire at Christ Church Priory, Canterbury, destroying the Cathedral and many manuscripts 1070; Stigand is represented on the Bayeux Tapestry.

Lanfranc (an Italian) Abbot of Caen (Normandy), Archbishop of Canterbury 1070–89.

Anselm (an Italian), Abbot of Bec (Normandy), Archbishop of Canterbury 1093–1109.

William of St Carilef (St Calais), Bishop of Durham 1081–96; exiled in Normandy 1088–96; d. 1096; gave fifty manuscripts to Library of Durham Cathedral.

*

THE most vivid and, it is believed, the most impartial account of the historical events culminating in the Norman invasion of England is found, surprisingly enough, not in literary but in pictorial form. The famous Bayeux Tapestry[1] is a strip narrative, in modern terminology, and can also be thought of as a documentary film featuring the story of this momentous event, so impartially told, however, that to this day no one is rash enough to state categorically that the Tapestry is either Saxon or Norman. The same dilemma exists in regard to other works of art produced during the second half of the eleventh century. It would seem, therefore, that whatever changes there were in government and church administration, and even in the arts, especially architecture, the styles followed in pictorial art as in literature retained a large measure of continuity with pre-Conquest forms.[2] After the Conquest, as before, there were two main stylistic currents in the stream of art; the indigenous Saxon decorative, linear style, and the recurrent style of painted figures originating in Carolingian art, which had been introduced into England through previous monastic contacts with Continental centres.[3] After the Conquest, it is true, Continental influence was greatly strengthened through increased contacts with Normandy and through the importation of Norman scribes and books, but these contacts were reciprocal in influence and carried much back to the Continent as well as away from it. Moreover, there are the further facts that Norman manuscript art before the Conquest was already deeply imbued with Saxon influence and that this art, when introduced into England as at Canterbury and later at Durham, was more congenial to English artists because of its Anglo-Saxon features; for this reason it fused more easily with current styles in England. There followed an accentuation of the phenomenon which was less noticeable in earlier periods, of a hybrid style in illuminated manuscripts with mixed Continental, i.e. Norman, and English flavour, and in a number of cases it is difficult if not impossible to determine whether the work was done by English or Norman artists, in England or in Normandy. It seems clear, however, that, whatever new motifs, designs, and colour schemes may have been introduced from Normandy, the vital, creative spirit of post-Conquest art in England was English and not Continental. But it is equally true, as Swarzenski[4] has pointed out, that 'English art needed constantly repeated stimulation from abroad to remain productive and creatively alive'. Pictorial art of the second half of the eleventh century illustrates well that fact.

In order to distinguish the new elements introduced into the Saxon style after the Norman Conquest, a brief survey of English mid-century style may be useful. As in the first half of the eleventh century, the centres of production of illuminated manuscripts were still largely in the south of England, notably at Winchester and Canterbury. The Winchester style as represented in the Benedictional of Æthelwold, even in the time of that Bishop, seems to have spread to the Fen country; about the middle of the eleventh century also there seems to be evidence of further productiveness of the style outside Winchester, perhaps at Thorney Abbey (Monte Cassino MS. BB. 437, 439). At New Minster, Winchester,[5] where the effect of the Utrecht style had been felt in the early part of the century, vigorous coloured outline drawing continues to flourish (Brit. Mus., Cott. MS. Tib. C.vi),[6] but in an outstanding example of undoubted New Minster production (Brit. Mus., Arundel MS. 60), a strange new, strongly Byzantine element appears. Likewise, two manuscripts connected with Hereford in the west of England (Brit. Mus., Cott. MS. Caligula A. xiv and Camb., Pembroke Coll., MS. 302) seem to be under the influence of a Continental painted figure style. The Canterbury manuscripts of this period, only recently the subject of a long-needed thorough investigation,[7] although showing more consistency in their linear decorative character, were subjected to more immediate and constant Norman influence through the two Norman Archbishops of Canterbury, Lanfranc and Anselm. It is in Canterbury that the historiated initial – a feature long to remain typical of English illumination – was fully developed, doubtless under Norman stimulus. Finally, a group of manuscripts at Durham, perhaps not all made there, the gift of the Norman, William of St Carilef, Bishop of Durham (1081–96) to the Cathedral, combine the technique of coloured line with heavy, acanthus foliage and figures of men and animals in a style which is found in manuscripts in Normandy.[8] More detailed distinctions between the local styles of this transitional period from Anglo-Saxon to Anglo-Norman will appear from the study of the individual manuscripts.

Pre-Conquest Manuscripts

About the middle of the eleventh century a new wave of influence from Reims seems to have been introduced into English illumination, not, however, in the form of the linear Utrecht Psalter technique, but in that of the impressionistic painting style. Three English manuscripts of about this date bear witness to this influence:[9] the Gospels of St Margaret (Bod. MS. Lat. liturg. f.5); the Monte Cassino Gospels (MS. BB. 437, 439); and a second Gospel Book, which was given by Countess Judith to Weingarten Abbey (Morgan MS. 708). All three manuscripts have full-page miniatures of writing Evangelists.

A small gospel lectionary[10] (Bod. MS. Lat. liturg. f.5) is closest to the impressionistic painting technique of Reims, the modelled figures and shaded draperies being only partially reduced to pattern. No symbols accompany the Evangelists (fol. 3 verso; Plate 48A). The colours are blue, green, and dark red; dull reddish gold is used for halo and book, and for details of the reading desk and bench and for the frame. The flat head and sharply broken contours of the figure, the broadly shaded draperies and curtains, and the humped ground line all recall, in simplified and conventionalized form, Reims painting such as is seen in the Ebbo Gospels. The background is the plain vellum, and there is no decorative border, which is unusual in English manuscripts.

The mid-eleventh century Gospel Book belonging to the library at Monte Cassino[11] (MS. BB. 437, 439) has Evangelists, who are writing, seated under decorated arches supported by columns with acanthus capitals and bases. Their symbols hover over them in fussy solicitation; the eagle of St John (page 166; Plate 45) perches familiarly on his head, and with bent neck and open beak seems to be exhorting the Evangelist as he writes. John leans over his desk, the drapery of his mantle folded around his body and falling in rich, but unnatural, linear patterns which are shaded with colour in the deep folds. The position of the figure is distorted; the feet and shoulders are in profile, the head, waist, and legs in three-quarters view. The background is painted with zigzag, streaky lines, probably to indicate sky. Many of these features suggest that the prototype of this manuscript also was a derivative of the Reims school: the ramping lions on the arch, the dynamic intensity of both Evangelist and symbol, the round-shouldered, distorted figure, the impressionistic background. Yet there is, also, a strong similarity to the Gospel Book made for Countess Judith (Morgan MS. 708).[12] Here, too, the figures are seated under arches, from the capitals of which spring stiff, interlaced foliage sprays in the manner of the earlier Trinity Gospels at Cambridge, as well as of some of the pages in the Benedictional of Æthelwold (cf. Plates 26 and 27). As compared with the Monte Cassino Gospels, the drawing in MS. 708 is stiffer and more stylized: the drapery folds are hard, and are indicated by uniform swathes of paint; the faces and hair are painted with strong colour (the John of fol. 66 verso has blue hair and beard and a pink face with red spots on the cheeks). It would seem to be a composite style resulting, perhaps, from a linear technique executed with brush and paint in place of pen and ink. Both this and the Monte Cassino manuscript represent the final stage of the Winchester style, as modified by a return influence from the Continent consisting of a mixture of Reims and Winchester elements.[13]

Coloured outline drawing of about the middle of the eleventh century is represented by a magnificent Psalter, Brit. Mus., Cott. MS. Tib. C.vi, the first known English example of a psalter containing a series of preliminary Bible pictures. These are full-page scenes mainly from the lives of David and of Christ, and beginning with the Creation (fols 2–18). In addition to these pages of drawings there are two painted miniatures: Christ in Majesty (fol. 18 verso) and David and the Musicians (fol. 30 verso). There are also painted foliage initials with decorative framework borders without animals or figures, in the general style of the much earlier New Minster Charter of King Edgar (Cott. Vesp. A.viii; Plate 25). The stylistic characteristics of all the illumination in Tib. C.vi, both outline drawing and painting, seem to be those of a single hand. The manuscript offers, therefore, exceptionally interesting material for a comparison of the same style as developed in the two techniques, for example, fols 10 and 30 verso (Plates 50 and 51).

The painted miniature of David and the Musicians (fol. 30 verso; Plate 51) was evidently copied from some good Carolingian original.[14] The figures are compact and well-proportioned, with thick, wig-like hair coloured red or blue. The drapery folds, though much stylized, are shaded with white or yellow for high-lights and darker tones accentuated with black or brown for the shadows. A curious bit of stylized light and shade is the use of circles or ovals of white pigment on David's elbow and on the abdomen and thigh of the musician Ethan. This feature occurs also on the knee of Christ in the other painted miniature (fol. 18 verso). Ornamental patterns consisting of quatrefoils, circles, and dots in bands are used on David's tunic. Similar patterns are found on the bars of the border framework of this page. The colours are light red, green, blue which when shaded with yellow produces a dull green – as in the tunic of the musician at the lower right – dull purple, and yellow used in place of gold for the crown and for the bars of the border framework. All the details of the composition are outlined with a broad, painted contour line of dull purple which has the effect of a shadow around the figure,[15] thus accentuating the effect of modelling. The foreground consists of a series of little humps painted blue and shaded with a yellow high-light in the centre of each.

Turning now to the coloured drawing of King David on fol. 10 (Plate 50), we can see the linear technique in all its precision and clarity unencumbered with the heavy, shaded pigments, and in consequence both freer and more monumental in the rendering of the figure. With the exception of the hands (which are in pale red outline and hardly show in the reproduction) all the drawing has been done in brown ink and the colour applied to the line with the shadow technique, described above in the painting; not, however, wholly to accentuate the modelling, but also to differentiate between the colour of the mantle, which is blue, and the tunic, which is dull reddish brown. On knees and elbow appear the round spots in dull red which are carried over from the high-lights of the shading technique. On other pages they often appear as blue or green spots (e.g. fol. 13 verso). The ornamental bands with circles and dots and the humpy foreground are used here as in the painting, but with much greater effectiveness in this swift, impressionistic style.

In spite of the totally different techniques of painting and of coloured drawing used in the two miniatures in Tib. C.vi the artist seems to have been one and the same person: the head and face – eyes, eyebrows, nose, ear – are identical in the two Davids. A curious difference in the manner of representing hair and beard is that in the painting they are very linear and stylized though washed over with colour; in the drawing they are shaded softly with colour and appear more natural. On the whole, there is no question that the artist was much more at home with the coloured drawing than with the painting.

In Brit. Mus., Arundel MS. 60, another fine psalter, made for New Minster c. 1060,[16] there are also two styles, one very much closer to a painted original than the other; but in this manuscript the illumination is certainly by two different hands, one perhaps later than the other. The first pages of the manuscript, illustrated with drawings of the signs of the zodiac, and a full-page Crucifixion on fol. 12 verso (Plate 52) seem to be the work of an uninspired copyist of the figures and technique of the outline drawings in Tib. C.vi.[17] The shadow outline technique, the stiff drapery folds, and the quatrefoil and circle ornamental patterns appear again here; but the line is flat and hard and has the meaningless complexity of a design that was copied without being well understood. The Christ in this miniature seems to have been taken, with some adaptation, from the Christ of the Crucifixion in Tib. C.vi (fol. 12 verso); the Virgin from Mary Magdalene of the Three Marys at the Tomb (fol. 13 verso); and John from an angel above the arches of the Easter Table on fol. 3. The clumsy folds of the Virgin's veil and the draped mantle of John are good examples of this copying of misunderstood drapery. In Arundel 60, as in Tib. C.vi, yellow replaces gold in the miniature and also in the decorative border.

The *Beatus* page (fol. 13) opposite the Crucifixion in Arundel 60 has a typical New Minster border with slender bars and twining foliage. The initial B is partly historiated with David playing the harp in the lower loop and 'gymnastic' with a figure climbing in the branches of the upper loop. The figure style is totally different from that of the Crucifixion miniature. Both the initial and the border are painted in brighter colours, with crisp, sharp outlines and jewel-like ornament.[18]

The second Crucifixion miniature on fol. 52 verso (Plate 53) is very different from the first and is probably somewhat later. The source of this style is clearly Byzantine, exaggeratedly stylized into an angular, formal linear pattern. The face shows a conventionalized modelling in pink lines and red spots on the cheeks. The hair and beard are dead black; the torso and limbs are reduced to an anatomical pattern of pink and blue lines; the drapery is pleated in flat geometric folds and bordered with a jewelled pattern. The sharp Z-curve of the crucified Christ is echoed in the swaying curve of the two flanking trees, which have pink trunks and branches, atop which are perched solid blue ovals patterned with foliage and red flowerets; the foreground consists of a series of blue and pink disks. Black outline is used around all the details of the composition. Except for the yellow bars of the framework border and the green backgrounds of the symbols of the Evangelists in the corner roundels, only vermilion, blue, and a dull pink are used. Yet the effect of the page is striking. Though the model may have been Byzantine,[19] this artist has injected into it a new element of powerful abstract pattern based on line and colour, which gives the miniature an eerie, other-worldly effect.

A different form of Byzantine influence is found in two stylistically related manuscripts of the mid eleventh century (Plate 49), and as in Arundel 60 probably was not introduced through direct contact with Eastern models but rather through Ottonian manuscripts, perhaps of the Reichenau school.[20] One of the two (Camb., Pembroke College, MS. 302), a Gospel Book, contains a description in Anglo-Saxon of the boundaries of the see of Hereford, and the manuscript itself may have been made there;[21] the other (Brit. Mus., Cott. MS. Caligula A.xiv), a troper,[22] is so close in style that it too has been assigned tentatively to Hereford.[23] Both manuscripts are remarkable for the boldness of their figure drawing and for their use of burnished gold and of strong, heavy colours, chiefly brick red and reddish purple, yellow, and dull green. With these colours, white, now oxidized, is used for the high-lights of the modelling. Backgrounds are painted in strong colour – sometimes purple, perhaps imitating a stained vellum leaf – with conventionalized wavy patterns representing clouds. The illustrations in Caligula A.xiv have crowded compositions more or less confined within formal frames (fol. 25; Plate 49A). Heads, hands, and feet are large, and features are boldly modelled. Characteristic of the heads are the stiffly curled coiffures, the strongly arched eyebrows, and the heavy square jowls. The drapery folds are so heavily stylized as to suggest stripes. Violent gestures and much use of long, swinging phylacteries intensify the excitement, as in the scene of the martyrdom of St Lawrence, and increase the complexity of the design.

The Evangelist miniatures in Pembroke 302 are also in long, narrow panels similar in proportions to those in Caligula A.xiv. Though the single figures appear more monumental in themselves there is the same extraordinary excitement in their poses and gestures (cf. Luke, fol. 60 verso; Plate 49B), and the same strong colours are used; the mantles are burnished gold, patterned with incised lines which were originally filled with some dark or perhaps black pigment or ink and give a niello-like effect. In the Luke miniature, the draped curtain of the background is light red shaded with white and darker red, and tucked into the folds are gold ball ornaments. Luke's hair and beard are blue, and red lines are used to model his face and hands. His tunic is light purple shaded with darker tone. The richness of the colouring and the strong shading are unusual in English illumination and are the characteristics that suggest Ottonian or late Carolingian figure style with strong Byzantine elements. It is noteworthy that the symbols of the Evangelists are not represented – an omission again suggestive of Eastern sources.[24]

Post-Conquest Manuscripts: Canterbury – The Bayeux Tapestry

After the Norman Conquest of England in 1066 the most conspicuous and far-reaching development in English illumination took place at Canterbury, particularly at Christ Church, where in 1070 Lanfranc accompanied by Norman monks undertook a 'regeneration' of monastic life on the Norman pattern. The change can be seen most clearly in the script.[25] In the illumination, also, modifications in the style and particularly in the colours are noticeable, though the continuity with the earlier Canterbury style is still evident. The impact of Norman influence on Canterbury after the arrival of Lanfranc was not that of a new and unfamiliar foreign style, but of a modified version of one long practised and wholly congenial to English artists.

The more prolific of the two Canterbury centres after the Conquest was Christ Church. Dodwell lists 76 illuminated manuscripts attributable to that scriptorium before 1200.[26] The techniques include both painting and coloured outline – a combination which has been noted in an earlier Christ Church manuscript, Arundel MS. 155 (Plates 40 and 41). In fact, this very manuscript is peculiarly important also because it seems to have directly influenced other manuscripts made at Canterbury in the second half of the eleventh century and thereby furnishes specific evidence for the survival of the earlier Canterbury style after the Conquest. Folio 133 of Arundel 155 (Plate 41) contains a seated figure of St Benedict with monks, which is found in a similar composition in Brit. Mus., Cott. MS. Tib. A.iii (fol. 117 verso), made at Canterbury c. 1040–70.[27] Also, in Arundel 155 there is another miniature (fol. 9 verso) showing St Pachomius receiving the Easter Tables from an angel, which is copied in Cott. MS. Caligula A.xv (fol. 122 verso), dating from about the same time as Tib. A.iii.

Even closer connexions exist between the later drawings[28] in Harl. 603 and those in earlier parts of the same manuscript. On fol. 17 verso is a sketch inserted in a blank space at the end of the text, which is a direct copy of three similar figures in one of the earlier miniatures on fol. 17. The copy (Plate 48B) is many times larger than the original, and the technique is much less free and illusionistic, but the style is pure Anglo-Saxon, such as developed under the influence of the Utrecht Psalter, in respect to the sureness of the line drawing, the vigour of the poses and gestures, and the use of coloured line in place of or in addition to the brown outline. The style of the sketch on fol. 17 verso is that of the latter part of the Harl. 603, fols 58 to the end. Thus this manuscript also is a direct carrier of the earlier Anglo-Saxon tradition into the post-Conquest period.

Finally, earlier English precedents can be pointed out also for the historiated initial which developed so vigorously at Canterbury after the Conquest: Vesp. MS. A.i (the eighth century Canterbury Psalter) contains some small ones; Royal MS. I D. ix (the Dunstan Gospels, late tenth century) has a Q (fol. 70) containing Christ in Majesty (Plate 28B); and Arundel MS. 155 (fol. 93) has a fully developed example (Plate 40) with David slaying Goliath. It is true, the initial letter in these early instances is used as a frame around the small picture, with little or no foliate ornament on the initial itself, as post-Conquest historiated initials have.

This type of historiated initial, that is, the decorative text initial containing a figure subject, seems to be a favourite Norman form, deriving perhaps from the Carolingian school of Corbie, and particularly from the Sacramentary of Drogo,[29] where it takes its place as the first letter of the text, instead of being treated, as in Arundel 155, as the central feature of a framed page. At Canterbury, as elsewhere in England, decorative initials had, of course, long constituted important ornamental features of the text page; at Canterbury, especially, animals, both naturalistic and fantastic, were familiar motifs among the foliate intricacies of the design of initials.[30] Occasionally even a human figure, climbing and jumping among the branches, replaced or accompanied the decorative animals, as in a tenth century manuscript, Bod. MS. Tanner 10;[31] but such examples are rare earlier, even in Canterbury work. The wholesale introduction of such human figures into the initial seems, therefore, to be one of the results of Norman influence on book art, and perhaps was introduced at Canterbury by Lanfranc. These human figures were used in two ways, sometimes both in the same initial; decorative, 'gymnastic' figures often naked, which were treated in the same manner as the ramping, clambering animals; and figures represented as actors in a scene which usually illustrates the text introduced by the initial.

Initials containing human figures can be associated with the St Augustine's scriptorium at Canterbury by means of one of the finest early examples of a manuscript containing only this kind of illumination, Brit. Mus., Cott. MS. Vit. C.xii, a martyrology with obits which seem to date it in the first decade of the twelfth century.[32] At the beginning of each month there is a KL monogram of the decorative foliage type and containing birds or animals or the sign of the Zodiac for the month. Only seven now survive: January, with animals and birds (fol. 114); February, with Aquarius, the January Zodiac sign, holding a water jug in one hand, while he warms the other over a fire, thus combining the sign of the Zodiac with the occupation of February (fol. 117 verso); March, with several little figures pruning the luxuriant vines which fill the letters (fol. 121); May, a dragon and foliage initial with a ram, the Zodiac sign for April, poised on top of the upright of the K (fol. 127); August, with a man fighting a dragon in the letter, and on top of the K, a lion biting its own tail – probably the Zodiac sign for July (fol. 134); September, with a fine coloured drawing of Virgo, the sign for August, in the best impressionistic outline style (fol. 139; Plate 46C); and finally October, with a woman holding the scales, which is the Zodiac sign for September. In all of these initials, the background is coloured, usually purple, more rarely blue and green. There is very little vermilion, but when used, its purpose is clearly to enliven, by its contrasting brightness, what is otherwise rather a dull colour scheme. The figures, both animal and human, are well drawn and shaded with colour; the initials are beautifully designed, with the delicate stems and foliage contrasting pleasingly with the solid or cross-hatched coloured backgrounds. In this manuscript the KL monogram is not set apart from the text, but serves both to introduce it and to enliven and beautify the page, which has no decorative border.

More elaborate in the number and kinds of decorated initials, yet so close in style as to suggest the same group of illuminators, is Brit. Mus., Arundel MS. 91, also a collection of Lives of the Saints, each of which is introduced by a decorative initial in the same colouring and technique as in Cott. Vit. C.xii. This manuscript, therefore, belongs likewise to the very early twelfth century, perhaps c. 1100. The initials are of all kinds; there are old-fashioned zoomorphic scroll initials[33] in red, blue, green, and purple; there are acanthus foliage and animal or dragon initials; there are plain initials containing 'histories', in this case, scenes illustrating the lives of the saints of which the text is introduced by the initial (fol. 188; Plate 46A); and there are initials composed of human figures. The figure style is extremely lively, the drawing is expressive and competent in its suggestion of violent action and of the excitement accompanying it. Indeed, there seems to be evidence that in some cases the colourist was less able than the draughtsman, for the flat solid colour of the backgrounds tends to obscure the clarity and precision of the outline.

Some features of the historiated initial T in Plate 46A should be noted because of their obvious kinship with the vigorous narrative style of the Bayeux Tapestry (see below). Chief among these are the spirited, well-drawn horses, especially the one which has fallen on its head, with feet and tail high in air; and the equally extraordinary figure of a knight still clutching his spear, while his shield falls downward ahead of him. Both horse and rider are very much in the spirit of the battle scenes of the Bayeux Tapestry (Plate 47B). So, too, is the idea of the strip narrative, which is especially well-fitted to the form of this initial T, and the disregard of the framing bands in the arrangement of the compositions, which push out over the edges and even beyond the limits of the initial, just as the scenes in the Bayeux Tapestry often continue beyond the main panel into the lower border.

The initial M in Arundel 91 (fol. 26 verso; Plate 46B) is an even better example than the T of the intricate design of a well-composed historiated initial. The subject – St Michael fighting the dragon – lends itself superlatively well to this type of illustration. The wings of both angel and beast, the flying drapery fold and the coiled tail are all most effective decorative elements to weave in and out of the initial frame. Even the body of Michael is used in this way. The figures are in brown outline tinted with red and green and silhouetted against a solid purple ground. A heavy purple contour line is painted around the outside of the initial letter and around parts of figures which are free of the background, as Michael's wings and the dragon's tail. The wings are shaded blue and green. It is an extremely fine, vigorous style which must be kept in mind for later comparison with that of the Durham Carilef manuscripts.

The decorative and historiated initial, taking its place in relation to the text and the layout of the page as in this manuscript, seems to satisfy in a peculiar way the decorative sense of the English illuminator, for the form persists, in greater or less degree, throughout the later history of English manuscripts.

The figure style of the historiated initials, as described above, comes, as we have seen, from the outline miniature; but in the St Augustine's manuscripts, and, in fact, in Canterbury illumination as a whole at the beginning of the twelfth century, there are very few freely designed miniatures such as were found in the earlier period under the influence of the Utrecht Psalter. One manuscript which does contain such miniatures on a full-page scale, and which can be associated with the scriptorium of St Augustine on the grounds of its figure style, is a copy of St Augustine's *De Civitate Dei*, MS. Plut. xii.17 in the Laurentian Library in Florence. The hand in which this manuscript is written looks like late eleventh century script,[34] but the illumination seems to be rather of the early twelfth. Dodwell thinks it can be attributed with certainty on stylistic grounds to Canterbury, and, less categorically, to St Augustine's.[35]

It contains illuminated initials in colour without gold, plain or with foliage and animal designs, at the beginning of each book; and prefixed to the text are four full-page miniatures with subjects as follows: fol. 1 verso, the Weighing of Souls; examples of sudden death, and a ploughing scene; fol. 2 verso, the City of God; fol. 3 verso, a large figure of St Augustine with monks (Plate 54); and on the facing page, fol. 4, a number of figures apparently in animated discussion with St Augustine (Plate 55). The figures are drawn in the firm, lively coloured outline style characterizing the Canterbury manuscripts of the post-Conquest period. St Augustine is silhouetted against a purple background powdered with patterns of dots and circles and two large circular ornaments filled with convention-alized leaves and other decorative motifs such as are found also in the framing bands of the miniature. St Augustine's vestments are richly ornamented with geometric designs some of which are used in other English manuscripts, as the Benedict of Arundel MS. 155 and David in Cott. MS. Tib. C.vi. The drapery folds of all the figures are amply represented with shaded lines, and the draperies themselves cling to the bodies or flap loose as though at the mercy of a violent wind. Hair also appears blown by the wind; faces are eager and animated, gestures are dramatic; even the ground line is whipped up into frothy hum-mocks. The draperies and the awkward, crossed-leg positions and the general liveliness of expression suggest French Romanesque sculpture of the school of Aquitaine, but these features are also characteristic of earlier Anglo-Saxon drawings, especially of Canterbury work. There may be Continental influence also in these miniatures, as the architectural framework of the border and the series of medallion heads suggest. The figure style, how-ever, has a good deal in common with the initials of Arundel MS. 91. The decorative initials in the Laurentian manuscript also are, apparently, English and close to initials in the Canterbury manuscripts, more particularly those made at St Augustine's.[36] Plain coloured backgrounds are used, against which the lively patterns of animals and grotesques, human figures and even heads in medallions stand out with striking decorative effect.

The Bayeux Tapestry (Plate 47) is a strip of embroidery over 230 feet long and about 20 inches wide; it is now displayed under glass in a special room in the town hall of Bayeux, but originally it hung on the wall of the Cathedral. The English provenance of the em-broidery, though still questioned, seems most plausible when we compare its lively illus-trative 'strip narrative' style with such manuscripts as the Cædmon Paraphrase (Bod., MS. Jun. 11; Plate 44) and with the historiated initials in later manuscripts of the post-Conquest Canterbury groups (Plate 46A). As for the animals of the border, as Kendrick remarks,[37] they 'might have come straight out of the Trinity Gospels, MS. B.10.4 (e.g. fol. 57)'; and the charming little hunting and agricultural scenes in the borders suggest Cott. MS. Julius A.vi and the Canterbury copy of the Utrecht Psalter (Harl. 603). The influence of the Utrecht Psalter style, which could in itself account for a great many in-dividual figures as well as for the general style of the embroidery, was, it is true, also felt on the Continent; it might be argued, therefore, that the design and style of the tapestry could be French as well as English; yet the fact remains that both English embroidery and English illumination seem to have been sufficiently known and admired on the Con-tinent to support the assumption, which the stylistic qualities suggest, that the design as well as the workmanship was English.[38]

The latest consensus seems to be that the Bayeux Tapestry was ordered in England by Bishop Odo, brother of the Conqueror, for his cathedral at Bayeux (consecrated in 1077 in 'the decade preceding 1083, when Odo was at the height of his power, a "second king" in England and at the same time keenly interested in his new Cathedral at Bayeux; ...'[39] In the latter part of the tapestry Odo figures prominently in a number of the scenes.[40]

The embroidery is on linen in wools, formerly of eight colours but now much faded: three shades of blue, two of green, red, yellow or buff, and grey, all used arbitrarily as in

English coloured outline miniatures.[41] The accuracy of the details, such as the distinction between the Normans and English by the difference in their haircut, the ships, the armour, and even the architecture – Westminster Abbey in the scene of the funeral of the Confessor – would indicate that the designer of the embroidery was thoroughly familiar with both Norman and Saxon characteristics and customs. This interest in details, together with the vivid narrative spirit, is an outstanding trait of English eleventh-century illumination. Probably the most dramatic and exciting scenes are those of the mêlée itself (Plate 47B) in which horses and riders fall headlong, and dead and dismembered soldiers fill the lower margin.

The two details of the Bayeux Tapestry reproduced in plate 47 are typical of the most frequently recurring motifs (horses and boats) but convey no idea of the impressiveness of the design as a whole. The principal actors in the drama appearing singly or in groups, in architectural settings, on horseback, or in boats, give accent to the pattern as the story unrolls, and incidents are set off from one another by decorative trees, which serve the purpose of dividing the epic into stanzas of unequal length. The rhythm is kept by the recurrence of these same few motifs. Seen as a whole, the design is astonishingly well-balanced, varied and interesting, and in the original bright colours with which the embroidery was done must have been startlingly gay and brilliant, though now it appears rather dull and uniform in tone.

Durham

More important even than the Canterbury manuscripts and the Bayeux Tapestry for the problem of English and Norman attribution of post-Conquest art, are some sixteen manuscripts with illuminations which formed part of a gift of about fifty by William of St Carilef (now St Calais), Bishop of Durham (1081–96), to the Cathedral Library.[42] The Carilef manuscripts fall into two groups: those made before his exile[43] in Normandy in 1088; and those made after that date, presumably in Normandy. Differences in the style of illumination can be distinguished, and it seems reasonable to assume that the style of the earlier group represents the survival in the north of England of pre-Conquest decorative elements with influence from the Continent, as at Canterbury, while manuscripts of the later group were perhaps illuminated in some Norman monastic scriptorium. For both of these assumptions the only evidence is stylistic.

The finest and most typical representative of the first group of Carilef manuscripts, made in great part before 1088, is the great Commentary of St Augustine on the Psalms, a manuscript in three volumes, of which it is recorded in a colophon of the last volume that it was written in Normandy. The second volume (MS. B.ii.13) contains on fol. 102 (Plate 56B) an initial I with a portrait of Bishop William under a bust of Christ Blessing, and in the bottom loop of the initial, a kneeling figure of a monk labelled 'Robertus Beniamin' who is assumed to be the illuminator. The decorative style of this and of several other initials in the volume (fol. 68; Plate 57A) consists of motifs drawn from earlier English initial style – animals and animal heads, interlace and acanthus leaves – all sprinkled liberally with rows of red dots. The designs are placed against solidly coloured backgrounds, as in the Canterbury post-Conquest initials. The English elements of this decorative style are the small, complete animals or animal heads of gentle and kittenish type – tame descendants from remote South English and Mercian ancestors – and the interlace patterned with dots. Foreign to this tradition are the fierce and gaping mask type of animal heads used as terminals, usually with acanthus leaves issuing from their mouths, and the coloured backgrounds. The colouring of the design also is new and may be foreign: much red and green in rather streaky lines and thin wash are used.

The figure style of the initial containing the two portraits is flat and linear and distinctly feeble. Characteristic of the heads are the enormous round eyes and heavy arched eyebrows; both the heads and the hands are too large for the body. If this work was typical of Robert Benjamin, he was not much of an artist, and the style would be of little interest were it not for its close relation to some similar work of bolder character which is thought to be the product 'of one and the same atelier'.[44] This second manuscript is a copy of St Jerome's Commentary on Isaiah (Bod. MS. 717) and contains at the end of the last page (fol. 287 verso) a small picture of a little man in a blue cowled and sleeved mantle over a white gown, with green hair, labelled: 'Hugo pictor' and 'imago pictoris et illuminatoris huius operis'. The manuscript contains, indeed, some fine pages of painting in the grand style: fol. v verso has a full-page miniature of the Prophet Isaiah seated under an arch draped with curtains and supported by marbled columns with acanthus capitals and bases. Above the arch is an elaborate display of architecture. The figure is dignified and well-proportioned and richly clothed, with much decorative pattern on the drapery. Opposite this page (fol. vi) is a miniature of Jerome and St Eustochium[45] also seated under arches which form part of a building. The figures are solidly drawn and delicately modelled, although the technique in both miniatures is more linear than painterly, and the colour is thin and shaded only with lines. The miniatures[46] are clearly the work of a painter and Hugo had reason to be proud to claim them. There are also in Bod. 717 two historiated initials with elaborate decorative designs (fol. vi verso; Plate 56A) which have many of the features of those in the Carilef St Augustine: the animals and huge animal heads with acanthus branches in their mouths, the acanthus foliage and the interlace; and within roundels formed by the branches, figures which are so similar to those of the initial I in the Durham manuscript that they could easily be by the same artist, in this case by 'Hugo pictor'. The question then arises whether Robertus Benjamin is, after all, the illuminator of the Durham manuscript, and it must be admitted that on this point there is no evidence. The Durham St Augustine portrait initial, therefore, might also be the work of the 'Hugo painter and illuminator' of the Bodleian manuscript. In view of the differences in style between the decorative initials of the Durham manuscript and the I containing the portraits, it may very well be that most of the initials were done by a 'native' artist, and that the initial with the portraits, which has much less fine decoration, was the work of a 'foreigner', that is, Hugo, who was perhaps a Norman.

The other group of illuminated Carilef manuscripts is best represented by a great Bible (Durham Cath. Lib., MS. A.ii.4), originally in two volumes of which the first is now lost. The illumination in this manuscript also consists of elaborate decorative and historiated initials in a style which is very different in many respects from that of the St Augustine.

Plate 57B illustrates one of the types of initials (fol. 87 verso), and Plate 58 another (fol. 65). All the initials are of large size and contain florid, rather coarse designs of acanthus foliage, and interlace terminating in enormous gaping dragon heads; there are also whole dragons swallowing acanthus leaves and waving their acanthus tails behind them. These are features, as we have seen, of the St Augustine, but the 'kitten' heads and the rows of dots and other smaller decorative details in the St Augustine are replaced in the Bible by the rank foliage and the writhing clawed and winged dragons who swallow everything they can get their mouths on. The backgrounds are strongly coloured – red, purple, green, or blue – and the design is drawn with a broad pen in brown, red, and green. The angel, symbol of Matthew (fol. 87 verso; Plate 57B), is a good example of the treatment of the figure, which is wholly linear, with the mantle painted in broad bands of red and blue and the tunic washed with flat vermilion and bordered in faun colour. Wings are gay with spots and lines of all colours, and the angel's hair is bright green. The background is painted with flat green and purple. The style is startling in its sharp contrasts of strong colour, but the drawing is bold and free and the initials constitute brilliant and varied ornament on a scale suitable to the great size of the pages.

One of the very finest of all is the B of the *Beatus* beginning the first psalm (fol. 65; Plate 58). The form and design of the initial may be compared with the Winchester style B of Harl. 2904 (Plate 21B): the upright of the letter with knots of interlace at top and bottom, terminating in a large animal head, corresponds fairly closely, but the loops of the B in the Durham Bible, instead of forming a frame for the panels of acanthus, are them-selves acanthus scrolls which coil and twist back and forth, catching their fleshy stems or curling leaf tips in the meshes of their own convolutions. Ramping in the midst of this whirling coil is a winged animal with curly tufted mane and leafy tail hardly to be distinguished either in form or in colour from the foliage around him. Below, seated on a curved branch, is David with his harp, a figure painted in streaks and washes, bold in drawing and strong in colour. The background shows in the interstices of the branches as flat areas of colour – alternately red, purple, blue, and green.

To evaluate properly this striking style one must see the originals, for the colour is an essential element of the design. Nothing like it can be seen in English illumination of an earlier date, and it seems not to have affected later English style, except as the decoration in initials tends to become increasingly large and heavy under the general influence of Romanesque painting. Recently, illuminated manuscripts in Normandy have been dis-covered which have so much in common with this flamboyant style that they would seem to have come from the same centre.[47] In drawing, in colouring, in figure and fiery dragon types, the style is almost identical; and although the provenance of the Norman manuscripts is not known, it seems to fit better with the hard linear version of the Win-chester style which developed in Normandy as a result of earlier importations from Eng-land than with the developments in England itself. This fact, in combination with the known sojourn of William of St Carilef in Normandy during the latter part of his life, points to the possibility if not the certainty that the Durham Bible style is Norman and not English. More precise attribution of this style to specific centres awaits further study of the Norman manuscripts.

Summary

The latter half of the eleventh century, especially after 1066, was primarily a period of political and monastic reorganization in England, hence it was one of the meagre periods for art, as to both quality and quantity. The Canterbury manuscripts, as produced at St Augustine's and Christ Church throughout the period, the Bayeux Tapestry produced no one knows where, and the Durham manuscripts probably made partly at Durham and partly in Normandy, are almost the sum total of pictorial art of the period. At Canterbury, as we have seen, Norman influence was direct and constant but not revolutionary in its effect; it served rather to stimulate the decoration of books with new forms of initials, especially the historiated initials which combined rich decorative designs and bright colours with representational subject matter. At Durham also the conservative tradition of animal ornament and interlace, with small patterns and a modest form of acanthus foliage, was perhaps the current style. Figure painting is limited in amount and its style probably stems from some other atelier, perhaps that of a Norman artist in England, or from Continental importations of miniatures. The later manuscripts of Bishop William of St Carilef are much closer to Norman than to current English work and may have originated in Normandy.

Thus in pictorial art the period is one of assimilation of new elements which fitted into the insular tradition, and of reorganization of new and old elements in readiness for the flowering of the great Romanesque Period which is to follow.

NOTES TO CHAPTER 3

p. 59   1. Sir Eric Maclagan, *The Bayeux Tapestry* (London, 1949): complete reproduction with eight plates in colour and introductory text with a summary of the evidence for its provenance and a bibliography. Kendrick supports the theory of English origin, *Late Saxon Art*, 128 ff. The question will be considered further later on in this chapter.

2. Wormald, 'The Survival of Anglo-Saxon Illumination', 127–45.

p. 60   3. See Chapter 2.

4. Hanns Swarzenski, 'Der Stil der Bibel Carilefs von Durham', *Form und Inhalt, Festschrift für Otto Schmitt* (Stuttgart, 1950), 92.

5. Cf. page 44.

6. The attribution of Tib. c.vi to New Minster is, however, not certainly established.

7. Dodwell, *The Canterbury School of Illumination.*

I am grateful to the author for allowing me to examine this book while it was still in proof.

8. Those closest in style to the Carilef manuscripts are Rouen, Bib. Pub., MS. A.85, made for St Ouen, and Bayeux Cathedral, MSS 57 and 58. Swarzenski, *op. cit.*, 94 ff. See also Boase, *Eng. Art 1100–1216*, plates 4 and 5.

9. This influence may have come to England from St-Bertin at St-Omer through connexions with this monastery under Abbot Bovo (d. 1065) whose pupil Foulkard came to Thorney Abbey.

10. Facsimile published by Forbes-Leith, *The Gospel Book of St Margaret.*

11. D. Maurus Inguanez, *Codicum Cassinesium Manuscriptorum Catalogus* (Monte Cassino, 1940–1).

12. Reproduced Harrsen, *op. cit.*, Figure 2. There are resemblances, too, with the slightly earlier Judith book, Morgan MS. 709 (plate 43).

13. A gospel book in Pembroke College Library, Cambridge (MS. 301) has illuminations by several hands, of which the St Matthew page (fol. 10 verso) is by far the best. It is daintily coloured, but the line is feeble and inconsequent, and all the vitality and power of the Winchester style have vanished.

14. The type of the composition is represented in the First Bible of Charles the Bald (Paris, Bib. Nat., MS. lat. 1) and the Golden Gospels of St Gall (reproduced Goldschmidt, *German Illum.*, I, plate 68A). For the technique, cf. also the St Augustine Psalter (Brit. Mus., Cott. MS. Vesp. A.i, Plate 10B), Harl. MS. 647, and its copy Tib. B.V (Plate 34B).

15. A similar contour line painted in green is used in the New Minster MS., Brit. Mus., Cott. Titus D. xxvii (Plate 37B).

16. Wormald, 'Survival,' 131, n. 2.

17. Homburger says they are by the same artist, but there is clearly a great difference in the dynamic quality of the outline; *op. cit.*, 68.

18. Reproduced in colour, Brit. Mus., *Schools of Illumination*, I, plate 16

19. It could be East German (Ottonian): cf. Sacramentary from Regensburg, 1102–14, Munich, Staatsbib. Cod. lat. 4456 (Cim. 60), fol. 15. Reproduced Goldschmidt, *German Illum.*, II, plate 75.

20. Swarzenski suggests Flemish influence, as Lüttich; *op. cit.*, 91.

21. Millar, *op. cit.*, 22 and 81.

22. Containing the 'tropi' or musical interpolations in the liturgy.

23. *Op. cit.*; Homburger, *op. cit.*, 6. It may be the troper given by Bishop Leofric to Exeter in the eleventh century. See W. H. Frere, *The Winchester Troper*, Henry Bradshaw Society, VIII (London, 1894), xxx and 99 ff. Two miniatures in this same style are found in a gospel book, made for Bishop Leofric while he was in exile. Swarzenski, *op. cit.*, 91. See also R. Schilling, 'Two Unknown Flemish Miniatures of the Eleventh Century', *Burl. Mag.*, XC (1948), 315 ff.

24. The earliest known representations of these symbols occur in mosaics of the fourth and fifth centuries in Naples, Baptistery of S. Giovanni in Fonte, and in Rome, Sta Pudenziana. It is thought that they may be western in origin.

25. Dodwell, *op. cit.*, 6. In Chapter 2 of this study the author demonstrates by many examples the post-Conquest continuity with pre-Conquest style.

26. *Op. cit.*, 119. Many have decorative initials only.   **p. 65**

27. F. Wormald, 'Two Anglo-Saxon Miniatures Compared', *Brit. Mus. Quart.*, IX, no. 4 (1935), 113–15. See also Wormald, *Eng. Drawings*, 45 ff. The two miniatures are on fol. 2 verso of Tib. A.iii and on fol. 56 verso of Durham Cath. Lib., MS. B.iii.32, which is copied from it except for the central figure of King Edgar which is omitted.

28. Wormald attributes these folios (58–73) to his Hands E and F of the second quarter of the eleventh century. There seems to be little difference in style between these and the sketch on fol. 17 verso.

29. Boinet, *op. cit.*, plates LXXXVI–XC.

30. Cf. MSS Tib. c.ii and Roy. 1 E. vi. An assortment is reproduced by Kendrick, *Late Saxon Art*, figure 1, and their survival in the tenth century manuscripts is discussed *op. cit.*, 30 ff.

31. Reproduced *op. cit.*, plate XXVIII 2, and discussed, 31 ff.

32. Wormald, 'Survival', 136.   **p. 66**

33. Kendrick, *Late Saxon Art*, 35 ff. and plate XXXI.

34. Guido Biagi, *Reproductions from Illuminated*   **p. 67** *MSS in the R. Medician Laurentian Library* (Florence, 1914). *New Pal. Soc.*, Series 1, plates 138–9 (fols 1 verso, 2 verso, and 5 reproduced).

35. Dodwell, *op. cit.*, 28.

36. Reproduced *New Pal. Soc.*, Series 1, plate 139   **p. 68** (fol. 5).

37. Kendrick, *Late Saxon Art*, 130.

38. *Op. cit.*, 128–31; Maclagan, *op. cit.*, 18 ff. Professor Loomis considers the tapestry to be Anglo-Saxon. *Art Bull.*, VI (1923–4).

39. Maclagan, *op. cit.*, 27.

40. For example, Maclagan, Nos 51 and 72. Lethaby once made the interesting suggestion that the aim of the Bayeux Tapestry was to show the fulfilment of God's judgement on Harold's violated oath. W. R. Lethaby, 'The Perjury at Bayeux', *Archaeol. Jnl*, LXXIV (1917), 136–8.

41. Dr Otto Pächt finds that the colour scheme   **p. 69** is similar to that of Norman painting, with the predominance of certain greens and reds, and that the architecture is represented much as in Norman miniatures.

42. Mynors, *Durham Cathedral Manuscripts*, Nos 30–45. Folio 1 of Vol. II of the great Bible (MS. A.ii. 4) contains a contemporary list of all the manuscripts given by Bishop Carilef.

p. 69   43. He was accused of having supported the conspiracy of Odo, Bishop of Bayeux, against William the Conqueror.

p. 70   44. Pächt, 'Hugo Pictor', 98.

45. A nun and follower of St Jerome, to whom he dedicated the commentary on Isaiah.

46. Swarzenski groups these miniatures and also the historiated initials on fol. vi verso and 2, with two miniatures in a gospel book, made for Bishop Leofric of Exeter, and ascribes both to 'the well-known Lüttich workshop which was also active at St Omer in the third quarter of the century'; *op. cit.*, 91. On the miniature of the Leofric Gospels, see note 23 above.

47. See note 8 above.

CHAPTER 4
ROMANESQUE ART OF THE TWELFTH CENTURY

*

HISTORICAL BACKGROUND:
ANGLO-NORMAN FEUDALISM AND MONASTICISM

POLITICAL

Henry I, King 1100–35. Organization of Anglo-Norman feudalism and internal law in England.

Stephen, nephew of Henry, crowned 1135; deposed 1141 (April); recrowned 1141 (December); died 1154. Political upheavals over the succession. Second Crusade 1147–8, in which many English took part.

Henry II, nephew of Henry I, King 1154–89. Married Eleanor of Aquitaine 1152; spent much time in France; his son Henry crowned king 1170; used style 'rex Anglorum et dux Normannorum et comes Andegavorum'. Died 1183.

ECCLESIASTICAL

Thomas Becket, Archbishop of Canterbury 1162–70; martyred 29 Dec. 1170; canonized 1173; translated 7 July 1220.

Henry of Blois, brother of King Stephen, brought up at Cluny (1110–26); Abbot of Glastonbury 1126–9; Bishop of Winchester 1129–71; journey to Rome 1151–2.

White monks (Cistercians) arrived at Waverley (Surrey) 1128; Rievaulx (Yorkshire) founded by Bernard of Clairvaux 1132; Fountains founded same year; 1135–67 (death of Ailred, Abbot of Rievaulx) Cistercians at their height; about forty houses founded in this time.

*

FOR twelfth century art in England, the reign of Henry I, and even the turbulent one of his nephew Stephen, were extremely important not only because of the close political and ecclesiastical connexions with France but even more because of the 'traditional relation with the Norman rulers of Sicily who were then planning a Mediterranean empire'.[1] Moreover, further direct connexions with the Continent followed upon the establishment in London by 1157 of German merchants, who imported goods from Constantinople via the Danube and the Rhine.[2] In England itself, 'the reign of Henry I was the heyday of Anglo-Norman monasticism', according to Knowles,[3] who continues: 'Norman and Anglo-Norman abbots continued to build, both materially, intellectually, and spiritually, upon existing foundations, and not only houses at important centres such as Canterbury and Winchester, and at shrines such as Bury, Malmesbury, and Durham, but also those in the remote fenland, such as Thorney and Croyland, became seats of an intense literary culture and schools of calligraphy and illumination.' Likewise, in the reign of Stephen there was an extraordinary exuberance of life among all the new religious bodies of men, and nunneries also were founded in great numbers. With the prohibition of further Cistercian houses in 1167, in the last decades of the twelfth century the rate of increase in religious foundations perceptibly slackened.

Of the two main sources of Continental influence noted above – Byzantine and Cistercian – the former was overwhelmingly more important in its effect on pictorial art.[4] The new stylistic elements characteristic of twelfth century art derive not from western monastic centres in France and Germany, as in the preceding period both before and after the Conquest, but from further east, from Byzantine art in Norman Sicily and from Constantinople itself through contacts opened up by the Crusades. Saxl[5] has summed up this Byzantine heritage received into English art under three heads: the idea of hieratic deity; the monumental style of wall painting inspired by Byzantine mosaics; the use in manuscripts of a framed composition with painted or gilded background and, within this frame, a well-defined and elaborated arrangement of figures.

In order to measure the effects of these new contacts on English art, we must look again into the art stream which, as we have seen in former periods, carries the continuity of English style. In the first decades of the twelfth century, as earlier, outline drawing remained a favourite form of artistic expression. This outline, as formerly, continued to follow and sometimes to combine the two established types: firm contour line with which pale washes were often used to suggest the colour and ornamental patterns of the draperies and even the modelling of the faces (as in Harl. MS. 2904) and the sketchy, broken outline in brown or coloured ink (as in Harl. MS. 603).

The firm, unbroken contour line in the early twelfth century seems to have been reinvigorated through new contacts with classical prototypes, or their Carolingian intermediaries. An early twelfth century Bestiary[6] (Bod., MS. Laud. Misc. 247), probably the earliest copy after illustrated Carolingian manuscripts of this text, has line drawings in brown ink, without colour or shading, which have the monumentality of classical modelled figures. This manuscript perhaps comes from Christ Church, Canterbury, and in Canterbury, as we have seen, other Carolingian manuscripts of classical type are known to have existed and been copied. Indeed, some of the animals in Bod. MS. 247 suggest, in the firmness of their technique, animals in the Harleian Aratus,[7] and its superb copy, Harl. MS. 2506. Another drawing in this same style, also from Canterbury, probably from St Augustine's Abbey, is the full-page figure of Christ which was added to the Bosworth Psalter (Brit. Mus., Add. MS. 37517), 'almost certainly ... copied from a pre-Conquest drawing',[8] towards the middle of the twelfth century.

An example of early twelfth century outline technique of the firm contour type, but painted in strong colours, can be seen in the pictures of the four Evangelists in a Gospel Book in the Morgan Library (MS. 777, fol. 24 verso; Plate 63B). The Evangelists are clearly derived from much earlier Carolingian models[9] in a curious representation showing them seated on their symbols, which is thought to come from oriental sources.[10] A rhythmic pattern is evolved from the contours, poses, gestures, and curling scrolls of these figures and their symbols; the heavy black contour line suggests twelfth century stained-glass technique. The colours, principally green, blue, and tan, are fine and clear, shaded only with lines, and are used quite arbitrarily for any detail;[11] faces, hands, and feet are outlined or lightly shaded with red. This manuscript also is thought to have been made at or near Canterbury.[12]

That the coloured outline style of the twelfth century is not merely a survival of earlier forms,[13] however, but is still a living type of expression rather than a formula to be applied, is demonstrated in an example of early twelfth century manuscript illustration which can be seen in process of evolution from painting to outline technique. The manuscript is a copy of Bede's Life of St Cuthbert (Oxford, Univ. Coll., MS. 165) and is fully illustrated in three different styles, all apparently, judging by peculiarities of detail, produced by the same artist. The styles are as follows: the miniature opposite fol. 1, of the author writing and presenting his book to the monks, in a completely painted style, with a blue background and a formal border containing stylized acanthus leaves. The colours are dull green and grey, with brown shading for drapery folds; faces have been painted with a pigment which has now turned black. On fols 1 and 5 are decorative initials in the painted style, on red and blue painted grounds; on fol. 4 verso is a miniature framed like the one above, but in outline; the figures, however, push out in all directions, as though the composition could not be contained within the limits of the frame; the technique is outline, in brown ink except for faces and hands which are in red; red or green shaded colour is used for garments, which are ornamented with bands of gold edged with white dots, or beads. The third and final stage in the evolution of this style, in which the artist obviously comes into his own in perfection of technique, appears on fol. 11 verso (Plate 59B), following several other tentative efforts to free himself from the formal, painted miniature style. The clear, fresh drawing on fol. 11 verso and thereafter is done in colours: red, green, and violet. Brown is used only for heads and hands. Though the composition of the picture suggests the rectangular form of a miniature, there is no frame; the pictures stand free, as illustrations of the text, in the manner of the Utrecht Psalter. In some of the later miniatures there is evidence that figures and architectural details are lacking which were present in the original miniatures, perhaps cut off at the sides, as in the Utrecht Psalter. Echoes of this earlier style can be seen also in the figure types, especially those in profile.[14]

Of two early twelfth century examples closer to the Utrecht style, one (Durham Cathedral Library, Hunter MS. 100) was executed before 1135 and perhaps even before 1128,[15] probably at Durham. The drawings illustrate the text, a collection of short pieces dealing with medicine, the Computus, and astronomy; they are partly tinted in red and green.

The other example of this same impressionistic style (Brit. Mus., Cott. MS. Titus D.xvi) contains (fols 1–36) Prudentius's *Psychomachia*, which is illustrated with much the same spirit as the eleventh century copies but in a different technique. It is dated *c.* 1100 and is particularly important because of a (contemporary?) inscription (fol. 37) stating its ownership by St Albans Abbey.[16] The figures (fol. 17 verso; Plate 59A) are very tall, slender, and lively, and are frequently represented in profile and poised for action, on tiptoe. Their faces are eager, their gestures are free and usually well and correctly drawn. The technique is coloured outline tinted in the deep drapery folds with thin colour used as a wash. The draperies are ragged in contour and whip round the figures revealing the shape and movement of the bodies. The faces are not modelled, but the hair is darkened around the face to suggest the soft, thick mass. The miniatures have no frames and almost no indication of ground line.

Finally, Professor Wormald calls attention[17] to a remarkable twelfth century 'copy' of the Harl. 2904 Crucifixion (cf. Plate 30) in a manuscript of the Chronicle of Florence of Worcester (Oxford, Corpus Christi Coll., MS. 157, fol. 77 verso; Plate 60) in which colour is used both for outline and for shading on the drapery and faces as in the earlier Harl. 2904. There is an amazing clarity and repose as well as a monumental solidity in the figures; but the emotional fervour of the Harleian Crucifixion has subsided. Drapery ends still fall in intricate linear patterns, but the curves are exaggerated and conscious; the figures are gracefully posed and stand firmly on their feet, but their faces are blank and they point with self-conscious moral purpose to the figure of Christ crucified, of which the accompanying text gives the symbolic explanation. This drawing is very much twelfth century in spirit; it may have been done as early as 1130, but seems to have been redrawn, as Dr Pächt has suggested, under the influence of mid-twelfth century style, such as is found in Bod. MS. Auct. F.2.13, an illustrated Terence[18] manuscript made at St Albans, of which we shall hear more later on in this chapter.[19]

The manuscripts of the first half of the twelfth century thus far discussed can be accounted for as variations on earlier English or Continental models tending towards a new monumentality characteristic of Romanesque art in general. Their subject matter, too, with one or two exceptions, is carried over from preceding periods, but the scale and magnificence of the psalters and gospel books and commentaries common in the earlier period is greatly increased in the second quarter of the twelfth century. This period has been called the 'first flush of Romanesque', and its style results from contacts with Byzantine art, probably in the first place through Continental intermediaries.[20]

The new elements first appear in a psalter written between 1119 and 1146 at the Abbey of St Albans, a manuscript which is generally known as the Albani Psalter,[21] now in the Library of St Godehard, Hildesheim. The Albani Psalter is fully and splendidly illuminated with calendar pictures, a fine *Beatus* initial (p. 72) and other initials introducing the principal psalms; following the Calendar are forty-six full-page miniatures of the life of Christ, and at the end (pp. 416 and 417) two additional pictures of the martyrdom of St Alban and of David and the musicians. In addition to the psalter, the Hildesheim manuscript contains (pp. 57–68) a poem on the life of St Alexis, with a picture, and three full-page pictures of the Emmaus story.

The illustration in the Albani Psalter is by three hands. The calendar pictures and the initials, except the *Beatus*, and the two miniatures now at the end of the psalter are certainly all by one hand, and were certainly executed at St Albans.[22] The preliminary miniatures are by a very different hand.[23] (Cf. Plates 61 and 62B.) The *Beatus* initial, and also the spirited sketch of a knightly combat in the upper part of the page (p. 72; Plate 62A), and the Alexis and Emmaus miniatures seem to be in a style which falls between that of the biblical miniatures and the psalter initials: it is flatter in modelling, more stylized and linear in treatment than the miniatures, and there is a good deal more emphasis on the decorative elements of the composition, such as the throne. The figure of David, however, especially the head, seems to be copied as closely as possible from that of the Christ in plate 61, except that in the David the artist has somehow missed the effect of foreshortening of the face on the far side, has increased the size and prominence of the ear, which hangs like a gypsy hoop ear-ring outside his hair, and has lost the expression in the eyes. These differences between the David of the initial and the figures in the miniatures seem to indicate that the competent painter of the miniatures had an assiduous follower who was striving to imitate the master's style. He was not, it would seem, the illuminator of the other initials, who also was affected by the style of the miniatures, but who understood much less well what it was all about. His figures (Plate 62B) are completely linear with thigh and drapery, hose and hair all heavily outlined and coloured with thin wash put on with a striped effect to suggest shading. Faces too are delineated with lines only, and all, except the frontal Christ, are seen in full profile. No ears at all are shown and hands are enormous. The decorative motifs in this initial are only interlace, also painted with the striped effect, and circles in the background. It is impossible to attribute the two initials on plate 62 to the same artist; yet, on the other hand, it is almost equally impossible to attribute the David to the painter of the preliminary miniatures. The most reasonable explanation of the differences in the style of the Albani illumination, therefore, seems to be two hands learning from the work of a very competent master whose style apparently was formed on Byzantine models.[24] The style of this master (Plate 61) is impressive, if rather heavy and solemn. His figures are tall, and thin in the shoulders, but have solid, fleshy thighs, long legs, and huge feet usually represented as though on tiptoe. The faces are elongated ovals with a firm, rounded chin. When seen in profile a suggestion is retained of the face beyond the nose; when in three-quarter view, the far side is foreshortened, but there is trouble with the far eye which gives the face a curious flattened contour. The drapery is painted in heavy solid colour, with high-lights in white lines which often are arranged in odd cobweb-like patterns, as over the thigh and arm. Deep shadows are indicated by heavy dark or black lines, and the ridges of folds between these deep lines are lighter than the foundation colour. The architectural setting is a Byzantine derivative, with twisted columns and domical cupolas with arcades and many openings shaded with dark and light areas and broad lines in the manner of conventionalized Byzantine buildings. The background is divided into compartments – by the architecture, in this miniature – which are coloured differently; but the figures are not kept within these panels, or even within the field of the miniature itself, toes and fingers protruding beyond the conventionalized foliage frame which surrounds the picture. The frame is treated somewhat like the border on a carved panel or book-cover, with the upper corners chamfered, but the lower band of ornament runs clear across the bottom, joining awkwardly the side panels.

Who was the fine artist of the preliminary miniatures and where did he come from? Swarzenski assumes that he was English and attributes to him, correctly, the miniatures in an apparently English manuscript in Verdun.[25] No other work by him is known. It is possible that the miniatures of the Albani Psalter were imported into St Albans from some Continental monastic centre where the influence of the great Reichenau school of illumination of a century earlier lingered on[26] and was further invigorated by fresh Byzantine contacts. Or it is possible that a Continental artist came to the scriptorium at St Albans among those who were invited by Abbot Paul (1077-93), of the Abbey of St-Étienne, Caen, of whom it is recorded that he collected scribes from everywhere to work in the St Albans scriptorium.[27]

Although the source of the Albani miniature style may never be determined, its influence is incontestable. Probably the first to register this influence is a magnificent manuscript with pictures and text of the Life and Miracles of St Edmund of East Anglia (New York, Morgan Lib., MS. 736), dated 1125-50 and perhaps even more closely before 1135.[28] The figures (fol. 9; Plate 65) have the same long, narrow bodies, heavy, shapeless legs, large feet and hands; and the faces show the same large wide-open eyes and drooping mouths. But the technique of the painting is less crisp than in the Albani miniatures, and there is much more interest in decorative detail, not only in the setting of the picture, but in the treatment of pattern on the clothing of Edmund and even of the skin garments of the petitioners, and in the stylization of the shading of the drapery folds. Yet it does not seem to be the thin, completely linear style of the artist of the initials in the Albani Psalter, but rather the hand of the competent and assiduous imitator, who painted the *Beatus* initial. In the St Edmund miniatures the solidity of the Albani miniatures has disappeared: ridged folds have become mere double lines; a rounded thigh has turned into an oval where a series of diagonal white lines are meant to suggest its roundness. Faces are seen in almost paper-flat profile, except that of Edmund which, though seen in three-quarter view, has the regular oval contour of a full front view. The decorative patterns of the frame are geometric linear motifs, as is also the design on the under side of the arch and on the buildings at the back and the details of decoration on the throne. This seems to be a faithful attempt on the part of the St Edmund artist to absorb the essentials of the figure technique as found in the preliminary miniatures of the Albani Psalter, but his medium of expression is so fundamentally linear that in applying the painted technique, he must needs regularize even the painted areas of the originals by confining them within hard lines.

The identification of the Edmund artist with the illuminator of the Albani *Beatus* initial seems to be confirmed by a comparison of the miniature (fol. 7 verso) of the Morgan manuscript representing the Battle with the Danes (Plate 66) with the very lively single combat scene above the B on the same *Beatus* page of the Psalter. The horses are identical, both in position and in the treatment of the heads, both ears showing, though the animal is seen in profile; and the riders, in the manner of representing their chain mail armour as well as in their violent gestures, seem too close to have been done by a different hand and certainly, if one can judge by the spirit of the drawing, are not copies. The Battle miniature in the Life of St Edmund is painted only with thin colour; the technique is fundamentally outline, and the figures are silhouetted against the magnificent plain blue ground with the clarity and effectiveness of a tapestry design. But it is to be noted that, as in the Albani miniatures, the figures will not be confined within the frame but partly disappear behind it and partly push out over its edges.

The superb draughtsmanship of the artist of the St Edmund manuscript shows to even better advantage in the few uncoloured full-page miniatures which precede a copy of the gospels given to Bury St Edmunds in the early thirteenth century, but believed to have originated there early in the preceding century (Camb., Pembroke Coll., MS. 120). The text, according to James,[29] was written in the first decades of the twelfth century, and is preceded by a series of twelve Bible pictures 'older by a good many years than the text'. But the drawings (fol. 5 verso; Plate 64) are without any doubt dependent on the style of the Albani Psalter miniatures, which would make a much earlier dating untenable. The characteristics that seem to betray the same hand as the St Edmund miniatures are the following: the exceedingly tall figures with cramped, narrow shoulders and heavy thighs and large feet and hands; the flat profiles, except for the Virgin in the upper picture, whose face is seen in unforeshortened oval though represented in three-quarter view; the large, wide-open eyes, long noses with a hump on the bridge, the drooping mouths and the decorative treatment of the architecture. It would appear that the drawings in Pembroke 120 were intended to be painted, since there is no indication whatsoever of shading in the drapery folds, and such pure contour drawing would be rare in England at this time.[30] In fact, the first few miniatures (fols 1–3) have been very badly painted in pale colours, certainly by a different hand, though perhaps not much later. The historiated initials in the text of Pembroke 120 were probably added at the time the manuscript was written, that is, the preliminary miniatures might have already existed in an unfinished condition; the initials show signs of being influenced by the preliminary drawings and might easily have developed out of this drawing style at Bury itself. What seems certain is that the miniatures were drawn by the artist who drew and painted the St Edmund miniatures, and that his style came directly out of the miniatures of the Albani Psalter.

Closely related to the Albani–Bury style are four large leaves[31] containing a long series of small scenes from the Nativity, Ministry, and Passion cycles of Christ. The leaves are thought to have been intended as preliminary leaves to a psalter, and on stylistic grounds have been assigned to Bury St Edmunds. There is, however, no documentary evidence for either provenance or dating, nor are there any indications as to the manuscript for which they might have been painted. They are now scattered among three different collections as follows:

New York, Morgan Library, MS. 724. Recto: twelve scenes from the lives of Moses and David. Verso: an additional two scenes from the life of David; the Jesse Tree; the Visitation, Birth of the Baptist, Naming of the Baptist, and the Nativity.

Brit. Mus., Additional MS. 37472. Recto: Shepherds, six scenes from the Magi story; Presentation of Christ, Angel appearing to Joseph, Flight into Egypt, Slaughter of the Innocents, and Death of Herod. Verso: Baptism: Wedding at Cana, Three Temptations of Christ, and a series of the Miracles.

New York, Morgan Library, MS. 521. Recto: continuation of the Ministry of Christ. Verso: early Passion cycle, through the Betrayal.

London, Victoria and Albert Museum, MS. 661. Recto: continuation of the Passion Cycle, ending with the Deposition. Verso: end of the Passion Cycle, the Appearances, the Commissioning of the Apostles, the Ascension, and Pentecost.

Each leaf is divided into twelve squares framed by borders consisting of double gold bands enclosing stylized leaf and other motifs; the whole page is surrounded by a similar border containing a different pattern at the top and bottom from that of the two sides. On the first leaf (Morgan 724) each square contains only one scene; on the verso, the Tree of Jesse occupies the space of several squares. The Infancy cycle on Add. MS. 37472 recto (Plate 67A) also contains one scene to a square; but on the verso of this leaf, the scenes of the Ministry occur two to a square, and this practice continues on the second Morgan leaf (MS. 521) and on the Victoria and Albert leaf (Plate 67B). Important scenes, however – the Crowning with Thorns, the Crucifixion, the Deposition, the Ascension, and Pentecost – occupy a whole square. The cycles are amazingly complete.[32] The inclusion of so elaborate a series of scenes of the Ministry and Miracles of Christ suggests the possible influence of Early Christian or Carolingian wall paintings; on the other hand, they recall a partial, surviving series of similar small scenes in rectangular panels found in the sixth or seventh century Gospels of St Augustine (Camb., Corpus Christi Coll., MS. 286) which was still at his abbey in Canterbury at this time. The fashion of prefixing Bible pictures to psalters, according to James, is not traceable earlier than Cotton manuscript Tib. C.vi and all the early examples known are English.

The Bible picture leaves are not all by the same hand, and this fact complicates their attribution on stylistic grounds to any one centre. The British Museum leaf, for example, is painted in a flat and linear 'old-fashioned' style, that is, the technique seems to be outline drawing with flat colour used to fill the area between the lines. The figures are more normally proportioned than in the miniatures of the Albani Psalter and more informally posed. Drapery is less deeply shaded for the folds, and when these are indicated, they are likely to form stylized patterns. The figures are not very lively in pose and gesture, and their heads are rather large for their bodies. The designs of the individual scenes are all planned in relation to the design of the whole page, with alternating colours used for backgrounds, and compositions balancing each other on the page. This is also true to a certain extent of other leaves, such as the one in the Victoria and Albert Museum, No. 661 (Plate 67B), but the compositions in this case do not always balance, since some are two to a square and others only one. But the style of the figures in the Victoria and Albert leaf is much livelier: the gestures are more violent, the bodies more roundly modelled, the actions and poses more exaggerated. Although the figures are not of the long, narrow type of the Albani and Bury style, they certainly have picked up somewhere the Byzantine type of drapery folds and the more modelled heads. The style of this page is, however, much more in the tradition which developed at Canterbury about the middle of the century, and culminated in the wonderful Lambeth Bible (Plate 73). There is the further fact that such a cycle of scenes as is found on the four Bible leaves, in the completeness of its subject matter and the absence of any decorative features except the formal framing bands, suggests wall paintings more than miniature pages in manuscripts; and it is at Canterbury that the most considerable remains of wall paintings of the twelfth century are found. While there is no more evidence for Canterbury provenance than for either Bury or St Albans, the Bible leaves seem to fit better stylistically into the painting tradition already established there.[33]

Even closer to the miniature style of the Albani Psalter, in the type of figures and in the manner of representing drapery folds with deep shadows and white lines, is an exceptionally fine psalter (Brit. Mus., Lansdowne MS. 383) made not later than the mid twelfth century for an abbey of nuns dedicated to St Edward at Shaftesbury (Dorset).[34] This manuscript has been shown[35] to represent the earliest example of the typical scheme of psalter illustration used in English psalters in the late twelfth and succeeding centuries. The principal features of this scheme are: a calendar illustrated with the signs of the zodiac and the labours of the months in small roundels (fols 1–12); full-page preliminary miniatures of New Testament subjects (fols 12 verso–15); three large historiated initials introducing Psalms 1, 51, and 109, and smaller initials introducing the other psalms. At the end of the Lansdowne Psalter there are two additional[36] full-page miniatures: the Virgin and Child with a kneeling nun (fol. 165 verso), and the Last Judgement represented by the Archangel Michael offering a napkin-full of souls to Christ (fol. 168 verso; Plate 68B).

The figure of St Michael, at least in such parts as the thigh and leg, is an extraordinary combination of modelled form revealed under the drapery, and surface pattern made by the drapery folds and ornamental bands applied like a bandage to the surface of the figure. As in the Albani miniatures, the drapery folds are painted with deep coloured and white areas and stripes, but in the Shaftesbury Psalter these are much more patternized. Again, in the type of folds there is anomaly: some of the edges lie long and straight, folded into stiff pleats, while others are lifted by an invisible wind and suspended in mid air in puffs and curls. The technique of treating the folds is, as we have seen in a different variation in the Edmund miniatures, Byzantine in origin, but the English artist once more has interpreted the modelled technique in terms of colour pattern, and has made a design which, although certainly effective as a decorative arrangement of the draped human figure, has little to do with modelling. The same treatment in the bust of Christ, in the roundel above, has resulted in an extremely hieratic type of frontal figure which, even more than the Michael, reminds us of a figure of Christ in an initial in the Albani Psalter (Plate 62B); that is, of the English artist's interpretation of this typical Byzantine figure. The background in the Shaftesbury miniature is striped with colour – purple, green, blue, and yellow – in a manner found in some Ottonian manuscripts derived from the Reichenau school[37] and ultimately stems from Byzantine 'skies' painted similarly in coloured stripes. Other interesting features betraying the English artist's love of ornament are the threading of the wing-tips of Michael through the gold bars of the frame, and the snail-like clouds on which he stands. The faces, hands, and feet are shaded with green and red, but all the figures are firmly outlined with a heavy black line.

Although the style and the iconography of some of the miniatures in Lansdowne 383 are related to the Albani Psalter, and the historiated initials are reminiscent of the earlier Canterbury style, the Lansdowne manuscript does not seem to be attributable to either of these centres, a fact which is borne out by the entries in the Calendar. Two other non-liturgical manuscripts, without Calendars for comparison, have been found,[38] however, which show close stylistic affinities with Lansdowne 383, and one of these which is now in Hereford (Cathedral Library, MS. O.5.xi) furnishes a possible clue to the localization of this style. Evidence that the style may have originated at Hereford at an earlier date is offered by certain peculiarities of the other of the two manuscripts stylistically associated with Lansdowne 383; namely, an illustrated Boethius in Oxford (Bod., MS. Auct. F.6.5). Folio 1 verso contains a full page miniature of Boethius in prison visited by Philosophy (Plate 68A). The peculiar facial type of Boethius with its strongly accented line from temple to chin joining at a sharp angle the drooping moustache, and the extremely heavy, arched eyebrows and stiffly curled hair, together with the strongly shaded, regular drapery folds and similar architectural details are found, though in less exaggerated form, in MS. Caligula A.xiv and its sister manuscript associated with Hereford, viz. Pembroke 302 (Plate 49B). The Boethius may thus represent the typical twelfth century hardening and formalizing of an earlier, freer style, showing no evidence of new influence of the Byzantine monumentality, as reflected in the Albani Psalter. The Oxford Boethius is placed by Farley and Wormald earlier than the Shaftesbury Psalter, and this dating is supported by its closer dependence on the earlier Hereford style of the Caligula and Pembroke manuscripts.

Between the Bodleian Boethius and Lansdowne 383, a new influence has intervened, patently that of the St Albans–Bury style. The miniatures in the Psalter are more formal and symmetrical in composition; the figures are more hieratic, draperies are flatter and more highly stylized and patterned. The historiated initials in Lansdowne 383 are even closer, in ornament and design, to the Boethius initials, since the figures in them show more liveliness and less hieratic symmetry than do those in the miniatures.

The third of this group, the Sermons of St John Chrysostom in the library of Hereford Cathedral, is also close to Lansdowne 383 in composition and figure types, but the technique is a reversion to the linear style of earlier Anglo-Saxon manuscripts, and thus something of the liveliness of this earlier style has been regained.[39]

A second wave of Byzantine influence which perhaps came direct and not by way of a Continental scriptorium, seems to have determined the style of the earliest of the fine twelfth century Bibles, the magnificent Bury Bible (Camb., Corpus Christi Coll., MS. 2), for which the illuminator Master Hugo apparently[40] was paid between 1121 and 1148. The decoration consists of miniatures and historiated initials, one or the other introducing each of the Books of the Bible. At the beginning of the manuscript (fol. 1 verso) is a very fine decorative initial F filled with scrollwork and lush acanthus leaves, with modelled human heads in profile and lively human figures among the vines, and also animals and birds. On the shaft of the initial are two roundels with a mermaid and a centaur – forebears of the progeny of grotesques that a little later are to people the pages of manuscripts. The page itself is often framed with double bands enclosing conventionalized acanthus and vine patterns in rich, heavy colours including much dark green.

The historiated initial with the prophet Amos (fol. 324; Plate 69A) is typical of the figure style, which retains something of the St Albans and Bury type of head but with less conventionalized modelling and more individualization. The modelling of the face, especially around the eyes, is heavy and greenish in colour; the hair and beard are treated as soft masses but the hair line is strongly marked by a black outline to separate it from the forehead. The shape of the face is oval, with a pointed chin. The type is monumental and impressive. The body, too, has much more solidity of form than the St Albans and earlier Bury figures, and the drapery, instead of being decorated with a conventionalized dark and white line pattern, is painted in sweeping folds that swing around the body following its contours and emphasizing its gestures. The folds themselves are still ridges but are handled more softly than in the Albani style.

These characteristics, together with the deep, rich colour and the free use of gold, suggest comparison with specific examples of Byzantine art – the mosaics of Norman Sicily,[41] and particularly with those of the Cappella Palatina at Palermo. Although the mosaics have the same flatness emphasized by firm, contour outlines as in the Bury Bible, the Bury master has still further reduced the pattern to a series of curved ridges; and although the faces may be derived from Byzantine mosaics, the conventionalized modelling has fallen into a formula of fixed patterns; for example, the hook between the eyes. Nevertheless, the style of Master Hugo is sufficiently reminiscent of characteristics of the Cappella Palatina mosaics to suggest that he may actually have seen them. Millar sums up the quality of the Bury Bible as follows: 'It is difficult to exaggerate the beauty of this book, which is ... unique, its deep rich colour and the firmness of its draughtsmanship alike placing it in the first rank of illuminated manuscripts of this or almost any century.'[42]

Meanwhile, c. 1150, at Christ Church, Canterbury, the text and illustrations of the Utrecht Psalter were again copied[43] in the current outline style (Camb., Trin. Coll., MS. R.17.1). The scribe was the monk Eadwine, whose portrait appears on fol. 283 verso (Plate 71). The psalter text is tripartite,[44] and each psalm and canticle has a decorative initial introducing each of the three versions, but the initial of the Gallican version is the largest and most elaborate (Plate 72B). Before each psalm there is an oblong picture extending the full width of the page, illustrating the text literally as in the Utrecht Psalter and its first copy, Harl. 603. Colour is used with the outline – blue, green, vermilion and brown – not in place of the ink line but following and shadowing it. The style is characteristically twelfth century, with a heavier, stiffer line, larger, coarser figures, and more formal detail stylized with decorative purpose.

The miniatures in plate 72, if compared with corresponding illustrations in the Utrecht Psalter or in Harl. MS. 603, show that the compositions have changed very little in the one hundred and fifty years since the first copy was made. The style, however, is quite a different matter. Features of the composition which are recognizable derivatives of the earlier versions are the tall, long-legged figures with their tiny heads, usually seen in profile, the curly ground lines, and the architecture – the classical temple in the upper miniature, the eastern type of tomb in the lower. But the poses of the figures, their gestures, their very clothes are different; they hardly seem to belong to the same race of men, so staid and sober have they become. The fact is that the lively spirit of the original, which was successfully transferred to the first copy by means of the sketchy technique, has been tamed or even almost completely eliminated by this tight, patterned rendering of figures and draperies, and conventionalized trees and landscape, and no matter how closely the poses and gestures may correspond to those in the original, in order that the meaning of the picture may not be lost, the rendering is clumsy and lifeless and without interest as a figure composition. However, from the point of view of decoration, the case is somewhat different, for the bright pure colours distributed in lines and bands of varying breadth over the surface produce a pleasing pattern which has more of the quality of illumination in relation to the text page than has either the earlier or the later copy (see Plate 91).

The initials are in the typical twelfth century Canterbury style: slender ribbon scrolls ending in acanthus leaves or stylized animal heads, against coloured grounds.

That the full-page miniature of Eadwine (Plate 71) is intended to be a portrait there can hardly be any doubt;[45] but his garb, though monastic, is painted, like Joseph's coat, in many colours. The use of colour in this miniature is exceptionally interesting since it serves three purposes and represents a kind of synthesis of all linear colour techniques thus far known in English art. Primarily, the colour, as is usual, accentuates the linear patterns of the drapery and the contours of the figure under it. It also is used heavily, not in lines but in areas, to model the face. And finally, it is used to produce an all-over pattern of decorative detail which includes fancy scrolls on the monkish robe itself, in the elaborate architectural setting and furniture, and in the formal border with scroll patterns and corner ornaments. The result is brilliant but rather over-ornate, and the colour technique of the modelling is distinctly odd: Eadwine's hair and beard are blue; there are bright green patches on his forehead and nose, around the eyes and on the cheeks and neck; also his tonsured head and his hands are shaded with green. The eyebrows and eyes are dark brown, and the eyes are suspended in the midst of the eye-socket and have a pop-eyed, wild expression. The drapery is tan with brown and green folds, and has a scrolled all-over pattern which matches that in the border of the miniature. The ground behind the figure, and the chair and desk are solid blue, and the details of architecture and furniture are picked out in red, green, and brown. The figure is outlined with a black or dark brown painted contour line. From this description, as well as from the reproduction, it is obvious that the picture is not a portrait in the accepted sense, but a fine *tour de force* in human figure drawing in the coloured outline technique. But there is more to the picture than this. The face is, after all, modelled with areas of colour and white – a technique which is foreign to that of coloured outline. It is obvious that the artist of the Eadwine portrait had knowledge, albeit somewhat confused, of the greenish flesh-tones such as we have seen in a much more intelligent and restrained application in the Amos picture of the Bury Bible. In other words, at Canterbury also, whether through direct contact with Byzantine art and techniques or through some intermediary such as the Bury Bible, the idea of building up flesh with coloured pigment had made its appearance. The result, as might be expected in the stronghold of coloured outline technique, is not from the standpoint of modelling exactly successful. But as decoration it is superb; and there is something about the great staring eyes with their strong green shadows which is neither flesh nor fowl in the technique of modelled figures but has an other-worldly quality that defies the beholder to ridicule or to ignore.

Whether or not the Bury Bible was the source of inspiration for the Eadwine portrait – the technique of this picture has hardly any relation to that of the illustrations of the Psalter itself – there is no doubt that the style of the Eadwine manuscript was powerfully effective in furthering the spread of the Byzantinesque fashion in miniature painting at Canterbury. Another great Bible with magnificent miniatures and historiated initials with strong Byzantine leanings both in drawing and in colour was made in the first decades after the middle of the twelfth century. The Dover[46] Bible (Camb., Corpus Christi Coll., MSS 3 and 4) seems to have been written at least in part by Eadwine, judging by the script and some very similar marginal drawings in the ink of the script, introduced in connexion with catchwords at the ends of quires.[47] The Dover Bible is in two volumes, of which the illumination of the second (MS. 4) is the earlier. Some miniatures are very similar in general type of figure to the Eadwine portrait and may have furnished models for it, as, for example, the Matthew (fol. 168 verso; Plate 70).

The Dover Bible style, however, is painting, not coloured outline. The figure is massive in proportions and solidly posed (cf. the cramped, stiff pose of Eadwine on the plate opposite); the head is thrust forward and the hands are stretched out eagerly offering the book of his Gospel which he holds in a hand covered by a veil. The strong twist of the torso, the thrust of the knees and the weight resting heavily on the left foot while the right drops lightly forward, are all characteristic of monumental painting, not of outline drawing style. The colour is rich and heavy. Matthew has blue hair, like Eadwine, and a gold halo; the drapery is bordered with burnished gold, as is the frame around the initial, and is painted in different tones of purple and blue, combined with orange. This colouring is markedly different from the red, green, and brown of the Eadwine picture, but much more like the Bury Bible of Master Hugo. The drapery folds are indicated by ridges, as in the Bury Bible, but the patterns in the Dover Bible tend to fall into more decorative motifs, in the form of parallels and zigzags, and delicate surface lines in formal designs fill up the spaces otherwise left plain by the fall of the drapery. The head is the most impressive feature of the miniature, and it is this which constitutes the closest link with the Eadwine portrait, except that the latter, strangely enough in view of the linear technique of the body, shows even fewer lines and a broader use of paint than does the Matthew of the Dover Bible. The Matthew has the same large eyes with very white eyeballs in which the dark pupils are suspended, and the same heavy shadowing in green under the eye. But the forehead is strongly lined, as is the nose, and the hair and beard are divided into separate sections by heavy black lines, whereas Eadwine's are treated as soft masses.

A strange type of figure replaces the typical Evangelist Luke at the beginning of his gospel in the Dover Bible (fol. 191 verso; Plate 63A). At first sight he appears to be murdering his symbol, the ox,[48] but recent opinion has it that the figure actually represents a priest performing a sacrifice. He holds what looks like an ink horn but must be a knife in his right hand, and with his left he lifts the head of the ox almost as though in the act of killing it. This curious figure is represented purely in contour outline; the pattern on his mantle is not at all affected by any drapery folds. The tunic is completely linear. But the head is modelled in the same manner as that of Matthew and looks strangely out of place with the ill-matched body and the unusual iconography. The Luke miniature is another one of those multiple instances in miniature painting where new-found access to an old archetype may interrupt or in a measure divert the stream of a developing style.

To sum up the techniques of these two outstanding Canterbury productions of about the middle of the twelfth century: the Eadwine artist seems to have been trying to reconcile, as others before him had done, two incompatible figure styles; while the artist of the Dover Bible had grasped the monumentality of the painted figure style and was competently translating it into linear idiom. His technique consists not of a thin contour or shading line, but of broad, ridge-like lines that carry and enforce the body contours of the massive figure. Some of the details of this type of linear design are introduced for the sake of sheer ornamental pattern, like the puffed or clinging drapery around the feet, yet even these are related to the intensity of the pose, and add to rather than detract from the monumentality of the composition as a whole. This feature we shall presently see much further developed at Canterbury.

In view of the prevalence in the twelfth century of figure compositions within frames, of the monumental scale of the figures, and of the general interest in the use of decorative pattern and strong, shaded colour, it is not surprising to find remains of extensive schemes of twelfth century wall painting in England.[49] As we have seen, the colour, the shaded technique, the framed miniature, and even the iconography and composition of some of the subjects in English twelfth century illumination are clearly derived from Byzantine mosaics such as were being produced in Sicily. Such fragments of wall painting as have survived in England demonstrate on the one hand their dependence on the style of contemporary illumination, and on the other, because of their monumental scale, an even closer correspondence to the mosaics.

At Canterbury, wall paintings were executed in various parts of the Cathedral at different times during the twelfth century. The earliest were probably in the apse of St Gabriel's Chapel in the crypt, and belong to the period of the completion of Conrad's choir, c. 1130. Since they were walled up before 1199, probably for structural reasons, the paintings that remain are in remarkably fine condition. In the centre of the vault is a large figure of Christ seated on a rainbow within an aureole supported by four flying angels,[50] and towards the west is the Heavenly Jerusalem with seraphs. In tiers on the walls are scenes, on the south side from the early life of Christ, and on the north from the life of St John. The theme is essentially apocalyptic, and it is worth noting that a similar scheme is to be found in other English twelfth century vault paintings, as at Kempley (Glos.), and there are comparable schemes in several Sussex churches, nearer to Canterbury.

The wall paintings in the apse of St Gabriel's Chapel display affinities with earlier and contemporary manuscript illumination in general, but a much closer stylistic correspondence can be observed in the single surviving figure on the wall of St Anselm's Chapel in Canterbury Cathedral. This painting, which is usually dated about mid twelfth century, represents St Paul and the viper[51] (Plate 76). Since the chapel was dedicated to Saints Peter and Paul, there may have been a corresponding figure of Peter on the opposite wall.[52] Again, the fine condition of the painting of Paul is the result of its protection by a buttress built across the apse in the thirteenth century and not removed until 1888.

The quality of the painting, as well as of the pigments used for it, marks a distinct advance over the work in St Gabriel's Chapel. The correspondence of the style of the St Paul to that of Amos in the Bury Bible (Plate 69A) points to a Byzantine source: the solidity of the rendering, in spite of the linear technique, in both figures suggests direct contact with Byzantine style, as it might be seen in the mosaics of Norman Sicily.[53] On the other hand, there is a tendency, already noted in the Matthew of the Dover Bible, towards mannerism in the drapery patterns, such as the cascading fold of the edge of the mantle, which suggests a stage further removed from the Byzantine prototype than the Bury Bible. The graceful S-curve formed by the heavily falling mantle from shoulder to hem, as Paul stoops forward, helps to stabilize the pose and keep the figure from seeming to pitch forward; but this axial line is also a central decorative feature of the complex pattern of ridged, curved folds. The contour, as usual at this time, is strongly marked by a black outline. The face is modelled with high-lights on forehead, nose, and cheek, in the Byzantine manner, but the eyebrows and wrinkles on the forehead are strongly linear. The colour is superb: the background is blue; St Paul wears a white gown shaded with grey and a tan mantle with brown shading and white high-lights. The cloud border is red and brown. The richness of the colour scheme and the competence of the painter in the representation of so monumental a figure suggests influence from some fine Continental centre, such as a Cluniac church,[54] where contacts with Italy were strong. In any case, no other English wall painting of this century can compare with the Canterbury St Paul in the sureness of the drawing and the beauty of the colouring.

The nave of St Gabriel's Chapel, in the crypt of the Cathedral, probably represents the latest phase of painting at Canterbury in the twelfth century. The best preserved fragments are in the vaulting divisions of the two western bays: medallions with branches and stems contain half length figures of (?) bishops and angels. The scheme suggests most closely the Jesse Tree of Lambeth MS. 3 (fol. 198), and the style, though probably later (c. 1184), retains something of the character of this manuscript.[55]

Other wall paintings have been found in recent years in Sussex, dating from the twelfth century. Since they were near Lewes Priory, the chief Cluniac house in England,[56] these, too, may be derived from Cluniac sources, although no record remains of wall paintings at Lewes itself. The earliest of the surviving paintings are at Hardham (Plate 75A) and are thought to date from c. 1125, when the church was built. The interior of the building was entirely covered with paintings of which a large portion survives. Above the chancel arch on the nave side are the Adoration of the Lamb and the Labours of the Months; continuing at the level of the upper zone, on the north and south walls are scenes from the Infancy of Christ; at the west end of the nave is a representation of the Torments of the Damned. In the second zone of the nave are the Baptism, Lazarus carried to Heaven, and the full story of St George. On the west wall of the chancel, over the arch, Adam and Eve (Plate 75A); on the east wall, Christ in Majesty, flanked by the Elders and the Apostles, on the north and south walls, in the upper zone. In the second zone are scenes from the Passion. The entire bottom zone in both chancel and nave seems to have been filled with painted draperies, now almost entirely destroyed. The scheme is formidable: the complete story of Salvation clearly and systematically presented, and one cannot help being reminded, as Tristram noted,[57] of the cycle and even of some individual drawings in the remarkable Cædmon manuscript in the Bodleian Library (MS. Junius 11; Plate 44).

The style of the Hardham painting is largely linear, though modelling of the heads is suggested by the use of white with the red outline, and by a few strokes of red for shading. There is no underpainting for the flesh. The most striking of the figures in their present state are the Adam and Eve (Plate 75A) on the west wall of the chancel, above the arch, and these figures show better than any others their dependence on Anglo-Saxon models of the Cædmon type. The figures are enormously tall and completely nude, the anatomy of the bodies being suggested by a schematized design of white and red lines. The Tempter at Eve's left hand is much more effective, perhaps because less clearly visible now than Adam and Eve. It seems to be a dragon-like creature with animal head and ears, wings, and a round body with legs. The style of the painting though crude has a certain naïve charm, especially in the faces.

The paintings at Clayton (Plate 75B) are somewhat later than those at Hardham; they are better preserved and of more monumental dignity. The scheme is an early version of the Last Judgement based on the Apocalyptic Vision of St John: over the chancel arch is Christ supported by angels with the twelve apostles; below, on the left side of the wall, Christ delivers the keys to St Peter; on the right, He gives the book to St Paul. The nave walls are divided into two zones of which the upper one is almost intact: on the north wall are an angel trumpeting, the death of Antichrist, the Blessed wearing crowns, and a group of laymen in short coats with bishops leading them, the Heavenly Jerusalem, and another angel trumpeting. On the south wall, corresponding scenes introduced by a trumpeting angel include souls awaiting judgement, an Apocalyptic rider, an angel receiving the souls, and others supporting the Cross. In the lower zones, the very fragmentary paintings include the general resurrection, the weighing of souls, and probably also Hell. The subject suggests one of the favourite themes of the church portal tympana of French Cluniac monasteries, as at Conques.[58] The technique is still linear, with the dark red outline and a second white line accentuating it, but black underpainting is used as a base for flesh tints. The figures are monumental in scale and extremely impressive. Particularly fine are the praying saint (Plate 75B) and some of the angels.[59] The scale of the figures and the sweeping draperies are much closer to Poitevin paintings, as at St-Savin-sur-Gartempe,[60] and it is obvious that influence from either mosaics or Continental wall painting has left its mark on the English outline style.[61]

At Kempley (Glos.) another small Norman church, dedicated to St Mary, contains a completely painted chancel, both barrel vault and walls. In the summit of the vault is a large Christ in Majesty in a triple Glory, his head towards the west, his feet resting on a rainbow. Surrounding him are the symbols of the Evangelists, the eagle on his right, the angel on his left above, the lion and the ox to right and left below. The Virgin and St Peter, two cherubim and two seraphim, the seven candlesticks and the sun and moon fill the remainder of the vault. On the walls below are the twelve apostles seated under arches (Plate 74), six to a side, looking up in adoration. At the end of the row, on one side is Bethlehem, on the other, Jerusalem. On the east wall of the apse are standing figures of a bishop, pilgrims, and angels. The scheme is again one of the grandiose themes found commonly in sculpture of the mid twelfth century, which probably were often inspired by manuscripts.[62] The painting at Kempley is in earth colours – red, yellow, and grey – with black and white for features and drapery folds. It is a bold, monumental style which has no connexion with English miniature art and must, it seems, have been done by some painter, perhaps a local artist, who was familiar with Continental wall painting. The

Kempley paintings belong to approximately the same period as the apse paintings in St Gabriel's Chapel at Canterbury Cathedral, although the fuller iconographic detail might suggest a slightly later date for Kempley.

From the foregoing survey of the few surviving[63] examples of twelfth century wall painting, it is obvious that with the exception of the St Paul at Canterbury, the medium has little to contribute to the development of Romanesque art in England. And it is to the manuscripts that we must turn once more for English Romanesque art in its maturity during the second half of the twelfth century.

At Canterbury, probably at Christ Church, another great Bible was made of which only the first volume[64] has survived intact (Lambeth Palace Lib., MS. 3). It is superbly illuminated in a style which, though obviously influenced in its origins by Byzantine models, illustrates well the new and startlingly dynamic type of linear figure design which was evolved. There are six large miniatures, each divided into two or three registers, the whole surrounded by a frame consisting of two plain gold bands usually filled with a conventionalized leaf pattern of a type used in the Albani Psalter (cf. Plate 61). The miniatures are in a continuous narrative style, with the scenes sometimes separated from each other by architecture, sometimes not (Plate 73). In addition to the miniatures, fine historiated initials introduce the Books of the Bible, and usually decorative initials introduce the Prologues.[65]

Most of the illumination, both miniatures and initials, appears to be by the same hand, which is represented on fol. 258 (Plate 73). The figures are effectively silhouetted against a plain background and their arrangement constitutes a lively over-all pattern which is dependent partly on the figure contours and partly on the manner of treating the drapery. The folds are drawn as ridges and lines, as in the Dover Bible, and all the areas between them are filled, as in the Eadwine portrait, with decorative surface ornament; but the figures vibrate as though charged with an electric current which had lifted them on their toes and set them aquiver. The drapery folds cling to the bodies, except where whipped out as by a gust of wind, yet reveal no modelling of the form beneath.

The inspiration for this extraordinary dynamic style can be seen, perhaps, in an initial by a different hand on fol. 284 verso (Plate 69B). The design of this figure too is linear, but instead of forming a dizzy surface pattern, the drapery folds have depth, and the lines which indicate them have some relation to the contours and movement of the body, even though they obviously are not determined by them, as in normal figures. The draperies are whipped about the prophet so violently that one can almost hear the crack of the flapping ends, and they are only kept from blowing clean off him, because they are caught round his heel and over his arm. The body faces left, and the head is bent back towards the right; a lock of fuzzy hair has been blown loose and stands out from his forehead; and the phylactery in his hand sweeps upward in a full curve, caught by the same violent wind. The closest analogy to this curiously unnatural yet powerful type of figure is found in the sculptures of Aquitaine, of which the prophet Isaiah at Souillac[66] is an outstanding example. The explanation of the difference between the two styles in the Lambeth Bible may lie in the fact that the principal master (Plate 73), working in the traditional Anglo-Saxon linear manner from some Byzantine model, had simply infused new life into the conventional linear patterns. The painter of the prophet Daniel (Plate 69B), however, belonged to a new school of artists who, with more complete understanding of the possibilities of the figure itself, not simply of its flat outer surface, had treated form and draperies as inseparable elements and evolved out of them a linear pattern with depth and consequently with greatly intensified dynamic life. The style of the Daniel is a forerunner of one of the styles of the Winchester Bible, and even influenced late twelfth century work in other media.[67]

The steps we have been following in the development of the typical English Romanesque style in painting have been localized chiefly in a very few centres, mostly in the south of England, that is, Canterbury and Sussex generally, and St Albans, Herts. Bury St Edmunds, the other great centre where the new style was germinating in the early part of the century, lay only a short sea journey from Canterbury, and stylistic interchange between the two great monasteries has already been noted in earlier periods. There is, however, also evidence that the new monumental linear style spread farther afield. Two fine examples of the new style in figures, expressed only in coloured outline, are a manuscript which belonged to and perhaps was made at Ramsey Abbey in the Fenlands (Camb., St John's Coll., MS. H.6), and a single leaf with a magnificent Madonna and Child prefixed to Bod. MS. 269.

The text of the Cambridge manuscript is Bede's Commentary on the Apocalypse. On folios ii and iii are four very fine full-page drawings: a bearded, nimbed apostle (John?); John vested as a bishop with a prostrate monk, 'scriptor libri', at his feet (fol. ii verso; Plate 77); a vaulted building with a tiled roof and three towers (Heavenly Jerusalem?) and beneath, the seven-branched candlestick; and Christ enthroned holding with both hands a sword which issues from his mouth. The figure of John as bishop is hieratic in pose and symmetrical in the formal patterning of the draperies. Yet the body is firmly modelled and the heavy drapery folds follow the contours of the form in the sinuous S-curves which characterize the magnificent figure of St Paul in St Anselm's Chapel at Canterbury (Plate 76). The face is lightly touched with colour to suggest the modelling under the eyes and on cheek and chin. The composition of the drawing as linear pattern is superb, with its well-ordered economy of line, yet the solidity of the figure has in no way been weakened by the reduction to linear techniques. The date is probably not earlier than the third quarter of the twelfth century.

The second of the two monumental drawings is perhaps slightly earlier.[68] It is a coloured drawing of the Madonna and Child on the recto of the first leaf of text of Augustine's Commentary on Psalms 101–50. It is of great size ($10\frac{3}{8}$ by $6\frac{1}{2}$ inches) and tremendous power (Plate 78). The colour is extraordinary because of the complete absence of blue; soft tones of vermilion, purple, and green are used both for the bands of the double mandorla and for the outline and wash-shading of the figures. Both Virgin and Child are extremely elongated figures with small heads but heavy bodies. The Virgin's draperies are not over-rich in folds but almost all of those indicated fall in long unbroken vertical lines over her shoulders and from behind her knees and seem to be so designed as to constitute a background pattern for the figure of the Child. The play of vertical and curved folds and the rounded figure contours repeatedly carry the eye through returning curves back to the central area and the focal figure, the Child, who is placed exactly at the intersection of the two circles. The arrangement of the colours in the central area repeats and intensifies this emphasis: the circular area behind the Virgin's shoulders is purple, as is the outer band of the lower circle; the inner band of the upper circle is green, as is the inner area behind the throne in the lower circle; and the striking band of vermilion which forms the outer band of the upper circle terminates exactly at the throne on which the Virgin and Child are seated. The drawing and the colour harmony constitute a masterpiece of mature twelfth century design and are wholly in the Romanesque tradition of monumental painting at its grandest. Unfortunately there is no indication of the centre where this consummate work was produced.

At St Albans, however, where the monumental style had made its first formal appearance in the first quarter of the century, other interesting developments were taking place. Not long after the middle of the century, a Terence manuscript (Bod. MS. Auct. F.2.13) was illustrated with drawings by four artists of whom the two distinguished by Morey[69] as A and B seem to have collaborated in the evolution of the monumental style at Winchester.[70] Some of the figures in the Terence miniatures are tall and thin, as in the Albani Psalter, but they have taken on an extraordinary liveliness (Plate 82), perhaps under the influence of the dramatic character of the scenes portrayed. The poses and gestures are stagy; and the masks which cover the faces introduce a new type of head with exaggerated features and grotesque, often coarse, expressions. From this source presumably evolved a liveliness of action in the representation of figures that is different from the optical liveliness produced by a linear surface pattern as in the Lambeth Bible.

The fusion of the styles of the Lambeth Bible and the Terence, perhaps in the person of a single artist, is responsible for most of the illumination in a magnificent psalter (Brit. Mus., Cott. MS. Nero C.iv) executed between 1150 and 1160, perhaps for Henry of Blois, Bishop of Winchester and a patron of the arts, either at the Cathedral Priory of St Swithin or at Hyde Abbey (formerly New Minster).[71] The psalter is preceded by a series of Bible pictures – thirty-eight full-page miniatures in two zones, almost all within frames of foliated and other conventional patterns and edged with bands of gold. Inserted in the midst of the series, and probably not forming part of the original manuscript, are two (later?) pictures, the Death (fol. 29) and the Enthronement of the Virgin (fol. 30; Plate 79) in Italo-Byzantine[72] style and colouring. In comparison with the other miniatures, fols 29–30 appear at first sight to be indeed by an Italian artist; but in spite of their more convincingly modelled figures and their richer, shaded colouring, they too are linear in technique. Although Italo-Byzantine characteristics have been noted in earlier English illumination, notably in the Albani Psalter and manuscripts influenced by it, nothing so strikingly Byzantine in feeling as these two miniatures in Nero C.iv has been found in earlier English work. The influence of this style was by no means limited to this one manuscript, as we shall see.

The Bible pictures in Nero C.iv have been extremely fine in colour, but most of the ultramarine pigment which originally covered their backgrounds has been removed, possibly for use elsewhere, the colours have become pale through the effect of damp, and most of the gold has disappeared. What remains, therefore, has to be judged primarily as drawing (fol. 12; Plate 80). The clinging 'damp' drapery with patterns formed by ridged folds are similar to those of the Lambeth Bible, but in Nero C.iv they have been further clarified and organized on the basis of fewer lines, and these more often of the contour and swinging S-curved type, such as characterize the painting of St Paul in St Anselm's Chapel at Canterbury Cathedral. The source, however, is probably to be sought not at Canterbury itself but in a common Byzantine prototype as represented in the miniatures of fols 29 and 30 of the Psalter. Likewise, from such a source are the large, solemn heads, almost always seen in three-quarter, not profile, view, with enormous eyes and heavy masses of hair and beard which contrast with the symmetrically curled locks and the pinched, tortured drapery edges of the Lambeth Bible. Architecture, too, is more elaborate and is used to form a stage setting for the scenes, to which the figures seem to have some spatial relation. In short, in contrast to the all-over patterned style of the Lambeth Bible, the composition of figures in Nero C.iv moves freely against open space or in a spatial relation to architectural setting.

The giant of twelfth-century English manuscripts – in scale, in quality, and in artistic importance – was produced at Winchester: the great Bible now in the Cathedral Library.[73] The manuscript was originally in two volumes, but has recently been rebound in four. In size (23 by 15¾ inches) and in the variety and magnificence of its illumination it surpasses even the fine Bibles made at Bury St Edmunds and Canterbury. It was probably begun *c.* 1160–70, i.e. during the lifetime of Henry of Blois. Before the illumination was completely finished, the manuscript was apparently obtained from Winchester by King Henry II for his new foundation at Witham, but it was returned to Winchester by St Hugh of Lincoln, then Prior of Witham.[74] At some time during its history a number of the historiated initials which introduce the Prologues and the Books of the Bible were cut out.[75] Somehow concerned with the making of the Bible is the single full-page miniature of unmistakable Winchester style now in the Morgan Library (MS. 619; Plate 86) which is believed to have been originally intended for inclusion in the Bible.[76] The only miniatures in the Bible, as differentiated from the historiated initials, are two full pages of drawings illustrating the apocryphal books of Judith (fol. 331 verso) and Maccabees (fol. 350 verso) in Vol. IV. The artist of these pages, who also drew some of the initials (as fol. 363; Plate 83A) has been designated as the Master of the Apocrypha Drawings.[77] At least five other artists have been distinguished: the Master of the Leaping Figures, whose style is represented by the historiated initial on fol. 148 (Jeremiah, Plate 83B); the Master of the Genesis Initial (fol. 209), Prologue to Zephaniah (Plate 84A); the Amalekite Master (fol. 69, Joshua, Plate 84B); the Master of the Morgan Leaf (fol. 190, Daniel; Plate 85A); the Master of the Gothic Majesty (fol. 131, Isaiah; Plate 85B).

The distinction between the styles of the six masters in their most typical work is fairly easy. The so-called Master of the Apocrypha Drawings is primarily a draughtsman. His principal work is the two pages of drawings composed like pictures without frames and with no decorative features. One initial only has been attributed to him (fol. 363; Plate 83A), preceding II Maccabees, and that is treated exactly as if it were a miniature, with architectural setting and no decorative elements except some interlace. It is true, the initial is not finished and undoubtedly was intended to be coloured; but this master's style is recognizable in the facial type, the stance, the drapery, and especially in the sensitive way in which he has sketched the contours of the limbs under the draperies. The gold borders on the draperies and the sharpening of the double line ridge-like folds appear to be preparation for the painting of the figure, perhaps by the Master of the Leaping Figures (cf. below). Another initial in the Bible, fol. 278 verso, at the beginning of Ecclesiasticus, with a wonderfully fine figure of Wisdom, seems to be another example of the Apocrypha Master's drawing[78] (cf. the equally impressive figure of King Antiochus, fol. 350 verso) with the gold borders and sharper drapery lines added as on fol. 363 by the Master of the Leaping Figures.

The Master of the Leaping Figures is well represented in the initial introducing the Book of Jeremiah (fol. 148; Plate 83B). He, too, is an extraordinary draughtsman, but his figures are designed not in normal lively activity but they sway and 'leap', with swinging draperies and wide-flung arms in a design that is primarily decorative in arrangement and emotional in tone. The colouring of this and other initials by the same Master is violent: strong red shaded with yellow and yellow with red, and much reddish purple, are used; blue is used for the ground; there are dull gold edges on the draperies (as noted above) as well as for the initial letters. The colouring undoubtedly derives from Byzantine painting, but as used by this artist it is strong if not beautiful.

The source of the Byzantine colouring and also of the type of facial modelling used by the Master of the Leaping Figures seems to be recognizable in the work of the artist who did the first two historiated initials in the Bible, the Genesis Master so-called from his fine initial to the Book of Genesis (fol. 5). His style is well illustrated in the initial on fol. 209 at the beginning of the Book of Zephaniah (Plate 84A). His modelling is heavy, his faces solemn, with sullen, almost baleful expressions resulting from the frowning wrinkled forehead, strong accentuation of the white of the eye, and mouths drawn down at the corners. Hands are broad and flat, and the open palm is modelled with a well-marked pattern. Drapery folds are designed in relation to the figure beneath, with no nonsense as to independent decorative patterns they could form on their own; they are heavy and tend to drag and impede the movements of legs and arms. This master's colouring also is strong, but the combinations of colour are more pleasing and the overpainting is more delicate than in the work of the Master of the Leaping Figures. A good deal of green is used, in the design and for shadowing the contour of the initial letter, outside. The gold used for backgrounds and for the letters is highly burnished, and in backgrounds is tooled with groups of tiny dots. The Christ head in the nimbus strongly suggests an Italo-Byzantine mosaic (cf. below, Morgan Master).

The fourth artist, the so-called Amalekite Master (Plate 84B), is a curious anomaly. His faces are painted in a yellowish flesh colour with strong high-lights and shadows, but according to a formula rather than as a well-understood technique of facial modelling. His figures are very active, in a clumsy, unstable way. The soldiers wear over their long chain mail hauberks a divided skirt or very long tunic which swings outward as they move. Their thighs are strongly outlined but the drapery folds are linear. The mushroom-like trees are extremely old-fashioned for this time. A striking feature of the decoration of the initial is the three fine profile heads of different types which are carefully modelled and differentiated. The persistent profiles and the long, thin shapeless yet lively figures suggest the style of the Bury St Edmunds Gospels (Pembroke 120; Plate 64); but something new has been added in the way of facial modelling. This could be the result of influence from the technique of the Genesis Master, but the influence is only superficial, for the technique of the miniature on the whole is linear.

The style of the Master of the Morgan Leaf is well represented in the Bible by the initial on fol. 190 (Plate 85A). His figures are of more nearly normal proportions, though the heads are perhaps a little too large for the bodies. They are roundly modelled in Byzantine light and shade technique softened and modulated by the exquisite colouring; all are outlined with heavy black line. The figures are dignified and restrained in action and gesture. The faces, which are usually seen in three-quarter view, are shaded around the eyes and cheeks, and are darkened on the far side to suggest foreshortening. There is little variety in the facial types and it is clear that the modelling is the result of a formula; yet the eyes are focussed and there is expression in them. The background is of burnished gold but the details of the setting – the table set for a feast, the figures seated behind it, and the servants in the foreground – are clearly arranged with some idea of spatial relationships. The table top is even foreshortened, so that the dishes do not appear to be sliding off it. This conception of a clearly organized spatial setting is something new in English illumination, and the Morgan Master in this respect is far ahead of his collaborators, except the Apocrypha Master (cf. Plate 83A) who seems to have had the same idea. The initial letter in the work of the Morgan Master also has a clarity of design and a crispness in form and colouring which is less marked in the rather overcrowded compositions of initials by the other Winchester artists. The rich colour effect of the initial as a whole is set off by the line of green paint surrounding it.

The fine style of the Morgan Master cannot be fully appreciated apart from the large full-page miniature which suggested his name (New York, Morgan Library, MS. 619; Plate 86). The puzzling problem of the origin and purpose of this leaf in relation to the Winchester Bible has been referred to, but no satisfactory solution offers itself. The subject comprises scenes from the life of David, and the miniature, if intended for the Bible, would probably have been placed before the Book of Samuel, which in the Bible is now introduced by an historiated initial. It is useless to suggest hypotheses to explain the existence of the leaf, but it is an extremely lucky accident which preserved it to us, for without it the full power and amazing beauty of the Morgan Master's style could never have been realized.

The page[79] is divided into zones: in the top zone, at the left, David is aiming a stone at an enormous Goliath who occupies the centre of the scene; at the right, Goliath lies on the ground with David holding his severed head. In the centre zone, at the left David is harping and dancing – at the same time, apparently – before a threatening Saul; at the right, David is anointed by Samuel. And in the lower zone is one of the most moving scenes of all, Absalom with his hair caught in the branches of a tree and David mourning his death. The backgrounds of the zones are painted in plain heavy colours, red, tan, and blue alternating. Against these backgrounds the wonderfully modelled figures stand out with almost sculpturesque clarity. The well-proportioned bodies, the softly shaded draperies which flow around them and reveal their form, and the powerful heads with broad, rounded foreheads and prominent cheek-bones correspond to these features in the Bible initial, but the monumental scale of the scenes on the Morgan leaf shows them off to the best advantage. The faces are painted with a yellowish flesh tone as a base, and the modelling is done largely with green. Otherwise, there is very little green used on the page, the dominant colours being red and blue.

The superb quality of the Morgan Master's style would inevitably have influenced the work of other artists[80] who might have seen it, and it seems to be reflected, though feebly, in the last of the Winchester artists to be distinguished, the Master of the Gothic Majesty, so called from his unfinished initial to Psalm CX with the imposing figures of the two Persons of the Trinity.[81] His painted style (fol. 131; Plate 85B) is interesting to compare with that of the Morgan Master included on the same plate. The proportions of the figures, the types of heads, even the manner of shading the drapery folds are all very similar to those of the Morgan Master, but the figures have somehow lost their substance and become silhouettes outlined with black line and covered with an arrangement of shaded patterns. The drapery of Christ and that of the servant on the right in the Morgan initial will illustrate the difference. The contour of the Morgan figure is clearly determined by the rounded shape of the thigh and leg; that of the Christ is apparently deliberately broken by the clumsy ridged folds which cut across it and swing outward at the bottom of the mantle, instead of clinging to and revealing the roundness of the leg as in the other picture. The faces, too, in the initial by the Gothic Master are flatter, less firmly modelled, and less intense in expression. The differences between the two styles, subtle though they are, in a sense are the differences between Romanesque and Gothic, the vigour and monumentality of the former contrasted with the suavity and grace of the latter. Yet, in itself, without comparison with the stronger style, the miniature by the Gothic Master is a very beautiful thing, with its gentleness and dignity, its pleasing arrangement of linear patterns, and its soft pink, blue, and grey colouring and brilliant burnished gold background. This style we shall meet again in the early manuscripts of the next century.

The six main illuminators of the Winchester Bible were all great masters, and it is not reasonable to imagine that they sprang fully formed out of an artistic void. The bold, intense facial style of the Genesis Master, it is true, seems foreign to previous English style and perhaps reflects further Continental influence resulting from the various contacts of Englishmen with Italy and the Byzantine East. The Master of the Leaping Figures is certainly the most dynamic artist at work on the Bible, and his style can be accounted for largely by two earlier English manuscripts. His damp draperies, for instance, with formal, ridged patterns and whipped edges, are found also in the Lambeth Bible; but the same type of drapery on more violently active figures, as in the Winchester Psalter (Nero C.iv), are much more like the 'leaping figures'. If we compare unpainted drawings by this Master with miniatures in Nero C.iv which have lost their colour, we can recognize the same patterns in the folds and the same lively, somewhat exaggerated poses and gestures. The other influence which helped to determine the Leaping Master's style was undoubtedly his association with the Master of the Apocrypha while he was illuminating the

Bodleian Terence (MS. Auct. F.2.13; Plate 82). It is apparently in this manuscript, perhaps because of the nature of the subject matter to be illustrated, that his violent theatrical gestures and poses were developed.[82] The other artists of the Bible, including the somewhat colourless Amalekite Master, were more or less influenced by the Genesis Master's technique of modelling and colour; but this is not wholly true of the Morgan Master who, as we have seen, displays an understanding of the modelled figure which perhaps came from first-hand contacts with Byzantine art, again perhaps in the mosaics of South Italy.[83]

The collaboration of a number of artists with individual styles on the same work in the Middle Ages usually not only resulted in the production of an outstanding monument but constituted the starting point for important new things to come, and in this respect the Winchester Bible was no exception. Its influence was felt immediately in several large Bibles comparable with it in the magnificence if not in the quality of their illuminations. Two of these are in the Bodleian Library: a great Bible illustrated with narrative scenes in miniatures or initials[84] (MS. Laud Misc. 752) and a two-volume Bible[85] (MS. Auct. E. infra 1 and 2) which has only a few historiated initials but a wealth of decorative letters in a fully developed Romanesque style – 'perhaps the greatest English repertory of Romanesque pattern'.[86] These Bibles, like the Winchester manuscript, were certainly illuminated by a number of artists over a considerable period. There is no evidence as to their provenance.

A large and splendid psalter dating from about the same time (i.e. c. 1175) can be assigned by means of its calendar to the diocese of York (Glasgow, Hunterian Museum, MS. U.3.2). The decoration consists of the usual calendar illustrations; twelve full pages of preliminary pictures – three each from the Old and the New Testament, the Ascension, Pentecost, and Christ in Majesty, and three subjects connected with the Death and Assumption of the Virgin; a full-page *Beatus* and eight large initials to the psalms of which two are historiated. The biblical pictures (Plate 81) are divided into two registers and surrounded by a formal frame, as in the miniatures of the Winchester Psalter (Plate 80), but the style is very unlike this manuscript although also a mixture of Byzantine modelling and linear drawing. In the York Psalter linear pattern is predominant. The figures are spread over the splendid gold tooled ground with complete indifference as to whether they are supposed to be in heaven or on earth, or as to what their spatial relation to each other may be. Wings, flying draperies, scrolls, ridged clouds are all arranged in a beautifully disposed surface pattern, which is still further enriched by the sinuous contours of the drapery and the elaborate design formed by the lines indicating their folds. Even the torso of Isaac in the lower scene and also the ram come in for their share of decorative treatment. Yet the figures themselves, especially the two representations of Abraham, are monumental in proportions and imposing in the type of head, which retains traces of modelling in the Byzantine manner around the eyes and on the cheek.

The final examples of twelfth century English manuscripts of great size are somewhat of an anti-climax when compared with the achievements of the Winchester scriptorium, though in scale and in the elaborateness of their decorative schemes they belong with the other great productions of the period. The four-volume Bible now in Durham Cathedral Library (MS. A.ii.1) was presented by Hugh de Puiset[87] (or Pudsey), Bishop of Durham

1153–95, but there is no indication as to whether it was made there or not. As in the Winchester Bible, each Book and Prologue had originally an illuminated initial, but the style both of the ornament and of the painting (fol. 173; Plate 87B) is on a much less lavish scale than in the Winchester manuscript. The initials were done by several hands, of which the one illustrated in the plate in some respects seems to have stylistic affinities with the Amalekite Master of the Winchester Bible, perhaps before he had been influenced by the Genesis Master's manner of modelling and colouring. At any rate, the figures in the initial introducing II Kings (Plate 87B) are in a much simpler, more wholly linear technique than any of the Winchester work, though the manner of treating the drapery folds and the types of the heads betray their Byzantine derivation. The poses are comical in their ineptness and the figures are flat in spite of the prominent shoulder, arm, and leg which are 'modelled' with oval patches forming part of the whole essentially linear pattern. The decoration of the initials is very simple and plain, with narrow bands constituting the shaft of the letter which ends in a scroll of conventionalized leaves. The background of the initials is of burnished gold and the colours are rather strong and bright.

Another illuminated manuscript, however, also given by Bishop Pudsey to Durham Cathedral (MS. A.ii.19 in the Cathedral Library), seems to establish some stylistic link between the Durham and the Winchester Bibles. Manuscript A.ii.19, a copy of the glossed epistles of St Paul, contains at the beginning of each epistle a fine historiated initial, usually on gold ground surrounded by a green painted line, as introduced into the Winchester Bible by the Genesis Master. The shaft of the initial is filled with conventionalized monochrome patterns as in the Winchester Bible, and the coloured ground is further decorated with dots and circles of white. Roundels containing lively animals are applied to the initial shafts. Some of the figures are strongly modelled in brown with white high-lights (fol. 87 verso; Plate 87A), and there is something of the vigour but little of the competence of the Winchester Byzantinesque style. The Pudsey manuscripts have certain stylistic affinities with manuscripts known to have been at St Albans at the beginning of the thirteenth century; hence the possibility that the Durham manuscripts might have been produced there, or at least under the influence of the St Albans scriptorium.

The source of the animal roundels in Durham MS. A.ii.19 is probably to be found in the twelfth century Bestiary, one of the most typically English medieval books. The finest Bestiary examples belong to the latter part of the century, and although only one can be localized – and that only as to ownership, not necessarily as to production – the style of the drawing in some of them points again to St Albans. (See Bod., MS. Ashmole 1511 below.)

Dr James[88] dealt with thirty-four English copies of the Latin prose text which forms the basis for the medieval Bestiary, the earliest dating from the eighth to the tenth centuries. Between these and the twelfth century manuscripts no intermediate copies are known, and the sudden popularity of the work in the twelfth century seems to have been due to the pictures which illustrate the text rather than to the text itself.

The earliest twelfth century manuscript is Bod. MS. Laud Misc. 247 with thirty-six chapters of text illustrated with lively pictures mainly in brown outline.[89] Later in the twelfth century, the text of a manuscript in Cambridge (Univ. Lib., MS. Ii.4.26) has expanded to 110 chapters, with a corresponding increase in the illustrations which in this manuscript were drawn first, the text then being written around them. The style is finer[90] than that of Bod. 247, though similar in that most of the drawings are uncoloured.

In the late twelfth century the illustrated Bestiary comes into its own. A fine painted manuscript in the Morgan Library (MS. 81) is said to be the one that was given to Radford Priory (now Worksop, in Nottinghamshire) in 1187 and, if so, was perhaps made there as early as *c.* 1170 (Plate 88B). Close to the end of the century and perhaps even finer in style is Bod. MS. Ashmole 1511 (fol. 14 verso; Plate 88A). The characteristics of the drawing and painting typical of the Bestiary illustration are well illustrated in these two examples, as is also the trend towards Gothic elegance in the linear patterns of the composition, which is characteristic of the later style.

Plate 88B illustrates the amusing fictitious procedure described for stealing a tiger cub, namely, throwing a mirror to the tigress who, seeing her own reflection, thinks it is her cub and therefore does not notice that the cub is being carried away.[91] The galloping horse, the flying cloak, and the tigress rearing up on her hind legs are the elements *par excellence* of a fine medieval design. The drawing is firm and is further accentuated by the black contour line and the strong colour. The choice of colours is far from realistic – the horse is blue and the tigers are vermilion – but they form a brilliant pattern against the gold background.

The illustration from Ashmole 1511 on the same plate (Plate 88A) represents the popular medieval story of the unicorn which, when hunted, could not be caught except when it took refuge with a virgin. The drawing here is even finer than that of Morgan 81 in the decorative handling of the design, yet it has lost nothing of the intense vitality of the representation. The technique is painting rather than drawing, yet line plays a dominant part in the arrangement of the design as a whole. The suave curves of the ground, trees, and figures are echoed in the violent gestures and tense expressions of both the hunters and the virgin. The colours are chiefly blue and vermilion with some pink, yellow, and green, against a burnished gold ground. This type of composition represents the turning point between Romanesque with the heavy serious faces and the exaggerated anatomy of the figures, and the linear elegance of the Gothic.

Bestiary pictures seem frequently to have copied each other or some common original. The Morgan Bestiary illustrated in plate 88B was apparently copied both as to text and pictures in the now imperfect manuscript in the British Museum, Royal 12 C. xix, of slightly later date and equally fine style; and to these two must be added the Leningrad Bestiary.[92] Bodleian MS. Ashmole 1511 likewise forms a trio with Bod. MS. Douce 151 and Aberdeen Univ. Lib., MS. 24.[93] Bodleian MS. 764 and Brit. Mus., Harl. MS. 4751, form a pair. Apart from their fine quality, particularly as to the drawing, the Bestiaries were very important from the end of the twelfth century as sources for animal subjects and even for grotesques, which became such a prominent feature of thirteenth century psalters. Animals and grotesques from the Bestiary are found too, though less commonly, in wall painting, tiles, and misericords of the thirteenth and fourteenth centuries in England.

Summary

In looking back over the productions of English art in the twelfth century, we find them to be considerable in number and high in quality even in a period of great art everywhere in Europe. The century began with outline drawing, often prettily coloured, still holding the field, until a fresh wave of Continental influence produced the revolutionary Albani Psalter. This was followed in unbroken succession by the magnificent Life of St Edmund in full colour, four very large, fine Bibles – Bury, Dover, Lambeth, and Winchester – and as many great psalters – Lansdowne, Eadwine, Winchester, and Glasgow; and the century ended with miniature painting on a monumental scale, in the work of the Morgan Master which, as we shall see, played an important part in the style of Continental as well as of English art at the turn of the century.

The outstanding accomplishment of English art in the twelfth century was the development of a dynamic figure style which differed from earlier styles less in spirit than in technique. Whereas in Anglo-Saxon art contour line was the principal means of expressing the form and movements of the human figure, in twelfth century English art the technique was that of modelled figures, learned from Byzantine sources, and transformed into linear pattern by the manipulation and arrangement of drapery folds, poses, and gestures. The figures themselves are solidly conceived and lively in a curious unrealistic sense; they live and move, as it were, in another world, charged with vitality and emotion and freed from the heaviness of earthly matter. In short, the twelfth century English artist has finally succeeded in mastering to his own satisfaction the problem of the modelled figure which had long plagued him, by converting it, modelling and all, into a dynamic decorative pattern.

NOTES TO CHAPTER 4

1. Saxl and Wittkower, *op. cit.*, 24.

2. *Op. cit.*

3. Dom David Knowles, *The Religious Houses of Medieval England* (London, 1940), 27 f.

4. The effect of Cistercian influence on English architecture was very marked, but since decoration in general was frowned on in Cistercian houses, pictorial art was little affected, except perhaps by the intensification of monastic fervour which so many new religious foundations would foster. However, Cistercian influence was reflected in the use of grisaille glass in windows, as in the Five Sisters in York Minster. See Chapter 5. An English Cistercian monk known as 'Pictor in Carmine' compiled an elaborate series of descriptions of subjects for painting. See Chapter 5, note 103.

5. Saxl and Wittkower, *op. cit.*, 24.

6. *English Romanesque Illumination* (Bodleian Picture Books 1), No. 7. On the Bestiary in general, see below 99 ff.

7. Harl. MS. 647. See Chapter 2, note 59. A tendency noticeable in Bod. MS. 247 to interlace the branches of trees and make curls of the ground has parallels in eleventh century manuscripts, such as the Ælfric Pentateuch and the Cædmon manuscript (*q.v.*), and is probably to be accounted for by Hiberno-Saxon heritage.

8. Dodwell, *op. cit.*, 34

9. The manuscript was formerly owned by A. Chester Beatty and is fully described by Eric Millar in the *Catalogue of the Library of A. Chester Beatty*, I (Western Manuscripts) (Oxford, 1927), No. 19. Millar suggests (74, n. 1) the Blois Gospels, the Ebbo Gospels, and the Bible of St Paul-outside-the-Walls

as representing the style of the prototype. The technique of the Morgan manuscript, however, is less impressionistic and more solid than any of these.

p. 76   10. Fritz Saxl, 'Beiträge zu einer Geschichte der Planetendarstellungen im Orient und im Okzident', *Der Islam*, III (1912), 151–77; Erwin Panofsky, 'Dürers Stellung zur Antike', *Wiener Jahrbuch für Kunstgeschichte*, I (1921–2), 43–92; cf. also Dimitris Tselos, *Art Bull.*, xxxiv (1952), 257–77.

p. 77   11. See Millar, *Catalogue of the Library of A. Chester Beatty*, coloured frontispiece to volume of plates (fol. 24 verso, Mark).

12. C. de Ricci, *Census of Medieval and Renaissance Manuscripts in the United States and Canada*, II, No. 777; Morgan Library, *Catalogue of an Exhibition of Illuminated Manuscripts*, 1934, 17, No. 29, plate 28.

13. Cf. Chapter 2, 39 f., for the development of these forms in the eleventh century.

14. For example, fol. 135; cf. Bodleian Library, *English Romanesque Illumination*, plate 6A.

15. Mynors, *op. cit.*, No. 57, plates 36 and 37.

16. Brit. Mus., *Schools of Illumination*, Part II, 6.

p. 78   17. Wormald, 'Survival', plate 7.

18. *Op. cit.*, 141, n. 2.

19. This manuscript is very important in relation to the style of the Winchester Bible. See Plate 82 and 157 ff. below.

20. Such as the Hitda Codex, Darmstadt, Landesbib. Cod. 1640; Goldschmidt, *German Illum.*, II, plate 86; Hans Jantzen, *Ottonische Kunst* (Munich, 1948), plates 64–7.

21. The only detailed study of this important manuscript to date was published by Goldschmidt, *Der Albanipsalter in Hildesheim*, 1895. Recently the miniatures have been completely rephotographed and a new study of the manuscript is in progress. The Psalter was connected with Cristina, the anchoress of Markyate. See Wormald, 'Development of English Illumination', 35. See also Boase, *English Art*, 102 ff.

22. On evidence based on the calendar and litany and on the importance of the miniature of the martyrdom of St Alban.

p. 79   23. It is possible that these miniatures come from another psalter. If the St Albans illuminator was influenced by the style of these miniatures, as seems evident, they would have to be contemporary or earlier than the initials of this Psalter.

24. Saxl and Wittkower, *op. cit.*, 26; the authors compare the Temptation of Christ with the somewhat later mosaic of the same subject in St Mark's, Venice.

25. Swarzenski, *The Berthold Missal*, 47 and figure 63. Swarzenski assumes that both this manuscript and the Albani Psalter miniatures are products of the St Albans scriptorium. On stylistic grounds, it would seem more reasonable to assume that either the illuminator or the miniatures were brought to St Albans from the Continent, since no parallels for this style in earlier English art are known.

26. Slight but significant evidence of this style is found on pages of the Albani Psalter where the border includes animals delicately etched in white line. Similar motifs are used in borders of some of the Reichenau manuscripts.

27. Swarzenski, 'Der Stil der Bibel Carilefs von Durham', 94.

28. On the grounds of an included letter referring to Henry I, who died in 1135. *New Pal. Soc.*, Series I, plates 113–15.

29. M. R. James, *Descriptive Catalogue of the Manuscripts in Pembroke College* (Cambridge, 1905). James noted that the pictures lack some of the characteristic marks of Anglo-Saxon art such as the fluttering draperies and sharp outlines.

30. Cf. Plates 77 and 78, which cannot be much later than this date.

31. See James, 'Four Leaves of an English Psalter'.

32. For comparative tables of this series with other nearly contemporary cycles, see *op. cit.*, 3–23.

33. The question arises whether the four leaves could represent a kind of artist's repertory of biblical compositions for use in wall paintings or miniatures, rather than themselves being intended as such preliminary miniatures. On the relationship between the four Bible-picture leaves and similar leaves in the Gospels of St Augustine, see F. Wormald, *The Miniatures in St Augustine's Gospels* (Cambridge, 1954), 12 f.

34. Mary Ann Farley and F. Wormald, 'Three Related English Romanesque Manuscripts', *Art Bull.*, xx (1940), 157–61.

35. *Op. cit.*, 158.

36. In later psalters these subjects are often included among the preliminary miniatures.

37. Again, the Hitda Codex of the Cologne School. See note 20 above.

38. Farley and Wormald, *op. cit.*, figures 1 and 2.

39. *Op. cit.*, figures 3–5.

40. M. R. James, *Cat. of the MSS in Corpus*

Christi Coll. Lib. (Cambridge, 1909), MS. 2. See also James, *On the Abbey of St Edmund at Bury* (Cambridge, 1895), 7. The Cambridge manuscript is the first volume only of the Bible, through the Book of Job.

41. Otto Demus, *The Mosaics of Norman Sicily* (London, 1950), 25–58, plates 16–18.

42. Millar, *op. cit.*, 31.

43. A facsimile of the Eadwine Psalter with his portrait reproduced in colour was published with an introduction by M. R. James, *The Canterbury Psalter*. The date of the manuscript can be closely determined between 1146–7 (the date of the recorded appearance of a comet which is referred to in a drawing on fol. 10) and 1170, the date of the death of Thomas Becket who is not included in the calendar. A detailed plan of Christ Church monastery on fols 284 verso–285 certainly localizes the manuscript there.

44. That is, it contains in three parallel columns the three versions of the text, Hebrew, Roman, and Gallican.

45. But not, as far as any evidence shows, a self-portrait, since Eadwine was only the scribe of the manuscript and his efforts at drawing do not seem to show much ability. See below and note 47.

46. So-called because it bears the pressmark of the Priory of St Martin at Dover, which was a dependent cell of Christ Church, Canterbury.

47. For example, fol. 144 of Trin. Coll. MS. R.17.1 and fol. 106 of Corpus Christi Coll. MS. 3.

48. This was James's interpretation, *Cat. of MSS in Corpus Christi Coll. Lib.*, I. A similar representation occurs in the Floreffe Bible (Brit. Mus., Add. MS. 17738, fol. 187), at the beginning of the gospel of Luke, as in the Dover Bible.

49. As also in Aquitaine, that part of France with which relations were particularly close during the middle decades of the century.

50. Tristram, *English Medieval Wall Painting*, I, 15 ff. Reproduced, Boase, *op. cit.*, plate 25.

51. This incident, related in Acts 28, is rarely depicted. It occurred shortly after Paul landed on Malta: he was building a fire with sticks when a viper attacked his hand.

52. Tristram, *op. cit.*, 21 ff. From surviving fragments of decoration on the stringcourse and window splay it would seem that originally the whole chapel was painted.

53. Saxl compares the Canterbury Paul with Paul in the scene of his conversion in the Cappella Palatina, Palermo. Saxl and Wittkower, *op. cit.*, No. 26, figures 1 and 2.

54. It may be remembered that Lewes Priory, a **p. 89** daughter of Cluny, was only a few miles from Canterbury. On painting connected with Lewes, see Baker, 'Lewes Priory and the Early Group of Wall Paintings in Sussex'. Little survives of Continental Cluniac painting, but its quality can be judged from the frescoes in St Hugh's Chapel, Berzé-la-Ville (Saône-et-Loire), dating from *c.* 1100. Joan Evans, *Cluniac Art of the Romanesque Period* (Cambridge, 1950), figures 21–4, 186, and 187.

55. Tristram, *op. cit.*, 20. For a description of Lambeth 3, see below.

56. *Op. cit.*, 27–36. The paintings are described and many are reproduced, plates 28–43. See also *Twelfth Century Paintings at Hardham and Clayton* with introduction by Clive Bell.

57. Tristram, *op. cit.*, 33. They may be compared also with the earlier Ælfric Pentateuch pictures (Plate 35).

58. On the façade of the Church of Sainte-Foy. **p. 90** Reproduced Arthur Gardner, *Medieval Sculpture in France* (Cambridge, 1931), figure 57.

59. *Twelfth Century Paintings*, plate 35.

60. See Henri Focillon, *Peintures romanes des églises de France* (Paris, 1938), 19–34, plates 1–39, especially some of the Old Testament pictures of the nave, as plates 6–23.

61. There are other wall paintings, or traces of them, in Sussex. At Coombes the walls of the tiny church were apparently covered with paintings which have recently been uncovered by Mr E. Clive Rouse. The subjects include scenes from the Infancy Cycle, Christ giving the key to St Peter and the book to St Paul, and a remarkable grotesque caryatid crouching in the soffit of the chancel arch. The style seems to be closer to Hardham than to Clayton; the paintings are probably early twelfth century.

62. See Émile Mâle, *L'Art religieux du XIIe siècle en France* (Paris, 1928), 378.

63. How much wall painting has been destroyed **p. 91** or is still hidden under plaster is, of course, impossible to guess. The discoveries of recent years, chiefly by Mr Rouse, suggest that more examples may yet come to light.

64. The second volume, sadly mutilated by having almost all the initials cut out, was identified by Millar in the Museum at Maidstone. Millar, *op. cit.*, 32.

65. Two historiated initials are reproduced, Nicolette Gray, *Jacob's Ladder* (London, 1949), plates

xviiid and xxvia. The text of this book was written for a child, but the plates consist entirely of reproductions from English manuscripts of the tenth to the twelfth centuries.

p. 91 66. Reproduced, Gardner, *Medieval Sculpture in France*, figure 52. Since this sculpture dates well before the middle of the twelfth century, it would seem that it might have influenced this style of painting; but on the other hand, there is much that is Byzantine in both the sculpture of Aquitaine and in the Lambeth Bible, and the most likely explanation seems to be a common Byzantine source, modified in both cases by the twelfth century propensity for powerful linear pattern.

p. 92 67. A small champlevé enamel plaque in the Victoria and Albert Museum has a Last Judgement in precisely this style; reproduced in a small booklet, entitled *Romanesque Art* (Victoria and Albert Museum, 1950), plate 21. The Last Judgement plaque is compared with miniatures from the Winchester Bible by H. P. Mitchell in *Burl. Mag.*, XLVII (1925), 163.

68. Professor Wormald dates the drawing in the second half of the twelfth century; see 'A Romanesque Drawing at Oxford', *Antiq. Jnl*, XII (1942), 17–21.

p. 93 69. L. W. Jones and C. R. Morey, *The Miniatures of the Manuscripts of Terence* (Princeton, 1931), 68–93.

70. Hand A is the so-called Master of the Apocrypha Drawings, Hand B the Master of the Leaping Figures. See *op. cit.*, 70 and 92–3.

71. The addition of the feast of the Dedication of the church of Shaftesbury indicates that it was given to Shaftesbury Abbey probably soon after its completion. Cf. Lansd. MS. 383 above, which was made for the same abbey.

72. Herbert, *op. cit.*, 137.

p. 94 73. No facsimile of the manuscript has been published but a small book by Oakeshott, *The Artists of the Winchester Bible*, distinguishes the various hands, names them from their principal characteristic miniatures, and reproduces many details of the illumination.

74. Millar, *op. cit.*, 34. The record is found in *Magna Vita S. Hugonis*, cap. xiii.

75. One of these was recently found and restored to its original place on fol. 203 verso, in vol. II, as bound at present.

76. Oakeshott, *Artists of the Winchester Bible*, 18 ff.

77. *Op. cit.*, 5 ff. Two details are reproduced,

Oakeshott, *The Sequence of English Medieval Art*, plates 27 and 28.

78. Oakeshott attributes this miniature to the Master of the Leaping Figures (*Artists of the Winchester Bible*, plates VII, VIII), but the figure seems too monumental in proportions and too quiet in mood for this master's style. King Antiochus is reproduced, *op. cit.*, plate XII.

79. The verso of the leaf contains scenes from the life of Samuel, certainly not by the same hand.

80. Perhaps even in other arts too. The fine Warwick (or Balfour) ciborium in the Victoria and Albert Museum has engraved figures so close to the drawing of the Morgan Master's figures as to suggest his hand in the drawing. Cf. especially the figure of Abraham in the Sacrifice of Isaac.

81. Reproduced, Oakeshott, *Artists of the Winchester Bible*, plate XXXVIII. It is the preliminary drawing for a painted initial.

82. A copy of the glossed Pauline Epistles in the Bodleian Library (MS. Auct. D.i.13) dated mid twelfth century may be an early work by this master. See *English Romanesque Illumination*, No. 16. The faces in this miniature even resemble the masks in the Terence miniatures.

83. Cf. fol. 169. The Pantocrator and a similar figure by the Genesis Master (Plate 84A above) both suggest direct influence from the Pantocrator in Italo-Byzantine apse mosaics, as at Cefalù; yet it is possible that the Morgan Master derived his type from the Genesis Master, rendering it in his own incomparable style.

84. A miniature of the Evangelist Mark and two historiated initials are reproduced, *English Romanesque Illumination*, plates 19 and 20.

85. *Op. cit.*, plates 12 and 17–18.

86. *Op. cit.*, 4.

87. Mynors, *op. cit.*, no. 147, plate 53.

88. James, *The Bestiary*.

89. *Op. cit.*, Suppl. plate 2. See above p. 76.

90. *Op. cit.*, a facsimile of this manuscript is included in James, *The Bestiary*.

91. See G. C. Druce, 'Mediaeval Bestiaries', *Jnl. Brit. Archaeol. Assn*, New series, XXV (1919–20), 52.

92. See Alexandra Konstantinowa, 'Ein englisches Bestiar', *Kunstwissenschaftliche Studien*, IV (Berlin, 1929).

93. James, *The Bestiary*, 55–9. See also James, 'The Bestiary in the University Library', *Aberdeen Univ. Bull.*, No. 36 (Jan., 1928).

THE THIRTEENTH CENTURY

*

HISTORICAL BACKGROUND

POLITICAL

Richard I (son of Henry II), King 1189–99; Third Crusade and captivity in Germany 1189–94; in France 1194–9.

John (brother of Richard), King 1199–1216; Magna Carta 1215; Fall of Constantinople 1204; loss of Normandy.

Henry III (son of John), King 1216–72; married Eleanor of Provence; great period of artistic activity under royal patronage 1230–50; veneration for Edward the Confessor; strong supporter of Pope's ambitions in England and Europe; brought in foreign craftsmen to work on new choir and shrine of the Confessor at Westminster Abbey 1245–70; Treaty of Paris 1259, all south-west France to Henry as vassal of Louis IX (d. 1270).

Edward I (son of Henry III), King 1272–1307; married Eleanor of Castile 1254; on Crusade 1270; beginning of Statutes in Parliament; Treaty of commerce with Flanders 1274.

ECCLESIASTICAL

New type of bishop, the 'University-trained professional secular'; Edmund Rich, Archbishop of Canterbury 1234–40.

Establishment of the four mendicant Orders: Dominicans 1221; Franciscans 1224; Carmelites c. 1240; Austin Friars 1248.

*

As the historical background suggests, the thirteenth, like the preceding century, is one in which foreign contacts play a large part in the formulation of artistic styles, but in this period England is no longer mainly at the receiving end. The monumental linear style evolved in the later twelfth century is still found in the earliest thirteenth century manuscripts in England, and also in the earliest thirteenth century French manuscripts, such as the Ingeborg Psalter.[1] Later in the century, the reign of Henry III saw the introduction into England of a number of foreign craftsmen working in other media, especially the mosaics and painting in the new choir of Westminster Abbey begun in 1245. Nevertheless, the pictorial style even of this Westminster School of artists displays a strong continuity with that of earlier thirteenth century English style, as it was represented in the paintings, now destroyed, of the Great Chamber of Westminster Palace; thus the Westminster or Court style, though Gothic, remained essentially independent of contemporary French work.

Several new features appear in English manuscripts during the first half of the thirteenth century. Most noticeable of all is the reduction in their size and consequently also in the scale of the script and of the illumination. Historiated initials, which in the twelfth century had consisted of a picture framed by a more or less formally designed letter, once again are treated as decorative features of the text or, as in the case of the great B of the *Beatus* page of psalters, as the sole decoration of a whole page. With the increase in importance of the initial, both decorative and historiated, new ornamental elements were introduced: scrollwork filling, diapered backgrounds, small scenes in roundels, and grotesques. Miniatures with conventionalized frames continue to be used for the preliminary series of Bible pictures in psalters and for illustrations in other texts, of which some new ones are apocalypses and chronicles. Psalter texts, which constitute by far the greatest number of illuminated manuscripts in this century, begin to introduce private devotional offices for the canonical hours, thus preparing the way for that most prolific type of medieval illuminated manuscript, the *Horae* or Books of Hours, which flooded the market in the later Middle Ages. In the thirteenth century, names of artists begin to appear more often, and in a few cases enough of their work can be identified to establish individual artistic styles. Chief among these illuminators are W., probably William, de Brailes and Matthew Paris; among painters, William of Westminster and Walter of Colchester.[2] Finally, in the thirteenth century not only do we have art in more media than previously, but there are clearer stylistic relations between the various forms.

This last feature, however, complicates considerably the matter of presentation of the material. The different forms, wall and panel painting, stained glass, manuscripts, embroideries, and decorative ceramic tiles, if discussed separately, lead one backward and forward in time, and besides fail to demonstrate the stylistic relations existing between them. A strictly chronological order is impossible, because we have not enough closely dated documentary evidence to constitute a reliable basis for tracing stages of development in any individual style. In any case, style seldom changed suddenly nor did it break completely with the past. A geographical arrangement is even more unsatisfactory, especially for manuscripts[3] which, as we have seen, cannot be assumed to have been made in centres where they were known to be in use. The most practical though perhaps the most difficult plan for dealing with this complex thirteenth century material seems to be to group it according to stylistic types in whatever medium they may occur. In some cases these can be localized or even associated with specific personalities,[4] but even where this is not true, they can be shown to mark the stages of development in Gothic art as they occurred in England.

The main headings in this scheme are:[5]

1. The survival and spread of the twelfth century figure and decorative style in various forms of art and in various parts of England *c.* 1200, but particularly at St Albans Abbey and Canterbury.

2. The evolution of Gothic decorative and illustrative style on a small scale, parallel to and sometimes influenced by French style of the second and third decades and found mainly in psalters and bibles and in stained glass – all produced chiefly in the south of England, notably at Canterbury.

3. The reincarnation of English outline drawing style, with figures firmly drawn on a large scale, and enriched with Gothic pattern, with or without colour; this is associated chiefly with Matthew Paris in illumination and Walter of Colchester in painting, both working at St Albans Abbey about the middle of the thirteenth century.

4. The emergence of a fully developed, typically English Gothic figure style characterized by linear contour drawing, vigorous modelling of faces, and richly shaded draperies; this is the achievement of the Westminster or Court School in the last third of the century.

1. The Monumental Painting Style of circa 1200

Two manuscripts of *c.* 1200 from St Albans Abbey,[6] and probably illuminated there, will serve to introduce the typical thirteenth century style in England: a Glossed Epistles of St Paul (Camb., Trin. Coll., MS. O.5.8), and a Glossed Gospels (MS. B.5.3). Of the two, the illumination in the Gospels is the finer in quality, although, apart from the Canon Tables, it is limited to the symbols of the Evangelists in foliated initials at the beginnings of the Gospel Books. The winged man, symbol of St Matthew in the tetramorph on fol. 4 verso (Plate 90A), is painted in a masterly style which, in the solidity of the figure, in the modelling of the head, and in the colouring – rich blue and red, and delicate pink and green – furnishes a link between the late twelfth century style as developed at Winchester, especially that of the Morgan and the Gothic Masters, and that of the five preliminary Bible pictures[7] of a psalter made for Westminster Abbey (Brit. Mus., Roy. MS. 2 A. xxii (fol. 12 verso; Plate 90B). In fact, the style of these two manuscripts is so similar that there seems little doubt that the pictures were painted by the same artist. The pictures of the Westminster Psalter also are very close in style and feeling to the work of the so-called Master of the Gothic Majesty of the Winchester Bible (cf. Plate 85B), and this suggests the possibility that the Winchester artist may later have worked at St Albans, to which centre Dr James[8] long ago tentatively attributed the Westminster Psalter.

The style of the Westminster miniatures is magnificent in the firmness and clarity of the drawing (fol. 14; Plate 89) and in the richness of the gold and colours. Against a burnished gold ground within a framed mandorla Christ is seated frontally on a red and green rainbow, his feet resting on a similar smaller one. He is clothed in a deep blue tunic having a red embroidered neck band and powdered with groups of tiny white dots. His mantle is pale tan shaded with deeper tones of the same. The border of the miniature is in blue monochrome. The flesh of the face, hands, and feet of Christ is modelled on a yellowish ground with shadows in brown or green; his hair and beard are reddish brown. The modelling of the figure is of the solid, bulky type of the Morgan Leaf, but the draperies are flatter and the contour line is irregular as in the style of the Master of the Gothic Majesty. Still, it is amazing what a convincing figure has been produced by means of the heavy black outline and the lightly shaded drapery folds. It is the drawing which is primarily responsible for the monumentality of this figure, as of the Trinity College Matthew.

Wherever the miniatures of Roy. MS. 2 A. xxii may have been painted, whether at St

Albans or elsewhere, two other psalters of only slightly later date must, it seems, have come out of the same atelier (Brit. Mus., Roy. MS. I D. x[9] and Arundel MS. 157). Both psalters are preceded by much fuller series of New Testament pictures than are found in Roy. 2 A. xxii; these series, though not corresponding with each other exactly, indicate a common archetype.[10] Of the two, Roy. MS. I D. x is the better in quality, and it is also closer to Roy. 2 A. xxii in style. But the faces show an exaggeration of the modelling lines and the expressions and gestures have crystallized into linear conventions; also the colouring is brighter than in Roy. 2 A. xxii. Still, the richly painted miniatures, the monochrome patterns of the frames, and the dotted ornament of the background link all three psalters closely in a style that seems to be associated with St Albans.

At Canterbury at the beginning of the thirteenth century large manuscripts were still being made. A psalter, the third and last of the copies made of the Carolingian Utrecht Psalter (Paris, Bib. Nat., MS. lat. 8846), was written and partly illustrated there[11] with framed miniatures which follow in general the subjects of the original and of the two other copies, but are painted in the monumental style of c. 1200. In addition to the psalter illustrations, the text is preceded by a series of magnificent Bible pictures in the same style.[12]

Plate 91 reproduces the miniature on fol. 90 verso illustrating Psalm 51 (52 in A.V. numbering), which can be compared with the Eadwine Psalter illustration for the same psalm in Plate 72A. The picture space is divided by an irregular formal band into two main compartments – Heaven and earth – following the idea of the rolling ground line used with the same purpose in the Eadwine Psalter. In Heaven, the half-length figure of the Deity appears in an oddly shaped frame, which was derived from the mandorla as in plate 72A but without its meaning; outside this frame is a conventionalized cloud-band. The other figures, 'the righteous' (verse 6) who see and laugh at the downfall of the wicked 'mighty man', are more solemn than in the Eadwine miniature; but their number is the same and they are in relatively similar positions. In the earth compartment, the wicked man sits in his 'tent' – a columned basilican building in Romanesque style, with a nave and aisles and a clerestory above the aisle roof – holding his sword and presumably giving orders for more wickedness. The figures are larger in the Paris miniature and they completely fill the spaces between the columns of the building; there is room for only three instead of four. The Psalmist and the 'green olive-tree' to which he likens himself occupy central positions in the lower compartment in both miniatures, and the Psalmist holds in his right hand the 'sharp razor' (verse 2) and points upward to God with his left hand.

Evidently the empty lower right corner in the Eadwine miniature did not please the artist of the Paris miniature, especially since the punishment of the wicked man found no place in the picture he was copying. So he introduces the offender again in this space and shows him falling on his head, 'rooted out of the land of the living' (verse 5), and in addition, true to the thirteenth century artist's *horror vacui*, he fills the lower corner of his miniature with more architecture, brightly coloured and shaded, to balance that on the other side.

The styles of the two miniatures are strikingly different. If the artist of the Eadwine Psalter sacrificed most of the excitement of the earlier models to his interest in coloured patterns, the artist of the Paris Psalter has deliberately eliminated what remained of its informal narrative interest and endowed the theme and the actors with the uncompromising solemnity of a justly administered judgement scene. The figures are marvellously painted, with heavy drapery swinging about them in bold sweeping curves, and with strongly modelled faces. The style was undoubtedly affected by the Winchester Bible and is perhaps closest to that of the Genesis Master (Plate 84A); but it is more linear. There is much of the imposing monumentality of the Dover and Lambeth Bibles but none of their stylization. This is mature Romanesque painting at its finest – in scale, in design, in technique, and in the rich colouring set off by the highly burnished plain gold background.

Several large illuminated Bibles of *c.* 1200 are also connected with Canterbury, but it is problematical whether their decoration was executed at Canterbury or in Normandy. The connexion with Canterbury is documented by a colophon in the three-volume 'Manerius Bible' in Paris (Bib. Ste-Geneviève MS. 8–10), written by 'Manerius scriptor cantuariensis'.[13] The illumination consists of historiated and decorative initials, painted in colour on gold grounds, but the style does not seem to tie up with the Canterbury style as represented by the Paris Psalter, and it may be Continental. Two related Bibles are in the Bibliothèque Nationale[14] in Paris (MSS lat. 11534–5 and 16743–6).

Another large Bible[15] (Morgan MS. 791) surpasses in scale and magnificence the Manerius Bible; it has similar initials which have been painted on separate pieces of vellum and pasted into spaces left for them in the appropriate text.[16] The full-page Trinity (fol. 4 verso; Plate 92) with choirs of angels, and creation scenes in roundels is a superb example of the style. The gold ground is very highly burnished and against it the richly coloured draperies of the figures, and the fine-coiled ribbon ornament with little animals crushed between the strands which fill the spaces between the roundels in the lower half of the page, give it a brilliance which is not surpassed in any other work of the period. The design is formal, arranged in compartments, like the miniatures in Paris MS. 8846. The central group of the Trinity has an unusual representation of Christ, the Second Person, as a small figure standing enclosed within the mantle of God the Father, and the Dove flying upward between them. It is particularly impressive because of the plain gold space surrounding it. Other interesting details of the page are the creation and fall of the angels, the four Continents – the names *Parse* and *Ethiopia* are legible – and the twelve prophets arranged in two rows of three on each side of the quatrefoil medallion containing the Trinity. The faces are modelled strongly with reddish brown colour and suggest the modelling of the Ste-Geneviève Bible; but the pale lovely colour of the Morgan Bible and the decorative designs constituting a well balanced all-over pattern seem closer to Paris MS. 8846 than to Ste-Geneviève MS. 8. On these grounds it seems likely that the Morgan Bible and the Paris Psalter may have been illuminated in Canterbury and the Manerius Bible and related manuscripts in Normandy. There is further evidence of the Canterbury attribution in the stylistic relation of the two manuscripts to stained glass.[17]

By far the greatest amount of English stained glass of late twelfth and early thirteenth century date is found at Canterbury. It all belongs to the period of rebuilding after the fire of 1174; there is nothing earlier.[18] The scheme of subject matter in the glass was elaborate. In the choir clerestory was a double row of figures representing the ancestors of Christ and Old Testament scenes dating from *c.* 1180. In the choir aisles were twelve theological windows, a concordance of Old and New Testament scenes of which fragments are now gathered in two windows of the north choir aisle (*c.* 1200–15). There were twelve windows in the aisles of the Chapel of the Holy Trinity with scenes of the miracles and probably of the life and martyrdom of Thomas Becket. Of these only the miracle scenes survive; they date from the second and third decades of the thirteenth century. In the Corona, at the extreme eastern end, are medallion windows[19] of *c.* 1220 with further scenes from the Old and the New Testaments.

The scenes of the genealogy and concordance in the earlier windows are in rectangular panels. One of the finest of these figures is Methuselah (Plate 93). The figure is monumental in its conception with the imposing proportions and gestures and the intense expression of the finest figures in the Byzantinesque late twelfth century style. The pose is conceived on a grand scale and magnificently rendered: one knee is drawn up, with the foot supported on the step of the seat and the elbow of the bent arm resting on the knee. Balance is maintained by the outstretched foot and the left hand tensely holding the left knee. The drapery is wrapped round the body in heavy folds which follow the curves of the figure and accentuate the balance of the composition as a whole. The loose fingers of the right hand stroking the beard and the gaze of the eyes turned away from the direction in which the head is facing give to the figure an overwhelming feeling of power and repose. The massiveness of the Methuselah figure is relieved by the bands of decorative pattern on the tunic, by the design of the cushion, and by the scrollwork in the spandrels of the arch under which he is seated. The colours are chiefly blue and red, with lighter tones in tan and a very little yellow and green.

The imposing style of the patriarch Methuselah, which is unquestionable Canterbury work, further supports the Canterbury attribution of the miniatures in the Paris Psalter and the Morgan Bible (cf. Plates 91 and 92). Especially striking are the similarity in the massive heads, in the poses, and in the thick, heavy draperies that swing about the body with no loose flying ends. The dignity and solemnity of the mood, though characteristic of Romanesque art in general, seems particularly consistent in the Canterbury manuscripts and glass. The designs of the fine late twelfth century figures in the glass at Canterbury may well have been drawn from a manuscript such as the Paris Psalter.

Two manuscripts in the British Museum dating from *c.* 1200 which show some evidence of intended use in other arts, painting and stained glass, are the fully illustrated lives of two saints: Bede's Life of St Cuthbert (Add. MS. 39943) made perhaps at Durham,[20] and Harl. Roll Y.6 containing eighteen outline drawings of the life of St Guthlac in roundels, made at or for Croyland Abbey, near Peterborough, in the Fenlands.[21]

Of the Cuthbert manuscript (Add. MS. 39943) there is a Durham record[22] that it was loaned to Richard le Scrope, Archbishop of York, presumably to serve as a model for a projected window dedicated to St Cuthbert in York Cathedral. Scrope was executed in 1405 and the window was not actually inserted until nearly a half-century later,[23] but there is further evidence that the Cuthbert manuscript was ultimately used for designs not of stained glass but of painting, in the choir stalls of Carlisle Cathedral in the late fifteenth century.[24] Forty-five pictures from the life of St Cuthbert now remain in Add.

39943 out of a probable fifty-five.[25] Among the many interesting scenes from the life of the Saint, the first miniature (fol. 1 verso; Plate 94B) stands out because of the fine quality of the painting and also for the general resemblance it bears to an earlier wall painting at Durham now, unfortunately, much restored.[26] The technique of the miniature is that of monumental painting. The Saint stands firmly and quietly against a panelled ground the centre of which is gold, while the pinkish border is powdered with groups of white dots. The modelling of the drapery and of the face is done with heavy pigments, much white being used on brownish flesh-tone for the face. The pigments are so thick that they have flaked off in places. The figure is well-proportioned and the hands and feet are drawn with skill and competence. The prostrate figure of a monk embracing the foot of the Saint is eloquent. Other miniatures in the manuscript show these same qualities of fine painting and tender devotional spirit. The manuscript is one of the best examples of the figure style at the time of transition between Romanesque and Gothic.

The Guthlac Roll (Plate 95B) is not painting but outline drawing with heavy, firm, continuous contours and very little use of colour. If the Cuthbert miniatures suggest wall painting, the Guthlac roundels suggest designs for stained glass (cf. Plate 95A) or possibly enamels.[27] The simple, flat canopy-like architecture with the figures in an undefined spatial relation to it; the tall, slender figures with long straight or elegantly curving drapery folds; the many lines used as shading on the figures as well as for contour; and the use of inscriptions to explain the scenes, place the compositions of the roundels in the category of glass painting, although no body colour is used. The form of the Guthlac Roll is almost unique in late medieval manuscripts, that is, the rotulus or roll rather than the codex or book form. It would seem that the pictures were indeed intended for use in some other form of art; but no evidence of what or where this may have been has come down to us.

2. The Gothic Small Scale Style (circa 1200–50)

The monumental painting style of the preliminary miniatures of the Westminster Psalter is not carried over into the initials, not even the great B of the *Beatus*. The initials are by a different hand and introduce the principal psalms. The B of the *Beatus* follows the general form which was established as early as the late tenth century (cf. Plate 21B), but the scrolled acanthus which earlier filled the letter has been reduced to a fine-sprung pattern of bare ribbon scrolls, overlapping and interlacing at intervals, and ending in conventionalized leaf motifs.[28] Within the scrolls, little animals clamber about. Another new feature is the introduction of roundels containing small scenes from the life of David in place of the interlace at the terminals of the upright of the B. The whole initial is on a patterned coloured ground surrounded by a green painted outline such as was first used, perhaps, in the initials of the Winchester Bible.

The style thus described in Roy. MS. 2 A. xxii has undergone some changes in the slightly later related psalters, Roy. MS. 1 D. x and Arundel MS. 157. The patterned background has been replaced by jewel-like diapering; the scrolls have become more tightly sprung, and the leaves have been reduced to the scale of the stems. Animals are livelier, even though often they are not true animals but only lacertine-like heads crushed between the coils of the spirals. There is brilliance and tautness in the intricate design of the initial, and the page with its rich diaper is well set off by the surrounding line of green. This style of *Beatus* pages we shall find repeated, with variations, in many other early thirteenth century English psalters.[29]

The fully developed English psalter style of *c.* 1220 was not confined to manuscripts made in the south of England. The Munich Psalter (Munich, Staatsbibl., Cod. lat. 835), according to liturgical evidence, was written and illuminated at Gloucester before 1222. Its *Beatus* page[30] has the slender interlacing ribbon coils with conventional leaves and animals, elaborate interlaced terminals[31] to the initial letter, and medallions and half medallions with scenes from the life of David applied to the border, which contains a version of Greek key pattern. Other illuminations consist of preliminary Bible pictures and historiated initials for the principal psalms.

Another very fine psalter of similar type and of about the same time was made, according to a thirteenth–fourteenth century inscription, for Robert de Lindesey, Abbot of Peterborough 1214–22.[32] On fols 35 verso and 36 of this psalter (London, Soc. of Antiquaries, MS. 59) are two full-page miniatures, the Crucifixion and Christ in Majesty,[33] painted in rich colour on patterned gold grounds, preceded by three pages each with two scenes from the life of Christ in brown and green tinted outline. A magnificent *Beatus* initial on fol. 38 verso (Plate 100) has eight roundels and two trefoil medallions with David and the Musicians and four prophets. The background is diapered in deep blue with white and red patterns. The richly shaded leaf motifs and the charming little rabbits and squirrels playing hide and seek among the branches give variety and life to the fine but otherwise rather formal designs.

It is high time now to introduce officially a significant new motif, the animal grotesque, which began to make its appearance in English psalter decoration in the early thirteenth century, and multiplied prodigiously during the course of the century. This curious form, which ultimately became almost a hallmark of English illumination, seems to have been evolved from two main sources. The lively little creatures, sometimes naturalistic, more often fantastic, which even as far back as the earliest Canterbury school of illumination[34] were climbing in and out of the foliage of the initial letters, by the end of the twelfth century had taken on new vigour and refused to be confined any longer within the limits of the decoration. About the same time, many more naturalistic animals recruited from the Bestiaries[35] began to swell the ranks of animal grotesques and, as they increased in number and variety, took on human attributes. The final outcome of this development was the use of the grotesque to caricature human and especially monkish frailties, which reached its climax at the end of the thirteenth and the beginning of the fourteenth century.

Perhaps the earliest examples of the grotesque clearly used with humorous intention are found in two early thirteenth century psalters (Brit. Mus., Harl. MS. 5102 and Lansd. MS. 420). Harley MS. 5102, which seems to be slightly the earlier of the two, has on fol. 3 a monkey in a cowl, on fol. 6 a human-animal-bird grotesque, and on fol. 13 verso a donkey playing a harp. Other pages show a fox in a cowl leaning on a crutch (fol. 46 verso), an ibex (fol. 50), and a goat playing a rebec (fol. 59). Similar musician animal grotesques are found in roundels on the *Beatus* page of Lands. MS. 420 (fol. 12 verso; Plate 94A): a donkey with a harp, a goat with a rebec, a lion, a monkey, a bear, a squirrel, a porcupine, an ibex, and a rabbit – most of these good Bestiary animals. In this same manuscript the grotesque is included in a new kind of marginal decoration which possibly resulted from French influence, namely, elaborate red and blue penwork containing a head, or an arm and hand, or most often a fish and occasionally a dragon. Towards the latter part of the manuscript, animals in human rôles, perhaps inspired by those in the *Beatus* initial, appear in the marginal penwork and in the line endings; among these are a goat's head wearing a mitre, and a fox with a crozier. The typical thirteenth century vogue for grotesque inventions is in full swing.

Harley MS. 5102 has neither preliminary Bible pictures nor Calendar,[36] but these may have been lost; however, five full-page miniatures, probably of contemporary date, have been inserted at intervals in the text.[37] Lansdowne MS. 420 has an elaborate series of preliminary Bible pictures showing close affinities in subjects with those of Roy. MS. 1 D. X and Arundel MS. 157, but the Lansdowne pictures are composed within roundels like the scenes in the *Beatus* page (Plate 94A) which suggest the influence of stained-glass medallions.[38] The background of the *Beatus* page is patterned with arabesque scrolls similar to those which are found in thirteenth century English stained-glass windows.

The later Canterbury glass windows are designed in medallions[39] (Plates 95A and 97), and both in the scale of the composition and in the type of the design they are more closely comparable to manuscript illumination than was twelfth century glass. The medallion in plate 95A has already been compared in certain respects with the medallion from the Guthlac Roll; but there are also many differences between the drawing technique of the Guthlac Roll and the richly coloured glass of the Canterbury medallion. To begin with, the background in the glass medallion is completely covered with an arabesque pattern in blue, and this ground appearing in all the interstices of the figure group and the architectural setting gives to the design that quality of all-over pattern which, with its balancing of colour areas, produces the finest stained-glass harmony. The details of the scene are scaled to the smaller size of the medallion and fitted with a minimum of empty space into the round shape. The liveliness of the figures, the brilliance of the colour, and the sparkling jewel-like effect of the medallion glass has much more of the quality of illumination in colour on gold than of outline drawing. There is even evidence that the Canterbury glass directly influenced the design of manuscript pages (cf. Plates 97 and 96) produced about the same time at Canterbury; this influence of stained-glass design on manuscripts becomes even more marked towards the middle of the thirteenth century.

The Bible of Robert de Bello[40] (Brit. Mus., Burney MS. 3; Plate 96) referred to above in connexion with the Canterbury medallion glass, illustrates well the thirteenth century trend towards smaller size in manuscripts and greatly reduced scale in figures and compositions as compared with manuscripts of the preceding centuries. Folio 5 verso, the Genesis page, has the initial filled with medallions, some overlapping, others linked together, containing scenes from Genesis and Exodus, and a Trinity. The figures are small and, though lively enough, are drawn and coloured with little attention to modelling.

The spaces around the medallions are filled with leafless stem scrolls such as are used also for other initials in the Bible. The influence of French manuscripts[41] was accountable for some characteristics of English manuscripts of this period, such as the flat, linear draperies, the white faces with features drawn in ink, the pale colouring, and the increase in decorative elements, especially the drolleries and ornamental penwork in red or blue introduced into the margins. There are other presumably English manuscripts of slightly later date which follow the contemporary French style so closely during this period as to be hardly distinguishable from them;[42] but in general there is greater liveliness and variety in the English figures and often a quaint unconventionality in the representations which distinguish them from the consistently meticulous but sometimes monotonously repetitious Parisian work.

To the third and fourth decades of the thirteenth century belongs the first work 'signed' by an English illuminator, W. de Brailes.[43] Three times his name appears beside the picture of a tonsured cleric: twice in the margins of a small book of Sarum Hours (Malvern, Dyson Perrins MS. 4), on fol. 43 with the words 'qui me depeint', and on fol. 47 the name alone; and once with the words, 'qui me fecit' on one of the six single leaves now in the Fitzwilliam Museum, containing the Last Judgement (Plate 99A). Other works recognized by their style as partly by him are a psalter in New College, Oxford (MS. 322), one historiated initial (for Psalm 109; Plate 99C) in a psalter in Sir Sydney Cockerell's collection (Kew, Surrey), and some initials in a small Bible in the Dyson Perrins Collection (MS. 5). To this list have been added in recent years twenty-seven small leaves unsigned (MS. 500 in the Walters Art Gallery, Baltimore) containing single miniatures with Old and New Testament subjects (Plate 99B) which Swarzenski suggests may have been prefixed originally to the Perrins Hours.[44] Seven additional leaves obviously from the same series were discovered later by Dr Millar in Paris.[45] The style in all of these illuminations is unmistakable, but they are certainly not all by the same hand, and it must be concluded that W. de Brailes directed a scriptorium or atelier in which there were a number of assistants.[46]

The characteristics of the 'signed' work may be taken as typical of de Brailes' style. They may be described briefly as the peculiar facial types, the unusual subjects, originality in the representations, and scrolls with Latin or French inscriptions. The facial types are well represented in plates 98 and 99: short, round faces with broad foreheads; long straight noses almost joining the mouths; eyes with accentuated whites and the iris crowded into one corner; and all the features strongly indicated with black lines. There is, however, some shading in white on the faces and in some cases considerable shading in dark tones and occasionally cross-hatching in white on the drapery. Colours are mainly pink and blue with a little red; the backgrounds are gold.

The originality of de Brailes' treatment of his subjects is well illustrated in his interpretation of the Fall of Man (Plate 98). In the top left roundel is recorded Adam's shamefaced excuse to an accusing God: 'The woman gave it me'; Eve's defence, top right: 'The serpent tempted me'; and the smug smile on the face of the serpent; God's 'no-nonsense now' manner as he puts shifts over the heads of his disobedient children; Adam's furious spade work and Eve's sullen and clumsy efforts to spin; Cain balefully watching his brother and plotting his murder which he executes with an evil leer, while Adam and Eve sit apart mourning over the tragedy; an inexorable God driving a remonstrating Cain out to be a wanderer and an outcast; and Cain's sad end, killed accidentally by his own grandson while hunting in the forest. The human tragedy in William de Brailes' eyes was evidently the story of a family disaster with a strong moral cast.

In the medallion from the Last Judgement (Plate 99A), de Brailes, looking none too happy, hopefully carries his credentials ('W. de Brailes me fecit') in his hand which is grasped firmly by a lusty angel flourishing a huge sword over the heads of the other shivering souls. De Brailes is a lively artist if not a great one; what his figures lack in monumentality they make up in originality of interpretation, with the result that in pictures by his hand there is never a dull moment.

Swarzenski suggests[47] a chronological order for the de Brailes manuscripts on the ground of the development of their style from Romanesque to Gothic; he places the Fitzwilliam leaves earliest and the Walters leaves last. The closeness of the style of these two manuscripts, however (Plates 98 and 99B), seems not to support this sequence. On the other hand, the decoration of the New College Psalter which, as Swarzenski notes, is very close to the Rutland Psalter dated about 1250, would suggest that the New College manuscript may be the most Gothic phase of de Brailes' style. Moreover, the fact that only the most showy of the miniatures in the New College manuscript are by his own hand seems to indicate a late date when richer decorative elements, perhaps influenced by the French Gothic style, have further affected the design of the miniatures.

These designs are clearly related to roundels of stained glass and wall painting; and it is interesting to note that several medallions containing single figures of apostles occur also in some contemporary paintings in the vaulting of the Chapter House of Christ Church Cathedral, Oxford, which have been attributed by James and Tristram[48] to de Brailes, or at least to designs by him. The condition of the paintings at present makes it difficult to establish any clear stylistic connexion, but the general form and the types of the figures seem to be similar to his style in the manuscripts.

Nothing is actually known of the provenance of the psalter belonging to the Duke of Rutland[49] (Belvoir Castle), though an obit occurs in the Calendar (May 24, fol. 3) of 'domini Edmundi de Laci', who may have been Edmund de Lacy, Earl of Lincoln (d. 1258). The Sarum Calendar (fols 1–6) contains the signs of the zodiac and the labours of the months in roundels. Every text page thereafter has a band down the left margin containing initials in gold or colour for each verse of every psalm. Folio 8 verso has a magnificent *Beatus* initial with David playing the harp and the Judgement of Solomon; and preceding six of the principal psalms are fine full-page biblical miniatures. But the glory and distinction of the Rutland Psalter is the wealth of marginal grotesques and the exquisite and lavish foliage decoration. (Cf. de Brailes, Plate 99C.)

Also contemporary with de Brailes but differing greatly from his style is a small group of very beautiful manuscripts executed *c.* 1240–60 for different monastic houses or for individuals in them and associated by Sir Sydney Cockerell[50] with the scriptorium of the new cathedral at Salisbury, built 1220–36. These are: (1) a Psalter made for a convent of nuns[51] (Oxford, All Souls Coll., MS. lat. 6); (2) a Psalter made for Wilton Abbey, near

Salisbury (London, Royal College of Physicians); (3) the 'Missal of Henry of Chichester' in the John Rylands Library in Manchester (MS. lat. R.24); and (4) the Bible of William de Hales in the British Museum (Roy. MS. I B. xii). The figure style of these manuscripts seems to be derived from the earlier Peterborough style of the Psalter of Robert de Lindesey and is more tranquil in mood and without the captiousness of William de Brailes. There is also a stronger feeling of Gothic elegance, particularly in the draperies. The All Souls Psalter has four preliminary miniatures representing the Annunciation (fol. 3), the Virgin nursing the Child (fol. 4), the Crucifixion (fol. 5; Plate 102), and Christ in Majesty (fol. 6). The Calendar (fols 7–12 verso) has no illustrations. On fol. 13 is a magnificent *Beatus* initial with a Tree of Jesse, a sybil, and prophets; and in roundels, small Old Testament scenes.

The Crucifixion is a very fine example of the style which uses line both for emphasis on contour and for decorative patterns, as on the thigh and shoulder of John. The figures are tall and slender and without solidity. The poses and gestures are unnatural, but are designed to express intense emotion; the swaying Virgin half turns away from the cross, with hands clasped tightly and head bowed in grief; John, nervously fingering the fold of his mantle with one hand, rests his cheek momentarily on the other as he strides towards the cross. Between these two is the dead Christ, quiet on the cross, emaciated and bleeding but sublime in features and form. Only the fluttering end of the knotted drapery shows life. The cross is the usual English form of lopped tree trunk. Above, God the Father, flanked by censing angels, receives the spirit of Christ represented by a dove. Below are the dead rising from the tomb, and at the sides the triumphant Church and the toppling Synagogue. The burnished gold background is incised with diamond patterns enclosing quatrefoils. The colour is intense – blue, pink, red, and green; the heavy contour lines are black.

The Crucifixion of the All Souls Psalter illustrates perfectly the balance between rich linear pattern and strong contour drawing in the figures, between symbolism and human emotion.

By contrast, this balance is rudely upset in the almost identical composition of the same subject in the Evesham Psalter (Brit. Mus., Add. MS. 44874, fol. 6, Plate 103). The very similarities in such details as the Tree-Cross, the poses and gestures of the figures, and the arrangement of the draperies serve to accentuate the differences between the two styles. Of these differences, the most striking are exaggeratedly English features in the Evesham Psalter, namely a total disregard of even the conventions of anatomy and an obsession with rich chiaroscuro patterns not only in the drapery but in the torso of the Christ; and a gripping emotional tension which is centred in the contrast between the suffering, drawn expression of the dying Christ and the wide-open, staring eyes of Mary and John. This emotion is reflected even in the faces of the sun and the moon held by the solemn angels who lean out of the picture above the cross. The technique is shaded line drawing, suggestive of the Matthew Paris style (see below) but crisper, harder, and much more patternistic owing to the deep angular drapery folds, the broken body contours, and the heavy shading. The colours are green, blue, brown, and red. The body of Christ and all the faces are modelled in brown with a red spot on the cheek. The background of the miniature is burnished gold except behind the cross where a design in flat red sprinkled with small white star and circle motifs follows the shape of the cross and extends down the sides and across the bottom of the miniature. A plain frame (contrasting with the ornate border with medallions in the All Souls miniature) surrounds the picture, but it is indicative of the dramatic character of the painting that the cross and the figures of Mary and John extend boldly out beyond the frame, overlapping it. The monumental scale of the composition, again as in the Matthew Paris style, suggests wall painting, but no work associated with Matthew Paris can compare with this in dynamic power. Eric Millar has rightly described the Evesham Crucifixion painting as 'reaching the high water mark of English illumination of the period'.[52]

On the verso of fol. 6 of the Evesham Psalter there is a fine vernicle which also suggests Matthew Paris in subject though not quite in spirit. The Calendar and the principal psalms of the Psalter are illustrated with small miniatures in what seems to be a somewhat different style, though it is possible that the smaller scale and the lighter character of the subject matter may account for the differences. Some of the historiated initials contain grotesques, mainly of the type with serpent body and human head, and even these are painted in the shaded technique. They lack, however, the variety and inventive humour of the grotesques in the Rutland Psalter.

Returning now to the other manuscripts of the Salisbury group, the Wilton Psalter,[53] which originally must have been as lavishly decorated as the All Souls manuscript and in much the same style, now retains only two of the large initials (fols 33 and 66 verso). But the 181 smaller historiated initials and 77 decorative ones plus a great number of decorative line endings indicate the richness of the manuscript.

The Manchester Missal has eight full-page miniatures and twelve fine historiated initials.[54] The Virgin and Child (fol. 150; Plate 104), with a votive figure[55] under a foliated arch and flanked by censing angels, is close in style to the exquisite Madonna and angels of the Chichester[56] roundel (Plate 105), dating from about the same time and not far removed geographically from Salisbury, where it is suggested that the Manchester Missal was made. The figures in the miniature, like those of the roundel, have the same completely flat, linear quality in the handling of the drapery which results in graceful curves but shows no evidence of the form under it. For example, the drawing of the knee of the votive figure in the miniature with the drapery dragged over it is so similar in treatment to that in the roundel that the same artist's hand might be suspected. The roundel was designed, apparently, as a unit of ornament on the wall of the chapel of the Bishop's Palace, not as part of a larger scheme of wall painting – the kind of design, therefore, which might very well be supplied by a miniaturist. The fineness of the decorative detail with its use of silver (now badly tarnished) also suggests the work of an illuminator. In spite of the fleur-de-lis in the blue background, the style seems to be wholly English, and the closest parallel to it is found in the Salisbury style,[57] especially as in the Manchester Missal.

The Bible of William de Hales, with small historiated initials at the beginnings of the Books, is a modest member of the Salisbury group.[58] It may even be by the same hand as the All Souls Psalter, perhaps an earlier or at any rate a less sumptuous example of his art.

From about the mid thirteenth century also come two manuscripts in the British Museum, a Bible and a small Book of Hours (Roy. MS. I D. i and Egerton MS. 1151), which show French influence though they are of undisputed English workmanship: Royal I D. i is signed in a colophon on fol. 540 verso by the scribe: 'Willelmus Devoniensis scripsit istum librum.' Egerton 1151 was obviously illuminated by the same artist.

The vellum of both these small books is very fine and thin as in French thirteenth century manuscripts, and the style is linear and flat and the faces have the features drawn in with black lines (Plate 101). The subject matter is extraordinary in its liveliness and humour. In the Genesis initial, scenes of the Creation and Fall and the Crucifixion are placed under canopies instead of in roundels (cf. MS. Burney 3; Plate 96); all manner of grotesque whimsies are represented in the margins. The borders are still simple in design and almost without foliage, thus differing from the borders in the Rutland Psalter. A miniature preceding fol. 5 in the Bible of William of Devon representing a Crucifixion and a Coronation of the Virgin, and a Virgin and Child flanked by Peter and Paul, contains, in the central panel, St Martin dividing his cloak with a beggar, and in the lower margin a kneeling monk or friar. The inclusion of St Martin in so important a position has led to the theory that the Bible may have been intended for someone at Canterbury, where this Saint was particularly venerated, and this theory is further borne out by the representation in a miniature prefixed to Psalms (fol. 321 verso) of the Martyrdom of St Thomas and some legendary incidents in his life. The French characteristics of the style would fit very well with a Canterbury origin.[59]

A third manuscript closely related to the style of these two is a psalter in the Morgan Library (MS. 756) also tentatively attributed to the 'neighborhood of Canterbury'.[60] This is the most richly illuminated of the three, having eight large miniatures and many smaller ones, twenty-three medallions in the Calendar, seven large and 176 smaller illuminated initials. The margins are filled with grotesques and hunting scenes, and the style has a strong French flavour as in the case of the other two.

3. Thirteenth-century Outline Drawings

From the first half of the thirteenth century there are only a few examples of outline drawing style, that most deeply rooted and most accomplished technique of the English artist in preceding periods. At the beginning of the century the Guthlac drawings carry on the tradition in pure outline without shading and almost without colour (Plate 95B). To the first quarter of the century belong some remarkable preliminary drawings[61] of Old Testament subjects prefixed to a Bestiary (Camb., Univ. Lib., MS. KK.4.25), in a shaded line technique with coloured washes applied over parts of the figure. The pictures suggest that the artist may have been copying the fine shaded painting style of the artists of the Winchester Bible, especially the Morgan Master (Plate 86). The figures are large and solid in their contour modelling and the drapery folds fall heavily over the body. Gold is used for haloes and decorative details of dress, but the drawings have no background and no borders. The technique is new in respect to the artist's obvious intention to accomplish with line shading what the late twelfth century painter did with pigments, and the

Cambridge drawings supply an intermediate step towards the remarkable work in a similar style which is associated with the mid-thirteenth century artist, Matthew Paris.

This artist, who, like W. de Brailes, identified himself by signing some of his work, has long been known as illuminator, painter, scribe, and historian. His influence at St Albans Abbey, where he was a monk, is reflected in the production of a great many illustrated manuscripts, but their very number precludes the probability that they were all the product of his own hand. Moreover, the styles, not only of the various manuscripts but of portions and even of individual pictures in them, demonstrate beyond a doubt that he had assistants. In fact, a careful stylistic analysis of the manuscripts most commonly accepted as his work[62] based on the only signed miniature (Roy. MS. 14 C. vii, fol. 6) could, it would seem, attribute to him only a very few of the large number of tinted and untinted drawings in his general style. They are the following: (1) the well-known and justly admired Virgin and Child, with a self-portrait bearing his signature, Frater Mathias Parisiensis (Plate 106); (2) two fine heads of Christ and one of the Virgin, all on fol. 281 (Plate 108) of the *Chronica Maiora* (Camb., Corpus Christi Coll., MS. 26);[63] (3) an even finer head of Christ (Vernicle), (Corpus Christi Coll., MS. 16, fol. 49 verso; Plate 110A); (4) all the drawing and some of the tinting in the illustrations of the lives of Saints Alban and Amphibalus (Dublin, Trin. Coll., MS. E.1.40, fol. 31; Plate 107A), perhaps Matthew Paris's earliest work; (5) some original sketches for marginal drawings in the two Cambridge manuscripts named above, e.g. fol. 215 in MS. 16 and p. 66 in MS. 26.

The first three drawings listed are examples of a monumental style based on late Romanesque painted figures such as in the preliminary miniatures of Roy. MS. 2 A. xxii (Plates 89 and 90B); the style may even have been derived from these very miniatures. Characteristic features of this monumental style are the firm, heavy proportions of the figures, the strong black contour lines which model the figure, the large, solid heads with solemn expressions, the thick, heavy draperies arranged in simple, broad, rhythmic curves and appearing to form a roll at the edges; and, finally, the shading with colour which reflects a painting technique rather than an all-over pattern. The *Historia Anglorum* (Roy. MS. 14 C. vii) was the last work of Matthew Paris. On fol. 218 verso is a picture by another artist of Matthew Paris lying on his deathbed, his elbow resting on a book inscribed 'Liber Cronicorum Mathei parisiensis', accompanied by an inscription, 'hic obit matheus parisiensis'. The date of the last item of the *Historia* written in his own hand is 1259, and it is assumed that this was the year of his death.

The extraordinary 'painterly' quality of the heads of Christ and of the Virgin in Corpus Christi College MSS 26 and 16 (Plates 108 and 110A) is evident when they are compared with the earlier wall paintings in the Chapel of the Holy Sepulchre, Winchester Cathedral (Plate 109). The head of Christ at Winchester might well have furnished the model for both the drawings by Paris, but especially the finer one (Plate 110A). The frontal facial type is the same, and the eyes, ears, and hair, and even the jewelled neckband (as in Plate 108) are alike. The other head of Christ on this page might have been drawn from the Deposition scene in the Winchester paintings. No close painted parallel for the Virgin and Child has been found, but the heads surrounded by clouds might come from a medallion such as those which still exist in the Chapel of the Holy Sepulchre at Winchester.

Although there is some evidence as to the ability of Matthew Paris as a panel painter, at St Albans, where we might expect to recognize his hand in some of the paintings on the piers of the nave, the work bears no resemblance to his style and, in fact, is known to have been done largely by another artist, Walter of Colchester[64] and his associates. At Windsor, however, in the cloister of St George's Chapel, there are remains of paintings of kings' heads which seem very close to the large-scale heads of Paris and perhaps may be attributed to him.[65]

Judging from the most obvious differences in style among the various miniatures attributed to him, Matthew Paris had at least two principal assistants, and probably there were other scribes and illuminators who participated in the large number of manuscripts to be ascribed, largely on a stylistic basis, to the scriptorium at St Albans. To one of the most competent of these assistants I should attribute at least part of the illustrations in *La Estoire de Seint Aedward le Rei*[66] (Camb., Univ. Lib., MS. EE.3.59; Plate 107B) and the five tinted pen drawings on fols 219 verso to 221 verso of Roy. MS. 2 A. xxii in the British Museum. These drawings are also on a monumental scale and clearly are inspired by Paris's style, if not copied from his own drawings.[67] The style of this assistant's work, however, seems to have a more irregular contour line, richer decorative detail, more painstaking execution, and less convincing figure modelling. The King (fol. 219 verso) and the Bishop (fol. 221) have something of the crispness and elegance of mid-thirteenth century French sculpture. Though wash colour is applied, it is not always used for shading to indicate depth of drapery folds or modelling of face or figure but often merely for decorative purposes.[68] The St Edward miniatures imitate most closely Paris's illustrative style as seen in the Life of St Alban (Dublin, Trin. Coll., MS. E.I.40; Plate 107A).

The second of Paris's recognizable assistants seems even closer to the Master's style in the thickset figures and the convincing gestures and expressions; but this assistant uses a linear formula which gives the pictures a monotonous sameness in figure types. To this second assistant I should attribute the marginal pictures which, with their text, may have been added later than the original writing, to Corpus Christi Coll., MSS 26 and 16. Some of this work is certainly by the Franciscan, Brother William the Englishman, whose picture appears on fol. 67 of MS. 16, and who signed a full-page picture of the Apocalyptic Christ (fol. 156) in the *Lives of the Offas* (Brit. Mus., Cott. MS. Nero D.i).[69]

It is inevitable to connect the tinted outline technique and the monumental figure style of Matthew Paris and his associates at St Albans with the similar style of a group of five out of some twenty illustrated manuscripts of the Apocalypse which were nearly all certainly produced in England in the first three-quarters of the thirteenth century.[70]

At the head of the whole group – the parent of them all in age, size, and artistic splendour – is the great Trinity College Apocalypse (Camb., Trin. Coll. Lib., MS. R.16.2) dated c. 1230.[71] This magnificent volume, measuring 17 by 12 inches, has richly painted miniatures on gold and coloured grounds which, although more than a quarter century later than the preliminary miniatures of Roy. MS. 2 A. xxii, have much in common with their 'painterly' style: the large heads and solid bodies strongly suggested under their draperies, the painted backgrounds decorated with dotted patterns, and the magnificent burnished gold and fine, strong colours. On the other hand, some of the figure types remind us of the ugly, open-mouthed profiles common in the earlier Bury manuscripts which were related to the Albani Psalter.

The miniatures in the Trinity College Apocalypse are by different hands, three or perhaps four,[72] which are distributed throughout the book; the last miniatures are not finished. The first two quires (fols 1–16) are heavily modelled in the fine painting style described above;[73] the Christ in Majesty (fol. 4) has a green face, hands, and feet, and is evidently reminiscent of the Byzantine manner, as are the fine, delicately modelled figures and the rich colouring. Folios 17–24 and other pages thereafter are by the artist who is closest in style to Matthew Paris. His figures are drawn in firm outline technique sometimes without colour, sometimes with deep shading in the painted drapery folds. Backgrounds and draperies are often patterned in small dots and circles or arabesques. The figures have very large round heads with broad foreheads, especially the angels with their close-cropped curly hair. In later phases of this master's style the figures tend to become somewhat coarse, but the faces in the miniature on fol. 27 (Plate 111) are delicately painted, with shading around the eyes and spots of pink on the cheeks. The faces are all very much alike in type and expression; all have the same very large, wide-open eyes and somewhat surprised expressions. The combination of the painted and the tinted outline techniques in the same miniature is a feature of this style. The miniatures do not seem to be the work of Matthew Paris himself, even in an early phase of his style. Perhaps they are by the second of his assistants who is here credited with the drawings in Brit. Mus. Nero D.i. The third artist's style can be seen on fol. 25 verso in one of the most magnificent pages, designed in a formal, decorative style in superb colours on a burnished, tooled gold ground. The figures are exquisitely drawn with a precision of detail and a flatness of colour which seem more French than English,[74] though the vigour of the poses and the eloquence of the gestures is in the English tradition. This style, and that of the first pages, can be distinguished clearly in the matter of colouring and technique from that of the second artist, who is closest to Matthew Paris; but it is likely that all were done in the same place, and that place probably was St Albans.

The grouping of the English Apocalypse manuscripts is based on two kinds of evidence: textual, according to which Delisle divided all the known manuscripts, not only the English, into 'families',[75] and stylistic, according to which James attempted at various times to establish clear-cut groups made at specific English centres. The difficulty that arises in reconciling the two kinds of evidence in relation to any one centre indicates that more than one textual archetype was available even within one stylistic group, resulting in what James called 'contamination' of one type of illustration by another. This shows most clearly in the introduction of scenes from the Life of St John – the number of scenes and their position in relation to the text of his Vision. Moreover, following the practice of other thirteenth century manuscripts, the two techniques of painting and outline drawing may be found in manuscripts of any one textual group, and even within the same manuscript as in Trin. Coll., R.16.2. Thus there remain, as distinctions between groups, only such stylistic characteristics as the types of faces and figures, of draperies and gestures, of compositions and their decorative elements.

The group which is closest to the great Trinity Apocalypse, but probably slightly later, is ascribed to St Albans. This contains five manuscripts which can be divided into a triplet and a pair. Paris, Bib. Nat., MS. 403, Bod., Auct. MS. D.4.17, and New York, Morgan MS. 524 (Plate 112) are three which are strikingly close in respect to the type of pictures, two to a page, with no accompanying text except the Latin inscriptions; the subjects, a long series of scenes from the Life of St John at the beginning and end of the Apocalypse illustrations, and the quality and style of the execution in beautiful, firm, outline drawing, delicately tinted in blue, red, and green, with plain coloured frames. Although the technique of these three manuscripts is the same, they do not all seem to have been done by the same hand, and a great scriptorium such as existed at St Albans under the tutelage of Matthew Paris could account for the differences. On the other hand, two of the three (Morgan MS. 524 and Bod. MS. Auct. D.4.17)[76] are replicas and these do seem to be the work of the same artist. The figure style of this group most nearly approximates the style of *La Estoire de Seint Aedward le Rei* (Camb., Univ. Lib., MS. EE.3.59; Plate 107B), here assigned to the most talented follower of Matthew Paris. The same style characterizes the illustrations of the other two members of the St Albans group: Malvern, Dyson Perrins MS. 10 and Brit. Mus., Add. MS. 35166, though in some miniatures both make more use of painting technique. These two Apocalypses contain some additional textual matter and also some extra scenes from the Life of St John. The Perrins and Additional manuscripts are a close pair stylistically; both are somewhat later in date.

The Canterbury group[77] is best represented by Lambeth Palace MS. 209 (Plate 113B) and by Douce MS. 180[78] in the Bodleian (Plate 113A). The Douce manuscript was made for Edward I and his wife, Eleanor of Castile, shortly before his accession to the throne in 1272; they are represented in an initial on fol. 1. The manuscript was possibly written in France and some of the illustrations, which are by more than one hand, have distinctly French stylistic characteristics such as are found also in another Apocalypse (Paris, Bib. Nat., MS. suppl. lat. 601), which is not listed by James as English. The drawing in both manuscripts is magnificent, and in the miniatures that were painted the colour is soft, delicate and harmonious.[79] The best explanation of the style of the Canterbury group may be that it is a mixture of French and English elements, such as we have found in other manuscripts executed there.

The chief differences in style between the two principal groups of Apocalypse manuscripts are the following: in the St Albans group, tinted outline is the technique used most generally, while in the miniatures of the Canterbury group the finished figures and even sometimes the backgrounds are painted; in the St Albans group the draperies are soft and clinging, and, even when deeply shaded, they usually hang softly around the body; in the Canterbury group the draperies are much more ample and form richer, more Gothic linear patterns. The faces in the St Albans group are rounded and delicately modelled, with large wide-open eyes; those in the Canterbury group are more irregular in contour, especially as to the foreshortened far cheek, and the features are drawn with line and not shaded.

Still another group of English Apocalypses, somewhat less closely integrated stylistically, points to the district of Peterborough[80] and may be significant in relation to a fine fourteenth century example (Dublin, Trin. Coll., MS. K.4.31) which is illuminated in one of the East Anglian styles (see Chapter 6; Plate 127).

4. The Court Style

The Court Style is a term used to describe paintings done under the patronage of King Henry III and of succeeding kings in connexion with the royal castles, palaces, and chapels. Much contemporary documentary evidence exists as to the painters, materials, and subjects[81] of these paintings, and a good deal of more or less detailed description has been recorded by persons who saw them, but of the paintings themselves little remains, and that little is not from the royal residences but from chapels or churches under royal patronage. Thus it is impossible to discuss comprehensively the thirteenth century Court style, though the best examples that survive, battered as they are, still bear witness to its superb quality. These examples are found at Windsor, in the Dean's cloister of St George's Chapel (Plate 110B); at Winchester Cathedral, in the Chapels of the Guardian Angels and the Holy Sepulchre in the choir (Plate 109); and at Westminster Abbey, in the panel now placed against the choir wall of the south ambulatory, the so-called 'Retable' (Plates 114 and 115B), in the wall paintings of the south transept (Plate 115A) and of the Chapel of St Faith.

The fine king's head at Windsor (Plate 110B) is painted in more than life-size on the wall of the south walk, about ten feet from the ground. The head is in full-front view like the Vernicles in the Matthew Paris style (Plate 110A); the hair and beard are white shaded with pale blue and grey; the face is pinkish white and the lips red; the crown is heavily outlined with brown and is studded with tiny spots of red for jewels. The features are so very similar to those of Paris's Vernicle in Cambridge, Corpus Christi MS. 16, that they would seem to have been designed by the same hand. If there is any surviving wall painting in England by Matthew Paris, it would seem to be this.

The scheme of the thirteenth century wall paintings at Winchester, which were extensive, is described in detail by Tristram.[82] Of those that survive, the finest are in the Chapel of the Holy Sepulchre and are dated about 1230. The best preserved portions are in the eastern bay; in the vaulting are the following subjects in medallions: Christ with the Symbols of the four Evangelists (not all visible); the Annunciation, the Nativity, the Annunciation to the Shepherds. On the east wall, below the half-figure of Christ in the vaulting, a Deposition and Entombment are the central features of this bay (Plate 109B); on the side walls are the Entry into Jerusalem and the *Noli me tangere*. In the western bay of the Chapel are the remains of what appear to be lives of saints. The paintings, says Tristram, 'seem to be the work of the hand which was responsible for the later miniatures in the Winchester Bible',[83] but nearly a half-century is perhaps too great a time lag for us to assume any direct connexion. What is true of the Winchester paintings is that their technique, like some of the work in the Bible, still displays characteristics of Byzantine painting, such as the greenish underpainting for flesh and the modelling of faces and drapery with strong high-lights. The figures are designed with swinging lines which are echoed in the long scrolls, the swaying trees, and the rolling ground (Plate 109B). The head of Christ (Plate 109A), which is amazingly Byzantine, may have furnished the model from which one of the heads was drawn (by Matthew Paris?) on the last leaf of Camb., Corpus Christi Coll. MS. 26 (Plate 108), but the linear technique of the drawing, as compared with the Winchester head makes it appear strikingly different. The bust of Christ in the Winchester vaulting against a blue ground forms part of the compositional scheme of the Deposition panel. The colours are chiefly red, yellow, and dull green.

The Chapel of the Guardian Angels at Winchester is somewhat later and may be the work of William of Westminster, who was appointed king's painter at Winchester by Henry III in 1239. The paintings[84] are in the vaulting and consist of busts of angels in medallions surrounded by scroll foliage and flowerets.

But the fact that the earlier paintings at Westminster, which may have been done by or under the supervision of William of Westminster,[85] between 1237 and 1239, have totally perished (as have also their repainted versions dating from after a fire in 1262) makes it impossible to judge whether any of the work at Winchester shows traces of the Court style. The paintings in the Great Chamber of Westminster Palace, even as restored in or after 1262, would have been of the very greatest importance for an account of English monumental painting of the thirteenth century. Unfortunately, all that remains of this splendid work are some copies made in the early nineteenth century,[86] before fire utterly destroyed them in 1834. Of the subject matter we have considerable knowledge, but of their style we know nothing.

The Westminster 'Retable' has been the subject of much discussion[87] as to its date, its attribution, and even its original purpose, but no certain conclusions have been reached. This is all the more strange, especially as regards the style of the painting, since the vicissitudes of its history, unhappy though it was,[88] have at least preserved to us in the surviving fragments the characteristics of the original style untouched by later restorations. The difficulty about agreement on an attribution of the style rests chiefly on two factors: the combination within the panel of elements which seem to be traceable only to quite different local sources; and the failure thus far to recognize any other example of painting where similar elements are combined. The panel is generally accepted as a work of the late thirteenth century, but the most recent opinion is that it may date[89] from c. 1270. Finally, disagreement as to the original purpose of the panel[90] adds to the difficulty of dating it more closely. All in all, therefore, the Westminster panel is one of the most prickly problems with which the historian of English painting has to deal.

The purpose of the present discussion which, in the absence of any new evidence relating to the panel, cannot hope to arrive at more definitive attribution than have previous studies, is to re-examine carefully all the stylistic features of the fragments that have survived and to attempt to explain them in the light of similar features, wherever they may be found. For this purpose, the style of the panel may perhaps best be considered under three main headings: the figure paintings – their subject matter, technique, and composition; the decorative detail introduced into the backgrounds and framing; the architectural framework – its design and its relation to the figured panels.

The fragments of the Westminster painting that have survived are all on a panel 11 feet long and 3 feet high. It is divided into five main parts: a central section consisting of three trefoiled arches each within a pointed enclosing arch under a gable, and flanked by tabernacles; both arches and tabernacles are supported by colonnettes. In the central compartment, which is considerably wider and higher than the others, is Christ standing in Majesty holding in his left hand the world, painted with a minute landscape with birds, fish, and animals, and blessing with his right. On his right side is the Virgin, on his left probably was the Apostle John; in thirteenth century iconography these two usually accompany the Crucifixion or Last Judgement. The panels at the two ends of the Retable have similar architectural frames of one arch each, and under the left arch is a standing figure of St Peter.[91] Between the architecturally framed panels the space is filled by four eight-pointed stars on each side, each containing a single scene; those which have survived represent miracles of Christ – the raising of Jairus's daughter, the healing of the blind man, and the feeding of the five thousand. We do not know the subjects of the other medallions. The subject matter is unusual for the Gothic west, and its fragmentary state makes it impossible even to surmise with what intention these small-scale figure subjects might have been chosen in the late thirteenth century.

The style of the painting (Plates 114B and 115B), as to both design and modelling of faces and drapery, is superb. The figures are tall and elegantly slender and stand in graceful swaying poses which are further accentuated by the swinging lines of the richly bordered drapery, the bent heads, and the somewhat mannered but sensitively modelled gesticulating hands with their nervous wiry fingers. The drapery is painted broadly with the heavy folds of thick material shaded in white high-lights, and this rich treatment is further carried out in the convolutions of the embroidered borders of tunic and mantle. The faces are modelled with a yellowish undertone for the flesh on which white high-lights and brown shadows are used, largely in a linear technique. The white lines are particularly noticeable at the corners of the eyes and on the foreheads, and they pick out individual hairs in eyebrows, moustaches, hair and beards. The mass of the soft, loose hair is suggested by broad treatment in solid colour with darker streaks and shadows in the thicker parts. The eyes are curiously shaped, with a tendency to elongate the outer corner and flatten the inner one, and to crowd the iris as far as possible into the far corner; the iris and the darker pupil are clearly distinguished. The three-quarter position of most of the heads shows a bulging forehead with no foreshortening and a flattened cheek which betrays the artist's lack of understanding of the skeletal structure of the head. Some heads are seen in profile, and at least one figure, in the scene of the Feeding of the Five Thousand, is in three-quarter back view with the head in a less than profile view. The groups of figures are closely composed and many show only the heads and the gesticulating hands; weaving in and out of the densely packed figures are the graceful patterned gold bands of the garments. The colouring of the draperies is rich and dark, with fine blues, deep red and some dark green. The grounds are gold, patterned with diamonds and dots.

The attribution of the figure style is difficult. The modelling and the heavy 'classical' drapery with its deep, broad folds are certainly more Italian than French or English: French drapery of the late thirteenth century tends to stand out in stiff, deeply and sharply undercut ridges on the sculptured figures, and the manuscripts, such as the French type of Apocalypse illustration, as Bod. MS. Douce 180 (Plate 113A), copy this deep, plastic drapery style; English drapery as seen in the manuscripts almost always produces a soft, rich surface pattern which has swinging curves but little weight (Plate 112). The decorative bands which are such a prominent feature of the style of the Retable and which carry the linear pattern, could be English, as could the tall, slender figures, however typical of Gothic art in general, and the somewhat linear treatment of the curly hair. Taken all together, the figure style seems to be a mixture of Gothic linear pattern and Italian light and shade technique. The variety in the poses of the figures, especially the three-quarter back view, and the prominence of the gesticulating hands, also suggest Italian influence. Such a combination of elements could be found in the second half of the thirteenth century both in France, especially in Paris and Avignon, and in Italy where the Pisan school of sculpture was furnishing a channel whereby French influence penetrated to Siena as early as 1265 and thence came to Rome through Arnolfo di Cambio at least by 1277.

Italian influence in specific motifs occurring in the decoration of the framework of the Westminster painting is more clearly identifiable. The tiny geometric motifs painted in blocks on a gold ground in the framework of the star-shaped medallions and in the borders of the larger panels, and covered with glass to simulate mosaic, if compared with the gold and coloured glass mosaic which lavishly decorates the tombs of both Edward the Confessor and Henry III in the Westminster sanctuary, leave no room for doubt as to the source of this decorative work. The tombs are of Italian workmanship; the tomb of the Confessor is said to have carried formerly an inscription which read as follows: 'Hoc opus est factum quod Petrus duxit in actum romanus cives.'[92] Pietro Oderisi, who is possibly the Petrus of the inscription, was an associate of Arnolfo di Cambio in several of his sculptured works at Rome. But whether or not a name can be attached to the Westminster tombs, the work is Italian and typically Roman, the so-called Cosmati work which is found in great abundance all over central and southern Italy. The patterns – diamonds, squares, circles, quatrefoils, sexfoils, and, most typical of Cosmati work, the eight-pointed Moorish star – are used in rich profusion in the frames of the Westminster painting. Moreover, interspersed with these geometric painted panels are imitations in gesso of antique cameos (Plate 114A) and gems in relief, which might well have had a direct influence on the types of painted heads.

Finally, we must consider the architectural framework itself of the Westminster panel. This is not, strictly speaking, architectural as to structure, but the decorative imitation of Gothic architectural style which is found at this time primarily in Italy, notably in the tabernacles and tomb canopies which combined Cosmati work with the Gothic architectural style introduced into Rome by Arnolfo. The closest similarities are found in the later examples in the environs of Rome, as the two tombs of Pope Clement IV and Adrian V in the church of S. Francesco at Viterbo.[93] The most striking feature which this architectural design has in common with the tombs is the steeply pointed trefoiled arch set within another arch under the gable which springs from the upper stage of the flanking tabernacles. In the tombs, the support of this whole superstructure is a single column; in the Westminster panel the columns form a cluster of three at the sides of the central panel, two bearing the two arches, the third and outer one supporting the tabernacle itself. The three colonnettes are carved so that they recess inward towards the figure of Christ. In the outer tabernacled panels the colonnettes are two in number, but also recessed, and the figure of Peter is slightly overlapped by the two inner shafts, as though the figure were not painted but carved, and standing within a tabernacle. But although the architectural framework of the Westminster panel is thought of spatially, the panel itself is surrounded by a flat rectangular border, and the space around the gables and pinnacle is filled with a diapered pattern.

The lateness of the dates of the Roman type of tabernacled tombs, like the lateness of the Italian painters whose style seems to have closest affinities with the painting of the Westminster Retable, namely Cavallini and Duccio,[94] raises the question of whether the panel could not be later than c. 1270. As far as our present documentary evidence goes, this could be so. On the grounds of the extremely accomplished painting style unmistakably evident in the Westminster fragments, a later date, perhaps in the last decade of the thirteenth century, would seem more acceptable. And this date would both fit the style better and bring the panel into a reasonable chronological relationship with other paintings in Westminster Abbey. It could in that case have been painted by an English artist under strong Italian influence.

The thirteenth century wall paintings that survive at Westminster Abbey are in the Chapel of St Faith which opens off the south transept and in the south transept itself. Those in the Chapel[95] may be dated c. 1280–90. The principal figure, St Faith, stands under a gabled trefoiled arch flanked, as in the Retable, by slender columns and pinnacles which fill the centre of a niche in the east wall, over the high altar. Below the saint is a predella containing eight-pointed star medallions (now empty) as in the Retable, and in the centre a Crucifixion with Mary and John. On the left splay of the niche is a kneeling Benedictine monk. The figure of St Faith has been drastically 'restored' and no reliable estimate can now be made either of the technique or of the quality of the original painting, which must have been very beautiful. The figure is extraordinarily attenuated, almost ten heads high, and the draperies fall in tortured convolutions. The colours are vermilion in the background, green for the Saint's gown and rose for her mantle, which is lined with vair. There are traces of gold and blue in the tracery of the canopy, and the ground outside it, now black, formerly was ornamented with gold fleur-de-lis.

The two paintings in the south transept, on the left side of the door opening into the Chapel of St Faith, are on an even larger scale than St Faith, the figures being nearly nine feet high. The subjects of the paintings are: left, the Incredulity of Thomas (Plate 115A); right, St Christopher and the Holy Child.[96] The style of these figures has the characteristic English flatness, with the draperies forming involved linear surface patterns, much less shaded than in the Retable. The backgrounds are red patterned with fleur-de-lis and green patterned with roses respectively. Though much of the colour of the faces and draperies has now flaked off, the accent in the figure drawing is on the broad aspects: hands and feet are enormous, and heads are unforeshortened and strongly outlined.

The three wall paintings at Westminster are all related to the Retable in many respects, but they are of much less fine quality and, perhaps by the same token, more typically English in their flat, linear technique. They have been attributed to Master Walter of Durham, the King's painter, who died in 1308.[97] They do not seem to be much earlier than 1300.

The Court style is represented not only in figure painting but also in decorative and figure sculpture, both painted. The spandrels of the arches of the triforium and other portions of the wall of the choir are covered with very beautiful diapered patterns, combined with foliage borders, all of which show traces of colour and gold. The famous angels in the spandrels at the ends of both transepts, and the figures of the Confessor and the Pilgrim in the south transept also were coloured and gilded. The effect of this colour and of the stained glass in the windows, of the gold and jewelled altar frontal and of the Cosmati pavement in the chancel and in the Chapel of the Confessor, together with the magnificent shrine itself, must have produced an unrivalled effect of splendour. There must also have been finely illuminated service books, and there are records of payments for rich embroidered vestments for use in the Abbey, as well as in St Stephen's Chapel.[98] Of neither manuscripts nor vestments of this period, however, are there any remains certainly identified as from Westminster, although the name of a woman embroiderer, Mabel of Bury St Edmunds, occurs eight times in the royal accounts of Henry III. The embroidered and jewelled altar frontal, now lost, has already been mentioned; it may have been the work of Mabel and her assistants.

Some fragments of embroidery which may date from this period, i.e. about the third quarter of the thirteenth century, may be seen in Worcester[99] and in London (Plate 116A). They are probably parts of a pair of buskins made for Walter de Cantelupe, Bishop of Worcester (1236–66), and they are embroidered with what appears to be a genealogy of Christ, the ancestor kings standing or sitting in circles formed by scrollwork with the same kind of rudimentary leaves and buds as are found in illuminated manuscripts of the earlier part of the century. The design suggests a typical late twelfth or early thirteenth century Jesse Tree, as found in manuscripts and in stained glass. The embroideries are perhaps not much later than *c.* 1250; similar foliage is found, it will be recalled, in the spandrels of the Chichester roundel (Plate 105). The embroidery in the Worcester fragments is in gold on silk and already exhibits the fineness of quality which is to give to English embroidery, the so-called *opus anglicanum*, its wide reputation during the late thirteenth and early fourteenth centuries.

A slightly later example of thirteenth century embroidery, probably dating from before 1284, is the so-called Clare Chasuble[100] in the Victoria and Albert Museum (Plate 117). The design is in barbed quatrefoils, and the spaces between them are filled with the slender scroll foliage as in the Worcester fragment. The areas outside the centre band contain also longer and more attenuated stems which twist in and out and enclose within medallions formed by them heraldic beasts, the lion and the griffin. The centre medallions contain a Crucifixion with Mary and John, a Virgin and Child resembling the Chichester roundel, the apostles Peter and Paul, and the martyrdom of Stephen. The technique of the design is similar to that of the Worcester fragments; the embroidery is in gold and colours on a deep blue satin ground. This is the earliest of many such ecclesiastical vestments in *opus anglicanum* with increasingly elaborate designs and subject matter, which will be discussed in the next chapter.

One other form of pictorial art reached a high point of development during the second half of the thirteenth century, that is, ceramic floor tiles.[101] The earliest of these, so far as can be judged from surviving examples, used simple geometric patterns of many varieties. The usual procedure was to design them in sets of four or multiples of four, the individual tiles being so planned that their arrangement would result in a variation of the patterns when laid on the floor. The Chapter House at Westminster still has a floor made up largely of the medieval tiles laid down between 1253 and 1258. Some are patterned with running scrolls and designs of window tracery, such as that of the great rose windows in the transepts of the Abbey. Others have heraldic and grotesque animals, while still others contain representations of everyday scenes and stories.

More famous even than the Westminster tiles are the remains of a tiled floor of similar style and workmanship formerly in Chertsey Abbey, near Windsor. Besides the more conventional patterns as used at Westminster, the Chertsey tiles contain illustrations of the romance of Tristram and of the story of Richard Cœur de Lion (Plate 116B). The vigour and sureness of the drawing is in the best outline tradition of the thirteenth century, as exemplified by Matthew Paris and the St Albans school. The figure of the King in combat is comparable to similar figures of horsemen in, for example, *La Estoire de Seint Aedward le Rei* or the many fine Apocalypses, especially those of the St Albans group. The circle of grotesques with foliage tails can be matched in the initial decoration of manuscripts of the mid thirteenth century, and the foliage ornament filling the corners, while somewhat stiffer and more formally designed, is of the type found in both manuscripts and embroideries.

Summary

The material which has been selected as representative of the various forms of English art in the thirteenth century includes only a part of the whole amount. By far the greatest proportion of this material consists of illuminated manuscripts, particularly psalters which, as we have seen, first follow the tradition of monumental figure painting as developed in the twelfth century, then diminish in scale under the influence of French thirteenth century style. The new element of decoration found in the psalters is the grotesques, which in English examples become ever freer in concept and more numerous as the century progresses. Some of these figures are fantastic, evolved out of earlier decorative animals; others are represented more naturalistically, perhaps under the influence of the Bestiary. But all, amusing and delightful as they are, represent only the preliminary stage of a development which was to come with the succeeding century in the East Anglian style.

Another feature of the illustrated psalters, which persists also in the next century, is the practice of introducing series of Bible pictures to precede the psalter proper. Some of these series have become separated from the psalter and exist now only as picture books without text except explanatory legends.[102] The monumental character of these pictures, with large-scale figures arranged as formal compositions in rectangles or roundels, suggests a connexion with wall paintings as to both design and subject matter. It seems likely that cycles of these pictures were available for copying, since many of the subjects included are the same. In the following century we shall find similar cycles in wall painting which, though surviving only in fragmentary form, demonstrate the existence of definite schemes.[103] The connexions between the design and the subject matter of the illuminated pages in the psalter itself with contemporary stained glass have been pointed out – a connexion which exists also between French manuscripts and glass. The relation of wall painting to manuscripts in English Gothic art, however, is not paralleled in French art, which always was more closely allied with goldsmith's work. This is one of the striking differences between the English and the French Gothic styles in painting.

Other characteristic features of the English Gothic style are the freedom from stylization in the play of the drapery patterns, the variety and liveliness of expression in the faces, and the freshness and originality in the interpretation of subject matter. An interest in naturalistic forms combined with a *penchant* for the humorously whimsical produced in English decorative borders a charm and variety which, though the workmanship is often less exquisite than in the finest French manuscripts, draws the eye from detail to detail and from page to page in an absorption which a comparable French manuscript cannot evoke. Some thirteenth century English work is excellent, while some is rough; but it is almost all interesting, more often than not amusing, and usually it is full of surprises as well as of riddles. These characteristics will help to explain the phenomenon of the East Anglian style which furnishes the theme of the following period.

NOTES TO CHAPTER 5

p. 105   1. The similarity between the Ingeborg Psalter (Chantilly, Musée Condé, MS. 1695) and the Westminster Psalter (Brit. Mus., Roy. MS. 2 A. xxii) has long been noted. It still is not established whether this fine manuscript was made in France or in England. For reproductions of the Ingeborg Psalter see J. Meurgey, *Les Principaux Manuscrits du Musée Condé* (Paris, 1930), plates X–XIII. Another psalter illuminated in similar style belonged to St Louis and is now in Leyden, MS. Lat. 76A in the Bib. de l'Université. This also is thought possibly to be English. Henri Omont, *Psautier de S. Louis* (Leyden, 1902).

p. 106   2. The work of these painters is, of course, not signed, but payments to them indicate that they were employed as masters in work which was known to be in progress at that time.

3. A geographical arrangement is more practicable for wall and panel painting, since much of it is *in situ*. See Tristram, *English Wall Painting*, II, 65–7. This book, which furnishes a corpus of thirteenth century English painting, will be referred to constantly in the present chapter.

4. This is not necessarily the same as localizing the origin of the style, since artists, even monks, did not remain stationary.

5. Not all the important examples of thirteenth

century English pictorial art will fit neatly under one or another of these headings, but the scheme will serve at least as a convenient basis for describing the representative examples of each phase, leaving the individual and nonconforming works to tie in where best they can.

6. The evidence for St Albans ownership of Trin. Coll. MSS B.5.3 and O.5.8 is, in both cases, an inscription on a fly-leaf, 'Hic est liber S. Albani', in an early hand.

7. The subjects are: the Annunciation, the Visitation, the Madonna and Child, Christ in Majesty, and David as Musician.

8. James, 'The Drawings of Matthew Paris', 24–6, plates XXVII–XXIX. The five coloured pen drawings in Matthew Paris style on the end fly-leaves may have been inspired in part by the preliminary leaves in Roy. MS. 2 A. xxii, which could have been seen by the later artist either at St Albans or at Westminster. The difference in date between the drawings and the preliminary leaves must be about half a century.

9. Herbert, 'A Psalter in the British Museum (Roy. MS. 1 D. x)'. On fol. 2 there is a vernicle in Matthew Paris style similar to that on fol. 221 verso of Roy. MS. 2 A. xxii. See below under Matthew Paris.

10. Preliminary series of Bible pictures had become established features of psalter illustration in the twelfth century, as we have seen. Two such series now existing unattached to any text are MS. I of the Dyson Perrins Collection at Malvern and MS. III.3.21 in Emmanuel College, Cambridge, both of *c.* 1200. Another elaborate series of 40 leaves precedes a psalter of *c.* 1200 in the Morgan Library (MS. 43, the Huntingfield Psalter). This manuscript is one of the most interesting and most lavishly illuminated of the late twelfth century psalters, but, alas, now badly damaged by water and with most of the blue of the backgrounds removed. An obit inserted in the Calendar for Roger de Huntingfield (d. 1204) connects the manuscript with Mendham Priory, Suffolk, founded by his father William in 1140. The text was apparently written in the last decade of the twelfth century and the original Calendar suggests Norfolk or Lincolnshire. Thompson, 'The Huntingfield Psalter' (*Proc. Soc. Antiq.*, XVI (1895–7), 219–20), thought the workmanship was not English and suggested the German border of Flanders as a possible source of the style. This, however, has some relation to that of the initials in Arundel 157 in its characteristic of combining tinted outline with solid colour ornamented with dotted patterns.

11. Millar, *op. cit.*, 46, plate 67: 'almost certainly executed at Canterbury'. This manuscript was not finished and the gaps were supplied by an Italian artist probably in Catalonia. See Millard Meiss, *Journal of the Walters Art Gallery*, IV (1941), 73 ff.

12. Facsimile published by Omont, *Psautier illustré*.

13. Millar, *op. cit.*, 36. See also *Bull. de la S.F.R.M.P.*, V (1921), 21 ff., plates IV–VIII.

14. Swarzenski, *The Berthold Missal*, 47, n. 80.

15. Seymour de Ricci, *Census*, II, 1503. The manuscript is from the collection of the Marquess of Lothian (1932) and was given to the Morgan Library in 1935.

16. The explanation of this practice, which was common in English manuscripts from *c.* 1200, is not known for certain. It might be interpreted as meaning that miniatures produced in lay or monastic centres were sold or given out for insertion at appropriate places in the text of a Bible or other familiar book. However, no such centre of production has been stylistically recognized. Some of the miniatures of the Lothian Bible are missing, having been removed, and others which remain crowd the spaces left for them in the text, partly overlapping it. An example of a similar practice of inserting miniatures is found in Brit. Mus., Add. MS. 39943 (see below).

The explanation may be (as Cockerell once suggested) the wish to finish a manuscript quickly, the unimportant miniatures being painted on separate pieces of vellum at the same time as the text was written or decorated. There also may be something in the idea of choosing softer, finer vellum, more suitable for the small-scale miniatures than the rougher quality generally used in large English manuscripts.

17. Cf. Brit. Mus., MS. Burney 3, and its relation to stained glass.

18. The Canterbury glass has been fully published by the Friends of Canterbury Cathedral, *The Ancient Glass of Canterbury*, with text by Bernard Rackham.

19. See p. 113 below.

20. Cf. an early twelfth century copy of Bede's Life of St Cuthbert probably made there (Bod. MS. 165, plate LIXB). The Additional manuscript miniatures are reproduced in *The Life of St Cuthbert*, edited by W. Forbes-Leith (London, 1888). This manuscript, which was formerly in the Yates Thompson Collection, is described in *A Descriptive Catalogue of Fifty MSS. from the Collection of Henry Yates Thompson*, Third Series, No. LXXXIV; see also plates V–XV in *Illustrations from 100 MSS. in the Library of H. Y. T.* (London, 1914).

21. For a complete reproduction, see Warner, *The Guthlac Roll*.

22. *Durham Catalogue* of 1416, published by the Surtees Society (Durham, 1838), 107.

23. See Harrison, *The Painted Glass of York*, 110–18. Only one subject in the window shows close resemblances in treatment to the corresponding miniature, but this is not surprising since the window is so much later. See Chapter 8 below.

24. Colgrave, 'The St Cuthbert Paintings on the Carlisle Cathedral Stalls', 17–21.

25. The practice of pasting in miniatures painted on separate pieces of vellum which was observed in Morgan MS. 791 was responsible for the loss of the remainder.

26. The full-length standing figure of a bishop, identified as Cuthbert, painted on the south jamb of the recess of the inner north aisle of the Galilee Chapel at Durham Cathedral, built by Bishop Pudsey *c.* 1175, is reproduced by Tristram, I, plate 86. The similarities in the figure are largely due to the dress and position, but the panelled background and the heavy painting technique are common to both the painting and the miniature.

p. 110

p. 111

p. 111   27. Such as the late twelfth century ciboria (two in the Victoria and Albert Museum and one in the Morgan Library) and a casket, all with roundels containing figure subjects. See Chamot, *English Medieval Enamels*, plates 4–8.

28. Reproduced Brit. Mus., *Reproductions from Illum. MSS.*, I, plate x. As forerunners of this decorative style cf. Bod. MS. 752, *English Romanesque Illumination*, plate 22. The style suggests a reversion to Celtic initials but may have appeared under Norman influence, perhaps at Canterbury where the lively little animals had long been at home. Two fine Canterbury manuscripts decorated only with initials of this type are Bod. MS. Auct. E. infra 6 (reproduced *op. cit.*, plate 21) and Cambridge, Trin. Coll., MS. B.5.4 – two parts of a glossed psalter by Herbert of Bosham.

p. 112   29. Uncoloured reproductions of these pages do not give any hint of their beauty. A fair coloured reproduction of the *Beatus* page (fol. 19) of Ar. 157 is found in *Schools of Illumination*, II, plate 8.

30. Reproduced Georg Leidinger, *Meisterwerke der Buchmalerei* (Munich, 1920), plate 19; see also *Orbis Pictus*, 8 (Miniatures du Moyen-Âge, Lausanne, 1950), plate 17. Closely related in style to the Munich Psalter is Cambridge, Trin. Coll., MS. B.11.4 (also before 1220), with earlier preliminary Bible pictures which seem to have influenced the subjects and style of the historiated initials of the Psalter. The *Beatus* page of this manuscript unfortunately is lost.

31. There is an unmistakable revival in these developed initials both in spirit and in design of Celtic calligraphic decoration, but the Psalter pages are much more brilliant in colouring owing to the lavish use of burnished gold grounds. Moreover, the initial and the background are not treated as one unified pattern as in the Celtic pages, but the letter and its decoration are set off sharply against the ground.

32. The Translation of St Thomas of Canterbury which occurred in 1221 is entered in the original hand of the Calendar.

33. Reproduced, Millar, *op. cit.*, plate 69. Closely related in style and perhaps also executed for the same Abbot Robert de Lindesey is a psalter in the Fitzwilliam Museum, Cambridge (MS. 12). Though somewhat plainer in style, the figures are painted with the same modelled technique in brown and white for the faces, and the same rich, soft draperies; the highly burnished gold grounds are patterned with dots and other motifs. The initials introducing the psalms are particularly close to those in the Lindesey Psalter. Compare, for example, the initial with David and Goliath, introducing Psalm 51 (52, A.V.) in both manuscripts.

34. Cf. plate 15 above. On the sources of monsters and animal grotesques see Boase, *op. cit.*, 84 ff.

35. Plates 87 and 88 above.

36. The Calendar, which takes on increased artistic importance in the thirteenth century, is usually illustrated with the signs of the zodiac and the occupations of the months, often in separate roundels in the margin of the page containing the appropriate month.

37. The folios and subjects are as follows: fol. 17, full-page miniature of the burial of Thomas Becket; fol. 32, a similar miniature, of the martyrdom of Thomas, perhaps the earliest known miniature of this subject; fol. 68, Sacrifice of Abraham; fol. 118, several saints; fol. 129, Peter walking on the water, and Christ and the Disciples. The style is very different from that of the rest of the manuscript and both in colouring and in technique does not look English.

38. Cf. the roundels in plates 92 and 96. Two late twelfth century stained-glass medallions have survived at York (Jesse and Daniel), and some thirteenth century ones at Canterbury (Plates 95A, 97).

39. So also were French windows, which used similar geometric forms, such as squares and circles. The medallions in thirteenth century glass were joined together by the iron armature which constituted the skeleton for the window. The designs composed by medallions in French windows tended to emphasize the central panels, on the axis of the light. In English windows the designs tended to be less closely integrated and the emphasis in them was spread more evenly over the whole of the window space. This is evident if one compares medallion windows at Chartres with those at Canterbury.

As to origins of the English glass, it is customary to attribute all good thirteenth century stained glass to France. Although there were close contacts between Canterbury and French art in this as in previous periods, the consensus now seems to be that the Canterbury windows, like those of York and Lincoln, are English in design and workmanship and in iconography. The glass itself, however, may have been imported from the Continent, since there is no record of the making of pot-metal glass in England, and in later times the best glass used in England was known to have been Continental (see Chapter 8 below). For a sensible discussion of the pros and cons for French origins of English glass, see Lafond, 'The Stained Glass Decoration of Lincoln Cathedral'.

40. Owned by Robert de Bello, Abbot of St Augustine's, Canterbury (1224–53).

41. The French pocket Bibles written in tiny script on the thinnest possible vellum are well known. English manuscripts never attained their minute scale or their fineness of workmanship.

42. Such as Brit. Mus., Roy. MS. 1 D. i. Egerton MS. 1151, written on the same fine vellum as Roy. 1 D. i, is decorated in a very similar style. See p. 118 f. below.

43. See Cockerell, *The Work of W. de Brailes*. The villages of Upper and Lower Brailes are about four miles east of Shipston-on-Stour and ten miles west of Banbury. A William de Brailes is listed among the many illuminators who in 1260 lived in Cat (or Catte) Street, Oxford. See Graham Pollard, *Notes for a Directory of Cat Street, Oxford, before 1500*. Unpublished manuscript in the Bodleian Library, G. A. Oxon 4°, 573.

44. Swarzenski, 'Unknown Bible Pictures by W. de Brailes'. The dimensions of the leaves are approximately the same but both have been trimmed. There is no conclusive evidence on this point.

45. Millar, 'Additional Miniatures by W. de Brailes'.

46. In support of this idea, the New College Psalter displays that curious phenomenon already noted in earlier manuscripts, of miniatures painted on separate pieces of vellum and pasted on the text pages.

47. Swarzenski, *op. cit.*, 63.

48. Reproduced and discussed, James and Tristram, 'Medieval Wall Paintings at Christ Church, Oxford', *Walpole Soc.*, VI (1927–8), 1–8. See also Tristram, *English Painting*, II, plates 83–92.

49. Published in facsimile by Millar, *The Rutland Psalter*.

50. B.F.A. Club, *Exhib. of Illum. MSS*, Nos. 41–2. See also Millar on the Wilton Psalter, *Bull. de la S.F.R.M.P.*, IV (1914–20), 62, plate LV, g and h. On the whole group see Hollaender, 'The Sarum Illuminator and His School', 230–62.

51. From the presence of St Melorius in the litany and calendar, it was suggested that the manuscript was written for the Abbey of Amesbury, perhaps for the nun who is kneeling in the miniature on fol. 4. There is no real evidence for this assumption.

52. *Brit. Mus. Quart.*, XI (1936–7), 22. The con-

nexion of the Psalter with Evesham is established by the Calendar entry on Nov. 13: 'Dedicatio ecclesie euesamensis'. The manuscript was purchased for the Museum in 1936 by the National Art Collections Fund. The fine *Beatus* page is reproduced in a *Diary* for 1954 issued currently by this foundation.

53. Prayers at the end of the litany (fol. 206) show that this manuscript was written for the Abbess of Wilton Abbey. B.F.A. Club, *Exhib. of Illum. MSS Cat.*, No. 42, plate 40. See also *Bull. de la S.F.R.M.P.*, IV (1914–20), 55, plates LIII–LV.

54. M. R. James, *A Descriptive Catalogue of the Latin Manuscripts in the John Rylands Library at Manchester*, I (Manchester, 1921), No. 24, 73–5, plates 51–7.

55. Perhaps Henry of Chichester. Hollaender, *op. cit.*, 232 ff.

56. Tristram, *op. cit.*, II, 302–3. Tristram's copy of the painting is reproduced in colour as the frontispiece.

57. Some medallion paintings in the vaulting of the choir at Salisbury Cathedral may also be related to the style of the Chichester roundel. The Salisbury roundels contain Calendar subjects (now repainted) and are surrounded by very beautiful scroll foliage, original bits of which are still visible. (Tristram, II, plates 65 and 66, and Suppl. plate 31.) The original colouring is delicate as in the Chichester roundel, suggestive of manuscript painting. Over the west doorway is a consecration cross in a quatrefoil within an incised circle, which may be compared with the medallion design at Chichester, which has a consecration cross adjoining it. For reproductions of the Calendar roundels see Borenius, 'The Cycle of Images', 44.

58. Interestingly enough, it is this manuscript which furnishes concrete evidence that the group can be attributed to Salisbury. According to a colophon, the Bible of William de Hales was written in 1254 for Thomas de la Wile on the occasion of his appointment as Master of the Salisbury schools. It is unlikely that the manuscript was produced elsewhere than in the scriptorium of the fine new cathedral which was in the last stages of completion. See Millar, *Bull. de la S.F.R.M.P.*, IV (1914–20), 62.

59. Another miniature in Roy. MS. 1 D. i (fol. 1) p 118 has an unusual if not unique representation of the four Orders of Friars in the margins, two of each order standing on pillars in the corners of the page. Most interesting are the Carmelites who are shown in their striped cloaks which were worn only until

1287 when they were changed to white as still worn. See *Speculum Carmelitarum*, vol. I, part II, 152. This detail unfortunately indicates only a date *ante quem* for the making of this manuscript.

p. 118 60. Known as the Cuerdon Psalter from the late owners, R. Townley Parker and R. A. Tatham of Cuerdon Hall. See Morgan Library, *Exhib. of Illum. MSS* (1934), No. 41, 22–3, plate 40.

61. Professor Wormald first called my attention to these drawings, which have not yet been published.

p. 119 62. See James, 'The Drawings of Matthew Paris', 1–26, with many reproductions. James lists nine as wholly or in part by Matthew Paris himself, but discusses only the first six: Cambridge, Corpus Christi Coll., MSS 16 and 26; Royal MS. 14 C. vii; Cott. MS. Nero D.i; additions to Royal 2 A. xxii; Cott. MS. Jul. D.vii; Dublin, Trin. Coll., MS. E.1.40; Cambridge, Univ. Lib., MS. Ee.3.59 (the only manuscript with a French text, *La Estoire de Seint Aedward le Rei*) and a fragment of the life of St Thomas of Canterbury now probably in a private collection in Belgium. Recently some additional drawings in the Bodleian Library (Ashmole MS. 304) have been attributed by Wormald to Matthew Paris, *Walpole Soc.*, XXXI (1942–3), 109 ff.

63. The attribution of these heads to Matthew Paris himself is to my mind the most questionable of those here listed. The technique is clearly related to that of painting, and they may represent either sketches from wall paintings or cartoons for them, in which case one is reminded of the many wall paintings at St Albans itself. For a discussion of these paintings and of the heads at Windsor which may be related to Paris's work, see below. In this connexion it is to be remembered that a painting of St Peter, now in the Oslo Museum, Norway, is attributed to Matthew Paris. See Andreas Lindblom, *La Peinture en Suède et en Norvège* (Stockholm, 1916). James accepts this attribution (*op. cit.*, 3). The painting as reproduced appears to be so damaged that no fresh study of it is possible.

p. 120 64. In addition to Walter of Colchester's brother Simon, his nephew Richard (Tristram, II, 318) is mentioned. It may be worth noting that, as Tristram remarks, St Albans supplied painters for Westminster (*op. cit.*, 329). The St Albans paintings are described and reproduced by Tristram, 325–30, plates 161–7. See also W. Page, 'The St Albans School of Painting', *Archaeologia*, LVIII (1902), 275–92.

65. Discussed under the Westminster or Court style, p. 123, plate 110B.

66. James, *La Estoire de Seint Aedward le Rei*.

67. Compare the head of Christ on fol. 221 verso and a similar one on fol. 2 of Arundel MS. 157, with the Vernicle on fol. 49 verso in Corpus Christi Coll. MS. 16: *Walpole Society*, XIV (1925–6), plate XXIX, for reproductions of fols 49 verso and 221 verso.

68. In plate 107B, compare the seated figure in the centre with the standing figure on the right. Even in the centre figure, it is not only the deep pockets that are shaded with colour.

69. As noted above, James attributes fols 1–4 of this manuscript to M. Paris, but the pictures do not seem to me to show the grasp of figure modelling which is typical of him. On Brother William see A. G. Little, *Franciscan History and Legend in English Mediaeval Art* (Manchester Univ. Press, 1937), 37.

70. The list and the grouping of the manuscripts are James's. See *The Apocalypse in Latin: MS. 10 in the Collection of C. W. Dyson Perrins* (Oxford, 1927). His grouping is as follows: St Albans – Paris 403, Bod. Auct. D.4.17, Morgan 524, Brit. Mus., Add. 35166, Dyson Perrins 10; Canterbury – Add. 42555, Lambeth 209, Douce 180; Westminster – Trin. Coll. B.10.2; Peterborough District – Bod. Canon. Bibl. 62, Camb., Magdalene Coll. 5, Bod., Tanner 184. In his book *The Dublin Apocalypse*, James suggests Peterborough as the most likely provenance for Trin. Coll. MS. K.4.31 since it is related textually to his Peterborough group.

71. James, *The Trinity College Apocalypse*. The provenance is still controversial: James was inclined to assign it to St Albans (Cockerell dissenting), and Lindblom thought it to be an early work of Matthew Paris himself. In his work on the Dyson Perrins Apocalypse, James still favoured a St Albans attribution for the Trinity College manuscript, *op. cit.*, 33.

72. See James, *Cat. of the MSS in Trinity Coll. Lib.*, No. 21.

73. *New Pal. Soc.*, Series I, plates 38 and 39 (fols 14 and 15 verso).

74. This artist, I believe, may have worked on the Dyson Perrins Apocalypse (Malvern, MS. 10) and perhaps was responsible for the French elements in apocalypses such as Douce 180.

75. See Leopold Delisle and P. Meyer, *L'Apocalypse en français au XIIIe siècle* (Paris, 1901).

76. Reproduced in coloured facsimile by Coxe, *The Apocalypse of St John ... from a MS. in the Bodleian Library*.

77. Perhaps the earliest member of the group is

Add. MS. 42555, the Abingdon Apocalypse dated before 1263, but much repainted. See *Brit. Mus. Quart.*, VI (1931–2), 71–3.

78. Reproduced in facsimile by James, *The Apocalypse in Latin and French*, Bodleian MS. Douce 180.

79. The Paris miniatures are not replicas but variants of those in Douce 180, chiefly differing in the freer and more vigorous compositions which tend to push out over the framework rather than remain within the confines of a well-ordered design. Cockerell also found these two manuscripts a stylistic pair, although he was never completely convinced that they were English.

80. James, *The Dublin Apocalypse*, 21. See note 70 above. Another apocalypse, Cambridge, Trin. Coll. MS. B.10.2, was attributed by James to Westminster on the grounds that its pictures of the late fourteenth century were partly copied in the sculptures of the fifteenth century choir screen in the Confessor's Chapel at Westminster. Noppen has suggested that these apocalypse pictures furnished models for the wall paintings in the Chapter House at Westminster. *Burl. Mag.*, LXI (1932), 146–59. For the frescoes, see Chapter 7 below.

81. Tristram, *op. cit.*, II, *Catalogue*, 497 ff. See also Borenius, 'The Cycle of Images in the Palaces and Castles of Henry III', 40–50.

82. Tristram, II, 611–17, plates 28–42. Some of the painting, as that in the Chapel of the Holy Sepulchre, replaced late twelfth century painting now visible only in a few places.

83. *Op. cit.*, 171 f.

84. *Op. cit.*, 168–71, plates 44–50.

85. *Op. cit.*, 94. The documents relating to William and others of the King's painters are given and interpreted by Tristram here and elsewhere in the book. The organization of the vast material in this massive volume, however, makes it exceedingly difficult to use. To extract all the facts one must usually comb through the whole volume.

86. Copies of the paintings were made in 1819–20 by C. A. Stothard and are in the library of the Society of Antiquaries, London. Some of them have been reproduced photographically by Tristram, *op. cit.*, suppl. plate 13; water colour copies and details by him, plates 16–25.

87. *Op. cit.*, 562–4. The Retable is reproduced in suppl. plates 1–6.

88. The panel, according to Vertue who first found it, was 'partly defaced after the reformation

manner', and later served as the top of a large press containing funeral effigies in the Abbey. George Vertue, *Notebooks* (1713–21), *Walpole Soc.*, XVIII (1929–30), 157. Additional damage to the Retable occurred later.

89. Wormald, 'Paintings in Westminster Abbey', 170 ff.

90. Tristram makes out what seems a good case for the use of the panel not as a retable but as one side of the 'coperculum' or wooden cover of the shrine of the Confessor. The date might still be about the time of the restoration of the shrine itself, before the translation of St Edward's relics in 1269. *Op. cit.*, 144–8.

91. It is probable that there was a corresponding p. 125 figure of Paul on the right side, but no evidence survives.

92. Antonio Muñoz, *Roma di Dante* (Milan, p. 126 Rome, 1921), 265 ff.

93. *Op. cit.*, 268, 269.

94. The earliest certain reference to Cavallini is p. 127 in 1291; see Raimond van Marle, *The Italian Schools of Painting*, I, 506. The earliest mention of Duccio is 1278, *op. cit.*, II, 2 f. The style of Cavallini is much closer to that of the Retable than the style of Duccio, which is strongly Byzantine.

95. The chevet, transepts, and crossing were dedicated in 1269 and probably also the Chapel of St Faith. It has been proposed that the painting in the transept is earlier than this, immediately after the completion of the Chapter House in 1253. See J. C. Noppen, 'The Westminster Painting and Master Peter', *Burl. Mag.*, XCI (1949), 305–9. Noppen suggests that the Retable was one of two *tabulae* sold by Master Peter to the King and paid for between 1256 and 1258. Lethaby's dating of 1270–5 for St Faith (*Burl. Mag.*, XXIX, 1916) has been quoted by Wormald, 'Paintings in Westminster Abbey', 166. St Faith is reproduced, Tristram, II, suppl. plate 12.

96. Reproduced, Tristram, II, plates 11 and 12.

97. Laurence Tanner, *Unknown Westminster Abbey* (London, 1948), 13.

98. Tristram includes records of some of these p. 128 furnishings, II, 78 ff.

99. Some of the fragments are in the British Museum, others in the Victoria and Albert Museum, and the remainder in the Chapter House of Worcester Cathedral.

100. Christie, *English Medieval Embroidery*, No. 44, 78–9.

p. 128   101. See Lethaby, 'The Romance Tiles of Chertsey Abbey', and 'The Westminster and Chertsey Tiles and Romance Paintings'.

p. 129   102. For example, Cambridge, Fitzwilliam Museum, MS. 370 (James, 'An English Picture-Book of the Late 13th Century', *Walpole Soc.*, XXV (1936–7), 23–30); Cambridge, St John's Coll., MS. K.26, B.F.A. Club, *Exhib. Illum. MSS*, No. 65.

103. In this connexion the remarkable treatise known as *Pictor in Carmine* should be remembered. This is a literary work compiled by an English Cistercian monk, containing the largest known collection of types and antitypes intended, as stated in the preface, for the guidance of painters, 'to supplement the faults of excessive levity by providing a supply of more excellent quality'. James, 'Pictor in Carmine', *Archaeologia*, XCIV (1951), 141–66. This paper was published posthumously, with the assistance of Eric G. Millar.

CHAPTER 6

THE EAST ANGLIAN PERIOD

*

HISTORICAL BACKGROUND

POLITICAL

The Plantagenets and the Rise of Nationalism in England. Edward I, son of Henry III and Eleanor of Provence, King 1272–1307; married Eleanor of Castile (d. 1290) and Margaret of France 1299; first 'English' king of England; reformed the laws; conquered Wales and temporarily Scotland; Model Parliament 1295.

Edward II, son of Edward I and Eleanor of Castile, King 1307–27; married Isabella of France; deposed 1327 and murdered.

Edward III, son of Edward II and Isabella, King 1327–77; Hundred Years' War with France begun 1337; Battle of Sluys (naval victory for English) 1340; Crécy 1346; capture of Calais 1347; Poitiers 1356; Treaty of Brétigny 1360; Order of the Garter founded 1348; Black Death 1348–9.

ECCLESIASTICAL

Increased wealth and worldliness among the clergy, both monastic and secular.

John Grandisson, Bishop of Exeter 1327–69, typical wealthy ecclesiastical patron of the arts.

*

THE half-century with which the present chapter will deal is one primarily of a national English taste which had formed itself during the preceding century on the love for rich decoration, for narrative in illustration, and for the bizarre and the fantastic in details. It is this last characteristic that gave fourteenth century manuscripts their peculiarly distinctive feature, the combination of the natural and the absurd in animal life that runs rampant over the pages. Foliage ornament, too, combines these two extremes of recognizable leaves and flowers, with conventionalized motifs of unknown species. Other arts also display these same characteristic elements.

Two aspects of English art of *c.* 1300 have become as well known, both in England and on the Continent, as Hiberno-Saxon and Winchester art of earlier periods; these are the East Anglian manuscripts and *opus anglicanum*[1] embroideries. These constitute the bulk of the material for the present chapter, although there are also in the period ending *c.* 1350 some few examples of good stained glass and a number of remains of wall and panel painting, mostly in bad condition and inferior in quality to the manuscripts and embroideries. It is significant that the two main typically English aspects of medieval pictorial art have much in common stylistically, and that both, during the half century under discussion, demonstrate the phenomenon of a quick flowering followed by a sudden decline in quality as well as in quantity of production. It has long been customary to explain this sudden decline, especially in the production of the manuscripts, by the ravages of the Black Death which took a heavy toll of all classes and professions of people, including, doubtless, scribes and illuminators.[2] The explanation is given further credence in the case of East Anglian manuscripts by the fact that many of them were, apparently, produced in monasteries, though not necessarily by the monks themselves but perhaps by a group or groups of travelling artists. In any case, the monasteries did suffer grievously under the plague,[3] and travelling craftsmen also must have been caught by it in one place or another, and have died. But a more careful examination of the products of East Anglian art in its later stages, that is, *c.* 1340, shows that actually the quality of the art had already deteriorated to such an extent that no sudden disaster is needed to explain its demise; a generation of gifted illuminators working in a style the origins of which are not yet fully understood came, in due time, to an end. On the other hand, the style did not wholly die, for we shall find in the second half of the fourteenth century survivals, particularly of its decorative features, which constitute recognizable components of later English style.

The relation of the successive styles in *opus anglicanum* to the manuscripts seems to be that of one medium following the developments in another; it is noteworthy in the case of the later embroideries that their designs seem to be taken not only from manuscripts but also from stained-glass windows, and they even reflect successive changes in window tracery and other architectural details.

The East Anglian Manuscripts

The roots of some of the characteristic features of the East Anglian style are found in thirteenth century English illumination, especially that of the fully illustrated English psalters. This is not strange in view of the fact that most of the East Anglian manuscripts are psalters, and thus their scheme of illustration follows that of the earlier books, namely, preliminary Bible pictures, Calendar with the signs of the Zodiac and the occupations of the months, and historiated initials, with particular emphasis on the *Beatus* page.

The new elements may be summed up under the following three heads: (1) a quite amazing growth in the naturalistic features of the borders, as leaves and flowers, birds and animals, that fill the margins of the pages; (2) a corresponding increase in the number and variety of grotesques which mingle on equal terms with the denizens of field and forest and which often, especially in the later examples, tend to become gross in size and coarse in humour; (3) the incorporation in the marginal decoration not only of the naturalistic and grotesque matter, but of illustrative material drawn from other sources, as the Bible, the Bestiary, the Apocalypse, and even the lives and miracles of saints, literary romances, and portraiture. The result of this indiscriminate tapping of all possible sources of illustrative material is, of course, a tremendously rich and interesting variety of subject matter which is still further enlivened by the artists' keen observation and extraordinary ability to represent things as they see or imagine them. Unfortunately this wealth of material is not always kept under control by a feeling for good design, and the tendency towards over-richness in amount and the lack of orderliness in arrangement of the marginal borders is an almost infallible criterion for distinguishing pure East Anglian from French work of the same period. The new characteristics, however, occur in English manuscripts in varying degrees; hence there are examples, as we shall see, which, though certainly more East Anglian than French, seem to have a modified character, approaching the French style.[4] The most outstanding of these is Queen Mary's Psalter (see below). The explanation of the variations in the East Anglian style seems to lie in the local provenance of the manuscripts. The principal centres where they were known to have been produced in the first quarter of the fourteenth century are the Diocese of Norwich, Peterborough, Bury St Edmunds, and York. In the second quarter of the century the style spread farther afield, and towards the middle of the century, manuscripts in the East Anglian style may have been made in London.

The beginnings of the style are found in the late thirteenth century. The earliest dated example is a psalter (Brit. Mus., Add. MS. 24686), begun for the marriage of Prince Alfonso,[5] son of Edward I, to Margaret, daughter of the Count of Holland, but not finished then, presumably because of the death of the Prince in 1284. Only the first quire of eight leaves in the Psalter (fols 11-18), including a magnificent *Beatus* page (Plate 118), is of this early date;[6] other leaves of this quire contain smaller historiated initials and borders with the naturalistic motifs characteristic of the East Anglian style. The quality of the work is exquisite, and the variety of flower, animal, and bird motifs attests to the artist's interest in natural life and his powers of observation and delineation of what he sees. There is reason to believe that the manuscript may have been begun at a Dominican house, possibly Blackfriars, London;[7] but the later part of the illumination is done in a style which we shall find to be characteristic of manuscripts made in Norwich. Whether the earlier style of the Alfonso Psalter was influenced directly by North French or Flemish illumination, or whether the new, freer style was the sole invention of English artists is a matter for conjecture.[8] But the fact remains that with the Alfonso Psalter the East Anglian style is fairly launched.

Closely related to the Alfonso Psalter and also early in date (between 1283 and 1300) is Brit. Mus., Roy. MS. 3 D. vi (Petrus Comestor's *Historia Scholastica*),[9] containing at the beginning of each book a large historiated initial and borders with naturalistic birds, animals, and grotesques, and heraldic shields. Millar again suggests Blackfriars, London, as a possible place of origin and notes[10] that French influence is strong in the manuscript. This influence, if indeed it is present, is again that of North France or Flanders, not Paris, and the naturalistic elements correspond to those in the Alfonso Psalter.

A third early manuscript with East Anglian characteristics but of unknown provenance is MS. 102 in the Morgan Library, New York – the 'Windmill Psalter' – so-called from the windmill introduced into the decoration on fol. 2 (Plate 119). This page is unusual because of the elaborate red and blue ornamental penwork surrounding the E, the second letter of the word *Beatus*,[11] of which the B with a Jesse Tree fills the whole of fol. 1 verso opposite. The remainder of the first words of the first psalm (*Beatus vir qui non*) are found on the scroll held by the flying angel. The combination of painted figures and penwork, and especially the use of pale green wash as shading on the latter, remind us of the mixed technique used in thirteenth century Apocalypse drawings.

The three early examples discussed above pose the problem of the origins of the East Anglian style; all three are certainly English,[12] yet in all three appear some elements of a new phase of English style: the charming informality of various kinds of naturalistic motifs, quaint, original types of grotesques, and exquisite draughtsmanship and colouring.

The earliest manuscript fully in this style and of certain provenance is the Peterborough Psalter[13] (Brussels, Bib. Roy., MS. 9961–2) dating from c. 1300. The decoration consists of the usual Calendar, a magnificent *Beatus* page (fol. 14; Plate 120) with David, and historiated initials with full borders for the principal psalms. An unusual additional feature is the series of types and antitypes, scenes from the Old and the New Testament, which are distributed throughout the manuscript and which are thought to have been copied from twelfth century paintings formerly in the choir of Peterborough Cathedral.[14] The best work in the manuscript is on fols 10–14 and recalls the finely drawn and spirited subjects of the Tenison Psalter and the Ashridge Priory Peter Comestor (see above). Folio 14 (Plate 120) has an elaborate border with animals and birds and amusing figures, one on stilts, among branches of oak leaves and acorns. A vivid hunting scene in the lower margin, and in the upper a cock riding a fox and a monkey[15] seated backward on a goat are among the many novel and diverting features of the decoration. The text of the Brussels Psalter is written throughout in gold, red, and blue letters. Originally the miniature pages must have been even more beautiful than at present; for a later French royal owner somewhat disfigured the backgrounds by adding gold fleur-de-lis and shields, thus overcrowding the compositions and margins. The style of the decoration in the Peterborough Psalter seems to have changed during the course of its illumination; on later pages (from fol. 26) there appears, among other new features, the foliage motif christened by Cockerell[16] the 'serrated cabbage leaf', which becomes a hallmark of the East Anglian style, especially that of the Norwich Diocese. The borders on these later pages resemble in design and motifs the Ormesby-Gorleston group (see below).

Another psalter (Camb., Corpus Christi Coll., MS. 53; Plate 122) not only shows evidence of Peterborough use in the Calendar and Litany, but contains the obit of a Prior of Peterborough and the Chronicle of Peterborough down to 1229.[17] There is evidence, however, that the manuscript was written for use in the Diocese of Norwich,[18] but whether it was illuminated there or in Peterborough is impossible to say.[19] Apart from the usual illustrated Calendar and historiated initials to the psalms, the manuscript contains two exceptionally interesting features: a set of twenty-four full-page miniatures, twelve of the life of Christ and of the Virgin, interspersed with twelve pairs of prophets and apostles. James[20] has pointed out the unusual, in fact unique, arrangement of these pictures in groups of four after the manner of small painted diptychs: the prophets and apostles, under paired trefoiled arches, are drawn on the vellum background and lightly tinted, and are so placed that they seem to form the outsides – actually the backs of the leaves – of two facing miniatures painted in colours upon a tooled gold ground. The painted subjects are grouped as the Joys and the Sorrows of the Virgin, with a dramatic link between the two in the group where the Coronation of the Virgin, the culminating

Joy, faces the Betrayal of Christ, the first of the Sorrows. If the subjects and their arrangement are correctly interpreted, the prototypes of the miniatures might have been a series of panel paintings of which unfortunately no comparable set survives.

The styles of the miniatures, both the tinted drawings and those in full colour (fol. 16, Plate 122), which are not apparently by the same artist, are characterized by the fine, careful drawing in the faces and by the long, graceful lines of the draperies which swing round the figures enveloping them in a pattern of rich, Gothic curves. The faces are tinted with pale colour and the hair is swept back from the forehead in a loose mass of curls with a wave over the ear. The gestures and, especially in the tinted drawings, the positions of the hands and feet are somewhat mannered, and the tall, slender figures themselves seem to swing and sway with the draperies. These characteristics are normal in early fourteenth century Gothic art; but the English figures are flatter and less modelled than the French, and the draperies are mere linear surface patterns. The facial types too have a delicate charm and variety which is typically English.

In the miniature reproduced (Plate 122) the Virgin and St Christopher stand under a double enclosing arch against a burnished and patterned gold ground. The incongruity of placing a grass plot under the Virgin's feet and a small pond with fishes, even an eel, swimming around the feet of Christopher has not troubled the artist. The tall, slender, graceful figures with their sweeping draperies, the rich yet soft colouring against the brilliant gold ground are strikingly effective.

The preliminary miniatures in Camb., Corpus Christi Coll., MS. 53 constitute only one of the two extraordinary features of this fine manuscript; the other is the addition, at the end of the Psalter, of a completely illustrated Bestiary by the artist of the tinted drawings. This part of the manuscript contains some of the most original work in it. Although, as we have seen, Bestiary subjects had long since been introduced into manuscript decoration, this is the first time that a series has been incorporated bodily as an integral part of the contents of a liturgical manuscript. This feature, together with the stylistic characteristics of the painted miniatures as pointed out above, forms the basis for the resemblance noted by Cockerell[21] between MS. 53 and Queen Mary's Psalter (Plate 123).

One more manuscript should be noted in connexion with the 'Peterborough style', although actually executed at Ramsey Abbey, a Benedictine monastery near Peterborough.[22] The date is *c.* 1300. The manuscript is now separated into two parts: five leaves painted on both sides with Bible pictures constitute MS. 302 in the Morgan Library (Plate 121); and the Psalter to which these leaves originally belonged, now in the Benedictine monastery of St Paul in the Lavanttal, Carinthia (MS. XXV.2.19). The Psalter has the usual illumination including the Calendar and the *Beatus* and other historiated initials, and shows the characteristic early East Anglian variety and charm in the decoration.

The miniature on fol. 8 (Plate 121) is in two registers. The ogee arches under which the two central scenes are placed are very like those of the miniatures in the Brussels Peterborough Psalter. The figure types also are extraordinarily close, especially in the use of a spot indicating modelling on the cheek and in the arrangement of the hair. It is possible that the same artist worked on both manuscripts. In the miniature of the Ramsey Abbey

Psalter the upper subject, the murder of St Thomas Becket, is flanked by a bishop holding a model of a church, and by St Paul. Below, a mitred abbot is seated with his feet on a ram, and a tonsured abbot rests his feet on a species of goat (?). Whether the ram is introduced in reference to the name 'Ramsey' can only be conjectured; such whimsies would not be foreign to the bizarre spirit of English medieval humour. The faces of all the figures in this and the other miniatures are eager in expression and the gestures are lively as in the Brussels Psalter. The colour is particularly fine, with deep ultramarine and lighter blues used for draperies, and for background, alternating with dull pink; the arabesque patterns are in white and the roses are gold. As usually in Peterborough work, the gold ground is tooled with squares or diamonds enclosing groups of dots.

The manuscript known as Queen Mary's Psalter[23] (Brit. Mus., Roy. MS. 2 B. vii; Plate 123) contains no evidence of its origin or early ownership. The date seems to be early fourteenth century. Its resemblance in certain features to Camb., Corpus Christi Coll., MS. 53 and the Peterborough manuscripts might suggest the Fen country as a possible place of origin. Millar considers it the 'central manuscript of the East Anglian group',[24] yet its decoration, apart from the wealth of miniatures and *bas de page*[25] illustrations, consists of fairly simple, often-repeated leaf and flower forms limited to groups of two or three attached to the corners of the rectangular miniatures which in this manuscript replace the usual large historiated initials at the beginnings of the principal psalms. The illumination seems to be wholly by one hand, even though the technique, like that of Corpus 53, is partly painting in full colour and partly tinted drawing. The artist, who was a consummate draughtsman, was primarily an illustrator rather than a decorator.

The illumination in Queen Mary's Psalter has been described so often and reproduced so widely that only a brief summary of the kinds of decoration it contains is necessary. The first sixty-six folios are filled with a long series of Old Testament scenes, from the Fall of Lucifer to the Death of Solomon, in the form of tinted drawings, usually two to a page, a total number of 223 drawings. Beneath each is a line of explanatory text in French. On fol. 67 verso is a full-page Tree of Jesse in a rectangular miniature. On fol. 68 are four miniatures representing the three Marys and the unusual subject of St Anne and her three husbands; there are also the Virgin and Child and Christ Enthroned. On fols 69 verso and 70 are two miniatures in six compartments, each with an apostle and a prophet (cf. Corpus MS. 53). The Calendar begins on fol. 71 verso and each month occupies two facing pages, with a miniature across the top of the leaf at the beginning of each month. The Psalter proper (fols 85–280) is illustrated with a series of miniatures from the life of Christ with a tinted drawing at the bottom of each page, the subjects drawn from all manner of sources (fol. 112 verso; Plate 123). Finally the Canticles (fols 280 verso– 302) are illustrated with scenes from the Passion in miniatures, and the Litany (fols 302 verso–318) with miniatures of saints. No other known psalter has such a complete and varied complement of illustrations, and no other English manuscript equals it in the sustained high quality of its workmanship.

The technique of Queen Mary's Psalter, whether in the miniatures using colour against gold or diapered grounds or in the delicately tinted drawings against the plain vellum ground, is almost purely linear. Features, hair, and drapery folds are indicated with lines, and only in the deep folds and on the cheeks is there a little shading in colour. In general, the scenes are represented on a very small scale, and in this respect the style differs from the Peterborough pictures, which suggest rather the scale of panel or wall painting. But many of the miniatures in Queen Mary's Psalter – in fact, all up to fol. 234 – are placed under architectural canopies, like the preliminary pictures in Cambridge MS. 53. The rich draperies and delicately modelled faces, the use of both painting and drawing technique, and even the incorporation of such new matter as the Bestiary subjects and the paired prophets and apostles, connect this Psalter, in some unexplained manner, with the Peterborough East Anglian style.

There are several other manuscripts illuminated partly or wholly by the artist of Queen Mary's Psalter. One is a Psalter (Malvern, Dyson Perrins, MS. 14) which belonged to Richard of Canterbury, a monk of St Augustine's Abbey.[26] Judging from the Calendar and Litany, the Psalter was made for use there, although not necessarily a product of that scriptorium. Its date is early fourteenth century, perhaps earlier than Queen Mary's Psalter.[27] Its decorative scheme is that of the conventional English psalter, with historiated initials for the fourteen more important psalms, but the partial borders have East Anglian naturalistic foliage and animal motifs. Another manuscript clearly in the style of Queen Mary's Psalter is a Bible (Cambridge, Univ. Lib., Dd. 1.14) with a fine Genesis initial decorated with a series of exquisite small scenes (fol. 5) and an historiated *Beatus* initial (fol. 179). Many of the decorative initials throughout the Bible are painted in gold and colours; others are pen-drawn.

The finest member of the Queen Mary's Psalter group, a copy of the Apocalypse with a French text (Brit. Mus., Roy. MS. 19 B. xv), was illuminated by three artists of whom the first was certainly the illuminator of Queen Mary's Psalter. A comparison of this style (fol. 5 verso; Plate 124) with fol. 112 verso (Plate 123) shows figures identical in the type of heads and of draperies. The shaded foliage in the Apocalypse can be matched in Queen Mary's Psalter, though the scale in the Apocalypse miniature is larger and the motifs are less naturalistically rendered. The background in the Apocalypse miniature is coloured red and blue as in many of the pictures in Queen Mary's Psalter, but it is plain, without diapering or other patterns, and the setting, though formal, has more suggestion of space than the architectural canopies or the barbed quatrefoil medallions in which the painted miniatures in Queen Mary's Psalter are usually placed. The Apocalypse, therefore, might appear to be somewhat later than Queen Mary's Psalter (*c*. 1320–30), the two techniques of painted miniature and free marginal drawing combining in these most lovely coloured drawings of typical English character.[28]

The styles of Corpus Christi Coll. MS. 53 and Queen Mary's Psalter represent only one branch of the main stream of development in East Anglian manuscript illumination;[29] the other branch is characterized by more lavish decorative elements, and appears to have been localized in the neighbourhood of Norwich. One of the earliest of the psalters in this style (Oxford, Bod. MS. Douce 366; Plates 125 and 126B) was written and perhaps partly illuminated at Bury St Edmunds[30] at the close of the thirteenth century. It was finished in successive stages during the early fourteenth century. It may still have been unbound when it was acquired by a monk of Norwich, Robert of Ormesby, and given to Norwich Cathedral *c.* 1325. Probably at this time the Psalter was given a second *Beatus* page and the earlier one was subsequently altered to receive the portraits of Robert himself and an abbot; the earlier style (*c.* 1300) can be seen in the remainder of the decoration on this page.[31] The tooled gold panels containing the two kneeling clerics have been placed over parts of the vine which enclosed further words on the opening text of the first psalm. The modelling of the faces and draperies in these portraits is much heavier than in other figures on the page, and there is a curious use of white pigment for the high-lights, which produces a strange, heavy-lidded, facial type with white on eyelids, nose, and around the mouth. This we shall meet again in later stages of the East Anglian style. The same technique is found in the figure of King David harping, which fills the second *Beatus* initial on fol. 10. The earlier style of the first *Beatus* page is found on some other pages of the Psalter, where historiated initials against gold or finely diapered grounds send out a rich foliage border, broken at intervals by interlaced knots and peopled by all manner of birds, animals, and human and animal grotesques. Subsequent pages slightly later in date (*c.* 1310) with historiated initials introducing the principal psalms (fol. 147 verso; Plate 125) have similar full-page borders containing a wealth of leaf, flower, animal, bird, insect, human, and grotesque motifs used in a variety of ways and perhaps with more spirit than good taste.

The subject of the initial D, God the Father and Christ the Son, seated side by side in an elaborate architectural setting, illustrates the text of Psalm 109 (A.V. 110): 'Dixit Dominus Domino meo: sede a dextris meis (The Lord said unto my Lord, sit thou at my right hand).' They are flanked by two seraphs and under the footstool of the figure on the left (Christ? on the right of God) five knights in full armour are kneeling. Flying about the initial are some most exquisitely drawn and painted birds, while in the border of the right hand margin an alternating series of butterflies and beetles forms the central motif of the bar-branch. In the upper margin an owl seated backward on a rabbit is pursued by a monkey, wearing falconer's gloves and riding on a greyhound. In the bottom margin a double fight rages fiercely: two naked men at fisticuffs are seated on a lion and a bear, and the lion has its teeth and claws buried in the neck of the bear. In the left margin, the most curious figure of all is shown: a semi-nude man sketchily draped is represented with the upper and lower parts of the body facing in opposite directions; he is blowing a trumpet from which a pennant flaps. The meaning of this strange figure, Pächt has suggested, may be found in certain phases of Italian influence.[32] Whatever their source, the lusty spirit of such drolleries as are found on this page is refreshing, and a study of these pages is its own reward in the light it throws on medieval fantasy and humour.

All the large initials on the pages of the Ormesby Psalter which were decorated *c.* 1310 were not done by the same hand. Plate 126B, reproducing a detail in actual size of fol. 131, shows much less variety in the foliage motifs, the principal one being a trefoil or cinquefoil which is large in size and is painted with spots of white intended to suggest shading as of plastic form. The facial types too are somewhat different and closer to those of another East Anglian manuscript, the Dublin Apocalypse (Plate 127). In the style illustrated on plate 126B the grotesques show a tendency towards exaggeration and coarseness which we shall see developing in subsequent decades. But the cat watching a rat just emerging from its hole, and the sentimental, sad-eyed dog seated between the young man with a falcon on his wrist and the lady holding her pet squirrel, are among the most charming of the natural animals represented in the Ormesby manuscript.

There are other manuscripts illuminated in one or more of the styles of the Ormesby Psalter; one of these furnishes a possible clue to the centre of their production. At Malvern, in the collection of Mr C. W. Dyson Perrins, is a psalter (MS. 13) in the Calendar of which is entered the Dedication of the church at Gorleston, Suffolk. In the fourteenth century MS. 13 was at the Cathedral Priory of Norwich.[33] The illumination, as in the Ormesby manuscript, consists of large historiated initials (Plate 126A) to the principal psalms, with bar borders of very great richness in both the number and the variety of the motifs and particularly in the lively and interesting animal scenes in the margins. An additional feature not found in the Ormesby manuscript is a full-page Crucifixion with Mary and John[34] painted in shaded colours including violet – unusual in English manuscripts – against a brilliantly diapered ground and surrounded by a frame containing the arms of England and medallions with portrait (?) heads. The date of the Gorleston Psalter must be close to that of the Ormesby middle style, that is, c. 1310–25 (cf. Plate 125). The Crucifixion page, however, is probably later and may have been added after the manuscript went to Norwich. The style on this page is a development of that of the Ormesby portraits which were added to the first *Beatus* page.[35]

The large historiated initial representing the Resurrected Christ appearing to King David (fol. 52 verso; Plate 126A) is remarkable for the extremely rich and varied patterning of the diapered and tooled gold background, outside and even inside the initial, in the arches over the figures. The initial itself consists entirely of slender interlaced bands ending in scrolls and leaves decorated with white spots. A grotesque of the more conventional French type appears in the margin. There is, in fact, something of the fineness of French technique in this style as a whole, as compared with the more painterly modelled style of the later work in the Ormesby Psalter (Plate 125). The richness of the design and the brilliance of the colouring on the most elaborate pages of the Gorleston Psalter, especially of the *Beatus* page (fol. 8), cannot be imagined from any reproduction.[36] It was matched in quality only by the slightly later Douai Psalter (now destroyed), which showed the same marvellous skill in draughtsmanship and the same exquisite balance of colour rivalling in its distribution over the page the rich mosaic effect of the best early French stained glass. The East Anglian style never surpassed the quality of the work in these two manuscripts, as in the first part of another one, very similar in style and only slightly inferior in quality, the St-Omer Psalter (Plate 129 below).

Several other manuscripts have illumination in the Ormesby–Gorleston style, perhaps by one or more of their several artists. Of these, the finest and most monumental in scale[37] is the Dublin Apocalypse (Trin. Coll., MS. K.4.31). The pictures which occupy half or more of the page (Plate 127) are designed in eight-foiled medallions placed against diapered grounds and surrounded by a rectangular frame filled with small geometric patterns. There are no foliage borders and the initials are of the plainest and simplest form, gold on pink and blue grounds. The figure compositions are on a large scale and almost completely fill the medallions. There is a suggestion of the technique of panel painting or perhaps even of sculpture in the scale and clarity of the drawing and in the strongly shaded colour, but the details necessary for the understanding of the scene, the temple, the altar, the grapevine which the angel with the sickle is about to cut down, are arranged in a purely decorative manner with no indication of spatial relationship. The application of the East Anglian style to large-scale drawing we shall meet again in manuscripts of slightly later date (cf. Arundel 83 below).

One other group of four manuscripts, three psalters and one Book of Hours, of the first quarter of the fourteenth century, having East Anglian characteristics, has been localized in central England, in the vicinity of Nottingham, where a group of lay illuminators may have been working. Two of the psalters, it is true, have Calendars pointing to Yorkshire (London, Lambeth Palace Lib., MS. 233, and Munich, Bayerische Staatsbib., Cod. gall. 16); the Hours (Camb., Fitz. Mus., MS. 242; Plate 128) has no Calendar; the third Psalter (New York, Pub. Lib., Spencer Colln, MS. 26) also has no Calendar but an inscription on fol. 1 refers to Brother John Tickhill, Prior of the Monastery of Worksop, near Notting-ham, 'who wrote this book ... and also gilded it ...'[38]

The illumination in these four manuscripts takes the usual form of historiated initials and borders; the Lambeth and Fitzwilliam manuscripts have the additional feature of a full-page miniature of Christ. The borders are less florid in design and in motifs than in most other manuscripts decorated in the East Anglian style. In three of the group, the motifs are chiefly variations of the trefoil form (cf. Plate 128), perhaps denoting Parisian influence on the style, such as has been detected in the iconography.[39] The Tickhill Psalter, however, introduces many types of foliate forms including a number of recognizable naturalistic ones.[40] Another characteristic feature of the Tickhill manuscript is the lavish use of inscribed scrolls explaining the pictures; in some cases they are so numerous as to mar the design. The illumination in this manuscript was left unfinished and on the later pages the order of successive processes in the drawing and painting of them can be followed.

Undoubtedly the most charming feature of decoration common to all the manuscripts in this group is the great number of *bas de page* and other marginal scenes, especially those with hunting and other animal subjects (Plate 128). Though lively, varied, and quaintly humorous, as the squirrel praying in the upper left margin, they are never vulgar and there is admirable freedom and skill in their rendering. The date of the Fitzwilliam Hours is *c.* 1308.[41]

The East Anglian style reached its height early in the second quarter of the fourteenth century in the illumination of two superb psalters known as the Douai and the St-Omer Psalters. The Douai Psalter most unfortunately was totally ruined by damp during the First World War and is now lost to us. The St-Omer Psalter formerly in the Yates Thompson Collection[42] is now in the British Museum (Add. MS. 39810). This fine manu-script was probably begun *c.* 1330, for members of the St-Omer family of Mulbarton, Norfolk, whose portraits appear on fol. 7; it was finished only in the fifteenth century for the famous bibliophile, Humphrey, Duke of Gloucester.[43] The early style, best repre-sented in the *Beatus* page (fol. 7; Plate 129), is profuse in the amount and infinitely varied in the elements of the decoration, both of the initial and of the full-page border; more-over, the vine branches and their motifs have become much smaller and more delicate in their rendering than they were in the Gorleston group. The design of the initial, a Jesse Tree as is usual, fills but does not overcrowd the space, and the tooled gold ground sets off effectively the vine scrolls and figures and is itself set off by the finely diapered blue and pink background of the square field. The gold ground continues all round the border of the page, filling the medallions and joining them together under the connecting interlaced panels. The leaf and flower motifs of the border are set closely on fine, hair-line or slender tapering stems which issue from the interlaced knots at intervals; the coloured motifs, red, blue, green, are interspersed with groups of round or oval gold leaves. The variety of subject matter is bewildering. Apart from the Old Testament scenes in the medallions, some of which seem to be parodied in the marginal figures, almost every kind of wild and domestic animal and bird – and a butterfly and a snail to boot – and a wide range of human activities are represented. Strangely enough, there are none of the human-animal grotesques such as are found in many other East Anglian manuscripts. The drawing is exquisite, the design is well-ordered, the colouring delicate, and the total effect inconceivably rich. The modelling of the heads and draperies, especially in the initial and in the medallions of the border, is of the type found in the portraits of Robert of Ormesby and the abbot added to the *Beatus* page of the Ormesby Psalter. Besides the *Beatus* page, the fourteenth century illumination in the St-Omer Psalter is found on three other pages with large historiated initials and full borders (fols 57 verso, 70 verso, and 120); still other pages show traces of the early decoration painted over in fifteenth century style. (See Chapter 8.)

Two final examples of East Anglian manuscripts dating from the later 1330s illustrate the trends of the style in its ultimate development. Both manuscripts are impressive in size (15 by 9 inches, and 14 by 9), in the amount of their decoration, and also in the scope of the subject matter treated. Both are now in the British Museum (Arundel MS. 83 and Add. MS. 42130).

Arundel MS. 83, known as the Psalter of Robert de Lisle,[44] is made up of two partial psalters, of which the first (fols 1–116) is perhaps twenty-five years earlier than the second. Some interesting preliminary pictures precede the first Psalter: a finely drawn and tinted seraph standing on a wheel (fol. 5 verso); a series of small pictures illustrating the twelve articles of the Apostles' Creed flanked by twelve apostles and twelve prophets (fol. 12); a page containing the seven acts of the Passion, flanked by representations of the seven canonical Hours and the seven last words of Christ (fol. 12 verso), and a symbolic Crucifixion explained by texts on scrolls (fol. 13). The *Beatus* page (fol. 14) has a large initial with a Tree of Jesse topped by a Crucifixion and a rich border containing heraldic shields and a hunting scene in the lower margin. There are historiated initials with simple borders for the principal psalms. The decorative style is of good quality, as in earlier East Anglian manuscripts, but the symbolic subject matter in its formal arrangement would be suitable for wall painting design.

The second part of the de Lisle Psalter consists only of a second Calendar and a great many pages of miniatures which, both in subject and in monumentality of scale, also suggest wall or panel paintings. Some of the more unusual subjects are worth noting, as the Twelve Properties of the Human State (fol. 126), the Ten Ages of Man (fol. 126 verso), the Three Living and the Three Dead, with inscriptions in English (fol. 127; Plate 130B), the ten Commandments with Christ and Moses (fol. 127 verso), the Tree of the Vices (fol. 128 verso) and of the Virtues (fol. 129, on facing pages), the Seven Spheres of the Wheel (fol. 129 verso), the Seraph on the Wheel (fol. 130 verso, cf. the same subject on fol. 5 verso). In addition to these didactic and symbolic pictures, there is a magnificent full-page Christ in Majesty (fol. 130) and an equally fine Virgin and Child (fol. 131 verso). A number of other pages are divided into panels or medallions containing scenes from the Nativity and Passion cycles of the life of Christ, and at the end of the book, full-page pictures on fols 133 verso–134 verso of the Ascension (Plate 130A), Pentecost, and the Coronation of the Virgin.

Two styles are easily distinguishable in miniatures of the second part of Arundel 83. Untinted outline drawing of exquisite delicacy (Plate 130B) is always used by this artist for the faces and sometimes for the draperies, though often the latter are painted and shaded heavily. There is a strong decorative emphasis in this work, which is seen in the elaborate architectural canopies and in the fine diapered patterns in the pages containing many scenes. This style, though certainly English, has a French delicacy in the technique and French good taste in the design.[45] The figures are not really modelled in spite of the shaded drapery and the strong firm contours.

The second style (fol. 133 verso; Plate 130A) which looks slightly later and is found mainly in the last pages of the book (except fol. 131 verso, which is by the first hand) has faces modelled in brownish flesh tone with white high-lights and touches of red on cheeks and lips. The draperies are exceedingly voluminous and richly shaded; the hands are especially well drawn and painted. There is certainly Italian influence in this style, which shows not only in the modelling and in the shaded draperies, but in the firmer conception of the figure under the draperies and in the grouping of the figures. By the same token, there is much less interest in the decorative patterning and less variety and precision in the ornamental patterns. It seems possible that the second style developed out of the first under some form of influence from Italian painting, or perhaps from a mixture of French and Italian elements.[46] The draperies in this second style are incredibly rich in colour, owing to the display of 'double-faced' or lined materials, that is, one colour for the outer side and another for the inner side of a garment, the change of colour showing in the convolutions of the folds. The colours chiefly used in this way are blue or tan with green 'lining' and green with tan lining. Other colours are clear red and grey.

The other final example of the East Anglian style (Brit. Mus., Add. MS. 42130), the famous Luttrell Psalter,[47] illustrates particularly well the breakup of the decorative and grotesque elements of the style and at the same time the increased emphasis on illustrative pictures in the margins (Plate 131). This latter feature we have seen, it is true, in Queen Mary's Psalter, but there the pictures were confined to delicately drawn vignettes in the bottom margins. In the Luttrell Psalter the pictures are not only in the bottom margins, but run up the sides and across the top of the pages as well, or even, as in the case of the often reproduced Travelling Coach for Ladies,[48] across two facing pages. The scale of these scenes and also of the monstrous, often hideous and vulgar grotesques is disproportionately large in relation to the borders, and even the motifs in the borders usually are too large and coarse to be beautiful. It has been suggested[49] that the manuscript was not decorated as planned when written; but the picture of the Luttrells on fol. 202 verso,[50] which can be dated not later than 1340, is in the same style as many other pages in the 'cheap and coarse' style noted by Millar. Certainly some pages are better than others, but too often even a reasonably good initial and border (fol. 169 verso; Plate 131B) is spoiled by a repulsive grotesque.

Without doubt the most interesting feature of the Luttrell Psalter is the series of scenes drawn from contemporary life, which have been used repeatedly to illustrate books on medieval English life.[51] There are, for instance, agricultural scenes,[52] scenes from home life, travel, sports and games, occupations and trades, animal life, and illustrations from romances. Though often crudely drawn and painted, these scenes display a lively realism in the actions and expressions of the figures and a close observation of details which give the pictures a very special value for understanding the conditions of medieval living. The technique of most of the painting is related to that of the two portraits added to the first *Beatus* page of the Ormesby Psalter and also to the early part of the St-Omer Psalter. The faces are modelled with much use of white, especially around the eyes and mouths, and the draperies are strongly shaded. The colours are somewhat different from those of earlier East Anglian manuscripts, in that a minimum of red and blue is used, and a considerable amount of violet and brown. The vigour of the modelling and the tendency to coarseness suggest a connexion with Flemish work, and it is obvious even in the earlier and better pages of this manuscript (Plate 131A) that the exquisite delicacy of the earlier East Anglian style has vanished and that whatever remains of its rich decoration and charming naturalism is far from producing such masterpieces as the Brussels Peterborough Psalter on the one hand, and the *Beatus* page of the St-Omer Psalter on the other.

Yet certain elements of the East Anglian style in its earlier phases do survive, and chief among these is the love of marginal illustrations which we have seen to be characteristic also of some earlier English manuscripts.[53] Two examples will serve to illustrate this trait: the so-called Taymouth[54] Hours (Brit. Mus., Yates Thompson MS. 13) and the Smithfield Decretals (Brit. Mus., Roy. MS. 10 E. iv; Plate 132). The outstanding feature of both these manuscripts, as of the Luttrell Psalter, is the amazing series of scenes illustrating all kinds of subjects in the bottom margins. Both manuscripts belong to the first half of the fourteenth century, probably near the middle. Neither can be considered fine illumination but both fall rather in the category of book illustration; the style is linear and the drawing, especially in the Decretals, is rather rough. There is very little border decoration in either, and only very few and simple leaf motifs are used.

The Smithfield Decretals, a large volume of the glossed decretals of Gregory IX, was written in Italy but illuminated in England, perhaps by the Canons of St Bartholomew's, Smithfield, in London.[55] The subject matter of the illustrations, some of which recalls that of the Luttrell Psalter, includes also Bible history and Lives of Saints, Romances and Fables, Allegories and scenes of everyday life (Plate 132). The technique is outline drawing filled in or shaded with flat colour. Although the drawing is for the most part rather carelessly executed, there is a tremendous liveliness and verve in both the animal and the human figures, and the pictures, like those in the Luttrell Psalter, have often been used to illustrate medieval life.

149

Also in the category of illustrated books is the Treatise of Walter de Milemete entitled *De Nobilitatibus Sapientiis et Prudentiis Regum* (Concerning the Nobility, Wisdom, and Prudence of Kings)[56] which was written and presented to Edward III *c.* 1326–7 (Oxford, Christ Church Lib., MS. E.11). In this volume every page of text has a full border filled with heraldic shields, small miniatures and grotesques. The subjects illustrated are concerned chiefly with the life of the king: the royal sport of hawking, the king with his knights, the king in court and council, and the king in battle (fol. 68; Plate 133). James distinguished four different artists,[57] of which the first painted the vigorous combat scenes in the borders beginning on fol. 60; his style, as James notes, is characterized by boldness of execution, and it is possible that his proper work was that of a mural painter. None of the artists are recognizable in any other manuscript and the source of the work is not known, but it probably was the product of a London shop. At the end of the book are some outline drawings, probably by the first artist, depicting engines of war, among them what is believed to be the earliest representation of a cannon.

Our final example of manuscript illumination in this chapter is, like the Walter de Milemete, more closely related to other forms of painting than to book decoration. This is the Bible Picture Book, formerly Holkham Hall MS. 666, but recently acquired from Lord Leicester by the British Museum (Add. MS. 47682). There is no evidence, other than stylistic, as to its dating, but it undoubtedly belongs to the first half of the fourteenth century, perhaps not much later than Queen Mary's Psalter. It consists of forty-two leaves containing some two hundred scenes which James [58] has divided into three sections: the beginnings of Old Testament History (fols 1–9); the Life of Christ (fols 10–38); and the Last Things (fols 39–42). The pictures begin by being full-page, then two registers are included on one page with several scenes in each register enclosed in lozenges with red hatched grounds. After fol. 9 few pages have these decorative grounds. The drawing of the faces and figures is broad and vigorous, not fine and meticulous as in the best illuminations; the colouring consists of washes of red and blue, with some green, yellow, and brown. The draperies are shaded but the faces show little modelling. In the Creation picture (fol. 2 verso; Plate 134) the imposing gesture of God in the act of creating the birds and animals has the effectiveness of monumental painting, but the poor little 'Noah's Ark' animals are lifeless compared with their charming prototypes in East Anglian manuscript borders. The birds are somewhat better.

The Holkham Bible Picture Book was apparently intended to be just that, namely, a book of pictures accompanied by a short explanatory French text sometimes in verse, sometimes in prose. On fol. 1 are represented, presumably, the artist and his employer who commissioned the book, a Dominican friar; an accompanying text, 'So I will, and if God grant me life, you will never see a better book than mine', suggested to James[59] that the book may have been illustrated by a professional artist in some other field, who was producing a set of copies from paintings which he knew or else following descriptions perhaps supplied by the Dominican. At any rate, the assortment of subjects represented is exceedingly wide and interesting, and the miniatures demonstrate the influence of the freshness and charm of the East Anglian style even though they lack its exquisite quality.

Opus Anglicanum

It is no accident that English embroidery, which also flowered magnificently in the late thirteenth and the first half of the fourteenth century, shows affinities in design and motifs with East Anglian manuscripts (cf. Plates 134 and 135). But whereas the manuscripts display local and individual variations in their decorative styles, the embroideries, as Mrs Christie has pointed out,[60] show certain systematic changes in design in the work of successive decades.

The principal stages in this evolution are three: (1) scroll work patterns, such as in the Worcester fragments (Plate 116A) of the late thirteenth century, related to similar patterns in late twelfth century wall painting and stained glass, and used as an all-over design; (2) geometrical panels, such as the barbed quatrefoils of the Clare Chasuble (Plate 117) and the medallions in thirteenth century stained glass, and the eight-point stars in the Westminster Retable; or other medallion forms, as plain or cusped circles; (3) architectural framework, which at first consisted of columns supporting foiled arches and gables, and later lost its architectural stability through the substitution of twisted stems for the columns; then, in the final phase, the arrangement of these stems to frame spaces of the desired shape and size for the figure subjects.

The three stages were by no means mutually exclusive nor is there any sharp chronological division between them; however, the order of their appearance is as given above, and the whole period covered by the evolution of the successive styles is little more than a half century. For example, the design of the Clare Chasuble consists of the characteristic features of both the first and second phases: scrollwork and barbed quatrefoil medallions simply arranged one above the other. In the last decades of the thirteenth century, the medallion designs began to appear more exclusively as, for example, on the cope in the Palazzo Comunale at Ascoli Piceno[61] in Italy, which was given by Pope Nicholas IV, 28 July 1288. The design is of the simplest geometric medallion type and consists of three rows of plain circles framing foiled circles enclosing the figure subjects. The shape of the cope using this design results necessarily in a number of partial medallions; there is, moreover, the problem of adapting the figure subjects not only to the shape of the medallion, but to their position on the cope when it is worn: the scenes cannot all be placed vertically in the medallions as they appear when the cope is laid out flat, because some of them would be upside down when it was worn. This type of design, therefore, rather quickly gave way to a more closely integrated arrangement – interlocked barbed quatrefoils as on the Vatican[62] and Syon[63] Copes (Plate 136), in which the figures could be arranged radially from the centre of the back. But this also resulted in some awkward problems, as can be seen in the apostle and angel figures at the sides, which stand diagonally in the panel. Where the circles are formed by the scrolls of the branches of the Jesse Tree[64] the problem is much simpler. Orphreys or any small panels of embroidery such as burses[65] take the quatrefoil medallions admirably. But for copes the basis of the design quickly changed into bands of architectural framework as in the Bologna Cope[66] (Plate 137), the columns of which could be spread at the bottom while the arches, narrowed in at the top, left a series of spandrels into which the angels with spread wings fit so beautifully. Between the two rows of arches a continuous band of star-shaped medallions[67] contains pairs of heads; a similar band tops the upper row of arches. The design thus divided into bands follows the semicircular shape of the cope, and while the arches all point towards the central area at the back of the neck, the effect of lines radiating from this centre is balanced by the circular bands of medallions which interrupt it; moreover, the arches in the lower band do not correspond in any fixed relation to those in the upper band. The advantage of composing the scenes in panels as in this design is the adaptability of the spaces. Architectural framework is suitable also for panels, as on orphreys[68] or altar dorsals (Plate 139), since they can be joined either vertically or horizontally as desired. The impressive figure of Christ Enthroned under such an arch probably formed part of an altar[69] frontal (Plate 135). The Annunciation above in similar architectural framework suggests that the design may have been affected by the frames of retables.

The final stage, the dissolution of the architectural framework into a radiating trellis-work of twisted branches which can be bent into any shape needed without breaking the unity of the design, is certainly the most satisfactory of all for ornamenting the cope; this design could be manipulated still further into what amounts to an all-over pattern, completely integrated yet allowing proper space for figures to stand upright in whatever part of the cope they might be placed. The twisted branch arcades developed, it seems, about 1325; good examples are the Pienza Cope,[70] the Butler Bowdon Cope,[71] and the chasuble matching it in the Metropolitan Museum, New York;[72] an example of the free vine pattern in all-over design is on the Steeple Aston Cope, on loan to the Victoria and Albert Museum.[73]

The subject matter usually found in ecclesiastical embroideries[74] was taken chiefly from the two main cycles of scenes from the life of Christ, the Nativity and the Passion, but the relative emphasis on these two series varies in different examples. The Bologna Cope (Plate 137) has seven scenes from the Passion in the upper tier of arcades, eleven scenes from the Nativity cycle and, in addition, the Martyrdom of St Thomas of Canterbury in the lower row. The central medallion of the upper band contains a head of Christ; in the other medallions are heads of apostles, saints, and prophets. The three central scenes of the Syon Cope (Plate 136) are the Coronation of the Virgin, the Crucifixion, and the Archangel Michael and the Dragon (Plate 138A). The Vatican Cope has a Madonna and Child in place of St Michael. In the lower rows of medallions in both copes are saints and apostles. Cherubs and seraphs standing on wheels (cf. Arundel MS. 83) fill the spaces between the medallions.

An unusual, in fact unique, subject is used for all but the three central medallions of the Ascoli Piceno Cope, namely, three groups of popes' heads, six martyred popes, six famed for their learning, and four nearly contemporary with Nicholas IV who held the See successively between 1242 and 1268. This cope was made to order for Pope Nicholas, between 1275 and 1280.

The techniques of English embroideries are clearly and fully explained with diagrams of the stitches in Mrs Christie's excellent book.[75] The workmanship in the early period generally is very good and the gold couching is used most effectively with the now faded but originally fresh and varied colours. It appears that much of the embroidery produced during this, the great, period of *opus anglicanum* was shop work of good quality.[76] The earlier work usually is all embroidered, figures and ground, with gold and coloured silks combined. Later work tends to embroider the figures with coloured silks against a patterned gold ground – a practice which suggests their relation to East Anglian miniatures. Gold and coloured silks and even pearls are used for the figures and decorative details on a greyish-blue silk twill background in the panel of Johannis de Thaneto (Plate 135); and a similar combination of gold pattern and coloured ground is used in the Metropolitan Chasuble, the Butler Bowdon Cope, and an altar dorsal in the Victoria and Albert Museum, all of which have red velvet grounds (Plate 139).

The closest stylistic relationship between the embroideries and East Anglian manuscript illumination is found in the later work, that is, in the first quarter of the fourteenth century. The similarities appear in the architectural frameworks with foliated crockets and finials, in the patterned gold grounds, and in animal and leaf motifs. Chief among these latter are oak leaves with acorns, and trefoil or cinquefoil leaves. The animals consist mainly of mask heads, lively little dragons, and even naturalistic animals, as on the Steeple Aston Cope. Heraldic animals also are used, probably often merely as decorative motifs, but sometimes in connexion with the arms of owners or donors.

In the earlier work and in the less fine later work, drapery on the figures is represented by completely linear patterns indicated by colour and by the direction of the stitches. The figures always have a strong dark outline when embroidered against a gold patterned ground; when the ground is not embroidered this is not so conspicuous. Some figures in the later work have the faces modelled in dark and light colour, while others show no modelling, the features being indicated in outline and colour used only in spots of pale pink on the cheeks. These two techniques were also used, as we have seen, in later East Anglian manuscripts (cf. Arundel MS. 83).

The present distribution of ecclesiastical vestments of *opus anglicanum* throughout Europe reflects the extent of the popularity and spread of this typical form of English art in the Middle Ages. The greatest number of fine embroidered copes exists in Italy, obviously the result of gifts to various popes by English kings, nobles, and ecclesiastics. A Vatican inventory of 1295 mentions *opus anglicanum* 113 times, greatly exceeding, says Christie, the number of embroideries of other specified workmanship. Outside Italy, fine examples of English embroideries still exist in Spain (Madrid, Toledo, Vich in Catalonia); in France at Lyons (in the Textile Museum) is a late thirteenth century Jesse Tree orphrey, and in the sacristy of the cathedral of Saint-Bertrand-de-Comminges are two fine copes presented to the cathedral by Pope John XXII in 1309. There are several examples of *opus anglicanum* in Brussels (Musée Cinquantenaire) and a cope in Stockholm, from Skå, and one in Uppsala. In England the most representative collection of examples is found in the Victoria and Albert Museum; there are also a few fragments in the British Museum. From the number of examples known to survive or mentioned in documents, the output must have been tremendous, and although no known centre has been established for the production of *opus anglicanum*, London has been suggested as the most likely. If, as Mrs Christie remarks, some of the pieces are no more than high grade hack work, this is not to be wondered at; yet in most of the surviving work of the great period (late thirteenth to early fourteenth century) one must be critical indeed to find flaws in either the workmanship or the designs.

Painting

Few examples of painting on wooden panels or on walls survive from the first half of the fourteenth century. Of the panel paintings the three most important are: two full-length figures of kings (Plate 142) out of an original four on the inside of the Sedilia in the choir at Westminster Abbey, and one king and a fragmentary Annunciation on the outside, all dated *c.* 1308; a retable at Thornham Parva[77] (Suffolk), also dated early in the fourteenth century, consisting of nine panels; in the centre, a Crucifixion with Peter and Paul (Plate 140), and in the four side panels on each side, standing figures of male and female saints under arches; and a long altar frontal or possibly the lid of a chest in the Musée de Cluny (Paris)[78] designed with four foiled medallions, each showing a scene from the life of the Virgin, in a peculiar order; left to right, Nativity of Christ (Plate 141A), Death of the Virgin, Adoration of the Magi, and Education of the Virgin (Plate 141B); the date, *c.* 1325–30.

The two last-named panel paintings are unquestionably closely related to the East Anglian manuscript style, the Thornham Parva Retable to the Norwich–Gorleston group, the Cluny panel to pages with similar medallions containing scenes from the early life of Christ[79] in Arundel MS. 83 (fols 124–5 verso). The style of the two panels shows some differences which may be due partly to their date. The medallion figures of the Cluny panel are extremely tall and slender, with rich shaded drapery, such as is characteristic of the later part of Arundel 83, painted before 1339. The faces have the smooth, oval shape of faces in this manuscript and some of them seem to be modelled; others, especially the women, have only a spot of pink on the cheek. The colours are duller and darker than in the manuscript, but this may be partly the result of prolonged exposure to light and dust. The Thornham Parva Retable is architectural in its general design, with the nine panels framed in the three sections of a triptych and separated from one another by slender half-columns which support a carved arcade. In the spandrels there is carved and gilded ornament; the columns and the patterned gesso backgrounds also are gilded. The total effect is very rich even though the individual colours tend to be rather dull – purples, greys, and browns prevailing. The total length of the Thornham Parva Retable is 12½ feet, its height about 3 feet.

The paintings of the Westminster Sedilia are probably by Master Thomas, son of Master Walter of Durham,[80] who is mentioned in the records as working for King Edward II *c.* 1308. He also was employed in restoring the Painted Chamber, and it has been suggested that the Sedilia figures resembled those in the Painted Chamber.[81] If there is a resemblance to surviving Westminster work, however, it would seem to be to the paintings in the south transept or even to the still earlier Westminster Retable from which the style of the south transept was perhaps derived (see Chapter 5). On the inside of the Sedilia there are two kings perhaps representing, according to Wormald, Sebert and

Ethelbert.[82] The figures are extremely tall and slender and the voluminous draperies lined with vair sweep about them in elegant, somewhat mannered curves. The colours are now darkened by the effect of varnishing about a hundred years ago. On the back of the Sedilia is the lower part of an Annunciation, discovered in 1922. The draperies have the same elegance and richness of linear pattern as those of the inside. On the two adjoining outside panels were figures of Edward the Confessor, of which the head only remains, and presumably of St John as a pilgrim to whom the King was offering the ring, as in the spandrel sculpture of the south transept.[83] The Sedilia paintings represent the later phase of the Court style initiated by William of Westminster in the first half of the thirteenth century.

Of the numerous traces of wall paintings from the first half of the fourteenth century, little survives which can give any clear idea of the style, but where it is possible to judge the quality, it would appear to have been on the whole rather poor. However, the schemes of wall decoration and the elaborate cycles of scenes represented evidently were fairly ambitious, and often the subjects and the novel manner of rendering them are very interesting. Four examples have been selected with typically elaborate schemes of mural painting dating from the first or second quarter of the fourteenth century. These are: Croughton (Northants), Chalgrove (Oxon), Peakirk (Northants), and Longthorpe (Northants). The dates are probably in this order: Croughton is dated c. 1300; Chalgrove and Peakirk at the end of the first or the beginning of the second quarter; Longthorpe in the second quarter of the century.

The Croughton and Chalgrove paintings were uncovered many years ago and have certainly deteriorated greatly since the descriptions of them were published;[84] Peakirk (near Peterborough), like the other two a tiny parish church (Plate 143A), was discovered[85] only in 1950–1; and Longthorpe, a private manor (Plate 143B) which is unique in having a tower with the walls completely painted with all kinds of subjects – religious, secular, allegorical, and purely decorative – was uncovered[86] in 1947. Chalgrove Church still shows a great many of the subjects which will be listed below as forming the scheme, though most of them are now faded, and without a key would perhaps scarcely be decipherable; the Croughton paintings, which must have been much finer in style than those of Chalgrove, now show only as dim shadows of scenes, with here and there a figure which can be identified. The paintings at Peakirk and Longthorpe are still as clearly visible as when first uncovered, and it is hoped that, with the methods now used to preserve them, they will remain so. Although all four of these places are geographically fairly close together, there seems to be no stylistic connexion between them. It is likely that the work in each case was done by a local painter, perhaps from some set of biblical pictures such as commonly precede the text of psalters,[87] but no basis for closely relating iconographically any two series of these or other known wall paintings has been found. It is true that in the case of the Longthorpe paintings, East Anglian features are present, especially in some of the foliage and animal motifs, and the work is good enough to have been done by an artist trained in so important an art centre as near-by Peterborough; but no stylistic connexions with any other known work, either manuscript or painting, have appeared.

Since little can now be seen of the style of the painting in the first two examples cited, their chief interest for the student of art is the scope and arrangement of the scheme. At Croughton the paintings cover both walls of the nave; the south wall is divided into three tiers, the north into two. The south wall has a very complete series of scenes from the life of the Virgin and the early life of Christ, beginning with the rejection of Joachim's offering in the temple, and ending with the Assumption of the Virgin. Two particularly interesting and rather unusual scenes in this series are the Virgin leaving her home, and her marriage. On the north wall is the Passion cycle ending with the Ascension and Pentecost, both now lost. Two additional scenes from the life of the Virgin are at the east end of the north aisle, in the Lady Chapel: the Annunciation and St Anne teaching the Virgin. Tristram, who apparently saw much more of the paintings than can be seen now, says they are 'executed with extraordinary certainty and sleight of hand; they are full of dramatic life, and give at the same time evidence of a very fine sense of line and composition'.[88]

The Chalgrove paintings have an even more complete scheme and a more balanced arrangement of individual scenes on the north and on the south walls. The north side begins with a Tree of Jesse, with the Annunciation figures in the window jamb adjoining; in two lower tiers in the centre of the wall are the Nativity, the Adoration of the Magi, the Massacre of the Innocents, and the Presentation in the Temple. Above these scenes, in the top tier, are four scenes from the Passion preceding the Crucifixion which is at the east end; below it, the Descent from the Cross and the Entombment. Two female saints, Helena and another, are in the east window jamb on this wall. In the chancel, on the north side: the Descent into Hell, the Resurrection, and the Ascension; flanking the east window, Peter and Paul; at the west end of the south wall, the Last Judgement in three zones; Bartholomew and perhaps Lawrence in the window jamb. In the middle sections, the Death, Funeral, and Entombment of the Virgin, the Miracle of the Jews, the Giving of her Girdle to St Thomas, her Assumption, and finally, at the east end of the south chancel wall, the Coronation of the Virgin, corresponding to Christ's Ascension on the north side. In the jamb of the remaining window on the south side are the two Saints John. The intention of planning a formal scheme with individual events in the lives of the Virgin and her Son is clear. The elaborate cycle of the Virgin's Death, especially the scene of the miracle at her funeral, may date the paintings, even apart from their style, later than those at Croughton (cf. Queen Mary's Psalter, with similar scenes in the marginal drawings). The style at Chalgrove was apparently less fine than at Croughton; the colours were yellow, red, and (?)blue; the figures were drawn in red outline. The subjects again evidently come from some picture book series, and the work is obviously that of local artists.

At Peakirk the workmanship is fairly crude, but the handling of the incidents and some of the unusual subjects make the paintings appealing and interesting. Most of the pictures are on the north nave wall, and except for some extraneous subjects, they all belong to one cycle, that of the Passion. An interesting and naïve feature of the arrangement is the placing of a huge St Christopher on the wall directly opposite the south doorway, actually interrupting the series of the Passion scenes in both the upper and the lower tier (Plate

143A). In the north aisle is an early example of a subject frequently found in later wall painting, namely, the Three Living and the Three Dead[89] (cf. Arundel MS. 83; Plate 130B). The three living kings are distinguished as to their ages. Over the north door is a scene which Mr Rouse[90] interprets as an allegorical representation of Gossip: two women in close converse, with a hairy devil leaning over their shoulders. The colours are the usual earth red, yellow, and dull green.

Of much better quality than anything that can now be seen in the other examples is the painting in the tower of Longthorpe, and unquestionably the finest single figure here is the king who stands behind the wheel of the five senses (Plate 143B), as identified by Mr Rouse (see note 86). The senses are symbolically represented by a monkey (taste), a vulture (smell), a spider in a web (touch), a boar (hearing), and a cock (sight). Mr Rouse suggests that this subject, together with the fashionable young man with his dog above the wheel, might be interpreted as the secular or worldly life contrasted with the contemplative or spiritual life on the wall opposite, which may be represented by some teaching figures and by the morality of the Three Living and the Three Dead, as was perhaps intended at Peakirk. Other subjects in this interesting scheme are the Wheel of Life with the Seven Ages of Man (cf. Arundel MS. 83 with the Ten Ages of Man, fol. 126 verso); pairs of Apostles, each with a portion of the text of the Creed (cf. Camb., Corpus Christi Coll. MS. 53); and several of the Labours of the Months, usually found in the Calendars of psalters and hours: January, a man warming himself at a fire, usually given to February; March, a man digging; December, killing a pig. In addition to these and other subjects only partially identified, there are a number of beautifully drawn and painted birds, several animals taken from the Bestiary, and some decorative foliage of the type found in East Anglian manuscripts. In fact, and this should surprise no one, the Longthorpe paintings have a great deal in common with the East Anglian style and, as already suggested, it seems likely that their artist was not a local dauber, but was trained in the school of Peterborough where we know paintings once adorned the choir and where the magnificent thirteenth century wooden ceiling of the nave with decorative designs, much repainted, can still be seen.[91]

Glass

Fourteenth century English glass, like that of the thirteenth, is neither plentiful nor has any of it survived without a great deal of mutilation, especially as to the heads of the principal figures, and without more or less questionable restoration. Moreover, in the fourteenth century as in the thirteenth most of the glass is localized, for the most part not in south England but in the North, primarily at York Minster, and in the Midlands, at Gloucester Cathedral and Tewkesbury Abbey. There is fourteenth century glass also in Somerset, notably at Wells Cathedral,[92] and a few isolated examples have even been preserved in small parish churches elsewhere, as at Deerhurst.

Unquestionably the richest collection of fourteenth century glass is found in York Minster,[93] and there may be an explanation for this in the fact pointed out by Knowles[94] that York is situated on a busy navigable river by which 'raw' glass – that is, sheets of coloured or white glass uncut and unpainted – could be and probably were brought into England across the Channel. For there is no positive evidence that the glassmaker's craft was practised at York or anywhere else in England during the Middle Ages.

At the beginning of the fourteenth century a number of innovations may be noted in respect to both the choice of colours and the design of stained glass windows, and in these developments it would seem that York took the lead. First in importance, perhaps, is the change in design from thirteenth century medallions with figure compositions[95] to panels with groups of figures or single figures under architectural canopies arranged in tiers in the long lights which were now unbroken by the formal patterns of the medallions as in earlier windows (cf. Plate 97).

Closely related to this fundamental innovation is another, the alternation in a single window light of coloured panels with grisaille panels containing shields or other small motifs. The arrangement of several lights in a single window in this alternation of coloured and grisaille panels gives the banded effect which is characteristic of fourteenth century windows (Plate 144).

These two new features are illustrated in the earliest fourteenth century glass at York Minster, the window in the north aisle of the nave,[96] given by Peter de Dene c. 1310 (Plate 144). Scenes from the life of St Catherine are arranged in two wide horizontal bands – two panels high, except for the central lower one containing the donor, which has three panels; between these bands and at the top and bottom are other bands of grisaille glass, one panel high, each enclosing a heraldic shield. The whole of each window light, the two tiers of coloured panels and the three of grisaille, is tied together by a coloured border containing heraldic devices and human and animal figures.

The third innovation to be noted in English fourteenth century glass is the discovery and subsequent excessive use of silver stain which, applied to white glass, colours it a rather strong yellow; this was used, apparently, to simulate gold in the tabernacle work of the canopies and also for details and sometimes for backgrounds. In the earlier windows, as the de Dene window at York, it is not excessive in amount, but the colour is usually too sharp to harmonize well with the duller red, blue, and green pot-metal glass. In another and later north aisle window at York Minster, the so-called Bell-Founders' or Tunnoc window, the yellow glass is used for dozens of bells hung in the tabernacle work and in the borders of each of the lights, which are banded like the de Dene window with grisaille and coloured panels. The date is before 1330.[97]

A fourth innovation in fourteenth century stained glass is first found in the Chapter House and Vestibule windows at York, dating from before 1335. This is the use of recognizable flower and leaf motifs treated naturalistically, such as the oak, maple, thorn, ivy, hop, and strawberry. Grotesque animals also are used, and this type of ornament reminds us at once of similar motifs used profusely in East Anglian manuscripts.[98] There is more grisaille glass in the Chapter House and Vestibule than coloured, and it seems possible that the influence of the near-by Five Sisters lancets filled with thirteenth century grisaille glass may be felt especially strongly here.

Finally, the great west window at York (c. 1338) illustrates well (Plate 146) the last fourteenth century innovation to be noted in glass, namely, the development of curvilinear patterns in the stone tracery of the upper part or head of the window. The earlier York windows described have foliated medallions of geometric plate-tracery in the heads, containing figure subjects (cf. Plate 144). Curvilinear tracery as in the York west window is designed in flowing lines which curve upward from vertical mullions of varying thickness and divide the window head into leaf-shaped lights. So irregular are most of these spaces that figure subjects and heraldic shields could not conveniently be fitted into them, and decorative patterns suggesting unsymmetrical leaf forms – at York white leaves against coloured grounds – are used with rich and pleasing effect. The eight lights of the west window contain single figures under tabernacles arranged in three or four bands of colour separated from each other by grisaille panels: eight archbishops are in the lower band, eleven apostles in the second band, and pairs of figures forming subjects in the third band and in the two central lights of the fourth. The subjects are, left to right: the Annunciation, the Nativity, the Resurrection, and the Ascension. In the two top centre lights is the Coronation of the Virgin.

The windows in the choir clerestory of Tewkesbury Abbey are little later than the York west window, though the style both of the tracery and of the glass is rather different. There are seven windows, five of five lights, two of four. The central window contains the Last Judgement, set under elaborate tabernacled canopies of white glass against coloured ground. In the bottom panels are heraldic shields. The four flanking side windows contain single figures of prophets, patriarchs, kings, and historical personages. The two windows having four lights – those nearest the crossing – contain single figures of knights who were lords of Tewkesbury (Plate 145B). The date[99] of the windows is c. 1344.

The knights are boldly drawn figures clad in armour that is transitional between chain mail and plate, and in blazoned surcoats. They stand against backgrounds of green, red, or blue, diapered or decorated with delicate arabesque patterns. Yellow is used for the chain mail and for the blazon of the surcoats and shields. In spite of much patterning, and some confusion due to restoration, the figures are among the most impressive found in English glass of the first half of the fourteenth century.

The final development of glass in this period is in the great east window of Gloucester Cathedral[100] (Plates 145A and 147) which in one unbroken wall of glass 78 by 38 feet commemorates the Battle of Crécy (1346) and the siege of Calais (1347); an examination of the heraldry has led to the conclusion that the window was in place by 1349. The window is wholly Perpendicular – in tracery, in design, and in colour – and it is the earliest known example of this style. The perpendicular and horizontal stone mullions and transoms divide the whole area into rows of rectangular panels each of which contains a single figure under a canopy. These separate figures, however, were conceived in relation to a single theme, the Coronation of the Virgin, of which they appear as witnesses, as in the great Italian Trecento altarpieces. The single figures are angels, apostles, saints, ecclesiastics, and kings. The three lowest rows are filled with quarried glass, each panel containing a star ornament and, in addition, those in the third row contain coats of arms.

The figure panels (Plate 145A) each contain a single figure in white glass under a white glass canopy, the side shafts of which extend into the light above and support the canopy there. The backgrounds are coloured, as are the borders of the draperies and the haloes:

ruby for the two central series of panels, and alternately ruby and blue for the outer tiers. Thus the colour effect in general is of vertical stripes of colour against a pattern of white figures and canopies.

The figures are beautifully drawn with full, rich draperies bordered by a pattern which curves in and out with the turn of the drapery folds. The position of the figures is strongly 'hip-shot' as in the latter part of Arundel MS. 83, but there is no suggestion of modelling of the body; the faces are carefully drawn, the hair and beard are thick and softly curling masses, the hands are delicately rendered with long, slender fingers. The drapery is shaded in the deep folds, as is the canopy, which has a certain suggestion of spatial depth partly because of this shading, partly because the cusps are made to project over portions of the figure. The style of the figure painting, like that of the window as a whole, shows progress as compared with Tewkesbury and York towards the clear and more natural rendering of the single figure, and heralds the plainer type of decorative painted glass which is characteristic of the late fourteenth and fifteenth centuries.

Summary

The first half of the fourteenth century well may be called the East Anglian period from the predominance of fine work produced there. As we have seen, the East Anglian style in general was marked by the variety of subject matter, by the originality with which it was treated, and by the rich and varied decorative elements. The sources of this style are partly to be found in the illustrated psalters, apocalypses, and bestiaries of preceding periods; but it would appear that some stimulating influence, perhaps from north France or Belgium, played a part in re-invigorating the older style. For the essence of the East Anglian style is its freshness, its earthiness, its pungent humour verging on vulgarity, and, above all, its fine colour and, in the later phase, the painterly technique of modelling the draperies. Many of these characteristics are found in a manuscript made about 1300 at Maastricht, Holland, a small Book of Hours (Brit. Mus., Stowe MS. 17) with miniatures and marginal scenes which, in lusty vigour and amusing originality as well as in type of decoration and general spirit, are closely related to East Anglian manuscripts of the early fourteenth century. Such examples as this may have influenced the East Anglian style. The English style, however, in the best period, is always much more lavish in its decoration; indeed, this profusion of ornamental features is perhaps its most strongly marked characteristic.

Whatever its origins, the East Anglian style quickly spread from manuscript illumination to the other arts in England; and from England to other parts of Europe. In the Lower Rhine, at Cologne, the Cathedral choir stalls are painted in a style which both in figures and in decoration shows signs of East Anglian influence. Even as far away as Bohemia its influence was felt and registered in the decorative style of a group of fine manuscripts made in the first half of the fourteenth century under the patronage of Johann von Neumarkt.

1. Both these terms have now become generic. Though the East Anglian manuscripts were largely produced in East Anglia (i.e. Norfolk and Suffolk), some examples of the style seem to have originated in other parts of England. The *opus anglicanum* (English work) in embroidery has not been localized anywhere; the name of a needlewoman, Mabel of Bury St Edmunds, mentioned frequently in the records between 1239 and 1244 as working for Henry III at Westminster, suggests an East Anglian connexion. See Christie, *English Medieval Embroidery*, 2, and Appendix I, 33–4.

2. See Millar, II, 24. On this question of the effect of the Black Death on the production of art, see Joan Evans, *English Art 1307–1461*, 74 ff.

3. Dom David Knowles, *Religious Houses of Medieval England* (London, 1940), 54.

4. The East Anglian style spread to the Continent but it also was affected by Continental, particularly French, influence even in England. See Georg Graf Vitzthum, *Die Pariser Miniaturmalerei* (Leipzig, 1907), 68–87.

5. Known as the Alfonso or the Tenison Psalter because of its later ownership by Archbishop Tenison (d. 1715). Saunders ascribes the Tenison Psalter to the Court School, but there are no known examples of the work of 'Court' illuminators at this time. Saunders, *Eng. Illum.*, I, 67.

6. The remainder of the Psalter and the Calendar containing obits of the mother, wife, and daughters of Edward I, were finished apparently for Elizabeth, Alfonso's sister, who married first John, Count of Holland, and later Humphrey de Bohun, Earl of Hereford. Prefixed to the Psalter are three leaves containing tiny miniatures of saints and scenes from the Passion, framed with borders containing the Bohun arms. The Bohun connexion is worth noting in view of the important group of fine illuminated manuscripts, some with strong East Anglian characteristics, made for members of the Bohun family in the third quarter of the fourteenth century. (See below, pp. 168 f.)

7. Millar, II, 63–4, 101–2.

8. *Op. cit.*, 63.

9. The manuscript seems to have been presented to Ashridge Priory (see inscription on fol. 1) by Edmund, Earl of Cornwall (d. 1300), who founded the Priory *c.* 1283. Edmund's arms occur on fol. 234. Reproduced, *op. cit.*, plate 95.

10. *Op. cit.*, 63.

11. Both pages (fols 1 verso–2) are reproduced, *op. cit.*, plate 99.

12. Cockerell, B.F.A. Club, *Exhib. Illum. MSS*, p. 140 22, says of Morgan MS. 102: 'It is unquestionably English, but there is something that suggests Parisian influence in the figures.'

13. See James, *A Peterborough Psalter and Bestiary*, 34 ff.; see also Van den Gheyn, *Le Psautier de Peterborough*. The manuscript was given by Abbot Godfrey de Croyland (1299–1321) to the French nephew of Pope John XXII.

14. *Op. cit.*, 34; see also James, 'On the Paintings formerly in the Choir at Peterborough', *Proc. Camb. Antiq. Soc.*, IX (1897), 178–94.

15. This is an early example of the so-called 'babewyns' which were so popular in the fourteenth century. See Evans, *op. cit.*, 38–44. Their invasion of the pages of liturgical manuscripts, whether made for clerics or laymen, is one of the most startling features of later medieval art.

16. Cockerell, *The Gorleston Psalter*, 1 ff.

17. James, *A Peterborough Psalter*, 13 and 15 ff.

18. The dedication of the church of Norwich was originally in the Calendar, but has been erased. I am indebted to Francis Wormald for this information.

19. A psalter which is almost certainly from Peterborough (Cambridge, Univ. Lib., MS. Dd.iv.17) is so close in style to Cambridge, Corpus Christi 53, as to suggest the same hand. Many of the compositions of the preliminary Bible pictures are the same. The technique of MS. Dd.iv.17, however, is a little less fine and the figures are less firmly drawn. It is possible that another artist was copying at Peterborough as closely as he could the pictures in MS. 53, which, whether made there or not, was certainly taken there. There is more evidence of another sort of the influence of MS. 53 and also of Dd.iv.17. A small silver pyx recently acquired by the Victoria and Albert Museum has on the outside of the lid an engraved figure of the Virgin and Child with a flower which is identical in design with this subject as represented in both Cambridge, Corpus Christi 53 (Plate 122) and Dd.iv.17: the drapery seems to

follow the arrangement of the Corpus Psalter, while the position of the Child is closer to that in DD.iv.17. The engraving is rather rough and there are traces of enamel still to be seen in the grooves. On the inside of the lid of the pyx is another subject which is obviously copied from MS. DD.iv.17: a Nativity. The connexion of the pyx with the University Library Psalter is not only stylistic but genealogical. See Charles Oman, 'The Swinburne Pyx', *Burl. Mag.*, XCII (1950), 337–41. Francis Wormald was the first to notice the stylistic relation between the pictures on the pyx and those in the manuscripts. Still another Peterborough Psalter with preliminary pictures in much the same style is Bod. MS. Barlow 22. See Millar, II, plates 22 and 23.

p. 140   20. James, *A Peterborough Psalter*, 18.

p. 141   21. *Ibid.*

22. See Robert Eisler, *Die illuminierten Handschriften in Kärnten*. Beschreibendes Verzeichnis der illuminierten Handschriften in Österreich, III (Vienna, 1907), No. 42, 83–9.

p. 142   23. Warner, *Queen Mary's Psalter*. The manuscript received this name from the fact that during her reign it was confiscated by English port authorities as it was about to be sent abroad, and was subsequently presented to her.

24. Millar, II, 13.

25. These marginal scenes and the general restraint in decorative elements suggest French influence in the style of Queen Mary's Psalter, as in the almost contemporary Pucelle manuscripts. Cf. L. Delisle, *Les Heures dites de Jean Pucelle* (Paris, 1910).

p. 143   26. Warner, *Descriptive Catalogue of Illuminated Manuscripts in the Library of C. W. Dyson Perrins* (Oxford, 1920), 57–9, plates XXI and XXII.

27. Cockerell dated it *c.* 1300; see B.F.A. Club, *Exhib. Illum. MSS*, 24, No. 50, plate 47.

28. A manuscript (*La Somme le roi*) in Cambridge (St John's College, MS. S.30) has a series of very fine historiated initials perhaps by the artist of Queen Mary's Psalter. See James, *Cat. of St John's Coll. Lib.*, No. 256. An Apocalypse in French bound with a copy of a French poem, 'La Lumiere as Lais' (Brit. Mus., Roy. MS. 15 D. ii), has miniatures and historiated initials close to Queen Mary's Psalter style but probably not by the same hand. This manuscript used to be attributed to Greenfield Nunnery (Lincs.). See Egbert, *The Tickhill Psalter and Related MSS*, 95–7.

29. For a general discussion of this second phase of East Anglian style see Cockerell, *The Gorleston Psalter*, 1–5.

30. *Summary Cat.*, V (1905), xxii–xxvii, a thorough examination of this manuscript and its history. See also Cockerell and James, *Two East Anglian Psalters*.

31. Reproduced Millar, II, plate 1.

32. Pächt, 'A Giottesque Episode in English Mediaeval Art', 54 ff. A carved figure of a trumpeter from a sarcophagus (reproduced, plate 15C) might be the model for the Ormesby trumpeter. This whole study of Italian influence on East Anglian and later English painting is most interesting and illuminating.

33. Cockerell, *The Gorleston Psalter*.

34. Reproduced, Millar, II, plate 14. See Pächt, *op. cit.*, plate 14, for Italian sources of this style. Italian influence, it will be remembered, was noticed at the end of the thirteenth century in the Westminster retable, both in the figure painting and in the patterned frames with cameo medallions.

35. This is in the Italianate 'modelled' style, described as 'Trecentesque' by Pächt, *op. cit.*, 51 ff. The stylistic history of the East Anglian phenomenon as a whole is still to be written, but Dr Pächt's article makes a promising beginning.

36. Millar, II, plate 15.

37. James, *The Dublin Apocalypse*. Two other manuscripts are related by James to the style: Bod. Ashmole MS. 1523 (the Bromholm Psalter) and Cambridge, Emmanuel Coll., MS. 112 (Gregory, *Moralia*).

38. Egbert, *The Tickhill Psalter*, 5. The other manuscripts of this group are also discussed by the author.

39. *Op. cit.*, 16–18.

40. *Op. cit.*, plates 87 and 88.

41. *Op. cit.*, 90 ff.

42. See *A Descriptive Catalogue of the Second Series of Fifty Manuscripts (Nos 51 to 100) in the Collection of Henry Yates Thompson* (Cambridge, 1902), MS. 58, 74–82.

43. On the fifteenth century additions, see Chapter 8 below.

44. Millar, II, plates 8–13; Warner, *Illum. MSS*, plate 31. The first psalter (fols 1–116 verso) was probably made for Sir William Howard of East Winch, near Lynn, Norfolk (d. 1308), or for his wife Alice de Fitton. At the end of the second Calendar is a note that Robert de Lisle gave this second psalter to his daughter Audere on 25 Nov. 1339.

8 45. On the relation of this miniature to a French manuscript, see R. Freyhan, 'English Influences on Parisian Painting of about 1300', *Burl. Mag.*, LIV (1929). But could the influence be reversed, that is, Paris on English?

Closely related to the style of the artist of the 'Three Living' is a single leaf belonging to the Staatliches Museum, Berlin (K.I.672), containing a superb painting of St Michael killing the Dragon. Reproduced, Oakeshott, *Sequence of English Medieval Art*, plate 35, opposite a coloured reproduction of the Three Living and the Three Dead from Ar. 83. The St Michael miniature was first published as East Anglian, by M. H. Bernath, 'An East Anglian Primitive in Germany', *Burl. Mag.*, LII (1928).

46. This is the time when Italian influence was very strongly felt in French miniatures of the Pucelle atelier. Cf. L. Delisle, *Les Heures dites de Jean Pucelle* (Paris, 1910).

47. E. G. Millar, *The Luttrell Psalter*.

48. *Op. cit.*, plates 115–16 (fols 181 verso–182).

9 49. *Op. cit.*, 5.

50. Reproduced in colour, *op. cit.*, frontispiece.

51. H. D. Traill and J. S. Mann, *Social England*, II (London, 1902); J. R. Green, *A Short History of the English People*, II (London, 1908); George M. Trevelyan, *An Illustrated English Social History*, I (London, 1949), and others.

52. A series of these has been reproduced in colour on post cards which are for sale at the British Museum.

53. As, for example, the Bury Psalter now in the Vatican Library; see above, pp. 50 f.

54. *Catalogue of Yates Thompson MSS*, Second Series, No. 57, 50–74, and *Illustrations from One Hundred MSS. in the Library of H. Y. Thompson* (London, 1914), plate LI. Pächt cites this manuscript as being 'the only one English MS. for the illumination of which Pucelle's style could have been the model', *op. cit.*, 53, n. 3.

55. A late fifteenth century inscription is found on fol. 1: Liber domus sancti Bartholomei in Smythfylde. The source of the illustration in this manuscript is suggested by Pächt to be Bolognese manuscripts, *op. cit.*, 55 ff.

50 56. James, *The Treatise of Walter de Milemete*.

57. *Op. cit.*, xxi–xxiv.

58. James, 'An English Bible-picture Book of the 14th Century (Holkham MS. 666), See also Léon Dorez, *Les Manuscrits à peinture de la bibliothèque de Lord Leicester* (Paris, 1908).

59. James, 'An English Bible-picture Book', 3.

60. Christie, *English Medieval Embroidery*, 7–9. p. 151

61. *Op. cit.*, 89–94, plates XLII–XLV; see also W. R. Lethaby, 'English Primitives: The Ascoli Piceno Cope and London Artists', *Burl. Mag.*, LIV (1929), 304–8.

62. Christie, *op. cit.*, 94–6, plates XLVI–XLIX.

63. *Op. cit.*, 142–8, plates XCV–C.

64. *Op. cit.*, 112–14, plates LXIII–LXIV.

65. *Op. cit.*, 139–40, plates XCI–XCII, and 152–5, plates CVI–CVII.

66. *Op. cit.*, 159–61, plates CXII–CXIII.

67. The shape of these medallions is the same as p. 152 those of the Westmister Retable.

68. *Op. cit.*, 176–8, plates CXXXVII–CXXXVIII.

69. The name 'Johannis de Thaneto' is inscribed on a silver frieze above the arch. His name is mentioned three times in a Canterbury Cathedral inventory of 1315. Christie, *op. cit.*, 134, plate LXXXVI (colour).

70. *Op. cit.*, 178–83, plates CXXXIX–CXLII.

71. *Op. cit.*, 167–71, plates CXXV–CXXIX.

72. *Op. cit.*, 172–5, plates CXXXI–CXXXIV.

73. *Op. cit.*, 161–4, plates CXIV–CXIX.

74. Few examples of non-ecclesiastical embroideries have survived from this period. *Op. cit.*, 6.

75. *Op. cit.*, 21–7.

76. *Op. cit.*, 17–19. p. 153

77. W. W. Lillie, 'A Medieval Retable at Thorn- p. 154 ham Parva'. It was clearly made for some Dominican house, since Saints Dominic and Peter Martyr are represented in the two end panels.

78. Borenius and Tristram, *op. cit.*, 19–20. The inside of the lid of a chest at Newport (Essex) is painted with a Crucifixion and saints, dating from the early fourteenth century. See Roy. Acad. Arts *Exhib. Brit. Prim. Paintings*, *Cat.* No. 10, plate VI. See also R.C.H.M.: *Essex*, I (1916) 200.

79. Reproduced, Millar, II, plate 12.

80. W. R. Lethaby, 'London and Westminster Painters', *Walpole Soc.*, I (1911–12), 69–75.

81. Borenius and Tristram, *op. cit.*, 18.

82. Wormald, 'Paintings in Westminster Abbey', p. 155 175. Professor Wormald compares the style of the

kings of the Sedilia with that of the Three Kings in Arundel MS. 83 (Plate 130B).

p. 155 83. A mid fourteenth century panel with this same subject was discovered by Tristram in the possession of V. W. York at Forthampton Court, near Tewkesbury. See *Burl. Mag.*, LXXXIII (1943), 160–5.

84. For Croughton see Borenius and Tristram, *op. cit.*, 20–2, plates 50–2; also Tristram and James, 'Wall-Paintings in Croughton Church, Northamptonshire'. For Chalgrove see W. Burges, 'On Mural Paintings in Chalgrove Church, Oxfordshire', *Archaeologia*, XXXVIII (1860), 431–8.

85. See E. Clive Rouse, *Illustrated London News* (29 Dec. 1951), 1074–5.

86. E. Clive Rouse, *Country Life* (4 April 1947), 604–8.

87. Cf. Chapter 5, note 103, above.

p. 156 88. Borenius and Tristram, *op. cit.*, 20.

p. 157 89. The same subject occurs in other wall paintings of about the same time, for example, in the church at Tarrant Crawford (Wilts.) and others. See Williams, 'Mural Paintings of the Three Living and the Three Dead in England', *Jnl Brit. Archaeol. Soc.*, 3rd series, VII (1942), 31–40.

90. E. Clive Rouse, *Illustrated London News* (29 Dec. 1951), 1075.

91. Tristram, I, 58–9.

92. Woodforde, *Stained Glass in Somerset*.

93. For coloured reproductions, see Harrison, *The Stained Glass of York Minster*.

94. Knowles, *The York School of Glass-Painting*, 3.

p. 158 95. It is true that the figure compositions within

thirteenth century medallions were placed under an architectural framework as at Canterbury (cf. Plate 95A). The change consists in the elimination of the medallion design and the further development of the canopy.

96. Peter de Dene became Canon of York in 1308. His adherence to Thomas of Lancaster caused him to retire hastily, after the latter's execution in 1322, to Canterbury. The window is not earlier than 1308 and surely not later than 1320. See Charles Winston and W. S. Walford, 'On an Heraldic Window in the North Aisle of the Nave of York Minster', *Archaeol. Jnl*, XVII (1860), 22–34; 133–48.

97. Richard Tunnoc, bell-founder, died in 1330. Knowles, *op. cit.*, plate XXI.

98. F. Harrison, *The Painted Glass of York*, 50. The same kind of naturalistic motifs are found in the glass of Wells Cathedral, cf. Woodforde, *Stained Glass in Somerset*, plate VIII. Knowles notes with surprise and without explanation the influence of Wells style on the glass of the parish church of St Denys at York (Knowles, *op. cit.*, 112 ff.) The so-called 'Golden Window' in the Lady Chapel at Wells was named from the extraordinary combination of yellowish tones (pot-metal and silver stain glass) with olive greens, harmonized in the Jesse Tree of the east window. The earliest of the windows in the north aisle of the church of St Denys exhibits, says Knowles, this same colour harmony.

99. Rushforth, 'The Glass in the Quire Clerestory of Tewkesbury Abbey'.

100. Rushforth, 'The Great East Window of Gloucester Cathedral'.

CHAPTER 7

THE INTERNATIONAL STYLE IN ENGLAND
⟨1350–1425⟩

*

HISTORICAL BACKGROUND

POLITICAL

Foreign Wars and Domestic Revolts

Edward III, King 1327–77; Treaty of Brétigny 1360 temporarily ended the war with France; King John of France a prisoner in England 1357–60, again in 1363; renewal of war 1369; death of Edward the Black Prince 1376.

Richard II, son of the Black Prince, King 1377–99 (deposed and died, perhaps murdered); Peasants' Revolt 1381; married Anne of Bohemia 1382 (d. 1394); alliance with William, Duke of Gelder, 1389; married Isabella daughter to King Charles VI of France 1396.

Henry IV, son of John of Gaunt, Duke of Lancaster, King 1399–1413; married Mary daughter of Humphrey de Bohun 1380 (d. 1394), and Johanna of Navarre 1403.

Henry V, son of Henry IV and Mary de Bohun, King 1413–22; married Katherine of Valois, daughter of Charles VI; Treaty of Troyes 1420; assumed title of heir and regent of realm of France.

Humphrey de Bohun, 7th Earl of Hereford, father of Mary and Eleanor, d. 1372–3; Psalters made for him contain his name in prayers; went to Italy 1368 for marriage of Lionel, Duke of Clarence, to Violanta Visconti, daughter of Duke of Milan.

John of Gaunt, Duke of Lancaster 1362–99.

John Beaufort, son of John of Gaunt, Earl of Somerset, d. 1409.

Eleanor de Bohun, Duchess of Gloucester, d. 1399.

ECCLESIASTICAL

Great Churchmen, Patrons of Art

Nicholas Lytlington, Abbot of Westminster 1362–86.

Simon Langham, Abbot of Westminster, Bishop of Ely, Archbishop of Canterbury 1366–1368; cardinal 1368; Bishop of Palestrina 1374; died at Avignon 1376, bequeathing books to Westminster Abbey.

Henry Despenser, Bishop of Norwich 1370–1406.

William of Wykeham, Bishop of Winchester 1367–1404; founded New College, Oxford, 1380; and Winchester College 1382.

Richard Mitford, Bishop of Salisbury 1395–1407.

Thomas Arundel, Archbishop of Canterbury 1396–7 and 1399–1414.

Henry Chichele, Archbishop of Canterbury 1414–43.

*

THE second half of the fourteenth century and the first quarter of the fifteenth were again a period of strong, continuous foreign contacts, politically through foreign wars and foreign marriages, and ecclesiastically through close relations with the papal court at Avignon. In art, this period was one of rich production in every form, stimulated no doubt by these foreign contacts, but also resulting naturally from the growth of personal power and wealth among both royal and noble, ecclesiastical and lay, patrons. At first the foreign influence was strongest from north Italy and south France; later, it came from Bohemia through the marriage of Richard with Anne; and still later, during the last decade of the century, the alliance of Richard with William, Duke of Gelder, against France brought England and the Low Countries into close relations. Finally, in the first quarter of the fifteenth century, the French marriages of Henry IV and Henry V introduced the influence of the International Style[1] from France and Burgundy where it had chiefly developed.

In England, the second half of the fourteenth century was a period of building. The Royal Chapel of St Stephen in the Palace of Westminster, rivalling the earlier Sainte-Chapelle of St Louis in Paris, was completely painted and the windows were filled with fine stained glass. In this period also the Chapter House of the Abbey of Westminster was entirely painted with a magnificent Last Judgement and a series of Apocalypse pictures which constitute the only known paintings of this subject in England. The splendidly imposing Westminster Hall with its superb hammerbeam roof and carved and painted angels was Richard's contribution to the Palace of Westminster. And in the last quarter of the century William of Wykeham began his two great college foundations: New College, Oxford, in 1380, and Winchester College in 1382. These are only a few of the many rich and important works sponsored by royal and ecclesiastical patrons. Many more have been discussed and referred to by Dr Joan Evans in the latest book to be published on English art of this period.[2] Although much of this art has perished, enough remains to indicate not only its amount but its generally high quality.

The period c. 1350 in England was, as we saw at the end of Chapter 6, rather sterile, the East Anglian style having nearly spent itself whether through the natural processes of growth and disintegration, or through the dying out of its practising artists, or both. In the meantime, however, the style had spread to the Continent and had been felt particularly in the Lower Rhine (Cologne) and as far east in Germany as Bohemia.[3] In France (Paris), on the other hand, the followers of Jean Pucelle were busy producing manuscripts which possess some decorative affinities with East Anglian style but probably are not directly influenced by them. The Pucelle mixture is French and Italian, under what specific circumstances has not been determined.[4]

Soon after the middle of the century, strong Italian influence begins to appear in the manner of modelling faces and draperies in English miniatures, while about the same time the more formal French ivy leaf border decoration is found in combination with East Anglian daisies. This mixture is illustrated in a psalter in the Vatican Library,[5] Rome (MS. Pal. lat. 537; Plate 148A). Many of the miniatures appear to have been inspired if not actually copied from those in Queen Mary's Psalter, but the manuscript is much more solidly painted as to figures and draperies, and the modelling of the faces in white paint over a dark, pinkish flesh tone, the great dark eyes, red lips, and reddish-yellow hair are certainly not East Anglian in origin. The border and initial are in typical French style, but the daisy buds introduced at the corners of the bar and occasionally elsewhere, like the figure composition, surely come from East Anglian manuscripts of the Queen Mary's Psalter type, which the illuminator of this manuscript must have seen either in England or on the Continent.

A similar French-Italian influence on English style can be seen in a Psalter (Paris, Bib. Nat., MS. lat. 765) made for the Fitzwarin family, having a Calendar with many East Anglian feasts and the first pages of its decoration in a rather debased version of the East Anglian style.[6] During the course of the illumination, however, Italian influence appeared in the richer draperies and the modelling of the faces in white on a dark flesh tone, sometimes, apparently, over the original East Anglian drawing. The colouring in this manuscript seems also to have been affected by Italian influence, the draperies being painted in richly shaded violet, pink, vermilion, and dull green. In the Fitzwarin Psalter a feature first appears, possibly from Continental sources, which becomes characteristic of some of the manuscripts to be discussed below, namely, the elaborate Late Gothic architectural settings (cf. Plate 150A).

In a third mid-century manuscript showing evidence of Continental influence (Camb., Fitz. Mus. MS. J.48), the Carew-Poyntz Hours,[7] the source seems to be almost entirely French, in the use of miniatures and bar borders with ivy-leaf motifs and in the *bas de page* scenes within frames at the bottom of the pages (Plate 148B). Again Italian influence appears in an accentuation of the features, especially the large black eyes under heavy lids, and in the heavily shaded draperies. Architecture, too, plays an important part in the scheme of decoration, and there is a certain awkward attempt at foreshortening and of spatial rendering in spite of the formal patterned backgrounds, which is absent in English examples of *bas de page* scenes of the preceding period (cf. Roy. 10 E. iv; Plate 132). There has been some later repainting in the miniatures of the Carew-Poyntz Hours, but the scene in Plate 148B (fol. 62 verso) represents fairly well the French-Italian-English mixture of the earlier decades of the second half of the fourteenth century.

This same French-Italian-English mixture of miniature styles with a Latin and French text written in an English hand and with English decoration and a Calendar and Litany pointing strongly to the diocese of Durham – all found in the M. R. James Memorial Psalter in the British Museum (Add. MS. 44949) – seems to settle the question of whether this style was produced in England or imported ready-made from abroad. The miniatures are by two hands, the first of which (fol. 4; Plate 150A) is closer to the Fitzwarin and Carew-Poyntz style, especially as to the white faces and beady black eyes. The colouring is less fine than in the Fitzwarin Psalter, with much green and dull yellow. The style is not very good; the stiff, uninteresting arcading and the coarsely-patterned diapered background do not seem to be quite suitable for the type of figure compositions which, in intention, follow the Italian Trecento principles[8] of spatial relationships and therefore use freely all possible views of the figures – frontal, profile, three-quarter, and back views. The artist, however, has not understood thoroughly what he was doing, and he combines in the same figure a side view of the feet of Christ in the scene with the Magdalene, a front view of his body from the waist up, and a three-quarter view of his head, which is turned in the opposite direction from that in which his feet are pointed. The Magdalene is seen in one of those extraordinarily inept kneeling back views which appear occasionally in miniatures by artists who have seen Italian paintings and don't understand how to represent this difficult foreshortened view. The body of the Magdalene, therefore, is shown as almost paper-flat and her legs are like bundles, the roundness of which the artist hoped to suggest by shading them to set them off from the rest of the body. The other group, Christ before Caiaphas, is somewhat better; but there is no depth to the three figures and no spatial relation between them and the profile view of Caiaphas. The feet of Christ in both miniatures are flat as though partially cut off by the frame of a picture as seen from below. The faces show a curious confusion of modelling conventions suggested by lines.

The Italianate type of heads in a mixed English Italianate style is illustrated in the two details in plate 150, B and C. The head at the left, from the wall painting formerly in St Stephen's Chapel, bears a strong resemblance to the head of David from one of the Bohun Psalters (Eg. 3277). The eyes and eyebrows are treated in very much the same manner, as are the pinched mouth and drooping moustache and beard. The style of the St Stephen's painting, like the Bohun style, seems to be derived directly from north Italian (Lombard) types; in the James Psalter, the influence seems to be more Sienese, perhaps the Franco-Sienese mixture which was current at Avignon. The James manuscript cannot be dated earlier than the third quarter of the fourteenth century[9] – a time when Avignon was greatly influencing painting done in France.

The strong, direct Italian influence which is evident in the foregoing manuscripts can be seen in the process of entering the English, that is, East Anglian, style in one of the earlier members of the group of eight or more manuscripts which, by means of inscriptions or coats of arms, can be associated with one or another of the Bohun family.[10] Humphrey de Bohun, 7th Earl of Hereford (d. 1372–3), seems to have been the patron for whom the Psalter in Vienna (Nationalbibl., MS. 1826*) was written, since his name, now erased, was mentioned in several of the prayers. The first part of the illumination, as far as fol. 49, has historiated initials in poor East Anglian style; but from fol. 50 onwards, Italian influence completely transforms the feebly-drawn figures and introduces a different kind of border motif.[11] Some other members of the Bohun group of manuscripts use this Italianized style;[12] but there are a few which seem to have had no such contacts, but to be illuminated in some version of French or possibly Flemish style, with small, linear figures and a formal border of one particular kind of cinquefoil leaf.[13]

Elements of both styles are illustrated in the Bohun manuscript most recently discovered (Brit. Mus., Egerton MS. 3277; fol. 123; Plate 149A), containing in five places in the borders the Bohun arms and the royal arms of England, and suggesting thereby that, although written for Humphrey de Bohun,[14] it may have been finished for Mary de Bohun, daughter of Humphrey, who married Henry of Lancaster, later Henry IV, in 1380. In this manuscript the north Italian influence is fully developed; its characteristics are the beady black eyes, the black hair and beards, the white faces and the richly shaded draperies.[15] The elaborate decorative style of the large historiated initials and their marginal borders is, however, fully English. The initial is divided into compartments having fine diapered or gold tooled grounds against which the figure subjects are placed. There is no interest in spatial representation, although a good deal of architecture is introduced and some elements of landscape – the green grass with East Anglian daisies growing in it. The East Anglian fondness for filling the margins with figures and decoration is here evident. It is a brilliant and extremely effective style with its fine burnished gold and strong, richly shaded colours, but little of the monumentality in the treatment of figures such as is found in Italian painting of the same time appears here.

The earliest date for the Bohun manuscripts is generally given as about 1370; judging from the style, the latest example may be a psalter made for Eleanor de Bohun (Edinburgh, Nat. Lib., MS. Adv. 18.6.5) who died in 1399. Where the Bohun manuscripts were made is unknown, although both Egerton MS. 3277 and the Eleanor de Bohun Psalter, in relation to certain other manuscripts, suggest a London provenance. The decorative style becomes less rich in the Eleanor de Bohun book, but the Italianate figure elements persist and even, it would seem, become more marked towards the end of the century, as can be seen in a Psalter in the British Museum (Add. MS. 16968; Plate 149B). Most of the illustrations in this manuscript are miniatures, but the text seems to have been written for historiated initials – the initial C of the first word, 'Crucifige', on this page is missing. The miniature contains foliated medallions such as occur in earlier English manuscripts (cf. Plate 130A) with interlaced frames placed on a rectangular panel. The figures are mainly behind the frames, but some of the feet extend into, or over, the framework. The background is burnished gold with no architectural setting indicated and no suggestion of depth in space, but the figures have the heavy-lidded, sullen faces of the Italianate Bohun style. The modelling is in white on a brownish flesh tone. This manuscript represents the fully developed late fourteenth century English style characteristic of two London manuscripts, the Lytlington Missal, made for Westminster Abbey, and some pages of the Carmelite Missal, probably made at Whitefriars (see below).

Further evidence that Italian influence was present in work done in London can be seen in the few fragments that survive of the series of wall paintings formerly in St Stephen's Chapel in the Palace of Westminster, now in the British Museum (Plate 151B). These paintings, though executed in fresco technique, are on a small scale and therefore easily comparable in style to the Italianate Bohun miniatures. It is difficult in the present battered and fragmentary state of the paintings to reconstruct the subjects as they were,[16] but enough remains to demonstrate Italianate characteristics apparently unmixed with French, and showing similarities to the figure style of Eg. MS. 3277 (see above). Characteristic of the St Stephen's frescoes are the richly gilded gesso backgrounds with patterns in relief, the architectural setting which is solidly and convincingly rendered, though without any real spatial depth, and the richly draped figures in three-quarter, profile, and full-face positions, with finely modelled features and expressive gestures. The style has neither the bulkiness of the Florentine nor the Gothic attenuation of the Sienese, but seems closer to the Lombard[17] style which developed at the end of the century in the frescoes of Altichiero and Avanzi at Padua.

The frescoes of St Stephen's Chapel can be dated on documentary evidence[18] in the

1350s and 60s. Two painters are named: Master Hugh of St Albans, appointed 1350, and William of Walsingham, mentioned as assisting Master Hugh in 1352 and apparently as replacing him in 1363. The fragments of painting which survive (Plate 151B) seem to be among the latest in date.[19]

There were fourteenth century wall paintings also at Westminster Abbey. The Chapter House walls were decorated with a great Last Judgement centred under the arcades on the east wall and extending into the adjoining walls on both sides. The date is variously given from mid fourteenth century to c. 1370; at any rate part of the work was ordered or directed by a Brother John of Northampton,[20] a monk of the Abbey, who said his first mass in 1375–6. In the centre of the Judgement composition can still be seen part of the figure of Christ in Majesty, displaying the wounds, his feet resting on the globe; flanking him are two standing seraphs (Plate 151A) on each side, feathered in the manner commonly found in East Anglian manuscripts. Little can be seen except the heads, so damaged are the paintings, but in so far as the style can de determined, it seems to have no direct connexion with either the Bohun style or with that of the St Stephen's frescoes. The oval faces of the angels with their round chins and straight brows and serious expressions perhaps suggest slightly the figures in the later part of Arundel MS. 83 (cf. Plate 130A), but since we do not know the provenance of this manuscript, it is of no help in localizing the source of the style of the Westminster Judgement. This is primarily decorative, as is seen in the haloes with a wheel window design and in the downward spreading wings with the patterned feathers. It must have been extremely beautiful, and very effective in its position facing the entrance to the Chapter House. The other walls also were entirely painted, apparently all at a later date; they will be discussed a little farther on.[21]

The paintings of St Stephen's Chapel and the Chapter House belong to the reign of Edward III, who died in 1377. To the following reign, that of his young grandson Richard who succeeded him, presumably belongs the much discussed Wilton Diptych (Plates 152–153), so-called from its sojourn at Wilton House before its acquisition by the National Gallery, London. Hardly any other art monument in England is known so well and valued so highly, yet offers such meagre information about itself. There is no documentary evidence at all as to either its date or the circumstances of its painting, though the literature setting forth theories on these points is voluminous.[22] The painting is in good condition and apparently has been little restored; it is in its original frame which is carved out of the same oak panels on which the two parts of the diptych are painted. The style of the painting is clear for anyone who wishes to try to attribute it, yet the fact is that in the course of the years it has been assigned to four different countries including England, all apparently with good stylistic reasons.

The panels represent King Richard as a young man or, as some claim, as a boy of eleven, which was his age at the time of his coronation in 1377; with him are his three patron saints, John the Baptist, Edward the Confessor, and Edmund of East Anglia, all three recommending him to the Virgin and Child in the midst of eleven angels on the opposite panel. The subject at first glance appears simple, but again controversy has arisen and continues to arise as to the interpretation and the occasion of the painting. The root of the difference of opinion as to the attribution of the painting lies in the fact that no other work has yet been found which is really close enough in style to indicate its provenance; the source of the difficulty in assigning a date and interpreting the meaning of the picture is the heraldry, namely, the broomscod collars and the white hart badges worn by Richard and the angels, and, in addition, the white banner bearing a red cross which might equally well, it seems, be the symbol of the resurrection of Christ and the banner of St George.[23]

The size of the Wilton Diptych ($14\frac{1}{2}$ by 21 inches including the frame) and the scale of the paintings suggest that the picture was either a portable altarpiece – but it is a little large for that – or was meant for the altar of a small chapel; it would appear insignificant on the altar of a large church. The scale of the painting also suggests the work of a miniature painter, and the arrangement of the panels like a book bears out this similarity in general idea. The technique, however, is that of panel painting in the Italian manner, tempera on a coating of gesso applied to oak boards.[24] The background of both panels is gold leaf stippled in delicate patterns. Gold is used also as a base for the brocaded robes of Richard and St Edmund; the pattern was probably produced by painting the ground around the motifs, which are stippled. The ground of Richard's robe is red patterned with a white hart lodged within a circle of broomscods and an eagle displayed; the ground of Edmund's robe is deep blue patterned with two long-tailed birds confronted, their necks encircled by a single crown with a star. The Christ Child is partly enveloped in a gold cloth, the folds of which are indicated by stippling; his halo is ornamented with a crown of thorns stippled on the gold and with three radiating pointed forms which have been identified as nails.

The colour scheme is extremely simple. The right panel is almost entirely in two tones of blue shaded and alternated so as to distinguish adjoining figures; the effect is of a shimmering pattern of lights and darks. The angels' wings are incredibly delicately shaded from white, through grey to black at the tips. Their hair is golden yellow painted with a glint on individual hairs and curls. Faces are modelled with thick pigments, white and pink on a greyish green base from which some of the overpainting has flaked off. In the opposite panel, Edward the Confessor is clad in a cream-coloured robe and mantle, shaded delicately in brown; John the Baptist wears a shaggy camel skin[25] mantle tied around the waist with a rope girdle. The surface of the mantle is painted meticulously, each individual hair showing; and the same technique is used in painting the fleece of the lamb. The rocky foreground on this panel is brownish with a dull green clump of trees. The foreground of the right panel is also dull green sprinkled with small growing flowerets and larger, stiffer flower heads, chiefly roses and lilies, scattered rather consciously in all the open spaces.

The two panels are designed as one composition, a strictly linear arrangement which is indicated mainly by the gestures and especially by the hands. Starting from the left side of the left panel, it moves downward by means of the hands of St Edmund and St Edward, passes across the shoulders of Richard and again upward to the opposite panel, where it is carried across the extended arms of the Child to the Virgin's head, and spreads right and left around the circle of angels. Here the main compositional line is carried by the pyramidal arrangement of the angels' heads, by their hands, and in the nearer ones, by the direction of the wings; the angels form an irregular hollow circle open at the front, within which the Virgin stands swaying slightly to the left as though about to move forward towards Richard. The body of the Child leaning in the same direction repeats this movement.

The mood, like the composition, includes both panels. Richard, proudly erect, kneeling well within the protective shelter of his patron saints, reaches out eager, trembling hands towards the Virgin and Child who both, separately, not as Mother and Child, incline graciously towards the suppliant. The heads and especially the eyes are painted so that their gaze apparently is directed towards one another, but on examination it is seen that no pair of eyes is actually focussed on the person or object towards which it is directed; this detail more than any other feature of the figure painting gives the panels the mystical dreaminess of mood harmonizing so perfectly with the cool colours and the softly falling draperies. In sharp contrast to this mood are the individually assertive but monotonously repetitive badges of the King's livery applied to each angel's shoulder, in such a clumsy manner that in some cases the badge renders movements of the arm nearly impossible. The badge of Richard is more awkwardly placed than any of the others, owing to his profile position; and his broomscod collar is hung clumsily around his neck in order that it may be fully visible. Add to these discordant details the apparently irrelevant banner, and the contradiction in mood is so marked that one cannot but wonder whether the heraldic insignia were not added to the panels later, with some change in intention – perhaps some years after they were first painted.[26]

The composition as described above, the technique of the painting, the decorative features of the panels, and the dreamy mystic mood which pervades the whole, belong to the earlier, not to the later, part of the period covered by the reign of Richard. They can be found in votive pictures in north Italy in the 1370s and 80s, where the Giottesque tradition of figure painting was relieved of some of its heaviness by the influence of the French Gothic linear style. Flat profile portraits[27] are common in this painting, as are votive figures 'recommended' by their patron saints. North Italian influence was present in the St Stephen's frescoes and was still strong in manuscripts some decades later. It would not be surprising therefore to find it in a contemporary English panel painting. But in the meantime, the Italian style had been modified by contacts with the Gothic North; it is this mixed Italian influence that seems to be reflected in the Wilton Diptych.

But the painter of the diptych was probably English, and neither French nor Italian. The simplicity and naïveté with which the figures are rendered, the informality of the composition, the tender, mystic mood, the exquisite delicacy of the workmanship are all characteristics that recur in English manuscript painting. English also is the flatness of the figures and faces which, in spite of the careful surface shading, could not be described as really modelled. The drapery, too, though Gothic in its linear pattern, is treated softly, with shallow folds and as surface ornament. This play of linear pattern wherever it is possible – even in the veins of the arms and foot of the Baptist and in the curls of the Confessor and of the angels, and in the strata of rock in the foreground – is a deeply rooted English trait. The style of the Wilton Diptych seems to represent the English version of the International style which was spreading over Europe in the later decades of the fourteenth century.

Two manuscripts belonging to Westminster Abbey, both probably made there in the early 1380s, show Italian influence but no close stylistic analogy to the Wilton Diptych nor, in fact, even to each other. One, a large missal executed[28] for Abbot Nicholas Lytlington in 1383–4, contains many historiated initials and a fine Crucifixion (fol. 157 verso; Plate 154) composed in the crowded, dramatic Italian manner. The figures are tall with ample draperies, some richly patterned, and with faces modelled somewhat in the manner of the Bohun manuscripts (cf. Plate 150c), but with brownish flesh and broad white highlights. Typical of the faces of the Lytlington Missal are the heavy eyelids and extremely arched eyebrows. There is considerable variety in the gestures and poses of the figures; one, Stephaton with the sponge, is represented with upturned head seen from behind – the curious, distorted position found in Italian pictures but little understood outside Italy.[29] The background of the Crucifixion is of tooled gold, with an entirely different pattern on the two sides of the cross. Bordering the picture is a wide frame consisting of small miniatures containing scenes from the Passion, and panels of very beautiful strapwork such as is found generally in English decorative work of the period. The marginal decoration consists of hair-line sprays containing gold balls and a few East Anglian motifs such as the daisy and the marigold, and oak and ivy leaves. In the corners are the symbols of the Evangelists, and in two panels at the bottom, the arms and monogram of Nicholas Lytlington. The colours are chiefly two shades of blue, pale vermilion, pink, brown, and tan; green is used for the foregrounds of the scenes. The quality of the painting is very good but the figure style is heavy and uninteresting, though the decorative effect of the page as a whole is exceedingly rich.

At about the same time as the Lytlington Missal, that is, probably shortly before or after Richard's marriage in 1382, the manuscript containing the order for the coronation of a king and a queen, the so-called *Liber Regalis*,[30] was made, perhaps at Westminster where it still is kept. The figure style of this manuscript (fol. 1 verso; Plate 155) is very different from that of the Lytlington Missal, as is also the technique of the painting; in some respects the technique is closer to that of the Wilton Diptych.[31] The heads are much more modelled than those of the Lytlington manuscript, with red and white high-lights on a greenish flesh tone; foreheads bulge, noses project boldly, eyeballs protrude, and necks are soft and flabby. The eyes roll to one side or the other and the enormous, misshapen hands gesticulate animatedly. The background is of tooled gold, as in the Lytlington Missal and on the Diptych, but the pattern is in flowing arabesques rather than in geometric motifs. The foreground shows a tiled pattern with no attempt at perspective in the rendering of the lines. The colour is extremely beautiful and in this respect also the *Liber Regalis* seems closer to the Wilton Diptych than to the Missal. The use of white as overpainting on the greenish base, heightened and enriched by pink and by soft red, gives an opalesque effect to the flesh and to some of the draperies. The figures are not strongly outlined to set them off from the gold ground, but internal detail of the accessories is sharply drawn in black line, and sometimes gilt paint is applied over the gold for greater richness. The deep ultramarine blue is shaded with white and occasionally cross-hatched. The technique, the figure types, and the colouring all suggest the style of Bohemian illumination of the late fourteenth century,[32] and it seems likely that some artist in the large train of Anne of Bohemia when she came to England painted the miniatures. No other illumination exactly like it is known in England either earlier or at this same time, but the influence of the style is evident in some slightly later English work.[33] The pictures have narrow frames decorated with conventional patterns, but attached to the frame are hair-line sprays containing gold balls and East Anglian daisies as in the Lytlington Missal. This and the decorative text initials are evidence that the *Liber Regalis*, like the Lytlington Missal, was probably executed at Westminster, though the miniature style is certainly foreign.

To the years immediately preceding 1398 belong the historiated initials in three different styles in the great Carmelite Missal probably written at Whitefriars, London. The great size of the manuscript and the elaborate and varied illumination which once filled the pages are matched by the high quality of the three figure-painting styles, certainly representing the work of the best artists available in England. Nothing is known about the circumstances of the making of this magnificent manuscript. In the nineteenth century it was cut up to make scrapbooks and only recently has been reconstructed into a semblance of its original splendour.[34]

One of the three styles is easily recognizable as what we may call the English style, as represented in the Bohun manuscripts and in the Lytlington Missal.[35] A second style (fol. 36 verso; Plate 156A) represents the closest approach in English illumination to the style of the *Liber Regalis*;[36] it may even be Bohemian in origin, somewhat modified by the English style of ornament, as in the decorative motifs and the fine interlace of the initial.[37] The technique of the figure painting uses the same greenish flesh tones with high-lights in white and shading in red and pink, and the white and paler colours have the same opalesque quality as in the *Liber Regalis*. The figure types are less queer in their expressions and gestures, but have the same misshapen hands, bulging foreheads, and sly eyes. Draperies swing in deep curves. The background is tooled in arabesque patterns, and the tiled foreground shows no interest in perspective even though interior architecture is represented, as in the setting of the baptismal scene. The colour is most beautiful against gold or coloured grounds, the latter decorated with arabesques in gilt paint. An outstanding feature of this style is the use of monochrome figures painted in blue or pink such as the angels in the Trinity scene. If this artist was English, he must have been greatly influenced by the *Liber Regalis* style; if, on the other hand, he was Bohemian, his style, as suggested above, evidently was modified by English work and possibly also by the style of the third artist in this same Carmelite Missal.

This third artist's style[38] has no parallel in earlier English work, but its influence changed the whole course of later English painting. More than either of the others, he is a figure painter. The scene of the Birth of the Virgin (fol. 138 verso; Plate 156B) illustrates his interest in solid and spatial form. The chapel-like house with its empty porch and its dim depths of interior space is, of course, not correctly rendered from the point of view of vanishing point perspective, but the use of light and shade in representing the solidity of the building, and the modification of its structural lines as they recede into the background as well as those of the tiled floor and the furniture, indicate clearly the artist's interest in the representation of space. The figures are closely grouped and bear a spatial relationship to each other; they – like the furnishings of the room – occupy space. The figures are modelled in light and shade, and the high-lights on the faces also are painted with white, often in the form of crosshatching, on a dark flesh tone. Lips, nostrils, and cheeks are touched with red, and on the far side of the face, a dark contour line silhouettes the foreshortened cheek against the background. The faces have the softness of flesh, the eyes the brilliance and expressiveness of life. The colours are rich, and varied by the use of overpainting. Two blues, ultramarine and a lighter slate blue, pale grey and dull green, with a minimum of brilliant vermilion and much use of white shaded with brown or blue for the folds, give the composition a deep brilliance lacking in both the Bohemian and the English painting styles. The architecture in the Birth of the Virgin is terra-cotta in colour shaded lighter and darker; the roof is slate blue; the bed canopy dark green, and the coverlet grey. A detail worth noting is the small bedside stool on which is a pewter candlestick and a candle, suggestive of similar details in Flemish interiors of the next century. The style of this artist is certainly Dutch;[39] there are traces in it of Italian and perhaps of Bohemian influence, but no signs of the French Gothic style either in the architecture or in the figures. The influence of this modelled style will be abundantly clear in early fifteenth century English illumination.

The more than life-size, full-length portrait of King Richard II in full regalia on his throne (Plate 162), which now hangs in the nave of Westminster Abbey, is still the subject of controversy as to authorship, though 'it is generally agreed that it was executed in England'.[40] The picture has suffered much from restoration and it is questionable whether its present state represents accurately the original painting.[41] Nevertheless, since it seems to be fairly consistent as to drawing, modelling, and details of hands and drapery, it must be judged on its characteristics as they now appear.

It is a magnificent painting. Richard is represented with a short two-pointed beard as on his tomb effigy;[42] but his face in the portrait is rounder, less sharp and drawn than in the effigy. It is the face of a young man but not a boy, evidently older by at least ten years than as he is depicted in the Wilton Diptych. The modelling of the face is softly done, in carefully graded shading from dark to light, not in white lines and cross-hatching as in the Diptych. The hair is bushy and soft, but there is less emphasis on the gleam of single hairs and strands and more depth in the mass. The upper part of the body is very slightly modelled under the mantle; the knees are thrust forward, but in a position which is not entirely convincing. The gown is patterned with a diamond-shaped motif composed of small conventional leaf forms, interspersed with crowned R's as on his tomb effigy. The folds of the mantle form a rich pattern of intricate curves, accentuated by the contrast of the ermine lining and the dark, soft red material. The throne is elaborate in design but curiously unsubstantial in construction owing to faulty perspective in the foreshortening. There is Gothic richness in the play of line in the drapery, but the modelling of the head is in a technique not generally found in French painting.[43] The hands with their curious tapering, widely separated fingers are reminiscent of those in the much earlier *Liber Regalis*, but certainly in the portrait they are less misshapen and awkward. A comparison of the portrait with the page from the *Liber Regalis* (Plate 155) will show how fundamental are the differences, in technique as in the rendering of the figure. But the Richard portrait does bear some resemblance to certain Bohemian panel paintings,[44] particularly as to the smooth modelling with areas of light and shade and the rich play of the drapery with its broad, deep folds. Even closer, perhaps, is the resemblance of the general style of the portrait to that of North German painting, which was strongly influenced by Bohemian style, as in the work of Meister Bertram.[45] The portrait of Richard seems to be less acceptable as the work of an English artist than is the Wilton Diptych; its connexions seem rather to be closer with the north of Europe than with either Italy or France.

Whoever the painter was, he has caught (if we can trust the painting as we see it to-day) something of the tragic character of King Richard – a man young in years and in the lineaments of his face but old in experience, though bitter and sad rather than wise in the acquiring of it. It has been suggested that the painting may have been done to commemorate an occasion in 1390 when the King and Queen in full regalia heard mass in the Abbey on St Edward's Day;[46] but there is no evidence to prove this, though the date may not be far wrong.

Another late fourteenth century panel painting is the Retable now displayed in the south choir aisle of the Cathedral at Norwich but originally made for the high altar;[47] it was probably given by a group of donors including Bishop Henry Despenser (1370–1406), whose arms are painted on the backs of some of the glass panels imitating enamel, which are inserted at intervals on the outer frame. The Retable consists of five oak panels, each with its own frame, at present less than three feet high; the total length is eight feet six inches. The subjects are: in the centre, a Crucifixion; on the left, the Flagellation and Bearing of the Cross; on the right, the Resurrection and Ascension (Plate 159A). The backgrounds are decorated with gilt gesso relief, with a running pattern of large vine leaves and tendrils in the centre and end panels, and in the other two, oak leaves and acorns in addition to vine leaves.

The figures are thin with narrow shoulders and large squarish heads. The modelling is somewhat stylized but is painted broadly, not in a linear technique. The eyes are shadowed with brown, and white is used for high-lights on nose, cheek, forehead, and chin. The eyes, many of which are blue, are large and remarkable for their variety of expression; Christ in the Resurrection scene looks straight out of the picture at the spectator, and the heads of the Apostles in the Ascension are tilted upward at different angles while the eyes are variously directed in their upward gaze. Draperies are soft and clinging and give the effect of being wrapped round the figures. The costume and armour are slightly fantastic as frequently represented in late fourteenth century painting. The colours are soft and shaded: Christ wears a purplish-red mantle lined with greenish blue. Other colours used are bluish green shaded with yellow or darker green, vermilion lightly shaded with madder, and dull blue shaded darker or with white. Many of the figures wear gowns or tunics of gold brocade. The Resurrection scene has a curious architectural structure in the background on which are two eagles displayed, each bearing on a cord around its neck an armorial shield, emblazoned with the symbols of the Passion. Christ wears a crown of thorns; his gold halo is cruciform with a scalloped border; the Apostles and the Virgin in the Ascension also have scalloped gold haloes. Christ in the Resurrection is stepping out from the tomb carrying the Resurrection banner and blessing with his right hand.

Like most work of this period, the style shows Italianate[48] elements in the shading of the draperies and in the figure types and composition. The drapery folds show no Gothic linear patterns. The bold, often brutal types of faces, as the sleeping soldiers in the Resurrection panel, suggest North German sources;[49] nevertheless, the work is almost certainly English, probably influenced by some phase of north European style.

Additional evidence for English workmanship in the Retable is furnished by two panels in almost identical style now incorporated with parts of a much later altarpiece in the church of St Michael-at-Plea, Norwich.[50] Two other small fragments of larger panels in much the same style are now in the Fitzwilliam Museum (Camb., Nos 706, 707; Plate 159B). The Norwich style as represented in all these paintings has no close stylistic relation to either the Westminster portrait of Richard or to the Wilton Diptych, even though the latter could be shown to be late enough in date. All are examples of different versions of International style as produced under various Continental influences, and flavoured locally in England.

In some respects, however, the Norwich paintings seem to show affinities with wall paintings in the Chapter House, Westminster, which form part of the Last Judgement composition but are certainly later in date than the principal group (Plate 151A). The heads in the two panels on the right side of the Judgement (Plate 160A) show a similar variety of positions and facial expressions to those in the Norwich Retable; they also have rather similar large, heavy-lidded eyes and squarish heads. But the Chapter House paintings, which are executed directly on the stone masonry, are rougher in technique and therefore not clear and sharp in details. Their date is late fourteenth century and they may be more closely related, in some unexplained manner, to the general style of one of the few English artists of the period whose name is known, the Dominican friar John Siferwas.

For the remainder of the decoration of the Chapter House, which is apparently still later, the subject is an elaborate series of illustrations of the Apocalypse (Plate 160B) in a different style from the Judgement groups and looking perhaps even less English, though many of the panels are now so damaged that it is difficult to see more than single figures or scenes here and there. The quality does not seem to be very good, and the same figures are repeated endlessly and almost without variation. The strong, crude colouring again suggests Low Country or perhaps German influence; the paintings, though interesting for the completeness of the subject matter[51] and for the fact that they represent the only known English wall or panel painting of the Apocalypse, are not very good and the application of yellowish varnish over the paint in modern times has not improved their appearance. The Apocalypse series may be dated[52] not later than 1400, but the large Bestiary animals with their names in English, which fill the lower part of the walls, are not earlier than sixteenth century.

More important stylistically than the Apocalypse paintings are those on the ceiling of the inner north aisle of the church of St Helen at Abingdon[53] (Berks), dating shortly after 1391. The subject is a Jesse Tree of a unique design: a series of panels 4 feet 9 inches tall and 9 inches wide containing alternately prophets and kings fill the slanting sides of the ceiling and are connected at the bottom of the panels by a running vine scroll. On the last two panels at the east end of the north side is a Crucifixion with the lily between the Virgin Annunciate and Gabriel. The figures are full-length (Plate 158) and are painted in a full range of colours on red ground, and further enriched by the use of gold for crowns and sceptres. At least two different hands can be distinguished (cf. Plate 158, A and B). The prophet and king at the left are drawn in awkward unsubstantial poses and the draperies are designed in rich meaningless convolutions. The hands are awkward and the eyes under their heavy white lids fail to focus. The figures in plate 158B are not markedly different in type and pose, but they seem to be better realized and more competently painted. It is probably the quality, and perhaps the present condition of the paintings, rather than differences in the style itself, that distinguish them one from another, but even the better ones do not seem to show close relationship to any other contemporary painting.[54]

It is obvious from the mediocre quality of the painting both in the Chapter House paintings and in the Abingdon ceiling, that this is not the medium in which any considerable developments towards a more realistic style in England are to be expected. English medieval painting at its best was never monumental in scale. And so at the turn of the fourteenth century, when greater interest in representation of form and space is everywhere appearing under the stimulus of Italian influence, in England the new elements again find expression in manuscript illumination. The beginnings of this new style we have seen in the Dutch artist's miniatures in the Carmelite Missal, and there is evidence that their influence on other work produced in England was immediately fruitful.[55] A number of different illuminators can be distinguished in manuscripts illustrated and decorated in this new style, but the names of only two are known to us. These are John Siferwas, who was mentioned above in connexion with the style of the Chapter House heads, and Herman Scheerre. Both were fine artists who worked contemporaneously in very different styles, and both seem to have had a considerable number of assistants. The manuscripts illuminated under the direction of these two artists include some of the finest examples produced in England in the later Middle Ages.

The signature of John Siferwas is found in two manuscripts datable in the two decades before and after 1400: the large missal made for and almost certainly at the Benedictine Abbey of Sherborne in Dorset between 1396 and 1407;[56] and a Gospel Lectionary executed as a gift to Salisbury Cathedral to the order of John, 5th Lord Lovell of Tichmarsh (d. 1408).

The Sherborne Missal, now in the Library of the Duke of Northumberland at Alnwick Castle,[57] in its present form measures 21 by 15 inches and was originally even larger, as the trimmed margins show. It must, therefore, have approximated the great Carmelite Missal in size and probably surpassed it in the amount, though certainly not in the quality, of its decoration. The Crucifixion (p. 380; Plate 161) of the Sherborne Missal, which it would have been interesting to compare with the corresponding page, now lost, in the Carmelite Missal, can probably be taken to represent the best work of Siferwas himself, who seems to have done most of the illumination in the earlier part of the book. The latter part is inferior in quality and was probably the work of several assistants.

The composition of the Crucifixion scene is of the dramatic Italian type which we have seen in the Lytlington Missal (cf. Plate 154) but much more crowded with figures, on foot and on horseback, and dressed in rich and somewhat fantastic costumes. The rendering of the figures is exceedingly lively but not correct either in anatomy or in pose and gestures.

Even the foreground group of the women and John, who are most carefully painted with respect to draperies and faces, is flattened against a richly patterned carpet in the midst of the rocky landscape foreground, with no understanding of the relation of the figures to the ground or to each other in the group. The background figures are disposed in a similar flat manner against a rising landscape with trees and architecture, and above it in place of sky is a patterned backdrop, in the upper corners of which appear monochrome angels in banks of cloud. But apart from this flat treatment of the composition, individual figures demonstrate considerable interest on the part of the artist in the modelling of the faces. Typical features are the large eyeballs painted solid black in the background figures, but in the nearer ones showing a dark iris in the lighter pupil, and the very heavy eyelids accentuated with white. The modelling of the faces depends for its effect on the use of a strong contrasting contour line of colour on the far side of the face. Foreheads, noses, and chins are touched with white; hair is pale yellowish brown with individual hairs lightened and the under parts of the mass shaded dark to give the effect of depth. The colours are somewhat strong with much use of patterning and of gold ornament, but the filmy veils of the women in the foreground are painted with great delicacy. The miniature is surrounded by a panelled frame shaded to represent wood, containing small figures, in medallions, of the Evangelists and scenes from the Old Testament, and also the Virtues, Peace, and Justice. These small figures are in the same style as the Crucifixion picture, but the minuteness of their scale gives them a vividness and liveliness which do not carry over when the figures are larger. Other pages with historiated initials and marginal borders with scenes and decorative figures including some magnificent birds[58] (Plate 165) are in the finer technique of the border scenes on the Crucifixion page. It is possible that Siferwas worked better on a small scale, and this theory is borne out by the illuminations in the other signed manuscript, the Lovell Lectionary.

Before leaving the Crucifixion miniature of the Sherborne Missal, a further comparison between the background figures and the group of heads in the Chapter House paintings (Plate 160A) may be suggested. The types of faces and the various positions of the heads, and even the manner of accentuating the features by strong shading, are very close in the styles of the two pictures; in both are the monochrome angels with spread wings. If the Chapter House heads were not painted by Siferwas or from his designs, certainly they were done by someone working in a very similar style. Or it might be that Siferwas himself was influenced by the paintings which, as we have seen, have certain resemblances to the Norwich Retable; the fantastic costumes worn by figures in the Sherborne Crucifixion also are related to those of the Norwich Retable. The only conclusion that can be drawn from these analogies is the distinction between this phase of English International style, for Siferwas seems certainly to have been an Englishman,[59] and the phase represented by the influence of the Dutch artist in the Carmelite Missal which we shall find in the group of manuscripts illuminated by Herman Scheerre and his associates.

The second manuscript signed by Siferwas illustrates even better his large-scale painting as compared to his miniature style. The Lovell Lectionary (Brit. Mus., Harl. MS. 7026) has lost many of its pages, but retains the dedicatory picture on fol. 4 verso (Plate 163)[60] representing Siferwas – his signature, Frater Johannes Siferwas, is at the bottom –

presenting his book to his patron Lord Lovell, who is named in the inscription on the scroll at the left of the picture. The faces, which look as though they were meant to be portraits, are painted with exaggerated attention to every detail, but the total effect is far from realistic. The eyes have the same bold protruding eyeballs and heavy lids as in the figures of the Sherborne Crucifixion, and the technique is wholly linear, with the modelling depending on the use of contrasting contours. The beauty of the drawing in Siferwas's style is again seen best in the smaller picture of the Coronation of the Virgin on the cover of the book which is represented in the miniature. Other pages in the Lectionary decorated with miniatures and marginal borders and figures show this same fineness and delicacy of workmanship, but all do not seem to be by Siferwas himself, or else some were done with much less meticulous care. The marginal decoration includes very beautifully painted angels, animals, and grotesques in the best English decorative style. The borders, like those of the Sherborne Missal, contain a great many different kinds of motifs some of which seem to come from East Anglian sources while others are very close to the feathery sprays and twisted acanthus scrolls in the borders of the Dutch artist's style in the Carmelite Missal. The colouring of the Lectionary like that of the Sherborne Missal is rich and strong, and heavily shaded; a very fine ultramarine blue is used freely with tooled gold or diapered coloured grounds.

The multiple sources of the Siferwas style are better understood from the fortunate preservation of an artist's sketchbook[61] (Camb., Mag. Coll., Pepysian Lib., MS. 1916) which contains material of many kinds collected, apparently, over a considerable period of time. The latest sketches are in late fourteenth century style, therefore contemporary with John Siferwas. Some of the drawings of birds and animals (Plate 164) even seem to have been used in the marginal decorations of the Siferwas manuscripts, notably the Sherborne Missal (as p. 388; Plate 165). The birds in the Sketchbook are particularly well drawn and coloured, even though the sketches were obviously intended merely to record the colours rather than to be finished pictures. The Sketchbook appears to have belonged to some atelier, but whether this was monastic or secular is problematical, since it includes all kinds of material, both secular and religious. An especially curious and interesting feature of the book is that its contents apparently were intended for use not only in manuscript illumination but for patterns of stained glass and embroideries, and even for larger figure compositions, like wall painting. On the page reproduced, besides birds of many recognizable species, there is a mermaid, a grotesque with a rabbit head, claw feet, and a fox's tail, and a tabby cat taking a bath.

The Siferwas style in the hands of a different artist[62] is recognizable in some of the miniatures illustrating the text of Marco Polo's Li Livres du Graunt Caam dating from c. 1400, which was added to an earlier manuscript of the Alexander Romance (Bod. Lib., MS. 264). On the opening page of the Marco Polo is a marvellously detailed panoramic view of Venice (fol. 218; Plate 157). Many of its well-known features are recognizable, as St Mark's Church with the four bronze horses, the Doge's Palace next to it, and the column with the lion of St Mark on the waterfront. The houses are medieval in their Gothic detail, but nearly all have stepped façades which were more typical of Flanders than of Italy. The shops and the street vendors, the galley ships and the small boats, the groups of well-dressed citizens and, in the lower right-hand corner, the rocky wilderness with lions and panthers, present a fascinating picture of Venice as the artist knew or imagined it at the turn of the century. But even such careful attention to the representation of countless details in this vivid manner has produced no illusion of space or of distance in the picture, for the background of the city, where sky should be, is still a coloured backdrop patterned delicately in gold. The artist was certainly English. His style savours of the various elements current in England at the end of the fourteenth century – Siferwas primarily, but also the Dutch artist of the Carmelite Missal, as shown by the sturdy figures with round faces and bright eyes. There is in addition something of the more delicate modelling of another illuminator whose name and style we know, Herman Scheerre, who seems to have brought into England from whatever part of the Continent he came – for he cannot be explained by English tradition alone – other elements to contribute to the mixture.

This mixed style, with hints of components from many sources and the curious contradictions of well observed details put together as a flat pattern with no grasp of spatial relations, is the current International Style of *c.* 1400. Its appearance in English painting is by no means unique, but the particular form which it took there is interesting, because it seems to have developed outside the sphere of influence from Paris, where Simone Martini and Sienese painting were greatly in vogue. The English International Style is not elegantly Gothic in its first phase but sturdily plain and matter of fact. It does not seem too much to infer that this was in great part due to the accident which brought the Dutch artist to work on the English Carmelite Missal in the last decade of the fourteenth century.

But neither the Dutch Carmelite miniatures, nor anything which smacks of the Siferwas style,[63] can account for the illuminator Herman Scheerre. For his style we turn first to an exquisite miniature of the Annunciation (Plate 166) painted on the verso of an inserted leaf (fol. 23) in a Book of Hours probably made for John Beaufort, Earl of Somerset, and Margaret de Holand whom he married in or before 1399.[64] The manuscript, which is known as the Somerset, Beaufort, or Grandison Hours, from obits of this family in the Calendar, is Brit. Mus., Roy. MS. 2 A. xviii. The Annunciation, which occupies the entire page, includes portraits thought to be John Beaufort and Margaret. In this miniature the architectural setting is exquisitely painted in white shaded with grey to suggest its three-dimensional form; without the gold decorative motifs and delicate hairline sprays which almost certainly were added later,[65] the architecture with the kneeling figures outside might suggest a small votive chapel within which the Annunciation takes place. The *prie-dieu* where the Virgin kneels is covered with a green cloth on which are diagonal bands with alternating scroll patterns and lettering which reads as follows:'omnia leuia sunt amanti; si quis amat non laborat; de daer.'[66] The baldaquin of the *prie-dieu* and the green and gold patterned backdrop are in fine contrast to the white architecture and the two very beautiful figures of the Virgin and Gabriel. The Virgin is clad in ultramarine blue and the angel in soft shaded pink. Their hair is pale gold with reddish high-lights; the floor is of the same colour slightly shaded with red towards the back to suggest depth. The faces are modelled in white and soft pink on a pale greyish-green flesh tone. The technique and quality of the modelling is closer to that of the Wilton Diptych than is any other known English painting; but the modelling itself is much softer and less linear, shading from light to dark with gentle gradations. All the faces, including the two kneeling donors, are seen in three-quarter view. The draperies flow about the figures in soft clinging folds revealing the forms beneath. It is difficult to exaggerate the delicacy of the drawing and modelling and the soft harmony of the colours in the Beaufort miniature; it is extremely accomplished painting and, in spite of the cryptic 'de daer' ending the inscription, it has usually been ascribed confidently to the illuminator, Herman Scheerre, who has been identified in several manuscripts containing miniatures in similar style. It is true that the Beaufort Annunciation was copied in these and other contemporary and later miniatures associated with Herman; nevertheless, the fine quality of the painting of the Beaufort miniature cannot quite be matched in any other English illumination of the period.[67]

Of Herman's own style there are a number of fine examples more or less certainly attributable on grounds of 'signatures' and mottoes as well as of style. Perhaps the earliest is the Book of Offices and Prayers in Latin and French (Brit. Mus., Add. MS. 16998) which contains his full name.[68] Part of the motto on the *prie-dieu* of the Beaufort miniature, 'omnia leuia sunt amanti', occurs also in Add. MS. 16998 (fol. 67). The other part, 'Si quis amat non laborat' followed by 'quod herman' is found on fol. 1 of the Breviary[69] which belonged to Archbishop Chichele (1414–43), now MS. 69 in the Library of Lambeth Palace. Whereas Add. MS. 16998 contains many small miniatures apparently all by Herman, the Chichele Breviary is illustrated with small historiated initials, only a few of which are by Herman himself. Herman's figure style as represented in these two manuscripts is characterized by long, thin faces most delicately modelled in brown on pale, almost white flesh colour, with touches of pale red on cheeks and lips. The technique of the modelling is fine and sensitive and the heads in many of the miniatures, though painted on a minute scale, are carefully differentiated as to type. The bodies and draperies are generally treated less carefully, but some of the gestures are eloquent.

One other manuscript contains Herman's name, the Psalter and Hours made for John, Duke of Bedford[70] (Brit. Mus., Add. MS. 42131). Curiously enough, the name Herman occurs only in line endings in this manuscript (fols 124 and 232 verso) and not on any of the miniatures. There is no basis, therefore, other than stylistic for determining how much of the illumination is to be attributed to Herman. None of the eleven large historiated initials seem to be in the exact style of the earlier, certainly identified Herman manuscripts, but some of the many small portrait heads enclosed in initials throughout the Psalter suggest Herman's delicate technique and sensitive rendering, as well as his wonderful skill in differentiating types. Many others of this series of heads, however, are obviously not by him, though they bear marks of his influence; these are probably the result of collaboration with other artists, as is the case with several other manuscripts in which Herman's style can be recognized.

There are three of these manuscripts. A Book of Hours formerly in the Chester Beatty Collection[71] contains the full motto as found in the Beaufort Annunciation; nevertheless the style does not seem to be that of Herman himself. A small but very beautiful Book of Hours in the Bodleian Library (MS. Lat. liturg. f.2) contains on fol. 19 verso a fragment of the motto beginning 'omnia'. The style of this manuscript looks early: the illuminations are miniatures, not historiated initials; the ornament around them consists of hair-line sprays with small gold motifs such as are found in some of the Dutch artist's miniatures in the Carmelite Missal. On internal evidence[72] the Bodleian manuscript can be dated between 1405 and 1413. One of the finest miniatures, almost certainly painted by Herman's sensitive hand, is the *Pietà* (fol. 10; Plate 169A). All the figures in this miniature show his typical pale modelling in brown and white, and have the characteristic serious expressions and simple, eloquent gestures. The background is painted with flat colour and a gold arabesque pattern, but the foreground is barren rock, reflecting the tragic mood of the picture. The colouring is chiefly fine ultramarine blue and soft shaded pink. There are seventeen of these full-page miniatures, of which many but not all are by Herman.[73]

The third manuscript to be attributed to Herman, at least in part as to execution and possibly wholly as to supervision, is the enormous Bible[74] (Brit. Mus., Roy. ms. 1 e. ix), popularly known as the 'Big Bible of Richard II', but certainly not executed before *c.* 1410. This manuscript closely approximates the Carmelite and Sherborne Missals both in size and in the amount of its decoration. The initials of all the Books of the Bible and most of the Prologues are historiated, the pictures varying in style and in quality. The two reproduced on plate 168 illustrate two different styles. The miniature representing the Baptism of Christ (fol. 262 verso; Plate 168B) is almost certainly by Herman. The wonderfully sensitive faces with their pale, soft modelling contrasting with the dark green of the landscape are typical of Herman; the Christ of the Baptism with his beautiful young body and eager, spiritual face may be compared with the tragic dead figure in the *Pietà* – both conceived with amazing spirituality, each in its own mood.

The most recent addition to the *œuvre* of Herman Scheerre, though bearing neither his name nor his motto, is a magnificent Crucifixion (Plate 167) painted on the verso of a large vellum leaf which is blank on the recto and evidently was intended to precede the *Te igitur* page of the Canon of the Mass in a great missal.[75]

The closest parallels to the figure style of this miniature are found in: Add. ms. 16998 which is signed (see note 68 above); Royal ms. 1 e. ix which contains his motto on fol. 229; and Bodleian ms. Lat. liturg. f.2 which contains a fragment of the motto on fol. 19 verso.[76] The technique of the Crucifixion miniature is soft as in a painter's style: the faces and hands, and the body of Christ, are lightly modelled in tones of brown. The eyes are pale brown with a darker iris; cheeks, lips, and nostrils are touched with light red; the hair is painted as a soft, shaded mass. The modelling of the figures is delicate yet firm, and they are wonderfully sensitive in gesture and expression. Outline is used only in places where the contour needs accentuation, as on the torso and the legs of Christ and for the profiles of Mary and John. No shading for drapery folds now appears, but there are drawing lines which must originally have been painted.[77] The outer side of Mary's mantle and the tunic of John are painted in flat, deep blue; John's tunic is powdered with groups of tiny white and pink dots. The Virgin wears a red gown which shows only at neck and wrist; and the lining of John's mantle also is red. The background, which in contemporary English manuscripts is usually of tooled gold, now is yellow with traces of red and blue patterns in the lozenges of the diaper.[78] The acanthus scrolls in the frame of the miniature are in blue monochrome, and the ribbon scrolls, now faded yellow, may have been pink originally. The only use of gold leaf is for the ground and the balls of the border sprays, which have very little stylistic connexion with the painted technique of the miniature and its frame and may have been added by another illuminator.

The miniature poses many problems. Its large scale – the figures are nearly 6 inches high – and its technique are those of panel painting. The composition is not of the usual late fourteenth century crowded Italian type, as in the Lytlington and Sherborne Missals (Plates 154 and 161), but of the mystic, meditative type more commonly found in the Low Countries.[79] The miniature is closely related in composition though not in style to the Crucifixion in an English Missal[80] dated 1398, which displays an unmistakable stylistic derivation from the Dutch artist's miniatures in the Carmelite Missal.

On the basis of this analogy the Herman Crucifixion might be the earliest of his works in England, i.e. soon after 1400. The technique of the drapery and especially the use of much white for the clothing, and the rich, rippling contour patterns are almost identical with those of Herman's miniatures in Royal MS. I E. ix (as fol. 2).[81] The modelling of the nude body of Christ in the Crucifixion is very close to that in the Baptism scene in this same manuscript (Plate 168B). The use of acanthus scrolls in English manuscripts occurs first in the Carmelite Missal (Plate 156B); but the combination of these with ribbon scrolls, twisted round a central rod, is found first in the Beaufort Annunciation (Plate 166) and on fol. 2 and other pages of Royal MS. I E. ix.

The new Herman miniature is of great importance for establishing this fine illuminator's origins in painting rather than in illumination. It also demonstrates beyond question the character of his style as distinguished from that of the painter of the Beaufort miniature.

The second important artist of Roy. MS. I E. ix painted the Genesis initial (fol. 3 verso; Plate 168A); it is very close in style to the Dutch artist of the Carmelite Missal, though it certainly is not by him; this same hand may have collaborated with Herman in the Chichele Breviary. The figures are short and stocky with large heads and heavily modelled faces. The draperies are rich and the colouring is vivid.

In addition to the two artists of the Bible represented in plate 168 there are others who show characteristics of the Siferwas or of the Herman style. Siferwas himself is not recognizable in any of the miniatures, however, and it would seem that a group of illuminators, perhaps working under the supervision of Herman, who painted the first miniature in the Bible, collaborated in its decoration. Many of the pages, large as they are, have marginal borders completely surrounding the text, and all the initials have more or less elaborate marginal sprays. In so much illumination there is bound to be considerable variation in the quality and originality of the work. An interesting feature of the Bible illumination is the fact that in some of the miniatures inscriptions in French are found; in others, inscriptions apparently in Low German. It would seem that the atelier which produced the Bible drew recruits also from the Continent. There is no indication as to the person for whom the Bible was made, nor where, but it seems likely that the atelier which produced it was a London shop.

Both Herman Scheerre and John Siferwas painted portraits, and the latter even painted and signed self-portraits[82] (cf. Plate 163). Herman undoubtedly painted some of the small portrait heads in the Bedford Psalter (Brit. Mus., Add. MS. 42131) though none of them is either named or signed. Siferwas also painted portraits of John Was, his scribe-collaborator on the Sherborne Missal, and of the Bishop of Salisbury and the Abbot of Sherborne Abbey who sponsored the work on that Missal. The double portrait in the Lovell Lectionary[83] is the most striking example thus far noted of an attempt at veri-similitude in representation, but owing to the conventions of representing the features, for example, the eyes in profile, it is impossible to judge whether Siferwas's eyes really protruded as unpleasantly as the picture suggests. In fact, the eyes, noses, mouths, and ears are almost identical as drawn in the two figures, and one wonders whether, in spite of the names, the artist was really trying to distinguish the appearance of the one from the other.

All the more remarkable, therefore, is a portrait of Geoffrey Chaucer painted by an unknown artist in an early copy of Hoccleve's *De Regimine Principum* (Brit. Mus., Harl. MS. 4866, fol. 88; Plate 169B) which stands beside a stanza of this poem, pointing to the lines in praise of Chaucer which say: 'that in order to remind other men of his personal appearance I have had his likeness made here to the end, in truth, that those who have least thought and memory of him may recall him by this painting'. The miniature must have been done some time after Chaucer's death in 1400 and therefore was painted either from memory by someone who had known Chaucer or from a picture made of him during his life. The remarkable thing about the picture is its suggestiveness of an individual man. There is age indicated in the white hair and thinning white beard and in the rather drawn features and tired eyes. His complexion is that of a fresh-faced old man with the colour showing through the pale, transparent skin. The face is thoughtful, intelligent, kindly – or does one read into the features the characteristics of the man as suggested by his writings? In any case, the fact is that the portrait, unlike the Lovell-Siferwas pictures, makes one think of an individual with a character as well as an outward appearance. This is the special virtue of the Chaucer portrait in Harl. 4866, and it is a characteristic that more than any other foreshadows the English Renaissance, an age of portrait painting.

The manuscript Harl. 4866 is a copy of what is perhaps the original manuscript of Hoccleve's *De Regimine Principum* (Arundel MS. 38) which, on a leaf now torn out, undoubtedly also contained a portrait of Chaucer. It would be most enlightening to know whether the two portraits were replicas. The picture on fol. 37 of the Arundel manuscript (Plate 169C) shows a presentation of his book by the author to Prince Henry; the date therefore must be shortly before 1413, the year of his coronation. In this miniature too it seems likely that the figures are intended to be portraits; certainly they are distinguished in age, in complexion, in features, and even in expression more clearly than the Lovell-Siferwas portraits. Henry is richly dressed in an ermine-lined blue gown with fashionable dagged sleeves hanging to the ground. A curious feature of the shading of the folds is the use of a golden yellow pigment which gives the effect of gilding; his girdle and coronet are gold. Hoccleve wears a madder pink gown with very high collar. His face is florid, in contrast to Henry's pale complexion; his hair is dark, Henry's golden brown; his mouth is firm with a bitter droop at the corners, Henry's is straight and thin-lipped. Again it would be most interesting to see the counterpart of this miniature which probably was on a leaf now missing at this place in Harl. 4866.

One more example of portraiture of this period is reproduced from a manuscript of Chaucer's *Troilus and Criseyde* (Camb., Corpus Christi Coll., MS. 61, fol. 1 verso; Plate 170). Chaucer is shown here as a much younger man than in Harl. 4866 and is reading to a company of richly and fashionably dressed nobles who sit or stand in various attitudes of attention. Though the facial types and attitudes of individual listeners are varied, the impression the picture gives is that the artist was more interested in the panoply of the scene than in the possibilities it offered for portraiture.[84] The style of this miniature is brilliant and highly decorative. The gold tooled background against which a fairy-tale castle is silhouetted, with figures conversing in the open windows and angels fluttering on the topmost turrets, reminds us of the Calendar pages in the *Très Riches Heures* of the Duc de Berry.[85] The style seems too elegant and sophisticated for typical English work, but the loose sprays of the border decoration with their softly curling shaded leaf and flower motifs can be matched in other English work[86] of about 1400 and will be met again in work of the next period, which can be assigned to a specific centre, Bury St Edmunds.

The preoccupation of the present chapter with manuscript illumination is not accidental, as was noted at the outset, since it was in that medium that the principal developments took place. Panel painting had a much smaller rôle in England, if surviving examples represent the accomplishment of the period. For notable though the Wilton Diptych and the Norwich Retable are, as compared with the manuscripts, they contribute little to the development of a more realistic painting style. Of stained glass also few examples have survived, and, though good of their kind, they are more interesting for the development of the design of the windows as a whole in relation to their tracery than for individual figures. Following the important innovations in colouring and design of stained-glass windows, which were introduced in the earlier part of the fourteenth century,[87] the later years have little to offer beyond further exploitation of the limited possibilities of composition within the rectangular panels formed by Perpendicular tracery.

Two examples of the best late fourteenth century glass are known to have been made in Oxford, where there is evidence of glass painting even earlier than this. The shop which produced the windows of the antechapel of New College, Oxford, also made and dispatched to Winchester[88] by cart the glass for the great east Jesse Tree window and the side windows of William of Wykeham's other foundation, Winchester College. The master of this shop was Thomas; his portrait with his name was included in one of the panels of the Winchester Jesse. The dates of the New College windows[89] are 1380–6; the Winchester College east window[90] can be dated *c.* 1393. The side windows in the Chapel were probably inserted not much later, because they were repaired[91] by Master Thomas in 1421–2.

New College as well as Winchester College had a Jesse window, but until recently it was believed to have been lost, having been replaced in the seventeenth century by a new window designed by William Peckitt. The old Jesse Tree window, it is recorded,[92] was given to Peckitt in part payment for his work. Peckitt came originally from York and he sent the old Jesse Tree glass back there; thus, eventually, some panels found their way into one of the windows in the south choir aisle of the Minster. Students of the glass have long been puzzled by the uncanny resemblance of these panels to the remains of the Winchester Jesse window (Plate 172A), but no explanation was forthcoming until a re-examination of the documents yielded this interesting and correct solution of the style of the York panels (Plate 172B). But the Winchester Jesse window had also suffered a disastrous fate. In the early nineteenth century it underwent a drastic 'restoration' which consisted in replacing all the old glass with copies, and – under what circumstances is not known – dispersing the old glass. For a hundred years the Winchester Jesse window was known only in this copy, but recently all the old fragments which could be collected in England were restored to the Chapel and are now placed in a large window in Thurbern's Chantry on the west wall of the College Chapel. The contrast between the rich and harmonious colouring of the old glass and that of its copy in the present east window of the Chapel is at once apparent.

We do not know exactly the design of the New College Jesse window, but at Winchester the copy has at least preserved the design in its entirety. In the centre of the lowest tier was Jesse, the stem issuing from his side; in the centre branches were David, Solomon, the Virgin and Child, and at the top, a strange addition to the traditional design, a Crucifixion with Mary and John. In the two rows of vine-branch panels on either side of the centre were sixteen kings and two prophets; and in the outer panels on each side the remaining ten prophets. From the similarity of the single figures surviving from the New College Jesse window, it is likely that the design followed in general that of Winchester.

The style of the two figure panels is indeed very close (Plate 172, A and B). The short, thickset figures with large heads holding their identifying scrolls and standing within the same sharp-elbowed loops of the vine could have stood side by side in the same window without suggesting any stylistic discrepancy. The features of both figures are painted with the same soft but firm modelling, the hair is treated in the same roughened manner, the drapery is decorated with an almost identical ornamental pattern. The vine leaves and the stiff bunches of grapes, and even the scrollwork of the background are identical in the two panels. Certainly one need not assume that the glass was all painted by the same hand even in the same window; but the similarities in style in these panels indicate unmistakably one workshop, that is, the shop of Master Thomas.

Some of the old glass still remains in the antechapel at New College.[93] The figures which fill six windows on each of two tiers include the prophets and patriarchs, the apostles and the Church Fathers, three Crucifixions and a group of holy women and penitents, all under elaborate architectural canopies against grounds powdered with the initials of their names. Under each figure is a scroll bearing the name and title. At the bottom of each window is a scroll containing the words: 'Orate pro Willelmo de Wykeham episcopo Wynton fundatore istius collegii'.

The figures in the windows of New College antechapel are taller than the Jesse Tree figures and better proportioned, with large heads and ample draperies. The faces are modelled with considerable understanding of features and expressions, and there is some variety in the types.

In Winchester College there were also large figures in the side windows. Three have survived and are now in the Victoria and Albert Museum (Plate 173A). They are similar in style to the Jesse figures but perhaps even more competently modelled as to the faces and, like the New College figures, better proportioned. The drawing of all the figures is extremely good and each figure is individually designed, without any apparent repetition of the same cartoon. The colouring in general is deep, rich, and varied, and a minimum of silver stain is used, and that only for borders and ornamental patterns on draperies. The backgrounds are coloured, red and blue, and a considerable amount of white is used in the draperies.

The connexion of William Peckitt with York which resulted in the Oxford glass finding its way there was not the first instance of the possible influence of the Oxford shop on York glass. John Thornton of Coventry, glazier, contracted in 1405 to glaze the great east window of the Minster and to finish the work within three years.[94] Coventry is in the Midlands, not far from Oxford, and it is conjectured from the characteristics of the style in the York glass that John Thornton may have learned his craft from the Oxford glaziers. However that may be, the great east window at York was the first of a large number of fifteenth century windows in the Minster and in the many parish churches of York, which furnish some of the finest and most interesting examples of later English glass.

The design of the York east window (Plate 171) is impressive, as is the scheme of its subject matter. The window, like that of Winchester, is divided into two halves by a gallery. In the upper half, under three equal arches each of three lights, is an elaborate scheme of many-shaped tracery panels; the lower half again is divided by a transom into two tiers, each of nine elongated panels with cusped heads. The tracery in the heads is Perpendicular, and there is a geometrical uniformity in the panels which is lacking in the flowing lines of Decorated tracery. On the other hand, the long unbroken lights below the tracery lend themselves admirably to a series of uniform panels, each one yard square, in which successive scenes of the Creation and Fall of Man and the Apocalyptic vision of his judgement and redemption unfold themselves with the continuity of a film strip. Above the gallery are twenty-seven scenes from Genesis and Exodus; in the lower half are eighty-one scenes from the Apocalypse and, in the lowest row of all, nine panels with figures of ecclesiastics and kings. Every panel is filled with coloured glass; the effect of the whole, therefore, is much more brilliant than that of the earlier east window at Gloucester.

The tracery panels contain half-length figures, of which the David (Plate 173B) may be compared with the Winchester and New College figures. The type of head is certainly very similar in proportions, in modelling, and in the treatment of the hair and beard. It would appear that the Oxford style of Master Thomas was carried over into York, where it flourished and spread, eventually to the Priory of Great Malvern, during the course of the fifteenth century.

Summary

The English International Style did not herald any Renaissance school of painting such as was in the making on the Continent, nor did it produce any great painters as in the Low Countries. The Wilton Diptych and the Westminster portrait of Richard are anonymous and unique of their kind in England. The 'New Style' in England at the beginning of the fifteenth century is confined to illumination and manifested itself both in the international character of the miniatures and in the rich new border ornament. Of the two illuminators whose names are known, Herman Scheerre was almost certainly a foreigner who brought new elements of style into England, and John Siferwas, who was English, apparently had contacts with Continental work either in England or on the Continent or both, which greatly affected his style. The source of the new miniature style and also of certain elements of the border decoration is identifiable in the work of the Dutch artist of the Carmelite Missal, whose name and specific origins we do not know. The influence of his style was so marked, however, that there can be no doubt as to the recognition in England of his outstanding ability and of the new elements which he introduced. The fine crop of richly illuminated manuscripts by a variety of hands bears witness to the stimulus resulting from international artistic contacts on English soil; it also represents the last flowering of the art of illumination in England.

NOTES TO CHAPTER 7

1. The mixture of Gothic and Italian painted figure styles which took place in the fourteenth century in various parts of Europe. On the International Style in general, see Raimond van Marle, *The Development of the Italian Schools of Painting*, VII (The Hague, 1926), 1–63.

2. *English Art 1307–1461*.

3. On the Influence of the East Anglian style in Germany, see Robert Freyhan, *Die Illustrationen zum Casseler Willehalm-Codex. Ein Beispiel englischen Einflusses in der rheinischen Malerei des XIV. Jahrhunderts* (Marburg, 1927). On the influence of East Anglian manuscripts on Bohemian illumination, see Jan Květ, *Iluminované Rukopisy Královny Rejčky* [The Illuminated Manuscripts of Queen Rejčka. A Contribution to the History of Czech Manuscript Painting in the fourteenth Century.] (Prague, 1931). The text is in Czech but includes a number of good plates for comparison of East Anglian and Czech border motifs.

4. In this connexion it may be recalled that some East Anglian manuscripts, such as the Ormesby Psalter (Plate 125), themselves show evidence of contacts with Italian painting in the first part of the fourteenth century. This shows chiefly in certain figure types and poses rather than in technique and composition. Cf. Pächt, 'A Giottesque Episode'.

5. Stephen Beissel, *Vaticanische Miniaturen* (Freiburg i.B., 1893), 41–2, plate XXIIIA.

6. Wormald, 'The Fitzwarin Psalter and its Allies', 71–9.

7. James, *Catalogue of the Manuscripts in the Fitzwilliam Museum*, 100, gives evidence for the date and ownership, as well as a description of the miniatures in detail. See also *op. cit.*, 73 and 79, plate 25C.

8. A detailed analysis of Italian, specifically of Giottesque influence, on English linear tradition is given by Pächt, *op. cit.*, 68 ff., in supporting the attribution of the Egerton Genesis to an English artist.

9. See Millar 'The Egerton Genesis and the M. R. James Memorial Manuscript', 1–5. A manuscript in Oxford discovered by Pächt (Bod. MS. Rawl. 185, dated before 1374) is very close in style to Add. MS. 44949 and may be partly by the same hand. Another manuscript illuminated in a mixed style (Brit. Mus., Egerton MS. 1894, the Egerton Genesis) seems to this writer not to be English in its style but rather a French-Italian mixture, since the technique is grisaille, which is found in many French manuscripts of the third quarter of the fourteenth century but in no known English ones of this time. James, *Illustrations of the Book of Genesis ... Egerton 1894*, believed the manuscript to be English, as does Millar. Pächt, as noted above, presents a well-reasoned and almost convincing case for an English origin, but the technique in its sculpturesque clarity seems more French than English.

p. 158

10. James and Millar, *The Bohun Manuscripts*. The manuscripts included are: Oxford, Exeter Coll., MS. 47; Oxford, Bod. MS. Auct. D.4.4; Vienna, Nationalbib., Cod. 1826*; Copenhagen, Thottsamml., MS. 547; and Riches Coll. (now in the Fitzwilliam

Museum, Cambridge). The Psalter in Edinburgh, National Lib., MS. Adv. 18.6.5, made for Eleanor de Bohun (d. 1399) was not included. Since the monograph appeared, two more manuscripts containing Bohun arms have been discovered: Brit. Mus., Roy. MS. 20 D. iv, a French text of *Lancelot du lac* with two earlier French miniatures painted over in the 'Bohun style', with Bohun arms added; and Brit. Mus., Eg. MS. 3277, bought by the British Museum in 1943 (see plate 149A).

p. 168   11. For illustrations and discussion of this infiltration of Italian style into Vienna MS. 1826★, see Rickert, *The Reconstructed Carmelite Missal*, 74 ff., and plate XL, a and b.

12. For example, Exeter Coll., MS. 47, also made for Humphrey de Bohun. James and Millar, *op. cit.*, plates I–XXII.

13. For example, Bod. MS. Auct. D.4.4, and Copenhagen, Thotts MS. 547. *Op. cit.*, plates XXIII–XXXVIII and LVII–LXI.

14. His name occurs in the same series of memorials as in three other Bohun manuscripts: Exeter MS. 47, Bod. Auct. D.4.4, and Vienna MS. 1826★.

15. The north Italian-English mixture of styles occurs also in a Book of Hours in Munich (Staatsbib. Cod. Lat. 23215) illuminated for Blanche of Savoy (d. 1387) by Giovanni da Como, *c.* 1378. In this case it would appear that an English illuminator was working in Italy.

p. 169   16. The paintings were in two registers of four scenes each on the north and the south walls of the chapel, under the windows. The subjects were the stories of Job (north side) and Tobit (south side). See Brit. Mus., *Guide to an Exhibition of English Art* (1934).

17. It is significant in this connexion to note that in the will of Hugh Payntour (1361), presumably Master Hugh of St Albans, is mentioned 'unam tabulam de VI peces de Lumbardy' which had cost £20. See W. R. Lethaby, 'London and Westminster Painters', *Walpole Soc.*, I (1911–12), 71.

18. An interesting sidelight is thrown on the painting at St Stephen's Chapel by a document of 1350 which appoints John Athelard, glazier and painter, to obtain painters for St Stephen's. Athelard himself continued to work at St Stephen's as a painter, possibly on cartoons for the windows. Salzman, 'The Glazing of St Stephen's Chapel, Westminster, 1351–2', 16.

p. 170   19. The paintings from the Chapel representing King Edward III and Philippa with their children, now entirely destroyed, are known only through copies made by Robert Smirke, now in the Society of Antiquaries, London. They seem to be earlier and much less Italianate in style. Reproduced, Evans, *op. cit.*, plate 27.

20. J. G. Noppen, 'The Westminster Chapter House Paintings', *Burl. Mag.*, LXI (1932), 146–59. See also Waller, *London and Middlesex Archaeol. Soc.*, IV (1871). The wording of the document is 'fieri fecit' (caused to be made) which precludes the assumption that Brother John was the painter.

21. As this book goes to press newly discovered wall paintings in fresco technique are being uncovered in a room over the gateway to the Byward Tower in the Tower of London. The subjects thus far visible are the Virgin and the Baptist (left), the Evangelist (?) and St Michael with the scales (right). The insertion of a Tudor fireplace destroyed the central subject. The figures are about half life-size and are exceptionally fine in technique and colour. The style and costume suggest a date *c.* 1380–90. For a sight of these paintings I am obliged to Mr B. H. St J. O'Neil, H.M. Chief Inspector of Ancient Monuments.

22. The principal discussions of the Wilton Diptych are the following: Scharf, *Description of the Wilton House Diptych* (London, 1882); W. G. Constable, 'The Date and Nationality of the Wilton Diptych', *Burl. Mag.*, LV (1929), 36–45; Sir Martin Conway, 'The Wilton Diptych', *op. cit.*, 209–12; M. V. Clarke, 'The Wilton Diptych', *op. cit.*, LVIII (1931), 283–94; Bodkin, *The Wilton Diptych*, Gallery Books, No. 16 (London, n.d.). The latest articles are: Tristram, 'The Wilton Diptych', *The Month*, New Series, I, No. 6 (1949); Joan Evans, 'The Wilton Diptych Reconsidered', *Archaeol. Jnl*, CV (1950), 1–5.

23. It is not proposed in this book either to support or to refute any of these theories about the Wilton Diptych, much less to invent any new theory about the date and provenance of the panels. The Wilton Diptych is primarily a work of art and not an historical document; it is, moreover, a masterpiece of its particular style.

24. The composition of the gesso can be seen clearly on the back of the right panel where it has been badly damaged.

25. The head and one foot of the animal can be seen, as in the representation of the Baptist in the Lytlington Missal (fol. 247 verso) made at Westminster 1383–4. See below.

26. Perhaps at the time of negotiations for the marriage in 1395, or even at the time of the trans-

ference of Richard's body from Langley to West-minster during the reign of Henry V.

27. For example, the frescoes at Lentate and Mocchirola. Reproduced, Pietro Toesca, *La pittura e la miniatura nella Lombardia* (Milan, 1912), figures 189–91, 193, and 196.

28. The expenses for making the Missal are listed in the Abbot's Treasurer's Roll for that year. See J. A. Robinson and M. R. James, *The Manuscripts of Westminster Abbey* (London, 1909), 7 ff.

29. Cf. examples which occur in Add. MS. 44949 (Plate 150A) and Egerton MS. 1894.

30. Reproduced, Earl Beauchamp, *Liber Regalis*, Roxburghe Club (London, 1870).

31. Scharf, *op. cit.*, 78, calls attention to the 'pre-dominance of blue in contact with gold, and the strong deep shadows on the faces' in the *Liber Regalis* as showing 'much affinity to the Wilton House Diptych'.

32. The best period of Bohemian illumination was somewhat earlier in the fourteenth century and is found in a group of manuscripts made for Johann von Neumarkt. See Max Dvořák, 'Die Illumina-toren des Johann von Neumarkt', *Jahrbuch der Kunst-hist. Sammlgn des allerhöchsten Kaiserhauses*, XXII (1901), 35–126. Later Bohemian manuscripts made for Wenzel, brother of Anne, have some of the ex-aggerated features found in the *Liber Regalis*. See Julius von Schlosser, 'Die Bilderhandschriften Königs Wenzel I', *op. cit.*, XIV (1893), 214–319.

33. For example, a manuscript of Statutes, after 1387, containing figures of English kings: Cam-bridge, St John's College, MS. A.7.

34. For a monograph on this manuscript with reproductions of all the important miniatures, see Rickert, *The Reconstructed Carmelite Missal*.

35. *Op. cit.*, plates XII–XVI, XIX b and c, XXXII, XXXIII, and colour plate D. The character and origins of this style are discussed in greater detail on 71–6 of the monograph.

36. *Op. cit.*, 76–80, plates II–VI, and colour plate B.

37. It may be remembered, however, that the East Anglian style of decoration had influenced the von Neumarkt manuscripts. See footnote 3 above. Particularly close to the border style of the Trinity miniature is that of the latest of this group, the Gospels of Johann von Troppau in Vienna (Nation-albib. MS. 1182). Ten full pages from this manuscript are magnificently reproduced in colour by Ernst

Trenkler, *Das Evangeliar des Johannes von Troppau* (Vienna, 1948).

38. Rickert, *op. cit.*, 80–90, plates I, VII–IX, XVII–XIXa, XX–XXXI, and colour plates A and C.

39. For parallel works establishing this origin of   p. 175 the style, see *op. cit.*, 83 ff.

40. Roy. Acad. Arts, *Exhib. Brit. Prim. Paintings, Cat.* No. 30. Borenius finds that 'the picture seems to offer such close parallels to the paintings of St Stephen's Chapel as to make it seem much more natural to look upon it as a work of the same school'. 'English Primitives', *Proc. Brit. Acad.*, XI (1924–5), 82.

41. The background, which is now plain gold, was originally decorated in some manner, probably with a tooled pattern, glimpses of which can still be seen through the openings in the tracery of the throne. At the time of the restoration there was, however, a gilt gesso pattern similar to that of the canopy or tester of the tomb of Richard and Anne in the Westminster Choir. This gesso ground was removed, but there does not seem to be complete agreement as to whether it was original or a later addition.

42. In the south choir aisle of the Abbey. The tomb was ordered in 1395, soon after the death of Anne in 1394. The contract for the work still exists and is published in Rymer's *Foedera*, VII (1709), 795–6. The master mason who designed it was Henry Yevele, for an account of whose life and work see John Harvey, *Henry Yevele* (London, 1944).

43. The portrait has been attributed to Beauneveu but seems to show no close resemblance to the work of this painter. See S. C. Cockerell, 'André Beau-neveu and the Portrait of Richard II at Westminster Abbey', *Burl. Mag.*, X (1906), 126–7.

44. Two late fourteenth century examples may be cited: the so-called Jerzen Epitaph and the Dube-čeker Altarpiece, both in Prague. Reproduced, Alfred Stange, *Deutsche Malerei der Gotik*, II (Ber-lin, 1936), plates 69–71; discussed 59 ff., 62 ff., and 65 ff.

45. *Op. cit.*, 132 ff.   p. 176

46. Borenius and Tristram, *op. cit.*, 26.

47. Roy. Acad. Arts *Exhib. Brit. Prim. Paint-ings, Cat.* No. 32. See also St John Hope, 'On a Painted Table or Reredos of the Fourteenth Century in the Cathedral Church of Norwich'. The boards comprising the Altarpiece run lengthwise. Only four of a probable five remain, the top one having been broken away, perhaps when it was

used, with the painted side down, as a table. At the same time the holes in the four corners were made for table legs. The upper part of the centre panel with the Crucifixion is cut off by the loss of the top board. It is not known what may have filled this space in the other panels.

p. 176 48. St John Hope, *op. cit.* See also Waller, 'On the Retable in Norwich Cathedral and Paintings in St Michael-at-Plea'. Waller says the Retable is Italian.

p. 177 49. Meister Bertram again comes to mind, rather in connexion with the figure types than with general style. Hanseatic influences on Norwich art would by no means be impossible. On the spread of Hanseatic art, see Stange, *op. cit.*, III, 196 ff. See also note 52 below.

50. Reproduced, Roy. Acad. Arts *Exhib. Brit. Prim. Paintings, Cat.* Nos 33, 34, plates xxa.

51. Noppen suggests that the model for the paintings was a late fourteenth century manuscript of the Apocalypse in Cambridge, Trinity College, MS. B.10.2. See 'The Westminster Apocalypse and its Source', 146–59. The manuscript is thought to have been made at Westminster. See Chapter 5, note 80, above.

52. *Op. cit.*, 159. Noppen thinks the Apocalypse paintings show strong German influence, as of the School of Meister Bertram. On this point, see Alexander Dorner, 'Ein Schüler des Meisters Bertram in England', *Jahrbuch der Preuss. Kunstsammlungen*, 58 (1937), 40 ff.

53. Borenius, 'An English Painted Ceiling of the Late Fourteenth Century'; see also Preston, 'The Fourteenth Century Painted Ceiling at St Helen's Church, Abingdon'.

p. 178 54. Borenius, *op. cit.*, 276, found that some of the kings resembled the portrait of Richard II at Westminster. As far as can be judged from their present state, the quality of even the better Abingdon figures is greatly inferior to that of the Richard portrait.

55. The most striking example of the influence of this new modelled style is in a large Crucifixion page in a missal in Corpus Christi College, Oxford, MS. 394, dated 1398. See Rickert, *op. cit.*, 93 ff., plate L. Another manuscript which is undated (Brit. Mus., Roy. MS. 20 D. V) not only shows strong influence of this style in the miniatures, but copies some of the Dutch artist's compositions in the Carmelite Missal, *op. cit.*, 93, plate LIIIa.

56. Joint patrons of the Sherborne Missal were Richard Mitford, Bishop of Salisbury (1395–1407)

and Robert Bruynyng, Abbot of Sherborne (1385–1415), who are represented frequently in pictures in this manuscript.

57. Herbert, *The Sherborne Missal*.

58. These occur most abundantly and with most precise ornithological intention between pages 363 and 393. Many are not only drawn and painted so accurately as to be recognizable, but in many cases are even labelled with their English names. A number are reproduced in the coloured frontispiece of Herbert's monograph.

59. Siferwas appears twice in documentary records. On 19 May 1380, F. John Cyfrewas, Friars Preachers, Guildford, was ordained acolyte at Farnham by the Bishop of Winchester (*Wykeham's Register*, ed. T. F. Kirby, *Hampshire Record Soc.*, I (1896), 296; 'Johannes Sifirwas, frater ordinis predicatorum' is named as the recipient of a pair of jet praying beads in the will of the widow Joan Elveden dated 4 Sept. 1421 (*Central Probate Registry*, Somerset House, P.P.C. Marche, fol. 52). These documents are quoted by Herbert, *op. cit.*

60. Reproduced in colour as frontispiece to Millar, II.

61. James, 'An English Medieval Sketchbook', plates I–XXIII.

62. He signed his name, Johannes, with the words 'me fecit' on another page, fol. 220. All the miniatures in this part of Bod. MS. 264 are not by this same artist, who, judging by his work, was perhaps the master of the group.

63. Another example of the Siferwas style, though certainly not by his hand, is a Book of Hours at Trinity College, Cambridge (MS. B.II.7), with a long series of miniatures. See Millar, II, plates 92 and 93.

64. Since the *Memoria* of St John of Bridlington is included in the manuscript the book was probably made between 1401 (when this Saint was canonized) and 1410. The miniature, however, may have been executed as early as 1399, the date given in the Royal Catalogue.

65. Parts of some of the sprays pass over the painting, as in the *prie-dieu* of the donor on the left side. The decoration is incongruous with the architectural framework of the miniature, and sets a style which was followed in the other miniatures by another hand in the same manuscript. This artist (known as the Master of the Beaufort Hours) also was influenced by this miniature. See Kuhn, 'Herman Scheerre and English Illumination of the Early Fifteenth Century'. Many of the attributions and

the chronology offered by Professor Kuhn do not seem to be supported by the characteristics of the styles.

66. The motto appears elsewhere, in illuminations done by the group with whom Herman was associated. The significance of the words 'de daer' is not known.

67. For a suggestion that this artist was foreign, see Rickert, *The Reconstructed Carmelite Missal*, 141.

68. He signed it, 'Hermannus Scheerre me fecit', on fol. 37. See Rickert, 'Hermann the Illuminator', *Burl. Mag.*, LXI (1935), 39 ff.

69. Evidence for a date before 1416 for the writing of the Breviary is based on the absence of offices for Saints David, Winifred, Chad, and John of Beverley, all ordered by Archbishop Chichele himself in 1416. *New Pal. Soc.*, Series II, plate 131. There is, however, no evidence that the manuscript was actually made for him, although the presence of his arms on the first page attests his ownership.

70. In a line ending on fol. 21 occur the words:'I pray God save the Duke of Bedford.'

71. Millar, II, Hand List No. 279. The manuscript is now said to be in America.

72. On fol. 146 verso is a miniature representing the beheading of Richard le Scrope, Archbishop of York, which took place in 1405, and on fol. 147 is the Office for him which was in use only till the death of Henry IV in 1413. The manuscript was perhaps intended for a York patron.

73. Some are certainly by the Master of the Beaufort Hours. See note 65 above.

74. All traces of some former inscriptions on the end fly-leaves have been so completely removed that nothing shows even under ultra-violet ray. Nothing at all is known, therefore, about its ownership or history. No donors and no coats of arms are represented anywhere in the manuscript. The dating is based wholly on stylistic considerations.

75. This leaf, now owned by Mr A. Wyndham Payne of Dartmouth, was evidently exposed for many years to the light which has faded some of the colours. Rusted holes around the edges of the leaf indicate that it was tacked to a panel and framed as a picture. Its present size is $14\frac{3}{4}$ by $10\frac{1}{4}$ inches, but the margins have been trimmed close to the border decoration. The possibility of its having been painted for the great Carmelite Missal cannot but suggest itself. This question and further stylistic considerations will be discussed more fully elsewhere.

76. Both are reproduced, Rickert, 'Herman the Illuminator', *Burl. Mag.*, LXI (1935), 39–40.

77. The original colour of the shading of the folds could have disappeared, since the surface of the miniature is so greatly damaged; but there is a possibility that the painting was never finished.

78. The background originally probably was a soft madder red, now faded to dull yellow. The diagonal lines forming the diaper and some of the patterns in the lozenges were in gilt paint, as is shown by particles still visible here and there. A miniature with precisely this pattern and suggested colouring is found on fol. 229 of Royal MS. I E. ix. This is the page, but not the miniature, which contains the Herman motto.

79. Such as the votive panel with the crucifixion and Hendrik van Rijn (d. 1363) in the Royal Museum, Antwerp. A miniature with a crucifixion very similar in composition to that of Herman precedes the Canon of the Mass in an early fifteenth century missal in the Seminary at Haaren. Reproduced, A. W. Byvanck and G. J. Hoogewerff, *La Miniature hollandaise* (The Hague, 1922–6), text volume, figure 12. p. 184

80. Given to the parish church at Lapworth, Warwickshire. See Rickert, *The Reconstructed Carmelite Missal*, 93 ff., plate L.

81. Reproduced, *op. cit.*, plate LIIIb.

82. Brit. Mus., Harl. MS. 7026, fol. 1 verso; and Sherborne Missal, 81, 216, and 276 with his name. On page 391 of this manuscript is a picture of a kneeling Dominican, which resembles more than any of the others the picture of Siferwas in the Lovell portrait. Reproduced, Herbert, *op. cit.*, plate XXV.

83. Plate 163 and pp. 179 f. above. p. 185

84. The portrait element has sufficiently impressed one scholar, however, to lure her into compiling from this miniature a complete roster of 'fourteenth century celebrities'. See Margaret Galway, 'The "Troilus" Frontispiece', *Mod. Lang. Review*, XLIV (April, 1949). p. 186

85. In the Musée Condé at Chantilly. See Comte Paul Durrieu, *Les Très Riches Heures du duc de Berry* (Paris, 1903).

86. For example, a psalter made for the Abbey of Bury St Edmunds, now in the Grammar School at Bury.

87. See Chapter 6, 157 ff.

88. Le Couteur, *Ancient Glass in Winchester*, 63,

quotes an entry from Wykeham's household accounts covering expenses for cartage; the date is
1393.

p. 186   89. New College was founded in 1380, and in
1386, when it was occupied, '... it may be assumed
that the windows of the chapel and hall were wholly
glazed ...', Christopher Woodforde, *The Stained
Glass of New College, Oxford*, 1.

90. Because there are no other payments after
1393, Le Couteur assumes that the glass was all in

place in 1394 when the College was handed over
by Wykeham, *op. cit.*, 63.

91. *Op. cit.*, 117, quoting entry of payment.

92. For documents referring to this transaction
and to the cost of transporting the Jesse glass to
York, see Woodforde, *op. cit.*, 20 ff.

93. Many of these figures are reproduced, Woodforde, *op. cit.*, plates I–XI and coloured frontispiece.

94. Harrison, *The Painted Glass of York*, 129.

CHAPTER 8

THE END OF THE MIDDLE AGES IN ENGLAND

*

HISTORICAL BACKGROUND

FOREIGN AND CIVIL WARS

Henry VI, son of Henry V, crowned at Paris 1431; reigned (with regencies) 1422–61 (deposed) and 1470–1; married Margaret of Anjou 1445.

John, Duke of Bedford, uncle of Henry VI, 1414–35; Regent of France 1422–35.

Humphrey, uncle of Henry VI, Duke of Gloucester 1414–47; married Jacqueline daughter of William, Count of Holland.

Battle of Castillon ended the Hundred Years War 1453.

Wars of the Roses between the Houses of Lancaster and York 1455–85.

Richard Neville, son-in-law of Richard Beauchamp, Earl of Warwick, 1439; 'Kingmaker' 1461–71.

Edward IV, son of Richard, 3rd Duke of York, King 1461–83; in exile in Flanders 1470–1; married Elizabeth Woodville 1464.

Edward V, son of Edward IV, King April–June 1483.

Richard III, son of Richard, 3rd Duke of York, King 1483–5.

Battle of Bosworth 1485.

Henry VII, great-great-grandson of John of Gaunt, Duke of Lancaster, King 1485–1509; united Houses of Lancaster and York by marrying Elizabeth of York, daughter of Edward IV 1486; his reign marks the transition between the Middle Ages and the Renaissance; his elder son, Prince Arthur, married Catherine of Aragon 1501; died 1502.

*

DURING the last three-quarters of the fifteenth century, English art was markedly affected by two waves of direct Continental influence, both initiated mainly by political events. The first was French, and occurred during the period of the regency of John, Duke of Bedford, uncle of the infant Henry VI (born 1421), who, soon after the death of his father in 1422, fell heir also to the kingdom of France through his mother, daughter of the King of France. The English tried to press the claim, and the regency established in Paris was temporarily successful. During this time the Duke took advantage of his opportunities to acquire many treasures from the royal collections, including illuminated manuscripts;[1] he also employed Parisian illuminators to make books for him, such as the magnificent Bedford Missal[2] (Brit. Mus., Add. 18850). French influence in illumination was not limited to work done in France, but French scribes and illuminators also came to England. The results of this French fashion are apparent in English illumination after 1425, in the more conventionalized types of figures and the formal border decoration. However, by the second quarter of the fifteenth century, French work under Flemish influence had incorporated many features of naturalism in composition, such as landscape and spatial concepts, and the influence of these also is reflected in English work. A good example of the new mixture of French and English can be seen in the later illumination of the St-Omer Psalter, which was finished for Humphrey, Duke of Gloucester (d. 1447), brother of the Duke of Bedford and of Henry V, and a famous bibliophile.

With the defeat and expulsion of the English from France, and the outbreak of the Wars of the Roses at home, the middle years of the century had little time or interest for the ordering or producing of art in England. They are very barren years, indeed, when the Franco-English style of illumination of the earlier part of the century dragged out a poor and on the whole undistinguished existence except for a few fine tinted drawings.

In other media, also, the middle years are lean, and the best representative of English art during this time is glass painting. Parish churches such as those of the dioceses of York and Norwich, chantry chapels such as Fromond's at Winchester and Beauchamp's at Warwick, and the Priory Church of Great Malvern (Worcs.) furnish the greatest amount of material for judging the style and the quality of English glass painting in the second half of the fifteenth century.

From the exile of Edward IV (1470–1), which was spent mostly in Bruges, came the second main stream of Continental influence on English art in the late fifteenth century; for Edward bought and ordered in Bruges manuscripts illuminated and painted in the highly realistic Flemish manner of the developed Northern Renaissance. It seems likely that English illuminators worked side by side with Flemish painters during this time, for there are many late fifteenth century manuscripts with Flemish miniatures and borders in the florid, rather coarse English manner. Certain it is that Flemish painters returned with Edward to England, and much work, both in manuscripts and in panels, and in painted glass[3] bear witness to their activities. If French influence was, on the whole, de-vitalizing in its effect on English work in the early part of the century – since the charm of English art ever depended on its originality and informality – Flemish realism of the end of the century was disastrous, for the English painter could neither assimilate it nor ignore it. With the advent of Flemish influence, therefore, English medieval painting came to an inglorious end.

The St-Omer Psalter (Brit. Mus., Add. MS. 39810), of which fol. 87 is illustrated in plate 174A, has been described (see Chapter 6) as being in its earlier parts one of the finest and most typical examples of the mature East Anglian style. The circumstances which interrupted the illumination of the manuscript are not known, but it appears from the book itself that the decoration was only about half finished in the earlier part of the fourteenth century. At what date it came into the hands of Humphrey, Duke of Gloucester, is not known, but it was finished for him in the style of the second quarter of the fifteenth century. Folio 87 contains an historiated initial with the central bar of the letter E eliminated, except for its truncated ends, in order to give the whole space to the picture of David playing the bells. Compared with the fine historiated initials of similar subject matter painted in the thirteenth and fourteenth centuries (cf. Plate 118), there is little to be said in praise of this curiously stiff, awkward figure seated precariously on a tilted bench in the foreground of a tiled floor, which shows no signs of foreshortening in the tiles or of recession into the background. The bells are hung awkwardly across the top of the initial, and the cramped position of David indicates only too clearly the artist's difficulty in achieving any spatial relationship between them. These problems in spatial composition had, it is true, been common to earlier artists, even in the late fourteenth century; in the miniatures of the Carmelite Missal and its successors, they had by no means been solved according to principles of true perspective. But the St-Omer miniature, judging by the decorative style of the border and the technique of shading one colour with another, cannot be much earlier than the 1430s, and should display greater competence in handling space. The style of the figure of David is an odd combination of hard outline and bright colouring intended to suggest modelling. The features are strongly accentuated with dark lines and white high-lights; yet there is no effect of roundness in the contours or of softness in the flesh, and the hands are shapeless. The border which surrounds the text page contains some motifs found earlier in East Anglian manuscripts, as the little round liver- and heart-shaped leaves; but the tendency of the illuminator was not to introduce many small, delicate naturalistic motifs but to increase greatly the size of cabbage-like forms developed from or related to the acanthus leaf, and to fill the roundels with them and twine them around the bar of the border in a writhing pattern which is rich and heavy but not beautiful. These coarse flower-leaf forms[4] are painted either in monochrome colours – blue, madder pink, or green – or in these colours striped with lines, most often in yellow or gilt paint on green and on dark or bright red. The sprays are heavy with tendrils ending in green dots. The whole design is overloaded and ugly, and its coarse scale dwarfs the historiated initial. This style is conspicuously out of step with the fine earlier pages of East Anglian work in the same manuscript, particularly where, as on some of the repainted pages like fol. 29 verso, the earlier design shows clearly through the later overpainting.

There is another interesting feature in the decoration of the St-Omer Psalter. Folios 152–67 in the latter part of the manuscript have borders which are completely French in style, and other pages before and after these are decorated in an English version of the French style: the French elements are the arrangement of the hair-line sprays in a formal border with even outside edges, and the use of many gold dots, sometimes tricked out with barbs drawn in black ink, and of tiny detached flowerets in pink and blue. The Calendar of the Psalter is decorated in this Franco-English style which is of Duke Humphrey's time.

The Franco-English mixture is documented not only by the elements of the style itself, but by internal evidence in other manuscripts. British Museum, Harl. MS. 4605, was written, according to the colophon, in London by a Frenchman and finished in 1434.[5] It is a copy of Christine de Pisan's *Le Livre des fays d'armes et de chevelrie* and contains at the beginnings of the four books miniatures in this curious, stiff, hybrid style. Folio 3 (Plate 174B), for example, if compared with the many similar portraits of the author found in French and Flemish copies of her books, demonstrates how far below Continental work this falls. The hard flat contour drawing and the feeble, patchy colouring of faces and hands and the strong ugly shades of pink, green, blue, and fiery red are such as would hardly be found in so unharmonious a combination in French work. At the same time, an English artist of the period, if uninfluenced by French models, probably would have drawn the figures with much greater freedom and coloured them more delicately. Certainly the French-English mixture as illustrated in the St-Omer Psalter and the Harleian Christine de Pisan has done the English style of the first quarter of the century no good.

Of different style but of exactly the same date is a most interesting manuscript of the *Metrical Life of St Edmund* by John Lydgate, which was written at Bury St Edmunds, where Lydgate was a monk, in 1433–4 (Brit. Mus., Harl. MS. 2278; Plate 175A). The pictures are framed miniatures, which, except for drawings, have always been infrequent in English illumination. The compositions are still lacking in perspective and show the high horizon characteristic of all late medieval pictures; but the figures themselves are arranged in groups which have some relation to the floor plan, tilted though this is, and it is noteworthy that outside the architectural enclosure, blue sky with floating white clouds can be seen. The figures in these miniatures in some respects remind us of the earlier miniature (Camb., Corpus Christi Coll., MS. 61; Plate 170), which shows characteristics of the Continental International style,[6] especially in the somewhat bizarre form which this took in Burgundy; and the Lydgate pictures display the same interest in rich and fantastic costumes, as illustrated in the figures at the back on the right side. The figures are modelled with considerable vigour; the faces are round, the flesh is soft, and the eyes are bright and lively with varied expressions. There are no sharp, hard contour lines visible. The style might be characterized as a soft modelled style in contrast to that of David in the St-Omer Psalter (Plate 174A). The source of this soft style seems to be found in contemporary Dutch miniatures rather than in French; and the style may have had some influence on a similar manner of painting figures with soft shadows, which is found in some of the York and Norwich glass of the second third of the fifteenth century.

The miniature reproduced in plate 175A is particularly interesting as depicting the presentation of the book by Lydgate and the monks of Bury to King Henry VI, for whom it was written. Another miniature (fol. 4 verso) commemorates a visit of the King to the shrine of St Edmund at Bury in 1433.

This same soft modelling and interest in the facial types in another technique appears in a copy of the *Desert of Religion*, of unknown provenance (Brit. Mus., Cott. MS. Faust. B.vi, Part 2; Plate 175B). This manuscript also is illustrated with miniatures, without borders, which are remarkable as examples of tinted drawing in a fully modelled technique. The figures, it is true, are often incorrectly drawn as to the proportions of the body, but the heads are magnificent. The bony contours of the cheeks, the well-drawn noses, eyes, and mouths, and most of all, the delicate gradations of shading on the flesh and the shadows on it are remarkably realistic. These characteristics stand out with increased vividness against the plain vellum background. The colours in the miniature are muted: white, soft grey, and mousy brown are the chief tints used on the faces, with only a touch of red wash on the lips and cheeks and of green in the landscape. It is an extraordinary style, like nothing known earlier in England;[7] but the tinted drawing technique itself is one in which the English artist had long been proficient, and in spite of the feeling that there is Dutch influence in the soft modelling, the work is almost certainly English, since the style appears in other manuscripts of undisputed English provenance a little later in the century. The date of this manuscript would not seem to be earlier than the second quarter of the fifteenth century.

The tinted outline style producing vividly modelled heads may originate in Bury St Edmunds. Another fine miniature which seems to be a developed example of it (Brit. Mus., Harl. MS. 4826, fol. 1; Plate 176) has been inserted as the fly-leaf of a copy on paper of Lydgate's poem, *The Pilgrim*. The miniature shows the author presenting his book to Thomas Montacute, Earl of Salisbury, to whom the poem was dedicated. The figures, which are more competently drawn than in the Cotton Faustina manuscript, have some of the same extraordinary sensitiveness in the delineation of the faces. Almost no colour is used, only faint washes – pink on the faces, green in the landscape. The profiles are rounder and less bony in contour than are those of the Faustina manuscript, and the drapery folds are carefully drawn with soft curves and some shading and cross-hatching in pen strokes. The landscape is very simply suggested by a horizon line with trees and a few flowerets in the foreground. The date of the miniature, judging from the armour and the high-cut hair, cannot be much before the middle of the fifteenth century.

The relation of this style, whatever its provenance, to that of the miniatures in a manuscript[8] containing works by Thomas Chaundler (Camb., Trin. Coll., MS. R.14.5) is so close as to suggest that the artist was trained in the same atelier. Chaundler's manuscript can be dated closely, since he speaks of himself as Chancellor of Oxford, a position he held only between 1457 and 1461. The manuscript contains a series of fifteen full-page miniatures illustrating the earlier of the tracts in the book. The presentation picture (fol. 8 verso; Plate 177) shows Chaundler offering the book to Bishop Bekynton, to whom it was dedicated. The technique is tinted outline of very delicate workmanship which, though English, shows more clearly recognizable French or Flemish feeling than does Harl. 4826. The figures are drawn with a firm, sure line and the drapery folds and the shading on the faces are indicated with cross-hatching. Only the palest colour is used on the faces and hands, but the tiled floor is painted red and green and the fringe of the baldaquin and also the framework of the miniature show a little colour. There is more detail in the Chaundler miniatures than in Harl. 4826: the carved ornament of the Bishop's chair, the leaded windows, and the patterned walls and canopy have the crispness and clarity of an engraved line. The drapery is represented with folds that are deeper and more sharply turned at the corners than in Harl. 4826, and suggest sculptured draperies rather than linear surface patterns – a characteristic of French rather than of English drawing. Other miniatures in the Chaundler manuscript are of comparable quality, but the sky in those with landscape backgrounds has been tinted, with spotty blue clouds, and the trees have been painted untidily with green, perhaps by a later hand.

In much the same type of figure style, but certainly by a less skilled hand, are four miniatures, ascribed, without any actual evidence, to Chaundler himself, in another manuscript containing works by him (Oxford, New College, MS. 288). The most interesting of these are three drawings of New College, Winchester, and Wells, of which the first is thought to have been done from observation. The miniatures in both Chaundler manuscripts represent English drawing style of the mid fifteenth century, under strong Continental influence from French or Franco-Flemish sources. They are to be distinguished from the purely Flemish drawings of the Beauchamp Pageants (see note 12 below) and possibly owe their Continental flavour more to French than to Flemish contacts.

An example of typically English painted style in manuscript illumination, dated[9] 1461 (Plate 178) shows that the earlier French-English mixture of stylistic elements has neither improved in quality nor developed any new features. A missal, now in two parts, made for Abingdon Abbey (Oxford, Bod., MS. Digby 227 and Trin. Coll., MS. 75) contains the usual full-page Crucifixion (fol. 113 verso) preceding the Canon of the Mass, painted in a style which is uninspired in drawing and ugly in colouring. The faces are stolid with solemn, heavy-lidded eyes, and the bodies are unmodelled under the draperies. The flat background is filled up with one thing and another – rays from the haloes, stars, and even old-fashioned arabesque patterns. The subject is really a Trinity, with God the Father above, and the Dove of the Spirit flying downward above the cross. The borders have the even outer edge seen in both of the earlier French-English manuscripts described above; the motifs are large and coarse, and the colouring is strong and ugly. The kneeling donor bearing his heraldic arms, and the angel above with a shield of the donor's arms introduce a worldly note into this most spiritual of all religious pictures, and give a fore-taste of the many donor portraits in religious settings which are a common feature of fifteenth century painted glass. In this, the high period of Flemish portraiture, there is not much to be said for the Abingdon Missal. In England these middle years are indeed lean ones for the fine art of painting.

A decade later, in the 1470s, two manuscripts interesting for their new subject matter but using an old technique were almost certainly illustrated by English artists. One of these (Morgan Library, MS. 775) the *Ordinances of Chivalry*[10], is illustrated with miniatures representing actual combats (fol. 2 verso; Plate 179) in which the knight, Sir John Astley, for whom the manuscript was written, took part. The pictures serve, therefore, as a record of events of which the artist may have been an eye-witness, and they have the authenticity of such a record, though the quality of the illustration is as mediocre as most other English work of the time. The second of the two manuscripts is a roll of arms, the so-called Warwick Roll, now in the College of Arms, London. It was drawn up and probably illustrated by one John Rous.[11] The opening picture in this Warwick Roll shows Rous writing and is usually described as a self-portrait of the author. Although it has the qualities of an individual, again the drawing is rough and it is in no wise a skilful or artistic work.[12]

Painting and Glass

The second and third quarters of the fifteenth century were marked in the manuscripts, as we have seen, by successive phases of Continental influence, first French, later Flemish. In panel and wall painting and in painted glass, of which a considerable quantity from the second third of the century has survived in England, these influences are not so clearly traceable as in the manuscripts. Towards the end of the century, Flemish glass painters working for Henry VII in King's College Chapel, Cambridge, revolutionized the traditional style of two-dimensional compositions for glass panels. The King's College glass is, therefore, not medieval in style, but Renaissance, as is most of the glass at Fairford.

In the mid fifteenth century, English windows were still made up of irregularly-shaped pieces of pot-metal and silver stained glass, but were no longer designed on the principle of the all-over pattern, or even on that of bands of colour and grisaille as in the first half of the fourteenth century, but to display the figure in clearly defined detail both of facial features, as in portraits, and of dress. The figures were represented either singly or in group compositions, with little if any background, and that little likely to introduce details of interior or exterior architecture or of landscape. Nevertheless, the design in English windows is flat, and there is no evidence of interest on the part of the painter-glazier in vanishing point perspective, correct foreshortening, or representations of three-dimensional form. This was true right through the century, until Flemish glass painting was introduced in the early sixteenth century.

In panel painting a similar situation holds, partly perhaps because fifteenth century panel painting is found principally in the rood screens which, being constructed with elaborate tracery framework, suggest an analogy in general design to the windows. Apart from the screens or other panels which are thought to have constituted parts of church furniture, no certainly English panel painting of the later fifteenth century is known. As for wall paintings, the remarkable series in Eton College Chapel executed, according to documentary evidence, at least partly by English artists, present a unique problem. Apart from these, English wall paintings of the later fifteenth century, though fairly numerous, as far as can be judged never reached a high level of execution. In subject matter, Dooms are repeated endlessly; the most frequently represented single saint is Christopher,[13] whose place opposite the south door of the church had long been established. The Doom regularly occupied the chancel arch, above the rood screen; in a unique instance at Wen-haston (Suffolk)[14] the Doom was painted on wooden boards fastened together and shaped to the chancel arch, and constituted the background for the rood, now lost, which was nailed to the boards.

The order of presentation of the varied material of fifteenth century English painting and glass in a stylistic sequence is difficult: the glass, except in a few instances, seems to reflect the styles of local schools, as at York and Norwich. The painted screens, a great number of which are found in East Anglia, although showing some basis for stylistic grouping, have little connexion with the style of the local glass. Nor is there any appreciable chronological development from the earlier to the later part of the century. In the absence of any better basis for grouping these works, however, the topographical arrangement has been followed. Thus we shall deal with East Anglian work first, as being greatest in amount; then with that of London and the Midlands; and finally with York and Great Malvern which are linked by some unexplained stylistic factor, though widely separated in distance. The choir stall paintings of Carlisle Cathedral of the end of the fifteenth century belong nowhere in contemporary relationships, but for subject matter and even for many of the compositions hark back to a Durham[15] manuscript of c. 1200 and furnish a striking example of the persistent traditional character of English medieval painting.

Nothing is actually known about the provenance of the two wooden panels now in the Society of Antiquaries, London, painted with four scenes from the Life of St Etheldreda (Plate 180). The panels are now framed together, but could originally have formed doors, as of an aumbry. They are said to have belonged to Ely Cathedral[16] and may be dated c. 1425. The painting is in tempera and perhaps oil, on a gesso ground; the gilded background is decorated with patterns in relief. The subjects of the panels from left to right, beginning at the top, are: the marriage of Etheldreda; the Saint leaving her husband and retiring to a convent; the Saint superintending the building of the church at Ely; and either her interment or her translation. The panels measure 46½ by 21 inches each.

The style of the painting in certain respects is related to that of the Bury manuscript of Lydgate's *Life of St Edmund* (Harl. 2278; Plate 175A). The figures are of much the same proportions, with rounded foreheads and bright eyes. The costumes, with their full, pleated skirts and bands of embroidery, are somewhat like those of the Lydgate, and in some cases have the rather bizarre character which is found in costumes represented in Burgundian art of the period. The poses are oddly unstable and stiff, and the gestures are unnatural. There is a French hardness and precision in the drawing; but the modelling is done with paint as in Dutch miniatures, not with lines, and it would seem that Burgundy might furnish a likely source for the mixture of elements which influenced this style.

That the style is not foreign to contemporary East Anglian painting is obvious when we compare with the St Etheldreda panels two others containing four saints, which are known to have formed part of a rood screen in the church of St John Maddermarket,[17] Norwich, now in the Victoria and Albert Museum (Nos 23, 24-1894). These panels bear the device and initials of Ralf Segrym, the donor, who was mayor of Norwich in 1451. Thus they are among the earliest examples of this form of English painting and one of the very few which can be dated.

The saints in one panel (Plate 181) are Leonard and Agnes (or Catherine); in the other panel they are Apollonia and William of Norwich. The panels are of oak, each 3 feet 4 inches high and 2 feet 5½ inches wide. The tracery which would have framed the panels is missing, but the background patterns which filled the cusped heads are still visible.

The style of the figures is to be associated with a group of East Anglian screens distinguished by Constable as belonging to the coastal area and having possible contacts with the Netherlands. The best example of the style of the group is the screen at Hempstead which, as he points out,[18] has as typical characteristics of the figures the small cheeks, protuberant foreheads, and fully modelled drapery, all of which are found in the Maddermarket panels. Moreover, the presence of St Leonard, who also occurs on the Hempstead screen and on only four others, connects the Maddermarket panels with this East Anglian group. The shaded draperies contrast pleasingly with the plain red or green grounds sprinkled with gold motifs, and the screen when complete with its remaining panels and its tracery framework gilded and coloured must have been brilliant.

A rood screen *in situ*, in the church of Barton Turf, dated after 1480 and belonging, according to Constable, to a different group,[19] is illustrated by the two panels (Plate 182) with figures of angels representing two orders of the angelic hierarchy,[20] namely thrones, holding a throne and scales, and archangels, dressed in armour, holding a mace, and standing within a castle. The backgrounds, of which little is seen behind the spread wings, are alternately red and green, and the costumes are usually complementary to the background. The haloes, feathers, and details of the mantles are gold. The figures are better proportioned and finer in drawing than those on the earlier panels, and this may be due to their later date. There is more careful modelling, especially of the figures and draperies, and more elegance and beauty in the design than in the Maddermarket panels. The rich tracery forms a canopy over the heads of the figures and a base under their feet. The contrast between the painted figures and the delicate carving of the woodwork is very effective.

A still later East Anglian screen of the finest quality is the one in Cawston Church, Norfolk. It consists of eight panels on each side of the chancel doors and contains pairs of apostles and saints. In the four panels of the doors themselves are the four Church Fathers. There are two distinct styles in the figure painting, both illustrated in plate 183. The Apostle Paul on the right is painted in a linear, stylized manner and stands in an awkward pose holding, without actually grasping, his sword and book. The figure is short and has a head too large for the body; there is no modelling of the form under the drapery. The Apostle Philip on the left stands easily in *contrapposto*, his body in profile, his head turned naturally and his gaze fixed on the spectator. The proportions of the head and body are good; the hair and face are softly modelled with gradations of light and shade, as is also the heavy drapery which is flung back over the shoulder. There seems little doubt of Flemish influence in this style, and it would appear that artists trained in two very different manners were working side by side on the same work. The date[21] of the Cawston screen can be ascertained from parish records as between 1490 and 1510.

Of about the same time, that is, just before the end of the fifteenth century, there was painted over the chancel arch in the little church of St Thomas of Canterbury at Salisbury, one of the largest Dooms[22] surviving in England (Plate 185). The exceptionally high space allowed for the inclusion of more detail than was usually introduced into such paintings, and this Doom must originally have been one of the finest of many examples of its kind in England.

In the upper part, under the flattened roof, is Christ in Judgement, seated on a rainbow and displaying the wounds, with the Virgin kneeling on his right and St John the Evangelist, holding a book, on his left. Below are the Apostles. On the spectator's left is the Resurrection of the Dead; on his right, Hell. In the lowest corners, left and right, are two saints, Osmund and a pilgrim, probably James the Greater. In the upper corners is an elaborate architectural representation of the Heavenly Jerusalem. The colours of the painting now are dull green, yellow, and red of various shades, with a little blue, as in the mantles of the Virgin and of some of the apostles. Red is used freely, as usual, in the representation of Hell. The repainted condition of the Doom makes it difficult to determine its original style or to evaluate its quality, but it would appear to be essentially English in its decorative composition, the details being spread loosely over the surface with no attempt to render space except for the more or less formal shading of the architecture. The two large saints in the lower corners of the arch stand in representations of carved and painted niches which suggest those of painted choir screens, as at Cawston. The figures show some evidence of Flemish influence in their more plastic rendering.

East Anglia in the latter half of the fifteenth century not only produced more and finer painted screens than any other part of England,[23] but it had a distinctive and apparently flourishing school of glass painting with its centre in Norwich.[24] The evidence for an identifiable local school, distinct in style from the glass produced elsewhere in England, rests on the peculiarly individual character of the glass in St Peter Mancroft at Norwich. At East Harling, south-west of Norwich and nearer to Bury St Edmunds, there is a quantity of glass very similar in style and undoubtedly from the same workshop. At Long Melford, south of Bury, in Suffolk, there are also considerable remains of fifteenth century glass, but the style here is both later and somewhat different. The characteristic figure style of the Norwich school suggests a possible Low Country derivation or at any rate foreign influence such as we have noticed already in the Bury manuscripts and in the St Etheldreda panels.

The glass now displayed in the east window of the chancel of St Peter Mancroft[25] at Norwich belongs to three periods, and undoubtedly has been collected there from windows elsewhere in the church which were glazed at different times. The subjects of the panels now in the great east window are the following: scenes from the Life of the Virgin, including both the Nativity Cycle and her later life, in a style which suggests a date of c. 1440; scenes from the life of St Peter, possibly originally in the east window since the church is dedicated to him, in a style of slightly later date, perhaps c. 1450; scenes from the Passion Cycle, and figures of saints and scenes from their lives, dating from c. 1480. Of the three periods, the two earlier ones are most characteristic of the Norwich style. The main features of the style are: well-proportioned figures set in architectural or landscape grounds, rather than against decorative patterned grounds; full, soft, well-rendered draperies; slight modelling of the bodies but great interest in the modelling of the heads, with attention to variety of position and expression. This last feature is especially prominent in the St Peter series. The painter's interest in literal detail in his representations is well illustrated in the Visitation panel (Plate 188A), where Elizabeth wears a maternity gown laced down the front, and carries over her arm a piece of scarlet cloth upon which, according to the legend,[26] she had been working when she heard of the Blessed Virgin's arrival. It is a charming, idyllic scene, full of homely interest rendered in a manner reminiscent of the miniature style in the Bury Lydgate of slightly earlier date.

In the East Harling glass, with some of the same subjects represented similarly but with variations in the style, the architecture shows patterned tiles in the foreground, and in the vaults overhead a peculiar stippling in black which is intended undoubtedly to suggest depth. The heavy draperies and the interest in faces observed in the Norwich glass appear also here. The donor portraits at East Harling[27] (Plate 188B) of the end of the century form a link with those at Long Melford,[28] which are almost all that is left of the large amount of glass formerly filling the perpendicular windows there. The interest in painting the faces is most noticeable in these portraits, and both at East Harling and at Long Melford there are some splendid examples of portraiture.

At Oxford, where at the end of the fourteenth century Master Thomas and his associates flourished so greatly under the patronage of William of Wykeham,[29] in the 1440s the art of glass painting was still in full swing. John Glazier is mentioned in connexion with executing the windows of the antechapel of All Souls College.[30] The glass of the four east windows dating from 1441–3 has survived, says Hutchinson, with less alteration than any other glass there. The four windows are designed on a very simple plan, with three lights each divided by a transom into two registers, thus providing panels for six figures each. The subjects are, in the upper rows, the twelve Apostles, and in the lower, twelve figures of holy women (Plate 187) standing on elaborate pedestals with tiled floors, under canopies which are strongly architectural in form and are supported by piers. The style is clear-cut and uncomplicated by details, the figures standing out sharply against the red and blue patterned backgrounds; the colours of the saints' garments are counter-changed with those of the background. The style carries over the earlier Oxford tradition of well-proportioned figures, amply draped, and with no complexities of ornament or detail. In the tracery above the top row the lights are filled with angels, the two centre openings having seraphs standing on wheels.

The so-called Royal window,[31] south of the great west window of the antechapel, now contains glass which formerly filled the windows of the old library of All Souls College. Here again the design of the double register is used, but in each light of each register there are two figures instead of one, representing kings. Although many of these have been wholly or partially renewed, the few original figures which remain are of particular interest because of the possibility that they may be the work of the famous Westminster glass-painter, John Prudde.[32] Certainly the glass of the Royal window differs from that of the others in the design of the canopies, in the style of the figures, in the amount of ornamental detail, and in the use of colour and pattern in the backgrounds; but whether or not this is the glass mentioned as the work of Prudde, the king's glazier, no one can say with certainty.

The only known surviving examples of John Prudde's work which are documented are the remains of the magnificent glass windows in the Beauchamp Chapel in the Collegiate Church of St Mary at Warwick. These were provided by the will of Richard Beauchamp,[33] Earl of Warwick (d. 1439), and inserted between 1447 and 1450. The angels with music scrolls in the tracery[34] in the east window and four full-length figures of saints (Plate 186) are original panels still *in situ*; a panel with the donor, now misplaced in the central light, was probably originally elsewhere in this window. The glass, according to the contract[35], was to be from 'beyond the seas and with no glass of England'; the colours were to be of the finest – blue, yellow, red, purple, crimson, and violet, and 'of white glasse, green glasse, and black glasse, he shall put in as little as shall be needful for the shewing and setting of the matters, images, and stories'. The cartoons for the designs were to be furnished to Prudde by the executors of the will, but these patterns were 'to be newly traced and pictured by another painter in rich colour, at the charges of the said glasier'.[36]

The two saints reproduced in Plate 186 are Thomas of Canterbury and Alban. Both are richly clothed, the one in pontifical robes, the other in white armour edged with gold, and a royal mantle lined with gold-patterned brocade and bordered with jewels. The

Archbishop's vestments are remarkable for the beauty of their ornament: the orphreys of the cope are embroidered with figures of prophets under canopies,[37] and have jewelled borders. These small figures are most beautifully rendered in painted coloured glass, and the jewels are tiny bits of glass set into the larger panels without leading. The backgrounds are red for Thomas and blue for Alban, and the quarries contain the chained bear and the ragged staff which are the armorial devices of the Beauchamps. The colour is indeed rich and brilliant and as little white, green, and black as possible actually is used, as stipulated in the contract. The faces are remarkably well delineated, with delicate line shading on the colourless glass. The fine contours of the faces, the well-proportioned figures, and the elegance and richness of the whole design support John Prudde's reputation as the most famous English glass-painter of his time.[38]

The series of monochrome paintings which occupy the north and south walls of the Chapel at Eton College are the most important remaining examples of fifteenth century wall painting in England. Their dates are known, 1479–80 to 1487–8, and the names of two painters, Gilbert, and William Baker, are mentioned in connexion with the work.[39] The names are English yet the style of the paintings seems to be more Continental than English.

The paintings are in two registers each six feet high separated by a two-foot border; the total length of the panels on each wall is about sixty-seven feet. Each tier is divided into eight panels five feet wide containing figure compositions representing the miracles of the Virgin,[40] separated from each other by single figures of female saints in the lower tiers and, in the upper, prophets standing on brackets under canopies. The technique is grisaille, that is, monochrome painting in tones of black and white on a red lead base which, now exposed in many places, gives the paintings a warm pinkish tinge. The painting is done in oils on a thin coating of gesso. The upper tier of subjects has almost entirely disappeared and the two centre panels of the lower tier are gone. Some of the lower tier paintings have deteriorated greatly, but of those that remain, it is possible to judge that the styles are not alike and that at least two artists must have painted the pictures; one executing those on the south side, the other, those on the north.

Plate 184 illustrates both styles. The upper picture includes the sixth and part of the seventh panel from the east on the north side, with the single figures of two saints, Etheldreda left, and Elizabeth right. The subjects of the panels are the Miracle of the Candle and the Miracle of the Woman who took the image of the Christ Child from the Madonna as hostage for her captive son.

Plate 184B represents the second panel from the west on the south side, the Miracle of the Empress who healed the knight's brother, and the single figure of Dorothy with her basket of flowers on the pedestal at the left.

The styles in these two panels are strikingly different. The north side paintings are composed with a strong feeling for space in the composition: an empty foreground except for the figures in niches, and a middle ground with figures in an architectural setting which is so planned and executed as to cut across the background and set it far back in shadow. On the back wall are windows with dark frames, on which the entering light casts shadows. The figures are arranged on a diagonal line leading into the far corner of the chapel.

The single figures stand on brackets which are represented as though seen from below, thus concealing the feet from the eye of the spectator; the canopies of the niches extend forward to correspond to the projection of the bracket, and the figure overlaps the colonnettes which flank the niche. The niche is thrown further into the background by deep shadows on one side. The spatial rendering is admirable – in the Flemish manner, depending upon the diagonal line of recession and the skilful placing of strong shadows and highlights. The figures are modelled, with draperies of heavy material arranged in rich patterns of deep folds, dark in the shadows, and white on the edges where the light catches them. The arrangement of the draperies of the kneeling woman in the Miracle of the Candle is strongly suggestive of similar figures in the paintings of Rogier van der Weyden, particularly those in grisaille representing carved figures. The composition, the poses, the setting, and the delicate modelling of faces and head-dresses are all those of Flemish painting of the second half of the fifteenth century, and it seems impossible that any artist but a Fleming could have shown himself so consummate a master in this technique.

The setting of the paintings on the south side is designed on the same scheme, with the panels set back by the architectural brackets and niches. But what a difference in the depth of the spatial rendering! The niche itself has no depth but is decorated with linear mouldings, ornamental colonnette capitals, and crocketed ogee-shaped gables with foliate finials – all in the best Tudor Gothic manner. The painting has suffered much damage and the background detail has almost disappeared, but it is evident from what remains that no such devices for representing depth in the setting have been used as in the other style. Although the figures are arranged on a shallow diagonal with the Empress at the point nearest the spectator in the exact centre of the group, there is no feeling that the other figures extend back into space. The poses are stiffer and more mannered than those on the other wall, the folds of the draperies are flatter and shallower, more complex in pattern and less realistic in texture. The faces, however, are carefully rendered with attention to the differentiation of types, as the two lepers at the left who are distinguished from the other healthy people at the right.

The technique of the two styles is very similar in the handling of the soft, muted tones of the grisaille, and the panels on the two sides of the chapel, therefore, match reasonably well. It has been suggested that the drawing may be the work of a single artist, the master, but the styles seem too far removed from each other for this to be true. It is more likely that a Fleming and an Englishman competent in Flemish technique were responsible for the two styles. It may be assumed that the Englishman was the William Baker mentioned in the documents.

The similarity of the Eton Chapel paintings to a series of wall paintings in the same technique in the Lady Chapel at Winchester Cathedral was pointed out by James,[41] who described the Winchester paintings as 'inspired' by the Eton pictures but not slavish copies of them. In style, the Winchester paintings are much closer to the Flemish master than to his presumed English collaborator.

The stained and painted glass of the later Middle Ages tells a similar story of English style, which was first influenced and finally superseded by Flemish work. The great St William window in the north choir transept of York Cathedral,[42] which can be dated *c.* 1421, belongs in point of time to the preceding chapter; but the close stylistic connexion between some of the figures in this window and those in the earliest windows at Great Malvern Priory Church makes the York window more suitable for discussion in relation to the latter part of the century. It seems likely that the glazing of the St William window, like that of the great east window of the York Minster choir, was supervised by John Thornton, who in 1410 was admitted a freeman in York and presumably established his shop there. Knowles[43] distinguishes four different styles of painting the faces, and conjectures that the enormous work was parcelled out to 'sub-contractors' in their own shops, possibly using cartoons furnished by the central shop run by John Thornton. Though it is difficult to see any striking connexion between the styles of the St William glass and that of the great east window, there is a general continuity between the work of Thornton and the later York windows (Plate 189).

The St William window is divided into four sections by three transoms; three of the sections consist of twenty-five panels each, and one of thirty, all with scenes from the life, translation, and miracles of the Saint. Across the bottom of the window are panels containing donors, members of the Ros family. There is some discrepancy in the sizes of the division of the window by the transoms, and Knowles offers the hypothesis that the St William window originally consisted of two separate windows, each of fifty panels, one in the north, and the other in the south choir transept, one containing scenes from the life, the other scenes from the miracles of St William. The incorporation of the two windows into one, he further suggests,[44] may have occurred when the St Cuthbert window, now in the south choir transept, was given about 1440. The windows now measure approximately the same in height, about 75 feet, and have a similar composition in panels, though the St Cuthbert style seems to be unrelated and is far inferior to that of the earlier St William window.

The style of the figures in some of the panels is extraordinarily fine (Plate 189A). The head in the detail of the Miracle of St William is well proportioned, the hair and beard are painted in a soft mass, the eyes are carefully delineated as to eyeballs and lids, the nostrils and lips are rounded. The heads are better than the bodies, the hands and feet in particular being clumsily drawn. Only details necessary for the representation of the scene are included, as the utensils on the bedside stand; the background behind the bed and the furnishings is decorated with an arabesque pattern of acanthus foliage; this is alternately blue and red in successive panels.

The three lights in the east window at All Saints, North Street, York,[45] are some twenty to twenty-five years later than the St William window, and the figure painting is much broader and less linear. St Christopher from one of the upper panels (Plate 189B) has a large, modelled head with soft, bushy hair and beard similar in type to the figure from the St William window. In spite of the difference in date and the better drawing in the St Christopher, there is considerable similarity to the St William. This is probably due not to any likelihood that the same craftsmen worked on the two windows, but that the figure tradition established by John Thornton in the east window of York Minster, either by means of cartoons or by a continuity in shopwork style, was carried over into other York glass. The coloured background with the running acanthus pattern is very close to that in the St William panels, and the elaborate buttresses, which are also present in the St William panels, dividing one panel from the other, are retained in the All Saints windows. But the feature of niches sheltering small figures of prophets of the same large-headed type as the principal figures is an innovation. The background of the Christopher panel is red; the Saint and the Christ Child both are clothed in white, patterned and bordered with gold. The colouring is not rich, but the contrast between figures and background gives to the painted figures some plasticity as in the panels of rood screens.

The other two lights of the east window of All Saints Church contain figures of St Anne teaching the Virgin, in the centre, against a blue ground, and John the Baptist, in the north light, wearing a gold-coloured camel's hair garment and a blue mantle, against a red ground corresponding to that of Christopher on the south side. All three lights have undergone considerable restoration, especially in the tracery and in the donor portraits in the lower parts of the window.

The stylistic connexion between the St William window and other windows in York churches can be explained more easily than can the relation between these and the style of the earlier windows in the Priory Church at Great Malvern, which has often been noticed but never accounted for. It may be merely the influence of the important York school of glass painting that reached as far afield as Malvern; but some unknown, more specific basis for a stylistic connexion between these two places seems likely.

The windows in the Priory Church at Great Malvern are in themselves an extraordinary phenomenon, not only because so much of the original glass has survived, though much moved about, but because of the fact that the glass represents more than a half century of uninterrupted development in style. The chronology of the original windows, as given by Rushforth,[46] is as follows:

Choir: east window and the adjacent clerestory windows, north side, with scenes from the Incarnation and the Passion, c. 1430–40 (Plate 190); remaining clerestory windows, c. 1460–70 (Plate 191).
Nave, originally the south clerestory, the north aisle, the west window, 1480–90.
North transept, north window, Magnificat window, 1501 (Plate 192).

Except for the choir, the greater part of the windows were inserted within the period when Richard Dene was Prior of Malvern (1457–91), and Rushforth suggests[47] that the scheme of the nave windows may be due to him, and that, since they have characteristics in common, they may represent work contracted for with a firm of glaziers. The subject of the nave windows was a concordance of Old and New Testament scenes.[48]

The finest glass in the church is found in the choir and in the Magnificat window of the north transept.

The east window originally contained twenty-four scenes from the Passion cycle, ending with Pentecost, besides the twelve Apostles, saints, and other subjects in the tracery lights. Many of the scenes are lost, badly damaged, or entirely reconstructed, but one of the few best preserved is the Last Supper (Plate 190), which shows, in comparison with the detail from the St William window (Plate 189A) unmistakable similarities in the style of the figure painting; the meticulous painting of the eyes, especially the eyeballs, the modelling of nose and lips, and the soft mass of hair and beard. The background has the same acanthus scroll pattern against a strongly coloured ground. But there are similarities also with the St Christopher in All Saints, York: the curving line at the corner of the eye, the oddly conventionalized drawing of the ear, and the richly patterned materials of the garments. The corkscrew curls of John in the Last Supper at Malvern resemble those of the Christ Child in the St Christopher panel, and the barred pattern of the table-cloth is like, though not identical with, that of the Christ Child's gown. The drapery technique seems to fall between the linear treatment of the St William window and the shaded technique of the All Saints panels, but is perhaps closer to the latter. On the grounds of these stylistic features, the date 1430–40 is very acceptable, and if Rushforth is correct in recognizing the arms of Beauchamp and Despenser, this date would be further supported, for Richard Beauchamp, Earl of Warwick, and Isabella Despenser his wife both died in 1439, and the window may have commemorated them.[49]

Of the surviving clerestory windows of the choir, the most interesting is the so-called Founders' window of *c.* 1460–70, containing, under canopies, figures of the founders of the Priory. Plate 191 reproduces a panel with St Wulstan, the last of the Saxon Bishops of Worcester, blessing Aldwin who holds a document bearing the great seal of the Priory. The style is clearly related to that of the east window but is less modelled and more linear in the contours and features of the heads and in the folds of the drapery. The figure is drawn on a larger scale, as is usual in clerestory windows, and the glass in these panels is better preserved than any other glass in the church.

The windows of latest date at Malvern are those of the north transept, of which the north window was glazed to commemorate the marriage of Prince Arthur, eldest son of Henry VII, to Catherine of Aragon in November 1501. The window still retains the kneeling figures of Arthur (Plate 192), his father, and three of the four knights originally there, with an inscription which asks for prayers for their 'good estate'. The window must have been made, therefore, before the death of Arthur in April 1502. It is called the Magnificat window from its subject, the Joys of Our Lady, which illustrate the verses of the Magnificat hymn in separate scenes in the main part of the window. The portrait of Prince Arthur reproduced in Plate 192 shows him in a coat of his blazon over armour, and wearing a coronet. He is kneeling before a *prie-dieu* on which is an open book, in a richly canopied recess. A choir of angels playing musical instruments surrounds the canopy. It is to be noted that they are not of the feathered seraph type familiar in English art throughout the fifteenth century, but young women with curly hair and dressed in long white gowns.

The style of the glass in this window is not only later but different from that in the other windows. The figures are better modelled, the colours richer and deeper in tone, and the drawing is more careful, especially as to the modelling of the faces. The Magnificat window may be the work of the king's glazier at Westminster.

With the later windows at Malvern Priory the story of English style in glass painting comes to an end. The differences between the earlier and the later Malvern windows probably can be accounted for by the influence of the more plastic Flemish style of Bruges which, it has been pointed out, was introduced in the manuscripts and paintings of the time of Edward IV.[50] Two other rich collections of stained glass, however, may be noted as an impressive postscript to the story of English medieval painting because of the rôle they play in marking the transition from late medieval style to that of the Renaissance in England. This glass is found in the parish church at Fairford (Glos.) and in the chapel of King's College, Cambridge.

The Fairford glass[51] is the earlier and dates from 1495 to 1505. There are twenty-eight windows in all, comprising a well-defined scheme of subject matter based, in general, on the Apostles' Creed. It begins in the first window west of the screen separating the Lady Chapel in the north choir aisle from the north aisle of the nave; the subjects of this first window are four Old Testament incidents representing types of the Incarnation of Our Lord: Eve Tempted in the Garden, Moses and the Burning Bush, Gideon and the Golden Fleece, and the Judgement of Solomon. In the Lady Chapel itself begins the series of events in the early life of the Virgin and of Christ, followed, in the great east window of the choir, by the Crucifixion and other scenes from the Passion Cycle. In the south choir aisle are the Appearances of Christ after the Resurrection, and the Ascension and Pentecost. The aisle windows contain the witnesses to the Faith – the Apostles on the south each with that text from the Creed which was traditionally attributed to him, and on the north, twelve prophets. The three west windows are filled with three Judgement pictures: the Judgement of Justice as represented by David and the Amalekite; the Last Judgement; and the Judgement of Truth or Mercy represented by the Judgement of Solomon. In the clerestory windows are figures of martyrs on the south side facing figures of persecutors of the Faith on the north. The scheme is not new, but the completeness and the systematic arrangement correspond to the popular late medieval literary compilations of similar material, such as the so-called *Biblia Pauperum*, or Poor Man's Bible.

The designs on the windows are of two kinds: single figures or, in a few instances, single scenes placed one to a window light under canopies of late Gothic perpendicular design, such as were common in earlier English windows; and elaborate scenes without canopies spreading over two or more lights or even over the whole of the window. Of the canopy type of design the Old Testament scenes in the first window outside the Lady Chapel are striking examples. In spite of the canopies, which look incongruous in relation to the pictorial scenes beneath them, especially the first three which take place in a landscape setting, the compositions are rendered more freely and with more naturalistic detail than anything we have yet seen in English work. The single figures in the aisle and clerestory lights also have taken on much more plasticity in the modelling and in the drapery, and stand with the heavy monumentality of Flemish figures.

More strikingly foreign to English style are the pictorial compositions which have no architectural canopies but spread freely over the window surface as though it were a canvas or a wall. Such are the two corresponding east windows in the Lady Chapel and in the Chapel of Corpus Christi, on the north and south sides of the choir respectively. In each case the central light contains the principal scene, the Assumption of the Virgin and the Transfiguration of Christ, while the two lights on each side are paired to receive a single scene with either a landscape background (as in the Flight into Egypt) or an architectural interior (as in the scene of Christ among the Doctors). The pictorial elements in both scenes are rendered without regard to the divisions of the window and with an attention to detail in costume and setting which is strikingly different from the more formal compositions characteristic of Gothic window design. The figures also, dressed in rich materials cut in contemporary fashions, have a plasticity, indicated by heavy shading, and a bulk and solidity which are not found in English glass painting even of the late middle ages. Certainly the dominating style of the Fairford windows is not English but Flemish, though the survival of the older canopied designs with single figures would suggest that English glaziers might also to some extent have assisted in the work.

The glass that formerly filled the windows in Henry VII's Chapel at Westminster Abbey may have been similar to that at Fairford,[52] but unfortunately none of it has survived. The splendid array of windows in the nearly contemporary chapel at King's College, Cambridge, however, offers a connecting link between the Flemish pictorial style without Renaissance detail, as found at Fairford, and the full-fledged Renaissance style with a whole new crop of decorative motifs, which is known to have been produced at least in part by Low-Country artists.[53] On the ground of ample documentary evidence the glass in the King's College Chapel can be dated between 1515 and 1531.

As in the windows at Fairford and probably also in those formerly in Henry VII's Chapel at Westminster, the subjects of the King's College Chapel glass[54] also constitute a cycle: according to the contract of 1526 apparently, as Harrison suggests,[55] echoing an earlier contract, they were to represent 'the story of the olde lawe and of the newe lawe', that is, scenes from the Old Testament chosen for their significance in connexion with scenes from the New Testament, or the long-familiar theme of a concordance. The relationship of the paired scenes, one to the other, is indicated by 'messenger' figures bearing scrolls with texts.

The King's College Chapel windows can be divided into two main chronological groups: four earlier windows executed by the Netherlander Barnard Flower and his assistants between 1515 and 1517; and a later group of twenty-one, including the east window but not the west, executed between 1526 and 1531. Names of a number of glaziers working on the later group are known:[56] Galyon Hone, John Nicholson, and Francis Williamson ('Willem Zoen') were Netherlanders or Flemings, and Symond Symondes, who was associated with Williamson, was probably English.

All the windows in the King's College Chapel have marked Renaissance characteristics both in style and in motifs, including a wealth of decorative detail. The chief differences between the earlier style of the Flower school and that of the successive later glaziers are in the nature and amount of this detail, and in the heaviness or delicacy of the painting itself; there are also certain individual characteristics of the styles which do not concern this present survey. However, the importance of the King's College Chapel glass as a whole for an understanding of the early stages and the spread of Renaissance influence in England cannot be overlooked.

Summary

In the fifteenth century English pictorial art was wholly at the receiving end of Continental influences; Europe was too intoxicated with the exploitation of its newly found stylistic expression to be aware of the sporadic and, for the most part, mediocre phenomena which registered superficially the influence of the new trends in England. The interesting thing is that this influence, which appeared during the century in all the arts – illumination, wall and panel painting, and stained glass – came primarily, as we have seen, from the Low Countries. This can be explained partly by the political and economic relations between England and Flanders during this period, and partly by a kinship of artistic temperament and tradition which had been apparent even throughout the Middle Ages and which greatly facilitated the transfer of Flemish style with its new Renaissance elements to England. These elements, which are manifest chiefly in the greater interest in observed detail and in concepts of spatial and atmospheric reality, had been stimulated previously in Flanders by influence from Italian painting at the turn of the century and during the fifteenth century flowered brilliantly in the so-called Northern Renaissance in Flanders and Holland. The interest in realistically rendered detail and its organization in an essentially decorative compositional scheme was the particular phase of the new style which the English artist could understand best. The curious fact is, however, that though accepting the new style with enthusiasm, he did not (perhaps could not) reconcile its modelled technique with his own fundamentally linear tradition. The arts of illumination and glass painting – both essentially linear in their best phases and both, but especially the former, the English artist's *forte* – fell foul of the new realistic tendencies, as witness Flemish miniatures of the early sixteenth century, which were no longer flat, as decorations of a text page should be, but opened up the page by inserting behind the border framework a picture conceived as a view through a window.[57] Similarly in stained glass, the flat composition suitable for the diffusion of light gave way to the figural composition in a spatial setting. With this concept of deep space the medieval English artist was not in sympathy, and when Flemish work of this type began to flood the market, the English illuminator and glass painter, being unwilling or unable to conform, could only retire from the scene. When next a vigorous painting style emerged in Britain, in the second third of the sixteenth century, two decisive factors had appeared to turn it into other channels: Hans Holbein had come to the court of Henry VIII, and the Reformation had swept away, almost overnight, a great part not only of existing medieval art but of the traditional subject matter upon which it had so richly drawn. Thus with the influx of the High Renaissance into England came new styles of painting and new subject matter which was mainly portraiture and themes taken from classical mythology. The story of this phase of English Art is told in another volume in this series.

p. 195 1. French influence on this period in England perhaps dates from the purchase of the Library of the Louvre by John Duke of Bedford in 1425. In 1427 a magnificent Livy manuscript (now Paris, Bib. Ste-Geneviève, MS. fr. 1.1) was sent by Bedford to his brother Humphrey Duke of Gloucester. Leopold Delisle, *Le Cabinet des manuscrits de la Bib. Nat.*, I (Paris, 1866), 52, n. 6.

2. Warner, *Illum. MSS*, plate 47.

p. 196 3. For example, the stained glass at Fairford (Glos.) and King's College Chapel, Cambridge. The panel portraits of kings in the Society of Antiquaries, London, seem to be more Flemish in style than English, as is also the martyrdom of St Erasmus in the same collection. For a suggestion that the St Erasmus might be English (perhaps Canterbury) see Sir Martin Conway, *Burl. Mag.*, XCI (1943), 129 ff.

p. 197 4. See M. Rickert, 'Illumination of the Chaucer Manuscripts', John M. Manly and Edith Rickert, *The Text of the Canterbury Tales*, I (1940), 561–605, with illustrations.

5. The colophon reads in part, 'un pater noster et un Ave Maria per mosseu Pey (or Rey?) de la fita, qui a escrivt a quest livre en l'an de nre sengr mil CCCCXXXIIIIO Et fut feit a londres a XV de May'.

p. 198 6. Similar in figure style but French in decoration is the very beautiful Psalter of Henry VI, Brit. Mus., Cott. MS., Dom. A.xvii. Warner, *Illum. MSS*, plate 48.

7. Another manuscript in similar style but slightly less fine in quality is Cambridge, Trin. Coll., MS. B.10.12, the *Meditations of St Bonaventura*. The heads are magnificent in this manuscript but the bodies are usually underdeveloped and misshapen. There is more colour used in this manuscript than in the Cotton Faustina, especially for backgrounds.

p. 199 8. Both this and Chaundler's other manuscript are discussed in the Roxburghe Club monograph by James, *The Chaundler Manuscripts*.

p. 200 9. On fol. 270 verso of the Bodleian volume is a colophon containing the date: '. . . annus millenus quadringenus tibi notus et sexagenus primus tunc ecce repletus.'

10. See Viscount Dillon, 'On a MS. Collection of Ordinances of Chivalry of the Fifteenth Century belonging to Lord Hastings'.

11. Archibald Russell, 'The Rous Roll', *Burl.*

Mag. XXX (1917), 23–31. Rous was attached throughout his life to the great Beauchamp family of Warwick and as a priest from *c.* 1445 held the chantry at Guy's Cliff founded by Richard Beauchamp (d. 1439). He wrote a number of books on the history of Warwick, of Guy's Cliff, and of the Warwick family.

12. A third of these historical-genealogical manuscripts, however, which was also written for the Beauchamps (Brit. Mus., Cott. MS. Jul. E.iv, art. 6) is a different matter as to the type and quality of its illustrations. The artist was undoubtedly Flemish, and it would be impossible to mistake and useless to deny the enormous difference in the fineness of the drawing and the skill in rendering figures, singly or in groups, and spatial compositions in this manuscript. For reproductions see Sir Edward Thompson, 'The Pageants of Richard Beauchamp, Earl of Warwick, Commonly Called the Warwick MS.', *Burl. Mag.*, I (1903), 151–64; also Viscount Dillon and W. H. St John Hope, *Pageant of the Birth, Life and Death of Richard Beauchamp, Earl of Warwick* (London, 1914).

13. Cf. H. C. Whaite, *St Christopher in English Mediaeval Wall Painting* (London, 1929).

14. Charles Keyser, 'On a Panel Painting of the Doom Discovered in 1892, in Wenhaston Church, Suffolk', *Archaeologia*, LIV (1895), 119–30.

15. See Colgrave, 'The St Cuthbert Paintings on the Carlisle Cathedral Stalls'. On the Durham manuscript see p. 110 f. above.

16. Roy. Acad. Arts *Exhib. of Brit. Prim. Paintings, Cat.* No. 38, plate XXII. A recent re-examination of the backs of the panels furnished no evidence as to their original use.

17. Victoria and Albert Museum, *Catalogue of English Furniture and Woodwork*, 2nd edition (1929). The figures have been much repainted.

18. Constable, 'Some East Anglian Rood Screen Paintings', 211–20, figures IX–X.

19. *Ibid.*, Constable suggests that the Barton Turf screen may have influenced the celebrated Ranworth Screen which he dates somewhat later.

20. The medieval hierarchy of the angels consisted of nine orders: Seraphim, Cherubim, Thrones, Dominations, Virtues, Powers, Principalities, Archangels, Angels. Barton Turf contains the finest surviving representations of the hierarchy.

21. *Op. cit.*, 290 ff. See also E. F. Strange, 'The Rood Screen of Cawston Church', *Walpole Soc.*, II (1912–13), 81–7, with coloured reproductions.

22. The reason for its size is that *c.* 1460–70 the present carved roof was added to the nave, the height of which was considerably raised at that time. The painting was coated with whitewash after the Reformation and only uncovered in 1819 when it was extensively 'restored' by Clayton and Bell, who also repainted the wall paintings in Salisbury Cathedral. See Hollaender, 'The Doom Painting of St Thomas of Canterbury, Salisbury'.

23. Other parts of England where painted screens may be found in numbers are the South Midlands, Devon and Cornwall, and Somerset. On the South Midlands screens see W. W. Lillie, *Jnl Brit. Archaeol. Assn*, 3rd series, IX (1944), 33–47. On the Devonshire screens see John Stabb, *Some Old Devon Churches*, I (London, 1908). One particularly fine example is at Ashton (South Devon), dating from the late fifteenth century. Reproduced, N. Pevsner, *The Buildings of England, South Devon* (London, 1952), plate 38A. The screens in South Devon and Cornwall are particularly rich in carving; the painted panels are usually found in the lower part of the screens.

24. Woodforde, *The Norwich School of Glass Painting in the Fifteenth Century.*

25. *Op. cit.*, 16–42.

26. *Op. cit.*, 24, and footnote 3.

27. *Op. cit.*, 42–55.

28. *Op. cit.*, 74–127.

29. See Chapter 7.

30. Hutchinson, *Mediaeval Glass at All Souls College.*

31. *Op. cit.*, 17 ff.

32. *Op. cit.*, 37 ff. See also below.

33. Philip B. Chatwin, 'Recent Discoveries in the Beauchamp Chapel, Warwick', *Birmingham Archaeol. Soc.*, LIII (1928), 145–66.

34. See William Bentley, 'Notes on the Musical Instruments Figured in the Windows of the Beauchamp Chapel, St Mary's, Warwick', *op. cit.*, 167–172. See also Charles F. Hardy, 'On the Music in the Painted Glass of the Windows of the Beauchamp Chapel at Warwick', *Archaeologia*, LXI (1909), 583–614.

35. The contract, which was first printed in Dugdale's *Antiquities of Warwickshire*, II (edition of 1656), is quoted by Le Couteur, *Ancient Glass in Winchester*, 104.

36. The patterns on paper referred to here may be the 'patrons otherwyse called A vidimus' mentioned in two of the contracts for the King's College glass. See footnote 55 below. On the meaning of the term 'vidimus', see further A. Van der Boom, *Burl. Mag.*, XCI (1949), 114.

37. Similar figures under canopies commonly p. 206 appear in fifteenth century embroidered orphreys which adorn vestments of rich materials, usually velvet. A number of examples can be seen in the Victoria and Albert Museum, London, notably the nearly contemporary Warwick Chasuble (No. 402–1907) bearing the arms of Henry de Beauchamp, Duke of Warwick (d. 1445). The ground of the vestments was usually *semé* with angels or seraphs on wheels, and heraldic emblems of the persons for whom they were made. Though rich in materials, fifteenth century vestments, in general, display workmanship in the embroideries which is far inferior to that of the earlier century.

38. Hutchinson, *op. cit.*, 38.

39. James and Tristram, 'Wall Paintings in Eton College Chapel and in the Lady Chapel of Winchester Cathedral'.

40. On the sources of the subject matter, see *op. cit.*, 19–36.

41. *Op. cit.*, 37 ff. p. 207

42. J. A. Knowles, 'Technical Notes on the St William Window in York Minster', *Jnl Brit. Soc. Master Glass-Painters*, X, No. 3 (1950), 118–131. The window was apparently given as a memorial to John, 8th Lord Ros (d. 1421), by his wife Margaret Despenser (distant cousin of Isabella Despenser, Countess of Warwick) who remarried in 1423. See Rushforth, *Mediaeval Christian Imagery*, 52.

43. Knowles, *op. cit.*, 122–4. p. 208

44. *Op. cit.*, 118 ff.

45. See P. J. Shaw, *An Old York Church: All Hallows in North Street* (York, 1908). In Chapter 3, 'Stained Glass Windows', by Charles P. D. Maclagan, these panels are reproduced in colour plates. The window is here dated *c.* 1440.

46. Rushforth, *Mediaeval Christian Imagery*, 1–3. p. 209

47. *Ibid.*

48. The glass that remains of the New Testament series is now collected in the north nave aisle, the second window from the east. The remains of the

Old Testament series are now in the south choir aisle (St Anna's Chapel). For a detailed listing of the subjects of all the original Malvern glass and its present location, see Hamand, *The Ancient Windows of Great Malvern Priory Church*.

p. 210   49. This is the Richard Beauchamp, Earl of Warwick, for whom the Beauchamp Chapel in St Mary's, Warwick, was built. See p. 205 above.

p. 211   50. Moreover, as early as 1449 a Fleming named John Utynam was employed by the King to 'make glass of all colours for the windows of Eton College and the College of St Mary and St Nicholas, Cambridge'. The document further states that 'because the said art' (of making glass) 'has never been used in England and John intends to instruct divers lieges of the king in many other arts never used in the realm beside the said art of making glass', provision is therefore made for a penalty to be imposed on any person who practises the art unlawfully. Public Record Office, *Calendar of Patent Rolls, 27 Henry VI*, part II, 255. In 1449–50 John Prudde, the King's glazier, was making 'storied glass' for the windows of Eton College Hall. Accounts *Empcio vitri* (1449–1450), printed in Willis and Clark, *Architectural History of the University of Cambridge*, I (Cambridge, 1886), 403.

51. For a detailed description of the windows, see Oscar G. Farmer, *Fairford Church and its Stained Glass Windows*, 5th edition (1938).

52. The manor of Fairford belonged to Henry VII and it might be expected that the King's glaziers would be responsible for both sets of windows.

53. Mr Kenneth Harrison, in the most recent publication on the King's College Chapel windows, has made out a very good case for the precedence of Flemish over Italian influence in the introduction of the full-fledged Renaissance style in England. *The Windows of King's College Chapel* (Cambridge, 1952), 19–35.

54. For a description of the subjects of the windows, see M. R. James, *A Guide to the Windows at King's College Chapel, Cambridge*, 3rd edition (revised) (Cambridge, 1951).

55. Harrison, *op. cit.*, 60. The contract is printed in full in Willis and Clark, *op. cit.*, I, 615 ff.

56. Harrison, *op. cit.*, 4 ff. See also the 'Tabular Summary' of windows attributed to the various glaziers on pp. 78–80.

57. See Otto Pächt, *The Master of Mary of Burgundy* (London, 1948), 25 ff.

EVALUATION

A T the conclusion of this survey of mediéval painting in Britain it may be well to look back over the ground it has covered and attempt to summarize and evaluate the accomplishments of English artists in more than eight centuries.

Perhaps the fact that stands out most clearly from the array of examples which form the basis of the survey is the predominance of illuminated manuscripts in the ratio of almost three to one over other forms of painting as illustrated in the plates. This proportion, astonishing as it may be, is essentially correct, in so far as our present knowledge of English painting in the Middle Ages is concerned. It is true that many additional examples of panel and wall paintings exist, and most of these are at least referred to in the text, though their damaged condition, or merely limitation of space, has necessitated their omission from our lists. But there are also uncounted numbers of illuminated manuscripts, some undoubtedly yet to be discovered in Great Britain and elsewhere, which would add very greatly to their number. It is doubtful whether any considerable additional examples of English stained glass will ever be found, but it is very probable that further *opus anglicanum* may exist in unsuspected places. But taken all in all, the count would still almost certainly be heavily in favour of the illuminated manuscripts.

The reasons for this are not far to seek. Manuscripts are portable and in time of danger or disaster can easily be transported to places of safety, where painting *in situ* must remain to face the vicissitudes of time and fortune. Moreover, manuscripts of good quality (that is, primarily, those decorated with gold leaf and fine colours) were normally considered by their owners as part of their treasure, not shelved in their libraries. Apparently, not even fine liturgical books were used commonly, but were brought out only for special occasions. These circumstances have resulted in the survival in almost perfect condition of a large body of painting which, instead of other forms where these have perished, or supplemented by them in whatever state they have survived, furnish the main body of evidence upon which our knowledge of medieval painting, in Britain as elsewhere, depends.

In the case of English medieval painting, the manuscripts are of peculiar importance; for, as must have become evident from the survey of its monuments, the fundamental characteristics of English pictorial art in all its forms are not those of painting but of outline drawing, and the technique of manuscript illumination at its best is linear. English drawing, it is true, in its developed stages makes use of colour even for purposes of shading or for filling in whole areas of a composition. But this is not the technique of true painting, which is rather the application of pigments of different tones to build up surfaces so that eventually the original drawing is partially or wholly obscured. The English technique of coloured outline, whether delicately shaded or evenly washed over with flat or shaded tones, never loses sight of the contour line; it is this fundamental characteristic which makes it possible to judge the style of painting in other forms by that of manuscripts; for in what has survived of wall and panel painting and of stained glass and embroidery, a similar technique is almost invariably used. We can assume, therefore, even without a comparable number of examples of the other arts, that the linear character of manuscript illumination determined their style. There is ample evidence for this assumption within the pages of this book.

Nevertheless, in the course of tracing stylistic developments throughout the Middle Ages, the term 'monumental' has frequently been applied to certain types of figure painting, as, for instance, the Winchester Bible, and even more aptly, the early glass represented by the Methuselah figure at Canterbury (Plate 93), and this term must now be explained in the light of the statements just made. 'Monumental' is used here to characterize one side in the recurrent swing of the pendulum between large-scale and small-scale painting or drawing. The monumental style therefore refers to a composition with few large figures nearly filling the space, thus leaving little, if any, room for decorative features. It also implies a figure type of imposing but approximately normal proportions, as contrasted with exaggeratedly tall or thin or distorted figures, as they were, in general, more often current in English figure painting and drawing. Thus there can be and is a monumental style in outline drawing, as witness some of the superb late tenth century miniatures such as the Crucifixion in the Harleian Psalter (Plate 30). The so-called small-scale style, in drawing or in painting, however, was much more to the English medieval artist's liking; it persists in one form or another, throughout every century, and it is upon this form that his greatest accomplishment was built. This is primarily the art of the illuminator.

On the technique of outline drawing in both of its forms rests the continuity of English painting in the Middle Ages, and this is true not only of figural compositions but of the decorative work as well. There are several kinds of line which have been distinguished in specific examples throughout this survey and which may now be summed up in relation to their effect on the development of English style as a whole.

Because the earliest examples of the art are primarily decorative, we must start with the use and effect of line in decoration. In Hiberno-Saxon manuscripts the line is firm, almost mechanically true and even, and it is used in wholly abstract designs. The decorative text pages of the early manuscripts as well as the entire pages of intricate linear ornament contain no representational elements and only an echo of symbolism in the occasional cross or the arrangement in a cross pattern. This harmony of technique and style is perfect in the early stages of the style; there is no discordant element to break it on the pages of the Book of Durrow; the simplicity of the colour scheme and the clarity of the linear patterns reign supreme.

But exclusively abstract patterns did not completely satisfy even the early artist of the Book of Durrow. There is a page or animal ornament (Plate 1) – animals they may be called by courtesy; for really they are only ribbons with heads, tails, and feet, and they are used in exactly the same manner as, but with more variety than, if the heads and appendages were amputated. But we must watch these little animals, for they will not always remain so tractable. In the early Hiberno-Saxon style they are a perfect complement to the abstract, linear patterns, and still the harmony is unbroken.

The introduction of the human form into this abstract style is one of the most interesting phenomena in the history of English art. For the temperament of the Celtic artist seems at this point to be distinguishable from his Anglo-Saxon contemporary by the manner in which he reacts to this totally extraneous element which he finds he must, in the interests of illustrating his book, incorporate into his repertoire. The Irish artist promptly makes of the figure a new and fascinating pattern, by reducing it to an organization of lines. The Anglo-Saxon artist, faced with the same problem (though perhaps not entirely with the same models to follow), rather worriedly transfers his painted model into an outline drawing of it; if he had been less an artist he would probably have traced it, as a child might do, and filled in the lines with colour. But there is evidence of analysis of the painted form and considerable intelligence as well as artistry in the selection of salient features to be included in his own picture. Thus in the very earliest stages of English pictorial art we have the beginnings of its two fundamental and persistently enduring elements: decorative linear pattern and figural drawing in outline.

The decoration did not long remain abstract and simple in motifs. Soon foliage of the vine and acanthus types was introduced from Continental sources, and the acanthus especially was received eagerly by Winchester artists, whence the style spread rapidly elsewhere in England. At Canterbury, there seemed to be a preference for animals of a much livelier variety than the earlier writhing lacertines. By the end of the twelfth century both types of decoration had settled down happily in the text initials which became larger and more imposing as the size of the manuscripts increased. Still Canterbury artists retained their preference for the ribbon-like scrolls and prancing animals, varied now by human figures climbing about among them. Winchester artists, on the other hand, took their decoration more seriously; the acanthus leaves became heavier and more boldly painted with heavy colours, as in the Winchester Bible, and foliage pendants to the initials extended into the margins. It was a sort of second spring for the acanthus of the earlier Winchester style, and the coarse plant flourished mightily.

In the midst of this lush and verdant growth, suddenly the whole style withered away and the next thing we know, at the very end of the twelfth century, is a new style in the Beatus initials in Psalters which, in its dizzy convolutions of ribbon coils and its wizened little animals crushed within the strands, reminds one not only of the earlier Canterbury style, but of its ancestor, the Hiberno-Saxon; but the complete harmony of animal and abstract pattern in this new style is lacking. The next step was inevitable. The scrolls put out leaves and buds, and the animals, released from their uncomfortable confinement, began to run about not only inside the decoration but out of bounds, in the margins of the page. Here the harmony begins to be restored, and when during the course of the thirteenth century the initial foliage grows out so that it surrounds the page forming a border for the animals to play in, all the elements are again in perfect accord. This is the East Anglian period, during which the foliage motifs become recognizable as particular species, and the animals also are amazingly drawn from nature, but introduced among them are also new species of hybrid and monstrous types. Again the inevitable happened: the monsters grew in size and monstrosity, the leaves and flowers became gigantic, and the whole style suddenly blew itself out, with only a few East Anglian daisies and marigolds surviving and an occasional grotesque showing its sad little face on the pages of otherwise monotonously repetitive bar borders bearing odd spoon and liver-shaped forms of nondescript variety. But hope was on the way. The ubiquitous acanthus at the end of the fourteenth century again displays its showy head and long trailing leaf, and mingling with current forms, produces at least new patterns and richer colouring. Characteristic of this phase of decoration are showers of fine hair-line sprays with small gold and coloured motifs which are interspersed among the heavier branches. This is the end of the development of English manuscript decoration.

As the decorative style developed primarily out of the Celtic ornamental style, so figural art traces a direct ancestry to Northumbrian, that is, Anglo-Saxon eighth-century manuscripts. The distinction of origins is unmistakable, but the reason for it is not clear: was it a matter of environment or temperament? At any rate, whereas Celtic figures show an increasing tendency towards a *reductio ad absurdum*, Anglo-Saxon figures, though often badly understood, always are unmistakably human. We have seen, in the survey, examples of the two main types of figures which were evolved by Anglo-Saxon artists out of two Continental prototypes: the monumental type which flourished especially at Winchester, and the lively, dramatically rendered narrative type which so quickly made itself at home at Canterbury. The monumental type associates itself with the heavily painted acanthus ornament of the Winchester style, or else appears completely free of ornament, in single miniatures in outline technique, as in the Harley Psalter; the restless Canterbury type, appearing in crowded scenes of miniatures at first, soon associated itself with the ornamental initials and the jumping animals. The mingling of figures and figure subjects with decorative motifs produced the form which suited most perfectly the English illuminator's taste and ideology, and this union occurred first at Canterbury. But it was the monumental figural style which produced late twelfth century wall painting and stained glass.

With the replacement of the heavy acanthus initials by the fine-line ribbon-scroll initials at the beginning of the thirteenth century, the small-scale figure comes into its own. Initials, and their relatives, medallions, were admirable places for composing a small but lively scene illustrating a story without violating the general ornamental effect. Designers of stained glass saw the possibilities of this style as combining a pleasing overall design for a panel with the lively interest and variety of a narrative. Thus manuscripts and stained glass drew very close together in this period, and again it was Canterbury which took the lead.

What new impulse produced the climax of this small-scale style in East Anglian art is still to be determined. Though some of its elements seem to have affinities with contemporary styles in north France and Flanders, there is no basis for believing that the style, or any of its essentials, was imported. In its underlying principles, its love of ornament, of variety, of exciting narrative, of the bizarre, and, above all, its harmony of figural and decorative features, it can be accounted for wholly in earlier phases of English painting. It is, as a matter of fact, in all respects the most characteristically English phase of medieval painting. This is important to remember in evaluating the art; for the East Anglian is the second and last great period of its development, and it is comparable in the quality of its best workmanship, as in the harmony and perfection of its elements, to the best Hiberno-Saxon work, though totally different in style and ideology. No wonder that this phase of English medieval painting, more than any other, spread abroad; it is reflected in the decorative style of Bohemia and in the figure style of the Lower Rhine and probably even of France. But the influence is a reflection only; it did not stimulate any new stylistic movements, partly because its great inventiveness had already exhausted almost all the possibilities of the style, and there was nothing much to do with it but to copy its motifs or debase it. Both happened, at home and abroad, and by the middle of the fourteenth century it was no longer productive.

Only one more phase need be noted in the development of English medieval painting, and that was the result mainly of influence from abroad. But it found congenial soil in England. The interest in facial expression had almost from his first figure painting interested the English artist, even though his modelling of the features was of the sketchiest nature. The faces of early votive figures, such as the St Dunstan at the feet of Christ (Plate 22), and Matthew Paris at the feet of the Virgin (Plate 106), show expressions of humility and devotion. The increase in the number of individual figures in association with various religious themes led to the introduction of individuals for their own sake, and this led, of course, for purposes of recognition, to portraiture. But the panel portraits of the later Middle Ages, such as King Richard in the Wilton Diptych and the large picture in Westminster Abbey, are painted in a technique which is not unmixed with Italian or other Continental influence, so that for examples of purely English skill in portraiture, we must turn again to manuscripts. In first rank, in the number of pictures as well as in their life-likeness, is the Bedford Psalter which contains dozens of small heads within initial letters, many painted so discerningly and skilfully that they must be considered portraits: some are almost certainly identifiable. The Bedford book is the work of a number of illuminators working together, perhaps under the direction of the illuminator Herman Scheerre. Out of the same atelier come the portraits reproduced in plate 169, B and C. The technique is linear, lightly coloured, and the artist's sensitiveness to his subject and his skill in depicting not so much what he sees as what he feels are evident. In view of the importance which portrait painting plays in later English art under the stimulus of Holbein and others from abroad, is it too much to suggest that this sensitive treatment of portraiture is also to be traced back to a continuity in the attitude of the English artist towards his subject?

For it must be remembered that his earliest experience in representations of free narrative were drawn from the lively illustrative scenes in the Utrecht Psalter, which he might have duplicated many times had his temperament been capable only of slavish copying. Instead, it is noteworthy that the model was re-born with each succeeding generation. The English medieval artist always seemed to need to express his individual reactions to whatever came to hand. This projection of his personality into the figural art is what gives his work, certainly its variety and interest, but more than that, its meaning. It was therefore possible for Continental manuscripts to be imported and even copied, in a manner of speaking, but the result would not be merely a duplication of the model, but a re-vivified version. It might not express the original artist's intention exactly, but it would certainly be the English artist's interpretation of the underlying facts or ideas in the representation before him. It was this constant awareness of the idea back of his model or subject that imparts to English medieval painting its significance as an art in its own right: it was fundamentally and intensely alive and creative. This independence of spirit also accounts in great part for the ability of English artists to be exposed without succumbing to those foreign influences which were constantly arriving from across the Channel throughout the Middle Ages. Even in the face of the strongest French influence, in the mid thirteenth century, when Paris was the hub of the art world and England even then was within easy reach of it, artists like Matthew Paris and William de Brailes, though showing evidence of knowledge of the wonderful new French style, quietly went their own way, using their own techniques and expressing their thoughts with characteristic independence. As long as English art remained sturdy and vigorous, it was safe from being stampeded by foreign styles. It is significant that in this same period of the climax of French international influence, it was English artists who painted in a variety of styles and with inimitable freshness and originality a long series of apocalypse pictures which are unsurpassed in medieval painting anywhere. Typically English too are the slightly earlier illustrated bestiaries with their marvellous renderings of tales about fabulous animals such as even their fertile imaginations would hardly have dreamed of without some stimulating model. This was grist for their mill, and their reaction to such eminently congenial material was not only magnificent drawing and fine though completely unnaturalistic painting, but the well-nigh inexhaustible stream of grotesques that poured out from the bestiary material into the borders of East Anglian manuscripts, and even into wall paintings and embroideries.

If there is no doubt about the vigour of English medieval style, what of the quality of its craftsmanship? In competition with the fine Paris style of the mid thirteenth century, English manuscripts are hopelessly lost. On this scale and within these more formal limitations, English work is less meticulous and exquisite, less strictly controlled by good taste in design as in subject matter, less uniform in quality, and, of course, it never reached the degree of diminutive size which the French pocket Bibles attained. It is probable that the very qualities that make English illumination interesting were responsible for the unevenness in their quality. For in Paris in the thirteenth century illuminators were trained and controlled by the guild system; in England even much later than the thirteenth century a great deal of work was still done in monasteries, either by monks or by lay illuminators who were brought in. As a matter of fact, we know very little about the training of English illuminators, but it would seem from the variations in their skill and manner of working that their training was far from systematic and may have been acquired largely by the method of trial and error. There is the interesting example of the early fourteenth century picture book (Plate 134) which contains an amazing series of illustrations drawn and painted in a manner which would have horrified a French illuminator of almost any period. They are certainly the work of some local genius who was an amateur in his craft.

This expression of individual skill, often very crude indeed, is most apparent in much of the surviving wall painting in England. It is true, that in its present battered state it would be difficult to evaluate the style of any artist; but Peterborough was a very important centre of art in the high Middle Ages, and the paintings in the manor at Longthorpe just outside the town (which are fairly well preserved) are certainly not the work of a highly skilled and trained painter, interesting though they are in their subject matter and its interpretation. Of panel painting there remains so very little outside the fine Court pieces and the East Anglian panels (where, naturally, we could expect to find at least moderately well-trained artists) that it is difficult to judge whether local artists often tried their hand at this kind of painting also. A few rather roughly painted chests, like one in Winchester Cathedral, would suggest that they did. The art of making stained-glass windows was, of course, necessarily too technical and difficult for amateurs; thus we find more artists showing evidences of training in such centres as Canterbury and York. Embroideries also show considerable similarity in the types of designs and figures, but in this art the technical skill which the designer might have shown in the original patterns would largely have vanished under the embroiderer's needle.

To sum up the picture of the accomplishment of English art in the Middle Ages, we can conclude that it demonstrates, in the variations of skill displayed, the same lack of uniformity that characterizes the interpretation of subject matter. But what is gain for the representational interest may be loss in the more formal and highly skilled technique. But rarely in either France or in England does one find both in equal measure.

This summary of the characteristic traits of English style has not so far taken account of the Continental influences in the later periods which were in some degree acceptable and accepted by English medieval artists. Of these the most congenial came from Flanders and the Low Countries. Italian influence and even, apparently, Bohemian had a limited effect on the technique, but were never really understood nor wholly accepted. There may be a reason for this.

Partly it was a matter of temperament. The more forthright, robust character of Flemish art in the late thirteenth century, with its less formal design and less controlled taste, appealed more strongly to the English artist and, within limits, he took it to his heart. A small Book of Hours in the British Museum, illuminated in Maastricht c. 1300, could almost be mistaken for English work and, in fact, does show some affinities with East Anglian manuscripts in the humour of its historiated initials, the lustiness of its grotesques and even in some of the decorative motifs. And yet the similarities seem to be rather of kind than of the influence of the one on the other. Another fourteenth century manuscript, a finely and fully illustrated copy of the Alexander Romance, in the Bodleian Library, written in Bruges c. 1338, could also (except, perhaps, for its technique) have been painted by an English illuminator. These two examples will serve to illustrate the strong affinities between English and Flemish style and interpretation. It would be no wonder, therefore, if Flemish influence were eventually found to be influential in the formulation of the East Anglian style, and yet in its earlier and finer phases, this style can, as we have seen, be well established as stemming from the continuity of English work. In its later phases, however, when a strange exaggerated type of modelling of faces and draperies makes its appearance in the larger and coarser motifs, and humour goes beyond the limits of the fantastic and becomes outright crude and vulgar, then, if we evaluate Flemish traits correctly, this phase may have been introduced into England from some Low Country source, for rarely does English humour allow itself the licence of such forms.

In the late fourteenth century a much more clear-cut contact with Netherlandish art is supplied by the work of a Dutch artist who, through what means we do not know, found himself in London and joined a group who were engaged in illuminating the great Carmelite Missal. The style of this artist can be matched in other late fourteenth century Netherlandish works, one of which was made for the Duke of Gelder, probably at Arnhem. So the style is authentically Dutch, and indeed contrasts strongly with that of his two collaborators on other pages. The interesting fact about this collaboration is that the Dutch style seems to have almost no effect on the other artists, but in some slightly later miniatures its influence is unmistakably apparent. The Dutchman was much more of a painter, in the true sense of the term, than any English artist whose work we know, and the effect of his heavy modelling, especially in the faces, and his stronger colouring and brilliant rendering of compositions of figures in architectural settings set up a whole new concept in late medieval English illumination. The companion volume to the great Missal, an enormous Bible with a full complement of historiated initials, many of which follow closely the Dutch artist's style, are evidence of his influence on English work. This influence might have been still more effective had not another artist appeared upon the scene, of unknown but certainly Continental origins, whose technique approached even more closely that of the traditional linear style. Herman Scheerre (the name suggests a Low Country origin) was a magnificent painter in the sensitive manner which was part and parcel of the English artist's temperament; but his technique, delicate and linear though it is, is based not on the outline style, but on a soft surface modelling in browns on a pale base. This technique appealed to the English artist more than the heavy, built-up modelling of the Dutch Carmelite artist, and became, in fact, the inspiration of a whole group of illuminators who had evidently learned from him. These two instances of a willingness to accept and incorporate into their traditional style new elements which were congenial are typical both of the English artists' independence and of their ability to assimilate what would enrich without radically altering their own manner of working.

The reaction of English artists to Italian styles of painting in the later Middle Ages is another matter, but is likewise indicative of their reluctance to yield to influences which they did not understand or approve. The spread of Italian influence everywhere in Europe in the second half of the fourteenth century was affecting the various local styles in such a marked manner that many examples of the so-called International Style cannot be assigned with certainty to any place of origin. Italian techniques were, however, particularly applicable to panel and wall painting, and since this form of art was not produced to any extent in England, we would not expect to find many examples of panel paintings in the International Style there. The one outstanding example is the Wilton Diptych (Plates 152 and 153). This is here attributed to this style solely on the grounds that there are elements of Italian technique which are not characteristic of English work; the composition and the mood, however, seem to be English. There may be further evidence of such a mixture of styles in the newly uncovered wall paintings in the Tower of London which, as far as they can be seen at present, appear to be in fresco technique and to have certain affinities with the Wilton Diptych in figure types and quality of colouring. But in this instance conclusions cannot be drawn until a thorough study of the paintings is possible.

The case for north Italian, or Lombard, influence has already been put for the source of these elements in the paintings from St Stephen's Chapel. It has also been pointed out that England had close political contacts with Lombardy in the third quarter of the century, which might have accounted for the introduction of Italian influence into England. A small piece of evidence of the practical contacts of one Englishman with Italian painting in Florence is furnished by the picture of a Knight of the Garter among the important foreground figures in the great fresco of the Church Triumphant in the Spanish Chapel in Sta Maria Novella in Florence. This man has been identified as one of the nobles who accompanied Lionel, Duke of Clarence, son of Edward III, on his journey to Lombardy on the occasion of his marriage in 1368 to an Italian princess. As an additional item in this connexion, Humphrey de Bohun, for whom some of the manuscripts showing strongest Italian influence were made, was one of the two men who made arrangements for this journey. There must have been a great many other visits of Englishmen to Italy, painters and illuminators among them. In fact, as we have seen, there is visible evidence of these contacts in English painting in such elements as the types of features or the modelling in faces and draperies, and the curiously misunderstood back view of figures as shown in plate 150A. These are only superficial details, and although, as we have seen, they do occur in a group of manuscripts, they do not imply much more than awareness of the Italian fashion. Nor could it really be otherwise, considering the fundamental differences between the Italian modelled style and the English linear style.

One more foreign influence should be looked at in the light of its acceptability by English artists in the late fourteenth century. There is much disagreement as to whether or not Bohemian artists came to England in the train of Anne of Bohemia at the time of her marriage to King Richard II. It must be admitted that there is no documentary evidence to support such a fact, but it will on the other hand be admitted by anyone who has studied the *Liber Regalis* (the Coronation Book of Kings, in Westminster Abbey Library) that it is painted in a style much more like that of Bohemian manuscripts than of any of English make. If it is the work of a Bohemian, it does not seem to have had much influence on English style, but an interesting sequel to its appearance in the *Liber Regalis* is its presence in a few of the miniatures in the Carmelite Missal. Whatever the source of this curious style may be, it seems to have been limited to these two examples, though traces of its influence, particularly in figure types, lingers in one or two other manuscripts made for Richard. The border decoration of the miniatures in the *Liber Regalis* is English and the book was probably made at Westminster. The decorative style of the 'Bohemian' miniatures in the Carmelite Missal has certain elements of East Anglian foliage, which could represent an echo of earlier East Anglian influences on Bohemian illumination.

All these various foreign contacts are indicated graphically in the Chart on pages 4–5 and discussed in the text; but it has seemed worth while to review them as a body because of the light they throw on the peculiar paradox of repudiation and acceptance by English artists of successive foreign influences to which they were exposed in the crucial period of the late Middle Ages. This determined attitude may have been both their weakness and their strength: certainly such examples of the International Style as the Broederlam altarpiece in Dijon illustrate what fine achievements became possible by the assimilation of Italian 'painterly' qualities; on the other hand, except for the Wilton Diptych, English late medieval art escaped the anonymity of much painting in the International Style by retaining its essential independence. Whatever was strong and deeply rooted in the English pictorial style remained fundamentally untouched by the feverish grasping after the representation of modelled form at the turn of the fourteenth century.

We know what that strong and deep root was, and also that it could still be fruitful, for in the middle of the fifteenth century it produced some of its finest, most mature examples in the style of tinted drawing (Plates 176 and 177). In these drawings the human figure in the hands of the English draughtsman at last reached its full realization through shaded line, and the faces, with characteristic portraiture in the most competent English manner, bear witness to the rightness of his resistance to overwhelming foreign influences.

That English painting was yet, in the end, caught by such a tide was due in great part to the fact that, fine as these late flowerings of the outline style were, it is obvious that the plant had lost its vigour. It almost seems as though English artists, dazzled by the wonderful new style which was flourishing so amazingly in Flanders, gave up the struggle, except, perhaps, for a few who for one reason or another were absorbed in the new style which flooded England in the late fifteenth century.

But our evaluation of painting in Britain in the Middle Ages should not end on such a sad note. For a just estimate of this phase of art we must turn back and remember the really vital force in earlier English pictorial art, namely, the techniques of dynamic outline which were evolved and adapted and survived so many centuries of growth and change. The forms which this creative force took on during its long history are the measure of the strength and the resilience of a technique capable of adapting itself to so many different purposes and yet retaining its fundamental character.

GLOSSARY

No claim is made as to either the completeness or the consistency of the terms included in this Glossary. The basis for selection has been solely their applicability to the present text.

Acanthus. Fleshy curling lobed leaf of a Greek plant, a favourite decorative motif especially in Roman art.

Addorsed. A term used in heraldry signifying figures placed back to back.

Animal interlace. Interlace (*q.v.*) formed of lacertines (*q.v.*) or other animal forms.

Arabesque (medieval). Ornamental pattern of stems and foliage in running curves or scrolls often including animals and birds within the coils. Cf. *Inhabited scroll.*

Baldacchino or baldaquin. A canopy over a seat or other place of honour.

Bar-branch. An ornamental motif in later medieval illumination consisting of a vertical or horizontal stem to which foliage is joined to form a marginal border. (*Below left.*)

Bar tracery. Decorative shapes given to stone-masonry in the head of a window or other opening to form a pattern. (*Above right.*)

Barbed quatrefoil. A four-lobed ornament having points between the lobes.

Benedictional. A liturgical service book containing episcopal benedictions for the great feasts of the Church year.

Book of Hours (Horae). A liturgical service book, used mainly for private devotions, containing the office in honour of the Virgin as recited in monasteries and churches after the Canonical Hours (*q.v.*) of the day. It often included also the Hours of the Holy Ghost and of the Holy Cross.

Breaks interlace see *Stopped-knot interlace.*

Breviary. A liturgical service book containing Offices for the Canonical Hours (*q.v.*).

Buskin. A covering for the foot and leg reaching to the calf or to the knee.

C-scroll. Two convergent spirals. (*Below left.*)

Cabbage head motif (so-called). A coarse floral or foliate ornament typical of fifteenth century illuminated border design; probably a descendant of the acanthus (*q.v.*). (*Above right.*)

Cable pattern. A two-strand flattened twist.

Calendar (ecclesiastical). The days of the months designated in relation to the Kalends, Nones, and Ides of the Roman calendar. The feasts and saints' days celebrated locally were entered in the Calendars of liturgical manuscripts. See also *KL monogram.*

Calendar pictures. Illustration of the twelve signs of the zodiac and the twelve labours or occupations suitable to the respective months.

Calligraphic style. A precise linear technique as developed in fine handwriting applied to decorative or pictorial art. Used particularly in connexion with Hiberno-Saxon manuscripts.

Camayeu or camaieu. Painting in monochrome, i.e. in tones of any single colour.

Canon Tables. A concordance of reference to parallel passages occurring in two or more of the four gospels. See also *Eusebian Canon Tables.*

Canonical Hours. The eight monastic church services prescribed for the twenty-four-hour day. They were:

Matins	three nocturns said during the night
Lauds	said at dawn
Prime	said at 6 A.M.
Terce	said at 9 A.M.
Sext	said at noon
Nones	said at 3 P.M.
Vespers	said at 6 P.M.

Compline said at nightfall

Champlevé. See *Enamel.*

Chasuble. A garment worn by the celebrant at Mass.

Cinquefoil. A five-lobed ornamental motif.

Cloisonné. See *Enamel.*

Codex Aureus. A manuscript book, usually the four gospels, written in gold.

Confronted. A term used in heraldry signifying figures placed face to face.

Cope. A bell-shaped outer garment worn by clergy during processions and at other important church functions.

Crested animal head. An animal head having an excrescence in the form of a curling lappet or ear or of an acanthus-type leaf form. Characteristic of South English and Mercian animal ornament.

Crockets. Projecting leaf ornaments placed on a frame or architectural member as an arch or gable. In the pictorial arts, used on frames of panel paintings and in representations of architectural detail.

Cross with interlace. Typical Celtic Christian stone monument decorated with a carved interlace pattern (*q.v.*).

Cross-hatching. Filling a space with two crossing systems of parallel lines in order to distinguish one space from another as to colour or tone.

Cruciform page. A decorative page in Hiberno-Saxon manuscripts, of which the central feature of the design is some form of cross.

Cusp. A projecting point formed by the meeting of two segmental curves in tracery. (*Below left.*)

Daisies (East Anglian, so-called). The common English daisy, a pink or white multi-petalled flower. In East Anglian ornament it was usually simplified to a rounded pinkish tip and a green calyx. (*Above right.*)

Dalmatic. A vestment worn by deacons, and (under their outer vestment) by bishops and certain other prelates when officiating at Mass.

Diagonal fret. A version of meander pattern (*q.v.*) running diagonally instead of vertically or horizontally.

Diaper work (medieval). Surface decoration composed of square or lozenge shapes which usually enclose small formal motifs.

Displayed. A term used in heraldry to describe an eagle or other bird represented with wings spread.

Dorsal (altar). A panel of material, often richly embroidered, hung against a wall behind an altar.

Easter Tables. Charts for the astronomical computations of the date of Easter.

Enamel, champlevé. A process of enamelling in which the ground of the metal is cut out to form the pattern and enamel is inserted in these hollows.

Enamel, cloisonné. A process of enamelling in which a flat metal surface is divided into compartments (cloisons) by the welding on to it of thin metal strips. The hollow cloisons are filled with enamel.

Eusebian Canon Tables. A concordance of references to parallel gospel passages compiled by Eusebius of Caesarea in the fourth century and commonly included in early medieval gospel books.

Finial. A carved ornament, usually resembling a conventionalized leaf or flower, used as a termination or finishing point of a gothic pinnacle, gable, or other architectural feature, or on frames as represented in pictorial art. (*Below left.*)

Fleuron. Decorative carved flower or leaf terminating a staff, a rod, or a sceptre. (*Above right.*)

Fresco painting. Mural painting executed on the fresh plaster, in which the pigments, suspended in a lime medium, bind with the plaster.

Frontal (altar). A decorative panel of rich cloth or embroidery, or of painted wood or precious metal and jewels, covering the front of an altar.

Gesso. A mixture of plaster of Paris and glue to form a hard smooth surface over wood, for use in panel painting.

Glossed text. Text which has been annotated with sources or parallel passages, for example, glossed epistles or gospels.

Gospel lectionary. Gospel book arranged according to liturgical order.

Granulation. Ornament in metalwork, consisting of tiny beads soldered to the surface.

Greek cross. Plain cross with four equal limbs, sometimes placed within a circle, as on early Irish monuments.

Grisaille. Painting done only with black, white, and the greys resulting from mixing them. Cf. *Camayeu.*

Grotesques. Systems of ornament representing fantastic subjects or extravagant figures and fanciful animals.

Guilloche. A system of ornament consisting of a loose, continuous twist or interlace, enclosing a series of equidistant circles.

Hatching. A system of parallel lines used to suggest tone or colour. See also *Cross-hatching*

Historiated initial. Initial letter at the beginning of an important text passage, enclosing a picture which illustrates or refers to the text it introduces.

Horae or Hours. See *Book of Hours.*

Inhabited scroll. An arabesque pattern with birds or animals among the branches.

Interlace. A general system of ornament consisting of lines or bands which pass over and under each other, like the threads in lace.

Key. See *Meander.*

KL monogram. A combination of the letters K and L from the Latin *Kalendae*, which stand at the beginning of each month in an ecclesiastical calendar.

Lacertine. A very elongated biped or quadruped with an eel-like body. The heads vary in type but usually have ears and a biting snout.

Lappets. Soft, curved ears found on many medieval animals.

Line endings or fillings. Ornament placed in the empty spaces left at the ends of lines which the writing does not completely fill.

Lodged. A term used in heraldry to describe an animal in repose, as the White Hart in the badge of Richard II.

Lozenge. A diamond shape used in diaper or other ornamental design to contain a motif.

Mandorla. The almond-shaped glory which surrounds Christ, the Virgin, or (rarely) saints ascending to Heaven.

Maniple. A band of embroidery worn by priests over the left hand or arm.

Mask (animal). A stylized animal head used as a decorative motif in classical art and carried over into Carolingian and later ornament.

Meander: also Key or Greek Key. A geometrical pattern formed by broken lines at right angles to one another.

Millefiori glass. A kind of mosaic glass used for mounts in metalwork. It was made by grouping several rods of different-coloured glass into a simple pattern, fusing them, and cutting the bundle crosswise so as to display the pattern. The technique was Roman, but it was used also by the Irish in the Late Celtic period.

Missal. A liturgical service book containing the texts and ceremonial for Masses for all the Sundays and for the various feast days throughout the whole year.

Niello. A process of incising in metal and filling the incised lines with a black compound which melts at a high temperature. When polished, the design appears as a black incrustation on the polished metal plate.

Ogee arch. An arch inscribed by means of four centres so as to be alternately concave and convex.

Orphreys. Decorative bands, usually embroidered, on ecclesiastical vestments.

Pelta. A classical ornamental motif formed by two converging curves joined by another line. The ancestor of the trumpet pattern (*q.v.*).

Phylactery. In Medieval Art, a long narrow band held or issuing from the mouth of a figure, intended to be inscribed with a text identifying the person or showing what he is saying.

Plaitwork. See *Interlace.*

Plate tracery. Pattern formed by piercing the solid masonry in the head of a window or other opening.

Pontifical. A liturgical book containing services to be celebrated by bishops.

Powdered (heraldic semé). Decorated with a number of small motifs scattered over a surface.

Psalter. A service book containing the psalms.

Quarried glass. Window panels divided into squares or diamonds, each containing an ornamental or heraldic motif.

Quatrefoil. Four-lobed ornamental form. Cf. *Barbed quatrefoil.*

Reserved edges. Spaces left around a painted ornament exposing the vellum of a manuscript page. In Hiberno-Saxon decoration the reserved edges aid in clarifying a complicated pattern of spirals or interlace.

Ribbon pattern. Sometimes used to describe plaitwork or strapwork; any flat ribbon-like ornament.

Rood. Cross or Crucifix.

Rood screen. See *Screen.*

Rosette. An ornament fitting into a circle and having six or more lobes or petals.

Roundel. A circular medallion containing ornaments or figures.

S-chain. An ornamental calligraphic pattern consisting of a series of connected S's, used to fill the space between large initials and smaller text letters in some early Hiberno-Saxon manuscripts.

Sacramentary. A liturgical service book containing the ritual for administering the sacrament; it is the predecessor of the much more complete missal *(q.v.).*

Sarum use. A form of liturgical use established by the thirteenth century at Salisbury (Sarum) and later adopted for use in English non-monastic churches.

Screen, parclose. The screen partially enclosing the choir and separating it from the remainder of the church.

Screen, rood. A screen between the choir and the nave of a church on the top of which was placed the rood or cross.

Scroll. See *Spiral.*

Seraph. The highest of the nine orders of angels. (For the other eight orders, see p. 214, note 20.) Seraphs were usually represented with six wings covered with human eyes.

Serrated cabbage leaf (so-called). An East Anglian decorative motif probably derived from the acanthus *(q.v.),* greatly elongated to form a graceful ribbon-like form with serrated edges.

Service books, liturgical. See *Benedictional, Book of Hours, Breviary, Gospel Lectionary, Missal, Pontifical, Psalter, Sacramentary,* and *Troper.*

Spandrel. The triangular space between two adjoining arches.

Spiral (Celtic). A pattern formed by a line revolving in a curve about a central point. See *C-scroll.*

Step patterns. Right-angled geometric patterns progressing in steps.

Stippled gold ground. Background of gold leaf on a miniature or painting which is decorated with patterns formed by a number of small dots punched on the surface with a pointed tool. Also called tooled. To be distinguished from stamped ground, where the motifs are pressed in with a die.

Stole. A narrow strip of material, often embroidered, worn by clerics around the neck, as a part of their ecclesiastical vestments *(q.v.).*

Stopped-knot interlace. The typically Celtic form of interlace, the strands being doubled back at intervals to form knots. Also called the breaks interlace.

Strapwork. A form of ornament consisting of bands or fillets interlaced or intertwined; a later offshoot of the Celtic interlace. (*Below left.*)

Terminal heads. Animal or human heads without bodies which are often attached to initial letters or other decorative forms as terminations. (*Above right.*)

Tetramorph. The union of the four symbols of the Evangelists – the angel, lion, ox, and eagle – into one figure.

Tooled ground. See *Stippled gold ground.*

Tracery. See *Bar tracery* and *Plate tracery.*

Trefoil. A three-lobed ornament.

Trefoiled arch. An arch shaped into three lobes.

Troper. A liturgical service book containing the musical interpolations or tropes.

Trumpet pattern. Two whorls (*q.v.*) joined across the open side by a curved line.

Twist. See *Cable pattern.*

Vair. Fur obtained from a variety of squirrel with grey back and white belly, used commonly in the Middle Ages for lining and trimming garments.

Vellum. Calf and other animal skins dressed and polished for use as writing material.

Vernicle. A term for the *Vera Icon* or true image of Christ's face traditionally impressed upon the *Sudarium* or cloth presented to Him by St Veronica on the road to Calvary.

Vestments. The robes worn by the clergy in the celebration of Mass and other church services and functions. See also *Chasuble*, *Cope*, and *Dalmatic.*

Vine scroll. Running arabesque pattern of grape or other vine stems with leaves and fruit.

Whorl. An elaboration of the spiral in which several lines curve in the same direction around a single centre.

BIBLIOGRAPHY

I

ENGLISH ART

GENERAL

BOASE, T. S. R. *English Art, 1100–1216.* Oxford, 1953. (Vol. III of The Oxford History of English Art.)

British Museum. *Guide to an Exhibition of English Art.* London, 1934.

EVANS, Joan. *English Art, 1307–1461.* Oxford, 1949. (Vol. V of The Oxford History of English Art.)

HARVEY, J. H. *Gothic England, a Survey of National Culture 1300–1550.* 2nd edition revised. London, 1948.

READ, Herbert. 'English Art', *Burl. Mag.,* LXIII (1933).

RICE, David Talbot. *English Art, 871–1100.* Oxford, 1952. (Vol. II of The Oxford History of English Art.)

SAUNDERS, O. E. *A History of English Art in the Middle Ages.* Oxford, 1932.

SAXL, Fritz, and WITTKOWER, Rudolf. *British Art and the Mediterranean.* Oxford, 1948.

Victoria and Albert Museum. *Exhibition of English Medieval Art, 1930* (Catalogue). London, 1930. 2nd edition, 1933.

PAINTING AND ILLUMINATION

BIRCH, Walter de Gray. *Early Drawings and Illuminations.* London, 1879.
Particular emphasis on subject matter.

BORENIUS, T., and TRISTRAM, E. W. *English Medieval Painting.* Florence and Paris, 1927.

British Museum. *Reproductions from Illuminated Manuscripts.* Series I–IV. London, 1923–8.

British Museum. *Schools of Illumination.* Parts I–IV, English. London, 1914–22.

Burlington Fine Arts Club. *Exhibition of Illuminated Manuscripts.* London, 1908.

DODWELL, C. R. *The Canterbury School of Illumination.* Cambridge, 1954.

FRY, Roger E. 'English Illuminated Manuscripts at the Burlington Fine Arts Club', *Burl. Mag.,* XIII (1908).

HARRISON, F. *Treasures of Illumination: English Manuscripts of the Fourteenth Century (c. 1250–1400).* London and New York, 1937.

HERBERT, J. A. *Illuminated Manuscripts.* London, 1911.
Chapters iv, vi, vii, x, xii, and xiii deal mainly with English Manuscripts.

JAMES, M. R. 'On Fine Art as Applied to the Illustration of the Bible in the Ninth and Five Following Centuries, Exemplified Chiefly by Cambridge Manuscripts', *Proceedings of the Cambridge Antiquarian Society,* VII (1888–91).

JAMES, M. R. 'Primitive Painting', *British Painting,* by C. H. Collins Baker. London, 1933.

KENDON, F. *Mural Paintings in English Churches during the Middle Ages.* London, 1923.

MILLAR, Eric G. *English Illuminated Manuscripts from the Xth to the XIIIth Century.* Paris and Brussels, 1926.

MILLAR, Eric G. *English Illuminated Manuscripts of the XIVth and XVth Centuries.* Paris and Brussels, 1928.

MYNORS, R. A. B. *Durham Cathedral Manuscripts to the End of the Twelfth Century.* Oxford, 1939.

OAKESHOTT, Walter. *The Sequence of English Medieval Art.* London, 1950.

Royal Academy of Arts. *Exhibition of British Primitive Paintings. 1923* (Catalogue). Oxford, 1924.

SAUNDERS, O. E. *English Illumination.* Florence and Paris [1928].

THOMPSON, D. V. *The Materials of Mediaeval Painting.* London, 1936.

THOMPSON, Sir Edward Maune. *English Illuminated Manuscripts.* London, 1895–6.

THOMPSON, Sir Edward Maune. 'Notes on the Illuminated Manuscripts in the Exhibition of English Medieval Painting', *Proceedings of the Society of Antiquaries of London,* 2nd series, XVI (1895–7).

TRISTRAM, E. W. *English Medieval Wall Painting.* I, *The Twelfth Century.* Oxford, 1944. II, *The Thirteenth Century.* Oxford, 1950.

WARNER, George F. *Illuminated Manuscripts in the British Museum.* London, 1903.

WORMALD, Francis. 'Decorated Initials in English MSS from A.D. 900 to 1100', *Archaeologia*, XCI (1945).

WORMALD, Francis. *English Drawings of the Tenth and Eleventh Centuries*. London, 1952.

STAINED GLASS

DRAKE, M. *A History of English Glass Painting*. London, 1912.

HARRISON, F. *Stained Glass of York Minster*. London, 1937.

HARRISON, F. *The Painted Glass of York*. London, 1927.

KNOWLES, J. A. *Essays in the History of the York School of Glass-Painting*. London, 1936.

LE COUTEUR, J. D. *English Mediaeval Painted Glass*. New York, 1926.

NELSON, P. *Ancient Painted Glass in England, 1170–1500*. London, 1913.

READ, Herbert. *English Stained Glass*. London, 1926.

WOODFORDE, Christopher. *Stained Glass in Somerset, 1250–1830*. Oxford, 1947.

EMBROIDERY

Burlington Fine Arts Club. *Exhibition of English Embroidery* (Catalogue). London, 1905.

CHRISTIE, A. G. I. *English Mediaeval Embroidery*. Oxford, 1938.

FARCY, L. de. *La Broderie du XIe siècle jusqu'à nos jours*. Angers, 1890. 1st Suppl. 1900. 2nd Suppl. 1919.

KENDRICK, A. F. *English Embroidery*. London, 1913.

Victoria and Albert Museum. *Catalogue of English Ecclesiastical Embroideries*. London, 1930.

ENAMELS

CHAMOT, Mary. *English Mediaeval Enamels*. London, 1930.

II

CHAPTER I

GENERAL

ÅBERG, Nils. 'The Occident and the Orient in the Art of the Seventh Century, the British Isles', *Kungl. Vitterhets, Historie och Antikvitets Akademiens Handlingar del. 56: 1*. Stockholm, 1943.
The study is written in English.

ALLEN, J. Romilly. *Celtic Art in Pagan and Christian Times*. 2nd edition. London, 1912.

BRØNDSTED, J. *Early English Ornament, the sources, development and relation to foreign styles of Pre-Norman ornamental art in England*. Translated from the Danish manuscript by A. F. Major. London and Copenhagen, 1924.

BROWN, G. Baldwin. *The Arts in Early England*. Vol. V. London, 1921.

BRUUN, J. A. *An Enquiry into the Art of the Illuminated Manuscripts of the Middle Ages*. Part I, *Celtic Illuminated Manuscripts*. Stockholm, 1897.

CLAPHAM, A. W. 'Notes on the Origins of Hiberno-Saxon Art', *Antiquity*, VIII (1934).

HENRY, Françoise. *Irish Art in the Early Christian Period*. 2nd edition. London, 1947.

HOVEY, W. R. 'Sources of the Irish Illuminative Art', *Art Studies*, VI (1928).

KENDRICK, T. D. *Anglo-Saxon Art to A.D. 900*. London, 1938.

MASAI, F. *Essai sur les origines de la miniature dite irlandaise*. Brussels, 1947.

NORDENFALK, Carl. 'Before the Book of Durrow', *Acta Archaeologica*, XVIII (1947).

ROBINSON, S. F. H. *Celtic Illuminative Art*. Dublin, 1908.

WESTWOOD, J. O. *Facsimiles of the Miniatures and Ornaments of Anglo-Saxon and Irish Manuscripts*. London, 1868.

MANUSCRIPTS

ABBOT, T. K. *Celtic Ornaments from the Book of Kells*. Dublin, 1895.

ALTON, E. H., and MEYER, Peter. *Evangeliorum Quattuor Codex Cenannensis. The Book of Kells*. Berne, 1950.
Facsimile in 2 vols. with many plates in colour. Vol. III (text), 1951.

DORAN, Joseph M. 'The Enamelling and Metallesque Origin of the Ornament of the Book of Durrow', *Burl. Mag.*, XIII (1908).

FRIEND, A. M. 'The Canon Tables of the Book of Kells.' *Medieval Studies in Memory of A. Kingsley Porter*, ed. W. R. W. Koehler, II. Cambridge, Mass., 1939.

KUYPERS, A. B. *The Book of Cerne*. Cambridge, 1902.

MILLAR, Eric G. *The Lindisfarne Gospels*. London, 1923.

SULLIVAN, Edward. *The Book of Kells*. 2nd edition. London, 1920.

CHAPTER 2
GENERAL

HARRSEN, Meta. 'The Countess Judith of Flanders and the Library of Weingarten Abbey', *Papers of the Bibliographical Society of America*, XXIV, Part I (1930).

HOMBURGER, Otto. *Die Anfänge der Malschule von Winchester im X. Jahrhundert*. Studien über Christliche Denkmäler. Leipzig, 1912.

KANTOROWICZ, E. H. 'The Quinity of Winchester', *Art Bulletin*, XXIX (1947).

KENDRICK, T. D. *Late Saxon and Viking Art*. London, 1949.

ROBINSON, J. A. *The Times of St Dunstan*. Oxford, 1923.

MANUSCRIPTS

ATKINS, Sir Ivor. 'An Investigation of Two Anglo-Saxon Calendars; the Missal of Robert of Jumièges and Saint Wulfstan's Homiliary', *Archaeologia*, LXXVIII (1928).

GAGE, John. 'A Dissertation on St Æthelwold's Benedictional', *Archaeologia*, XXIV (1832).

GASQUET, F. A., and BISHOP, E. *The Bosworth Psalter*. London, 1908.

GOLLANCZ, Sir Israel. *The Cædmon Manuscript*. London, 1927.

NIVER, Charles. 'The Psalter in the British Museum, Harley 2904', *Medieval Studies in Memory of A. Kingsley Porter*, ed. W. R. W. Koehler, II. Cambridge, Mass., 1937.

TOLHURST, J. B. L. 'An Examination of Two Anglo-Saxon Manuscripts of the Winchester School: the Missal of Robert of Jumièges and the Benedictional of Saint Æthelwold', *Archaeologia*, LXXXIII (1933).

WARNER, G. F., and WILSON, H. A. *The Benedictional of Saint Æthelwold, Bishop of Winchester 963–984*. Roxburghe Club, Oxford, 1910.

WARREN, F. E. *The Leofric Missal*. Oxford, 1883.

EMBROIDERY

BROWN, G. Baldwin, and CHRISTIE, Mrs Archibald. 'St Cuthbert's Stole and Maniple at Durham', *Burl. Mag.*, XXIII (1913).

CHAPTER 3
GENERAL

PÄCHT, Otto. 'Hugo Pictor', *Bodleian Library Record*, III, No. 30 (1950).

WORMALD, Francis. 'The Survival of Anglo-Saxon Illumination after the Norman Conquest', *Proceedings of the British Academy*, XXX (1944).

MANUSCRIPT

FORBES-LEITH, W. *The Gospel Book of St Margaret*. Edinburgh, 1896.

BAYEUX TAPESTRY

BELLOC, Hilaire. *The Book of the Bayeux Tapestry*. London, 1914.

LEVÉ, A. *La Tapisserie de la reine Mathilde dite la tapisserie de Bayeux*. Paris, 1919.

LOOMIS, Roger S. 'The Origin and Date of the Bayeux Embroidery', *Art Bulletin*, VI (1923–4).

MACLAGAN, Eric. *The Bayeux Tapestry*. London, 1949.

Victoria and Albert Museum. *Guide to the Bayeux Tapestry*. 3rd edition. London, 1931.

CHAPTER 4
GENERAL

BAKER, Audrey. 'Lewes Priory and the Early Group of Wall Paintings in Sussex', *Walpole Society*, XXXI (1942–3). Published 1946.

Bodleian Library. *English Romanesque Illumination*. Bodleian Picture Books, I. Oxford, 1951.

WORMALD, Francis. 'The Development of English Illumination in the Twelfth Century', *Journal of the British Archaeological Association*. 3rd Series, VIII (1943).

MANUSCRIPTS

GOLDSCHMIDT, Adolf. *Der Albanipsalter in Hildesheim und seine Beziehung zur symbolischen Kirchenskulptur des XII. Jahrhunderts*. Berlin, 1895.

JAMES, M. R. 'Four Leaves of an English 12th Century Psalter and an English Picture-Book of the Late 13th Century', *Walpole Society*, XXV (1936–7).

JAMES, M. R. *The Canterbury Psalter*. London, 1935.

OAKESHOTT, Walter. *The Artists of the Winchester Bible*. London, 1945.

PAINTING

BELL, Clive. *Twelfth Century Paintings at Hardham and Clayton*. Introduction by Clive Bell. Lewes (Sussex), 1947.

CHAPTER 5

GENERAL

BORENIUS, T. 'The Cycle of Images in the Palaces and Castles of Henry III', *Journal of the Warburg and Courtauld Institutes*, VI (1943).

HOLLAENDER, Albert. 'The Sarum Illuminator and His School', *Wiltshire Archaeological and Natural History Magazine*, L (1943).

MANUSCRIPTS

COCKERELL, S. C. *The Work of W. de Brailes.* Roxburghe Club, Cambridge, 1930.

COXE, H. O. *The Apocalypse of St John the Divine* (Bod. MS. Auct. D.4.17). Roxburghe Club, London, 1876.

HERBERT, J. A. 'A Psalter in the British Museum' (Roy. MS. I D X), *Walpole Society*, III (1913–1914).

JAMES, M. R. *The Apocalypse in Latin and French* (Bod. MS. Douce 180). Roxburghe Club, Oxford, 1922.

JAMES, M. R. *The Apocalypse in Latin* (MS. 10 in the collection of C. W. Dyson Perrins, F.S.A.). Oxford, 1927.

JAMES, M. R. *The Bestiary* (Camb. Univ. Lib. MS. li.4.26). Roxburghe Club, Oxford, 1928.

JAMES, M. R. 'The Drawings of Matthew Paris', *Walpole Society*, XIV (1925–6).

JAMES, M. R. *La Estoire de Seint Ædward le Rei* (Camb. Univ. Lib. MS. Ee. 3.59). Roxburghe Club, Oxford, 1920.

JAMES, M. R. *The Trinity College Apocalypse.* (Camb. Trin. Coll. MS. R.16.2). Roxburghe Club, London, 1909.

JAMES, M. R., and TRISTRAM, E. W. 'Medieval Wall Paintings at Christ Church, Oxford', *Walpole Society*, XVI (1927–8).

MILLAR, Eric G. 'Additional Miniatures by W. de Brailes', *Journal of the Walters Art Gallery*, II (1939).

MILLAR, Eric G. *The Rutland Psalter.* Roxburghe Club, Oxford, 1937.

OMONT, Henri. Psautier illustré (Bib. Nat. MS. lat. 8846), Paris, n.d.

SWARZENSKI, Hanns. 'Unknown Bible Pictures by W. de Brailes', *Journal of the Walters Art Gallery*, I (1938).

WARNER, Sir George. *The Guthlac Roll.* Roxburghe Club, Oxford, 1928.

PAINTING

LETHABY, W. R. 'Medieval Paintings at Westminster', *Proceedings of the British Academy*, XIII (1927).

WORMALD, Francis. 'Paintings in Westminster Abbey and Contemporary Paintings', *Proceedings of the British Academy*, XXXV (1949).

STAINED GLASS

LAFOND, Jean. 'The Stained Glass Decoration of Lincoln Cathedral in the Thirteenth Century', *Archaeological Journal*, CIII (1946).

RACKHAM, Bernard. *The Ancient Glass of Canterbury Cathedral.* London, 1949.

TILES

LETHABY, W. R. 'English Primitives – IV "The Westminster and Chertsey Tiles and Romance Paintings"', *Burl. Mag.*, XXX (1917).

LETHABY, W. R. 'The Romance Tiles of Chertsey Abbey', *Walpole Society*, II (1912–13).

CHAPTER 6

GENERAL

PÄCHT, Otto. 'A Giottesque Episode in English Medieval Art', *Journal of the Warburg and Courtauld Institutes*, VI (1943).

WILLIAMS, E. Carlton. 'Mural Paintings of the Three Living and the Three Dead in England', *Journal of the British Archaeological Association*. 3rd series, VII (1942).

MANUSCRIPTS

COCKERELL, S. C. *The Gorleston Psalter.* London, 1907.

COCKERELL, S. C., and JAMES, M. R. *Two East Anglian Psalters at the Bodleian Library, Oxford.* Roxburghe Club, Oxford, 1926.

EGBERT, D. D. *The Tickhill Psalter and Related Manuscripts.* New York, 1940.

GHEYN, J. van den. *Le Psautier de Peterborough.* Brussels [1905].
Le Musée des Enluminures, fasc., 2, 3.

JAMES, M. R. 'An English Bible-picture Book of the Fourteenth Century (Holkham MS. 666)', *Walpole Society*, XI (1922–3).

JAMES, M. R. *The Dublin Apocalypse.* Roxburghe Club, Cambridge, 1932.

JAMES, M. R. *A Peterborough Psalter and Bestiary of the Fourteenth Century.* Roxburghe Club, Oxford, 1921.

JAMES, M. R. *The Treatise ... De nobilitatibus, sapientibus et prudentiis regum.* Roxburghe Club, London, 1913.

MILLAR, Eric G. *The Luttrell Psalter.* London, 1932.

WARNER, Sir George. *Queen Mary's Psalter.* London, 1912.

PAINTING

LILLIE, W. W. 'A Medieval Retable at Thornham Parva', *Burl. Mag.*, LXIII (1933).

LILLIE, W. W. 'The Retable at Thornham Parva', *Proceedings of the Suffolk Institute of Archaeology and Natural History*, XXI (1933).

TRISTRAM, E. W., and JAMES, M. R. 'Wall-Paintings in Croughton Church, Northamptonshire', *Archaeologia*, LXXVI (1927).

STAINED GLASS

RUSHFORTH, G. MacN. 'The Great East Window of Gloucester Cathedral.' *Bristol and Gloucestershire Archaeological Society, Transactions.* XLIV (1922).

RUSHFORTH, G. MacN. 'The Glass in the Quire Clerestory of Tewkesbury Abbey.' *Bristol and Gloucestershire Archaeological Society, Transactions.* XLVI (1924).

CHAPTER 7

GENERAL

KUHN, Charles. 'Herman Scheerre and English Illumination of the Early Fifteenth Century', *Art Bulletin*, XXII (1940).

SHAW, W. A. 'The Early English School of Portraiture', *Burl. Mag.*, LXV (1934).

WOODFORDE, Christopher. 'English Stained Glass and Glass-painters in the Fourteenth Century', *Proceedings of the British Academy*, XXV (1939).

WORMALD, Francis. 'The Fitzwilliam Psalter and Its Allies', *Journal of the Warburg and Courtauld Institutes*, VI (1943).

MANUSCRIPTS

HERBERT, J. A. *The Sherborne Missal.* Roxburghe Club, Oxford, 1920.

JAMES, M. R., *Illustrations of the Book of Genesis.* Roxburghe Club, Oxford, 1921.

JAMES, M. R. 'An English Medieval Sketchbook, No. 1916 in the Pepysian Library, Magdalene College, Cambridge.' *Walpole Society*, XIII (1924–1925).

JAMES, M. R., and MILLAR, E. G. *The Bohun Manuscripts.* Roxburghe Club, Oxford, 1936.

MILLAR, Eric G. 'The Egerton Genesis and the M. R. James Memorial MS.', *Archaeologia*, LXXXVII (1937).

RICKERT, Margaret. *The Reconstructed Carmelite Missal.* London, 1952.

PAINTING

BODKIN, Thomas. *The Wilton Diptych.* Gallery Books, No. 16. London, n.d.

BORENIUS, T. 'An English Painted Ceiling of the Late Fourteenth Century', *Burl. Mag.*, LXVIII (1936).

HOPE, W. H. St John. 'On a Painted Table or Reredos of the Fourteenth Century in the Cathedral Church of Norwich', *Norfolk Archaeology*, XIII (1898).

NOPPEN, J. G. 'The Westminster Apocalypse and its Source', *Burl. Mag.*, LXI (1932).

PRESTON, Arthur. 'The Fourteenth Century Painted Ceiling at St Helen's Church, Abingdon', *Berkshire Archaeological Journal*, XL (1936).

SCHARF, George. *Description of the Wilton House Diptych.* London, 1882.

TRISTRAM, E. W. 'The Wilton Diptych', *The Month*, New Series, I, No. 6 (1949).

WALLER, J. G. 'On the Retable in Norwich Cathedral and Paintings in St Michael-at-Plea', *Norfolk Archaeology*, XIII (1898).

STAINED GLASS

LE COUTEUR, J. D. *Ancient Glass in Winchester.* Winchester, 1920.

SALZMAN, L. F. 'The Glazing of St Stephen's Chapel, Westminster, in 1351–2', *Journal of the British Society of Master Glass-Painters*, I, No. 4 (1926).

WOODFORDE, Christopher. *The Stained Glass of New College, Oxford.* London, 1951.

CHAPTER 8

GENERAL

CONSTABLE, W. G. 'Some East Anglian Rood Screen Paintings', *Connoisseur*, LXXXIV (1929).

WOODFORDE, Christopher. *The Norwich School of Glass Painting in the Fifteenth Century*. London, 1950.

MANUSCRIPTS

DILLON, Harold Arthur, Viscount. 'On a Manuscript Collection of Ordinances of Chivalry of the Fifteenth Century belonging to Lord Hastings', *Archaeologia*, LVII (1900).

JAMES, M. R. *The Chaundler Manuscripts*. Roxburghe Club, London, 1916.

PAINTING

COLGRAVE, Bertram. 'The St Cuthbert Paintings on the Carlisle Cathedral Stalls', *Burl. Mag.*, LXXIII (1938).

HOLLAENDER, Albert. 'The Doom Painting of St Thomas of Canterbury, Salisbury', *Wiltshire Archaeological and Natural History Magazine*, L (1944).

JAMES, M. R., and TRISTRAM, E. W. 'The Wall Paintings in Eton College Chapel and in the Lady Chapel of Winchester Cathedral', *Walpole Society*, XVII (1928–9).

STAINED GLASS

HAMAND, L. A. *The Ancient Windows of Great Malvern Priory Church*. St Albans, 1947.

RUSHFORTH, G. MacN. *Mediaeval Christian Imagery*. Oxford, 1936.

HUTCHINSON, F. E. *Medieval Glass at All Souls College*. London, 1949.

Hiberno-Saxon (Northumbria?): Decorative Page, from Book of Durrow.
Seventh century (second half). 9⅝ by 6⅛ in. *Trinity College, Dublin*

(B) Hiberno-Saxon (Northumbria?): Symbol of St John, from Book of Durrow. Seventh century (second half). 9⅝ by 6¼ in. *Trinity College, Dublin*

(A) Hiberno-Saxon (Northumbria?): Symbol of St Matthew, from Book of Durrow. Seventh century (second half). 9⅝ by 6¼ in. *Trinity College, Dublin*

D

B

C

A

(A) Anglo-Saxon: Great Buckle, Sutton Hoo Treasure. Seventh century (first half). $5\frac{1}{4}$ by $2\frac{1}{8}$ in. *Department of Medieval Antiquities, British Museum*

(B) Anglo-Saxon: Hanging Bowl Escutcheon, Sutton Hoo Treasure. Seventh century (first half). $2\frac{5}{8}$ in. diameter. *Dept. of Medieval Antiquities, Brit. Mus.*

(C) Anglo-Saxon: Gold Clasp, Sutton Hoo Treasure. Seventh century (first half). $2\frac{1}{2}$ by $2\frac{1}{8}$ in. *Department of Medieval Antiquities, British Museum*

(D) Hiberno-Saxon (Northumbria?): Decorative Page, from Book of Durrow. Seventh century (second half). Detail approx. actual size. *Trinity Coll., Dublin*

3

Northumbrian (Lindisfarne): Cruciform Page, from Lindisfarne Gospels. 698–721.
13½ by 9¾ in. *British Museum*

Northumbrian (Lindisfarne): Text Page, from Lindisfarne Gospels. 698–721.
13½ by 9¾ in. *British Museum*

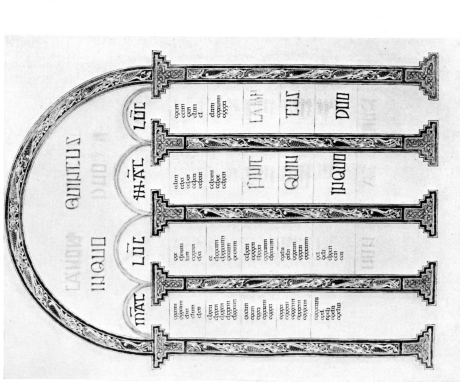

(B) Irish (Iona and Kells): Canon Table Page,
from Book of Kells. 760–820. 13 by 9¼ in. *Trinity College, Du*

(A) Northumbrian (Lindisfarne): Canon Table Page,
from Lindisfarne Gospels. 698–721. 13½ by 9¾ in. *British Museum*

(A) Northumbrian (Lindisfarne): St Matthew, from Lindisfarne Gospels. 698–721. 13½ by 9¾ in. *British Museum*

(B) South Italian (?): The Scribe Ezra, prefixed to Northumbrian Bible. Late sixth century. 19⅞ by 13 in. *Biblioteca Medicea Laurenziana, Florence*

(B) Northumbrian (made at Echternach?):
St Matthew, from Echternach Gospels. Eighth century (first half).
Miniature 10¼ by 7⅝ in. *Bibliothèque Nationale, Paris*

(A) Irish (Northumbria?):
St Luke, from Gospel Book of Chad. Early eighth century.
Miniature 9¾ by 7¼ in. *Cathedral Library, Lichfield*

8

(B) Irish: St Mark, from Gospels. c.750–60.
Miniature 9¼ by 7 in. *Stiftsbibliothek, St Gall*

(A) South English: St Mark, from Cutbercht Gospels. Eighth
century. Miniature 10¼ by 8½ in. *Nationalbibliothek, Vienna*

9

(B) Canterbury: David as a Musician, from Psalter. Mid eighth century. 9¼ by 7 in. *British Museum*

(A) Northumbrian: David as a Warrior, from Cassiodorus, *Commentary on Psalms. c.*725. Miniature 14⅞ by 10¾ in. *Cathedral Library, Durham*

(A) Canterbury: St Matthew, from Gospels. c. 760.
Miniature 12½ by 10⅛ in. *Royal Library, Stockholm*

(B) Mercian(?): St Matthew, from Rome Gospels, c. 800.
13½ by 10⅛ in. *Biblioteca Apostolica Vaticana, Rome*

II

Mercian (?): XPI Page, from Rome Gospels, *c.* 800. 13½ by 10⅜ in.
Biblioteca Apostolica Vaticana, Rome

Irish (Iona and Kells): XPI Page, from Book of Kells. 760–820. 13 by 9½ in.
Trinity College, Dublin

Irish (Iona and Kells): St Matthew, from Book of Kells. 760–820. 13 by 9½ in.
Trinity College, Dublin

Canterbury: Decorative Text Page, from Bede, *Ecclesiastical History*. Late eighth century.
Detail approx. actual size. *British Museum*

Canterbury: St Luke, from Gospels. *c.* 800. 18½ by 13⅝ in.
British Museum

Mercian: St Luke, from Gospel Book of Cerne. 818–30 (?). 9⅛ by 7⅜ in.
University Library, Cambridge

(A) Unknown (Winchester?):
Daniel, from Embroidered Stole. 909–16.
Detail actual size.
Cathedral Library, Durham

(B) Unknown (Winchester?):
Peter Deacon, from Embroidered Maniple.
909–16. Detail actual size.
Cathedral Library, Durham

Unknown: Presentation of the Book to Pope Gregory, from Rabanus Maurus,
De Laude Crucis. Tenth century. 16½ by 13½ in. *Trinity College, Cambridge*

(B) Winchester: Christ Enthroned, from Æthelstan Psalter. Tenth century (first third). Approx. actual size.
British Museum

(A) Unknown (Winchester): Athelstan presenting the Book to St Cuthbert, from Bede, *Life of St Cuthbert. c.* 930. 11½ by 7⅞ in. *Corpus Christi College, Cambridge*

(B) Ramsey Abbey (?): Beatus Initial, from Psalter.
Late tenth century. Initial 6¾ by 5½ in. *British Museum*

(A) Canterbury: Beatus Initial, from Bosworth Psalter.
Late tenth century. Initial 6¾ by 3⅞ in. *British Museum*

Glastonbury (?): Christ and St Dunstan, prefixed to a Composite Volume.
Mid tenth century. 9¾ by 7¼ in. *Bodleian Library, Oxford*

Canterbury or Sherborne Abbey?: God the Son, from Sherborne Pontifical. *c.*992–5.
12½ by 8 in. *Bibliothèque Nationale, Paris*

Canterbury or Sherborne Abbey?: Crucifixion, from Sherborne Pontifical. *c.* 992–5.
12½ by 8 in. *Bibliothèque Nationale, Paris*

Winchester: King Edgar offering Charter to Christ, from New Minster Charter. Dated 966. 8⅛ by 6⅜ in. *British Museum*

Winchester or Ely: Annunciation, from Benedictional of Æthelwold. *c.* 975–80.
11½ by 8½ in. *Devonshire Collection, Chatsworth*

Winchester or Ely: Death of the Virgin, from Benedictional of Æthelwold. *c.* 975–80.
11½ by 8½ in. *Devonshire Collection, Chatsworth*

(B) Canterbury (?): Historiated Initial with Majesty, from Gospels.
Early eleventh century. 13¾ by 10¾ in. *British Museum*

(A) Canterbury (?): Christ in Majesty, from Gospels.
Late tenth century. 12¾ by 9¼ in. *Trinity College, Cambridge*

(B) Winchester: Death of the Virgin, from Benedictional of Archbishop Robert. 900–1037 (?). 12⅝ by 9⅛ in. *Bibliothèque Publique, Rouen*

(A) Glastonbury: 'Vita', from Leofric Missal. Before 979. 8⅞ by 5⅞ in. *Bodleian Library, Oxford*

Ramsey Abbey (?): Crucifixion, from Psalter. Late tenth century. Miniature 9¼ by 7⅛ in.
British Museum

Ely (?): Nativity, from Missal of Robert of Jumièges. 1006–23. 13¼ by 8¾ in.
Bibliothèque Publique, Rouen

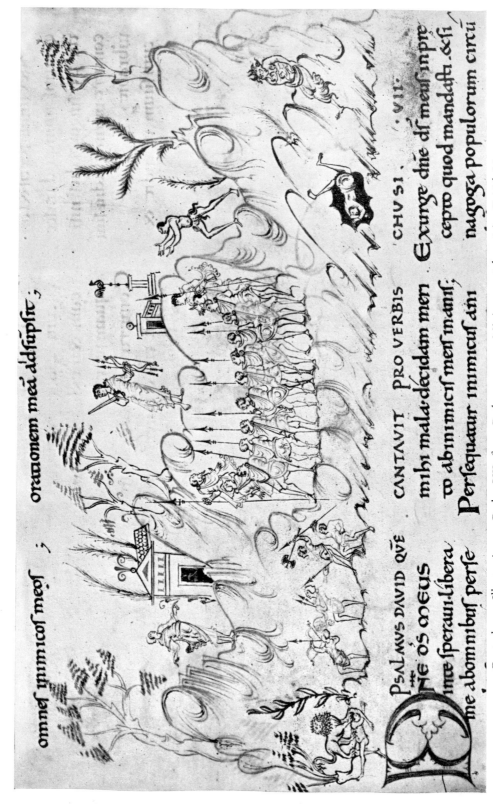

Canterbury: Illustration to Psalm VII, from Psalter. c. 1000. Miniature 4¼ by 9¾ in. *British Museum*

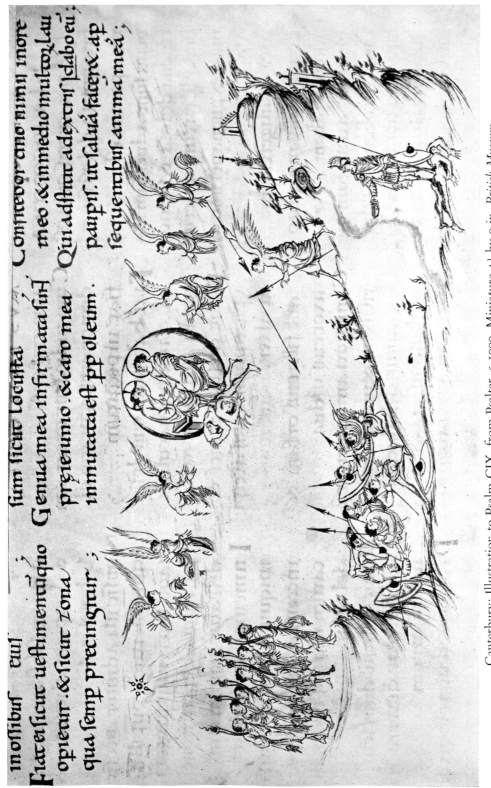

Canterbury: Illustration to Psalm CIX, from Psalter. c. 1000. Miniature 4½ by 9 in. *British Museum*

33

(A) Canterbury (?): Ploughing, from Hymnal. Early eleventh century.
Miniature 1¼ by 4 in. *British Museum*

(B) Canterbury: Ploughing, from Astronomical Treatises. Early eleventh century.
Miniature 2¾ by 7⅝ in. *British Museum*

Canterbury: Building the Tower of Babel, from Ælfric, *Metrical Paraphrase of Pentateuch*.
Eleventh century (second quarter). 12⅞ by 8¾ in. *British Museum*

(B) Winchester: St John, from Grimbald Gospels.
Early eleventh century. 12¾ by 9¼ in. *British Museum*

(A) Winchester: St Luke, from Grimbald Gospels.
Early eleventh century. 12¾ by 9¼ in. *British Museum*

(B) Winchester: Crucifixion, from New Minster Offices.
1023–35. 5 by 3⅞ in. *British Museum*

(A) Winchester: Knut and Ælfgyfu, from New Minster
Register. 1020–30. 10⅛ by 5¾ in. *British Museum*

(A) Unknown: Aldhelm and Nuns of Barking, from Aldhelm, *De Virginitate*. Late tenth century. Miniature 3⅝ by 6¼ in. *Lambeth Palace Library, London*

(B) Malmesbury: 'Luxuria', from Prudentius, *Psychomachia*. Beginning of eleventh century. Miniature 4¼ by 7⅝ in. *Corpus Christi College, Cambridge*

(A) Bury St Edmunds:
Christ Victorious, from Bury Psalter.
Eleventh century (second quarter).
Detail approx. 9 in. high.
Biblioteca Apostolica Vaticana, Rome

(B) Bury St Edmunds:
Psalmist on Mt Sion, from Bury Psalter.
Eleventh century (second quarter).
Detail approx. 9 in. high.
Biblioteca Apostolica Vaticana, Rome

Canterbury: Historiated Initial with David and Goliath, from Psalter. *c.* 1012–23. 11½ by 8½ in. *British Museum*

Canterbury: St Benedict and Monks of Canterbury, from Psalter. *c.* 1012–23.
11½ by 8½ in. *British Museum*

Croyland (?) or Ely (?): Christ Triumphant, from Psalter. Eleventh century
(second quarter). 10½ by 6½ in. *Bodleian Library, Oxford*

Winchester (?): Crucifixion, from Weingarten Gospels. Eleventh century (second quarter).
11½ by 7½ in. *Pierpont Morgan Library, New York*

Canterbury (?): Noah's Ark, from Cædmon's Poems. Eleventh century
(second quarter). Miniature 9 by 7¾ in. *Bodleian Library, Oxford*

Winchester Style (Fen Country?): St John, from Gospels. *c.* 1050–60. 10 by 6¾ in.
Monte Cassino Library

(A) Canterbury: Historiated Initial with Scenes
from the Life of St Cesarius, from Martyrology.
c. 1100. Detail 4½ by 3¾ in. *British Museum*

(B) Canterbury:
St Michael, from Martyrology. *c.* 1100.
Initial 3¼ by 2½ in. *British Museum*

(C) Canterbury: Zodiac Sign 'Virgo',
from Martyrology. Twelfth century
(first decade). 3½ by 3 in. *British Museum*

(A) Anglo-Norman: Landing Horses, from Bayeux Tapestry. *c.* 1073–83.
Detail 1 ft 9 in. by 2 ft 11 in. *Town Hall, Bayeux*

(B) Anglo-Norman: Battle of Hastings, from Bayeux Tapestry. *c.* 1073–83.
Detail 1 ft 9 in. by 2 ft 11 in. *Town Hall, Bayeux*

(A) Unknown: St Matthew, from Gospel Lectionary. Mid eleventh century. 6⅝ by 4⅜ in. *Bodleian Library, Oxford*

(B) Canterbury: The Psalmist between an Angel and a Devil, from Psalter. Eleventh century (second half). Detail 6¼ by 3½ in. *British Museum*

(B) Hereford (?): St Luke, from Gospels. Mid eleventh century. 7¾ by 4 in.
Pembroke College, Cambridge

(A) Hereford (?): Scenes from Life of St Lawrence, from Troper. Mid eleventh century. 6⅜ by 3⅝ in.
British Museum

49

Unknown: David, from Psalter. *c.* 1050. 10 by 6 in. *British Museum*

Unknown: David and Musicians, from Psalter. *c.* 1050. 10 by 6 in. *British Museum*

Winchester: Crucifixion, from Psalter. *c.* 1060. 12 by 7½ in.
British Museum

Winchester: Crucifixion, from Psalter. Eleventh century (third quarter). 12 by 7½ in.
British Museum

Canterbury: St Augustine, from Augustine, *De Civitate Dei*. Early twelfth century.
13¾ by 9⅞ in. *Biblioteca Medicea Laurenziana, Florence*

Canterbury: Clerics Discussing, from Augustine, *De Civitate Dei*. Early twelfth century. 13¾ by 9⅞ in. *Biblioteca Medicea Laurenziana, Florence*

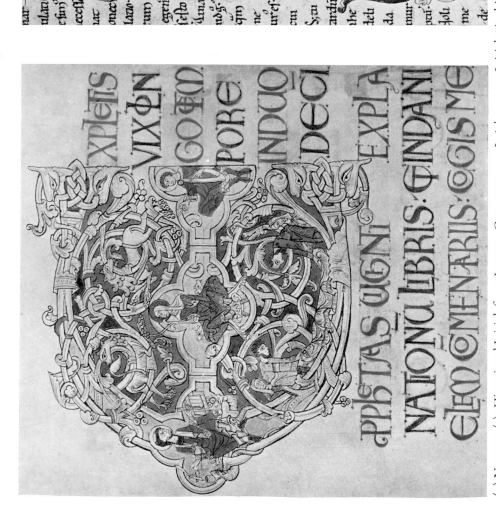

(A) Norman (?): Historiated Initial, from Jerome, *Commentary on Isaiah. c.* 1100. Initial 6 in. high. *Bodleian Library, Oxford.*

(B) Durham (?): Initial with Robertus Benjamin, from Augustine, *Commentary on Psalms.*
Before 1088. Initial 7⅞ in. high. *Cathedral Library, Durham*

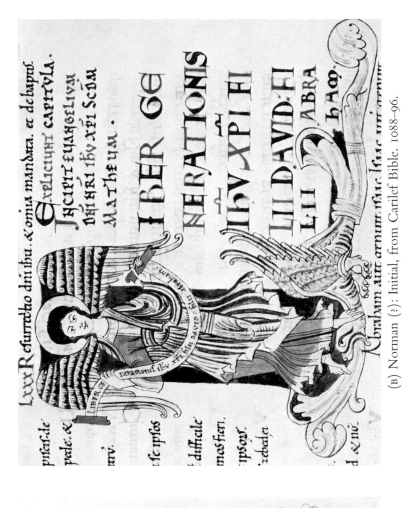

(B) Norman (?): Initial, from Carilef Bible. 1088–96.
Initial 4⅞ by 5⅝ in. *Cathedral Library, Durham*

(A) Durham (?): Initial, from Augustine.
Commentary on Psalms. Before 1088. Initial 4½ by 4¼ in.
Cathedral Library, Durham

Norman (?): Beatus Initial, from Carilef Bible. 1088–96. Actual size.
Cathedral Library, Durham

Ingemuit tā triste nefas forassima uirtus
Sobrietas. dextā socios dededit cornu
Inunctāq; manū quondā sine cede pire.

(A) St Albans (?): Sobriety, from Prudentius, *Psychomachia*.
Early twelfth century. Approx. actual size. *British Museum*

que pascebat dñis : monastiū pete decreunt.
Quoin te facien cibos dño, peurante pceperit.

Cunq; noyy yrre ccanencion ingressū
sedulo iā corde meditaret : affuit gra
supna que animū ei arti inpposito firma

(B) Durham (?): St Cuthbert's Horse finds Bread for the Saint,
from Bede, *Life of St Cuthbert*. Early twelfth century.
Actual size. *University College, Oxford*

St Albans (?): Crucifixion, from Florence of Worcester's Chronicle. *c.* 1130.
Miniature approx. 8½ by 5¾ in. *Corpus Christi College, Oxford*

St Albans: Adam and Eve driven from Paradise, from Albani Psalter. 1119–46. 10⅞ by 7¼ in.
Library of St Godehard, Hildesheim

(A) St Albans: Beatus Page, from Albani Psalter. 1119–46. 10⅞ by 7¼ in. *Library of St Godehard, Hildesheim*

(B) St Albans: Initial to Psalm LXV, from Albani Psalter. 1119–46. Initial 7¼ in. high. *Library of St Godehard, Hildesheim*

(A) Canterbury: St Luke, from Dover Bible.
Twelfth century (third quarter). Initial 4¼ in. diameter
Corpus Christi College, Cambridge

(B) Unknown: St Mark, from Mostyn Gospels.
Early twelfth century. 10⅜ by 6⅝ in.
Pierpont Morgan Library, New York

Bury St Edmunds (?): Ascension, Decollation of the Baptist, from Bury Gospels.
Early twelfth century. 16¼ by 10¾ in. *Pembroke College, Cambridge*

Bury St Edmunds: St Edmund feeding the Hungry, from *Life of St Edmund*.
1125–50. 10¾ by 7¼ in. *Pierpont Morgan Library, New York*

65

Bury St Edmunds: Fight with the Danes, from *Life of St Edmund*. 1125–50.
10¾ by 7¼ in. *Pierpont Morgan Library, New York*

(A) Unknown: Scenes from Infancy of Christ, from Bible Picture Leaf.
Mid twelfth century. Detail 7¾ by 11 in. *British Museum*

(B) Unknown: Scenes from the Passion, from Bible Picture Leaf. Mid twelfth century.
Detail 7¾ by 11 in. *Victoria and Albert Museum, London*

(B) Hereford (?): St Michael, from Lansdowne Psalter. Mid twelfth century. 8⅞ by 5⅜ in. *British Museum*

(A) Hereford (?): Boethius in Prison, from Boethius, *De Consolatione Philosophiae*. Twelfth century (second quarter). 8 by 5 in. *Bodleian Library, Oxford*

(A) Master Hugo: Prophet Amos, from Bury Bible. 1121–48.
Initial approx. $3\frac{7}{8}$ by $3\frac{3}{4}$ in.
Corpus Christi College, Cambridge

(B) Canterbury: Prophet Daniel, from Lambeth Bible.
Twelfth century (second half). Initial $3\frac{1}{2}$ in. diameter.
Lambeth Palace Library, London

Canterbury: St Matthew, from Dover Bible. Twelfth century (third quarter).
Initial 5½ by 4 in. *Corpus Christi College, Cambridge*

Canterbury: Portrait of the Scribe Eadwine, from Eadwine Psalter. *c.*1150.
18 by 13 in. *Trinity College, Cambridge*

(A) Canterbury: Illustration for Psalm LI, from Eadwine Psalter. *c.* 1150.
Miniature 5 by 11½ in. *Trinity College, Cambridge*

(B) Canterbury: Illustration for Psalm XV, from Eadwine Psalter. *c.* 1150.
Miniature 5½ by 11½ in. *Trinity College, Cambridge*

Canterbury: Moses and Israelites, from Lambeth Bible. Twelfth century (second half).
Miniature 10⅛ by 8⅝ in. *Lambeth Palace Library, London*

Unknown: Apostles, from Apocalypse Paintings. Mid twelfth century. Detail approx. 5 by 12 ft.
North Chancel Wall, Church of St Mary, Kempley, Gloucestershire

(B) Cluniac (?): Praying Saint, from Wall Paintings.
Twelfth century (first half). Detail approx. 2 ft 6 in. high.
North Wall of Nave, Clayton Church, Sussex

(A) Cluniac (?): Adam and Eve, from Wall Paintings. c. 1125.
Figs. approx. 4 ft high.
West Wall of Chancel, Hardham Church, Sussex

Canterbury: St Paul and the Viper, Wall Painting. Mid twelfth century. 5 ft 9 in. by 5 ft 6 in.
East Wall, St Anselm's Chapel, Canterbury Cathedral

Ramsey Abbey (?): St John, from Bede, *Commentary on the Apocalypse*. Twelfth century
(third quarter). 10⅝ by 7 in. *St John's College, Cambridge*

77

Unknown: Madonna and Child, prefixed to Augustine, *Commentary on Psalms*.
Twelfth century (second half). 10⅜ by 6½ in. *Bodleian Library, Oxford*

Italo-Byzantine (?): Virgin Enthroned, from Psalter. Twelfth century (third quarter). 12¾ by 9 in. *British Museum*

Winchester: Adoration of the Magi, from Psalter. 1150–60. 12¾ by 9 in.
British Museum

York (?): Sacrifice of Abraham, Bible Picture from Psalter. *c.* 1175. 11⅜ by 7⅜ in.
Hunterian Museum, Glasgow

St Albans: Terence Comedies. Mid twelfth century. Detail 6½ by 8½ in. *Bodleian Library, Oxford*

(A) Winchester: Initial for II Maccabees, from Bible. c.1160–70.
Initial $4\frac{1}{4}$ by $3\frac{1}{2}$ in. *Cathedral Library, Winchester*

(B) Winchester: Initial for Jeremiah, from Bible. c.1160–70.
Initial $4\frac{3}{8}$ by 5 in. *Cathedral Library, Winchester*

(B) Winchester: Initial for Joshua, from Bible. c. 1160–70. Initial 5¼ by 5½ in. *Cathedral Library, Winchester*

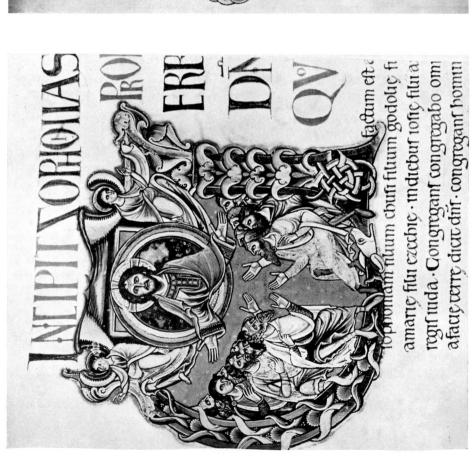

(A) Winchester: Initial for Zephaniah, from Bible. c. 1160–70. Initial 4⅝ by 4½ in. *Cathedral Library, Winchester*

(B) Winchester: Initial for Isaiah, from Bible. c. 1160–70.
Initial 4⅜ by 4⅝ in. *Cathedral Library, Winchester*

(A) Winchester: Initial for Daniel, from Bible. c. 1160–70.
Initial 4¾ by 4⅜ in. *Cathedral Library, Winchester*

85

Winchester: Scenes from Life of David, from Bible Picture Leaf. Twelfth century
(third quarter). 22⅝ by 15¼ in. *Pierpont Morgan Library, New York*

(A) Durham (?): Initial for Corinthians,
from Pauline Epistles. 1153–95.
Detail 15 by 5¼ in.
Cathedral Library, Durham

(B) Durham (?): Initial for II Kings,
from Pudsey Bible. 1153–95.
Detail approx. 9 by 3 in.
Cathedral Library, Durham

(A) Unknown: The Unicorn, from Bestiary. Late twelfth century.
Miniature 4⅛ by 4½ in. *Bodleian Library, Oxford*

(B) Radford Priory (?): Tiger, from 'Worksop' Bestiary. Before 1187 (?).
Miniature 3½ by 4 in. *Pierpont Morgan Library, New York*

St Albans or Westminster (?): Christ in Majesty, from Westminster Psalter. *c.* 1200.
9 by 6¼ in. *British Museum*

(B) St Albans or Westminster (?): Annunciation, from
Westminster Psalter. c. 1200. 9 by 6¼ in. *British Museum*

(A) St Albans: Symbol of St Matthew, from Glossed Gospels.
c. 1200. Approx. actual size. *Trinity College, Cambridge*

Canterbury: Illustration for Psalm LI, from Psalter. c.1200. Miniature 6⅜ by 11½ in. *Bibliothèque Nationale, Paris*

Canterbury (?): Trinity, from Lothian Bible. *c.* 1200. 14 by 10 in.
Pierpont Morgan Library, New York

Canterbury: Methuselah, Panel from Stained Glass Window.
Late twelfth century. 5 ft by 2 ft 5 in.
Clerestory, South-West Transept, Canterbury Cathedral

(B) Durham (?): St Cuthbert, from Bede, *Life of St Cuthbert.*
c.1200. 5⅝ by 3⅞ in. *British Museum*

(A) Unknown: Beatus Page, from Psalter.
Early thirteenth century. 12 by 8¼ in. *British Museum*

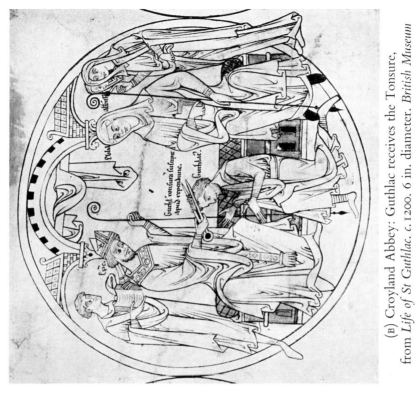

(B) Croyland Abbey: Guthlac receives the Tonsure, from *Life of St Guthlac. c. 1200. 6 in. diameter. British Museum*

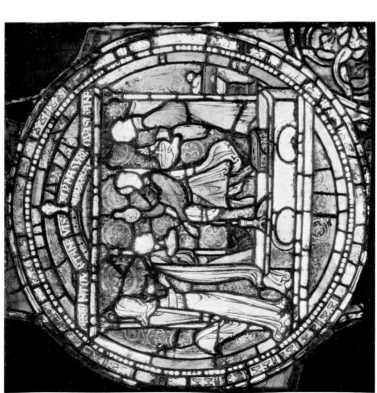

(A) Canterbury: Medallion, from Stained Glass Window. *c.* 1220. Detail approx. 3 ft diameter. *Trinity Chapel, Canterbury Cathedral*

95

Canterbury: Genesis Initial, from Bible of Robert de Bello. 1224–53. 10⅞ by 7⅞ in.
British Museum

Canterbury: Biblical Scenes, from Stained Glass Window. *c.* 1220.
Detail approx. 11 by 7 ft. *Corona, Canterbury Cathedral*

W. de Brailes: Scenes from Genesis, Bible Picture Leaf. *c.* 1230–50. 9⅞ by 6⅞ in.
Fitzwilliam Museum, Cambridge

(A) W. de Brailes (signed):
Portrait of W. de Brailes, from Last
Judgement. *c.* 1230–50. Detail 1¼ in.
diameter. *Fitzwilliam Museum,
Cambridge. Reproduced by permission
of the Syndics*

(B) W. de Brailes: Christ walking on the Water,
from Bible Pictures. *c.* 1230–50. 5¼ by 3⅞ in.
Walters Art Gallery, Baltimore

(c) W. de Brailes: Initial with Trinity for Psalm CIX, from Psalter. *c.* 1230–50.
Actual size. *Sir Sydney Cockerell, Kew, Richmond*

Peterborough: Beatus Page, from Psalter of Robert de Lindesey. 1214–22. 9½ by 6 in.
Society of Antiquaries, London

Canterbury (?): Genesis Page, from Bible of William of Devon.
c. mid thirteenth century. 12⅜ by 8 in. *British Museum*

Salisbury (?): Crucifixion, from Psalter. *c.* mid thirteenth century. 12 by 8½ in.
All Souls College, Oxford

Evesham (Worcestershire): Crucifixion with a Bishop as Donor, from Psalter.
Mid thirteenth century. 12⅜ by 8 in. *British Museum*

Salisbury (?): Virgin and Child, from Missal 'of Henry of Chichester'. Mid thirteenth century.
12½ by 8 in. *John Rylands Library, Manchester*

Salisbury (?): Virgin and Child, Painted Roundel. Mid thirteenth century. 2 ft 6 in. diameter. *Chapel of the Bishop's Palace, Chichester*

Matthew Paris (signed): Virgin and Child, from Matthew Paris,
Historia Anglorum. Before 1259. 14 by 9⅜ in. *British Museum*

nun ad... par le nerd... de pl... il eftur fun eff... Amphibal la ceox dure Agenoillie, Suspire e plore
ich en bone terre de fun. vgeeur le fegeet Se tresible ne dour ne fume. ke il ne aie sa cuftume.

I ia e repruua. laidir e efcharni   C vimanr. kar de moi eft ia tut acumpli
G efkau fane efpandre de efcurgief bati   T rembla treftur li mundz. folail enoblcuri
V es paumes ala face crucnment feri   V n granez veilz du temple defira e rumpi
E nun fuft dræfæ. autre cnfuers vmi   F roifirenr peref. e la lune enpali

(A) Matthew Paris: Alban watching Amphibalus kneeling before the Cross,
from *Lives of Saints Alban and Amphibalus*. Mid thirteenth century.
Detail 4¼ by 6½ in. *Trinity College, Dublin*

E puis li dift. amis ceo apent   A edward languift. sitz cuftord P   ar mal fa gueitent mult deget
A deu meimes omnipotent   I at dift il kar fuffe mort   O   ut en auerott oi eargent
P t crauf tdee z mne e change   G il remaiu de nun liguage   R   t af danoit en teff prefent
N egnef puuez a hume eftrange   ocif funt p grett fanfage   A   uein le augueire deneucher

(B) Matthew Paris, assistant: Brihtwold, Bishop of Winchester relates his Vision,
the Young Edward praying, from *L'Estoire de Seint Aedward le Rei*.
Thirteenth century (third quarter). Detail 5¼ by 7¾ in. *University Library, Cambridge*

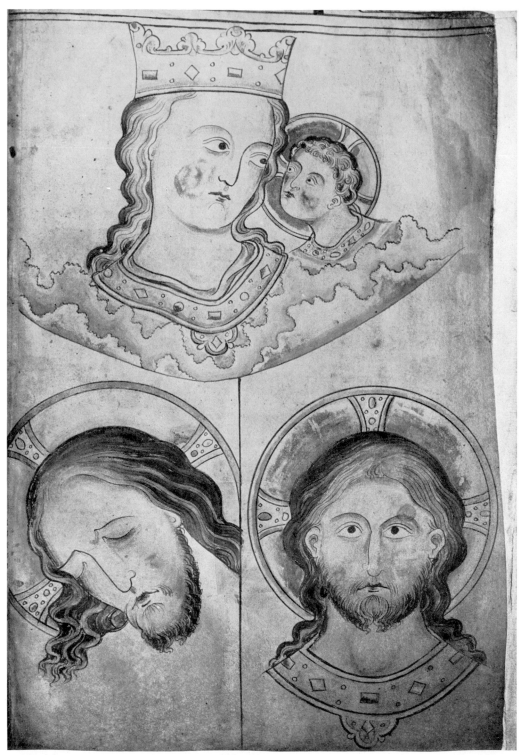

Matthew Paris: Heads of Christ and the Virgin, from Matthew Paris, *Chronica Maiora*.
Mid thirteenth century. 14¼ by 9⅜ in. *Corpus Christi College, Cambridge*

(A) Court Style (?): Majesty, Wall Painting. *c.* 1230.
Figure 3 ft 4 in. high. *Vault, Chapel of the*
Holy Sepulchre, Winchester Cathedral

(B) Court Style (?): Deposition, Wall Painting. *c.* 1230. Detail 4 ft 11 in.
by 7 ft 6 in. *East Wall, Chapel of the Holy Sepulchre, Winchester Cathedral*

(B) Matthew Paris (?): Head of a King, Wall Painting.
Mid thirteenth century.
Over life-size. Cloister, Windsor Castle

(A) Matthew Paris: Head of Christ, from Matthew Paris,
Chronica Minora. Mid thirteenth century. Miniature 5¾ by 6 in.
Corpus Christi College, Cambridge

St Albans (?): St John and the Angel, from Apocalypse. c. 1230. Miniature 4½ by 8¼ in. *Trinity College, Cambridge*

St Albans: The Apocalyptic Woman, St Michael and Dragon, from Apocalypse.
Mid thirteenth century. 10¾ by 7⅝ in. *Pierpont Morgan Library, New York*

(A) Canterbury: St John and the Angel, from Apocalypse. *c.* 1270. Miniature 4½ by 5¾ in. *Bodleian Library, Oxford*

(B) Canterbury: St John and the Angel, from Apocalypse. Thirteenth century (third quarter). Miniature 4½ by 6 in. *Lambeth Palace Library, London*

(B) Court Style: Feeding the Five Thousand, from Retable. Thirteenth century (last quarter). Detail approx. actual size.

South Ambulatory, Westminster Abbey, London

(A) Court Style: Gesso Head imitating Cameo, from Frame of Retable. Thirteenth century (last quarter). 1 in. across.

South Ambulatory, Westminster Abbey, London

(B) Court Style: St Peter, from Retable.
Thirteenth century (last quarter). Detail approx. actual size.
South Ambulatory, Westminster Abbey, London

(A) Master Walter of Durham: The Incredulity of Thomas.
Detail of Wall Painting. *c.* 1300. 8 ft 9 in. high.
South Transept, Westminster Abbey, London

(B) Court Style (?): Richard Cœur de Lion, Tile from Chertsey Abbey.
Thirteenth century (second half). 16 in. square.
Edward VII Gallery, British Museum

(A) Worcester (?): Kings, from Fragment of
Worcester Embroideries. 1236–66. Detail 12⅞ by 10½ in.
Edward VII Gallery, British Museum

Unknown: Crucifixion, Madonna, Saints Peter and Paul, and Martyrdom of Stephen.
Clare Chasuble. Before 1284. 3 ft 3½ in. by 2 ft 8 in. *Victoria and Albert Museum, London*

London (?): Beatus Page, from Tenison Psalter. Before 1284. 9½ by 6½ in.
British Museum

in confilio impiorum: & in uia pec
catorum non ftetit: & in cathedra pe
ftilentie non fedit. Sed in lege domini uoluntas eius:
& in lege eiufmeditabit dic ac nocte.
Et erit tanquam lignum qd plan
tatum eft fecus decurfus aquaru

East Anglian: Ornamental Text Page, from Windmill Psalter. Late thirteenth century.
12⅝ by 8½ in. *Pierpont Morgan Library, New York*

East Anglian (Peterborough): Beatus Page, from Peterborough Psalter. *c.* 1300.
11¾ by 7⅝ in. *Bibliothèque Royale, Brussels*

East Anglian (Ramsey Abbey): Martyrdom of St Thomas Becket, Bible Picture from a
Psalter. *c.* 1300. 10 by 6⅝ in. *Pierpont Morgan Library, New York*

East Anglian (Peterborough or Norwich): Virgin and St Christopher, from Peterborough Psalter. Early fourteenth century. 13⅝ by 9¼ in. *Corpus Christi College, Cambridge*

East Anglian (?): Adoration of the Magi, from Queen Mary's Psalter.
Early fourteenth century. 10⅞ by 6⅞ in. *British Museum*

East Anglian (Artist of Queen Mary's Psalter): St John and the Angel, from Apocalypse.
*c.*1320–30. Miniature 5¼ by 5 in. *British Museum*

East Anglian (Norwich): Illustration to Psalm CIX, from Ormesby Psalter. *c.* 1310–25.
14⅞ by 10 in. *Bodleian Library, Oxford*

(A) East Anglian (Gorleston): Resurrected Christ appearing to David, from Gorleston Psalter. *c.* 1310–25. Detail approx. 4 in. square. *C. W. Dyson Perrins, Malvern*

(B) East Anglian (Norwich): Grotesques from Ormesby Psalter. *c.* 1310–25. Detail 3½ by 10 in. *Bodleian Library, Oxford*

Et aluis angls exunt de templo qd; i celo hiis z yxx sal
ee acuta · et aluis angle exyt de altari eq halet potestate sup
igne· et clamaut uoce magna ad eii eq halet falce acuta dicet
auttre falce tua acuta et uindemia botros umee tre qm matur
fiit uue eius·

East Anglian (Gorleston ?): Angel with the Sickle, from Apocalypse. Early fourteenth century.
14½ by 8⅛ in. *Trinity College, Dublin*

East Anglian (Midlands?): Initial with Christ blessing, Border with Grotesques, from Book of Hours. *c.* 1308. 9½ by 6 in. *Fitzwilliam Museum, Cambridge. Reproduced by permission of the Syndics*

eatus uir
qui non a
buit in con
silio impi
orum. ⁊ in
uia pceoru
non stetit:
⁊ incathe

dra pstilencie non sedit.
Sed in lege domini uoluntas eius: et in
lege eius meditabitur die ac nocte.
Et erit tamquam lignum quod planta
tum est secus decursus aquarum:quod fruc
tum suum dabit in tempore suo.
Et folium eius non defluet: et omnia q̄
cumq̄ faciet prospterabuntur.
Non sic impii non sic: sed tamquam pul
uis quem proicit uentus a facie terre.

East Anglian: Beatus Page, from St Omer Psalter. *c.* 1330. 13⅛ by 8¼ in.
British Museum

129

(B) East Anglian: 'The Three Living', from Psalter of Robert de Lisle. Before 1339. Miniature 4⅝ by 3¾ in. *British Museum*

(A) East Anglian: Ascension, from Psalter of Robert de Lisle. Before 1339. Miniature 11 by 7¼ in. *British Museum*

(A) East Anglian: Beatus Initial, from Luttrell Psalter. *c.* 1340.
Detail 7⅜ by 9⅝ in. *British Museum*

(B) East Anglian: Marginal Scene and Grotesque, from Luttrell Psalter. *c.* 1340.
Detail 7 by 9⅝ in. *British Museum*

(A) London (St Bartholomew's, Smithfield?): Fox killed by Geese, from Smithfield Decretals. Mid fourteenth century or earlier. Detail 3⅜ by 5¾ in. *British Museum*

(B) London (St Bartholomew's, Smithfield?): Monk and Lady in Stocks, from Smithfield Decretals. Mid fourteenth century or earlier. Detail 2⅜ by 6⅜ in. *British Museum*

(C) London (St Bartholomew's, Smithfield?): The King's Messenger, from Smithfield Decretals. Mid fourteenth century or earlier. Detail 2¼ by 5⅝ in. *British Museum*

sona non fit infnturo talia eis di
tura. amozes lominum caute att
huntur. t anim ad benundlenac af
fecconem fozaus inclinantur. Et
et nunc ad nictone expecedonem. et
lpoltium opprestione malaus unit
tentuil ❧ Et eos unficando eis ostm
dtis inam lenignitatem. t fami
harcatis nirtutem. eos oppzelamo
ut inim mainnenant lonoze. ad
pspium eonum romeduin. t fiaturi
cuiditum ❧ Iam et hijs potenttise
onum amozes ad nos allico. t
mozem ab eis amouere ❧ Et eos
ad pzelii delidnum fozt aiat. t osta
tes t andnees saptenter face. ❧ Et
tunc scmp tene expediunt. cum lie
aus mon quam fugere uellent ❧
Et tunc sup inimicos In leuitis in
tozram t expecconem cumnphile.

Unknown: Creation of the Birds and Animals, from Holkham Bible Picture Book.
Fourteenth century (first half). 11¼ by 8¼ in. *British Museum*

134

Canterbury (?): Christ in Majesty, Embroidered Panel. Early fourteenth century.
3 ft 3½ in. by 16½ in. *Victoria and Albert Museum, London*

Unknown: The Syon Cope. c. 1300. 9 ft 8 in. by 4 ft 10 in. *Victoria and Albert Museum, London*

Unknown: Embroidered Cope. Early fourteenth century. 10 ft 7 in. by 4 ft 10 in. *Museo Civico, Bologna*

(B) Unknown: Coronation of the Virgin, from Vatican Cope. *c.* 1300. Detail approx. 27 in. high. *Museo Sacro, Biblioteca Apostolica Vaticana, Rome*

(A) Unknown: Crucifixion, St Michael, and Angels, from Syon Cope. *c.* 1300. Detail approx. 2 ft high. *Victoria and Albert Museum, London*

138

Unknown: Scenes from the Life of the Virgin. From Embroidered Altar Dorsal. Fourteenth century (first quarter). Detail approx. 10½ by 13 in. *Victoria and Albert Museum, London*

East Anglian (?): Crucifixion with Peter and Paul, Centre Panels of Painted Retable. Early fourteenth century.
Detail 4 ft 6 in. by 3 ft. *Thornham Parva Church, Suffolk*

(B) East Anglian (?): Education of the Virgin, from Painted Panel.
c. 1325–30. Detail approx. 3 ft square. *Musée de Cluny, Paris*

(A) East Anglian (?): Nativity of Christ, from Painted Panel.
c. 1325–30. Detail approx. 3 ft square. *Musée de Cluny, Paris*

Court School (Master Thomas?): Two Unidentified Kings, Sedilia Paintings. *c.* 1308.
Each panel 9 ft by 2 ft 8 in. *South Side of Choir, Westminster Abbey, London*

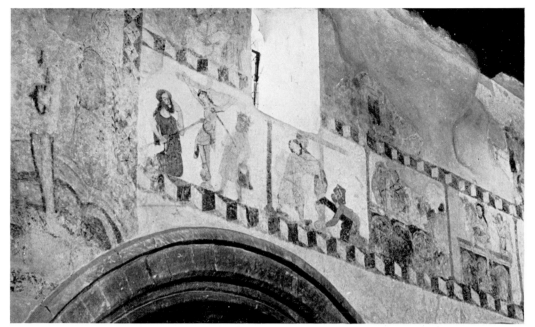

(A) Influence of Peterborough (?): Scenes from the Passion, Wall Paintings. Fourteenth century (second quarter). Approx. 22 ft. *North Wall of Nave, Peakirk*

(B) Influence of Peterborough (?): Wheel of the Five Senses, from Wall Paintings. Fourteenth century (second quarter). Detail approx. 6 ft high. *East Wall, Tower, Longthorpe Manor*

York School: Peter de Dene Stained Glass Window. *c.* 1310. Detail approx. 16 by 10 ft.
North Aisle, York Minster

(A) Unknown:
St Peter, from Great East Window.
c. 1349. Detail approx. 9 by 3 ft.
East Wall, Choir, Gloucester Cathedral

(B) Unknown:
Knight, from Clerestory Window.
c. 1344. Detail approx. 4 ft high.
Choir, Tewkesbury Abbey

York School: Coronation of the Virgin, and other Subjects,
Stained Glass Window. *c.* 1338.
54 ft 3 in. by 25 ft 3 in. *West Wall, Nave, York Minster*

Unknown: Coronation of the Virgin, and other Subjects,
Great East Window. *c.* 1349.
78 by 38 ft. *East Wall, Choir, Gloucester Cathedral*

147

(B) Italianate-English: The Angel Gabriel, from Carew Poyntz Hours. Fourteenth century (second half). $7\frac{7}{8}$ by $4\frac{5}{8}$ in. *Fitzwilliam Museum, Cambridge. Reproduced by permission of the Syndics*

(A) Italianate-English: Creation, from Psalter. Fourteenth century (second half). $8\frac{3}{8}$ by $4\frac{7}{8}$ in. *Biblioteca Apostolica Vaticana, Rome*

(A) 'Bohun MSS Style': Scenes from the Life of Christ, from a Bohun Psalter. *c.* 1370–80. Initial 4⅝ by 5¼ in. *British Museum*

(B) 'Bohun MSS Style': Christ carrying the Cross, and Adoration of the Magi, from Psalter. Late fourteenth century. Miniature 4⅞ by 2½ in. *British Museum*

(A) Italianate-English: Scenes from the Passion, from the
M. R. James Memorial Psalter. Late fourteenth century.
Miniature 4⅜ in. square. *British Museum*

(B) Italianate-English: Head.
Detail of Wall Painting, from St Stephen's
Chapel. Fourteenth century (third quarter).
Head 2⅝ in. high. *British Museum*

(C) 'Bohun MSS Style': Head, from
Bohun Psalter. *c.* 1370–80. Detail 1⅞ by 1¼ in.
British Museum

(A) Court School: Seraph from Last Judgement Wall Painting.
Fourteenth century (third quarter). Detail approx. 4 ft wide.
Chapter House, Westminster Abbey, London

(B) Italianate-English: Story of Job, Wall Painting, from St Stephen's Chapel,
Westminster. Fourteenth century (third quarter).
Detail approx. 10¾ by 12¼ in. *King Edward VII Gallery, British Museum*

English (Court School?): Richard and his Patron Saints, Left Side of Wilton Diptych. 1380–90 (?). 14½ by 10½ in. *National Gallery, London*

English (Court School?): Madonna among Angels, Right Side of Wilton Diptych.
1380–90 (?). 14½ by 10½ in. *National Gallery, London*

London (Thomas Rolf?): Crucifixion, from Lytlington Missal. 1383–4.
20¾ by 14½ in. *Westminster Abbey Library, London*

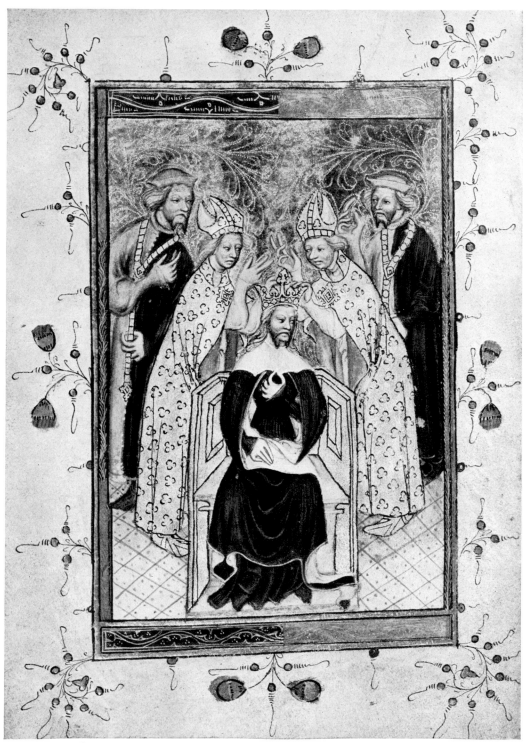

London (Westminster?): Coronation of a King, from *Liber Regalis. c.*1382.
10½ by 7 in. *Westminster Abbey Library, London*

(B) London (Whitefriars?): Birth of the Virgin, from Carmelite Missal. 1393–8. Initial 4½ in. square. *British Museum*

(A) London (Whitefriars?):
Trinity and Baptism, from Carmelite Missal. 1393–8.
Initial 4½ in. square. *British Museum*

'Johannes': View of Venice, from Marco Polo, *Li Livres du Graunt Caam.* c. 1400. Detail 9¼ by 12½ in. *Bodleian Library, Oxford*

Unknown: Kings and Prophets, from Painted Ceiling. Fourteenth century (last decade).
Single figures approx. 4 ft 9 in. high. *Lady Chapel, St Helen's Church, Abingdon*

(A) East Anglian (?): Resurrection and Ascension, from Painted Retable.
Late fourteenth century. Detail approx. 2 ft 10½ in. by 3 ft 5 in.
South Choir Aisle, Norwich Cathedral

(B) East Anglian (?): Christ before Pilate, fragment from Painted Panel.
Late fourteenth century. Detail 12¾ by 11 in. *Fitzwilliam Museum, Cambridge.*
Reproduced by permission of the Syndics

(A) Siferwas School (?): Group of Men from Last Judgement. Wall Painting. Late fourteenth century. Detail approx. 4 ft square.
Chapter House, Westminster Abbey, London

(B) Meister Bertram School (?): Apocalypse. Wall Painting. Before 1400. Detail approx. 4 ft square. *Chapter House, Westminster Abbey, London*

John Siferwas: Crucifixion, from Sherborne Missal. 1396–1407. 21 by 15 in.
Duke of Northumberland, Alnwick Castle

Unknown: Portrait of King Richard II. Fourteenth century (last decade).
7 ft by 3 ft 7 in. *South Side of Nave, Westminster Abbey, London*

John Siferwas: Lord Lovell and John Siferwas, from Lovell Lectionary. Before 1408.
Miniature 11¾ by 7¼ in. *British Museum*

163

Unknown: Sketches of Birds and Animals, from Pepysian Sketch Book. Late fourteenth century. 9$\frac{13}{16}$ by 7$\frac{13}{16}$ in. *Pepysian Library, Magdalene College, Cambridge*

John Siferwas: Detail of Marginal Border, from Sherborne Missal. 1396–1407.
Detail approx. 12½ by 9 in. *Duke of Northumberland, Alnwick Castle*

'de daer': Annunciation, from Beaufort Hours. 1401–10. 8½ by 5¼ in.
British Museum

Herman Scheerre (?): Crucifixion, Single Leaf from a Missal. Early fifteenth century.
14¾ by 10¼ in. *A. Wyndham Payne, Dartmouth*

(A) Associate of Herman Scheerre: Creation of the Animals, from Bible. *c.* 1410.
Initial approx. 3½ in. square. *British Museum*

(B) Herman Scheerre (?): Baptism of Christ, from Bible. *c.* 1410. Initial approx.
4 in. square. *British Museum*

(A) Herman Scheerre (?): Pietà,
from Book of Hours.
1405–13. 5⅞ by 4⅞ in.
Bodleian Library, Oxford

(B) Unknown: Portrait of Geoffrey
Chaucer, from Hoccleve, *De Regimine
Principum*. Early fifteenth century.
Miniature 3 by 1½ in. *British Museum*

(C) Unknown Follower of Herman Scheerre:
Prince Henry and Hoccleve, from Hoccleve,
De Regimine Principum. Before 1413.
Detail 5⅜ by 4 in. *British Museum*

Bury St Edmunds (?): Chaucer reading, from Chaucer, *Troilus and Criseyde*.
Early fifteenth century. 12½ by 8⅝ in. *Corpus Christi College, Cambridge*

John Thornton of Coventry: Apocalypse, Stained Glass Window. 1405–8.
72 by 31 ft. *East Wall, Choir, York Minster*

(B) Master Thomas of Oxford: Prophet Amos, from Jesse Window. 1380–6. Detail approx. 3 by 2 ft. *South Aisle Choir, York Minster. Formerly in Antechapel, New College, Oxford*

(A) Master Thomas (signed) of Oxford: Prophet Nathan, and Fragments including hand of Jesse, from Jesse Window. *c.*1393. Detail 3 ft 2 in. by 2 ft 1 in. *Thurbern's Chantry, West Window, Winchester College Chapel*

(A) Master Thomas of Oxford:
Prophet Zephaniah and St James, Stained Glass Panels
from Winchester College Chapel, Clerestory. *c.* 1400.
Each panel approx. 5 ft 1 in. by 1 ft 9 in.
Victoria and Albert Museum, London

(B) John Thornton of Coventry:
David, from Great East Window. 1405–8.
Detail approx. 3 ft high.
East Wall, Choir, York Minster

173

(A) Unknown: David Playing Bells, from St Omer Psalter. Fifteenth century (second quarter). Initial 3⅝ by 3¾ in. *British Museum*

(B) London (?): The Author Writing, from Christine de Pisan, *Le Livre des fays d'armes*. Dated 1434. Miniature 4⅜ by 5½ in. *British Museum*

(A) Bury St Edmunds: King Henry VI receiving the Book,
from Lydgate, *Life of St Edmund*. 1433–4.
Miniature 4 by 4⅜ in. *British Museum*

(B) Unknown: Richard the Hermit,
from *Desert of Religion*.
Fifteenth century (second quarter).
Detail 6½ by 3¾ in. *British Museum*

Bury St Edmunds (?): The Earl of Salisbury receiving the Book, from Lydgate, *The Pilgrim*. Mid fifteenth century. Miniature 7⅛ by 5 in. *British Museum*

Ihumilis thomas. C. alme Vniuersitatis Oxonie ꝑ ecclesie Ca
thedralis Wellñ Cancellari9: ad insigne dominū ꝑ beatissimū psule
Dominū thomā de bekintona Wellñ et bathoñ pontificem
seipm cū psenti opusculo ꝓ sua omnia .ꝑ

Oxford (?): Bishop Bekynton receiving the Book, from Chaundler, *Works*.
1457–61. 10⅛ by 8 in. *Trinity College, Cambridge*

177

Oxford (?): Crucifixion with Bishop as Donor, from Abingdon Missal. Dated 1461.
14⅛ by 9½ in. *Bodleian Library, Oxford*

178

Unknown: Tournament, from *Ordinances of Chivalry*. *c.* 1470. 9⅝ by 6⅝ in.
Pierpont Morgan Library, New York

Ely (?): Life of St Etheldreda, Painted Panels. *c.* 1425. Each panel 3 ft 10½ in. by 1 ft 9 in.
Society of Antiquaries, London

East Anglian: St Leonard and Female Saint, from Painted Screen,
formerly in St John Maddermarket, Norwich. 1451. 3 ft 4 in. by 2 ft 5½ in.
Victoria and Albert Museum, London

East Anglian: Two of the Nine Orders of Angels, from Painted Screen. After 1480.
Each panel approx. 2 ft 3½ in. by 7 in. *Barton Turf Church, Norfolk*

East Anglian: Apostles Philip and Paul, from Painted Screen. 1490–1510.
Each panel approx. 1 ft 7¾ in. by 5¾ in. *Cawston Church, Norfolk*

(A) William Baker (in part): Miracle of the Candle, from Wall Painting. 1479–88.
Detail 4 ft 10 in. by 6 ft 4 in. *North Wall, Eton College Chapel. (Copyright Country Life)*

(B) William Baker (in part): Healing of the Knight's Brother,
Wall Painting. 1479–88. Detail approx. 4 ft 10 in. by 3 ft.
South Wall, Eton College Chapel. (Copyright Country Life).

Unknown: Doom, Wall Painting. *c.* 1500. Approx, 22 ft wide. *Chancel Arch, St Thomas, Salisbury*

John Prudde (documented): Saints Thomas of Canterbury and Alban,
from Stained Glass Window. 1447–50. Each panel 4 ft 5 in. by 1 ft 8½ in.
East Window, Beauchamp Chapel, St Mary's Church, Warwick

'John Glazier': Saints Etheldreda, Catherine, and Sativola, from Stained Glass Window.
1440–50. Each light 6 ft 9½ in. by 1 ft 3½ in.
South Window, East Wall, Antechapel, All Souls College, Oxford

(B) Norwich School:
Donor Portrait, from Stained Glass Window.
Late fifteenth century. 2 ft 7 in. by 1 ft 6 in.
East Window, East Harling Church, Norfolk

(A) Norwich School:
Visitation, from Stained Glass Window. *c.* 1440.
Detail 2 ft 6 in. by 1 ft 8 in.
East Window, St Peter Mancroft, Norwich

(B) York School: St Christopher, from Stained Glass Window. *c.*1440–50. 4 ft 6 in. by 1 ft 10 in. *East Window, All Saints in North Street, York*

(A) York School: Miracle of St William, from St William Window. *c.*1421. Detail 2 ft 2 in. by 1 ft 6 in. *North Choir Transept, York Minster*

York School (?): Last Supper, from Stained Glass Window. *c.* 1430–40.
Detail 4 ft 6 in. by 2 ft 6 in. *East Window, Choir, Priory Church, Gt Malvern*

York School (?): Bishop Wulstan, from Founders' Window. *c.* 1460–70.
Detail 7 ft 6 in. by 2 ft 6 in. *North Clerestory, Choir, Priory Church, Gt Malvern*

London (?): Prince Arthur, from Magnificat Window. 1501. Detail
4 ft 2 in. by 2 ft. *North Transept, Priory Church, Gt Malvern*

GENERAL INDEX

Numbers in italics refer to plates. Only the more important of the notes are indexed: in such cases the page on which the note appears, and the number of the note, are given, thus: 192[54]. Manuscripts are indexed, by their location, in the separate Index of Manuscripts which follows this index: the popular names of manuscripts which are mentioned in the text are included in this index, with a cross-reference to the location and number under which they will be found in the Index of Manuscripts.

A

Abingdon (Berks), St Helen, 177–8, 192[54]; *158*

Abingdon Apocalypse, *see* London, British Museum, Add. MS. 42555

Abingdon Missal, *see* Oxford, Bodleian MS. Digby 227, and Oxford, Trinity College MS. 75

Acanthus ornament, 6, 19, 35, 36, 39, 41, 43, 53[10],[18], 54[32], 71, 184, 197, 217, 220

Ada school, 21, 22, 23, 37, 38, 43, 52

Adrian V (Pope), tomb of, 126

Ælfgyfu, 33, 48; *37a*

Ælflæda, 33, 53[11]

Ælfric, *Metrical Paraphrase of Pentateuch and Joshua*, *see* London, British Museum, Cotton MS. Claudius B.iv

Ælfwin, 48, 57[83]

Ælfwius, 57[81]

Æthelgar, Archbishop, 55[50]

Æthelred the Unready, 33

Æthelstan, 24, 33, 35, 36, 37; Psalter of, *see* London, British Museum, Cotton MS. Galba A.xviii and Oxford, Bodleian MS. Rawl. B.484

Æthelwold, 34, 42, 44

Æthelwold, Benedictional of, *see* Chatsworth, Devonshire Collection

Æthelwulf, 33

Aidan, St, 9, 10, 28[24]

Ailred, St, 75

Alban and Amphibalus, SS., Lives of, *see* Dublin, Trinity College, MS. E.I.40

Albani Psalter, *see* Hildesheim, Library of St Godehard

Aldhelm, St, 10; *De Laude Virginitatis*, *see* London, British Museum, Roy. 5 F. iii; London, Lambeth Palace Library, MS. 200

Alfonso, Prince, 139

Alfonso Psalter, *see* London, British Museum, Add. MS. 24686

Alfred, King, 33, 34, 35

Alfred Jewel, 35

Alphege, 55[52]

Altichiero, 169

Amalekite Master (Winchester Bible), 94, 95–6, 98, 99; *84b*

Amesbury Abbey, 133[51]

Amiatinus, Codex, *see* Florence, Biblioteca Laurenziana

Amos (Bury Bible) ,84–5, 88–9; *69a*

Angelic Hierarchy, 202–3, 214[20]

Anglo-Saxon Chronicle, 33

Anglo-Saxon style, 6–7, 18 ff., 34 ff.; and Irish, distinguished, 26, 218–19, 220

Animal ornament, 12, 19, 20, 22, 24, 25, 36, 53[5], 218; on embroidery, 153; *see also* Birds, biting; Grotesques, animal; Lacertines

Anne of Bohemia, 166, 173

Annunciation (Beaufort Hours), 181–2; *166*

Anselm, St, 59, 60

Antwerp, Royal Museum, votive panel, 193[79]

Apocalypse: manuscripts, 120–2, 134[70]; paintings: Clayton, 90; Kempley, 88, 90–1; Westminster Chapter House, 166, 177, 192[51-2]; *160*; *see also* Cambridge, Trinity College Library, MSS B.10.2, R.16.2; Dublin, Trinity College Library, MS. K.4.31; London, British Museum, MSS Add. 42555, Roy. 15 D. ii, Roy. 19 B. xv; London, Lambeth Palace Library, MS 209; Malvern, Dyson Perrins Collection, MS. 10; New York, Pierpont Morgan Library, MS. 524; Oxford, Bodleian Library, MSS Auct. D.4.17, Douce 180; Paris, Bibliothèque Nationale, MS. 403

Apocrypha Drawings, Master of the (Winchester Bible), 94–5, 97 f., 104[70]; *83a*

Aquitaine, 91, 103[49]

Aratus, *see* London, British Museum, MSS Harl. 647, Harl. 2506

Ardagh Chalice, 27[7]

Armagh, Book of, *see* Dublin, Trinity College Library, MS. 52

Arnolfo di Cambio, 125, 126

Arthur, Prince, 210; *192*

Arundel, Thomas, Archbishop of Canterbury, 165

Arundel Psalters, *see* London, British Museum, MSS Arundel 60, Arundel 155

Ascension, 148; *64*, *130a*

Ascoli Piceno, cope, 151, 152

Ashridge Priory, 161[9]

Ashton (S. Devon), 215[23]

Asser, 33

Astley, Sir John, 200

Athelard, John, 190[18]

Athelstan, King, see Æthelstan

Augustine, St (of Canterbury), 9

Augustine, St, Gospels of, see Cambridge, Corpus Christi College Library, MS. 286

Augustine, St, Psalter of, see London, British Museum, MS. Cott. Vesp. A.i

Augustine, St (of Hippo), Commentary on the Psalms, see Durham, Cathedral Library, MS. B.ii.13; Oxford Bodleian MS. 269

Augustine, St, De Civitate Dei, see Florence, Biblioteca Laurenziana, MS. Plut. xii, 17

Aureus, Codex, see Stockholm, Royal Library

Avanzi, 169

Avignon, 168

B

Babewyns, 161[15]

Baker, William, 206, 207

Balfour Ciborium, 104[80]

Barking Abbey, 10, 49

Barton Turf, 202–3, 214[19]; 182

Bayeux Cathedral Library, MSS 57 and 58, 72[8]

Bayeux Tapestry, 59, 67, 68–9, 73[38-41]; 47

'Beatus' page in Psalters, 39, 41, 51, 63, 71, 78–9, 106, 111, 112, 113, 115, 116, 132[29], 139, 140, 144, 146, 147, 219; 21a, 21b, 58, 62a, 94a, 100, 118, 120, 129, 131a

Beauchamp, Henry de, Duke of Warwick, 215[37]

Beauchamp, Richard, Earl of Warwick, 205, 210, 214[12], 215[49]

Beaufort, John, Earl of Somerset, 165, 181

Beaufort Hours, see London, British Museum, MS. Roy. 2 A. xviii

Beaufort Hours, Master of, 192[65], 193[73]

Beauneveu, André, 191[43]

Becket, see Thomas Becket

Bede, St (Venerable), 10, 27[11]; Commentary on the Apocalypse, see Cambridge, St John's College Library, MS. H 6; Ecclesiastical History, see London, British Museum, MS. Cotton Tib. C.ii; Life of St Cuthbert, see Cambridge, Corpus Christi College, MS. 183; London, British Museum, MS. Add. 39943; Oxford, University College Library, MS. 165

Bedford, John, Duke of, 182, 195, 214[1]

Bedford Hours, see London, British Museum, MS. Add. 42131

Bedford Missal, see London, British Museum, MS. Add. 18850

Bedford Psalter, see Bedford Hours

Bekynton, Bishop, 199; 177

Belgae, 9

Bell-founders' Window, see York Minster

Benedict Biscop, St, 10, 17

Bertram, Meister, 176, 192[49, 52]

Berzé-la-Ville, St Hugh's Chapel, 103[54]

Bestiary, 99–100, 112, 141, 222; 88; see also Aberdeen, University Library, MS. 24; Cambridge, Corpus Christi College, MS. 53; Cambridge, University Library, MSS Kk.4.25, Ll.4.26; London, British

Museum, MSS Harl. 4751, Roy. 12 C. xix; New York, Pierpont Morgan Library, MS. 81; Oxford, Bodleian Library, MSS 764, Ashmole 1511, Douce 151, Laud Misc. 247

Bewcastle Cross, 27[17], 30[46]

Bible: Charles the Bald, First Bible of, 53[12, 14], 73[14]; French Pocket, 133[41], 222; 'St Paul-outside-the Walls', of, 101[9]; see also Amiatinus, Codex; Bury Bible; Carilef Bible; Dover Bible; Lambeth Bible; Lothian Bible; Manerius Bible; Pudsey Bible; Robert de Bello, Bible of; William of Devon, Bible of; William de Hales, Bible of; Winchester Bible, Cambridge, University Library, Dd.1.14; London, British Museum (Big Bible), Roy. 1 E. ix; Malvern, Dyson Perrins Collection, MS. 5; Paris, Bibliothèque Nationale, MSS lat. 11534–5, 16743–6

Bible pictures (preceding Psalter), 106, 129; see also Baltimore, Walter Gallery, MS. 500; Cambridge, Emmanuel College, MS. iii.3.21; Cambridge, Fitzwilliam Museum, MSS 330, 370; Cambridge, St. John's College, MS. K.26; London, British Museum MSS Add. 37472, 47682; London, Victoria and Albert Museum, MS. 661; Malvern, Dyson Perrins Collection MS. 1; New York, Pierpont Morgan Library, MSS 302, 521, 619; Winchester Psalter; York Psalter

Biblia Pauperum, 211

Birds, biting, 16, 28[25], 29[34], 35

Black Death, 138

Blackfriars (London), 139

Blanche of Savoy, Hours of, 190[15]

Blois Gospels, 101[9]

Bobbio, 9

Boethius, see Oxford, Bodleian Library, MS. Auct. F.6.5

Bohemia, 8, 160, 166, 173, 175, 189[3], 191[32, 37, 44], 225

Bohun, Eleanor de, Duchess of Gloucester, 165, 169, 189[10]

Bohun, Humphrey de, 7th Earl of Hereford, 165, 168

Bohun, Mary de, 168

Bohun family, 8, 161[6]; see also Bohun MSS

Bohun manuscripts, 167, 168–9, 189[10]

Bohun Psalter, see Cambridge, Fitzwilliam Museum, Riches Collection; Copenhagen, Thottsammlung, MS. 547; Edinburgh, National Library, MS. Adv. 18.6.5; London, British Museum, MS. Egerton 3277; Oxford, Bodleian Library, MS. Auct. D.4.4; Oxford, Exeter College Library, MS. 47; Vienna, Nationalbibliothek, Cod. 1826*

Bologna cope, 151, 152; 137

Bosworth Psalter, see London, British Museum, MS. Add. 37517

Bovo, Abbot of St Bertin, 72[9]

Bradford on Avon, 54[31]

Brailes, Upper and Lower, 133[43]

Brailes, W. de, 3, 106, 133[43], 222; Bible picture leaves, 98; 99a, 99b; Psalters, 99c; see also Kew, Surrey, Sir Sydney Cockerell MS.; Oxford, New College, MS. 322; Hours, Malvern, Dyson Perrins Collection, 4

Bromholm Psalter, *see* Oxford, Bodleian Library, MS. Ashmole 1523

Bruges, 8, 196, 210, 211

Brussels, Musée Cinquantenaire, 153

Bruynyng, Robert, Abbot, 192[56]

Burgundy, 8, 166, 202

Bury St Edmunds, 7, 50, 75, 81, 92, 139, 143, 186, 198, 199

Bury Bible, *see* Cambridge, Corpus Christi College, MS. 2

Bury St Edmunds, Psalter, 193[86]

Butler Bowdon cope, 152, 153

Byzantine art and influence, 7, 8, 19, 35, 64, 76, 79, 83, 84, 86, 93, 123

C

C-scrolls, 28[28]

Cabbage leaf, serrated, 140

Cædmon, *see* Oxford, Bodleian Library, MS. Junius 11

Calais, Siege of, 159

Calendars, 132[36]; occupational, 46–7, 56[59], 66; *34*

Calligraphic ornament, 6, 12 ff., 24

Cambridge, Fitzwilliam Museum, 706, 707; painted panels, 177; *159b*

Cambridge, King's College Chapel, 201, 212, 214[3], 216[53]

Cannon, 150

Canon Tables, 11, 16, 20, 22, 23, 27[4], 43; *6*

Cantelupe, Walter de, *see* Walter de Cantelupe

Canterbury, 6, 7, 10, 18, 19–20, 45, 52, 72, 75, 106, 109, 118, 219, 220; glass at, 2, 7, 109–10, 113, 132[39]; *93, 95a, 97*; Christ Church, 24, 44, 45, 59, 64–5, 76; St Anselm's Chapel, 88; *76*; St Augustine's Abbey, 20, 47, 66, 67, 76, 143; St Gabriel's Chapel, 88–9

Canterbury Psalter, *see* London, British Museum, MS. Cotton Vesp. A. i

Carew-Poyntz Hours, *see* Cambridge, Fitzwilliam Museum, MS. J.48

Carilef, William de, 59, 60, 69; Manuscripts of, 69–71; *see also* Durham Cathedral Library

Carlisle Cathedral, choir stalls, 110, 201

Carmelite Missal, *see* London, British Museum, Add. MSS 29704–5

Carmelites, 133[59]

Carolingian Renaissance, 1, 6, 34

Cassiodorus, *Commentary on the Psalms, see* Durham Cathedral Library, MS. B.ii.30

Catalonia, 131[11]

Cathach, 27[12]; of St Columba, 12–13; *see* Dublin, Royal Irish Academy

Catherine, St, 158

Cats and Rats, 24, 144–5

Cavallini, Pietro, 126, 135[94]

Cawston (Norfolk), 203; *183*

Cefalù, 104[83]

Celtic, *see* Irish

Ceolfrid, 10, 29[30]

Cerne, Book of, *see* Cambridge, University Library, MS. Ll.i.10

Chad, St, 10; Gospels of, *see* Lichfield Cathedral Library

Chalgrove (Oxon), 155–6

Chartres, 132[39]

Chaucer, Geoffrey, 1; portraits of, 185–6; *Troilus and Criseyde, see* Cambridge, Corpus Christi College, MS. 61

Chaundler MSS, *see* Cambridge, Trinity College Library, MS. R.14.5; Oxford, New College, MS. 288

Chertsey Abbey, tiles, 129; *116b*

Chester Beatty Hours, 182

Chester-le-Street, 35

Chichele, Henry, Archbishop of Canterbury, 165, 182, 193[69]

Chichele Breviary, *see* London, Lambeth Palace Library, MS. 69

Chichester Roundel, 117, 128, 133[57]; *105*

Christ Betrayed (Book of Kells), 23

Christ Enthroned (Altar frontal), 152; *135*

Christina (anchoress), 102[21]

Christine de Pisan, *Le Livre des fays d'armes, see* London, British Museum, MS. Harl. 4605

Christopher, St, 201; *see also* Peakirk

Chronica Maiora, see Cambridge, Corpus Christi College Library, MS. 26

Ciboria, 132[27]

Cistercians, 75, 76, 101[4]

Clare Chasuble, 128, 151; *117*

Clayton, 90; *75h*

Clement IV, Pope, tomb of, 126

Cluny, 33; Cluniac painting, 89, 103[54]

Cluny, Musée de, painted panels, 154; *141a*

Cnut, *see* Knut

Cologne, 8, 166; cathedral, choir stalls, 160

Colour, use in MSS, 2, 11, 14, 22–3, 36, 41, 86, *et passim*; use in medieval painting, 3

Columba, St, Psalter of, 12–13, 27[13]; *see also* Cathach

Comestor, Petrus, *Historia Scholastica, see* London, British Museum, MS. Roy. 3 D. vi

Conques, Sainte-Foy, 90, 103[58]

Continent, *see* Europe

Coombes (Sussex), 103[61]

Copes, 151 ff.

Coptic influence, 27[7, 17], 53[7]

Corbie, 65

Coronation Oath-books, 54[19]

Coronation of Virgin, *see* Virgin

Cosmati work, 126

Court style, 8, 105, 107, 123 ff.

Coventry, 188

Crécy, battle of, 159

Croughton (Northants), 155–6

Croyland Abbey, 51, 75, 110

Crucifixion, 16, 21; *see also* Abingdon Missal, *178*; All Souls Psalter, *102*; Bologna Cope, *137*; Dartmouth (Scheerre), *167*; Evesham Psalter, *103*; Florence of Worcester, *60*; Harleian Psalter, *30*; Lytlington Missal, *154*, New Minster Offices, *37b*; Sherborne Missal, *161*; Sherborne Pontifical, *24*; Syon Cope, *138a*; Thornham Parva Retable, *140*; Weingarten Gospels, *43*; Winchester Psalter, *52, 53*

Crundale sword pommel, 28[18]

Crusades, 7, 76

Cuerdon Psalter, see New York, Pierpont Morgan Library, MS. 756

Cul Dremhne, Battle of, 27[13]

Cutbercht Gospels, see Vienna, Nationalbibliothek, MS. lat. 1224

Cuthbert, St, 9, 36, 131[26]; Life of, see Bede, Carlisle Cathedral, and York Glass; Vestments, see Durham Vestments

D

David, 18, 62, 79, 96, 196–7; *10, 40, 50, 51, 58, 62a, 86, 118, 120, 131a, 173b, 174a*

De Laude Virginitatis (Aldhelm), see Aldhelm

Deerhurst, glass, 157

Dene, Peter de (York Minster), 158, 164[96]; *144*

Dene, Richard, 209

Desert of Religion, see London, British Museum, MS. Cotton Faust. B.vi

Despenser, Henry, Bishop of Norwich, 165, 176

Despenser, Isabella, 210

Despenser, Margaret, 215[42]

Development, periods of, 6

Dimma, Book of, see Dublin, Trinity College, MS. 59

Dooms, 201, 203–4

Dorsals, altar, 152, 153; *139*

Dots, red, 12, 14, 25

Douai Psalter, 145, 146

Double-faced draperies, 148

Dover Bible, see Cambridge, Corpus Christi College Library, MS. 3–4

Drogo, Sacramentary of, 30[47], 42, 65

Dubečeker Altarpiece, see Prague

Dublin Apocalypse, see Dublin, Trinity College Library, MS. K.4.31

Duccio, 126, 135[94]

Dunstan, St, 34, 38, 54[33]

Dunstan Gospels, see London, British Museum, MS. Roy. 1 D. ix

Dunstan Pontifical, see Paris, Bibliothèque Nationale, MS. lat. 943

Durham, 7, 60, 72, 75, 110, 111, 131[26]

Durham Book, see Lindisfarne Gospels

Durham Ritual, see Durham Cathedral Library, MS. A.iv.19

Durham Vestments, 35–6; *18*

Durrow, Book of, see Dublin, Trinity College Library, MS. 57 (A.4.5)

E

Eadfrith, 10, 13

Eadwine, 85, 86; *71*

Eadwine Psalter, see Cambridge, Trinity College Library, MS. R.17.1

East Anglia, screens, 201 ff.; glass, 204; MS. illumination, 8, 137 ff., 166, 169, 219–20, 225

East Harling, 204; *188b*

Ebbo Gospels, 61, 101[9]

Echternach, 10; Echternach Gospels, see Paris, Bibliothèque Nationale, MS. lat. 9389

Edgar, King, 33, 42; *25*

Edmund, Life of St, see New York, Pierpont Morgan Library, MS. 736

Edmund (Rich), St, 105

Edmund, Earl of Cornwall, 161[9]

Edward the Confessor, St, 33, 59, 105, 122, 135[80, 90], 170, 171

Edward the Elder, 33

Edward I, King, 105, 122, 137

Edward II, King, 137

Edward III, King, 137, 150, 165, 170

Edward IV, King, 195, 196

Edward V, King, 195

Egbert, King, 9

Egerton Genesis, see London, British Museum, MS. Egerton 1894

Ellendun, Battle of, 9

Ely, St Etheldreda's, 44, 202

Embroidery, see Bayeux Tapestry, Cuthbert vestments, and opus anglicanum

Enamelling, 9

Enamels, see Alfred Jewel, Ciboria, Last Judgement Plaque, Sutton Hoo Burial

Erasmus, St, Martyrdom of, see London, Society of Antiquaries

Estoire de Seint Aedward le Rei, see Cambridge, University Library, MS. Ee.3.59

Etchmiadzin Gospels, 23

Ethelbert, King, 155

Etheldreda, St, panels, see London, Society of Antiquaries

Ethelwald, Bishop, 25, 31[77]

Eton College Chapel, frescoes, 201, 206–7; *184*; glass, 216[59]

Europe, influence from, 3–8, 36–7, 38–9, 52, 60, 75–6, 78 ff., 84, 98, 104[83], 114, 160, 161[4], 166 ff., 195 ff., 223 f.; opus anglicanum in, 153

Eusebian Canon Tables, see Canon Tables

Evangelists, symbols and pictures of, 11, 17, 21, 22–3, 25, 26[3], 28[29], 61; *2, 7a, 8, 9, 11, 14, 16, 17, 36, 45, 48a, 49b, 63, 70*; see also under Gospels and names of Evangelists

Evesham Psalter, see London, British Museum, MS. Add. 44874

Ezra, 15, 29[31]; *7b*

F

Fahan Mura, 27[17]

Fairford, 201, 211, 212, 214[3], 216[52]

Faith, St, see Westminster Abbey

Fall of Man (W. de Brailes), 114; *98*

Fitton, Alice de, 162[44]

Fitzwarin Psalter, see Paris, Bibliothèque Nationale, MS. lat. 765

'Five Sisters', see York Minster

Flanders, influence of, 8, 196, 200 ff., 203, 204, 223; see also Low Countries

Fleury, 34, 42

Floreffe Bible, 103[48]

Florence of Worcester, Chronicle, *see* Oxford, Corpus Christi College Library, MS. 157

Flower, Barnard, 212

Foliage ornament, 137

Forms of medieval art, 2

Forthampton Court (Tewkesbury), 164[83]

Foulkard, 72[9]

Fountains, 75

France, influence of, 166–7, 195 ff., 221–2; *see also* Europe

Franco-Saxon style, 6

Fresco, 2–3

Frithestan, Bishop of Winchester, 33, 53[11]

Fromond Chapel, *see* Winchester, Fromond Chapel

Fulda, 37, 54[23]

Fulk, Archbishop of Reims, 34, 56[62]

G

Gelder, William, Duke of, 166

Gelderland, 8

Genesis Initial, Master of the (Winchester Bible), 94, 95, 97, 98, 104[83]; *84a*; Genesis scenes, *61*, *75a*, *92*, *96*, *98*, *101*, *129*, *134*, *148a*, *168a*

German merchants, 75

Germany, 189[3]; North, 176, 177, 192[49, 52]

Gero, Sacramentary of, 55[45]

Gilbert (painter at Eton), 206

Giovanni da Como, 190[15]

Glass, grisaille, 101[4], 158; millefiori, 27[7]; making, 3; stained, 2, 3, 7, 109–10, 132[39], 157 ff., 186, 196, 204 ff.; *see also* Cambridge, King's College Chapel; Canterbury; Deerhurst; East Harling; Eton College Chapel; Fairford; Gloucester; Lincoln; London, Victoria and Albert Museum (Winchester panels); Malvern (Gt); Long Melford; Norwich, St Peter Mancroft; Oxford; Tewkesbury; Warwick, St Mary's; Wells; Westminster Palace; St Stephen's Chapel; Winchester College Chapel; York

Glastonbury, 34, 38, 54[33]

Glazier, John, 205; *see also* Flower, Barnard; Hone, Galyon; Nicholson, John; Prudde, John; Thomas, Master; Thornton, John; Symondes, Symond; Utyman, John; Williamson, Francis

Gloucester, Duke of, *see* Humphrey

Gloucester, 112; Cathedral, glass, 157, 159–60; *145a*, *147*

Godescalc Gospels, 21, 30[60]

Godfrey, Abbot of Croyland, 161[13]

Gold, use in MSS, 2

Golden Gospels, of St Gall, 73[14]

Gorleston Psalter, *see* Malvern, Dyson Perrins Collection, MS. 13

Gospels, 1, 10, 191[37], Etchmiadzin Gospels, 23; Godescalc Gospels, 21, 30[60]; Lorsch Gospels, 55[45]; Poussay Gospels, 55[46]; Rabula Gospels, 22; York Gospels, 56[66]; *see also* Armagh, Book of; Cerne, Book of; Cutbercht Gospels; Dimma, Book of; Durrow, Book of; Echternach Gospels; Grim-

bald Gospels; Johann von Troppau, Gospels of; Lindisfarne Gospels; MacDurnan Gospels; Mac-Regal Gospels; Mostyn Gospels; Mulling, Book of; St. Augustine's Gospels (Cambridge, Corpus Christi College Library, MS. 286); St Chad, Gospels of (Lichfield Cathedral Library); St Margaret, Gospels of; Weingarten Gospels; *see also* Cambridge, Pembroke College Library, MSS 120, 301, 302; Trinity College Library, MSS B.53, B.10.4; Durham Cathedral Library MS. A.ii.17; London British Museum, MSS Cott. Tib. A.ii, Roy. 1 D.ix, Roy. 1 E. vi; Monte Cassino, Abbey Library, BB.437,439; New York, Pierpont Morgan Library, MSS 708, 777; Rome, Biblioteca Apostolica Vaticana, MS. Barb. lat. 570; St Gall, Abbey Library, MS. 51

Gothic Majesty, Master of the (Winchester Bible), 94, 97, 107; *85b*

Gothic style, 7–8, 106 ff.

Gower, John, 1

Grandison Hours, *see* Beaufort Hours

Grandison, John, Bishop of Exeter, 137

Greenfield Nunnery (Lincs.), 162[28]

Gregory I, St, *Moralia*, *see* Cambridge, Emmanuel College Library, MS. 112; *Pastoral Care*, 33; *see also* Oxford, Bodleian Library, MS. Hatton 60

Grimbald, 33, 34, 42

Grimbald Gospels, *see* London, British Museum, MS. Add. 34890

Grisaille painting, 189[9], 206

Grotesques, 100, 112–13, 129, 132–4, 138, 139, 140, 144, 158

Guthlac, St, 10, 110

Guthlac Roll, *see* London, British Museum, MS. Harl. Y.6

H

Haaren, Seminary, Crucifixion in Missal, 193[79]

Hanseatic art, 192[49]

Hardham, 89–90; *75a*

Hempstead, 202

Henry I, 59, 75

Henry II, 75, 94

Henry III, 105, 123, 161[1]

Henry IV, 165, 166

Henry V, 165, 166, 185

Henry VI, 195

Henry VI, Psalter of, *see* London, British Museum, MS. Cotton Dom. A.xvii

Henry VII, 195; Chapel of, 212

Henry of Blois, Bishop of Winchester, 75, 93

Henry of Chichester, Missal of, *see* Manchester, John Rylands Library, MS. Lat. R.24

Herbert of Bosham, 132[28]

Hereford, 64

Hiberno-Saxon style, 6, 9 ff.

Historia Anglorum, *see* London, British Museum, MS. Roy. 14 C. vii

Hitchin, Escutcheon from hanging bowl, 28[19]

Hitda Codex (Darmstadt, Landesbibliothek, Cod. 1640), 102[20, 37]

Hoccleve, 1; *De Regimine Principum, see* London, British Museum, MSS Arundel 38, Harl. 4866

Holand, Margaret de, 181

Holbein, Hans, 213

Holkham Bible Picture Book, *see* London, British Museum, MS. Add. 47682

Hone, Galyon, 212

Horae, *see* Hours, Books of

Hours, Books of, 106; *see also* Beaufort Hours; Bedford Hours; Cambridge, Fitzwilliam Museum, MS. 242; Cambridge, Trinity College Library, MS. B.ii.7; Carew-Poyntz Hours; Chester Beatty Hours; London, British Museum, MSS Egerton 1151; Maastricht Hours; Malvern, Dyson Perrins Collection, MS. 4; Oxford, Bodleian Library, MS. Lat. liturg. f.2; Taymouth Hours

Howard, Sir William, 162[44]

Hugh of Lincoln, St, 94

Hugh of St Albans, Master, 170, 190[17]

'Hugo pictor', 70

Hugo, Master, 84, 85

Human figure, Hiberno-Saxon treatment, 26; 12th century treatment, 101; *et passim*

Humphrey, Duke of Gloucester, 146, 195, 196, 214[1]

Huntingfield Psalter, *see* New York, Pierpont Morgan Library, MS. 43

Hyde Abbey, *see* Winchester

I

Illuminators, identity of, 3; *see also,* Brailes, William de; Hugo Pictor; Hugo, Master; Johannes; Paris, Matthew; Rolf, Thomas; Scheerre, Hermann; Siferwas, John

Ingeborg Psalter, *see* Chantilly, Musée Condé, MS. 169

Inhabited scroll, 36

Initials, decorated, 36, 53[5], 112, 132[31], *et passim*; historiated, 19, 45, 55[51], 60, 65, 67, 106, 145; *28b, 40, et al.*; human figures in, 65-6

Interlace, Celtic, 6, 12, 27[17]

Iona, 9, 10, 21

Ireland, 9

Irish and Anglo-Saxon traits, distinction, 26, 219, 220

Irish Manuscripts, 20-4

Irish monks, 10-11

Italian influence, 8, 125, 126, 127, 144, 148, 162[32, 34, 35], 163[46], 166-9, 172-3, 176, 178, 189[4, 8], 224-5

Italy, opus anglicanum in, 153

J

James Psalter, *see* London, British Museum, MS. Add. 44949

Jarrow, 10, 15, 18

Jerome, St, Commentary on Isaiah, *see* Oxford, Bodleian Library, MS. 717

Jerzen Epitaph, 191[44]

Jesse Tree, in embroideries, 128, 151, 153; *116a*; in glass, 132[38], 186-7; *172*; in manuscripts, 81, 139; *129*

Johann von Troppau, Gospels of, 191[37]

Johannes (of Bodleian MS. 264), 192[62]

Johannis de Thaneto, 153, 163[69]; *135*

John, King, 105

John, St, symbol of, 11; *2b; see also* Evangelists

John of Bridlington, St, 192[64]

John Chrysostom, St, Sermons, *see* Hereford Cathedral Library, MS. O.5.xi

John XXII, Pope, 153

John of Gaunt, 165

John of Northampton, 170

Judith, 33, 34

Judith of Flanders, 57[81], 61

K

Kells, Book of, *see* Dublin, Trinity College Library, MS. A.1.6

Kempley (Glos), 88, 90-1; *74*

Knotted ornament, 27[17]

Knut, 33, 48; *37a*

L

Labours of the months, 157; *see also* Calendars, occupational

Lacertines, 11-12, 16, 29[34]; *1*

Lacy, Edmund de, Earl of Lincoln, 115

Lambeth Bible, *see* London, Lambeth Palace Library, MS. 3

Lancelot du lac, see London, British Museum, MS. Roy. 20 D. iv

Lanfranc, 59, 60, 64, 66

Langham, Archbishop Simon, 165

Lapworth Missal, *see* Oxford, Corpus Christi College, MS. 394

Last Judgement Plaque (London, Victoria and Albert Museum), 104[67]

Last Judgement: Tewkesbury window, 159; W. de Brailes, 115; Westminster Chapter House, 166, 170, 177; *151a, 160a*

La Tène art, 9

Leaping Figures, Master of the (Winchester Bible), 94, 95, 97, 104[70, 78]; *83b*

Leningrad Bestiary, 100

Lentate, 191[27]

Leofric, 73[23]

Leofric Missal, *see* Oxford, Bodleian Library, MS. 579

Leonard, St, 202

Lewes Priory, 89, 103[54]

Liber Regalis, see London, Westminster Abbey Library

Liber Vitae (New Minster), *see* London, British Museum, MS. Stowe, 944

Life of Christ; Nativity Cycle, *see 26, 31, 67, 90b, 123, 141, 166, 188a*; Passion Cycle, *67, 109b, 149, 150a, 159, 168b, 169b, 190; see also* Crucifixion and Ascension

Lincoln, glass at, 132[39]

Lindesey, Robert de, Abbot of Peterborough, 112, 132[33]; *see also* Cambridge, Fitzwilliam Museum, MS. 12; London, Society of Antiquaries, MS. 59 (Lindesey Ps.)

Lindisfarne, 9, 10

Lindisfarne Gospels, see London, British Museum, MS. Cotton Nero D.iv

Line drawing technique, 2, 6, 7, 26, 46, et passim

Lisle Psalter, see London, British Museum, MS. Arundel 83

Livy, Paris, Bibliothèque Sainte-Geneviève, MS. fr. 1.1, 214[1]

Llanalet Pontifical, see Rouen, Bibliothèque Publique, MS. A.27

Lobbes, Abbey of, 54[19]

Lombardy, 169, 190[17]

London style, 3

London, British Museum, see Chertsey Abbey tiles; Manuscripts; St Stephen's Chapel frescoes; Sutton Hoo Burial, and Worcester Embroideries

London, National Gallery, see Wilton Diptych

London, Society of Antiquaries: Martyrdom of St Erasmus, 214[3]; Panel portraits of kings, 214[3]; St Etheldreda panels, 202, 214[16]; 180

London, Tower of, Byward Tower wall paintings, 190[21]

London, Victoria and Albert Museum: altar dorsal, 153; 139; ciboria, 132[27]; glass from Winchester, 187–8; 173a; panels from Norwich, St John Maddermarket, 202; 181; pyx, 161[19]; opus anglicanum, 153; Steeple Aston cope, 152; Warwick chasuble, 215[37]; Warwick (Balfour) ciborium, 104[80]; see Clare chasuble; see also Manuscripts and Winchester College Glass

Long Melford, 204

Longinus, 16, 21

Longthorpe (Northants), 155, 157; 143b

Lorsch Gospels, 55[45]

Lothaire Gospels, Paris, Bibliothèque Nationale, Lat. 266, 42

Lothian Bible, see New York, Pierpont Morgan Library, MS. 791

Louis, St, 105; Psalter of, 130[1]

Lovell, Lord, 180

Lovell Lectionary, see London, British Museum, MS. Harl. 7026

Low Countries, 166, 175, 177, 184, 204, 213

Luke, portraits or symbols of, 17, 20, 25, 64, 87, 103[48]; 16, 17

Lumière as lais, La, and Apocalypse, see London, British Museum, MS. Roy. 15 D. ii

Luttrell Psalter, see London, British Museum, MS. Add. 42130

Lydgate, John, 1; Metrical Life of St Edmund, see London, British Museum, MS. Harl. 2278; The Pilgrim, see London, British Museum, MS. Harl. 4826

Lyons, Textile Museum, orphrey, 153

Lytlington, Nicholas, Abbot of Westminster, 3, 165, 173

Lytlington Missal, see London, Westminster Abbey Library

M

Maastricht, Book of Hours, Stowe MS. 17, 160, 223

Mabel of Bury St Edmunds, 128, 161[1]

MacDurnan, Gospels of, see London, Lambeth Palace Library

MacRegal Gospels, see Oxford, Bodleian Library, MS. Auct. D.2.19

Majesty, see 20b, 25, 28, 37a, 89, 109a, 135

Malmesbury, 49, 75

Malvern (Great), Priory, 188, 196, 208–10, 215[48]; 190–2

Manerius Bible, see Paris, Bibliothèque Sainte-Geneviève, MS. 8–10

Margaret, Gospels of St, see Oxford, Bodleian Library, MS. Lat. liturg. f.5

Mark, St, Portraits and symbols of, 17, 20, 21; 9; see also Evangelists

Martin, St, 118

Martini, Simone, 181

Matthew, St, Portraits and symbol of, 11, 15, 17, 19a, 23, 25, 87; 2a, 7a, 11, 14; see also Evangelists

Medallions, glass, 113–14, 132[39], 158, 164[95], 220; 95a, 97

Meditations of St Bonaventura, see Cambridge, Trinity College Library, MS. B.10.12

Mediterranean influence, 15–16

Melorus, St, 133[51]

Mendham Priory (Suffolk), 131[10]

Mendicant Orders, 105, 133[59]

Mercia, 9, 24, 25, 35

Metalwork, 9, see enamels

Methuselah, 110, 218; 93

Michael, St, 67, 83, 152, 190[21]; miniature, see Berlin, Staatliches Museum, MS. K.1.672; see also 46b, 68b, 112, 136, 138a

Middle Ages, dates of, 1

Milemete, Walter de, see Walter de Milemete

Miniatures, 25; inserted, 109, 131[16], 133[46]

Mitford, Richard, Bishop of Salisbury, 165, 192[56]

Mocchirola, 191[27]

Models, 54[27]

Moklebust, 27[7]

Monkwearmouth, see Wearmouth

Montacute, Thomas, Earl of Salisbury, 199

Monte Cassino Gospels, see Monte Cassino, Abbey Library

Morgan Leaf, see New York, Pierpont Morgan Library, MS. 619

Morgan Leaf, Master of the (Winchester Bible), 94, 96, 97, 98, 101, 104[80]; 85a, 86

Mosaics, 85, 88

Mulbarton, 146

Mulling, Book of, see Dublin, Trinity College Library, MS. 69

Munich Psalter, see Munich, Staatsbibliothek, Cod. lat. 835

N

Naples, San Giovanni in Fonte, 73[24]

Netherlands, see Low Countries

Neumarkt, Johann von, 160, 191[32]

Neville, Richard, Earl of Warwick, 195

New Minster Abbey, see Winchester

New Minster Charter, *see* London, British Museum, MS. Cotton Vesp. A.viii

Newport (Essex), chest-lid, 163⁷⁸

New York, Metropolitan Museum, chasuble, 152, 153

Nicholas IV, Pope, 151, 152

Nicholson, John, 212

Noah's Ark, 52; *44*

Normandy, 60, 71, 109

Normans, arrival of, 7, 59 ff.

Northern Renaissance, 213

Northumbria, 9, 10, 15–19

Norwich, 139, 140, 143, 145, 196, 204; retable, 176–7, 179, 191⁴⁷; *159a*

Norwich, St John Maddermarket, 202; *181*

Norwich, St Michael-at-Plea, 177

Norwich, St Peter Mancroft, glass, 204; *188a*

Nottingham, 146

O

Oderisi, Pietro, 126

Odilo, St, Abbot of Cluny, 33

Odo, St, Abbot of Cluny, 34

Odo, Bishop of Bayeux, 68

Offa, 9

Offas, Lives of the, see London, British Museum, MS. Cotton Nero D.1

Opus anglicanum, 2, 8, 36, 127–8, 137, 138, 151–4; 161¹, 215³⁷; *116, 117, 135, 136, 137, 138, 139*

Ordinances of Chivalry, *see* New York, Pierpont Morgan Library, MS. 775

Ormesby, Robert of, 143

Ormesby Psalter, *see* Oxford, Bodleian Library, MS. Douce 366

Orphreys, 215³⁷

Oslo Museum: St Peter (attr. Matthew Paris), 134⁶³

Oswald, St, of Worcester, 34

Oswald, King, 9

Oswy, 9

Otto I, Emperor, 37

Outline, coloured and tinted, 39–41, 46, 76; drawings, 13th century, 118 ff., 218, 226; *see also* line drawing

Oxford, 3, 133⁴³; glass painting at, 186, 204–5; All Souls College, 205; *187*; painting at Christ Church Chapter House, 115; New College, 166; glass at, 186–7, 194⁹²; *see also* York Minster

P

Padua, 169

Painted Chamber, *see* Westminster Palace

Painter-Glaziers, 3

Painters, *see* Baber, William; Gilbert; Hugh of St Albans; Peter, Master; Simon of Colchester; Thomas, Master; Walter of Colchester; Walter of Durham

Palermo, Cappella Palatina, 85, 103⁵³

Panel paintings, 2, 200, 201; *see also* Abingdon, Barton Turf; Cambridge, Fitzwilliam Museum, 706,

707; Carlisle Cathedral; Cawston; Forthampton; London, Society of Antiquaries; Norwich Cathedral; Norwich, St John Maddermarket; Norwich, St Michael-at-Plea; Oslo Museum; Paris, Musée de Cluny; Ranworth; Thornham Parva; Westminster Abbey; Wilton Diptych; *see also* Rood screens

Paris, 8, 114, 181; Musée de Cluny, Altar frontal, 154; *141*; Sainte-Chapelle, 166

Paris, Matthew, 3, 8, 106, 107, 118–20, 129, 130⁸, 134⁶²⁻³, 222; *106, 107, 108, 110*

Passion cycle, wall paintings, 156

Patrick, St, 9

Paul, St, and the Viper, 88–9, 103⁵¹⁻³; *76*

Paul, Abbot of St Albans, 80

Payntour, Hugh, *see* Hugh of St Albans

Peakirk (Northants), 155, 156–7; *143a*

Peckitt, William, 186, 188

Peter, Master, 135⁹⁵

Peterborough, 122, 134⁷⁰, 139, 140–1, 157, 161¹⁹; Cathedral, 140, 157

Peterborough Psalters, *see* Brussels, Bibliothèque Royale, MS. 9961–2; Cambridge, Corpus Christi College, MS. 53

Petrus, sculptor, *see* Oderisi, Pietro

'Pictor in carmine', 101⁴, 136¹⁰³

Pienza cope, 152

Pisan school, 126

Polo, Marco, *Li Livres du Graunt Caam, see* Oxford, Bodleian Library, MS. 264

Portraits, 184–5, 221; *163*; *see also under names*

Poussay, Gospels of, 55⁴⁶

Prague, Dubečeker altarpiece, 191⁴⁴

Prudde, John, 205–6, 216⁵⁰

Prudentius, *Psychomachia*; *see* Cambridge, Corpus Christi College Library, MS. 23; London, British Museum, MSS Add. 21499, Cotton Cleop. C.viii, Cotton Titus D.xvi

Psalters, 106, 145, 146; preliminary Bible pictures, 106, 129; typical illustrations scheme, 83; East Anglian, 138 ff., Ingeborg Psalter, 105, 130¹; St Louis, Psalter of, 130¹; *see also* Æthelstan Psalter; Albani Psalter; Alfonso Psalter; Bedford Psalter; Bohun Psalters; Bosworth Psalter; Brailes, William de, Psalters; Bromholm Psalter; Canterbury Psalter; Columba, St, Psalter of; Cuerdon Psalter; Eadwine Psalter; Evesham Psalter; Fitzwarin Psalter; Gorleston Psalter; Henry VI, Psalter of; Huntingfield Psalter; James Psalter; Lindesey Psalter; Lisle Psalter; Munich Psalter; Ormesby Psalter; Peterborough Psalters; Queen Mary's Psalter; Ramsey Abbey Psalter; Rutland Psalter; St-Omer Psalter; Shaftesbury Psalter; Tickhill Psalter; Westminster Psalter; Wilton Psalter; Windmill Psalter; York Psalter; *see also* Cambridge, Fitzwilliam Museum, MS. 12; Trinity College Library, MS. B.11.4; University Library, MS. Dd.4.17; London, British Museum, MSS Add. 16968, Arundel 60, 155, 157, Nero C.iv, Tib. C.vi, Harl. 603, 2904, 5104, Lansd. 420, Roy. 1 D. x; Lambeth Palace Library, MS. 233;

Malvern, Dyson Perrins Collection, MS. 14; Oxford, All Souls College, MS. Lat. 6; Bodleian Library, MSS Barlow 22, Douce, 296, Junius 27, Rawl. 185; Paris, Bibliothèque Nationale, MSS Lat. 8824, 8846; Rome, Biblioteca Apostolica Vaticana, MSS Pal. lat. 537, Reg. lat 12

Pucelle, Jean, 163[54], 166

Pudsey, Bishop, see Puiset

Puiset, Hugh de, Bishop of Durham, 98–9; see also Durham Cathedral Library MSS

Pyx, silver (Victoria and Albert Museum), 161[19]

Q

Queen Mary's Psalter, see London, British Museum, MS. Roy. 2 B. vii

R

Rabanus Maurus, 37, 38, 54[23]; see also Cambridge, Trinity College, MS. B.16.3

Rabula Gospels, 23

Radford Priory (Notts), 100

Ramsey Abbey, 92, Psalter, 141; 121; see also New York, Pierpont Morgan Library, MS. 302, and Lavanttal, Carinthia, Benedictine Abbey, MS. xxv.2.10

Ranworth, 214[19]

Ravenna, Sant' Apollinare Nuovo, 35

Reculver, 55[54]

Redwald, King, 13

Reformation, 213

Regensburg, 73[19]

Registrum Gregorii (Chantilly, Musée Condé), 55[46]

Reichenau, 55[45, 46], 79, 83, 102[26]

Reims, 7, 52, 56[58], 62

Retables, see Panel paintings

Rich, Edmund, see Edmund

Richard I, 105, 128; 116b

Richard II, 165, 166, 170–2; tomb, 175, 191[41-2]; Westminster Abbey portrait, 175–6, 191[40-3]; 162

Richard of Canterbury, Psalter, 143

Richard of Colchester, 134[64]

Rievaulx, 75

Ringerrike ornament, 58[83]

Robert, Archbishop (of Rouen), 55[49], see also Rouen, Bibliothèque Publique, MS. Y.6

Robert de Bello, Bible of, see London, British Museum, MS. Burney 3

Robert Benjamin, 69–70

Robert of Jumièges, Missal of, 55[49]; see also Rouen, Bibliothèque Publique, MS. Y.6

Robert de Lindesey, Abbot of Peterborough, see Lindesey, Robert de

Robert of Ormesby, see Ormesby and Ormesby Psalter

Rolf, Thomas, 154

Romanesque style, 7, 75 ff.

Rome, Vatican cope, 151, 152; 138b

Rome, Santa Pudenziana, 73[24]

Rome Gospels, see Rome, Biblioteca Apostolica Vaticana, MS. Barb. lat. 570

Rood screens, 201, 202–4, 214[19], 215[23]; 181, 182, 183

Ros, John, 8th Lord, 215[42]

Roses, Wars of the, 195, 196

Rosette motif, 19

Rossano Gospels, 28[29]

Rotulus MSS 111, 200

Rouen 'Benedictional', see Rouen, Bibliothèque Publique, MS. Y.7

Rous, John, 200, 214[11]

Rushworth Gospels, see Oxford, Bodleian Library, MS. Auct. D.2.19

Ruthwell Cross, 27[17], 29[42], 30[46]

Rutland Psalter, see Belvoir Castle

S

S-chain ornament, 12–13, 14, 16

St Albans, 7, 8, 77, 78, 84, 99, 106, 107, 118, 119, 120, 121, 122, 129, 130[8], 134[63, 64, 70, 71]

Saint-Bertrand-de-Comminges, 153

St Gall, 9, 20

St Gall Gospels, St Gall Abbey Library, MS 51

St-Omer Psalter, see London, British Museum, MS. Add. 39810

St-Omer, St Bertin, 72[9]

Saint-Savin-Gartempe, 90

Salisbury, 115, 116, 117, 133[58]; Cathedral roundels, 133[57]

Salisbury, St Thomas of Canterbury, 203–4, 215[22]; 185

Salzburg, 20

Scheerre, Herman, 178, 179, 181–4, 189, 221, 224

Screens, see Rood screens

Scrope, Archbishop Richard le, 110, 193[72]

Sebert, King, 154

Sedilia, see Westminster Abbey

Segrym, Ralf, 202

Seraph on the Wheel, 148, 152; 151a, 170

Settings, 1

Seven Ages of Man, 157

Seven Spheres of the Wheel, 148

Shaftesbury, 104[71]

Shaftesbury Psalter, see London, British Museum, MS. Lansd. 383

Sherborne Missal, see Alnwick Castle Library

Sherborne Pontifical, see Paris, Bibliothèque Nationale, MS. lat. 943

Sicily, 75, 76, 85

Siferwas, John, 177–80, 181, 184–5, 189, 192[59]

Silver stain, for glass, 158, 164[98], 201

Simon (Brother of Walter of Colchester), 134[64]

Skå, 153

Sketchbook, see Cambridge, Magdalene College, Pepysian Library, MS. 1916

Smithfield Decretals, see London, British Museum, MS. Roy. 10 E. iv

Somerset Hours, see Beaufort Hours

Somme le roi, La, see Cambridge, St John's College, MS. S.30

Souillac, 91, 104[66]

Stained glass, see Glass

Steeple Aston cope, 152, 153
Stephaton, 16, 21, 173
Stephen, King, 75
Stephen's (St) Chapel, see Westminster, Palace of
Stigand, 34, 59
Stockholm, 153
Stonyhurst College, 30[46]
'Stopped-knot' design, 12
Sutton Hoo burial, 13, 28[25], 35; *3a, 3b, 3c*
Swegn, 33
Swinburne pyx, 161[19]
Symondes, Symond, 212
Syon cope, 151, 152; *136, 138a*

T

Tara brooch, 27[7]
Tarrant Crawford (Wilts), 164[89]
Taymouth Hours, see London, British Museum, Yates
    Thompson MS. 13
Techniques, of medieval painting, 2–3
Ten Ages of Man, 147, 157
Ten Commandments, 148
Tenison, Archbishop Thomas, 161[5]
Tenison Psalter, London, British Museum, Add. MS.
    24686
Terence, see Oxford, Bodleian Library, MS. Auct.
    F.2.13
Tewkesbury Abbey, glass, 157, 159; *145b*
Theodore of Tarsus, Archbishop, 10
Thomas Becket, St, 75, 110, 118, 132[32, 37], 152; *121,
    186*; Life of (MS. Belgium), 134[62]
Thomas, Master (painter at Westminster), 154
Thomas, Master (Oxford glass-worker), 186, 187, 204
Thomas of Lancaster, 164[96]
Thomas de la Wile, 133[58]
Thorney Abbey, 60, 75
Thornham Parva (Suffolk), retable, 154, 163[77]; *140*
Thornton, John, 188, 208
Three Living and Three Dead, 148, 157, 163[45], 164[89];
    130b
Tickhill, John, 146
Tickhill Psalter, see New York, Public Library,
    Spencer Collection, MS. 26
Tiles, floor, 2, 128–9; *116b*
Toledo, 153
Tours, school of, 35, 37, 51, 53[14]
Tree of the Vices, 148
Tree of the Virtues, 148
Très Riches Heures du duc de Berry (Chantilly, Musée
    Condé), 186, 193[85]
Trewhiddle style, 35, 53[8]
Trinity, see *92, 99c, 125, 156a*
Trinity College Apocalypse, see Cambridge, Trinity
    College, MS. R.16.2
Trinity Gospels, see Cambridge, Trinity College, MS.
    B.10.4
Troper, 73[22, 23]; see also London, British Museum,
    Cotton MS. Calig. A.xiv
Tunnoc, Richard, 164[97]
Twelve Properties of Human State, 147

U

Uppsala, 153
Utrecht Psalter, 6–7, 45–6, 52, 55[53-4], 56, 57–8[60], 221;
    copies of, see Cambridge, Trinity College, R.17.1;
    London, British Museum, MS. Harl. 603; Paris,
    Bibliothèque Nationale, MS. lat. 8846
Utynam, John, 216[50]

V

Vatican, see Rome
Venice, 180–1; *157*; St Mark's, 102[24]
Verdun, 79, 102[25]
Vernicles, 119, 122, 123
Vestments, see Opus anglicanum
Vich, 153
Vikings, 9, 34, 58[53]
Vine, as ornamental form, 6, 22, 23, 26, 30[46, 65], 36,
    53[10], 219
Virgin, Coronation of, 150, 152; *136, 138b, 146, 147*
Virgin, Life of, cycle, wall paintings, 156; see also *27,
    29b, 136, 138a, 139, 141, 156b*
Virgin and Child: Book of Kells, 23; Bodleian MS.
    269; *78*; Missal of Henry of Chichester, *104*;
    Chichester roundel, *105*; Matthew Paris, *106*;
    Lisle Psalter, 148; Wilton Diptych, *153*
Viterbo, San Francesco, 126

W

Wall paintings, technique, 2–3; 12th century, 88 ff.;
    13th century, 123–4, 127; 14th century, 155 ff.,
    169–70; 15th century, 206–7; see also Canterbury
    Cathedral; Chalgrove; Chichester; Clayton;
    Coombes; Croughton; Eton College Chapel;
    Hardham; Kempley; London, Tower of; Long-
    thorpe; Oxford, Christ Church Chapter House;
    Peakirk; Salisbury, St Thomas; Westminster
    Abbey; Westminster Palace; Winchester; Wind-
    sor
Walter de Cantelupe, Bishop of Worcester, 128
Walter de Milemete, *De Nobilitatibus*, see Oxford,
    Christ Church, MS. E 11
Walter of Colchester, 106, 107, 134[64], 120
Walter of Durham, 127, 154
Warwick, Earl of, see Beauchamp; Neville
Warwick, St Mary's, Beauchamp Chapel, glass at,
    196, 205–6; *186*
Warwick chasuble, 215[37]
Warwick ciborium, 104[80]
Warwick Manuscript, 214[12]
Warwick Roll, see London, College of Arms
Was, John, 185
Waverley, 75
Wearmouth, 10, 17
Weingarten Abbey, 57[81], 61; Gospels of, see New
    York, Pierpont Morgan Library, MS. 709
Wells Cathedral, glass, 157, 164[98]
Wenhaston (Suffolk), 201
Wenzel of Bohemia, 191[32]
Wessex, 9, 33, 34

Westminster Abbey, 105, 127 f.; Chapel of St Faith, 127, 135[95]; chapter house, 129, 135[80], 166, 170, 177, 179, 192[51-2]; *151a*, *160*; choir, 7, 105; Henry VII's Chapel, 212; 'Retable', 123, 124–7, 135[88 ff.], 151; *114*, *115b*; Richard II portrait, *see* Richard II; Sedilia, paintings of, 154–5; *142*; South Transept, 127; *115a*; Tomb and Shrine of St Edward, 126, 135[90]; Tomb of Henry III, 126; Tomb of Richard II, *see* Richard II

Westminster Hall, 166

Westminster, Palace of: Painted Chamber, 105, 123, 154; St Stephen's Chapel, 128, 166, 168, 169–70, 190[16, 18, 19]; *150b*, *151b*

Westminster Psalter, *see* London, British Museum, MS. Roy. 2 A. xxii

Westphalia, 8

Weyden, Rogier van der, 207

Wheel of Life, 157

Whitby, Synod of, 9

William, St, *see* York Minster

William I, 59

William II, 59

William de Brailes, *see* Brailes, William de

William, Duke of Gelder, 166

William of Devon, 117; Bible of, *see* London, British Museum, MS. Roy. 1 D. i

William the Englishman, 120

William de Hales, Bible, of, *see* London, British Museum, MS. Roy. 1 B. xii

William of St Carilef, *see* Carilef

William of Walsingham, 170

William of Westminster, 106, 124, 155

William of Wykeham, 165, 166, 187, 205

Williamson, Francis, 212

Willibrord, St, 10, 29[38]

Wilton Abbey, 133[53]

Wilton Diptych, 170–2, 190[26], 226; *152–3*

Wilton House, 170

Wilton Psalter, *see* London, Royal College of Physicians

Winchester, 37, 42, 75; Hyde Abbey (New Minster Abbey), 33, 42, 47–9, 55[50], 60, 93

Winchester, Fromond Chapel, 196

Winchester, St Swithin's (Old Minster), 42, 44, 52, 93, 94

Winchester Bible, *see* Winchester Cathedral Library

Winchester Cathedral: Chapel of Guardian Angels, 123, 124; Chapel of Holy Sepulchre, 119, 123–4, 135[82]; *109*; Lady Chapel, 207

Winchester College, 166; glass at, 186–8; *172a*, *173a*

Winchester Psalter, *see* London, British Museum, MS. Cotton Nero C.iv

Winchester style, 3, 6, 42 ff., 220

Windmill Psalter, *see* New York, Pierpont Morgan Library, MS. 102

Windsor, St George's Chapel, cloister, 120, 123, 134[63]; *110b*

Witham, 94

Worcester embroidery fragments, 128, 151; *116a*

Worksop, 146

X

XPI monogram (Book of Kells), 23; *13*; (Rome Gospels), 25; *12*

Y

Yevele, Henry, 191[42]

York, 139, 196

York, All Saints North Street, 208–9; *189b*

York, St Denys, 164[98]

York Minster: glass, 132[38], 157–9; Bell-founders' Window, 158, 164[97]; Cuthbert, St, window, 110, 208; Dene, Peter de, window, 158, 164[96]; *144*; East window, 188, 208; *171*, *173b*; Five Sisters window, 101[4], 158; Jesse window, 186–7, 188; *172b*; West window, 158–9; *146*; William, St, window, 207–9, 215[42]; *189a*

York Psalter, *see* Glasgow, Hunterian Museum, MS. U.3.2

York Gospels, 56[66]

Yorkshire, Calendars, *see* London, Lambeth Palace 233; Munich, Staatsbib., Cod. gall. 16

INDEX OF MANUSCRIPTS

Numbers in italics refer to plates. Only the more important of the notes are indexed: in such cases the page on which the note appears, and the number of the note, are given, thus: 192[56]. Manuscripts frequently referred to by specific names are entered under their classification numbers in the collections that contain them: cross-references from the names will be found in the General Index.

ABERDEEN, University Library
  24 (Bestiary): 100
ALNWICK CASTLE LIBRARY
  Sherborne Missal: 178–9, 192[56-8]; *161, 165*

BALTIMORE, Walters Art Gallery
  500 (Bible Picture Leaves, W. de Brailes): 114, 133[44]; *99b*
BELVOIR CASTLE
  Rutland Psalter: 115, 118
BERLIN, Staatliches Museum
  K.1.672 (Single Leaf: St Michael): 163[45]
BRUSSELS, Bibliothèque Royale
  9961–2 (Peterborough Psalter): 140, 161[13]; *120*

CAMBRIDGE
  Corpus Christi College Library
    2 (Bury Bible): 84–5, 86, 87, 101; *69a*
    3–4 (Dover Bible): 86–8, 101; *63a, 70*
    16 (*Chronica Minora*): 119, 120, 123, 134[67]; *110a*
    23 (Prudentius, *Psychomachia*): 49, 57[71-2]; *38b*
    26 (*Chronica Maiora*): 119, 120, 123, 134[62-3]; *108*
    53 (Peterborough Psalter and Bestiary): 140–1, 161[18-19]; *122*
    61 (Chaucer, *Troilus and Criseyde*): 186, 193[84]; *170*
    183 (Bede, *Life of St Cuthbert*): 36, 39; *20a*
    286 (Gospels of St Augustine): 9, 10, 18, 29[43], 82
  Emmanuel College Library
    112 (Gregory, *Moralia*): 162[37]
    III.3.21 (Preliminary Bible Pictures from Psalter): 131[10]
  Fitzwilliam Museum
    330 (Bible Picture Leaves, W. de Brailes): 114, 115; *98, 99a*
    Riches Collection (Bohun Psalter): 189[10]
    J 48 (Carew-Poyntz Hours): 167; *148b*
    12 (Psalter): 132[33]
    242 (Hours): 146; *128*
    370 (Bible Pictures): 136[102]
  Magdalene College Library
    Pepysian Library, 1916 (Sketchbook): 180; *164*
  Pembroke College Library
    120 (Gospels): 81, 96; *64*
    301 (Gospels): 73[13]
    302 (Gospels): 60, 64; *49b*

St John's College Library
  A 7 (statutes): 191[33]
  H 6 (Bede, *Apocalypse*): 92; *77*
  K 26 (Bible Pictures): 136[102]
  S 30 (*La Somme le roi*): 162[28]
Trinity College Library
  B.5.3 (Glossed Gospels): 107, 130[6]; *90a*
  B.5.4 (Glossed Psalter): 132[28]
  B.10.2 (Apocalypse): 134[70], 135[80], 192[51]
  B.10.4 (Gospels): 44, 55[50], 68; *28a*
  B.10.12 (*Meditations of St Bonaventura*): 214[7]
  B.11.4 (Psalter): 132[30]
  B.11.7 (Hours): 192[63]
  B.16.3 (Rabanus Maurus, *De Laude Crucis*): 37; *19*
  O.5.8 (Glossed Epistles): 107, 130[6]
  R.14.5 (Chaundler): 199, 214[8]; *177*
  R.16.2 (Apocalypse): 120–1, 134[71]; *111*
  R.17.1 (Eadwine Psalter): 85–6, 101, 103[43-5], 108; *71, 72*
University Library
  Dd.1.14 (Bible): 143
  Dd.4.17 (Psalter): 161[19]
  Ee.3.59 (*Estoire de Seint Aedward*): 120, 122, 134[62]; *107b*
  Ii.4.26 (Bestiary): 99–100
  Kk.4.25 (Bestiary): 118–19
  Ll.1.10 (Book of Cerne): 25; *17*
CHANTILLY, Musée Condé
  169 (Ingeborg Psalter): 105, 130[1]
CHATSWORTH, Devonshire Collection
  Benediction of Æthelwold, 42–4, 55[43], 60; *26, 27*
COPENHAGEN, Thottsammlung
  547 (Bohun Psalter): 189[10], 190[13]

DARTMOUTH, Collection of Mr A. Wyndham Payne
  Crucifixion: 183–4, 193[75], [77-8]; *167*
DUBLIN, Royal Irish Academy
  Cathach of St Columba (Psalter): 12–13
DUBLIN, Trinity College Library
  52 (Book of Armagh): 24
  57 (A.4.5) (Book of Durrow): 11–13, 26[2] ff.; *1, 2, 3d*
  59 (Book of Dimma): 24
  69 (Book of Mulling): 24
  A.1.6 (Book of Kells): 16, 21–4, 30[62] ff.; *6b, 13, 14*

E.1.40 (*Lives of SS Alban and Amphibalus*): 119, 120, 134⁶²; *107a*
K.4.31 (Apocalypse): 122, 144, 145–6; *127*
DURHAM, Cathedral Library
A.ii.i (Pudsey Bible): 98–9; *87b*
A.ii.4 (Carilef Bible): 70–1; *57b, 58*
A.ii.17 (Gospels): 16, 21
A.ii.19: 99; *87a*
A.iv.19 (Ritual): 36, 39, 53⁵
B.ii.13 (St Augustine, *Commentary on the Psalms*): 69–70; *56b, 57a*
B.ii.30 (Cassiodorus): 18; *10a*
Hunter 100: 77

EDINBURGH, National Library
Adv. 18.6.5 (Psalter): 169, 189¹⁰

FLORENCE, Biblioteca Laurenziana
Amiatinus, I (Bible): 10, 15, 18, 29³⁰ ff.; *7b*
Plut. xii.17 (St Augustine, *De Civitate Dei*): 67, 68; *54, 55*

GLASGOW, Hunterian Museum
U.3.2 (York Psalter): 98, 101; *81*

HEREFORD, Cathedral Library
O.5.xi (Sermons of St John Chrysostom): 83, 84
HILDESHEIM, Library of St Godehard
Albani Psalter, 78–80, 91, 101, 102²¹ ff.; *61, 62*

KEW, Sir Sydney Cockerell Collection
Psalter (W. de Brailes): 114; *99c*

LAMBETH PALACE LIBRARY, *see under* LONDON *below*
LAVANTTAL (Carinthia), Benedictine Abbey
xxv.2.19 (Ramsey Abbey Psalter): 141–2
LICHFIELD, Cathedral Library
Gospels of St Chad: 10, 16–17; *8a*
LONDON
British Museum
Add. 16968 (Psalter): 169; *149b*
Add. 16998 (Offices): 182
Add. 17738 (Floreffe Bible): 103⁴⁸
Add. 18850 (Bedford Missal): 195
Add. 21499 (Prudentius, *Psychomachia*): 49, 57⁷⁴
Add. 24686 (Alfonso or Tenison Psalter): 139, 161⁵⁻⁶; *118*
Add. 29704–5 (Carmelite Missal): 169, 174–5, 181, 184, 189, 193⁷⁵, 197; *156*
Add. 34890 (Grimbald Gospels): 47–8, 56⁶²⁻⁴, 66; *36*
Add. 37472 (Bible Picture Leaf): 81–2, 102³³; *67a*
Add. 37517 (Bosworth Psalter): 39, 76; *21a*
Add. 39810 (St-Omer Psalter): 145–7, 149, 196–8; *129, 174a*
Add. 39943 (Bede, *Life of St Cuthbert*): 110–11, 131²⁰; *94b*
Add. 42130 (Luttrell Psalter): 147, 148–9; *131*
Add. 42131 (Bedford Psalter and Hours): 182, 185, 221

Add. 42555 (Abingdon Apocalypse): 134⁷⁰
Add. 44874 (Evesham Psalter): 116–17, 133⁵²; *103*
Add. 44949 (James Psalter): 167–8, 191²⁹; *150a*
Add. 47682 (Holkham Bible Picture Book): 150, 222; *134*
Arundel 38 (Hoccleve, *De Regimine Principum*): 185; *169c*
Arundel 60 (Psalter): 60, 63; *52, 53*
Arundel 83 (Lisle Psalter): 147–8, 152, 154, 162⁴⁴, 163⁴⁵, 170; *130*
Arundel 91 (Martyrology): 66–7; *46*
Arundel 155 (Psalter): 49–50, 65; *40, 41*
Arundel 157 (Psalter): 108, 111, 132²⁹
Burney 3 (Bible of Robert de Bello): 113–14, 131¹⁷, 133⁴⁰; *96*
Cotton Calig. A.xiv (Troper): 60, 64, 73²³, 84; *49a*
Cotton Calig. A.xv: 25
Cotton Claud. B.iv (Ælfric): 47; *35*
Cotton Cleop. C.viii (Prudentius, *Psychomachia*): 49
Cotton Dom. A.xvii (Psalter of Henry VI): 214⁶
Cotton Faust. B.vi (*Desert of Religion*): 198, 199; *175b*
Cotton Galba A.xviii (Psalter): 37, 38; *20b*
Cotton Jul. A.vi (Hymnal): 46–7, 56⁵⁹, 68; *34a*
Cotton Jul. D.vii (Matthew Paris): 134⁶²
Cotton Jul. E.iv (Warwick Manuscript): 214¹²
Cotton Nero C.iv (Winchester Psalter): 93–4, 97, 101; *79, 80*
Cotton Nero D.i (*Lives of the Offas*): 120, 134⁶², 134⁶⁹
Cotton Nero D.iv (Lindisfarne Gospels): 10, 13–16, 24, 28²⁴ ff.; *4, 5, 6a, 7a*
Cotton Tib. A.ii (Gospels): 36–7, 54¹⁹
Cotton Tib. A.iii: 65
Cotton Tib. B.v (Astronomical Treatises): 46–7, 56⁵⁹, 73¹⁴; *34b*
Cotton Tib. C.ii (Bede): 20, 30⁵⁴; *15*
Cotton Tib. C.vi (Psalter): 60, 62, 63, 72⁶, 82; *50, 51*
Cotton Titus D.xvi (Prudentius, *Psychomachia*): 77–8; *59a*
Cotton Titus D.xxvi and xxvii (New Minster, Prayers and Offices): 48–9, 73¹⁵; *37b*
Cotton Vesp. A.i (Canterbury Psalter): 18–19, 20, 55⁵¹, 65, 73¹⁴; *10b*
Cotton Vesp. A.viii (New Minster Charter): 33, 38, 42, 43; *25*
Cotton Vit. C.xii (Martyrology): 66; *46c*
Egerton 1151 (Hours): 118, 133⁴²
Egerton 1894 (Genesis): 198⁸, ⁹, 191²⁹
Egerton 3277 (Bohun Psalter): 168–9, 189¹⁰; *149a, 150c*
Harl. 603 (Utrecht Psalter copy): 45–6, 68, 76, 85; *32, 33, 48b*
Harl. 647 (Aratus): 55⁵³, 56⁵⁹, 73¹⁴, 76
Harl. 2278 (Lydgate, *Life of St Edmund*): 198, 202; *175a*
Harl. 2506 (Aratus): 55⁵³, 56⁵⁹, 76

Harl. 2904: 39, 40–1, 55⁵³, 71, 78, 218; *21b, 30*
Harl. 4605 (Christine de Pisan): 197–8, 214⁵; *174b*
Harl. 4751 (Bestiary): 100
Harl. 4826 (Lydgate, *The Pilgrim*): 199; *176*
Harl. 4866 (Hoccleve, *De Regimine Principum*): 185; *169b*
Harl. 5102 (Psalter): 112–13, 132³⁷
Harl. 7026 (Lovell Lectionary): 179–80, 163, 185
Harl. Y 6 (Guthlac Roll): 10, 110, 111, 113, 118; *95b*
Lansd. 383 (Shaftesbury Psalter): 83, 84; *68b*
Lansd. 420 (Psalter): 112–13; *94a*
Roy. 1 B. xii (Bible of William of Hales): 117, 133⁵⁸
Roy. 1 D. i (Bible of William of Devon): 118, 133⁴², ⁵⁹; *101*
Roy. 1 D. ix (Dunstan Gospels): 45, 56⁶⁵, 65; *28b*
Roy. 1 D. x (Psalter): 108, 111
Roy. 1 E. vi (Gospels): 19–20, 30⁵³; *16*
Roy. 1 E. ix (Big Bible): 183, 184, 193⁷⁴, ⁷⁸; *168*
Roy. 2 A. xviii (Beaufort Hours): 181–2, 192–193⁶⁴⁻⁶, ⁷³; *166*
Roy. 2 A. xxii (Westminster Psalter): 107–8, 111, 119, 120, 130⁷⁻⁹, 134⁶²; *89, 90b*
Roy. 2 B. vii (Queen Mary's Psalter): 139, 142–3, 148, 156, 162²³, 166; *123*
Roy. 3 D. vi (Petrus Comestor): 139
Roy. 5 F. iii (Aldhelm, *De Laude Virginitatis*): 53⁵
Roy. 10 E. iv (Smithfield Decretals): 149–50, 163⁵⁵, 167; *132*
Roy. 12 C. xix (Bestiary): 100
Roy. 14 C. vii (Matthew Paris, *Historia Anglorum*): 119, 134⁶², 221; *106*
Roy. 15 D. ii (*La Lumière as lais and Apocalypse*): 162²⁸
Roy. 19 B. xv (Apocalypse): 143; *124*
Roy. 20 D. iv (*Lancelot du lac*): 189¹⁰
Roy. 20 D. v (Gregory, Sermons): 192⁵⁵
Stowe 944 (New Minster *Liber Vitae*): 48; *37a*
Yates Thompson 13 (Taymouth Hours): 149, 163⁵⁴
College of Arms
  Warwick Roll: 200, 214¹¹
Lambeth Palace Library
  3 (Bible): 82, 89, 91–2, 93, 101, 103⁶⁴⁻⁷; *69b, 73*
  69 (Chichele Breviary): 182, 184, 193⁶⁹
  200 (Aldhelm, *De Laude Virginitatis*): 49; *38a*
  209 (Apocalypse): 122, 134⁷⁰; *113b*
  233 (Psalter): 146
  Gospels of MacDurnan: 24
Royal College of Physicians
  Wilton Psalter: 117, 133⁵³
Society of Antiquaries
  59 (Lindesey Psalter): 112, 132³³; *100*
Victoria and Albert Museum
  661 (Bible Picture Leaf): 81–2, 102³³; *67b*
Westminster Abbey Library
  Liber Regalis: 173–4, 175, 191³¹, 225; *155*
  Lytlington Missal: 169, 172–3, 174, 178, 190²⁵, 191²⁸; *154*

MALVERN, Dyson Perrins Collection
  1 (Preliminary Bible Picture from Psalter): 131¹⁰
  4 (Hours, W. de Brailes): 114
  5 (Bible): 114
  10 (Apocalypse): 122, 134⁷⁰, ⁷⁴
  13 (Gorleston Psalter): 145; *126a*
  14 (Psalter): 143
MANCHESTER, John Rylands Library
  Lat. R.24 (Missal): 116, 117, 133⁵⁵; *104*
MONTE CASSINO ABBEY LIBRARY
  BB.437,439 (Gospels): 60, 61; *45*
MUNICH, Staatsbibliothek
  Cod. gall. 16 (Psalter): 146
  Cod. lat. 835 (Munich Psalter): 112, 132³⁰

NEW YORK
  Pierpont Morgan Library
  43 (Huntingfield Psalter): 131¹⁰
  81 (Bestiary): 100; *88b*
  102 (Windmill Psalter): 139–40, 161¹²; *119*
  302 (Preliminary Bible Pictures from Ramsey Abbey Psalter): 141–2; *121*
  521,724 (Bible Picture Leaves): 81–2, 102³³
  524 (Apocalypse): 122, 134⁷⁰; *112*
  619 (Bible Picture Leaf): 96–7; *86*
  708,709 (Gospels): 51, 57⁸¹, 61; *43*
  736 (*Life of St Edmund*): 80, 101; *65, 66*
  756 (Cuerdon Psalter): 118, 134⁶⁰
  775 (Ordinances of Chivalry): 200; *179*
  777 (Mostyn Gospels): 76; *63b*
  791 (Lothian Bible): 109, 110, 131¹⁵; *92*
  Public Library
  Spencer Collection 26 (Tickhill Psalter): 146

OXFORD
  All Souls College
    lat. 6 (Psalter): 116; *102*
  Bodleian Library
    264 (Marco Polo): 180–1, 192⁶²; *157*
    269 (St Augustine, *Commentary on Psalms*): 92–3; *78*
    579 (Leofric Missal): 40, 58⁸⁵; *29a*
    717 (St Jerome on Isaiah): 70; *56a*
    752: 132²⁸
    764 (Bestiary): 100
    Ashmole 304: 134⁶²
    Ashmole 1511 (Bestiary): 99, 100; *88a*
    Ashmole 1523 (Bromholm Psalter): 162³⁷
    Auct. D.1.13 (Pauline Epistles): 104⁸²
    Auct. D.2.19 (Rushworth or MacRegal Gospels): 24
    Auct. D.4.4 (Bohun Psalter): 189–90¹⁰, ¹³, ¹⁴
    Auct. D.4.17 (Apocalypse): 122, 134⁷⁰
    Auct. E. infra 1 and 2 (Bible): 98
    Auct. E. infra 6 (Glossed Psalter): 132²⁸
    Auct. F.2.13 (Terence): 78, 93, 98; *82*
    Auct. F.4.32 (Composite Text): 37–8, 53⁵, 54²⁵⁻⁷, 221; *22*
    Auct. F.6.5 (Boethius): 84; *68a*
    Barlow 22 (Psalter): 161¹⁹
    Digby 227 (Abingdon Missal): 200, 214⁹; *178*

Douce 151 (Bestiary): 100
Douce 180 (Apocalypse): 122, 125, 134[70, 74]; *113a*
Douce 296 (Psalter): 51, 57[79]
Douce 366 (Ormesby Psalter): 143–4, 149, 162[32], 189[4]; *125, 126b*
Hatton 60 (St Gregory, *Cura Pastoralis*): 35
Junius 11 (Cædmon): 51–2, 57[82-3], 58[85], 89; *44*
Junius 27 (Psalter); 39, 54[32]
Latin liturg. f.2 (Hours): 182–3, 193[72-3]; *169a*
Latin liturg. f.5 (Gospels of St Margaret): 61; *48a*
Laud Misc. 247 (Bestiary): 76, 99
Laud Misc. 752 (Bible): 98, 104[84]
Rawl. 185 (Psalter); 189[9]
Rawl. B 484 (Leaf from Æthelstan Psalter): 37
Tanner 10: 65
Christ Church, Library
E 11 (Walter de Milemete): 150; *133*
Corpus Christi College
157 (Florence of Worcester): 78; *60*
394 (Lapworth Missal): 184, 192[55], 193[80]
Exeter College
47 (Bohun Psalter): 189–90[10, 12, 14]
New College
288 (Chaundler): 199–200, 214[8]
322 (Psalter, W. de Brailes): 114, 115, 133[46]
Trinity College
75 (Abingdon Missal): 200
University College
165 (Bede, *Life of St Cuthbert*): 77, 131[20]; *59b*

PARIS
Bibliothèque Sainte-Geneviève
8–10 (Manerius Bible): 109
Bibliothèque Nationale
403 (Apocalypse): 122, 134[70]

lat. 765 (Fitzwarin Psalter): 167
lat. 943 (Dunstan or Sherborne Pontifical): 38–9, 56[65]; *23, 24*
lat. 8824 (Psalter): 56[60]
lat. 8846 (Utrecht Psalter copy): 108–9, 110; *91*
lat. 9389 (Echternach Gospels): 17, 29[38]; *8b*
lat. 11534–5 (Bible): 109
lat. 16743–6 (Bible): 109
suppl. lat. 601 (Apocalypse): 122, 135[79]

ROME, Biblioteca Apostolica Vaticana
Barb. lat. 570 (Gospels): 20, 24–5, 31[75]; *11b, 12*
Pal. lat. 537 (Psalter): 166–7; *148a*
reg. lat. 12 (Psalter): 50–1; *39*
ROUEN, Bibliothèque Publique
A 27 (Llanalet Pontifical): 57[83]
A 85: 72[8]
Y 6 (Missal of Robert of Jumièges): 34, 45, 55[52]; *31*
Y 7: (Benedictional of Archbishop Robert): 44; *29b*

ST GALL, Abbey Library
51 (Gospels); 20–1, 23; *9b*
STOCKHOLM, Royal Library
Codex Aureus: 19, 30[48, 49]; *11a*

VIENNA, Nationalbibliothek
Cod. 1826★ (Bohun Psalter): 168, 189[10], 190[11, 14]
MS. lat. 1224 (Cutbercht Gospels): 20; *9a*

WESTMINSTER ABBEY LIBRARY, *see under* LONDON *above*
WINCHESTER, Cathedral Library
Winchester Bible: 7, 94–8, 101, 104[73 ff.], 218; *83–5*